Fifth Edition

Microprocessors and Microcomputers
Hardware and Software

Ronald J. Tocci
Monroe Community College

Frank J. Ambrosio
Monroe Community College

PRENTICE HALL
Upper Saddle River, New Jersey

Columbus, Ohio

Library of Congress Cataloging-in-Publication

Tocci, Ronald J.
    Microprocessors and microcomputers : hardware and software /
Ronald J. Tocci, Frank J. Ambrosio. —5th ed.
      p.   cm.
    Includes index.
    ISBN 0-13-010494-9
    1. Microprocessors.   2. Microcomputers.   I. Ambrosio, Frank J.
II. Title.
    QA76.5.T556   2000
    004.16—dc21   98-47317
                                      CIP

Publisher: Charles Stewart
Associate Editor: Kate Linsner
Production Editor: Rachel Besen
Design Coordinator: Karrie Converse-Jones
Cover Designer: Kurt Besser
Production Manager: Deidra Schwartz
Marketing Manager: Ben Leonard

This book was set in Times Roman by Clarinda Company and was printed and bound by R.R.D. Donnelley & Sons Company. The cover was printed by Phoenix Color.

©2000, 1997, 1987, 1982, 1979 by Prentice-Hall, Inc.
Pearson Education
Upper Saddle River, New Jersey 07458

Photo Credits: Photo Researchers, Inc.

Printed in the United States of America

10 9 8 7 6 5 4 3 2 1

ISBN: 0-13-010494-9

Prentice-Hall International (UK) Limited, *London*
Prentice-Hall of Australia Pty. Limited, *Sydney*
Prentice-Hall of Canada, Inc., *Toronto*
Prentice-Hall Hispanoamericana, S. A., *Mexico*
Prentice-Hall of India Private Limited, *New Dehli*
Prentice-Hall of Japan, Inc., *Tokyo*
Prentice-Hall (Singapore) Pte. Ltd., *Singapore*
Editora Prentice-Hall do Brasil, Ltda., *Rio de Janeiro*

For my Mom Tomaselli, who, even in her sickness and suffering, showed us how to love and care for each other.

Ronald J. Tocci

To my family:
My loving wife, Ana, my wonderful son, Filip, and my caring mother, Georgina. Thank you for the love, support, and prayers.

Frank J. Ambrosio

Preface

This book was written to provide a comprehensible introduction to microprocessors and microcomputers for a broad range of readers. It can serve as a textbook in electronic technology, computer technology, and computer science programs from the vocational school to four-year college level. It can also be used by computer hobbyists as well as practicing technicians and engineers. A significant portion of the text requires a basic knowledge of digital principles and circuits. For this reason, a comprehensive review of this material is presented in the first three chapters to help those readers who have only a minimal background or who have been away from the field for a while.

The major philosophy that has been followed in this book is that the principles and techniques of microprocessors and microprocessor-based systems are the most important concepts to understand, and it is not necessary to survey the whole field of available microprocessors and microprocessor applications. We believe that the best pedagogical approach is to use a currently popular, powerful, yet easy-to-understand microprocessor chip as the vehicle for teaching these concepts. We also believe that since 8-bit microprocessors are simple and easy to understand, this makes them an appropriate choice for an introductory textbook. As such, we have chosen to use the **68HC11** microprocessor as that vehicle. The 68HC11 is one of the most powerful and flexible 8-bit microprocessors in general use, and it contains all of the elements and features that need to be part of an introduction to microprocessors and microprocessor applications. Everything the reader learns and understands using this representative device can be readily transferred to other microprocessors and applications, including the more complex 16-bit and 32-bit devices.

This fifth edition retains all of the valuable learning aids of the previous editions, including (1) extensive use of clearly explained illustrative examples to provide immediate reinforcement; (2) clear, uncluttered diagrams to enhance the understanding of the written material; (3) liberal use of flowcharts; (4) glossaries of important terms at the end of each chapter for easy review of chapter contents; (5) more than 400 end-of-chapter questions and problems of varied complexity; and (6) an extensive appendix containing a detailed description of each of the 68HC11's available instructions.

The major enhancement to this edition is the inclusion of material intended to give the reader basic principles and techniques of digital systems troubleshooting. This includes the following:

- *Chapter 2.* Addition of material on troubleshooting digital systems, internal and external digital IC faults, and test equipment used to troubleshoot digital systems.
- *Chapter 5.* Inclusion of a Troubleshooting Case Study of a typical RAM decoding logic in a 68HC11-based circuit.
- *Chapter 8.* Addition of a Troubleshooting Case Study of a circuit using switches and LEDs connected as I/O devices for entering and displaying single-byte data.
- *Chapter 9.* Inclusion of a Troubleshooting Case Study of a hex keyboard interface for a software scanning technique using a 68HC11 MCU-based circuit.
- Expansion of end-of-chapter questions and problems in Chapters 2, 5, 8, and 9 to cover the newly introduced material on troubleshooting.
- Considerable expansion of Appendix A to include a complete Op Code vs. Instruction Cross Reference.

In preparing this fifth edition, the very helpful comments and suggestions of several users of the fourth edition were considered and acted upon. The authors particularly wish to acknowledge Vernon Seier, who assisted in this capacity.

Ronald J. Tocci
Monroe Community College

Frank J. Ambrosio
Monroe Community College

Contents

1

Number Systems and Codes

OBJECTIVES

Upon completion of this chapter, you will be able to:

- Understand the binary, octal, and hexadecimal number systems.
- Convert between hexadecimal and decimal numbers.
- Convert between hexadecimal and binary numbers.
- Express decimal numbers using the BCD code.
- Have a basic understanding of alphanumeric codes, especially the ASCII code.
- Use the parity method for error detection during the transfer of binary-coded information.
- Perform addition, subtraction, multiplication, and division on two binary numbers.
- Add and subtract signed binary numbers by using the 2's-complement system.
- Add and subtract hexadecimal numbers.
- Use negation to convert a positive binary number to its negative equivalent or a negative binary number to its positive equivalent.
- Understand the concept of an arithmetic overflow when adding two binary numbers.

INTRODUCTION

Computers of all sizes have one thing in common—they handle *numbers.* In digital computers, these numbers are represented by binary digits. A *binary digit* is a digit that can take on only the values of 0 or 1, and no other value. The major reason why binary digits are used in computers is the simplicity with which electrical, magnetic, and mechanical devices can represent binary digits. Because the term "binary digit" is used so often in computer work, it is commonly abbreviated to *bit.* Henceforth, we shall use the latter form.

▶ 1.1 DIGITAL NUMBER SYSTEMS

Although actual computer operations use the binary number system, several other number systems are used to communicate with computers. The most common are the decimal, octal, and hexadecimal systems.

Decimal System

The *decimal system* is composed of the 10 symbols or digits: 0, 1, 2, 3, 4, 5, 6, 7, 8, and 9; using these symbols, we can express any quantity. The decimal system, also called the *base 10 system,* because it has 10 digits, has evolved naturally as a result of the fact that human beings have 10 fingers. In fact, the word "digit" is derived from the Latin word for "finger."

The decimal system is a *positional-value system,* in which the value of a digit depends on its position. For example, consider the decimal number 453. We know that the digit 4 actually represents 4 *hundreds,* the 5 represents 5 *tens,* and the 3 represents 3 *units.* In essence, the 4 carries the most weight of the three digits; it is referred to as the *most significant digit* (MSD). The 3 carries the least weight and is called the *least significant digit* (LSD).

The various positions relative to the decimal point carry weights that can be expressed as powers of 10. This is illustrated below, where the number 2745.214 is represented. The decimal point separates the positive powers of 10 from the negative powers. The number 2745.214 is thus equal to

$$(2 \times 10^{+3}) + (7 \times 10^{+2}) + (4 \times 10^{+1}) + (5 \times 10^{+0})$$
$$+ (2 \times 10^{-1}) + (1 \times 10^{-2}) + (4 \times 10^{-3})$$

In general, any number is simply the sum of the products of each digit value times its positional value; see Fig. 1.1.

Decimal Counting   The number 9 is the largest digit value in the decimal system. Thus, as we are counting in decimal, a given digit will progress upward from 0 to 9. After 9, it goes back to 0 and the next higher digit position is incremented (goes up by 1). For example, note the digit changes in the following counting sequences: 25, 26, 27, 28, 29, 30; 196, 197, 198, 199, 200.

For a given number of digits, N, we can count decimal numbers from zero up to $10^N - 1$. In other words, with N digits we can have 10^N different numbers, including zero.

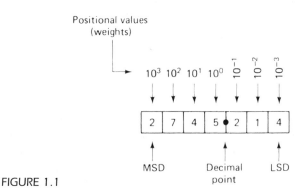

FIGURE 1.1

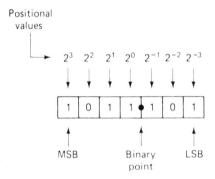

Positional values

MSB   Binary point   LSB

FIGURE 1.2

To illustrate, with three decimal digits, we can count from 000 to 999, a total of 1000 different numbers.

Binary System

In the *binary system* there are only two symbols or possible digit values, 0 and 1. Even so, this *base 2 system* can be used to represent any quantity that can be represented in decimal or other number systems. In general, though, it will take a greater number of binary digits to express a given quantity.

All the statements made earlier concerning the decimal system are equally applicable to the binary system. The binary system is also a positional-value system, wherein each bit has its own value or weight expressed as a power of 2, as shown in Fig. 1.2.

In the number expressed above, the positions to the left of the *binary point* (counterpart of the decimal point) are positive powers of 2; the leftmost bit carries the most weight and is referred to as the *most significant bit* (MSB). The positions to the right of the binary point are negative powers of 2; the rightmost bit carries the least weight and is referred to as the *least significant bit* (LSB). The binary number 1011.101 is represented above, and its equivalent decimal value can be found by taking the sum of the products of each bit value (0 or 1) times its positional value.

$$1011.101_2 = (1 \times 2^3) + (0 \times 2^2) + (1 \times 2^1) + (1 \times 2^0)$$
$$+ (1 \times 2^{-1}) + (0 \times 2^{-2}) + (1 \times 2^{-3})$$

$$= 8 + 0 + 2 + 1 + .5 + 0 + .125$$

$$= 11.625_{10}$$

Notice in the preceding operation that subscripts (2 and 10) were used to indicate the base in which the particular number is expressed. This convention is used to avoid confusion whenever more than one number system is being employed.

Binary Counting The largest digit value in the binary system is 1. Thus, when counting in binary, a given digit will progress from 0 to 1. After it reaches 1, it recycles to 0 and the next higher bit position is incremented. (See Fig. 1.3.)

Note in this example that the least-significant-bit (LSB) position changes value at each step in the counting sequence. The next higher bit (2^1) changes value every

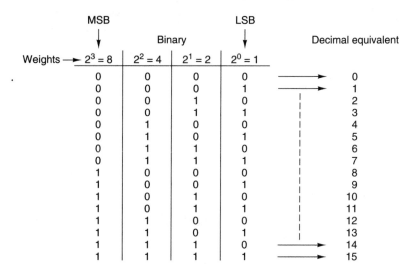

FIGURE 1.3

two counts, the 2^2 bit changes value every four counts, and the 2^3 bit changes every eight counts.

In the binary system, using N bits, we can count through 2^N different numbers, including zero. For example, with 2 bits, we can count 00, 01, 10, 11 for four different numbers. Similarly, with 4 bits, we can count from 0000 up to 1111, a total of $2^4 = 16$ different numbers. The largest number that can be represented by N bits is always equal to $2^N - 1$ in decimal. Thus, with 4 bits, the largest binary number is 1111_2, which is equivalent to $2^4 - 1 = 15_{10}$.

Binary/Decimal Conversions   As explained earlier, the binary number system is a positional system where each bit carries a certain weight based on its position relative to the binary point. Any binary number can be converted to its decimal equivalent simply by summing together the weights of the various positions in the binary number that contain a 1. To illustrate:

$$1 \quad 1 \quad 0 \quad 1 \quad 1 \text{ (binary)}$$
$$2^4 + 2^3 + 0 + 2^1 + 2^0 = 16 + 8 + 2 + 1$$
$$= 27_{10} \text{ (decimal)}$$

The same method is used for binary numbers that contain a fractional part.

$$1 \quad 0 \quad 1 \,.\, 1 \quad 0 \quad 1 = 2^2 + 2^0 + 2^{-1} + 2^{-3}$$
$$= 4 + 1 + .5 + .125$$
$$= 5.625_{10}$$

The following conversions should be performed and verified by the reader:

(1.) $1 \quad 0 \quad 0 \quad 1 \quad 1 \quad 0_2 = 38_{10}$

(2.) $0 \,.\, 1 \quad 1 \quad 0 \quad 0 \quad 0 \quad 1_2 = .765625_{10}$

(3.) $1 \quad 1 \quad 1 \quad 1 \quad 0 \quad 0 \quad 1 \quad 1 \,.\, 0 \quad 1 \quad 0 \quad 1_2 = 243.3125_{10}$

There are several ways to convert a decimal number to its equivalent binary system representation. A method that is convenient for small numbers is just the reverse of the process described in the preceding section. The decimal number is simply expressed as a sum of powers of 2 and then 1s and 0s are written in the appropriate bit positions. To illustrate:

$$13_{10} = 8 + 4 + 1 = 2^3 + 2^2 + 0 + 2^0$$
$$= 1 \quad 1 \quad 0 \quad 1_2$$

Another example:

$$25.375_{10} = 16 + 8 + 1 + .25 + .125$$
$$= 2^4 + 2^3 + 0 + 0 + 2^0 + 0 + 2^{-2} + 2^{-3}$$
$$= 1 \quad 1 \quad 0 \quad 0 \quad 1 \quad . \quad 0 \quad 1 \quad 1_2$$

For larger decimal numbers, the foregoing method is laborious. A more convenient method entails separate conversion of the integer and fractional parts. For example, take the decimal number 25.375, which was converted above. The first step is to convert the integer portion, 25. This conversion is accomplished by repeatedly *dividing* 25 by 2 and writing down the remainders after each division until a quotient of zero is obtained.

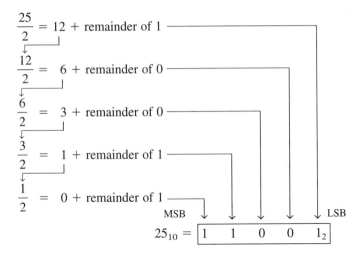

$$25_{10} = \boxed{1 \quad 1 \quad 0 \quad 0 \quad 1_2}$$

The desired binary conversion is obtained by writing down the remainders, as shown above. Note that the *first* remainder is the LSB and the *last* remainder is the MSB.

The fractional part of the number (.375) is converted to binary by repeatedly *multiplying* it by 2 and recording any carries into the integer position.

$$.375 \times 2 = .75 = .75 \text{ with carry of } 0$$
$$.75 \times 2 = 1.50 = .50 \text{ with carry of } 1$$
$$.50 \times 2 = 1.00 = .00 \text{ with carry of } 1$$

$$.375_{10} = \boxed{.0 \quad 1 \quad 1_2}$$

Note that the repeated multiplications continue until a product of 1.00 is reached,* since any further multiplications result in all zeros. Notice here that the *first* carry is written in the first position to the right of the binary point.

Finally, the complete conversion for 25.375 can be written as the combination of the integer and fraction conversions.

$$25.375_{10} = 1 \quad 1 \quad 0 \quad 0 \quad 1 . 0 \quad 1 \quad 1_2$$

The reader should apply this method to verify the following conversion:

$$632.85_{10} \approx 1 \quad 0 \quad 0 \quad 1 \quad 1 \quad 1 \quad 1 \quad 0 \quad 0 \quad 0 . \quad 1 \quad 1 \quad 0 \quad 1 \quad 1_2$$

Octal Number System

The *octal number system* has a *base of eight,* meaning that it has eight possible digits: 0, 1, 2, 3, 4, 5, 6, and 7. Thus, each digit of an octal number can have any value from 0 to 7. The digit positions in an octal number have weights that are powers of 8:

$$\longleftarrow\!-\!- \boxed{8^4 \quad 8^3 \quad 8^2 \quad 8^1 \quad 8^0 \; . \; 8^{-1} \quad 8^{-2} \quad 8^{-3} \quad 8^{-4} \quad 8^{-5}} \!-\!-\!\longrightarrow$$

octal point ⌋

An octal number, then, can be easily converted to its decimal equivalent by multiplying each octal digit by its positional weight. For example,

$$372_8 = 3 \times (8^2) + 7 \times (8^1) + 2 \times (8^0)$$
$$= 3 \times 64 + 7 \times 8 + 2 \times 1$$
$$= 250_{10}$$

Another example:

$$24.6_8 = 2 \times (8^1) + 4 \times (8^0) + 6 \times (8^{-1})$$
$$= 20.75_{10}$$

Counting in Octal The largest octal digit is 7, so when counting in octal, a digit is incremented upward from 0 to 7. Once it reaches 7, it recycles to 0 on the next count and causes the next higher digit to be incremented. This is illustrated in the following sequences of octal counting: 64, 65, 66, 67, 70; 275, 276, 277, 300.

With N octal digits, we can count from zero up to $8^N - 1$, for a total of 8^N different counts. For example, with three octal digits we can count from 000_8 to 777_8, which is a total of $8^3 = 512_{10}$ different octal numbers.

Conversion between Octal and Binary The primary advantage of the octal number system is the ease with which conversions can be made between binary and octal num-

---

*Most of the time, 1.00 will not occur and the process is terminated after a suitable number of places in the binary fractional number is reached.

bers. The conversion from octal to binary is performed by converting *each* octal digit to its 3-bit binary equivalent. The eight possible digits are converted as follows:

Octal Digit	0	1	2	3	4	5	6	7
Binary Equivalent	000	001	010	011	100	101	110	111

Using these conversions, any octal number is converted to binary by individually converting each digit. For example, we can convert 472_8 to binary as follows:

$$
\begin{array}{ccc}
4 & 7 & 2 \\
\downarrow & \downarrow & \downarrow \\
100 & 111 & 010
\end{array}
$$

Hence, octal 472 is equivalent to binary 100111010. As another example, consider converting 54.31_8 to binary.

$$
\begin{array}{ccccc}
5 & 4 & . & 3 & 1 \\
\downarrow & \downarrow & \downarrow & \downarrow & \downarrow \\
101 & 100 & . & 011 & 001
\end{array}
$$

Thus, $54.31_8 = 101100.011001_2$.

Converting from binary to octal is simply the reverse of the foregoing process. The binary digits are grouped into groups of 3 on each side of the binary point, with zeros added on either side if needed to complete a group of 3 bits. Then, each group of 3 is converted to its octal equivalent. To illustrate, consider the conversion of 11010.1011_2 to octal:

$$
\begin{array}{cccccccccc}
0\ 1\ 1 & 0\ 1\ 0 & . & 1\ 0\ 1 & 1\ 0\ 0 & \text{(binary)} \\
\downarrow & \downarrow & & \downarrow & \downarrow & \\
3 & 2 & . & 5 & 4 & \text{(octal)}
\end{array}
$$

Note that 0s were added on each end to complete the groups of 3 bits. Here are two more examples: $11110_2 = 36_8$, $10011.01_2 = 23.2_8$.

Usefulness of Octal System   The ease with which conversions can be made between octal and binary make the octal system attractive as a shorthand means of expressing large binary numbers. In computer work, binary numbers with up to 36 bits are not uncommon. These binary numbers, as we shall see, do not always represent a numerical quantity but often are some type of code that conveys nonnumerical information. In computers, binary numbers might represent (1) actual numerical data, (2) numbers corresponding to a location (address) in memory, (3) an instruction code, (4) a code representing alphabetic and other nonnumerical characters, or (5) a group of bits representing the status of devices internal or external to the computer.

When dealing with a large quantity of binary numbers of many bits, it is convenient and more efficient for us to write the numbers in octal rather than binary. Keep in mind, however, that the digital system works strictly in binary and we are using octal only as a convenience for the operators of the system.

TABLE 1.1

Hexadecimal (Hex)	Decimal	Binary
0	0	0000
1	1	0001
2	2	0010
3	3	0011
4	4	0100
5	5	0101
6	6	0110
7	7	0111
8	8	1000
9	9	1001
A	10	1010
B	11	1011
C	12	1100
D	13	1101
E	14	1110
F	15	1111

Hexadecimal Number System

The *hexadecimal system* uses *base 16*. Thus, it has 16 possible digit symbols. It uses the digits 0 through 9 plus the letters A, B, C, D, E, and F as the 16 digit symbols. Table 1.1 shows the relationships among hexadecimal, decimal, and binary. Note that each hexadecimal digit represents a group of four binary digits. It is important to remember that hex (abbreviation for hexadecimal) digits A though F are equivalent to the decimal values 10 through 15.

Hex-to-Decimal Conversion

A hex number can be converted to its decimal equivalent by using the fact that each hex digit position has a weight that is a power of 16. The LSD has a weight of $16^0 = 1$, the next higher digit has a weight of $16^1 = 16$, the next higher digit has a weight of $16^2 = 256$, and so on. The conversion process is demonstrated in the examples that follow.

$$356_{16} = 3 \times 16^2 + 5 \times 16^1 + 6 \times 16^0$$
$$= 768 + 80 + 6$$
$$= 854_{10}$$
$$2AF_{16} = 2 \times 16^2 + 10 \times 16^1 + 15 \times 16^0$$
$$= 512 + 160 + 15$$
$$= 687_{10}$$

Note that in the second example, the value 10 was substituted for A and the value 15 for F in the conversion to decimal.

Decimal-to-Hex Conversion

Recall that decimal-to-binary was done using repeated division by 2, and decimal-to-octal can be done using repeated division by 8. Similarly, decimal-to-hex conversion can be done using repeated division by 16. The examples below will illustrate. Note how the remainders of the division process form the digits of the hex number. Also note that any remainders that are greater than 9 are represented by the letters A through F.

EXAMPLE 1.1

Convert 423_{10} to hex.

Solution

$$\frac{423}{16} = 26 + \text{remainder of } 7$$

$$\frac{26}{16} = 1 + \text{remainder of } 10$$

$$1 = 0 + \text{remainder of } 1$$

$$423_{10} = \boxed{1 \quad A \quad 7}_{16}$$

EXAMPLE 1.2

Convert 214_{10} to hex.

Solution

$$\frac{214}{16} = 13 + \text{remainder of } 6$$

$$\frac{13}{16} = 0 + \text{remainder of } 13$$

$$214_{10} = \quad D \quad 6_{16}$$

Hex-to-Binary Conversion

Like the octal number system, the hexadecimal number system is used primarily as a "shorthand" method for representing binary numbers. It is a relatively simple matter to convert a hex number to binary. *Each* hex digit is converted to its 4-bit binary equivalent (Table 1.1). This is illustrated on page 10 for $9F2_{16}$.

$$9F2_{16} = \quad 9 \qquad F \qquad 2$$

$$\overbrace{1001} \quad \overbrace{1111} \quad \overbrace{0010}$$

$$= 100111110010_2$$

Binary-to-Hex Conversion

This conversion is just the reverse of the process above. The binary number is grouped into groups of four bits and each group is converted to its equivalent hex digit.

$$101110100110_2 = \underbrace{1011} \quad \underbrace{1010} \quad \underbrace{0110}$$

$$B \qquad A \qquad 6$$

$$= B \, A \, 6_{16}$$

To perform these conversions between hex and binary, it is necessary to know the 4-bit binary numbers (0000–1111) and their equivalent hex digits. Once these are mastered, the conversions can be performed quickly without the need for any calculations. This is why hex (and octal) numbers are so useful in representing large binary numbers.

Counting in Hexadecimal

When counting in hex, each digit position can be incremented (increased by 1) from 0 to F. Once a digit position reaches the value F, it is reset to 0 and the next digit position is incremented. This is illustrated in the following hex counting sequences:

1. 38, 39, 3A, 3B, 3C, 3D, 3E, 3F, 40, 41, 42
2. 6F8, 6F9, 6FA, 6FB, 6FC, 6FD, 6FE, 6FF, 700

Note that when there is a 9 in a digit position, it becomes an A when it is incremented.

▶ 1.2 CODES

When numbers, letters, words, or other information is represented by a special group of symbols, the process is called *encoding* and the group of symbols is called a *code.*

We have seen that any decimal number can be represented by an equivalent binary number. The group of 0s and 1s in the binary number can be thought of as a code representing the decimal number. When a decimal number is represented by its equivalent binary number, we call it *straight binary coding.* If the decimal number is represented by its octal equivalent, we call it *octal coding,* and similarly for *hex coding.* Each of these types of coding is really just a different number system. In digital systems, many codes are used that do not fall into this classification.

BCD Code

Digital systems all use some form of binary numbers for their internal operation, but the external world is decimal in nature. This means that conversions between the decimal and binary systems are being performed often. These conversions between decimal and binary can become long and complicated for large numbers. For this reason, another means of encoding decimal numbers which combines some features of both the decimal and binary systems is sometimes used.

If *each* digit of a decimal number is represented by its binary equivalent, this produces a code called *binary-coded decimal* (hereafter abbreviated BCD). Because a decimal digit can be as large as 9, 4 bits are required to code each digit (binary code for 9 is 1001).

To illustrate the BCD code, take a decimal number such as 874. Each digit is changed to its binary equivalent as follows:

$$
\begin{array}{ccc}
8 & 7 & 4 \\
\downarrow & \downarrow & \downarrow \\
1000 & 0111 & 0100
\end{array}
$$

As another example, let us change 94.3 to its BCD-code representation.

$$
\begin{array}{cccc}
9 & 4 & . & 3 \\
\downarrow & \downarrow & \downarrow & \downarrow \\
1001 & 0100 & . & 0011
\end{array}
$$

Once again, each decimal digit is changed to its straight binary equivalent.

The BCD code, then, represents each digit of the decimal number by a 4-bit binary number. Clearly, only the 4-bit binary numbers from 0000 through 1001 are used. The BCD code does not use the numbers 1010, 1011, 1100, 1101, 1110, and 1111. In other words, only 10 of the 16 possible 4-bit binary code groups are used. If any of these "forbidden" 4-bit numbers ever occurs in a machine using the BCD code, it is usually an indication that an error has occurred.

EXAMPLE 1.3

Convert the BCD number 0110100000111001 to its decimal equivalent.

Solution

$$
\begin{array}{cccc}
0110 & 1000 & 0011 & 1001 \\
6 & 8 & 3 & 9
\end{array}
$$

EXAMPLE 1.4

Convert the BCD number 011111000001 to its decimal equivalent.

Solution

$$
\begin{array}{ccc}
0111 & \underbrace{1100} & 0001 \\
7 & & 1
\end{array}
$$

↳ forbidden code group indicates error in BCD number

Comparison of BCD with Straight Binary It is important to realize that a BCD number is *not* the same as a straight binary number. A straight binary code takes the *complete* decimal number and represents it in binary; the BCD code converts *each* decimal *digit* to binary individually. To illustrate, take the number 137 and compare its straight binary and BCD codes:

$$1 \quad 3 \quad 7_{10} = 1 \quad 0 \quad 0 \quad 0 \quad 1 \quad 0 \quad 0 \quad 1_2 \quad \text{(binary)}$$

$$1 \quad 3 \quad 7_{10} = 0001 \quad 0011 \quad 0111 \qquad \text{(BCD)}$$

The BCD code requires 12 bits to represent 137, whereas the straight binary code requires only 8 bits. It is always true that the BCD code for a given decimal number requires more code bits than the straight code. This is because BCD does not use all possible 4-bit groups, as pointed out earlier.

The main advantage of the BCD code is the relative ease of converting to and from decimal. Only the 4-bit code groups for the decimal digits 0 through 9 need be remembered. This ease of conversion is especially important from a hardware standpoint because in a digital system, it is the logic circuits that perform the conversions.

BCD is used in digital machines whenever decimal information is either applied as inputs or displayed as outputs. Digital voltmeters, frequency counters, and digital clocks all use BCD because they display output information in decimal. Electronic calculators use BCD because the input numbers are entered in decimal via the keyboard and the output numbers are displayed in decimal.

Alphanumeric Codes

If it is to be very useful, a computer must be capable of handling nonnumeric information. In other words, a computer must be able to recognize codes that represent numbers, letters, and special characters. These codes are classified as *alphanumeric codes.* A complete and adequate set of necessary characters includes (1) 26 lowercase letters, (2) 26 uppercase letters, (3) 10 numeric digits, and (4) about 25 special characters, including +, /, #, and %.

This totals up to 87 characters. To represent 87 characters with some type of binary code would require at least 7 bits. With 7 bits, there are $2^7 = 128$ possible binary numbers; 87 of these arrangements of 0 and 1 bits serve as the code groups representing the 87 different characters. For example, the code group 1010101 might represent the letter U.

The most common alphanumeric code is known as the American Standard Code for Information Interchange (ASCII) and is used by most minicomputer and microcomputer manufacturers. Table 1.2 shows a partial listing of the 7-bit ASCII code. For each character, the octal and hex equivalents are also shown. The ASCII code is used in the transmission of alphanumeric information between a computer and external input/output devices like a printer or video display terminal (VDT).

Parity

The process of transferring binary-coded information is subject to error, although modern equipment has been designed to reduce the probability of errors occurring. However, even relatively infrequent errors can cause useless results, so it is desirable to detect them when-

TABLE 1.2   Partial Listing
            of ASCII Code

Character	7-Bit ASCII	Octal	Hex
A	100 0001	101	41
B	100 0010	102	42
C	100 0011	103	43
D	100 0100	104	44
E	100 0101	105	45
F	100 0110	106	46
G	100 0111	107	47
H	100 1000	110	48
I	100 1001	111	49
J	100 1010	112	4A
K	100 1011	113	4B
L	100 1100	114	4C
M	100 1101	115	4D
N	100 1110	116	4E
O	100 1111	117	4F
P	101 0000	120	50
Q	101 0001	121	51
R	101 0010	122	52
S	101 0011	123	53
T	101 0100	124	54
U	101 0101	125	55
V	101 0110	126	56
W	101 0111	127	57
X	101 1000	130	58
Y	101 1001	131	59
Z	101 1010	132	5A
0	011 0000	060	30
1	011 0001	061	31
2	011 0010	062	32
3	011 0011	063	33
4	011 0100	064	34
5	011 0101	065	35
6	011 0110	066	36
7	011 0111	067	37
8	011 1000	070	38
9	011 1001	071	39
Blank	010 0000	040	20
.	010 1110	056	2E
(	010 1000	050	28
+	010 1011	053	2B
$	010 0100	044	24
*	010 1010	052	2A
)	010 1001	051	29
−	010 1101	055	2D
/	010 1111	057	2F
,	010 1100	054	2C
=	011 1101	075	3D

ever possible. One of the most widely used schemes for error detection is the *parity method.*

A *parity bit* is an extra bit that is attached to a code group that is being transferred from one location to another. The parity bit is made either 0 or 1, depending on the number of 1s that are contained in the code group. Two different methods are used.

In the *even-parity method,* the value of the parity bit is chosen so that the total number of 1s in the code group (including the parity bit) is an *even* number. For example, suppose that the code group is 1000011. This is the ASCII character C. The code group has *three* 1s. Therefore, we will add a parity bit of 1 to make the total number of 1s an even number. The *new* code group, including the parity bit, thus becomes

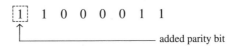

If the code group contains an even number of 1s to begin with, then the parity bit is given a value of 0. For example, if the code group is 1000001 (the character A), the assigned parity bit would be 0, so the new code, including the parity bit, would be 01000001.

The *odd-parity method* is used in exactly the same way except that the parity bit is chosen so that the total number of 1s (including the parity bit) is an *odd* number. For example, for the code group 1000001, the assigned parity bit would be a 1. For the code group 1000011, the bit would be a 0.

Regardless of whether even parity or odd parity is used, the parity bit becomes an actual part of the code word. For example, adding a parity bit to the 7-bit ASCII code produces an 8-bit code.

The parity bit is used to ensure that during the transmission of a character code from one place to another (for example, VDT to computer), any *single* errors can be detected. Thus, if odd parity is being used and the recipient of the transmitted character detects an *even* number of 1 bits, clearly the character code must be in error.

Obviously, the parity method has limitations insofar as it can only detect single errors and it cannot detect which bit is in error. There are more elaborate schemes used not only to check for multiple errors but also to detect where the errors are and to correct them. The error-correction schemes are not important to our study of microcomputers, so they are not discussed in this book.

▶ 1.3 BINARY ARITHMETIC

Arithmetic operations can be performed on binary numbers in exactly the same way as on decimal numbers. In some cases, however, certain binary operations are done differently from their decimal counterparts because of hardware considerations.

Binary Addition

The addition of two binary numbers is performed in exactly the same manner as the addition of decimal numbers. In fact, binary addition is simpler since there are fewer cases to learn. Let us first review a decimal addition.

$$
\begin{array}{r}
3\ 7\ 6 \quad \text{LSD} \\
+4\ \ 6\ \ 1 \\
\hline
8\ \ 3\ \ 7
\end{array}
$$

The least-significant-digit (LSD) position is operated on first, producing a sum of 7. The digits in the second position are then added to produce a sum of 13, which produces a *carry* of 1 into the third position. This produces a sum of 8 in the third position.

The same general steps are followed in binary addition. However, there are only four cases that can occur in adding the binary digits (bits) in any position. They are:

$$0 + 0 = 0$$

$$1 + 0 = 1$$

$$1 + 1 = 0 \text{ plus a carry of 1 into the next position}$$

$$1 + 1 + 1 = 1 \text{ plus a carry of 1 into the next position}$$

This last case occurs when the two bits in a certain position are 1 and there is a carry from the previous position. Here are several examples of the addition of two binary numbers:

$$
\begin{array}{r}
0\ 1\ 1\ (3) \\
+\ \ 1\ 1\ 0\ (6) \\
\hline
1\ 0\ 0\ 1\ (9)
\end{array}
\qquad
\begin{array}{r}
1\ 0\ 0\ 1\ (\ 9) \\
+\ \ 1\ 1\ 1\ 1\ (15) \\
\hline
1\ 1\ 0\ 0\ 0\ (24)
\end{array}
\qquad
\begin{array}{r}
1\ 1\ .\ 0\ 1\ 1\ (3.375) \\
+\ \ 1\ 0\ .\ 1\ 1\ 0\ (2.750) \\
\hline
1\ 1\ 0\ .\ 0\ 0\ 1\ (6.125)
\end{array}
$$

Addition is the most important arithmetic operation in digital systems because the operations of subtraction, multiplication, and division as they are performed in many modern digital computers and calculators actually use only addition as their basic operation.

Binary Subtraction

In many large computers and in most microcomputers, the operation of subtraction is performed using the operation of addition. This process requires the use of the *2's-complement form.*

The 2's-complement of a binary number is obtained by replacing each 0 with a 1, and each 1 with a 0, then adding 1 to the resulting number. The first step of changing each bit is called *1's-complementing.* For example, the 1's-complement of 10110110 is 01001001.

The 2's-complement of a binary number is formed by adding 1 to the 1's-complement of the number. For example, the 2's-complement of 10110110 is obtained as follows:

$$
\begin{array}{ll}
\text{original number} & 10110110 \\
\text{1's-complement} & 01001001 \\
\text{add 1} & +1 \\
\hline
\text{2's-complement} & 01001010
\end{array}
$$

The operation of subtraction can be performed by converting the *subtrahend* (the number to be subtracted) to its 2's-complement and then *adding* it to the *minuend* (the number being subtracted from) and disregarding any carry. To illustrate, consider subtracting the number 1001 from 1100 (decimal 9 from decimal 12).

Normal subtraction		2's-complement subtraction	
Minuend	1100	Minuend	1100
Subtrahend	−1001	2's-complement of subtrahend	+0111
Difference	0011	Sum	10011
		disregard final carry	

Thus, the final result is 0011 (decimal 3).

We will say more about 2's-complement subtraction after we introduce signed numbers.

Signed Numbers

In binary machines, the binary numbers are represented by a set of binary storage devices (for example, flip-flops). Each device represents one bit. For example, a 6-bit flip-flop register could store binary numbers ranging from 000000 to 111111 (zero to 63 in decimal). This represents the *magnitude* of the number. Because digital computers and calculators must handle negative as well as positive numbers, some means are required for representing the *sign* of the number (+ or −). This is usually done by adding another bit to the number, called the *sign bit*. In general, the common convention that has been adopted is that a 0 in the sign bit represents a positive number and a 1 in the sign bit represents a negative number. This is illustrated below. This number is divided into two parts: the leftmost bit is the sign bit, which is 0, indicating +; the other 7 bits are the value of magnitude of the number. Thus, the number is $+52_{10}$.

$$\boxed{0}\ 0\ 1\ 1\ 0\ 1\ 0\ 0_2 = +52_{10}$$

sign bit

In the same manner, the following number is -52_{10}.

$$\boxed{1}\ 0\ 1\ 1\ 0\ 1\ 0\ 0_2 = -52_{10}$$

sign bit

This method for representing signed numbers is called the *true-magnitude form* because the true value of the binary number is used for both + and − numbers and only a sign bit is added.

Computers that use the 2's-complement system represent positive numbers as described above; however, a different technique is used for representing *negative* numbers. Instead of using the true magnitude of the number, the 2's-complement of the number is used. This is illustrated as follows for the number -52_{10}.

$$\begin{array}{l} \boxed{0}\ 0\ 1\ 1\ 0\ 1\ 0\ 0 = +52_{10} \\ \boxed{1}\ \underbrace{1\ 0\ 0\ 1\ 1\ 0\ 0}\ = -52_{10} \end{array}$$

sign bit ⟶↑   2's-complement
                     of 0110100_2

Negation

Negation is the operation of converting a positive number to its equivalent negative number or a negative number to its equivalent positive number. When signed binary numbers are represented in the 2's-complement system, *negation* is performed simply by performing the 2's-complement operation. To illustrate, let's start with +9. Its signed representation is 01001. If we 2's-complement this, we get 10111. Clearly, this is a negative number since the sign bit is 1. Actually, 10111 represents −9, which is the negative equivalent of the number we started with. Likewise, we can start with the representation for −9, which is 10111. If we 2's-complement this, we get 01001, which we recognize as +9. These steps are diagrammed below:

$$\text{start with} \rightarrow \quad 01001 = +9$$

$$\text{2's-complement (negate)} \rightarrow \quad 10111 = -9$$

$$\text{negate again} \rightarrow \quad 01001 = +9$$

So we negate a signed binary number by 2's-complementing it. This negation changes the number to its equivalent of opposite sign.

EXAMPLE 1.5

Represent each of the following signed decimal numbers as signed binary numbers in the 2's-complement system. Use a total of 5 bits including the sign bit.
(a) −6   **(b)** −1   **(c)** −8

Solution

(a) Start by writing +6 using 5 bits:

$$\begin{array}{ll} +6 = 00110 & \\ \quad\ \ 11001 & \text{(1's-complement)} \\ \underline{+\ 00001} & \text{(add 1)} \\ \quad\ \ 11010 & \text{(2's-complement representation of } -6) \end{array}$$

(b) Start with +1:

$$\begin{array}{ll} +1 = 00001 & \\ \quad\ \ 11110 & \text{(1's-complement)} \\ \underline{+\ 00001} & \text{(add 1)} \\ \quad\ \ 11111 & \text{(2's-complement representation of } -1) \end{array}$$

(c) Start with $+8$:

$$+8 = 01000$$
$$10111 \quad \text{(1's-complement)}$$
$$+ \ 00001 \quad \text{(add 1)}$$
$$11000 \quad \text{(2's-complement representation of } -8)$$

EXAMPLE 1.6 _____

Each of the following numbers is a signed binary number in the 2's-complement system. Determine the decimal value in each case:

(a) 01110   **(b)** 10100   **(c)** 11110

Solution

(a) The sign bit is 0, therefore the number is *positive* and the other 4 bits represent the true magnitude of the number. That is, $01110_2 = +14_{10}$. Thus, the decimal number is **+14.**

(b) The sign bit is 1, therefore we can see that the number is *negative* but we cannot tell what the magnitude of the number is. We can find the magnitude by *negating* (2's-complementing) the number to convert it to its positive equivalent.

$$10100 \quad \text{(original negative binary number)}$$
$$01011 \quad \text{(1's-complement)}$$
$$+ \ 00001 \quad \text{(add 1)}$$
$$01100 \quad (+12)$$

Since the result of the negation is $01100_2 = +12_{10}$, the original number 10100_2 must be equivalent to -12_{10}.

(c) Follow the same procedure as in (b):

$$11110 \quad \text{(original negative binary number)}$$
$$00001 \quad \text{(1's-complement)}$$
$$+ \ 00001 \quad \text{(add 1)}$$
$$00010 \quad (+2)$$

Thus, $11110_2 = -2_{10}$.

▶ 1.4 ADDITION USING SIGNED NUMBERS

Now we will investigate how the operations of addition and subtraction are performed in digital computers that use the 2's-complement representation for negative numbers. In the various cases to be considered, it is important to remember that the sign-bit portion of each number is operated on the same as the magnitude portion. A 5-bit representation including the sign bit is used in the following examples.

Case I: Two Positive Numbers

The addition of two positive numbers is straightforward. Consider the addition of $+9$ and $+4$.

```
   +9  ⟶  0  1  0  0  1 (augend)
+(+4)  ⟶  0  0  1  0  0 (addend)
          --------------
          0  1  1  0  1 (sum = +13)
          ↑
          └ sign bits
```

Note that the sign bits of the *augend* and *addend* are both 0 and the sign bit of the sum is 0, indicating that the sum is positive.

Case II: Positive Number and Smaller Negative Number

Consider the addition of +9 and −4. Remember that the −4 will be in its 2's-complement form.

```
            ┌ sign bits
            ↓
   +9  ⟶    0  1  0  0  1
+(−4)  ⟶    1  1  1  0  0
            --------------
         1̸  0  0  1  0  1
         ↑
         └ this carry is disregarded, so the
           result is 00101 (sum = +5)
```

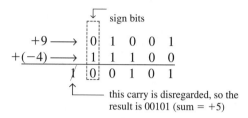

In this case, the sign bit of the addend is 1. Note that the sign bits also participate in the addition process. In fact, a carry is generated in the last position of addition. *This carry is disregarded,* so the final sum is 00101, which is equivalent to +5.

Case III: Positive Number and Larger Negative Number

Consider the addition of −9 and +4.

```
   −9  ⟶ 1  0  1  1  1
+(+4)  ⟶ 0  0  1  0  0
         --------------
         1  1  0  1  1 (sum = −5)
```

The sum here has a sign bit of 1, indicating a negative number. Because the sum is negative, it is in 2's-complement form, so the last four bits (1011) represent the 2's-complement of 0101 (equivalent to decimal 5). Thus, 11011 is equivalent to −5, the correct expected result.

Case IV: Two Negative Numbers

```
   −9  ⟶  1  0  1  1  1
+(−4)  ⟶  1  1  1  0  0
          --------------
       1̸  1  0  0  1  1
       ↑
       └ this carry is disregarded, so the
         result is 10011 (sum = −13)
```

The final result is again negative and in 2's-complement form with a sign bit of 1.

Case V: Equal and Opposite Numbers

$$
\begin{array}{r}
-9 \longrightarrow 1 \quad 0 \quad 1 \quad 1 \quad 1 \\
+(+9) \longrightarrow 0 \quad 1 \quad 0 \quad 0 \quad 1 \\
\hline
\not{1} \quad 0 \quad 0 \quad 0 \quad 0 \quad 0
\end{array}
$$

↰— disregard, so the result is 00000
(sum = +0)

The final result is obviously "plus zero," as expected.

▶ 1.5 SUBTRACTION IN THE 2'S-COMPLEMENT SYSTEM

The subtraction operation using the 2's-complement system actually involves the operation of addition and is really no different from the cases considered in the preceding section. When subtracting one binary number (the *subtrahend*) from another binary number (the *minuend*), the procedure is as follows:

1. Take the 2's-complement of the subtrahend, *including* the sign bit. If the subtrahend is a positive number, this will change it to a negative number in 2's-complement form. If the subtrahend is a negative number, this will change it to a positive number in true binary form. In other words, we are changing the sign of the subtrahend.
2. After taking the 2's-complement of the subtrahend, it is *added* to the minuend. The minuend is kept in its original form. The result of this addition represents the required *difference*. The sign bit of this difference determines whether it is + or − and whether it is in true binary form or 2's-complement form.

Let us consider the case where +4 is to be subtracted from +9.

$$\text{minuend} \quad (+9) \longrightarrow 0\,1\,0\,0\,1$$

$$\text{subtrahend} (+4) \longrightarrow 0\,0\,1\,0\,0$$

Change subtrahend to its 2's-complement form (11100). Now add this to the minuend.

$$
\begin{array}{r}
0 \quad 1 \quad 0 \quad 0 \quad 1 \\
+1 \quad 1 \quad 1 \quad 0 \quad 0 \\
\hline
\not{1} \quad 0 \quad 0 \quad 1 \quad 0 \quad 1
\end{array}
$$

↰— disregard, so the result is 00101 = +5

When the subtrahend is changed to its 2's-complement, it actually becomes −4, so we are adding +9 and −4, which is the same as subtracting +4 from +9. This is the same as Case II of the preceding section. Any subtraction operation, then, actually becomes one of addition when the 2's-complement system is used. This feature of the 2's-complement system has made it the most widely used method, since it allows addition and subtraction to be performed by the same circuitry.

The reader should verify the results of using the foregoing procedure for the following subtractions.

1. $+9 - (-4)$
2. $-9 - (+4)$
3. $-9 - (-4)$
4. $+4 - (-4)$

Remember: When the result has a sign bit of 1, it is negative and in 2's-complement form.

Overflow

In each of the previous addition and subtraction examples, the numbers that were added consisted of a sign bit and 4 magnitude bits. The answers also consisted of a sign bit and 4 magnitude bits. Any carry into the sixth bit position was disregarded. In all of the cases considered, the magnitude of the answer was small enough to be represented by 4 binary bits. Let's look at the addition of $+9$ and $+8$.

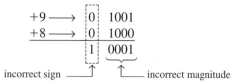

$$\begin{array}{cccc}
+9 \longrightarrow & 0 & 1001 \\
+8 \longrightarrow & 0 & 1000 \\
\hline
& 1 & 0001 \\
\end{array}$$

incorrect sign ⟶   ⟶ incorrect magnitude

The answer has a negative sign bit, which is obviously incorrect. The answer should be $+17$, but the magnitude 17 requires more than 4 bits and therefore *overflows* into the sign-bit position. This overflow condition always produces an incorrect result, and its occurrence is detected by examining the sign bit of the result and comparing it with the sign bits of the numbers being added. In a computer, a special circuit is used to detect any overflow condition and to signal that the answer is erroneous.

▶ 1.6 MULTIPLICATION OF BINARY NUMBERS

The multiplication of binary numbers is done in the same manner as multiplication of decimal numbers. The process is actually simpler since the multiplier digits are either 0 or 1, so that at any time we are multiplying by 0 or 1 and no other digits. The following example illustrates:

$$\begin{array}{ccccccc}
& & & 1 & 0 & 0 & 1 & \longleftarrow \text{multiplicand} = 9_{10} \\
& & & 1 & 0 & 1 & 1 & \longleftarrow \text{multiplier} = 11_{10} \\
\hline
& & & 1 & 0 & 0 & 1 & \\
& & 1 & 0 & 0 & 1 & & \\
& 0 & 0 & 0 & 0 & & & \\
1 & 0 & 0 & 1 & & & & \\
\hline
1 & 1 & 0 & 0 & 0 & 1 & 1 & \longleftarrow \text{final product} = 99_{10} \\
\end{array}$$

partial products

In this example the multiplicand and multiplier are in true binary form and no sign bits are used. The steps followed in the process are exactly the same as in decimal multiplication. First, the LSB of the multiplier is examined; in our example it is a 1. This 1 multiplies the multiplicand to produce 1001, which is written down as the first partial product. Next, the second bit of the multiplier is examined. It is a 1, so 1001 is written for the second partial product. Note that this second partial product is *shifted* one place to the left relative to the first one. The third bit of the multiplier is 0, so 0000 is written as the third partial product; again, it is shifted one place to the left relative to the previous partial product. The fourth multiplier bit is 1, so the last partial product is 1001, shifted again one position to the left. The four partial products are then summed up to produce the final product.

Most digital machines can add only two binary numbers at a time. For this reason, the partial products formed during multiplication cannot all be added together at the same time. Instead, they are added together two at a time; that is, the first is added to the second and their sum is added to the third, and so on. This process is illustrated for the preceding example.

```
         ⎧    1  0  0  1 ←——— first partial product
    add  ⎨ 1  0  0  1       ←——— second partial product shifted left
         ⎩ ───────────
         ⎧  1  1  0  1  1 ←——— sum of first two partial products
    add  ⎨ 0  0  0  0       ←——— third partial product shifted left
         ⎩ ────────────
         ⎧   0  1  1  0  1  1 ←——— sum of first three partial products
    add  ⎨ 1  0  0  1          ←——— fourth partial product shifted left
         ⎩ ───────────────────
           1  1  0  0  0  1  1 ←——— sum of four partial products, which
                                    equals final total product
```

▶ 1.7 BINARY DIVISION

The process for dividing one binary number (the *dividend*) by another (the *divisor*) is the same as that which is followed for decimal numbers, what we usually refer to as "long division." The actual process is simpler in binary because when we are checking to see how many times the divisor "goes into" the dividend, there are only two possibilities, 0 or 1. To illustrate, consider the following examples of division:

```
              0  0  1  1
      1  1 ⟌ 1  0  0  1          (9 ÷ 3 = 3)
              0  1  1
              ─────────
              0  0  1  1
```

```
              0  0  1  0 . 1
    1  0  0 ⟌ 1  0  1  0 . 0      (10 ÷ 4 = 2.5)
              1  0  0
              ─────────
                    1  0  0
                    1  0  0
                    ─────────
                          0
```

In most modern digital machines, the subtractions that are part of the division operation are usually carried out using 2's-complement subtraction, that is, complementing the subtrahend and adding.

▶ 1.8 HEXADECIMAL ARITHMETIC

Hex numbers are used extensively in machine language computer programming and in conjunction with computer memories (that is, addresses). When working in these areas, there will be situations where hex numbers have to be added or subtracted. We will be adding and subtracting hexadecimal numbers throughout this text, so it is important to review the basic hex arithmetic operations.

Hex Addition

This can be done in much the same manner as decimal addition, as long as we remember that the largest hex digit is F instead of 9. To illustrate, let us add the hex numbers 58 and 24.

$$
\begin{array}{r}
58 \\
+24 \\
\hline
7C
\end{array}
$$

Adding the LSDs (8 and 4) produces 12, which is C in hex. There is no carry into the next digit position.

Now let us add 58_{16} and $4B_{16}$.

$$
\begin{array}{r}
58 \\
+4B \\
\hline
A3
\end{array}
$$

Here the addition of 8 and B can be thought of as $8 + 11 = 19_{10}$ (remember that $B_{16} = 11_{10}$). Since $19_{10} = 1 \times 16^1 + 3 \times 16^0 = 13_{16}$, we write down the 3 digit and carry a 1 into the next position. This carry is added to the 5 and 4 digits to produce A (remember that $A_{16} = 10_{10}$).

Here is another example:

$$
\begin{array}{r}
3AF \\
+23C \\
\hline
5EB
\end{array}
$$

The sum of F and C can be considered to be $15 + 12 = 27_{10}$. Since $27_{10} = 1 \times 16^1 + 11 \times 16^0 = 1B_{16}$, the sum digit is B and there is a carry of 1 into the second digit position.

Hex Subtraction

Remember that hex numbers are just an efficient way to represent binary numbers. Thus, we can subtract hex numbers using the same method as that used for binary numbers. The hex subtrahend will be 2's-complemented and then *added* to the minuend, and any carry out of the MSD position will be disregarded.

How do we 2's-complement a hex number? One way is to convert it to binary, 2's-complement the binary equivalent, and then convert it back to hex. This process is illustrated below.

$$
\begin{array}{lll}
\text{73A} & \longleftarrow \text{hex number} \\
0111 \quad 0011 \quad 1010 & \longleftarrow \text{convert to binary} \\
1000 \quad 1100 \quad 0110 & \longleftarrow \text{2's-complement it} \\
\text{8C6} & \longleftarrow \text{convert back to hex}
\end{array}
$$

There is a quicker procedure. Subtract *each* hex digit from F, then add 1 to the LSD. Let us try this for the same hex number from the example above.

$$
\begin{array}{ccc}
\text{F} & \text{F} & \text{F} \\
-7 & -3 & -A \\
\hline
8 & C & 5 \\
 & & +1 \\
\hline
8 & C & 6
\end{array}
$$

←— subtract each digit from F
←— add 1 to LSD
←— hex equivalent of 2's-complement

Try either of the foregoing procedures on the hex number E63. The correct result for the 2's-complement is $19D_{16}$.

EXAMPLE 1.7

Subtract $3A5_{16}$ from 592_{16}.

Solution   First, convert the subtrahend (3A5) to its 2's-complement form by using either method presented above. The result is C5B. Then add this to the minuend (592).

$$
\begin{array}{r}
592 \\
+ \ \text{C5B} \\
\hline
\cancel{1}\text{1ED}
\end{array}
$$

←— disregard carry

Ignoring the carry-out of the MSD addition, the result is $1ED_{16}$. We can prove that this is correct by adding $1ED_{16}$ to $3A5_{16}$ and checking to see that it equals 592_{16}.

Hex Negation

Negation of a hexadecimal number is the same as finding the 2's-complement of the binary equivalent of that hexadecimal number. If a hex number has its MSB (most significant bit) equal to 0, the hex number is positive. If a hex number has its MSB equal to 1, the hex number is negative. To negate a hex number we will use the same procedure that was used to negate a binary number to its equivalent of opposite sign.

EXAMPLE 1.8

Negate the following hexadecimal numbers using both methods:
(a) 63A   (b) 8AC

Solution

(a) *One way:* Start by writing the binary equivalent of $63A_{16}$.

$$63A_{16} \longrightarrow \begin{array}{l} 0110\ 0011\ 1010 \\ 1001\ 1100\ 0101 \\ 0000\ 0000\ 0001 \\ + \underline{\hspace{3.5cm}} \\ 1001\ 1100\ 0110 \end{array}$$

(positive hex number since MSB = 0)
(1's-complement)
(add 1)

(Negation of $63A_{16} = 9C6_{16}$)

Another way:

$$\begin{array}{ccc} F & F & F \\ \underline{-6} & \underline{-3} & \underline{-A} \\ 9 & C & 5 \\ & & +1 \\ \hline 9 & C & 6 \end{array}$$

← subtract each digit from F_{16}

← add 1 to LSD

← hex equivalent of 2's-complement

Thus, by using either method, the negation of the *positive* hex number $63A_{16}$ results in **$9C6_{16}$.** Clearly, $9C6_{16}$ is a *negative* number since its MSB = 1.

(b) Start by writing the binary equivalent of $8AC_{16}$.

$$8AC_{16} \longrightarrow \begin{array}{l} 1000\ 1010\ 1100 \\ 0111\ 0101\ 0011 \\ 0000\ 0000\ 0001 \\ + \underline{\hspace{3.5cm}} \\ 0111\ 0101\ 0100 \end{array}$$

(negative hex number since MSB = 1)
(1's-complement)
(add 1)

(Negation of $8AC_{16} = 754_{16}$)

Another way:

$$\begin{array}{ccc} F & F & F \\ \underline{-8} & \underline{-A} & \underline{-C} \\ 7 & 5 & 3 \\ & & +1 \\ \hline 7 & 5 & 4 \end{array}$$

← subtract each digit from F_{16}

← add 1 to LSD

← hex equivalent of 2's-complement

Thus, by using either method, the negation of the *negative* hex number $8AC_{16}$ results in **754_{16}.** Clearly, 754_{16} is a *positive* number since its MSB = 0.

GLOSSARY

Alphanumeric Codes Codes that represent numbers, letters, and operation characteristics (e.g., ASCII code).

BCD Code Binary-coded-decimal system, in which each digit of a decimal number is encoded in its 4-bit binary equivalent.

Binary Number System Number system that uses only the digits 0 and 1.

Bit Abbreviation for "binary digit."

Hexadecimal Number System Number system that uses the digits 0 through 9 and the alphabet letters A through F.

Negation The operation of converting a positive number to its equivalent negative number or a negative number to its equivalent positive number.

Octal Number System Number system that uses the digits 0 through 7.

1's-Complement Result obtained by taking a binary number and changing each bit to its opposite value.

Overflow When in the process of adding signed binary numbers a carry of 1 is generated from the MSB position of the number into the sign bit position.

Parity Bit Extra bit that is attached to a code group to make the number of 1s conform to a predetermined form (odd or even).

2's-Complement Result obtained by adding 1 to the 1's-complement of a binary number.

QUESTIONS AND PROBLEMS

Section 1.1

1. Convert each binary number to decimal:
   (a) 10110 (b) 10001101 (c) 100100001001 (d) 1111010111
2. Convert the following decimal values to binary:
   (a) 37 (b) 14 (c) 189 (d) 205 (e) 2313
3. What is the largest decimal value that can be represented by an 8-bit binary number? A 16-bit number?
4. Convert each octal number to its decimal equivalent.
   (a) 743 (b) 36 (c) 3777 (d) 257
5. Convert each decimal number to octal:
   (a) 59 (b) 372 (c) 919 (d) 65536
6. Convert each of the octal values from Problem 4 to binary.
7. Convert the binary numbers in Problem 1 to octal.
8. List the octal numbers in sequence from 165_8 to 200_8.
9. When a large decimal number is to be converted to binary, it is sometimes easier first to convert it to hex, and then from hex to binary. Try this procedure for 2313_{10} and compare it to the procedure used in Problem 2(e).
10. Convert each hex value to decimal:
    (a) 92 (b) 1A6 (c) 37FD (d) 2C0
11. Convert each decimal value to hex:
    (a) 75 (b) 314 (c) 2048 (d) 25619
12. Convert the binary numbers in Problem 1 to hexadecimal.
13. Convert the hex values in Problem 10 to binary.
14. In most microcomputers the *addresses* of memory locations are specified in hexadecimal. These addresses are sequential numbers that identify each memory circuit.

(a) A particular microcomputer can store an 8-bit number in each memory location. If the memory addresses range from 0000_{16} to $FFFF_{16}$, how many memory locations are there?

(b) Another microcomputer is specified to have 4096 memory locations. What range of hex addresses does this computer use?

15. List the hex numbers in sequence from 280_{16} to $2A0_{16}$.

Section 1.2

16. Encode each decimal number in BCD:
    (a) 47   **(b)** 962   **(c)** 187   **(d)** 42689627

17. How many bits are required to represent the decimal numbers in the range from 0 to 999 using straight binary code? Using BCD code?

18. The following numbers are in BCD. Convert them to decimal.
    (a) 1001011101010010   **(b)** 000110000100

19. Represent the statement "X = 25/Y" in ASCII code.

20. Attach an *even* parity bit to each of the ASCII codes for Problem 19 and give the results in hex.

21. The following code groups are being transmitted. Attach an *even*-parity bit to each group.
    (a) 10110110   **(b)** 00101000   **(c)** 11110111

22. Convert the following decimal numbers to BCD code and then attach an *odd*-parity bit.
    (a) 74   **(b)** 38   **(c)** 165   **(d)** 9201

Sections 1.3–1.8

23. Convert each decimal number to an 8-bit signed number in the 2's-complement system.
    (a) -31 **(b)** $+76$ **(c)** -1 **(d)** $+254$

24. Each of the numbers below is a signed number in the 2's-complement system. Determine the decimal equivalent of each.
    (a) 01101011   **(b)** 11101110   **(c)** 10000001

25. Negate each of the signed binary numbers of Problem 24. Determine the decimal equivalent of each.

26. Perform the following operations using the 2's-complement system representing each number with 5 bits including the sign bit.

(a) $+10$	**(b)** $+11$	**(c)** $+15$	**(d)** -10	**(e)** -7
$+(+\ 5)$	$+(-\ 6)$	$-(+\ 5)$	$+(+\ 5)$	$-(-8)$

27. Determine which of the following additions of signed binary numbers will result in an *overflow* condition.
    (a) $10011 + 00111$ **(b)** $10110 + 10001$ **(c)** $01000111 + 01000110$

28. Perform each hexadecimal operation.

(a) 597_{16} (b) 849_{16} (c) A3B (d) A3B
$+612_{16}$ $-5F4_{16}$ $+0C6$ $-0C6$

29. Convert $+75_{10}$ to its equivalent signed 8-bit binary number. Then, convert the signed 8-bit number to its hex equivalent. Finally, represent -75_{10} in hex by using hex negation.

2

Digital Circuits

OBJECTIVES

Upon completion of this chapter, you will be able to:

- Cite the differences between parallel and serial transmission.
- Understand the basic digital gates and tri-state logic.
- Understand several types of flip-flops including the SC flip-flop, the edge-triggered D flip-flop, the JK, and D-Type latch.
- Recognize synchronous and asynchronous flip-flop inputs.
- Analyze clock signals that are used by various types of computers and microcomputers.
- Understand the importance of the manufacturer's required Setup and Hold times for edge-triggered flip-flops.
- Analyze flip-flop registers used in parallel and serial data transfers.
- Cite the requirements and precautions that must be taken when connecting digital circuits using the data bus concept.
- Understand the operation of Decoders, Encoders, and Multiplexers.
- Analyze the basic operation of a typical arithmetic logic unit.
- Use the basic troubleshooting rules of digital systems.

INTRODUCTION

The circuitry of digital systems and digital computers is designed to operate on voltage signals that are digital in nature; that is, these signals can have only two possible values at any time. Figure 2.1 shows a typical digital waveform that goes between the levels of 0 volts (V) and +5 V. These voltage levels are assigned the binary values 0 and 1, respectively. These 0 and 1 representations are called *logic levels.* Although the logic levels in Fig. 2.1 are shown as exactly 0 V and +5 V, in practical systems each logic level will represent a range of voltages. For example, logic 0 (also referred to as a LOW) might be any voltage between 0 V and +0.8 V, and logic 1 (also called a HIGH) might range from +2 V to

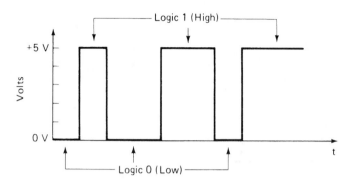

FIGURE 2.1   Typical digital signal.

+5 V. Incidentally, these are the logic-level ranges for the transistor–transistor logic (TTL) family of integrated circuits.

In digital computers, the digital voltage signals can represent different things. A single digital voltage signal can represent one bit of a binary number, one bit of some binary code (for example, BCD, ASCII), a logic or control level that signals the status of some situation, or several other possibilities. Regardless of what these digital or logic signals represent, the circuits that operate on these signals are called *digital logic circuits*. This chapter reviews all the logic circuits needed to understand and use computers.

▶ 2.1 PARALLEL AND SERIAL TRANSMISSION

It is generally necessary to transmit signals representing complete binary numbers consisting of several bits from one part of a system to another. There are basically two ways of doing this: parallel transmission and serial transmission.

In *parallel representation* or *transmission* of binary numbers or codes, each bit is derived from a separate circuit output and transmitted over a separate line. Figure 2.2A illustrates the arrangement for a 5-bit number. Each circuit output represents one binary digit (bit) and can be either 0 V (binary 0) or 5 V (binary 1). The five circuit outputs are present simultaneously, so at any time the complete binary number is available at the outputs. In Fig. 2.2A, the binary number 10110 is represented.

In *serial transmission,* which is illustrated in Fig. 2.2B, only *one* signal output line is used to transmit the binary number. This output line transmits the various bits one at a time in sequence, generally starting with the least significant bit. It should be apparent that some sort of timing is needed to be able to distinguish among the various bits. In the figure, a *clock signal* is used to provide the sequencing. A clock signal is an important part of most digital systems and is used to provide accurate timing of operations. In serial transmission, each time a clock pulse occurs, the output signal changes to the next bit of the binary number. In Fig. 2.2B, the output sequences through the bits 01011 (note that time increases from left to right). The actual binary number being transmitted is 11010, since the LSB is transmitted first.

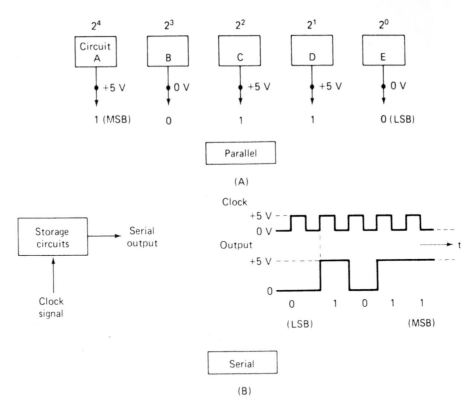

FIGURE 2.2   Parallel and serial transmission of binary numbers.

▶ 2.2 LOGIC GATES

Logic gates are digital circuits that have two or more logic inputs and produce a single output with a logic level determined by the logic levels present at the inputs. Figure 2.3 shows each of the basic logic gates, the mathematical expressions for their operation, and a table showing the output level for each combination of input levels.

AND Gate   The AND gate operates such that the output will be at the 1 level *only when all* inputs are 1. The mathematical expression for the two-input AND gate is written as $X = AB$, the same as ordinary multiplication. For a three-input gate, it would be $X = ABC$, and so on for more inputs.

OR Gate   The OR gate produces a 1 output when *any* input is at the 1 level. Its mathematical expression is $X = A + B$, where the $+$ stands for the OR operation and not normal addition. For a three-input OR gate, it would be $X = A + B + C$, and so on.

NOT Gate   This is actually not a gate since it can have only one input. It is commonly called an *inverter,* and it produces an output whose logic level is always the *opposite* of the input logic level. The mathematical statement of its operation is $X = \overline{A}$. The overbar always indicates the inversion (NOT) operation.

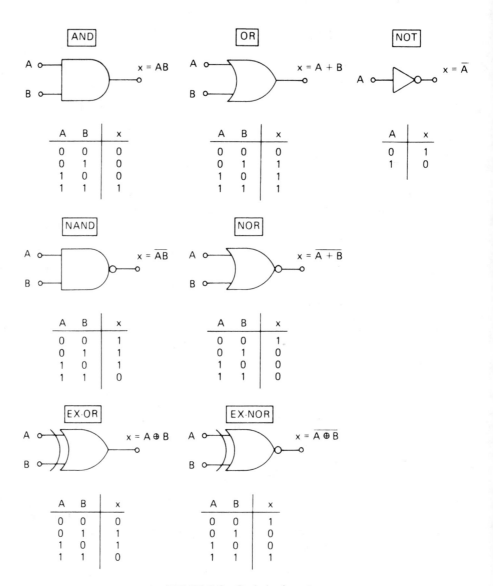

FIGURE 2.3   Basic logic gates.

NAND Gate   The NAND gate combines the AND and NOT operations, such that the output will be 0 *only when all* inputs are 1. Its logic expression is $X = \overline{AB}$, which indicates that inputs *A* and *B* are first ANDed and then the result inverted. Thus, a NAND gate always produces an output that is the inverse (opposite) of an AND gate.

NOR Gate   The NOR gate combines the OR and NOT operations such that the output will be 0 when *any* input is 1. Its logic expression is $X = \overline{A + B}$, which indicates that *A* and *B* are first ORed and then the result inverted. A NOR gate always gives an output logic level that is the inverse of an OR gate.

EXCLUSIVE-OR Gate   The EX-OR gate produces a 1 output only when the two inputs are at *different* logic levels. An EX-OR gate always has two inputs, and its output expression is $X = A\overline{B}+\overline{A}B$ which is often expressed as $X = A \oplus B$.

EXCLUSIVE-NOR Gate   This gate is the inverse of the EX-OR gate. It produces a 1 output only when the inputs are at the *same* logic level. The EX-NOR output expression is $X = \overline{A \oplus B} = \overline{A\overline{B}+\overline{A}B} = AB+\overline{A}\,\overline{B}$.

▶ 2.3 TRI-STATE (THREE-STATE) LOGIC

The development of *bus-organized* computers (discussed later) led to the development of a type of logic circuitry that has *three* distinct output states. These devices, called *tri-state logic* devices, have a third output condition in addition to the normal HIGH and LOW logic voltage levels. This third condition is called the *high-impedance,* or *high-Z* state.

Figure 2.4 shows the symbol and operation for a tri-state buffer equivalent to a 74HC125. The ENABLE input determines the output operation so that the output acts either as a normal output (ENABLE=0) or as a high-Z output (ENABLE=1). In the *enable* condition, the circuit behaves exactly as any logic buffer gate, producing an output voltage

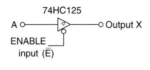

Operating Conditions

ENABLE ($\overline{E}$)	OUTPUT
HIGH	**Disabled**: output is Hi-Z state. Input A has no effect
LOW	**Enabled**: operates as a buffer

(A)

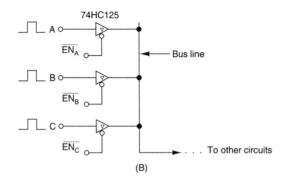

(B)

FIGURE 2.4   (A) Tri-state buffer; (B) typical bus arrangement.

level equivalent to the input logic level. In the *disable* high-Z state, the output terminal acts as if it were disconnected from the buffer; in other words, think of it as a virtual open circuit.

The ENABLE input ($\overline{E}$) in Fig. 2.4A is active-LOW, as indicated by the small circle on the device symbol. This means that the buffer output is enabled when ENABLE is LOW. Some tri-state buffers, such as the 74HC126, have an active-HIGH ENABLE input, so that their outputs are enabled when ENABLE is HIGH.

Tri-state buffers are often used in applications where several logic signals are to be connected to a common line called a *bus*. Although we examine this in more detail later, we can get the basic idea from Fig. 2.4B. This arrangement permits us to transmit any one of the three signals (A, B, or C) over the bus line to other circuits by enabling only that buffer corresponding to the desired signal. If more than one buffer is enabled at one time, then two or more buffer outputs will be active; this will produce a signal on the bus that is some combination of the two signals. This situation is usually not desirable and is called *bus contention*. It may also result in damage to the buffer's output circuitry because of the excess current flow when one output is trying to go LOW while the other is trying to go HIGH.

Many types of logic circuits are currently available with tri-state outputs. Another common one is the *tri-state inverter,* which operates exactly like the buffer in Fig. 2.4, except that it produces the inversion operation in the enabled state. Its symbol is the same as shown in Fig. 2.4, except that there is a circle on the output.

Other tri-state circuits include flip-flops, registers, memories, and almost all microcomputer and microprocessor interface chips.

▶ 2.4 FLIP-FLOPS

Logic gates produce outputs that depend on the *current* logic states of the inputs. Digital systems of almost any degree of complexity also require logic circuits that can produce outputs that depend on the *previous* states of the inputs, in other words, circuits with memory. The most widely used memory circuit is the *flip-flop* (FF).

Flip-flops are logic circuits that have two outputs, which are the inverse of each other. Figure 2.5 indicates these outputs as Q and $\overline{Q}$ (actually any letter could be used, but Q is the most common). The Q output is called the normal FF output and $\overline{Q}$ is the inverted FF output. When a FF is said to be in the HIGH (1) state or the LOW (0) state, this is the condition at the Q output. Of course, the $\overline{Q}$ output is always the inverse of Q.

There are two possible operating states for the FF: (1) Q = 0, $\overline{Q}$ = 1; and (2) Q = 1, $\overline{Q}$ = 0. The FF has one or more inputs, which are used to cause the FF to switch back and forth between these two states. Once an input signal causes a FF to go to a given state, the

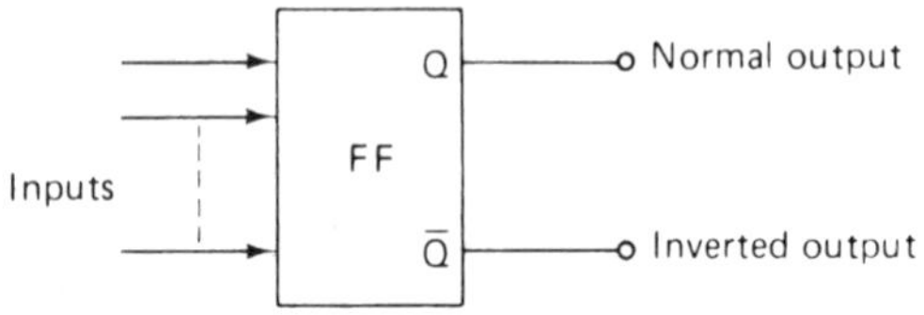

FIGURE 2.5.   *General flip-flop symbol.*

FF will remain in that state even after that input signal is terminated. This is its memory characteristic.

The flip-flop is known by several other names, including bistable multivibrator, latch, and binary, but we will generally use flip-flop because it is the most common designation in the digital field.

Basic FF Circuit

Figure 2.6 shows how two cross-coupled NAND gates are arranged to form the basic SET/CLEAR FF (SC FF). The circuit has two active-LOW inputs, $\overline{SET}$ and $\overline{CLEAR}$. These inputs are normally both 1. If the $\overline{SET}$ input is brought to 0, the Q output goes to the 1 state (and $\overline{Q} = 0$). Even if $\overline{SET}$ returns to 1, Q will remain at 1, owing to the internal feedback. This is called *setting* the FF. Similarly, when the $\overline{CLEAR}$ input is brought to 0, Q will go to the 0 state and stay there. This is called *clearing* the FF. The table in Fig. 2.6 summarizes this FF's operation. Note that $\overline{SET}$ and $\overline{CLEAR}$ should not go LOW simultaneously, or an ambiguous output state will result.

It should be mentioned here that the $\overline{CLEAR}$ input is often called the $\overline{RESET}$ input, and resetting the FF is the same as clearing the FF.

The FF of Fig. 2.6 has limited usefulness in itself, but it is the basic building block of many types of IC FFs. These IC FFs all utilize a *clock* input to synchronize the changing from one state to another. We will describe clocked FFs after a brief look at clock signals.

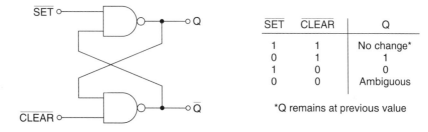

SET	CLEAR	Q
1	1	No change*
0	1	1
1	0	0
0	0	Ambiguous

*Q remains at previous value

FIGURE 2.6   Basic SC flip-flop made from NAND gates.

▶ 2.5 CLOCK SIGNALS

Most digital systems operate as *synchronous sequential systems*. What this means is that the sequence of operations that takes place is synchronized by a *master clock signal*, which generates periodic pulses that are distributed to all parts of the system. This clock signal is usually one of the forms shown in Fig. 2.7; most often it is a square wave (50 percent duty cycle), such as the one shown in Fig. 2.7B.

The clock signal is the signal that causes things to happen at regularly spaced intervals. In particular, operations in the system are made to take place at times when the clock signal is making a transition from 0 to 1 or from 1 to 0. These transition times are pointed out in Fig. 2.7. The 0-to-1 transition is called the *rising edge* or *positive-going edge* of the clock signal; the 1-to-0 transition is called the *falling edge* or *negative-going edge* of the clock signal.

The synchronizing action of the clock signal is the result of using *clocked flip-flops,* which are designed to change states on either (but not both) the rising edge or the falling edge of the clock signal. In other words, the clocked FFs will change states at the appropriate clock transition and will rest between successive clock pulses. The frequency of the clock pulses is generally determined by how long it takes the FFs and gates in the circuit to respond to the level changes initiated by the clock pulse, that is, the propagation delays of the various logic circuits.

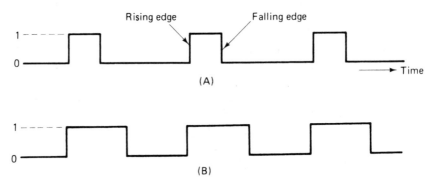

FIGURE 2.7   Clock signals.

The microcomputer we'll use in this textbook utilizes a single clock signal (E), but some computers, including many microcomputers, have their timing controlled by two or more clock signals. One common combination shown in Fig. 2.8 utilizes two clock signals identified by the symbols ϕ_1 and ϕ_2 (phase 1 and phase 2). This more complex clocking arrangement provides four different edges and three different states per period, compared to only two edges and two states per period for a single clock signal.

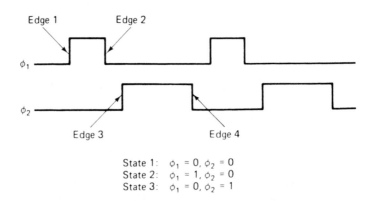

State 1: $\phi_1 = 0, \phi_2 = 0$
State 2: $\phi_1 = 1, \phi_2 = 0$
State 3: $\phi_1 = 0, \phi_2 = 1$

FIGURE 2.8   Two-phase clock signals.

Clocked FFs all have at least two types of inputs: a clock input (abbreviated CLK) and one or more control inputs. The control inputs are used to determine what state the FF output will go to when a signal is applied to the CLK input. The signal at the CLK input is the actual triggering signal that causes the FF to respond according to the control inputs.

Edge-Triggered D Flip-flop

Figure 2.9A shows the symbol and truth table for an edge-triggered D FF equivalent to a 7474. It is so called because it has a single control input, D. This FF operates such that the logic level present at the D input is transferred to the Q output *only* on the positive-going edge of the CLK input signal. The D input has no effect on Q at any other time, as illustrated by the example waveforms shown in Fig. 2.9B.

Note that the negative-going edge of the CLK signal has no effect on the FF output. There are edge-triggered D FFs that trigger *only* on the negative-going edge of the CLK input. These otherwise operate exactly the same and have the same symbol except for a small circle on the CLK input to indicate negative-edge triggering.

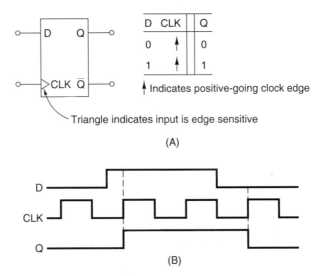

(A)

(B)

FIGURE 2.9   Positive edge-triggered D FF.

Edge-Triggered JK Flip-flop

The edge-triggered JK flip-flop is the most versatile type of FF available. As shown in Fig. 2.10, it uses two control inputs, J and K. These determine what will happen to the Q output when the positive edge of the CLK signal occurs, according to the accompanying truth table.

J = K = 0: If this condition is present when the positive edge of the CLK signal occurs, there will be no change in the state of the FF (see the waveforms in Fig. 2.10B).

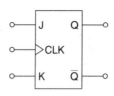

J	K	CLK	Q
0	0	↑	Q_0 (no change)
1	0	↑	1
0	1	↑	0
1	1	↑	$\overline{Q_0}$ (toggles)

Q_0 is state Q just prior to ↑ of CLK.

(A)

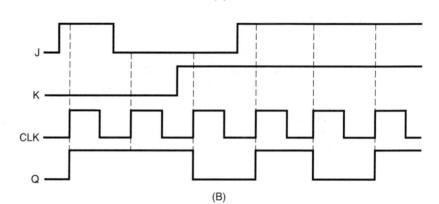

(B)

FIGURE 2.10   Edge-triggered JK FF.

J = 1, K = 0: This condition always produces Q = 1 on the occurrence of the positive edge of the CLK signal.

J = 0, K = 1: This always produces Q = 0 on the occurrence of the positive edge of the CLK signal.

J = 1, K = 1: If this condition is present when the positive edge of the CLK signal occurs, the Q output will switch to its opposite state (toggle).

Again, note that nothing happens to Q except on the positive edge of the CLK signal. There are negative edge-triggered JK FFs, whose operation is otherwise exactly the same. A small circle on the CLK input symbolizes negative-edge triggering.

D-Type Latch

The edge-triggered FFs can change states only when the appropriate edge of the CLK signal occurs. The D-type latch is similar to the edge-triggered D FF except that it can change states during the HIGH portion of the ENABLE signal. Figure 2.11 shows the D-type latch symbol and operation. As long as the ENABLE is HIGH, output Q will follow changes in the D input. When ENABLE goes LOW, Q will store (or latch) its last value, and the D input has no further effect.

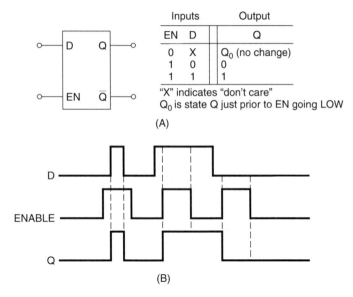

Inputs		Output
EN	D	Q
0	X	Q_0 (no change)
1	0	0
1	1	1

"X" indicates "don't care"
Q_0 is state Q just prior to EN going LOW

(A)

(B)

FIGURE 2.11   D-Type latch.

▶ 2.7 SYNCHRONOUS AND ASYNCHRONOUS FF INPUTS

For the clocked flip-flops that we have been studying, the J, K, and D inputs have been referred to as *control inputs.* These inputs are also called *synchronous inputs,* because their effect on the FF output is synchronized with the CLK input. As we have seen, the synchronous control inputs must be used in conjunction with a clock signal to trigger the FF.

Most clocked FFs also have one or more *asynchronous inputs,* which operate independently of the synchronous inputs and clock input. These asynchronous inputs can be used to set the FF to the 1 state or clear the FF to the 0 state at any time, regardless of the conditions at the other inputs. Stated in another way, the asynchronous inputs are *override* inputs, which can be used to override all the other inputs in order to place the FF in one state or the other.

Figure 2.12 shows a clocked JK FF with present ($\overline{PRE}$) and clear ($\overline{CLR}$) inputs. These active-LOW asynchronous inputs are activated by a 0 level, as indicated by the small circles on the FF symbol. The accompanying truth table indicates how these inputs operate. A LOW on the $\overline{PRE}$ input *immediately* sets Q to the 1 state. A LOW on the $\overline{CLR}$ *immediately* clears Q to the 0 state. Simultaneously LOW levels on $\overline{PRE}$ and $\overline{CLR}$ are forbidden, since this leads to an ambiguous condition. When neither of these inputs is LOW, the FF is free to respond to the J, K, and CLK inputs, as previously described.

It is important to realize that these asynchronous inputs respond to dc levels. This means that if a constant 0 is held on the $\overline{PRE}$ input, the FF will remain in the Q = 1 state regardless of what is occurring at the other inputs. Similarly, a constant LOW on the $\overline{CLR}$ input holds the FF in the Q = 0 state. Thus, the asynchronous inputs can be used to hold the FF in a particular state for any desired interval. Most often, however, the asynchronous

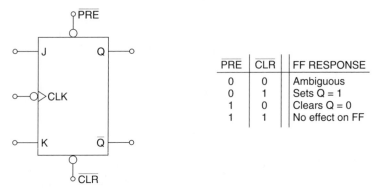

PRE	CLR	FF RESPONSE
0	0	Ambiguous
0	1	Sets Q = 1
1	0	Clears Q = 0
1	1	No effect on FF

FIGURE 2.12   Clocked JK FF with asynchronous inputs.

inputs are used to set or clear the FF to the desired state by application of a momentary pulse.

▶ 2.8 SETUP AND HOLD TIMES

Two timing requirements must be met if a clocked JK FF is to respond reliably to its control inputs when the active CLK transition occurs. These requirements are illustrated in Figure 2.13 for a JK FF that triggers on a PGT (positive-going transition).

The *setup time, t_S,* is the time interval immediately preceding the active transition of the CLK signal during which the synchronous input has to be maintained at the proper level. IC manufacturers usually specify the minimum allowable setup time $t_S(min)$. If this time requirement is not met, the FF may not respond reliably when the clock edge occurs.

The *hold time, t_H,* is the time interval immediately following the active transition of the CLK signal during which the synchronous input has to be maintained at the proper level. IC manufacturers usually specify the minimum acceptable value of hold time $t_H(min)$. If this time requirement is not met, the FF may not trigger reliably.

Thus, to ensure that a clocked JK FF will respond properly when the active clock transition occurs, the synchronous inputs must be stable (unchanging) for at least a time interval equal to $t_S(min)$ *prior* to the clock transition, and for at least a time interval equal to $t_H(min)$ *after* the clock transition.

IC flip-flops will have minimum allowable t_S and t_H values in the nanosecond range. Setup times are usually in the range 5 to 50 ns while hold times are generally from 0 to 10 ns. Notice that these times are measured between the 50 percent points on the transitions.

These timing requirements are very important in synchronous systems, because, as we shall see, there will be situations where the synchronous inputs to a FF are changing at approximately the same time as the CLK input.

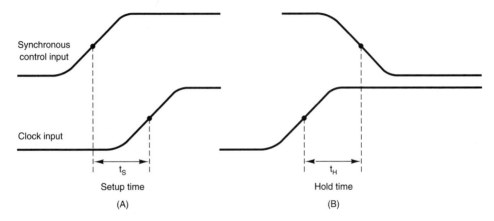

FIGURE 2.13 Control inputs have to be held stable for (A) a time, t_S, prior to active clock transition and for (B) a time, t_H, after the active clock transition.

▶ 2.9 FF REGISTERS

A simple *register* is a group of memory devices used to store binary information. More complex registers can modify the stored information in some manner. The most common register device is the FF, and a counter is an example of an FF register. Two other types of FF registers are buffer (storage) registers and shift registers.

As we will see, registers play a significant role in digital computer systems. In fact, in its simplest form, a computer is a system of registers in which binary information is transferred from one register to another register, operated on in some way, and then transferred to another register. For the time being, we will concentrate on the operation of transferring information from one register to another.

Parallel Transfer

Figure 2.14 shows two 3-bit registers. The X register consists of FFs X_1, X_2, and X_3; the Y register consists of FFs Y_1, Y_2, and Y_3. Each FF is an edge-triggered D FF. The TRANSFER pulse applied to the CLK inputs of the Y register causes the value of X_1 to be transferred to Y_1, X_2 to Y_2, and X_3 to Y_3. This transfer of the contents of the X register into the Y register is a *parallel* transfer, since the 3 bits are transferred simultaneously. Since we will be dealing with register-to-register transfers quite a bit, we will use the following shorthand notation to indicate such a transfer:

$$[X] \to [Y]$$

The symbol [X] will mean the contents of the X register, and similarly for [Y]. The arrow indicates the direction of the transfer.

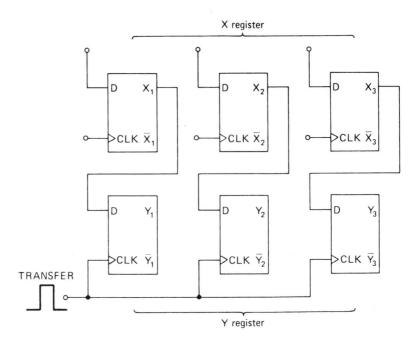

FIGURE 2.14   Parallel transfer from X register to Y register.

Serial Transfer

Serial transfer from one register to another occurs 1 bit at a time. Before examining serial transfer, we will look at the operation of a shift register. Figure 2.15 shows a 3-bit shift register using edge-triggered JK FFs. The FFs are connected such that the current content of each FF is transferred to the FF on its right when the negative edge of a SHIFT pulse occurs. In addition, the level present on the serial input S is transferred into FF X_2.

To illustrate, assume that the X-register contents are $X_2 = 1$, $X_1 = 0$, $X_0 = 1$. Using the shorthand notation, we can write this as [X] = 101. Also, assume that S = 0. Each of these logic levels is setting up the succeeding FF to take on its value when the SHIFT pulse occurs. Thus, after the occurrence of the negative edge of the SHIFT pulse, the register contents are [X] = 010; that is, the level on S has shifted to X_2, the *previous* level of X_2 has shifted to X_1, and the *previous* level of X_1 has shifted to X_0. The *previous* value of X_0 is lost.

If S is now changed to 1 and a second SHIFT pulse occurs, the result is [X] = 101. With S = 1, a third SHIFT pulse produces [X] = 110; and so on.

Figure 2.16 shows two 3-bit shift registers connected so that the contents of the X register will transfer serially into the Y register. The complete transfer requires *three* SHIFT pulses, one per bit. The complete transfer sequence is shown in the diagram, assuming that S = 0, [X] = 101, and [Y] = 011.

Serial transfer requires more time than parallel transfer because of the need to shift 1 bit at a time. On the other hand, serial requires fewer interconnections between the two registers.

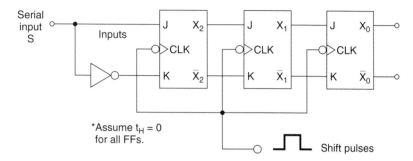

FIGURE 2.15   Shift register.

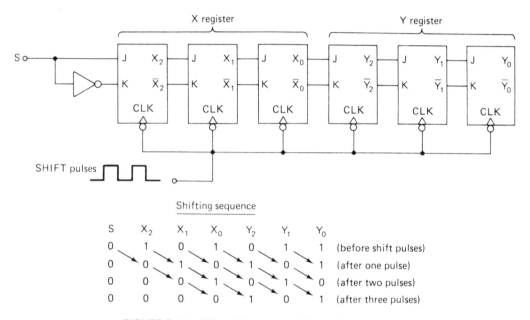

Shifting sequence

S	X₂	X₁	X₀	Y₂	Y₁	Y₀	
0	1	0	1	0	1	1	(before shift pulses)
0	0	1	0	1	0	1	(after one pulse)
0	0	0	1	0	1	0	(after two pulses)
0	0	0	0	1	0	1	(after three pulses)

FIGURE 2.16   [X] → [Y] using serial transfer.

▶ 2.10 IC REGISTERS

It is rarely necessary to construct registers from individual FFs because of the availability of a wide variety of integrated-circuit registers. We will not attempt to show all the numerous variations but will concentrate on the basic types used in microcomputer applications.

Data-Latching Registers

The data-latching type of register uses the D-type latches discussed earlier. Figure 2.17 shows the representation for a 4-bit latching register. The ENABLE input is common to each latch and causes the data outputs Q_3, Q_2, Q_1, and Q_0 to respond to the data inputs D_3, D_2, D_1, and D_0 as follows:

1. While ENABLE is HIGH, each Q output follows the logic levels present on its corresponding D input (for example, Q_3 follows D_3).
2. When ENABLE goes LOW, each Q output latches (holds) the last D value and cannot change even if the D input changes.

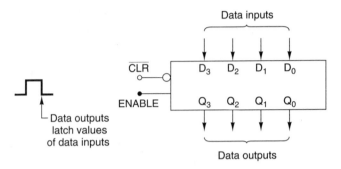

FIGURE 2.17   Four-bit latching register.

The CLEAR input is used to clear each output to 0 simultaneously on a LOW level.

Edge-Triggered Registers

The edge-triggered type of register (Fig. 2.18) uses edge-triggered D FFs so that the data inputs only affect the data outputs at the instant when CLK makes a *low-to-high* transition. At that time, the levels present on the D inputs transfer to the Q outputs. Variations in the D input levels will cause no change in the Q outputs, but for proper data transfer to occur, it is necessary that the D inputs be stable when the CLK transition occurs.

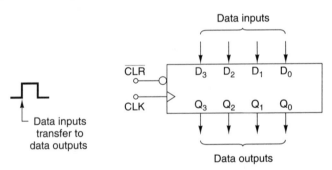

FIGURE 2.18   Four-bit edge-triggered register.

Tri-state Registers

In most modern computers the transfer of data takes place over a common set of connecting lines called a **data bus**. In these bus-organized computers, many different devices can have their outputs and inputs tied to the common data bus lines. Because of this, the devices that are tied to the data bus will often have tri-state outputs, or they will be tied to the data bus through tri-state buffers such as the one in Fig. 2.4.

Some of the devices that are commonly connected to a data bus are (1) microprocessors, discussed in Chapter 6; (2) semiconductor memory chips, covered in Chapter 3; (3) numerous types of microcomputer peripherals such as analog-to-digital converters (ADCs), digital-to-analog converters (DACs), universal asynchronous receiver transmitters (UARTs), peripheral interface adapter (PIA), just to mention a few, discussed in Chapter 9.

Almost always, the devices connected to a data bus will contain registers that hold their data. The outputs of these registers will have tri-state buffers to allow data busing. There are many IC registers available that include the tri-state buffers on the same chip. One of these is the TTL 74173 (and its CMOS counterpart, the 74HC173), whose logic symbol is shown in Fig. 2.19.

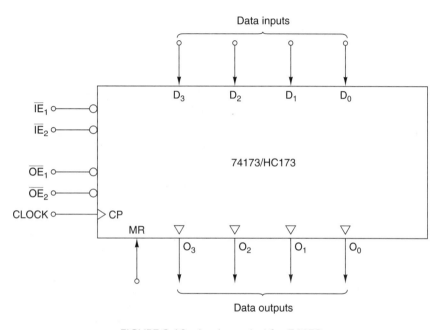

FIGURE 2.19   Logic symbol for 74173.

The 74173 is a 4-bit register with parallel in/parallel out capability. There are four FF outputs that are internally connected to tri-state buffers, which are *enabled* when $\overline{OE}_1 = \overline{OE}_2 = 0$ and provide the chip outputs 0_0–0_3. If either $\overline{OE}_1$, $\overline{OE}_2$, or both are equal to a 1, the chip outputs 0_0–0_3 are in the high-Z state. The data applied to the chip inputs on D_0–D_3 are connected to the D inputs of the register FFs through internal logic. This logic circuitry allows for two modes of operation: (1) *load data:* When $\overline{IE}_1 = \overline{IE}_2 = 0$, the data at the D_0–D_3 inputs are transferred into the FFs on the *positive-going transition* of the clock pulse at CP; (2) *hold data:* When $\overline{IE}_1$, $\overline{IE}_2$, or both are equal to 1, the data stored in the FF register remain the same when the *positive-going transition* of CP occurs. It should be noted that the load operation can take place even if the outputs are in a high-Z state. Also, when MR = 1, the contents of the register FFs are cleared *asynchronously* regardless of the logic states on $\overline{IE}_1$, $\overline{IE}_2$, $\overline{OE}_1$, and $\overline{OE}_2$.

▶ 2.11 DATA BUSING

Figure 2.20 illustrates a typical situation in which a microprocessor (the CPU chip in a microcomputer) is connected to several devices over an 8-line data bus. The data bus is simply a collection of conducting paths over which digital data are transmitted from one device to another. Each device provides an 8-bit output that is sent to the inputs of the

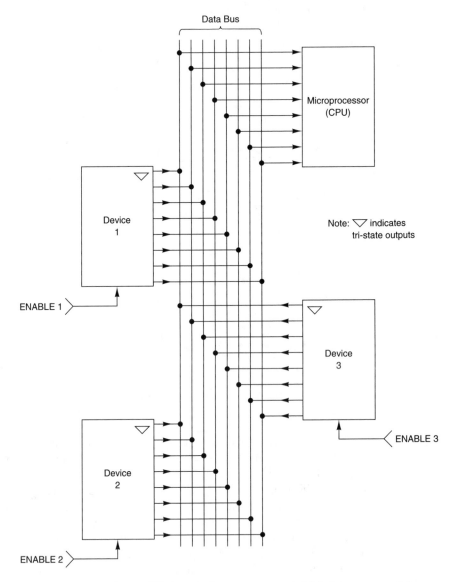

FIGURE 2.20   Three different devices can transmit 8-bit data over an 8-line data bus to a microprocessor; only one device at a time is enabled so that bus contention is avoided.

microprocessor over the 8-line data bus. Clearly, since the outputs of each of the three devices are connected to the same microprocessor inputs over the data bus conducting paths, we have to be aware of bus contention problems (Section 2.3) where two or more signals tied to the same bus line are active and are essentially fighting each other. Bus contention is avoided if the devices have tri-state outputs or are connected to the bus through tri-state buffers (Section 2.3). The enable inputs to each device (or its buffer) are used to ensure that no more than one device's outputs are active at a given time.

EXAMPLE 2.1

(a) Refer to the circuit of Fig. 2.20, and describe the conditions necessary to transmit data from device 3 to the microprocessor.

(b) What will be the status of the data bus when none of the devices is enabled?

Solution

(a) ENABLE3 has to be activated; ENABLE2 and ENABLE1 must be in their inactive state. This will put the outputs of device 1 and device 2 in the high-Z state and essentially disconnect them from the bus. The outputs of device 3 will be activated so that their logic levels will appear on the data bus lines and be transmitted to the inputs of the microprocessor. We can visualize this by covering up device 1 and device 2 as if they were not part of the circuit; then we are left with device 3 alone connected to the microprocessor over the data bus.

(b) If none of the device enable inputs is activated, all of the device outputs are in the high-Z state. This disconnects all device outputs from the bus. Thus, there is no definite logic level on any of the data bus lines; they are in the indeterminate state. This condition is known as a *floating* bus, and each data bus line is said to be in a *floating* (indeterminate) state. An oscilloscope display of a floating bus line would be unpredictable. A logic probe would indicate an indeterminate logic level.

▶ 2.12 DATA BUS OPERATION

The data bus is very important in computer systems, and its significance will not be appreciated until our later studies of memories and microprocessors. For now, we will illustrate the data bus concept for register-to-register data transfer. Figure 2.21 shows a bus-organized system for three 74173 tri-state registers. Note that each register has its pair of $\overline{OE}$ inputs tied together as one $\overline{OE}$ input, and similarly for the $\overline{IE}$ inputs. Also note that the registers will be referred to as registers A, B, and C from top to bottom. This is indicated by the subscripts on each input and output.

In this arrangement, the data bus consists of four lines labeled DB_0–DB_3. Corresponding outputs of each register are connected to the same data bus line (for example, O_{3A}, O_{3B}, and O_{3C} are connected to DB_3). Because the three registers have their outputs connected together, it is imperative that only one register has its outputs enabled while the other two register outputs are in the high-Z state. Otherwise, there will be

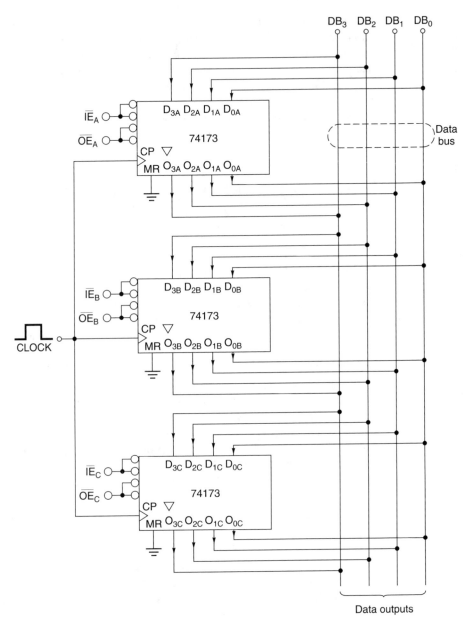

FIGURE 2.21   Tri-state registers connected to data bus.

"bus contention" (two or more sets of outputs fighting each other) and possible chip damage.

Corresponding register inputs are also tied to the same bus line (for example, D_{3A}, D_{3B}, and D_{3C} are tied to DB_3). Thus, the levels on the bus will always be ready to be transferred to one or more of the registers depending on the $\overline{IE}$ inputs.

Data Transfer Operation

The contents of any one of the three registers can be parallel-transferred over the data bus to one of the other registers through the proper application of logic levels to the register ENABLE inputs. In a typical system, the control unit of a computer (that is, the CPU) will generate the signals that select which register will put its data on the data bus, and which one will take the data from the data bus. Example 2.2 will illustrate this. Note that in Example 2.2 and throughout the text we will use brackets to indicate "the contents of"; for instance, [A] represents "the contents of register A."

EXAMPLE 2.2

Describe the input signal requirements for transferring $[A] \rightarrow [C]$.

Solution   First, only register A should have its outputs enabled. That is, we need

$$\overline{OE}_A = 0, \overline{OE}_B = \overline{OE}_C = 1$$

This will place the contents of register A onto the data bus lines.
      Next, only register C should have its inputs enabled. For this we want

$$\overline{IE}_C = 0, \overline{IE}_A = \overline{IE}_B = 1$$

This will allow only register C to accept data from the data bus when the *positive-going transition* of the clock signal occurs.
      Finally, a clock pulse is required to actually transfer the data from the bus into the register C FFs.

It is easy to see how we can add more registers to the data bus so that a greater number of register-to-register data transfers are possible. Of course, each register adds two more ENABLE inputs that have to be controlled for each data transfer. Each register also adds data inputs that have to be driven by the outputs of the register that is putting data on the bus. In systems where a large number of registers (or other devices) are connected to the bus, the register outputs may have to be buffered by circuits that are called *bus drivers*. Even when the devices have high input impedances, the total capacitive load connected to each bus line will deteriorate the transition times of the level changes on each bus line. A bus driver IC will have very low output resistance in either logic state and will be able to charge and discharge the bus capacitances more rapidly than a normal IC.

Bus Signals

The timing diagram in Fig. 2.22 shows the various signals involved in the transfer of the data 1011 from register A to register C. The $\overline{IE}$ and $\overline{OE}$ lines that are not shown are assumed to be in their inactive HIGH state. Prior to time t_1, the $\overline{IE}_C$ and $\overline{OE}_A$ lines are also HIGH, so that all of the registers' outputs are disabled and none of the registers will be placing their data on the data bus lines. In other words, the data bus lines are in the high-Z or "floating" state as represented by the hatched lines on the timing diagram. The high-Z state does not correspond to any particular voltage level.

At t_1 the $\overline{\text{IE}}_\text{C}$ and $\overline{\text{OE}}_\text{A}$ inputs are activated. The outputs of register A are enabled, and they start changing the data bus lines DB_3 through DB_0 from the high-Z state to the logic levels 1011. After allowing time for the logic levels on the data bus to stabilize from invalid logic levels to valid logic levels (t_1–t_2), the PGT of the clock is applied at t_2. This PGT will transfer these logic levels into register C, since $\overline{\text{IE}}_\text{C}$ is active. If the PGT occurs before the data bus has valid logic levels, unpredictable data will be transferred into C.

At t_3, the $\overline{\text{IE}}_\text{C}$ and $\overline{\text{OE}}_\text{A}$ lines return to the inactive state. As a result, register A's outputs go to the high-Z state. This removes the register A output data from the bus lines and the bus lines return to the high-Z state.

Note that the data bus lines show valid logic levels only during the time interval when register A's outputs are enabled. At all other times, the data bus lines are floating, and there is no way to easily predict what they would look like if displayed on an oscilloscope. A logic probe would give an "indeterminate" indication if it were monitoring a floating bus line. Also note the relatively slow rate at which the signals on the data bus lines are changing. Although this effect has been somewhat exaggerated in the diagram, it is a characteristic common to bus systems and is caused by the capacitive load on each line. This load consists of a combination of parasitic capacitance and the capacitances contributed by each input and output connected to the line.

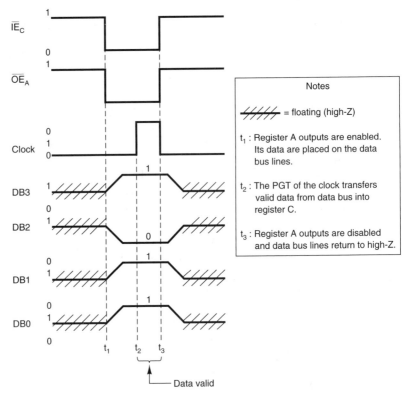

FIGURE 2.22 Signal activity during the transfer of the data 1011 from register A to register C.

Simplified Bus Timing Diagram

The timing diagram in Fig. 2.22 shows the signals on each of the four data bus lines. This same kind of signal activity occurs in digital systems that use the more common data buses of 8, 16, or 32 lines. For these larger buses, the timing diagrams like Fig. 2.22 would get excessively large and cumbersome. There is a simplified method for showing the signal activity that occurs on a set of bus lines that uses only a single timing waveform to represent the complete set of bus lines. This is illustrated in Fig. 2.23 for the same data transfer situation depicted in Fig. 2.22. Notice how the data bus activity is represented. Especially note how the *invalid* data are shown on the diagram during the t_1–t_2 and t_3–t_4 intervals. Note also, how the *valid* data 1011 are indicated on the diagram during the t_2–t_3 interval. We will generally use this simplified bus timing diagram from now on.

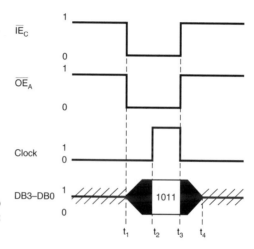

FIGURE 2.23   Simplified way to show signal activity on data bus lines.

Expanding the Bus

The data transfer operation of the four-line data bus of Fig. 2.21 is typical of the operation of larger data buses found in most computers and other digital systems, usually 8-, 16-, or 32-line data buses. These larger buses generally have many more than three devices tied to the bus, but the basic data transfer operation is the same: *One device has its outputs enabled so that its data are placed on the data bus; another device has its inputs enabled so that it can take these data off the bus and latch them into its internal circuitry on the appropriate clock edge.*

The number of lines on the data bus will depend on the size of the data **word** (unit of data) that is to be transferred over the bus. A computer that has an 8-bit word size will have an 8-line data bus, a computer that has a 16-bit word size will have a 16-line data bus, and so on. The number of devices connected to a data bus will vary from one computer to another and depends on factors such as how much memory the computer has and the number of input and output devices that must communicate with the CPU over the data bus.

All device outputs must be tied to the bus through tri-state buffers. Some devices, like the 74173 register, have these buffers on the same chip. Other devices will need to be connected to the bus through an IC called a **bus driver.** A bus driver IC has tri-state outputs with a very low output impedance that can rapidly charge and discharge the bus capacitance. This bus capacitance represents the cumulative effect of all the parasitic capacitances of the different inputs and outputs tied to the bus, and can deteriorate the bus signal transition times if they are not driven from a low-impedance signal source. Figure 2.24 shows a 74HC541 octal bus driver IC connecting the outputs of an 8-bit analog-to-digital converter (ADC) to a data bus. The bus driver's two enable inputs are tied together so that a LOW on the common enable line will allow the ADC's outputs through the buffers and onto the data bus from where they can be transferred to another device.

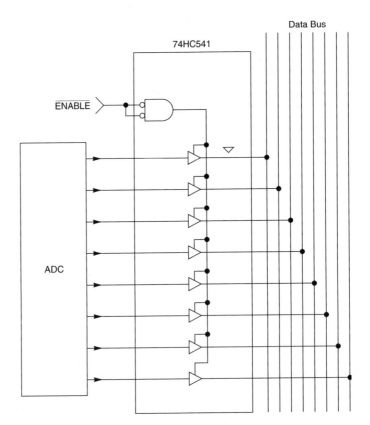

FIGURE 2.24 A 74HC541 octal bus driver connects the outputs of an analog-to-digital converter (ADC) to an 8-line data bus.

Simplified Bus Representation

Usually many devices are connected to the same data bus. On a circuit schematic this can produce a confusing array of lines and connections. For this reason, a more simplified representation of data bus connections is often used on block diagrams and in all but the most detailed circuit schematics. This simplified representation is shown in Fig. 2.25 for an 8-line data bus.

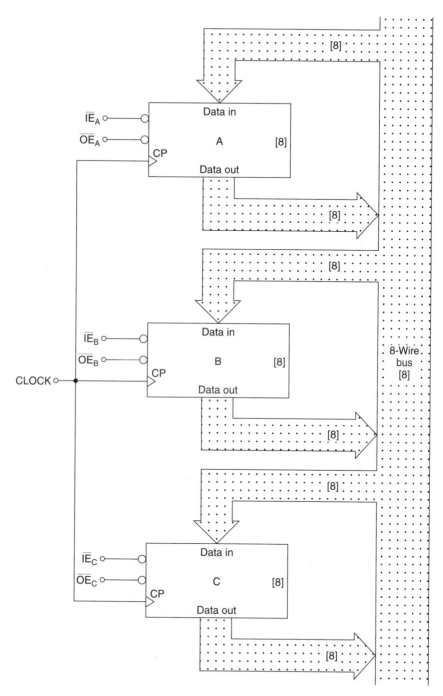

FIGURE 2.25 Simplified drawing of bus arrangement.

The connections to and from the data bus are represented by wide arrows. The numbers in brackets indicate the number of bits that each register contains, as well as the number of lines connecting the register inputs and outputs to the bus.

Another common method for representing buses on a schematic is presented in Fig. 2.26 for an 8-line data bus. It shows the eight individual output lines from a 74HC541 octal bus driver labeled D_7–D_0 *bundled* (not connected) together and shown as a single line. These bundled data output lines are then connected to the data bus, which is also shown as one line (i.e., the eight data bus lines are bundled together). The "/8" notation indicates the number of lines represented by each bundle. This *bundle method* is used to represent the connections from the data bus to the eight microprocessor data inputs.

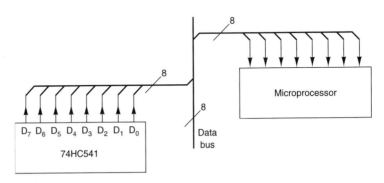

FIGURE 2.26   Bundle method for simplified representation of data bus connections. The "/8" denotes an 8-line data bus.

Bidirectional Busing

Each register in Fig. 2.21 has both its inputs and its outputs connected to the data bus, so that corresponding inputs and outputs are shorted together. For example, each register has output O_2 connected to input D_2 because of their common connection to DB_2. This, of course, would not be true if bus drivers were connected between the register outputs and the data bus.

Because inputs and outputs are often connected together in bus systems, IC manufacturers have developed ICs that connect inputs and outputs together *internal* to the chip in order to reduce the number of IC pins. Figure 2.27 illustrates this for a 4-bit register. The separate data input lines (D_0–D_3) and output lines (O_0–O_3) have been replaced by input/output lines (I/O_0–I/O_3).

Each I/O line will function as either an input or an output depending on the states of the ENABLE inputs. Thus, they are called *bidirectional data lines*. The 74LS299 is an 8-bit register with common I/O lines. Many memory ICs and microprocessors have bidirectional transfer of data.

We will return to the important topic of data busing in later chapters of this textbook.

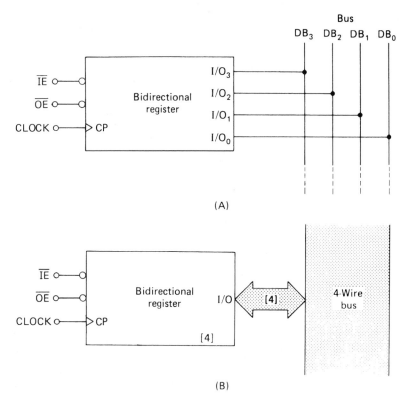

(A)

(B)

FIGURE 2.27 (A) Bidirectional register; (B) simplified diagram.

EXAMPLE 2.3

Redraw Fig. 2.27A using the bundled line representation.

Solution See Fig. 2.28.

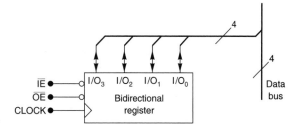

FIGURE 2.28 Bundled line representation of a bidirectional register.

▶ 2.13 DECODERS

In digital computers, binary codes are used to represent many different types of information, such as instructions, numerical data, memory addresses, and control commands. A code group that contains N bits can have 2^N different combinations, each of which repre-

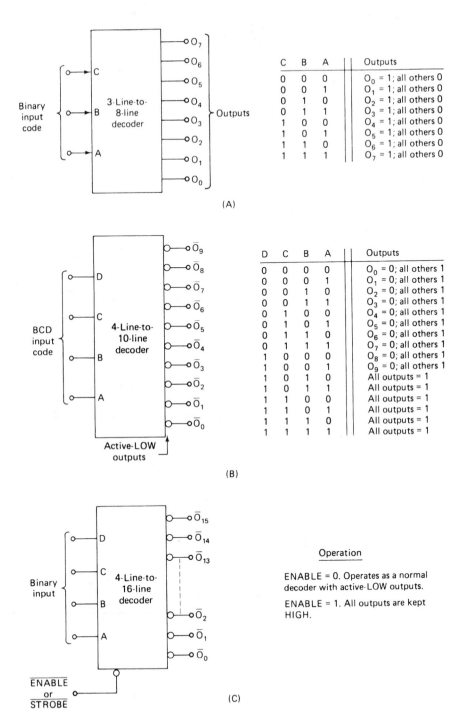

C	B	A	Outputs
0	0	0	$O_0 = 1$; all others 0
0	0	1	$O_1 = 1$; all others 0
0	1	0	$O_2 = 1$; all others 0
0	1	1	$O_3 = 1$; all others 0
1	0	0	$O_4 = 1$; all others 0
1	0	1	$O_5 = 1$; all others 0
1	1	0	$O_6 = 1$; all others 0
1	1	1	$O_7 = 1$; all others 0

(A)

D	C	B	A	Outputs
0	0	0	0	$O_0 = 0$; all others 1
0	0	0	1	$O_1 = 0$; all others 1
0	0	1	0	$O_2 = 0$; all others 1
0	0	1	1	$O_3 = 0$; all others 1
0	1	0	0	$O_4 = 0$; all others 1
0	1	0	1	$O_5 = 0$; all others 1
0	1	1	0	$O_6 = 0$; all others 1
0	1	1	1	$O_7 = 0$; all others 1
1	0	0	0	$O_8 = 0$; all others 1
1	0	0	1	$O_9 = 0$; all others 1
1	0	1	0	All outputs = 1
1	0	1	1	All outputs = 1
1	1	0	0	All outputs = 1
1	1	0	1	All outputs = 1
1	1	1	0	All outputs = 1
1	1	1	1	All outputs = 1

(B)

Operation

ENABLE = 0. Operates as a normal decoder with active-LOW outputs.

ENABLE = 1. All outputs are kept HIGH.

(C)

FIGURE 2.29   Various IC decoders.

56

sents a different piece of information. A logic circuit is required which can take the N-bit code as logic inputs and then generate an appropriate output signal to identify which of the 2^N combinations is present. Such a circuit is called a *decoder*.

Most integrated-circuit decoders can decode 2-, 3-, or 4-bit input codes. Several examples shown in Fig. 2.29 illustrate the characteristics of decoder circuits. The top diagram is a 3-line-to-8-line decoder. It has a 3-bit input code (C, B, A) and, therefore, $2^3 = 8$ possible combinations. The eight output lines, 0 through 7, indicate which combination is present. This is shown in the accompanying truth table. For example, if the input code is CBA = 100 (binary equivalent of 4_{10}), then output 4 will be a 1, while all other outputs are 0. Thus, one and only one output will be active (HIGH) depending on which input code is present. This particular decoder is also called a *binary-to-octal* decoder, since it takes a binary input code and produces *eight* outputs.

The decoder in Fig. 2.29B is a 4-line-to-10-line decoder. Although it has a 4-bit input, only the 10 BCD input codes (0000–1001) are used. Thus, there are only 10 output pins. Each output pin is active-LOW, which means that it is normally HIGH and goes LOW only when the corresponding input code is present. Note the small circles and the overbars on the outputs (for example, $\overline{O_3}$) indicating active-LOW operation. This decoder is commonly called a *BCD-to-decimal* decoder, since it converts a BCD-coded input into a decimal output.

The decoder in Fig. 2.29C utilizes all 16 possible combinations of the four inputs, so it has 16 active-LOW outputs. A special control input called $\overline{\text{ENABLE}}$ (also called $\overline{\text{STROBE}}$) is used to control the decoder's operation. The small circle on this input indicates that it is active-LOW, meaning that a 0 on $\overline{\text{ENABLE}}$ *enables* the decoder to operate normally; a 1 on the $\overline{\text{ENABLE}}$ input *disables* the decoder, and all outputs remain HIGH independent of the binary input code.

▶ 2.14 ENCODERS

A decoder takes an input code and activates the one corresponding output. An *encoder* performs the opposite operation; it generates a binary output code corresponding to which input has been activated. A commonly used IC encoder is represented in Fig. 2.30. It has eight active-LOW inputs, which are kept normally HIGH. When one of the inputs is driven to 0, the binary output code is generated corresponding to that input. For example, when input $\overline{I_3} = 0$, the outputs will be CBA = 011, which is the binary equivalent of decimal 3. When $\overline{I_6} = 0$, the outputs will be CBA = 110.

Priority Encoders

What happens if more than one of the encoder inputs is made LOW? For some encoders, the outputs would be garbage. For a *priority encoder*, the outputs would be the binary code for the *highest*-numbered input that is activated. For example, assume that the encoder of Fig. 2.30 is a priority encoder and that inputs $\overline{I_4}$ and $\overline{I_7}$ are simultaneously made LOW. The output code will be CBA = 111, corresponding to input $\overline{I_7}$. No matter how many inputs are activated, the code for the highest one will appear at the output.

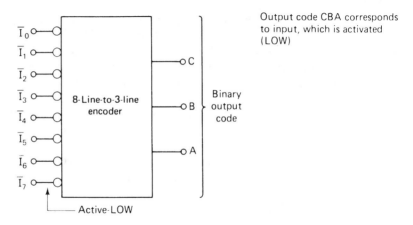

FIGURE 2.30   Typical IC encoder.

▶ 2.15 MULTIPLEXERS (DATA SELECTORS)

A *multiplexer* or *data selector* is a logic circuit that accepts several data inputs and allows only *one* of them at a time to get through to the output. The routing of the desired data input to the output is controlled by SELECT inputs (sometimes referred to as ADDRESS inputs). Figure 2.31 shows a general multiplexer. In this diagram, the inputs and outputs are drawn as large arrows to indicate that they may be one or more lines.

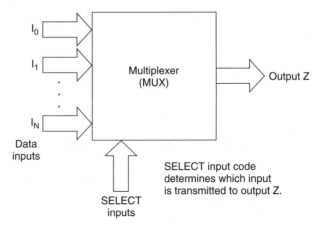

FIGURE 2.31   General diagram of digital multiplexer.

There are many IC multiplexers with various numbers of data inputs and SELECT inputs. Because the basic operation is similar for all of these, we will only look at one representative example (Fig. 2.32). This is called a *four-input, 2-bit multiplexer.* Each set of inputs consists of 2 bits, and there are four sets of inputs called *input ports.* For instance, A_1 and A_0 are one input port, and B_1 and B_0 are another. There is only one set of outputs (output port), Z_1 and Z_0, whose logic levels at any time will be identical to the logic levels present at *one* of the input ports as selected by the SELECT inputs S_0 and S_1.

To illustrate, with $S_1 = S_0 = 0$, the A input port is selected so that $Z_1 = A_1$ and $Z_0 = A_0$. Similarly, with $S_1 = 1$ and $S_0 = 0$, the C input port is selected so that $Z_1 = C_1$ and $Z_0 = C_0$. Only the selected inputs will affect the output. Clearly, this multiplexer behaves like a multipole, multiposition switch whose position is controlled by the logic levels at S_1 and S_0.

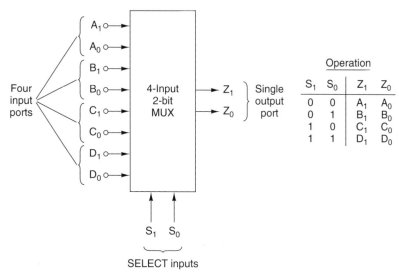

FIGURE 2.32   Four-input, 2-bit multiplexer.

▶ 2.16 ARITHMETIC CIRCUITS

A computer is capable of performing arithmetic, logical, and data manipulation operations on binary numbers. The circuitry that performs these operations is internal to the computer and is not normally accessible to the user. For this reason, we choose not to spend any time showing how logic circuits can be arranged to act as adders, subtracters, and so on. Instead, we will consider the collection of these arithmetic circuits as a single unit called the *arithmetic/logic unit* (ALU).

A typical ALU is diagrammed in Fig. 2.33 together with its associated registers. The ALU portion consists of logic circuitry that will perform operations such as addition, subtraction, multiplication, division, square roots, exponentials, data manipulations (for example, shifting), and logical operations (AND, OR, etc.) on the *two* binary numbers contained in the two input registers. Some or all of these operations are available in any computer, depending on its sophistication and complexity. Larger, more expensive computers have an ALU that can do all of these functions and even more. Small, cheap microcomputers have an ALU that can do only a few simple operations. However, through proper programming even these simple computers can be made to perform the more complex operations but at a sacrifice in speed compared to the more complex computers.

The two registers feed the two binary numbers on which the ALU will operate. These numbers are referred to as *operands* and the ALU operates on them in accordance with the control inputs. For example, one operand is stored in the *data buffer register* (B)

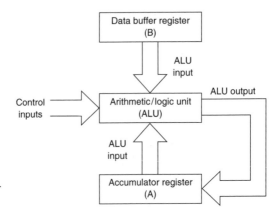

FIGURE 2.33 Typical computer arithmetic/logic unit.

and the other operand is stored in the *accumulator register* (A). The control inputs determine what the ALU will do with these operands. The results of the operation appear at the ALU output and are then immediately transferred to the accumulator. In other words, the results of any ALU operation end up stored in the accumulator.

Much more will be said about the ALU and its operations in later chapters.

▶ 2.17 TROUBLESHOOTING DIGITAL SYSTEMS

It requires special equipment and knowledge to troubleshoot and repair microcomputer-based systems. The most basic level of troubleshooting and repair of digital systems requires identifying the defective device or printed circuit card and then replacing it. This is often referred to as *basic card swapping*. The next level up in troubleshooting requires the technician to determine the exact nature of the anomaly. Once the exact malfunction is determined, it may require the replacement of an individual component or the repair of a printed circuit board. This is called *simple signal checking* troubleshooting, or *troubleshooting to the component level*. To do simple signal checking troubleshooting requires a trained electronic technician with detailed knowledge of electronics and digital systems. Moreover, the technician must have hands-on experience with certain basic electronic troubleshooting tools such as the *logic probe, logic pulser, current tracer, logic analyzer,* and *oscilloscope*. Of course, the most important and effective troubleshooting tool is the technician's brain, and that is the tool we are hoping to develop here by presenting troubleshooting principles and techniques, examples, and problems in this and the following chapters.

We will focus on the *simple signal checking* method of troubleshooting in all of the Troubleshooting Case Studies and examples that we will be doing in this book, and we will assume that the technician has the aforementioned troubleshooting tools.

▶ 2.18 INTERNAL DIGITAL IC FAULTS

Digital IC faults may be classified as either internal or external faults. We begin our discussion with internal faults.

Internal Digital IC Faults

There are basically four types of internal IC failures:

1. Malfunction in internal circuitry
2. Inputs or outputs shorted to ground or V_{CC}
3. Inputs or outputs open-circuited
4. Short between two pins (other than ground or V_{CC})

An example of each type of failure follows.

Malfunction in Internal Circuitry This is usually caused by one of the internal components failing completely or operating outside its specifications. When this happens, the IC outputs do not respond properly to the IC inputs. There is no way to predict what the outputs will do, because it depends on which internal component failed.

Input Shorted to Ground or V_{CC} This type of failure will cause an IC input to be stuck to either a logic HIGH or a logic LOW. Figure 2.34(a) shows input B of a NAND gate shorted to ground within the IC. This will cause pin 2 to always be in the LOW state. If this input pin is being driven by a logic signal B, it will effectively short B to ground. Thus, this type of fault will affect the output of the device that is generating the B signal. Similarly, an IC input pin could be internally shorted to +5 V as in Figure 2.34(b). This would keep pin 1 stuck in the HIGH state. If this input pin is being driven by a logic signal A, it will effectively short A to +5 V.

Output Shorted to Ground or V_{CC} This type of failure will cause an IC output to be stuck to either a logic HIGH or a logic LOW. Figure 2.34(c) shows output pin 3 of a NAND gate shortened to ground within the IC. This will cause pin 3 to always be in the LOW state. Therefore, the output of the NAND gate will not respond to the conditions applied to inputs at pins 1 and 2; in other words, logic inputs A and B will have no effect on output X.

An IC output pin can also be shorted to +5 V within the IC as shown in Figure 2.34(d). This forces the output 3 to be stuck HIGH regardless of the state of the signals at the input pins.

Open-Circuited Input or Output An open circuit can result from a break in the very fine wire that connects an IC pin to the IC's internal circuitry. Sometimes, an open circuit can also result from a bent or broken pin in an IC package. Occasionally, an open trace on a printed circuit board will cause an input/output to behave as an open circuit.

In applications where the IC belongs to the TTL logic family, an open input/output will act as a logic HIGH. Devices belonging to the CMOS logic family will respond erratically and may even become damaged from overheating when one or more inputs is open.

Short Between Two Pins An internal short between two pins of an IC will force the logic signals at those pins to always be identical. Whenever two signals that are supposed to be different show the same logic-level variations, there is a good possibility that the signals are shorted together. Consider the circuit in Figure 2.35, where pins 5 and 6 of the NAND gate are internally shorted together. The short causes the two INVERTER output pins to be connected together so that the signals at Z1 pin 2 and Z1 pin 4 must be identical

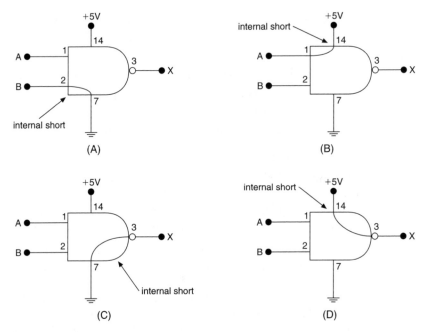

FIGURE 2.34 (a) IC input internally shorted to ground; (b) IC input internally shorted to V_{CC}; (c) IC output internally shorted to ground; (d) IC output internally shorted to V_{CC}.

even when the two INVERTER input signals are trying to produce different outputs. To illustrate, consider the input waveforms shown in the diagram. Even though these input waveforms are different, the waveforms at outputs Z1–2 and Z1–4 are the same.

During the interval t_1 to t_2 both INVERTERs have a HIGH input and both are trying to produce a LOW output, so that their being shorted together makes no difference. During t_4 to t_5, both INVERTERs have a LOW input and are trying to produce a HIGH output, so that again their being shorted has no effect. However, during the intervals t_2–t_3 and t_3–t_4, one INVERTER is trying to produce a HIGH output while the other is trying to produce a LOW. For this reason the actual voltage level that appears at the shorted outputs will depend on the internal IC circuitry. For TTL devices it will usually be a voltage in the high end of the logic 0 range (i.e. close to 0.8 V), although it may also be in the indeterminate range. For CMOS devices it will often be a voltage in the indeterminate range. Whenever you see a waveform like the Z1–2, Z1–4 signal in Figure 2.35 with three different levels, you should suspect that two output signals may be shorted together.

▶ 2.19 EXTERNAL FAULTS

We have seen how to recognize the effects of various faults internal to digital ICs. Many more things can go wrong external to the ICs; we will describe the most common types of external faults in this section.

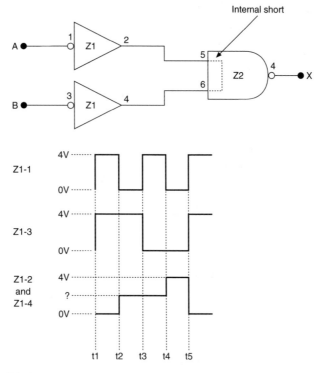

FIGURE 2.35 When two input pins are internally shorted, the signals driving these pins are forced to be identical, and usually a signal with three distinct levels results.

Open Signal Lines

This category includes any fault that produces a break or discontinuity in the conducting path such that a voltage level or signal is prevented from going from one point to another. Some of the causes of open signal lines are:

1. Broken wire
2. Poor solder connection; loose wire-wrap connection
3. Crack or cut trace on a printed circuit board (some of these are hairline cracks that are difficult to see without a magnifying glass)
4. Bent or broken pin on an IC
5. Faulty IC socket such that the IC pin does not make good contact with the socket
6. Components inserted into the printed circuit board in the wrong orientation

This type of circuit fault can often be detected by careful visual inspection and then verified by disconnecting power from the circuit and checking for continuity with an ohmmeter between the two points in question.

Shorted Signal Lines

This type of fault has the same effect as an internal short between IC pins. It causes two signals to be exactly the same. A signal line may be shorted to ground or V_{CC} rather than to another signal line. In those cases the signal will be forced to the LOW or the HIGh state. The main causes for unexpected shorts between two points in a circuit are as follows:

1. *Sloppy wiring.* An example of this is stripping too much insulation from ends of wires that are in close proximity.
2. *Solder bridges.* These are splashes of solder that short two or more points together. They commonly occur between points that are very close together, such as adjacent pins on a chip.
3. *Incomplete etching.* The copper between adjacent conducting paths on a printed circuit board is not completely etched away.

Again, a careful visual inspection can very often uncover this type of fault, and an ohm-meter check can verify that the two points in the circuit are shorted together.

Faulty Power Supply

All digital systems have one or more dc power supplies that supply the V_{CC} and V_{DD} voltages required by the chips. A faulty power supply or one that is overloaded (supplying more than its rated amount of current) will provide poorly regulated supply voltages to the ICs, and the ICs either will not operate or will operate erratically.

A power supply may go out of regulation because of a fault in its internal circuitry, or because the circuits that it is powering are drawing more current than the supply is designed for. This can happen if a chip or a component has a fault that causes it to draw much more current than normal.

It is a good troubleshooting practice to check the voltage levels at each power supply in the system to see that they are within their specified ranges. It is also a good idea to check them on an oscilloscope to verify that there is no significant amount of ac ripple on the dc levels and to verify that the voltage levels stay regulated during the system operation.

One of the most common signs of a faulty power supply is one or more chips operating erratically or not at all. Some ICs are more tolerant of power supply variations and may operate properly, while others are not. You should always check the power and ground levels at each IC that appears to be operating incorrectly.

Output Loading

When a digital IC has its output connected to too many IC inputs, its output current rating will be exceeded, and the output voltage can fall into the indeterminate range. This effect is called *loading* the output signal (actually it's *overloading* the output signal) and is usually the result of poor design or an incorrect connection.

▶ 2.20 COMMON TEST EQUIPMENT USED IN THE TROUBLESHOOTING OF DIGITAL SYSTEMS

Besides the usual analog test equipment, such as VOMs, oscilloscopes, frequency counters, signal generators, etc., digital troubleshooting requires some specialized equipment.

The following list includes a brief operational description of the basic troubleshooting tools used in all of the Troubleshooting Case Studies and troubleshooting examples in this book.

Logic Probe

A logic probe is a small hand-held instrument with a pointed metal tip that is applied to the specific point you want to test. The logic level that is present at the probe tip will be indicated by the status of an indicator light or LED in the probe. The four possibilities are given in the table of Figure 2.36.

Note that an indeterminate logic level produces a *dim* indicator light. This includes the condition where the probe tip is applied to a point in a circuit that is open or floating—that is, not connected to any source of voltage. This logic state is often referred to as HI-Z. Note that not all logic probes are designed to detect an indeterminate logic level. Many logic probes can detect only logic levels HIGH, LOW, and PULSING signals.

When the tip of the logic probe is touching a point where a logic level HIGH is present, the indicator light in the probe will be ON (bright). Conversely, when the tip of the logic probe is touching a point where a logic level LOW is present, the indicator light in the probe will be OFF.

Logic probes are also capable of detecting signals that change between a logic level HIGH and a logic level LOW (i.e. a clock). The logic probe shows a PULSING indicator light when this condition is detected.

Logic Pulser

A logic pulser is a testing and troubleshooting tool that generates a short-duration pulse when manually activated, usually by pressing a button. Some logic pulser models have a switch that allows the user to inject a burst of short-duration pulses into a circuit node. The logic pulser shown in Figure 2.37 has a needle-shaped tip that is applied to the circuit node that is to be pulsed. The logic pulser is designed so that it senses the existing voltage level at the node and produces a voltage pulse in the opposite direction. In other words, if the node is LOW, the logic pulser produces a narrow positive-going pulse; if the node is HIGH, it produces a narrow negative-going pulse.

In the circuit of Figure 2.37, every time the button on the logic pulser is depressed flip-flop Q will toggle and the state of its Q output will be shown by the indicator light on the logic probe.

Current Tracer

A current tracer is a troubleshooting tool that can detect a *changing* current in a wire or printed circuit board trace without breaking the circuit. The current tracer has an insulated tip that contains a magnetic pickup coil. When the tip is placed at a point in the circuit, it

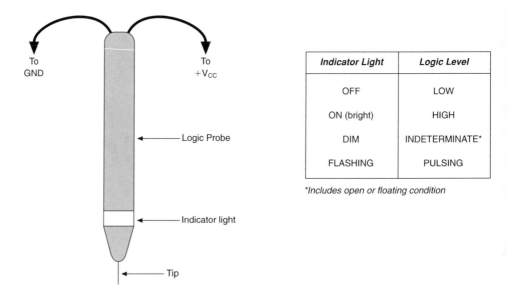

Indicator Light	Logic Level
OFF	LOW
ON (bright)	HIGH
DIM	INDETERMINATE*
FLASHING	PULSING

*Includes open or floating condition

FIGURE 2.36 A logic probe and its four possible status conditions.

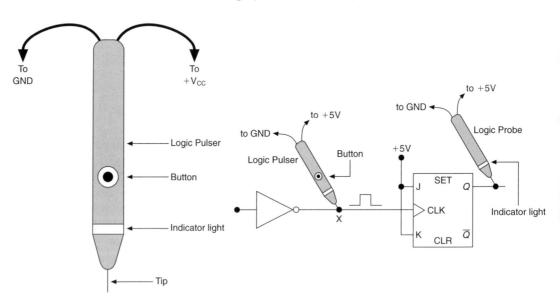

FIGURE 2.37 A logic pulser can inject a pulse at any node that is not shorted directly to ground or V_{CC}.

senses a changing magnetic field produced by a changing current and causes a small indicator LED to flash. The current tracer does not respond to static current levels, no matter how great the current may be. It responds only to a change in current level.

A current tracer is used with a logic pulser to trace the exact location of shorts to ground or V_{CC}. This is illustrated in Figure 2.38, where node X is shorted to ground through the internal short at gates 2's input. If the logic pulser is touched to X and its button is pressed, no voltage pulse will be detected, because of the short to ground. However, there will be a pulse of current flowing from the pulser's output to ground through the short (Isc). This current pulse can be detected by a current tracer.

In Figure 2.38(a), the current tracer is placed to the left of X, and the logic pulse is pulsed. The tracer will indicate no current pulse through the path that it is monitoring. In Figure 2.38(b), the tracer is moved to the other side of X. This time when the logic pulser is pulsed, the current tracer will indicate the occurrence of a current pulse through the path that it is monitoring. This proves that the short to ground is inside gate 2's input rather than gate 1's output.

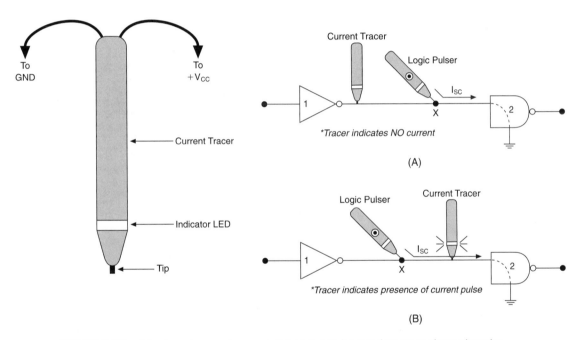

FIGURE 2.38 A logic pulser and a current tracer can be used to trace shorted nodes.

Logic Analyzer

There are many different types of logic analyzers used to aid in the troubleshooting of digital systems. Like all oscilloscopes, all logic analyzers perform basically the same function. It is not our intent here to teach how to use a logic analyzer, since it is a fairly complex troubleshooting instrument. We believe that the teaching of such a complex instrument is better accomplished in a laboratory environment. Nevertheless, some of the troubleshooting exercises in this book will require some limited usage of a logic analyzer. Consequently, a brief explanation of the basic operation of the logic analyzer is required.

A logic analyzer is a digital instrument that can store and display several channels of digital data. The logic analyzer, after it is properly triggered, stores data in memory first, then causes the data to be continually displayed on its CRT screen. Thus, the data that the logic analyzer displays has already occurred and it is not real-time like that displayed by a non-storage oscilloscope. Logic analyzers can display many channels of digital data. We will assume that the logic analyzer used in our troubleshooting examples is a 24-channel logic analyzer. Therefore, we will be able to display 24 different digital signals simultaneously. The digital data can be displayed in a *tabular format,* using binary, octal, or hexadecimal characters, as well as in *timing diagram* format. Figure 2.39(a) and (b) shows two typical logic analyzer displays in the tabular format.

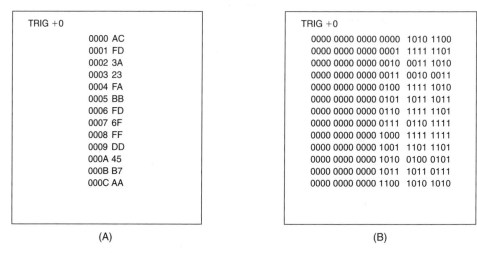

(A)   (B)

FIGURE 2.39(a) Logic analyzer's hexadecimal display in tabular format. (b) Logic analyzer's binary display in tabular format.

GLOSSARY

Accumulator Register   Location where the results of any ALU operation are stored.

Arithmetic/Logic Unit (ALU)   Collection of arithmetic and logic circuits used to perform arithmetic, logical, and data manipulations on binary numbers in a computer.

AND Gate   Digital circuit that implements the AND operation. The output of this circuit is HIGH (logic level 1) only if all of its inputs are HIGH.

Asynchronous FF Inputs   Inputs that override all other inputs to place the FF in the Set or Cleared state.

Bidirectional Bus   Sharing of common bus lines by input and output. Depending upon the state of the disable inputs, information can flow as an output or an input.

Bundled Method   See Bundling.

Bundling   Method for efficiently representing groups of bus lines on a circuit diagram.

Bus   Group of wires used as a common path connecting all the inputs and outputs of several registers so that data can be easily transferred from any one register to any other using various control signals.

Bus Contention   Two or more sets of outputs on the same bus trying to take control (enabled) at the same time. This can result in possible chip damage.

Bus Drivers   Circuits that buffer the outputs of devices connected to a common bus; used when a large number of devices share a common bus.

Clock Signal   Signal used to synchronize the operations of digital systems.

Clocked FF   FF that will respond to the control inputs only on the occurrence of the appropriate clock signal.

Control Inputs   Input signals synchronized with the active clock transition that determine the output state of an edge-sensitive flip-flop.

Current Tracer   A current tracer is a troubleshooting tool that can detect a *changing* current in a wire or printed circuit board trace without breaking the circuit.

D-Type Latch   Level clocked D flip-flop. When the ENABLE is HIGH, Q (output) follows D (input); when the ENABLE goes LOW, the data present at the time of the negative-going edge are stored (latched).

Decoder   Logic circuit that can take an N-bit code representing instructions, data, or control commands as its logic inputs and generate an appropriate output signal to identify which of the 2^N combinations is present.

Edge-Triggered Flip-Flop   Manner in which a flip-flop is activated by a signal transition. A flip-flop may be either a positive or a negative edge-triggered flip-flop.

Encoder   Logic circuit that generates a binary output code corresponding to the input which was activated.

Exclusive-NOR Gate   Two-input logic circuit that produces a HIGH output only when the inputs are equal.

Exclusive-OR Gate   Two-input logic circuit that produces a HIGH output only when the inputs are different.

Flip-Flop   Logic circuits with memory; in other words, a logic circuit capable of storing a logic level 1, or a logic level 0.

Floating Bus   When all outputs connected to a data bus are in the high-Z state.

High-Z State   Logic output state that is neither a logic HIGH nor a logic LOW. In other words, an output in the high-Z state acts as if it were a virtual open circuit.

Hold Time   Time interval immediately following the active transition of the clock signal during which the control input has to be maintained at the proper level.

Invalid Data   Logic levels on a data bus that are changing unpredictably from one state to another.

INVERTER   See NOT Gate.

Logic Analyzer   A logic analyzer is a digital instrument that can store and display several channels of digital data. The digital data can be displayed in a *tabular format,* using binary, octal, or hexadecimal characters, as well as in *timing diagram* format.

Logic Probe   A logic probe is a small hand-held instrument with a pointed metal tip that is applied to the specific point you want to test. The logic level (HIGH, LOW, or HI-Z) that is present at the probe tip will be indicated by the status of an indicator light or LED in the probe.

Logic Pulser   A logic pulser is a testing and troubleshooting tool that generates a short-duration pulse when manually activated, usually by pressing a button. The logic pulser is designed so that it senses the existing voltage level at the node and produces a voltage pulse in the opposite direction.

Multiplexer   Logic circuit that selects one of several inputs to become its output. The input selected is dependent on the state of the SELECT inputs.

NAND Gate   Logic circuit that operates like an AND gate followed by an INVERTER. The output of a NAND gate is LOW (logic level 0) only if all inputs are HIGH (logic level 1).

NOR Gate   Logic circuit that operates like an OR gate followed by an INVERTER. The output of a NOR gate is LOW (logic level 0) when any or all inputs are HIGH (logic level 1).

NOT Gate   Also referred to as an INVERTER; logic circuit that implements the NOT operation. A NOT gate has only one input, and its output logic level is always the opposite of its input's logic level.

OR Gate   Digital circuit that implements the OR operation. The output of this circuit is HIGH (logic level 1) if any or all of its inputs are HIGH.

Override Inputs   Synonymous with "asynchronous flip-flop inputs."

Parallel Transmission   Transfer of binary information during which all bits of a word are transferred at the same time and over individual lines.

Priority Encoder   Encoder that responds by giving the binary output code for the highest numbered input which is activated if more than one input is activated simultaneously.

Register   Group of memory devices (FFs) used to store binary information.

Serial Transmission   Transfer of binary information where the bits of a word are transmitted sequentially over a single output line.

Setup Time   Time interval immediately preceding the active transition of the clock signal during which the control input has to be maintained at the proper level.

Synchronous Flip-Flop Inputs   See Control Inputs.

Tri-state Logic   Logic circuits that operate as normal digital devices when enabled and high-Z (disconnected) when disabled.

Valid Data   Logic levels on a data bus that are stable.

QUESTIONS AND PROBLEMS

Sections 2.1–2.3

1. (a) How many different logic outputs are required to represent an 8-bit binary number using *parallel* representation? (b) How many are required using *serial* representation?
2. Look at the logic symbols in Fig. 2.40. Which one will produce a HIGH output when any input goes LOW?
3. Which gate in Fig. 2.40 will have a LOW output when any of its inputs is HIGH?

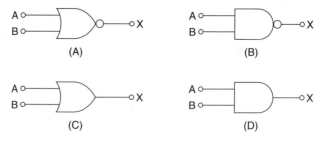

FIGURE 2.40

4. The device in Fig. 2.41 is a tri-state INVERTER. Fill in the truth table.

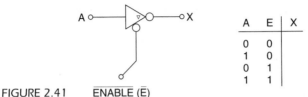

A	E	X
0	0	
1	0	
0	1	
1	1	

FIGURE 2.41 $\overline{\text{ENABLE}}$ ($\overline{\text{E}}$)

Sections 2.4–2.12

5. Explain the difference between an edge-triggered D flip-flop and a D-type latch.
6. What type of input is common to all edge-triggered flip-flops?
7. Explain the difference between flip-flop synchronous and asynchronous inputs.
8. Refer to the edge-triggered JK flip-flop of Fig. 2.10. Assume that the JK flip-flop is a negative edge-triggered flip-flop and is set before the CLK is applied. Draw output waveform Q.
9. A certain clocked flip-flop has a minimum $t_S = 10$ ns and $t_H = 5$ ns.
   (a) How long must the control inputs be stable prior to the active clock transition?
   (b) How long must the control inputs be stable after the active clock transition?
10. Compare the relative advantages of parallel and serial transfer of data between two registers.
11. An 8-bit shift register holds the data word 10110010. What will the register contents be after *three left* shifts? (Assume that serial input = 0.)
12. What is meant by the term "data bus"?
13. What is "bus contention," and what must be done to prevent if from occurring?
14. What is the function of a bus driver?
15. What is the principal reason for having registers with common I/O lines?
16. What logic conditions are needed to cause the transfer of data from register C to register B in Fig. 2.21?
17. What is the difference between a data bus that is in the high-Z state and a data bus that is floating?
18. Using the simplified bus representation, draw the diagram of a bus system arrangement that includes two 8-bit registers with separate input and output lines, and two 8-bit bidirectional registers. Use bundling to represent data lines.

Sections 2.13–2.16

19. Match the device in column I with its function from column II.

I	II
(A) Decoder	(1) Produces binary-coded output corresponding to the activated input.
(B) Encoder	(2) Activates one output corresponding to the binary input code.
(C) ALU	(3) Switches one of several input channels to a single output channel.
(D) Multiplexer	(4) Collection of arithmetic and logic circuits used to perform all of the arithmetic and logic operations in a computer.

20. What are the functions of the accumulator register in a computer arithmetic/logic unit?

Sections 2.17–2.20

21. Refer to the circuit of Figure 2.42. A technician uses a logic probe to determine the conditions at the various IC pins. The results are recorded in the figure. Examine these results and determine whether the circuit is working properly. If not, suggest some of the possible faults and what troubleshooting tool or tools you would use to troubleshoot the circuit.

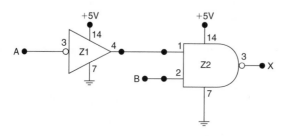

Pin	Condition
Z1-3	Pulsing
Z1-4	LOW
Z2-1	LOW
Z2-2	HIGH
Z2-3	HIGH

FIGURE 2.42

3

Memory Devices

OBJECTIVES

Upon completion of this chapter, you will be able to:

- Understand and correctly use the terminology associated with memory systems.
- Describe the difference between READ/WRITE memory and READ-ONLY memory.
- Discuss the difference between volatile and nonvolatile memory.
- Determine the capacity of a memory device from its inputs and outputs.
- Outline the steps that occur when the CPU reads from or writes to memory.
- Distinguish among the various types of ROMs and cite some common applications.
- Understand the timing requirements of ROMs and EEPROMs.
- Understand and describe the organization and operation of static and dynamic RAMs.
- Compare the relative advantages and disadvantages of MROM, EPROM, EEPROM, and flash memory.
- Combine memory ICs to form memory modules with larger word size and/or capacity.

INTRODUCTION

One of the major advantages that digital systems have over analog systems is the ability to easily store large quantities of digital information and data for short or long periods of time. This memory capability is what makes digital systems so versatile and adaptable to many situations. For example, in a digital computer the internal main memory stores instructions that tell the computer what to do under *all* possible circumstances so that the computer will do its job with a minimum amount of human intervention.

This chapter is devoted to a review of the most commonly used types of memory devices and systems. We have already become very familiar with the flip-flop, which is an electronic memory device. We have also seen how groups of FFs called registers can be used to store information and how this information can be transferred to other locations. FF registers are high-speed memory elements that are used extensively in the internal

73

operations of a digital computer where digital information is continually being moved from one location to another. Advances in LSI and VLSI technology have made it possible to obtain large numbers of FFs on a single chip arranged in various memory-array formats. These bipolar and MOS semiconductor memories are the fastest memory devices available, and their cost has been continuously decreasing as LSI technology improves.

Digital data can also be stored as charges on capacitors, and a very important type of semiconductor memory uses this principle to obtain high-density storage at low power requirement levels.

Semiconductor memories are used as the **internal memory** of a computer (Fig. 3.1), where fast operation is important. A computer's internal memory—also called its *main memory* or *working memory*—is in constant communication with the central processing unit (CPU) as a program of instructions is being executed. A program and any data used by the program reside in the internal memory while the computer is working on that program. RAM and ROM (to be defined shortly) make up internal memory.

Another form of storage in a computer is performed by **auxiliary memory** (Fig. 3.1), which is separate from the internal working memory. Auxiliary memory—also called *mass storage*—has the capacity to store massive amounts of data without the need for electrical power. Auxiliary memory operates at a much slower speed than internal memory, and it stores programs and data that are not currently being used by the CPU. This information is transferred to the internal memory when the computer needs it. Common auxiliary devices are magnetic disk, magnetic tape, and semiconductor magnetic bubble memory (MBM). Semiconductor *flash memory*—with its higher speed, its lower power requirements, smaller size, and nonmechanical operation—shows promise as a major competitor to disk memories.

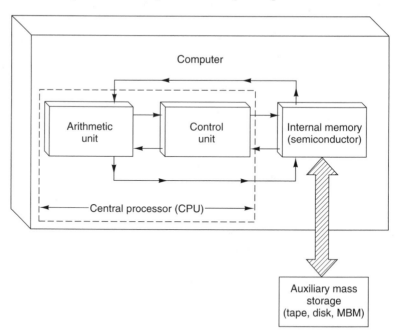

FIGURE 3.1   *A computer system normally uses high-speed internal memory and slower external mass memory.*

We will take a detailed look at the characteristics of the most common memory devices used as the internal memory of a computer. First we define some of the common terms used in memory systems.

▶ 3.1 MEMORY TERMINOLOGY

Memory Cell   This is a device or electrical circuit used to store a single bit (0 or 1). Examples of memory cells include a flip-flop, a single magnetic core, and a single spot on magnetic tape or disk.

Memory Word   This is a group of bits (cells) in a memory that represents information or data of some type. For example, a register consisting of eight FFs can be considered to be a memory that is storing an 8-bit word. Word sizes in modern computers typically range from 4 to 64 bits, depending on the size of the computer.

Byte   This is a special term used for an 8-bit word. A byte always consists of 8 bits, which is one of the most common word sizes in microcomputers.

Nibble   A 4-bit binary number. Half of one byte.

Capacity   This is a way of specifying how many bits can be stored in a particular memory device or complete memory system. To illustrate, suppose that we have a memory that can store 4096 20-bit words. This represents a total capacity of 81,920 bits. We could also express this memory's capacity as 4096×20. When expressed this way, the first number (4096) is the number of words, and the second number (20) is the number of bits per word (word size). The number of words in a memory is often a multiple of 1024. It is common to use the designation "1K" to represent 1024 when referring to memory capacity. Thus, a memory that has a storage capacity of $4K \times 20$ is actually a 4096×20 memory.

The development of larger memories has brought about the designation "1M" or "1 meg" to represent $2^{20} = 1,048,576$. Thus, a memory that has a capacity of $2M \times 8$ is actually one with a capacity of $2,097,152 \times 8$. The designation "G" or "giga" refers to $2^{30} = 1,073,741,824$. For example, a hard disk with a capacity of 2 gigabytes (2GB) can store 2,147,483,648 bytes of data.

EXAMPLE 3.1

A certain semiconductor memory chip is specified as $2K \times 8$. How many words can be stored on this chip? What is the word size? How many total bits can this chip store?

Solution

$$2K = 2 \times 1024 = 2048 \text{ words}$$

Each word is 8 bits (one byte). The total number of bits is therefore

$$2048 \times 8 = 16,384 \text{ bits}$$

Density   Another term for *capacity*. When we say that one memory device has a greater density than another, we mean that it can store more bits in the same amount of space. It is more dense.

Address   This is a number that identifies the location of a word in memory. Each word stored in a memory device or system has a unique address. Addresses are always specified as a binary number, although octal, hexadecimal, and decimal numbers are often used for convenience. Figure 3.2 illustrates a small memory consisting of eight words. Each of these eight words has a specific address represented as a 3-bit number ranging from 000 to 111. Whenever we refer to a specific word location in memory, we use its address code to identify it.

READ Operation   This is the operation whereby the binary word stored in a specific memory location (address) is sensed and then transferred to another location. For example, if we want to use word 4 of the memory of Fig. 3.2 for some purpose, we have to perform a READ operation on address 100. The READ operation is often called a *fetch* operation, since a word is being fetched from memory. We will use both terms interchangeably.

Addresses

0 0 0	Word 0
0 0 1	Word 1
0 1 0	Word 2
0 1 1	Word 3
1 0 0	Word 4
1 0 1	Word 5
1 1 0	Word 6
1 1 1	Word 7

FIGURE 3.2   Each word location has a specific binary address.

WRITE Operation   The operation whereby a new word is placed into a particular memory location. It is also referred to as a *store* operation. Whenever a new word is written into a memory location, it replaces the word that was previously stored there. The old word is lost in the process of writing into this memory location.

Access Time   This is a measure of a memory device's operating speed. It is the amount of time required to perform a READ operation. More specifically, it is the time between the memory receiving a READ command signal and the data becoming available at the memory output. The symbol t_{ACC} is used for access time.

Cycle Time   Another measure of a memory device's speed. It is the amount of time required for the memory to perform a read or write operation and then return to its original state ready for the next command. Cycle time is normally longer than access time.

Volatile Memory   This refers to any type of memory that requires the application of electrical power in order to store information. If the electrical power is removed, all information stored in the memory will be lost. Many semiconductor memories are volatile, whereas all magnetic memories are nonvolatile, which means they can store information without electrical power.

Random Access Memory (RAM)   This refers to memories in which the actual physical location of a memory word has no effect on how long it takes to read from or write into that location. In other words, the access time is the same for any address in memory. Most semiconductor memories and magnetic core memories are RAMs.

Sequential Access Memory (SAM)   A type of memory in which the access time is not constant, but varies depending on the address location. A particular stored word is found by sequencing through all address locations until the desired address is reached. This produces access times which are much longer than those of random access memories. Examples of sequential access memory devices include magnetic tape, disk, and magnetic bubble memory.

READ/WRITE Memory (RWM)   Any memory that can be read from or written into with equal ease.

READ-Only Memory (ROM)   Refers to a broad class of semiconductor memories designed for applications where the ratio of READ operations to WRITE operations is very high. Technically, a ROM can be written into (programmed) only once, and this operation is normally performed at the factory. Thereafter information can only be read from the memory. Other types of ROM are actually READ-mostly memories (RMM), which can be written into more than once, but the WRITE operation is more complicated than the READ operation and it is not performed very often. All ROM is nonvolatile. The various types of ROM will be discussed later.

Static Memory Devices   Semiconductor memory devices in which the stored data will remain permanently stored as long as power is applied, without the need for periodically rewriting the data into memory.

Dynamic Memory Devices   Semiconductor memory devices in which the stored data *will not* remain permanently stored, even with power applied, unless the data are periodically rewritten into memory. The latter operation is called a REFRESH operation.

Internal Memory   Also referred to as the computer's *main* or *working memory*. It stores instructions and data the CPU is currently working on. It is the highest-speed memory in the computer and is always a semiconductor memory.

Auxiliary Memory   Also referred to as *mass storage* because it stores massive amounts of information external to the internal memory. It is slower in speed than internal memory and is always nonvolatile. Magnetic tape and disk are common auxiliary memory devices.

▶ 3.2 GENERAL MEMORY OPERATION

Although each type of memory is different in its internal operation, there are certain basic operating principles that are the same for all memory systems. An understanding of these basic ideas will help in our study of individual memory devices.

Every memory system requires several different types of input and output lines to perform the following functions:

1. Select the address in memory that is being accessed for a READ or WRITE operation.
2. Select either a READ or WRITE operation to be performed.
3. Supply the input data to be stored in memory during a WRITE operation.
4. Hold the output data coming from memory during a READ operation.
5. ENABLE (or DISABLE) the memory so that it will (or will not) respond to the address inputs and read/write command.

Figure 3.3 illustrates these basic functions in a simplified diagram of a 32 × 4 memory that stores 32 4-bit words. Since the word size is 4 bits, there are four data input lines, I_0–I_3, and four data output lines O_0–O_3. During a WRITE operation the data to be stored into memory have to be applied to the data input lines. During a READ operation the word being read from memory appears at the data output lines.

This memory has 32 different storage locations and therefore 32 different addresses, ranging from 00000_2 to 11111_2 (0 to 31 in decimal). Thus, we need *five* address inputs A_0–A_4, to specify one of the 32 address locations. To access one of the memory locations for a READ or WRITE operation, a 5-bit address code for that particular location has to be applied to the address inputs.

The READ/WRITE ($R/\overline{W}$) input controls which memory operation is to take place: read (R) or write (W). The input is labeled $R/\overline{W}$; since there is no bar over the R, this indicates that the READ operation occurs when $R/\overline{W} = 1$. The bar over the W indicates that the WRITE operation takes place when $R/\overline{W} = 0$. There are other labels that are often used for this input. Two of the more common ones are $\overline{W}$ (WRITE) and $\overline{WE}$ (WRITE ENABLE). Again, the bar indicates that the WRITE operation occurs when the input is LOW. It is understood that the READ operation occurs for a HIGH.

Many memory systems have some means for completely disabling all or part of the memory so that it will not respond to the other inputs. This is represented in Fig. 3.3 as the MEMORY ENABLE input, although it can have different names in the various memory systems. It is an active-HIGH input that enables the memory to operate normally when it is kept HIGH. A LOW on this input disables the memory so that it will not respond to the address and $R/\overline{W}$ inputs. This type of input is useful when several memory modules are combined to form a larger memory. We will examine this idea later.

EXAMPLE 3.2

A certain memory has a capacity of 256K × 8.

(a) How many data input and data output lines does it have?

(b) How many address lines does it have?

(c) What is its capacity in bytes?

Solution

(a) Eight of each, since the word size is eight.

(b) The memory stores 256K = 256 × 1024 = 262,144 words. Thus, there are 262,144 memory addresses. Since 262,144 = 2^{18}, it requires an 18-bit address code to specify one of 262,144 addresses.

(c) A byte is 8 bits. This memory has a capacity of 262,144 bytes.

The example memory in Fig. 3.3 illustrates the important input and output functions common to most memory systems. Of course, each type of memory will often have other input and output lines that are peculiar to that memory. These will be described as we discuss the individual memory types.

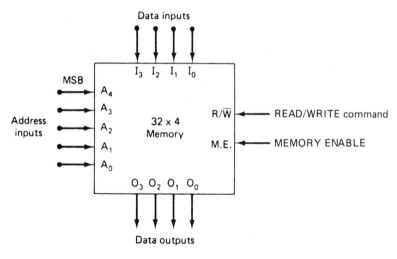

FIGURE 3.3   General diagram for a 32 × 4 memory.

▶ 3.3 READ-ONLY MEMORIES

This type of semiconductor memory is designed to hold data that are either permanent or will not change frequently. During normal operation, no new data can be written into a ROM, but data can be read from ROM. For some ROMs the data that are stored have to be entered in during the manufacturing process; for other ROMs the data can be entered electrically. The process of entering data is called *programming* the ROM. Some ROMs cannot have their data changed once they have been programmed; others can be *erased* and reprogrammed as often as desired. We will take a detailed look at these various types of ROMs later. For now, we will assume that the ROMs have been programmed and are holding data.

ROMs are used to store data and information that are not to change during the operation of a system. A major use for ROMs is in the storage of programs in microcomputers. Because all ROMs are *nonvolatile,* these programs are not lost when the microcomputer is turned off. When the microcomputer is turned on, it can immediately begin executing the program stored in ROM. ROMs are also used for program and data storage in a wide range of microprocessor-controlled equipment, such as calculators, appliances, security systems, automobiles, etc.

ROM Block Diagram

A typical block diagram for a ROM is shown in Fig. 3.4A. It has three sets of signals: address inputs, control input(s), and data outputs. From our previous discussions we can determine that this ROM is storing 16 words, since it has $2^4 = 16$ possible addresses, and each word contains 8 bits, since there are eight data outputs. Thus, this is a 16 × 8 ROM. Another way to describe this ROM's capacity is to say that it stores 16 bytes of data.

The data outputs of most ROM ICs are either open-collector or tri-state outputs to permit the connection of many ROM chips to the same data bus for memory expansion. The most common number of data outputs for ROMs are 4 bits and 8 bits, with 8-bit words being the most common.

The control input $\overline{\text{CS}}$ stands for *chip select*. This input is essentially an ENABLE input that enables or disables the ROM outputs. Some manufacturers use different labels for the control input, such as CE (chip ENABLE) or OE (output ENABLE). Many ROMs have two or more control inputs that have to be activated in order to enable the data outputs. The $\overline{\text{CS}}$ input shown in Fig. 3.4A is active LOW. Note that there is no R/$\overline{\text{W}}$ (READWRITE) input because the ROM cannot be written into under normal operating circumstances.

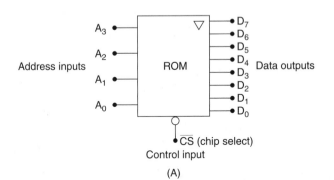

(A)

Word	A_3	A_2	A_1	A_0	D_7	D_6	D_5	D_4	D_3	D_2	D_1	D_0
0	0	0	0	0	1	1	0	1	1	1	1	0
1	0	0	0	1	0	0	1	1	1	0	1	0
2	0	0	1	0	1	0	0	0	0	1	0	1
3	0	0	1	1	1	0	1	0	1	1	1	1
4	0	1	0	0	0	0	0	1	1	0	0	1
5	0	1	0	1	0	1	1	1	1	0	1	1
6	0	1	1	0	0	0	0	0	0	0	0	0
7	0	1	1	1	1	1	1	0	1	1	0	1
8	1	0	0	0	0	0	1	1	1	1	0	0
9	1	0	0	1	1	1	1	1	1	1	1	1
10	1	0	1	0	1	0	1	1	1	0	0	0
11	1	0	1	1	1	1	0	0	0	1	1	1
12	1	1	0	0	0	0	1	0	0	1	1	1
13	1	1	0	1	0	1	1	0	1	0	1	0
14	1	1	1	0	1	1	0	1	0	0	1	0
15	1	1	1	1	0	1	0	1	1	0	1	1

(B)

Word	A_3	A_2	A_1	A_0	D_7-D_0
0	0				DE
1	1				3A
2	2				85
3	3				AF
4	4				19
5	5				7B
6	6				00
7	7				ED
8	8				3C
9	9				FF
10	A				B8
11	B				C7
12	C				27
13	D				6A
14	E				D2
15	F				5B

(C)

FIGURE 3.4   (A) ROM block diagram; (B) programmed data; (C) hex data.

The READ Operation

Let us assume that the ROM has been programmed with the data shown in the table of Fig. 3.4B. There are 16 different data words stored at the 16 different address locations. For example, the data word stored at location 0011 is 10101111. Of course, the data are stored in binary inside the ROM, but often we use hexadecimal notation to show the programmed data efficiently. This is done in Fig. 3.4C.

To read a data word from ROM, it is necessary to do two things: Apply the appropriate address inputs, and then activate the control inputs. For example, if we want to read the data stored at location 0111 of the ROM in Fig. 3.4, we have to apply $A_3A_2A_1A_0 = 0111$ to the address inputs, and then apply a LOW to $\overline{CS}$. The address inputs will be decoded inside the ROM to select the correct data word, 11101101, that will appear at the D_7–D_0 outputs. If $\overline{CS}$ is kept HIGH, the ROM outputs will be disabled and will be in the high-Z state.

▶ 3.4 ROM ARCHITECTURE

The internal architecture (structure) of a ROM IC is very complex, and it is not necessary to be familiar with all of its detail. It is instructive, however, to look at a simplified diagram of the internal architecture such as that shown in Fig. 3.5 for the 16 × 8 ROM. There are four basic parts: *row decoder, column decoder, register array,* and *output buffers.*

Register Array

The register array is the section that stores the data that have been programmed into the ROM. Each register contains a number of memory cells equal to the word size. In this case, each register stores an 8-bit word. The registers are arranged in a square matrix array that is common to many semiconductor memory chips. We can specify the position of each register as being in a specific row and specific column. For example, register 0 is in row 0/column 0, and register 9 is in row 1/column 2.

    The eight data outputs of each register are connected to an internal data bus that runs through the entire circuit. Each register has two ENABLE inputs (E) that have to be HIGH in order for the register's data to be placed on the bus.

Address Decoders

The applied address code $A_3A_2A_1A_0$ determines which register in the array will be enabled to place its 8-bit data word onto the bus. Address bits A_1A_0 are fed to a 1-of-4 decoder, which activates one row select line, and address bits A_3A_2 are fed to a second 1-of-4 decoder, which activates one column select line. There will be only one register that is in both the row and the column selected by the address inputs, and this is the one that will be enabled.

EXAMPLE 3.3

What register will be enabled by input address 1101?

Solution $A_3A_2 = 11$ will cause the column decoder to activate the column 3 select line, and $A_1A_0 = 01$ will cause the row decoder to activate the row 1 select line. This will place HIGHS at both ENABLE inputs of register 13, thereby causing its data outputs to be placed on the bus. Note that the other registers in column 3 will only have one ENABLE input activated; similarly for the other row 1 registers.

EXAMPLE 3.4

What input address will enable register 10?

Solution   The ENABLE inputs of this register are connected to the row 2 and column 2 select lines, respectively. To select row 2, the A_1A_0 inputs have to be at 10, and to select column 2, the A_3A_2 inputs have to be 10. Thus, the required address will be $A_3A_2A_1A_0 = 1010$.

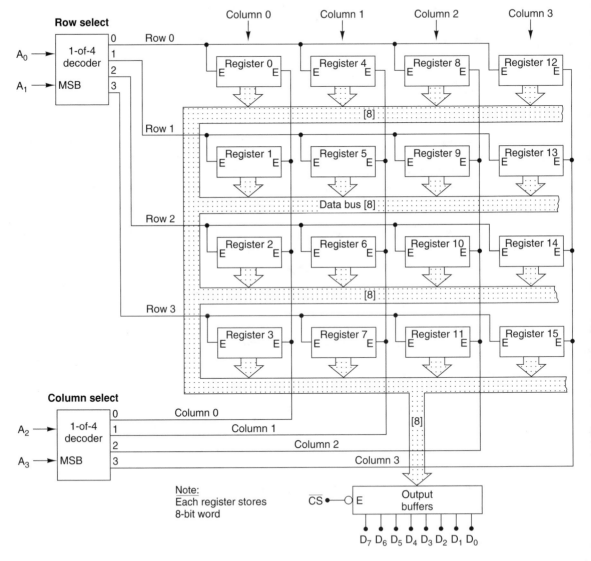

FIGURE 3.5   Architecture of 16 × 8 ROM.

Output Buffers

The register that is enabled by the address inputs will place its data on the data bus. These data feed into the output buffers, which will pass the data to the external data outputs provided that $\overline{CS}$ is LOW. If $\overline{CS}$ is HIGH, the output buffers are in the high-Z state, and D_7-D_0 will be floating.

The architecture shown in Fig. 3.5 is similar to that of most IC ROMs. Depending on the number of stored data words, the registers in some ROMs will not be arranged in a square array. For example, the Intel 2708 is a MOS ROM that stores 1024 8-bit words. Its 1024 registers are arranged in a 64-by-16 array. In practice, ROM capacities typically range from 32 to over 1 M bytes.

EXAMPLE 3.5
_____

Describe the internal architecture of a ROM that stores 4K bytes and uses a square register array.

Solution 4 K is actually $4 \times 1024 = 4096$, so this ROM holds 4096 8-bit words. Each word can be thought of as being stored in an 8-bit register, and there are 4096 registers connected to a common data bus internal to the chip. Since $4096 = 64^2$, the registers are arranged in a 64-by-64 array; that is, there are 64 rows and 64 columns. This requires a 1-of-64 decoder to decode six address inputs for the row select, and a second 1-of-64 decoder to decode six other address inputs for the column select. Thus, a total of 12 address inputs are required. This makes sense since $2^{12} = 4096$, and there are 4096 different addresses.

▶ 3.5 ROM TIMING

There will be a propagation delay between the application of a ROM's inputs and the appearance of the data outputs during a READ operation. This time delay, called *access time,* t_{ACC}, is a measure of the ROM's operating speed. A graphical description of access time is shown by the waveforms in Fig. 3.6.

The top waveform represents the address inputs, the middle waveform is an active LOW chip select, $\overline{CS}$, and the bottom waveform represents the data outputs. At time t_0, the address inputs are all at some specific level, some HIGH, and some LOW. $\overline{CS}$ is HIGH, so that the ROM data outputs are in their high-Z state (represented by the hash-mark line).

Just prior to t_1, the address inputs are changing to a new address for a new READ operation. At t_1 the new address is valid; that is, each address input is at a valid logic level. At this point, the internal ROM circuitry begins to decode the address inputs to select the register that is to send its data to the output buffers. At t_2 the $\overline{CS}$ input is activated to enable the output buffers. Finally, at t_3, the outputs change from the high-Z state to the valid data that represent the data stored at the specified address.

The time delay between t_1, when the new address becomes valid, and t_3, when the data outputs become valid, is the access time t_{ACC}. Typical bipolar ROMs will have access times in the range 30 to 90 ns, while MOS ROMs will range from 200 to 900 ns.

Another important timing parameter is the *output enable time,* t_{OE}, which is the delay between the $\overline{CS}$ input and the valid data output. Typical values of t_{OE} are 20 ns for bipolar ROMs and 25-100 ns for MOS ROMs. This timing parameter is important in situations where the address inputs are already set to their new values, but the ROM outputs have not yet been enabled. When $\overline{CS}$ gets LOW to enable the outputs, the delay will be t_{OE}.

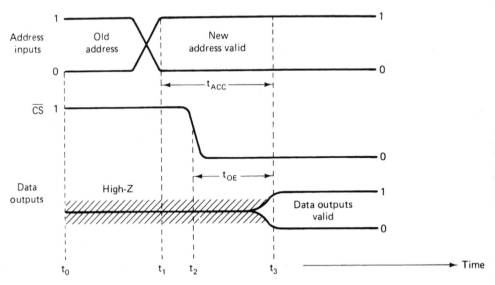

FIGURE 3.6   Typical timing from a ROM READ operation.

▶ 3.6 TYPES OF ROM

Now that we have a general understanding of the internal architecture and external operation of ROM devices, we will take a brief look at the various types of ROMs to see how they differ in the way they are programmed and in their ability to be erased and reprogrammed.

Mask-Programmed ROM

The mask-programmed ROM has its storage locations written into (programmed) by the manufacturer according to the customer's specifications. A photographic negative called a *mask* is used to control the electrical interconnections on the chip. A special mask is required for each different set of information to be stored in the ROM. Since these masks are expensive, this type of ROM is economical only if you need a very large quantity of the same ROM. Some ROMs of this type are available as off-the-shelf devices preprogrammed with commonly used information or data such as certain mathematical tables and character generator codes for CRT displays. A major disadvantage of this type of ROM is that it cannot be reprogrammed in the event of a design change requiring a modification of the stored data. The ROM would have to be replaced by a new one with the desired data written into it. Several types of user-programmable ROMs have been developed to overcome this disadvantage. Mask-programmed ROMs, however, still represent the most economical approach when a large quantity of identically programmed ROMs are needed.

Mask-programmed ROMs are commonly referred to as just ROMs, but this can be confusing since the term ROM actually represents the broad category of devices that, during normal operation, are only read from. We will use the acronym MROM whenever we refer to mask-programmed ROMs.

Figure 3.7 shows the structure of a small bipolar MROM. It consists of 16 memory cells arranged in four rows of four cells. Each cell is an NPN bipolar transistor connected in the common-collector configuration (input at base, output at emitter). The top row of cells (ROW 0) constitutes a 4-bit register. Note how some of the transistors (Q_0 and Q_2) have their bases connected to the ROW 0 enable line, while others (Q_1 and Q_3) do not. The same is true of the cells in each of the other rows. The presence or absence of these connections determines whether a cell is storing a 1 or a 0, respectively. The condition of each base connection is controlled during production by the photographic mask based on the customer-supplied data.

Note that cells that are in corresponding positions in each row (register) have their emitters connected to a common output. For instance, the emitters of Q_0, Q_4, Q_8, and Q_{12} are connected together as data output D_3. As we shall see, this will present no problem because only one row of cells will be activated at one time.

The 1-of-4 decoder is used to decode the address inputs $A_1 A_0$ to select which row (register) is to have its data read. The decoder's active-HIGH outputs provide the ROW enable lines that are the base inputs for the various rows of cells. If the decoder's enable input, $\overline{EN}$, is held HIGH, all of the decoder outputs will be in their inactive-LOW state, and all of the transistors in the array will be off because of the absence of any base voltage. For this situation, the data outputs will all be in the LOW state.

When $\overline{EN}$ is in its active-LOW state, the conditions at the address inputs determine which row (register) will be enabled so that its data can be read at the data outputs. For example, to read ROW 0, the $A_1 A_0$ inputs are set to 00. This places a HIGH at the ROW 0 line; all other row lines are at 0 V. This HIGH at ROW 0 turns on transistors Q_0 and Q_2, but not Q_1 and Q_3. With Q_0 and Q_2 conducting, the data outputs D_3 and D_1 will be HIGH; outputs D_2 and D_0 are still LOW. In a similar manner, application of the other address codes will produce data outputs from the corresponding register. The table in Figure 3.7 shows the data for each address. You should verify how this correlates with the base connections to the various cells.

Bipolar MROMs are available in several low capacities. One of the more popular ones is the 74187. It is organized as a 256×4 memory, and has an access time of 40 ns. Its outputs are open-collector types which require external pull-up resistors. Another bipolar ROM is the 7488A, which has a capacity of 32×8 and an access time of 45 ns.

MOS MROMs have an internal structure similar to Figure 3.7 except that the cells are MOSFETs rather than bipolar transistors. The TMS47256 is an NMOS version that has a capacity of $32K \times 8$, an access time of 200 ns, and a standby power of 82.5 mW. The CMOS version, the TMS47C256, has an access time of 150 ns and a standby power of only 2.8 mW.

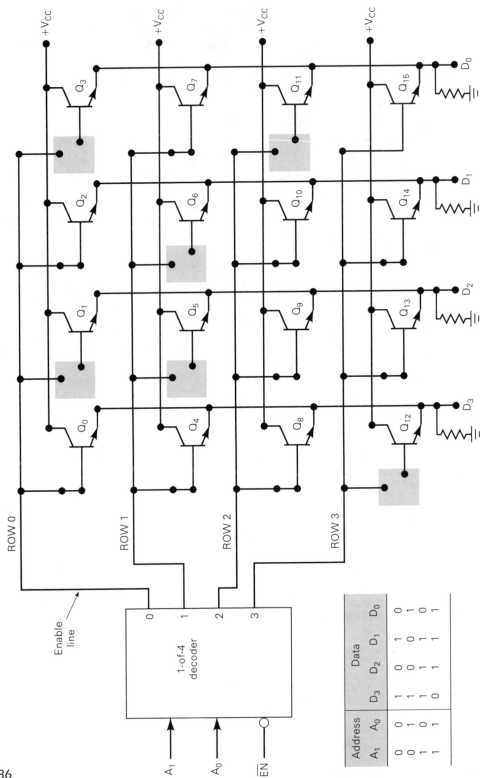

FIGURE 3.7   Structure of a bipolar MROM shows one bipolar transistor used for each memory cell. An open base connection stores a "0"; a closed base connection stores a "1".

Programmable ROMs (PROMs)

A mask-programmable ROM is very expensive and would not be used except in high-volume application, where the cost would be spread out over many units. For lower-volume applications, manufacturers have developed **fusible-link** PROMs that are user-programmable; that is, they are not programmed during the manufacturing process but are custom-programmed by the user. Once programmed, however, a PROM is like an MROM in that it cannot be erased and reprogrammed. Thus, if the program in the PROM is faulty or has to be changed, the PROM has to be thrown away. For this reason, these devices are often referred to as "one-time programmable" ROMs.

The fusible-link PROM structure is very similar to the MROM in that certain connections either are left intact or are opened in order to program a memory cell as a 1 or a 0, respectively. In the MROM of Figure 3.7 these connections were from the enable lines to the transistor bases. In a PROM each of these connections is made with a thin fuse link that comes intact from the manufacturer (see Fig. 3.8).

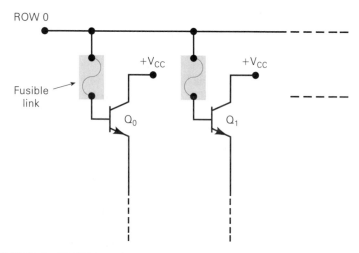

FIGURE 3.8   PROMs use fusible links that can be selectively blown open by the user to program a logic 0 into a cell.

The user can selectively *blow* any of these fuse links to produce the desired stored memory data. Typically, data is programmed or "burned" into an address location by applying the address to the address inputs, placing the desired data at the data pins, and then applying a high-voltage pulse (10–30 V) to a special programming pin on the IC. This causes a large current to flow through each selected fuse link, burning it open and permanently storing a logic 0 in that cell. Once all address locations have been programmed in this manner, the data are permanently stored in the PROM and can be read over and over again by accessing the appropriate address. The data will not change when power is removed from the PROM chip, because nothing will cause an open fuse link to become closed again.

The process of programming a PROM and verifying that the stored data are correct is rarely done manually; rather, it is done automatically by a special apparatus called a *PROM programmer*. Typically, the PROM chip is plugged into a socket on the PROM programmer. The programmer circuitry selects each address of the PROM, burns in the correct data at that address, verifies the data, and sequences to the next address to repeat the process. The data to be burned into the PROM are input to the programmer from a keyboard, from a disk drive, or transferred from a computer. The latter operation, called *downloading,* allows the user to develop and test the program/data on a computer and then, when it is finished and working, transfer it from the computer's memory to the PROM programmer, which will "burn it" into the PROM.

A popular bipolar PROM IC is the 74186, which is organized as sixty-four 8-bit words and has a typical access time of 50 ns. Another one is the TBP28S166, which is a 2K × 8 chip. MOS PROMs are available with much greater capacities than bipolar devices. The TMS27PC256 is a CMOS PROM with a capacity of 32K × 8 and a standby power dissipation of only 1.4 mW. It is available with maximum access times ranging from 120 to 250 ns.

Erasable Programmable ROM (EPROM)

An EPROM can be programmed by the user and it can also be *erased* and reprogrammed as often as desired. Once programmed, the EPROM is a *nonvolatile* memory that will hold its desired data indefinitely. The process for programming an EPROM involves the application of special voltage levels (typically in the 10- to 25-V range) to the appropriate chip inputs for a specified amount of time (typically 50 ms per address location). The programming process is usually performed by a special programming circuit that is separate from the circuit in which the EPROM will eventually be working. The complete programming process can take up to several minutes for one EPROM chip.

The storage cells in an EPROM are MOS transistors with a silicon gate that has no electrical connections (i.e., a *floating gate*). In its normal state, each transistor is off and each cell is storing a logic 1. A transistor can be turned on by the application of a high-voltage programming pulse that injects high-energy electrons into the floating-gate region. These electrons remain trapped in this region once the pulse is terminated, since there is no discharge path. This keeps the transistor on *permanently* even when power is removed from the device, and the cell is now storing a logic 0. During the programming process, the EPROM's address and data pins are used to select which memory cells will be programmed as 0s, and which ones will be left as 1s.

Once an EPROM cell has been programmed, it can be erased by exposing it to ultraviolet (UV) light applied through a window on the chip package. The UV light produces a photocurrent from a floating gate back to the silicon substrate, thereby removing the stored charges, turning the transistor off, and restoring the cell to the logic 1 state. This erasing process typically requires 15 to 20 minutes of exposure to UV rays. Unfortunately, there is no way to erase only selected cells; *the UV light erases all cells at the same time* so that an erased EPROM stores all 1s. Once erased, the EPROM can be reprogrammed.

EPROMs are available in a wide range of capacities and access times; devices with a capacity of 128K × 8 and an access time of 45 ns are commonplace. The Intel 2732 is an example of a typical EPROM. The 2732 is a 4K × 8 NMOS EPROM that operates from a single +5 V power source during normal operation. Figure 3.9A is the logic symbol for the 2732. Note that it shows 12 address inputs, since $2^{12} = 4096$, and eight data outputs. It has two control inputs. $\overline{CE}$ is the chip ENABLE input that is used to place the device in a

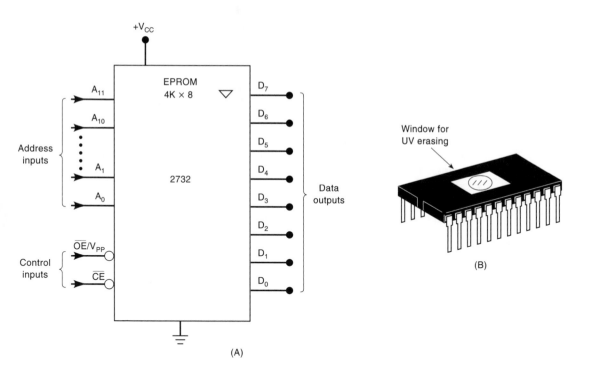

FIGURE 3.9 (A) Logic symbol for 2732 EPROM; (B) typical EPROM package showing ultraviolet window; (C) 2732 operating modes.

standby mode where its power consumption is reduced. $\overline{OE}/V_{PP}$ is a dual-purpose input whose function will depend on the device operating mode. $\overline{OE}$ is the output ENABLE and is used to control the device's data output buffers so that the device can be connected to a microprocessor data bus without bus contention. V_{PP} is the special reprogramming voltage required during the programming process.

The 2732 package in Figure 3.9B shows the characteristic "window," which allows the internal circuitry to be exposed to UV light when the complete memory contents are to be erased. A sticker is placed over the window after erasure and reprogramming to protect against accidental erasure from ambient light.

The 2732 has several operating modes that are controlled by the $\overline{CE}$ and $\overline{OE}/V_{PP}$ pins as presented in Figure 3.9C. The program mode is used to write new data into the

EPROM cells. This is most often done on a "clean" EPROM, one that has previously been erased with UV light so that all cells are 1s. The programming process writes one 8-bit word into one address location at one time as follows: (1) the address is applied to the address pins; (2) the desired data are placed at the data pins, which function as inputs during the programming process; (3) a high voltage, nominally 21 V, is applied to V_{PP}; and (4) $\overline{CE}$ is pulsed LOW, typically for 50 ms. This process is repeated for all memory locations. If done manually, this can take several hours. Usually, however, it is done automatically with a commercial EPROM programmer much like the PROM programmers described above. A clean EPROM can be programmed in a few minutes once the desired data have been entered, transferred, or downloaded into the EPROM programmer.

The Intel 27C512 is a 64K $\times$ 8 EPROM that can be programmed much more rapidly than the 2732. The 27C512 requires a $\overline{CE}$ pulse for only 100 μs to write a single byte, as compared to 50 ms for the 2732; this translates into a total chip programming time of 8 to 10 s. The 27C512, like all EPROMs, is erased by exposure to UV light for up to 15 to 20 min.

EPROMs were originally intended for use in research and development applications where the need to alter the stored program several times is very common. As they became more reliable and less expensive, they became attractive for inclusion in low- and medium-volume products and systems. Today, millions of EPROMs are still in use. However, they have several major drawbacks that have been overcome by the newer EEPROMs and flash memory devices, so EPROMs are not being used in many new applications and designs. These drawbacks include (1) they have to be removed from their circuit to be erased and reprogrammed; (2) the ERASE operation erases the entire chip—there is no way to select only certain addresses to be erased; and (3) the erase and reprogramming process can typically take 20 min. or more.

Electrically Erasable PROM (EEPROM)

The disadvantages of the EPROM were overcome by the development of the *electrically erasable PROM* (EEPROM) as an improvement over the EPROM. The EEPROM retains the same floating-gate structure as the EPROM, but with the addition of a very thin oxide region above the drain of the MOSFET memory cell. This modification produces the EEPROM's major characteristic—its electrical erasability. By applying a high voltage (21 V) between the MOSFET's gate and drain, a charge can be induced onto the floating gate, where it will remain even when power is removed; reversal of the same voltages causes a removal of the trapped charges from the floating gate and erases the cell. Since this charge-transport mechanism requires very low currents, the erasing and programming of an EEPROM can be done *in circuit* (i.e., without a UV light source and special PROM programmer unit).

Another advantage of the EEPROM over the EPROM is the ability to electrically erase and rewrite *individual* bytes (8-bit words) in the memory array. During a WRITE operation, internal circuitry automatically erases all the cells at an address location prior to writing in the new data. This byte erasability makes it much easier to make changes in the data stored in an EEPROM. Additionally, an EEPROM can be programmed more rapidly than many EPROMs; typically, it takes 5 ms to write into an EEPROM location, compared to 50 ms for an EPROM, though newer EPROMs are much faster (100 μs).

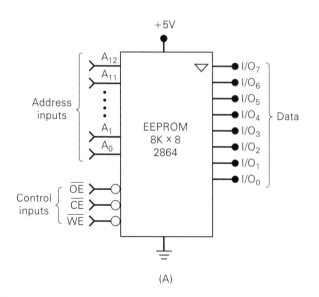

(A)

	Inputs			
Mode	$\overline{CE}$	$\overline{OE}$	$\overline{WE}$	I/O pins
READ	LOW	LOW	HIGH	DATA$_{OUT}$
WRITE	LOW	HIGH	LOW	DATA$_{IN}$
STANDBY	HIGH	X	X	High Z

(B)

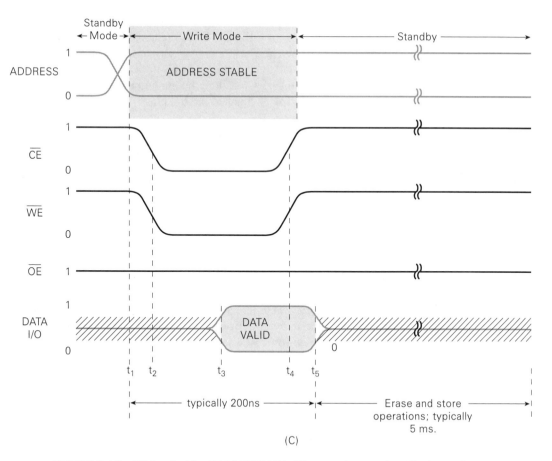

(C)

FIGURE 3.10   (A) Symbol for 2864 EEPROM; (B) operating modes; (C) timing for write operation.

The early EEPROMs, such as Intel's 2816, required appropriate support circuitry external to the memory chips. This support circuitry included the 21-V programming voltage (V_{PP}), usually generated from a +5-V supply through a dc-to-dc converter, and circuitry to control the timing and sequencing of the erase and programming operations. The newer devices, such as the Intel 2864, have integrated this support circuitry onto the same chip with the memory array, so that it requires only a single 5-V power pin. This makes the EEPROM as easy to use as the READ/WRITE memory we will be discussing shortly.

The byte erasability of the EEPROM and its high level of integration come with two penalties: density and cost. The memory cell complexity and the on-chip support circuitry place EEPROMs far behind an EPROM in bit capacity per square millimeter of silicon; a 1-Mbit EEPROM requires about twice as much silicon as a 1-Mbit EPROM. So, despite its operational superiority, the EEPROM's shortcomings in density and cost-effectiveness have kept it from replacing the EPROM in applications where density and cost are paramount factors.

The logic symbol for the Intel 2864 is shown in Figure 3.10A. It is organized as an 8K × 8 array with 13 address inputs ($2^{13} = 8192$) and eight data I/O pins. Three control inputs determine the operating mode according to the table given in Figure 3.10B. With $\overline{CE}$ = HIGH the chip is in its low-power standby mode, in which no operations are being performed on any memory location and the data pins are in the high-Z state.

To read the contents of a memory location, the desired address is applied to the address pins, $\overline{CE}$ is driven LOW, and the OUTPUT ENABLE pin, $\overline{OE}$, is driven LOW to enable the chip's output data buffers. The WRITE ENABLE pin, $\overline{WE}$, is held HIGH during a READ operation.

To write into (program) a memory location, the output buffers are disabled so that the data to be written can be applied as inputs to the I/O pins. The timing for the WRITE operation is diagrammed in Figure 3.10C. Prior to t_1 the device is in the standby mode. A new address is applied at that time. At t_2 the $\overline{CE}$ and $\overline{WE}$ inputs are driven LOW to begin the WRITE operation; $\overline{OE}$ is HIGH so that the data pins will remain in the high-Z state. Data are applied to the I/O pins at t_3 and written into the address location on the rising edge of $\overline{WE}$ at t_4. The data are removed at t_5. Actually, the data are first latched (on the rising edge of $\overline{WE}$) into an FF buffer memory that is part of the 2864 circuitry. The data are held there while other circuitry on the chip performs an erase operation on the selected address location in the EEPROM array, after which the data byte is transferred from the buffer to the EEPROM array and stored at that location. This ERASE and STORE operation typically takes 5 ms. With $\overline{CE}$ returned HIGH at t_4 the chip is back in the standby mode while the internal ERASE and STORE operations are completed.

The 2864 has an enhanced write mode that allows the user to write up to 16 bytes of data into the FF buffer memory, where it is held while the EEPROM circuitry erases the selected address locations. The 16 bytes of data are then transferred to the EEPROM array for storage at these locations. This process also takes about 5 ms.

▶ 3.7 FLASH MEMORY

EPROMs are nonvolatile, offer fast read access times (typically 120 ns), and have high density and low cost per bit. They do, however, require removal from their circuit/system to be erased and reprogrammed. EEPROMs are nonvolatile, offer fast read access, and allow rapid in-circuit erasure and reprogramming of individual bytes. Their drawbacks are lower density and much higher cost than EPROMs.

The challenge for semiconductor engineers was to fabricate a nonvolatile memory with the EEPROM's in-circuit electrical erasability, but with densities and costs much closer to EPROMs, while retaining the high-speed read access of both. The response to this challenge was the **flash memory.**

Structurally, a flash memory cell is like the simple single-transistor EPROM cell (and unlike the more complex two-transistor EEPROM cell), being only slightly larger. It has a thinner gate-oxide layer that allows electrical erasability but can be built with much higher densities than EEPROMs. The cost of flash memory is considerably less than for EEPROM, although not yet as close to EPROM as it will be as flash technology improves.

Flash memories are so-called because of their rapid erase and write times. Most flash clips use a *bulk erase* operation in which all cells on the chip are erased simultaneously; this bulk erase process typically requires hundreds of milliseconds compared to 20 min. for UV EPROMs. Some newer flash memories offer a *sector erase* mode, where specific sectors of the memory array (e.g., 512 bytes) can be erased at one time. This prevents having to erase and reprogram all cells when only a portion of the memory needs to be updated. A typical flash memory has a write time of 10 μs per byte compared to 100 μs for the most advanced EPROM and 5 ms for EEPROM (which includes automatic byte erase time).

Memory manufacturers everywhere are working on developing and improving flash memory devices, and each has its own approach as to what features and performance characteristics are the most important. We will not attempt to survey the vast array of manufacturers and devices here. Instead, we present a representative flash memory IC from one of the leading memory manufacturers and use it as a vehicle for learning the main aspects of flash memory operation. By looking at this representative device we will also get exposed to the use of *command codes* as a means by which we can control the internal operations of the more complex logic chips. This will serve as a good introduction to the many types of command-controlled ICs that are part of most microprocessor-based systems.

The 28F256A CMOS Flash Memory IC

Figure 3.11A shows the symbol for Intel Corporation's 28F256A CMOS flash memory chip, which has a capacity of 32K × 8. The diagram shows 15 address inputs (A_0–A_{14}) needed to select the different memory addresses; that is, $2^{15} = 32K = 32,768$. The eight data input/output pins (DQ_0–DQ_7) are used as inputs during memory WRITE operations and as outputs during memory READ operations. These data pins float to the high-Z state when the chip is deselected ($\overline{CE}$ = HIGH) or when the outputs are disabled ($\overline{OE}$ = HIGH). The write enable input ($\overline{WE}$) is used to control memory WRITE operations. Note that the chip requires two power-supply voltages: V_{cc} is the standard +5 V used for the logic circuitry; V_{PP} is the erase/programming power-supply voltage, nominally +12 V, which is needed for the erase and programming (write) operations.

The control inputs—$\overline{CE}$, $\overline{OE}$, and $\overline{WE}$—control what happens at the data pins in much the same way as for the 2864 EEPROM, as the table in Figure 3.11B shows. These data pins are normally connected to a data bus. During a WRITE operation data are transferred over the bus, usually to the microprocessor. It is important to note that if the V_{PP}

pin is not held at a high voltage (over 6.5 V), WRITE operations cannot be performed, and the chip can only be read from; so it acts as a read-only memory (ROM) and the memory contents cannot be altered.

The operation of this flash memory chip can be better understood by looking at its internal structure. Figure 3.12 is a diagram of the 28F256A showing its major functional blocks. You should refer to this diagram as needed during the following discussion. The unique feature of this structure is the *command register,* which is used to manage all the chip functions. Command codes are written into this register to control which operations take place inside the chip (i.e., erase, erase verify, program, program verify). These command codes usually come over the data bus from the microprocessor. State control logic examines the contents of the command register and generates logic and control signals to the rest of the chip's circuits to carry out the steps in the operation. Let's look at how this works for some of the commands.

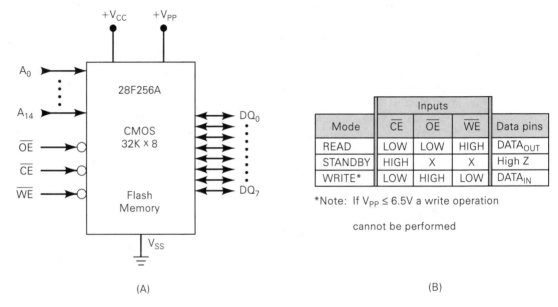

	Inputs			
Mode	$\overline{CE}$	$\overline{OE}$	$\overline{WE}$	Data pins
READ	LOW	LOW	HIGH	$DATA_{OUT}$
STANDBY	HIGH	X	X	High Z
WRITE*	LOW	HIGH	LOW	$DATA_{IN}$

*Note: If $V_{PP} \leq 6.5V$ a write operation

cannot be performed

(A)

(B)

FIGURE 3.11   (A) Logic symbol for 28F256A flash memory chip; (B) control inputs $\overline{CE}$, $\overline{OE}$, $\overline{WE}$ control the device's data pins.

Read Command

To set up the chip for READ operations, it is necessary first to WRITE all 0s ($00000000_2 = 00_{16}$) into the command register. This is done by applying 00_{16} to the data pins and pulsing $\overline{WE}$ LOW while $\overline{CE}$ = LOW and $\overline{OE}$ = HIGH (as shown in the table in Fig. 3.11B). The address inputs can be in any state for this step because the input data will automatically be routed to the command register. Once this is done, the device is set up to have data READ from the 262,144-bit (32,768-byte) memory matrix (array). Memory data are read in the usual way: (1) apply the address to be read from; (2) set $\overline{WE}$ = HIGH, $\overline{CE}$ = LOW, and pulse $\overline{OE}$ = LOW to enable the output buffers to pass data from the cell matrix to the data output pins. The READ access time for the 28F256A is 120 ns, maximum. The

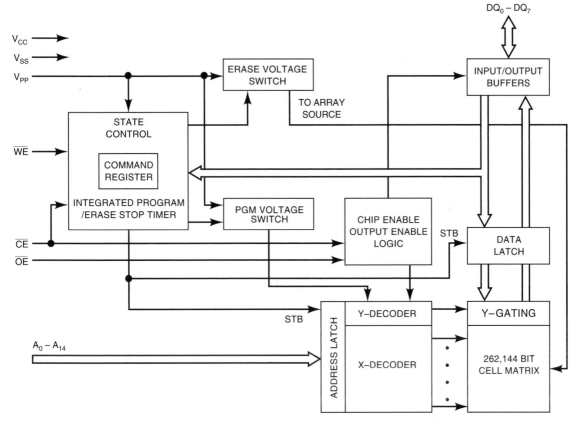

FIGURE 3.12 Functional diagram of 28F256A flash memory chip. (Courtesy of Intel Corporation.)

device remains enabled for memory reads as long as the command register contents remain at 00_{16}.

Set Up ERASE/ERASE Commands

To erase the entire contents of the memory array requires two steps: (1) writing the code 20_{16} to the command register to set up the chip for the ERASE operation; and (2) again writing the code 20_{16} to the command register to begin the ERASE operation. This two-step sequence makes it less likely that the memory contents will be erased accidentally. After the second command code has been written, the 12 V from V_{PP} is used to erase all cells in the array. This process takes about 10 ms.

Erase-Verify Command

After the ERASE operation, it is necessary to verify that all memory cells have been erased; that is, all bytes = 11111111_2 = FF_{16}. The erase-verify operation must be done for each byte address. It is initiated by writing AO_{16} to the command register. Then a READ operation is done on the address to be verified and the output data are checked to see that it equals FF_{16}. These two steps are done for each address, and the total time to verify all addresses is about 1 s. If the data at an address do not show up as FF_{16}, the chip must be erased again using the erase command sequence above.

Set Up Program/Program Commands

The device can be set up for byte programming by writing the code 40_{16} to the command register. This is followed by writing the data that are to be programmed to the desired address.

Program Verify Command

After a byte has been programmed into an address, the content of that address must be verified to ensure that it has been programmed successfully. This is done by first writing the code CO_{16} to the command register to set up the verify operation. This is followed by a READ operation, which will cause the chip to output the data from the address that was just programmed so that it can be compared to the desired data.

The complete process of programming and verifying each address location takes about 500 ms for the 28F256A.

▶ 3.8 ROM APPLICATIONS

With the exception of MROM and PROM, most ROM devices can be reprogrammed, so technically they are not *read-only* memories. However, the term ROM can still be used to include EPROMs, EEPROMs, and flash memory, because during normal operation the stored content of these devices is not changed nearly as often as it is read. So ROMs are taken to include all semiconductor, nonvolatile memory devices, and they are used in applications where nonvolatile storage of information, data, or program codes is needed, and where the stored data rarely or never change. Here are some of the most common application areas.

Firmware

The most widespread application of ROMs is in the storage of data and program codes that must be available on power-up in microprocessor-based systems. These data and program codes are called *firmware* because they are firmly stored in hardware (i.e., ROM chips) and are not subject to change during normal system operation. Some PCs, business computers, and laptop computers store their operation system programs and language interpreters (e.g., BASIC, Pascal) in ROM firmware so that the computer can be used immediately after power is turned on.

In addition to the familiar microcomputers, there are many other microprocessor-based systems that use ROM firmware. Consumer products such as automobiles, VCRs, CD players, and microwave ovens, as well as all kinds of production machinery have embedded microcontrollers which consist of a microprocessor that controls and monitors the operation according to programs and data that are stored in ROM.

In all of these systems, system operation depends to a great degree on what is stored in the ROM, and changes in system operation are usually made by changing the contents of ROM. With EPROMs, this requires either removing the chips from the system for erasure and reprogramming, or replacing them with new ones. This necessitates suspension of system operation for anywhere from a few minutes to an hour. The use of EEPROMs, and better still, flash memory, cuts this down considerably since they can be rapidly erased and reprogrammed in-system.

Bootstrap Memory

Many microcomputers and most large computers do not have their operating system programs stored in ROM. Instead, these programs are stored in external mass memory, usually magnetic disk. How, then, do these computers know what to do when they are powered on? A relatively small program, called a *bootstrap program*, is stored in ROM. (The term *bootstrap* comes from the idea of pulling oneself up by one's own bootstraps.) When the computer is powered on, it will execute the instructions that are in this bootstrap program. These instructions typically cause the CPU to initialize the system hardware. The bootstrap program then loads the operating system programs from mass storage (disk) into its main internal memory. At that point the computer begins executing the operating system program and is ready to respond to the user commands. This startup process is often called "booting up the system."

Data Tables

ROMs are often used to store tables of data that do not change. Some examples are trigonometric tables (i.e., sine, cosine, etc.) and code-conversion tables. Several standard ROM "look-up" tables are available with trig functions. One, The National Semiconductor MM4220BM, stores the sine function for angles between 0 and 90°. This ROM is organized as a 128×8, with seven address inputs and eight data outputs. The address inputs represent the angle in increments of approximately 0.7°. For example, address 0000000_2 is 0°, address 0000001_2 is 0.7°, address 0000010_2 is 1.41°, and so on, up to address 1111111_2, which is 89.3°. When an address is applied to the ROM, the data outputs will represent the approximate sine of the angle. For example, with input address 1000000_2 (representing approximately 45°) the data outputs will be 10110101_2. Since the sine is less than or equal to 1, these data are interpreted as a fraction; that is, $.10110101_2$ which when converted to decimal equals .707 (the sine of 45°).

Data Converter

The data converter circuit takes data expressed in one type of code and produces an output expressed in another type. Code conversion is needed, for example, when a computer is outputting data in straight binary code and we want to convert it to BCD in order to display it on 7-segment LED readouts.

One of the easiest methods of code conversion uses a ROM programmed so that the application of a particular address (the old code) produces a data output that represents the equivalent in the new code. The 74185 is a TTL ROM that stores the binary-to-BCD code conversion for a 6-bit binary input. To illustrate, a binary address input of 100110 (decimal 38) will produce a data output of 00111000, which is the BCD code for decimal 38.

Function Generator

The function generator is a circuit that produces waveforms such as sine waves, sawtooth waves, triangle waves, and square waves. Figure 3.13 shows how a ROM look-up table and a DAC (digital-to-analog converter) are used to generate a sine-wave output signal.

The ROM stores 256 different 8-bit values, each one corresponding to a different waveform value (i.e., a different voltage point on the sine wave). The 8-bit counter is continuously pulsed by a clock signal to provide sequential address inputs to the ROM. As the counter cycles through the 256 different addresses, the ROM outputs the 256 data points to the DAC. The DAC output will be a waveform that steps through the 256 different analog voltage values corresponding to the data points. The low-pass filter smoothes out the steps in the DAC output to produce a smooth waveform.

Circuits such as this are used in some commercial function generators. The same idea is employed in some speech synthesizers, where the digitized speech waveform values are stored in ROM.

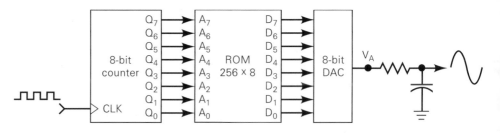

FIGURE 3.13   Function generator using a ROM and a DAC.

Auxiliary Storage

Because of their nonvolatility, high speed, low power requirements, and lack of moving parts, flash memory modules have become feasible alternatives to magnetic disk storage. This is especially true for lower capacities (5 Mbytes or less) where flash is cost-competitive with magnetic disk. The low power consumption of flash memory makes it particularly attractive for laptop and notebook computers which use battery power. We can expect to see more and more of these "semiconductor disk drives"—that is, flash memory cards made up of several flash ICs and control logic—being used in place of the slower, bulkier, less reliable, and more power-hungry disk drives.

▶ 3.9 SEMICONDUCTOR RAMS

Recall that the term *RAM* stands for *random access memory,* meaning that any memory address location is as easily accessible as any other. Many types of memory can be classified as having random access, but when the term RAM is used with semiconductor memories it is usually taken to mean READ/WRITE memory (RWM) as opposed to ROM. Because it is common practice to use RAM to mean semiconductor RWM, we will do so throughout the following sections.

RAMs are used in computers for the *temporary* storage of programs and data. The contents of many RAM address locations will be changing continually as the computer executes a program. This requires fast READ and WRITE cycle times for the RAM so as not to slow down the computer operation.

A major disadvantage of RAMs is that they are volatile and will lose all stored information if power is interrupted or turned off. Some RAMs, however, use such small amounts of power in the standby mode (no READ or WRITE operations taking place) that they can be powered from batteries whenever the main power is interrupted. Of course, the main advantage of RAMs is that they can be written into and read from with equal ease.

The following discussion of RAMs will draw on some of the material covered in our treatment of ROMs, since many of the basic concepts are common to both types of memory.

▶ 3.10 RAM ARCHITECTURE

As with the ROM, it is helpful to think of the RAM as consisting of a number of registers, each storing a single data word and each having a unique address. RAMs typically come with word capacities of 1K, 4K, 8K, 16K, or 64K, and word sizes of 1, 4, or 8 bits. As we will see later, the word capacity and word size can be expanded by combining memory chips.

Figure 3.14 shows the simplified architecture of a RAM that stores 64 words of 4 bits each (that is, a 64×4 memory). These words have addresses ranging from 0 to 63_{10}. In order to select one of the 64 address locations for reading or writing, a binary address code is applied to a decoder circuit. Since $64 = 2^6$, the decoder requires a 6-bit input code. Each address code activates one particular decoder output, which, in turn, enables its corresponding register. For example, assume an applied address code of

$$A_5 A_4 A_3 A_2 A_1 A_0 = 011010$$

Since $011010_2 = 26_{10}$, decoder output 26 will go HIGH, selecting register 26 for either a READ or a WRITE operation.

READ Operation

The address code picks out one register in the memory chip for reading or writing. In order to *read* the contents of the selected register, the READ/WRITE (R/$\overline{W}$)* input must be a 1.

---

*Some IC manufacturers use the symbol $\overline{WE}$ (WRITE/ENABLE) instead of R/$\overline{W}$ for READ/WRITE control input. In either case, the operation is the same.

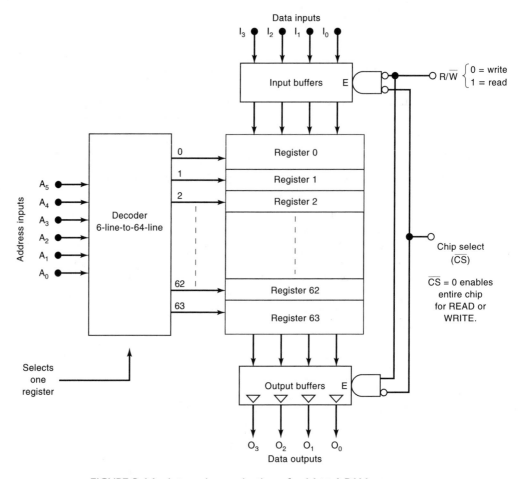

FIGURE 3.14 Internal organization of a 64 × 4 RAM.

In addition, the *CHIP SELECT* ($\overline{CS}$) input must be activated (a 0 in this case). The combination of R/$\overline{W}$ = 1 and $\overline{CS}$ = 0 enables the output buffers so that the contents of the selected register will appear at the four data outputs. R/$\overline{W}$ = 1 also *disables* the input buffers so that the data inputs do not affect the memory during a READ operation.

WRITE Operation

To write a new 4-bit word into the selected register requires that R/$\overline{W}$ = 0 and $\overline{CS}$ = 0. This combination *enables* the input buffers so that the 4-bit word applied to the data inputs will be loaded into the selected register. The R/$\overline{W}$ = 0 also *disables* the output buffers, which are tri-state, so that the data outputs are in their high-Z state during the WRITE operation. The WRITE operation, of course, destroys the word that was stored previously at that address.

Chip Select

Most memory chips have one or more CS inputs that are used to enable the entire chip or disable it completely. In the disable mode all data inputs and data outputs are disabled (high-Z) so that neither a READ nor a WRITE operation can take place. In this mode the contents of the memory are unaffected. The reason for having CS inputs will become clear when we combine memory chips to obtain larger memories. Note that many manufacturers call these inputs *CHIP ENABLE* (*CE*). When the CS or CE inputs are in their active state, the memory chip is said to be *selected;* otherwise it is said to be *deselected.* Many memory ICs are designed to consume much lower power when they are deselected. In large memory systems, for a given memory operation, one or more memory chips will be selected while all others are deselected. More will be said on this later.

Common Input/Output Pins

In order to conserve pins on an IC package, manufacturers often combine the data input and data output functions using common input/output pins. The R/$\overline{\text{W}}$ input controls the function of these I/O pins. During a READ operation, the I/O pins act as data outputs that reproduce the contents of the selected address location. During a WRITE operation, the I/O pins act as data inputs.

We can see why this is done by considering the chip in Fig. 3.12. With separate input and output pins, a total of 18 pins is required (including ground and power supply). With four common I/O pins, only 14 pins are required. The pin savings become even more significant for chips with larger word size.

The architecture illustrated in Fig. 3.14 for a 64 × 4 RAM will be somewhat different for larger capacity RAMs. The registers would be arranged in a matrix such as that shown for the ROM architecture in Fig. 3.5. The address decoders would select the row and column of the register that is being accessed for a READ or WRITE operation. This matrix architecture reduces the size of the decoding circuitry required.

EXAMPLE 3.6

The 2147H is an NMOS RAM that is organized as a 4K × 1 with separate data input and output, and a single active-LOW CHIP-SELECT input. Draw the logic symbol for this chip, showing all its functions.

Solution   The logic symbol is shown in Figure 3.15A.

EXAMPLE 3.7

The MCM6206C is a CMOS RAM with 32K × 8 capacity, common I/O pins, an active-LOW CHIP-ENABLE, and an active-LOW OUTPUT-ENABLE. Draw the logic symbol.

Solution   The logic symbol is shown in Figure 3.15B.

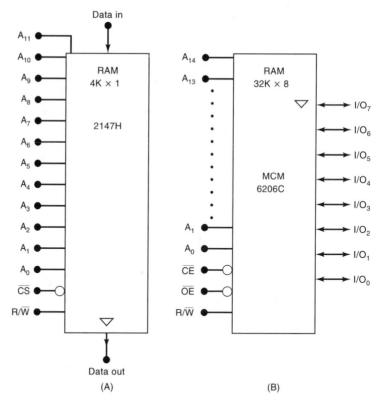

FIGURE 3.15   (A) Logic symbol for 2147H RAM chip; (B) MCM6206C RAM.

▶ 3.11 STATIC RAM

The RAM operation that we have been discussing up to this point applies to a *static* RAM. A static RAM is one that can store data as long as power is applied to the chip. Static RAM memory cells are essentially flip-flops that will stay in a given state (store a bit) indefinitely, provided that power to the circuit is not interrupted. Later we will describe *dynamic* RAMs, which store data as charges on capacitors. With dynamic RAMs the stored data will gradually disappear because of capacitor discharge, so it is necessary to periodically refresh the data (that is, recharge the capacitors).

Static RAMs are available in bipolar, MOS, and BiCMOS technologies. BiCMOS is a recent logic series that combines the best features of bipolar and CMOS technologies. However, the vast majority of applications use NMOS or CMOS RAMs. Nevertheless, bipolars have the advantage in speed (although CMOS and BiCMOS are gradually closing the gap), and MOS devices have much greater capacities. Figure 3.16 shows a typical bipolar static memory cell and a typical NMOS static memory cell just for the purposes of comparison. The bipolar cell contains two bipolar transistors and two resistors, while the NMOS cell contains four N-channel MOSFETs. The bipolar cell requires more chip area than the MOS cell because a bipolar transistor is more complex than a MOSFET, and because the bipolar cell requires separate resistors whereas the MOS cell uses MOSFETs as resistors (Q_3 and Q_4). A CMOS memory cell would be similar to the NMOS cell except that it would use P-channel MOSFETs in place of Q_3 and Q_4. This results in lower power consumption but increases the chip complexity, so that CMOS capacities fall somewhere between bipolar and NMOS.

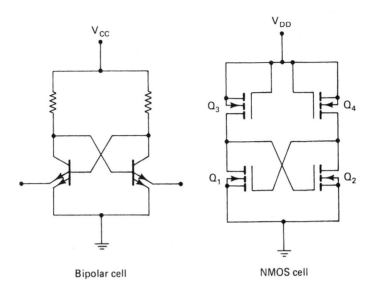

Bipolar cell   NMOS cell

FIGURE 3.16 Typical bipolar and NMOS static RAM cells.

Static RAM Timing

RAM ICs are most often used as the internal memory of a computer. The CPU (central processing unit) continually performs READ and WRITE operations on this memory at a very fast rate determined by the limitations of the CPU. The memory chips that are interfaced to the CPU have to be fast enough to respond to the CPU READ and WRITE commands, and a computer designer has to be concerned with the RAM's various timing characteristics.

Not all RAMs have the same timing characteristics, but most of them are similar, so we will use a typical set of characteristics for illustrative purposes. The nomenclature for the different timing parameters will vary from one manufacturer to another, but the meaning of each parameter is usually easy to determine from the memory timing diagrams on the RAM data sheets. Figure 3.17 shows the timing diagrams for a complete READ cycle and complete WRITE cycle for a typical RAM chip.

The waveforms in Fig. 3.17A show how the address inputs, chip select input, $R/\overline{W}$ input, and data outputs behave during a READ cycle. Note that the $R/\overline{W}$ line stays HIGH throughout the READ cycle. In most memory systems, $R/\overline{W}$ is normally kept HIGH and is driven LOW only during a WRITE cycle. The READ cycle starts at t_0 when the address inputs change to the new address from which data are to be read; the READ cycle ends at t_3 when the address inputs change to a different address to begin the next READ cycle. Thus, the t_0–t_3 interval defines the READ cycle time, t_{RC}.

The access time, t_{ACC}, occurs within the t_{RC} interval, and it represents the time required for the memory chip to produce valid data outputs. Of course, the $\overline{CS}$ input has to be driven LOW. The timing parameter t_{CO} is the time it takes for the memory outputs to go from high-Z to valid data after $\overline{CS}$ goes LOW. The time interval, t_{OD}, is the time it takes for

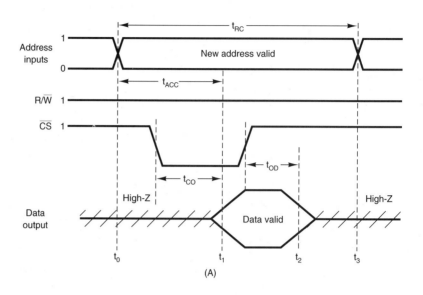

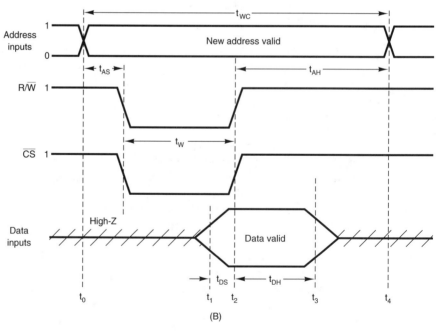

FIGURE 3.17   Typical timing for static RAM: (A) READ cycle; (B) WRITE cycle.

the outputs to return to the disabled (high-Z) state after $\overline{CS}$ returns HIGH. Thus, the memory outputs hold valid data between t_1 and t_2, during which time the data can be transferred to another circuit. Any attempt to transfer the memory data prior to t_1 will produce invalid results. In many microcomputer systems, the positive-going transition of $\overline{CS}$ is used to clock the valid memory data into a CPU register.

Figure 3.17B shows the signal activity for a WRITE cycle that begins when the CPU supplies a new address to the RAM at a time t_0. The CPU drives the $R/\overline{W}$ and $\overline{CS}$ lines LOW after waiting for a time t_{AS}, called the *address setup time*. This gives the RAM's address decoders time to respond to the new address. $R/\overline{W}$ and $\overline{CS}$ are held LOW for a time interval t_W, called *write-time* interval.

During this write-time interval at time t_1 the CPU applies valid data to the data bus to be written into the RAM. These data have to be held at the RAM input for at least a time interval t_{DS} prior to, and for at least a time interval t_{DH} after, the deactivation of $R/\overline{W}$ and $\overline{CS}$ at t_2. The t_{DS} interval is called the *data setup time*, and t_{DH} is called the *data hold time*. Similarly, the address inputs have to remain stable for the *address hold-time* interval, t_{AH}, after t_2. If any of these setup- or hold-time requirements are not met, the WRITE operation will not take place reliably.

The complete *WRITE cycle time*, t_{WC}, extends from t_0 to t_4 when the CPU changes the address lines to a new address for the next READ or WRITE cycle.

The *READ cycle time*, t_{RC}, and WRITE cycle time, t_{WC}, are what essentially determine how fast a memory chip can operate. For example, in an actual application, a CPU will often be reading successive data words from memory one right after the other. If the memory has a t_{RC} of 50 ns, the CPU can read one word every 50 ns, or 20 million words per second; with $t_{RC} = 10$ ns, the CPU can read 100 million words per second. Table 3.1 shows the minimum READ and WRITE cycle times for some representative static RAM chips.

TABLE 3.1   Minimum READ and WRITE Cycle Times

Device	t_{RC} (min) (ns)	t_{WC} (min) (ns)
CMOS MCM6206C, 32K $\times$ 8	15	15
NMOS 2147, 4K $\times$ 1	35	35
BiCMOS MCM6708A, 64K $\times$ 4	8	8

▶ 3.12 DYNAMIC RAM

Dynamic RAMs are fabricated using MOS technology and are noted for their high capacity, low power requirement, and moderate operating speed. As we stated earlier, unlike static RAMs, which store information in FFs, dynamic RAMs store 1s and 0s as charges on a small MOS capacitor (typically a few picofarads). Because of the tendency for these charges to leak off after a period of time, dynamic RAMs require periodic recharging of the memory cells; this is called **refreshing** the dynamic RAM. In modern DRAM chips, each memory cell must be refreshed typically every 2, 4, or 8 ms, or its data will be lost.

The need for refreshing is a drawback of dynamic RAM as compared to static RAM because it may require external support circuitry. Some DRAM chips have built-in refresh control circuitry that does not require extra external hardware but does require special timing of the chip's input control signals. Additionally, as we shall see, the address inputs to a DRAM have to be handled in a less straightforward way than SRAM. So, all in all, designing with and using DRAM in a system is more complex than SRAM. However, their much larger capacities and much lower power consumption make DRAM the memory of choice in systems where the most important design considerations are keeping down size, cost, and power.

For applications where speed and reduced complexity are more critical than cost, space, and power considerations, static RAMs are still the best. They are generally faster than dynamic RAMs and require no refresh operation. They are simpler to design with, but they cannot compete with the higher capacity and lower power requirements of dynamic RAMs.

Because of their simple cell structure, DRAMs typically have four times the density of SRAMs. This allows four times as much memory capacity to be placed on a single board, or alternatively, requires one-fourth as much board space for the same amount of memory. The cost per bit of dynamic RAM storage is typically one-fifth to one-fourth that of static RAMs. A further cost saving is realized because the lower power requirements of dynamic RAM, typically one-sixth to one-half those of a static RAM, allow the use of smaller, less expensive power supplies.

The main applications of SRAMs are in areas where only small amounts of memory are needed (up to 64K), or where high speed is required. Many microprocessor-controlled instruments and appliances have very small memory capacity requirements. Some instruments, such as digital storage oscilloscopes and logic analyzers, require very high-speed memory. For applications such as these, SRAM is normally used.

The main internal memory of most personal microcomputers (e.g., IBM PC or Apple) uses DRAM because of its high capacity and lower power consumption. These computers, however, sometimes use some small amounts of SRAM for functions requiring maximum speed such as video graphics and look-up tables.

▶ 3.13 DYNAMIC RAM STRUCTURE AND OPERATION

The dynamic RAM's internal architecture can be visualized as an array of single-bit cells as illustrated in Fig. 3.18. Here there are 16,384 cells arranged in a 128×128 array. Each cell occupies a unique row and common position within the array. Fourteen address inputs are needed to select one of the cells ($2^{14} = 16,384$); the lower address bits, A_0 to A_6, select the row, and the higher-order bits, A_7 to A_{13}, select the column. Each 14-bit address selects a unique cell to be written into or read from. The structure in Figure 3.18 is a $16K \times 1$ DRAM chip. DRAM chips are currently available in capacities of $4096K \times 1$ ($4M \times 1$) and $1 M \times 4$. DRAMs with a 4-bit word size have a cell arrangement similar to Figure 3.18 except that each position in the array contains four cells, and each applied address selects a group of four cells for a READ or a WRITE operation. As we will see later, larger word sizes can be attained by combining several chips in the appropriate arrangement.

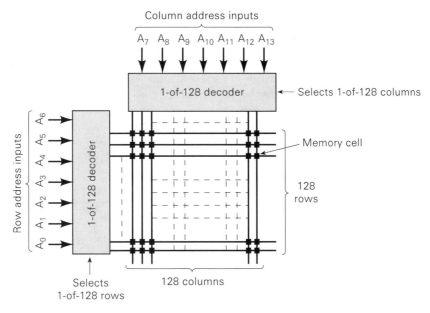

Column address inputs

A_7 A_8 A_9 A_{10} A_{11} A_{12} A_{13}

1-of-128 decoder ◄— Selects 1-of-128 columns

Memory cell

128 rows

128 columns

Row address inputs

A_6 A_5 A_4 A_3 A_2 A_1 A_0

1-of-128 decoder

Selects 1-of-128 rows

FIGURE 3.18   Cell arrangement in 16K × 1 dynamic RAM.

Figure 3.19 is a symbolic representation of a dynamic memory cell and its associated circuitry. Many of the circuit details are not shown, but this simplified diagram can be used to describe the essential ideas involved in writing to and reading from a DRAM. The switches S1 through S4 are actually MOSFETs that are controlled by various address decoder outputs and the R/$\overline{W}$ signal. The capacitor of course, is the actual storage cell.

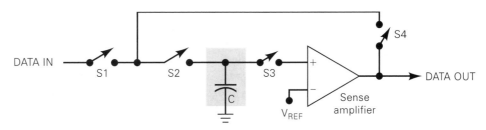

DATA IN — S1 S2 C S3 + Sense amplifier S4 DATA OUT V_{REF} −

FIGURE 3.19   Symbolic representation of a dynamic memory cell. During a WRITE operation, semiconductor switches S1 and S2 are closed. During a READ operation, all switches are closed except S1.

To write data to the cell, signals from the address decoding and READ/WRITE logic will close switches S1 and S2, while keeping S3 and S4 open. This connects the input data to C. A logic 1 at the data input charges C, and a logic 0 discharges it. Then the switches are open so that C is disconnected from the rest of the circuit. Ideally, C would retain its charge indefinitely, but there is always some leakage path through the off switches, so that *C* will gradually lose its charge.

To read data from the cell, switches S2, S3, and S4 are closed and S1 is kept open. This connects the stored capacitor voltage to the *sense amplifier*. The sense amplifier compares the voltage with some reference value to determine if it is a logic 0 or 1, and produces a solid 0 V or 5 V for the data output. This data output is also connected to *C* (S2 and S4 are closed) and refreshes the capacitor voltage by recharging or discharging. In other words, the data bit in a memory cell is refreshed each time it is read.

Address Multiplexing

The 16K × 1 DRAM array depicted in Fig. 3.18 has 14 address inputs. A 64K × 1 DRAM array would have 16 address inputs. A 1M × 4 DRAM needs 20 address inputs; a 4M × 1 needs 22 address inputs. High-capacity memory chips such as these would require many pins if each address input required a separate pin. In order to reduce the number of pins on their high-capacity DRAM chips, manufacturers utilize *address multiplexing* whereby each address input pin can accommodate two different address bits. The savings in pin count translates to a significant decrease in the size of the IC packages. This is very important in large-capacity memory boards, where you want to maximize the amount of memory that can fit on one board.

We will use the 4116, a 16K × 1 DRAM, to illustrate the address multiplexing idea. A simplified diagram of this chip's internal architecture is shown in Fig. 3.20A. It contains an array of cells arranged as 128 rows by 128 columns. There are a single data input line, a single data output line, and an R/$\overline{W}$ input. There are seven address inputs, and each one has a dual function (e.g., A_0/A_7 will function as both A_0 *and* A_7). Two address **strobe** inputs are included for loading the row and column addresses into their respective on-chip registers. The **row-address strobe** $\overline{RAS}$ clocks the 7-bit row address register, and the **column address strobe** $\overline{CAS}$ clocks the 7-bit column address register.

A 14-bit address is applied to this DRAM in two steps using $\overline{RAS}$ and $\overline{CAS}$. The timing is shown in Fig. 3.20B. Initially, $\overline{RAS}$ and $\overline{CAS}$ are both HIGH. At time t_0, the 7-bit row address (A_0 to A_6) is applied to the address inputs. After allowing time for the setup-time requirements (t_{RS}) of the row address register, the $\overline{RAS}$ input is driven LOW at t_1. This NGT (negative-going transition) loads the row address into the row address register so that A_0 to A_6 now appear at the row decoder inputs. The LOW at $\overline{RAS}$ also enables this decoder so that it can decode the row address and select one row of the array.

At time t_2, the 7-bit column address (A_7 to A_{13}) is applied to the address inputs. At t_3, the $\overline{CAS}$ input is driven LOW to load the column address into the column address register. $\overline{CAS}$ also enables the column decoder so that it can decode the column address and select one column of the array.

At this point the two parts of the address are in their respective registers, the decoders have decoded them to select the one cell corresponding to the row and column address, and a READ or a WRITE operation can be performed on that cell just as in a static RAM.

You may have noticed that this DRAM does not have a CHIP-SELECT (CS) input. The $\overline{RAS}$ and $\overline{CAS}$ signals perform the CHIP-SELECT function since they must both be LOW for the decoders to select a cell for reading or writing.

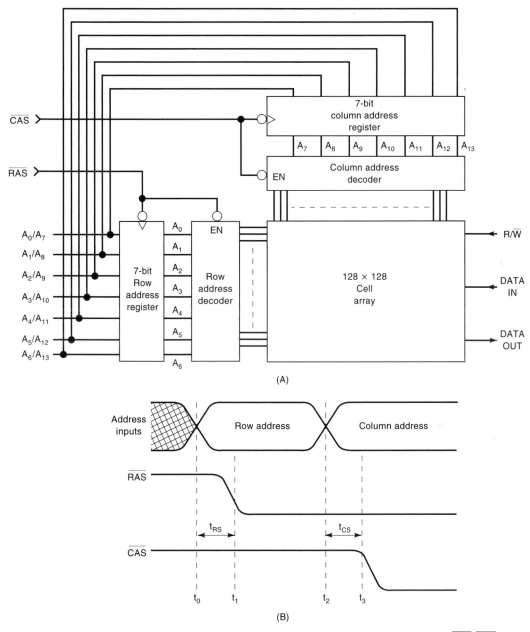

FIGURE 3.20 (A) Simplified architecture of the 4116, a 16K × 1 DRAM; (B) $\overline{RAS}/\overline{CAS}$ timing.

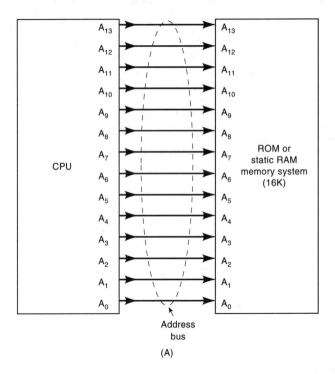

(A)

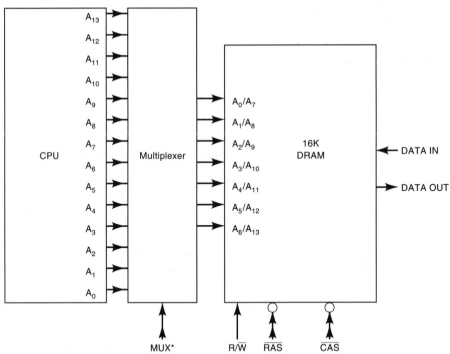

*MUX = 0 transmits CPU addresses
$A_0 - A_6$ to DRAM. MUX = 1 transmits
$A_7 - A_{13}$ to DRAM.

(B)

110   FIGURE 3.21 (A) CPU address bus driving ROM or static RAM memory; (B) CPU addresses driving a multiplexer that is used to multiplex the CPU address lines into the DRAM.

EXAMPLE 3.8

How many pins are saved by using address multiplexing for the 4M × 1 DRAM?

Solution   Eleven address inputs are used instead of 22; $\overline{RAS}$ and $\overline{CAS}$ are added; no $\overline{CS}$ is required. Thus, there is a net saving of *ten* pins.

In a typical computer system, the address inputs to the memory system come from the central processing unit (CPU). When the CPU wants to access a particular memory location, it generates the complete address and places it on address lines that make up an **address bus.** Figure 3.21A shows this for a memory that has a capacity of 16K words and therefore requires a 14-line address bus going directly from the CPU to the memory.

This arrangement works for ROM or for static RAM, but it has to be modified for DRAM that uses multiplexed addressing. If the memory is DRAM, it will have only 7 address inputs. This means that the 14 address lines from the CPU address bus have to be fed into a multiplexer circuit that will transmit 7 address bits at a time to the memory address inputs. This is shown symbolically in Figure 3.21B. The multiplexer select input, labeled *MUX,* signal has to be synchronized with the $\overline{RAS}$ and $\overline{CAS}$ signals that clock the addresses into the DRAM. This is shown in Fig. 3.22. *MUX* has to be LOW when $\overline{RAS}$ is pulsed LOW so that address lines A_0 to A_6 from the CPU will reach the DRAM address inputs to be loaded on the NGT of $\overline{RAS}$. Likewise, *MUX* has to be HIGH when $\overline{CAS}$ is pulsed LOW so that A_7 to A_{13} from the CPU will be present at the DRAM inputs to be loaded on the NGT of $\overline{CAS}$.

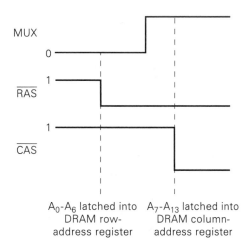

FIGURE 3.22   Timing required for address multiplexing.

A_0-A_6 latched into DRAM row-address register A_7-A_{13} latched into DRAM column-address register

▶ 3.14 DRAM READ/WRITE CYCLES

The timing of the READ and WRITE operations of a DRAM is much more complex than for a static RAM, and there are many critical timing requirements that the DRAM memory designer has to consider. At this point, a detailed discussion of these requirements would probably cause more confusion than enlightenment. We will concentrate on the basic timing sequence for the READ and WRITE operations for a typical DRAM system like that of Fig. 3.21B.

DRAM READ Cycle

Figure 3.23 shows typical signal activity during the READ operation. It is assumed that R/$\overline{\text{W}}$ is in its HIGH state throughout the operation. The following is a step-by-step description of the events that occur at the times indicated on the diagram.

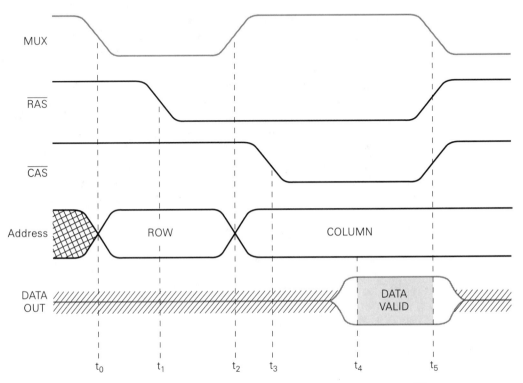

FIGURE 3.23 Signal activity for a READ operation on a dynamic RAM. The R/$\overline{\text{W}}$ input (not shown) is assumed to be HIGH.

t_0: *MUX* is driven LOW to apply the row address bits (A_0 to A_6) to the DRAM address inputs.

t_1: $\overline{RAS}$ is driven LOW to load the row address into the DRAM.

t_2: *MUX* goes HIGH to place the column address (A_7 to A_{13}) at the DRAM address inputs.

t_3: $\overline{CAS}$ goes LOW to load the column address into the DRAM.

t_4: The DRAM responds by placing valid data from the selected memory cell onto the DATA OUT line.

t_5: *MUX, $\overline{RAS}$, $\overline{CAS}$,* and DATA OUT return to their initial states.

DRAM WRITE Cycle

Figure 3.24 shows typical signal activity during a DRAM WRITE operation. Here is a description of the sequence of events.

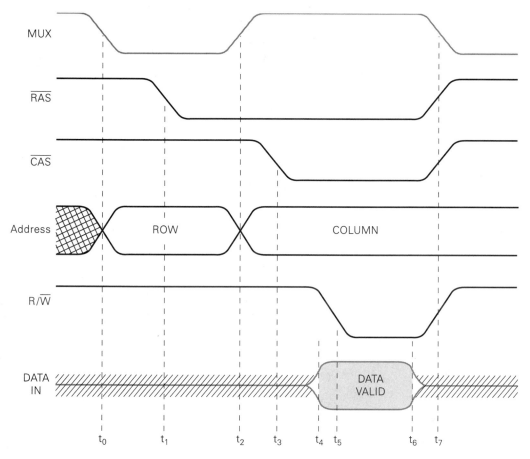

FIGURE 3.24   Signal activity for a WRITE operation on a dynamic RAM.

t_0: The LOW at *MUX* places the row address at the DRAM inputs.

t_1: The NGT at $\overline{RAS}$ loads the row address into the DRAM.

t_2: *MUX* goes HIGH to place the column address at the DRAM inputs.

t_3: The NGT at $\overline{CAS}$ loads the column address into the DRAM.

t_4: Data to be written are placed on the DATA IN line.

t_5: $R/\overline{W}$ is pulsed LOW to write the data into the selected cell.

t_6: Input data are removed from DATA IN.

t_7: *MUX*, $\overline{RAS}$, $\overline{CAS}$, and $R/\overline{W}$ are returned to their initial states.

▶ 3.15 DRAM REFRESHING

A DRAM cell is refreshed each time a READ operation is performed on that cell. Each memory cell has to be refreshed periodically (typically, every 4 ms) or its data will be lost. This requirement would appear to be extremely difficult, if not impossible, to meet for large-capacity DRAMs. For example, a 1M × 1 DRAM has 2^{20} = 1,048,576 cells. To ensure that each cell is refreshed within 4 ms, it would require that READ operations would have to be performed on successive addresses at the rate of one every 4 ns (4 ms/1,048,576 ≈ 4 ns). This is much too fast for any DRAM chip. Fortunately, manufacturers have designed DRAM chips so that

whenever a READ operation is performed on a cell, all the cells in that row will be refreshed.

Thus, it is only necessary to do a READ operation on each *row* of a DRAM array once every 4 ms to guarantee that each *cell* of the array is refreshed. Referring back to the 128 × 128 structure of Figure 3.18, this means that each time a READ operation is performed on any row—say, row 1101011—all 128 cells in that row will be refreshed.

Clearly, this row-refreshing feature makes it easier to keep all DRAM cells refreshed. However, during the normal operation of the system in which a DRAM is functioning, it is unlikely that a READ operation will be performed on each row of the DRAM within the required refresh time limit. Therefore, some kind of refresh control logic is needed either external to the DRAM chip or as part of its internal circuitry. In either case, there are two refresh modes: a *burst* refresh and a *distributed* refresh.

In a burst refresh mode, the normal memory operation is suspended, and each row of the DRAM is refreshed in succession until all rows have been refreshed. In a distributed refresh mode, the row refreshing is interspersed with the normal operations of the memory.

The most common method for refreshing a DRAM is the $\overline{RAS}$-**only refresh.** It is performed by strobing in a row address with $\overline{RAS}$ while $\overline{CAS}$ and R/$\overline{W}$ remain HIGH. Figure 3.25 illustrates how $\overline{RAS}$-only refresh is used for a burst refresh of a 16K DRAM. A **refresh counter** is used to supply 7-bit row addresses to the DRAM address inputs starting at 0000000 (row 0). $\overline{RAS}$ is pulsed LOW to load this address into the DRAM and this refreshes row 0. The counter is incremented and the process is repeated up to address 1111111 (row 127). The complete burst refresh takes about 50 μs.

While the refresh counter idea seems easy enough, we must realize that the row addresses from the refresh counter cannot interfere with the addresses coming from the CPU during normal READ/WRITE operations. For this reason, the refresh counter addresses have to be multiplexed with the CPU addresses, so that the proper source of DRAM addresses is activated at the proper times.

Some of the newer DRAM chips have on-chip refreshing capabilities that eliminate the need to supply external refresh addresses. For example, the Intel 21256 is a 256K × 1 DRAM arranged as a 512 × 512 array. It has on-chip refresh control logic and a refresh counter that are used as part of a refresh method called $\overline{CAS}$-**before-**$\overline{RAS}$ **refresh.** In this method the $\overline{CAS}$ signal is driven LOW and held there as $\overline{RAS}$ is pulsed LOW. When the on-chip refresh control logic senses this sequence, an internal refresh operation takes place automatically at the row address given by the on-chip counter (not the externally applied address). The counter is internally incremented in preparation for the next $\overline{CAS}$-before-$\overline{RAS}$ cycle.

There are other refresh methods, but in general the $\overline{RAS}$-only and the $\overline{CAS}$-before-$\overline{RAS}$ are the preferred methods. Regardless of what method is used and what the source of the refresh address, the system designer has to see to it that the refresh cycles occur often enough to ensure that each row is refreshed within the specified time.

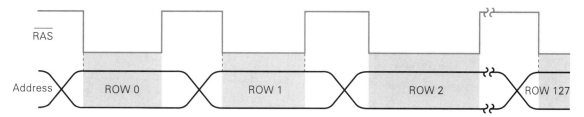

* R/$\overline{W}$ and $\overline{CAS}$ lines held HIGH

FIGURE 3.25   The $\overline{RAS}$-only refresh method uses only the $\overline{RAS}$ signal to load the row address into the DRAM to refresh all cells in that row. The $\overline{RAS}$-only refresh can be used to perform a burst refresh as shown here. A refresh counter supplies the sequential row addresses from row 0 to row 127 (for a 16K × 1 DRAM).

▶ 3.16 EXPANDING WORD SIZE AND CAPACITY

In most IC memory applications the required memory capacity or word size cannot be satisfied by one memory chip. Instead, several memory chips have to be combined to provide the desired capacity and word size. We will see how this is done through several examples that illustrate all the important concepts that will be needed when we interface memory chips to a microprocessor.

Expanding Word Size

Suppose we need a memory that can store sixteen 8-bit words and all we have are RAM chips arranged as 16 × 4 memories with common I/O lines. We can combine two of these 16 × 4 chips to produce the desired memory. The configuration for doing so is shown in Fig. 3.26. Examine this diagram carefully and see what you can find out from it before reading on.

Since each chip can store sixteen 4-bit words and we want to store sixteen 8-bit words, we are using each chip to store *half* of each word. In other words, RAM-0 stores the four *higher*-order bits of each of the 16 words, and RAM-1 stores the four *lower*-order bits of each of the 16 words. A full 8-bit word is available at the RAM outputs connected to the data bus.

Any one of the 16 words is selected by applying the appropriate address code to the four-line *address bus* (AB_3, AB_2, AB_1, AB_0). For now, we will not be concerned with where these address inputs come from.* Note that each address bus line is connected to the

---

*Typically, the address lines come from the CPU portion of a computer.

corresponding address input of each chip. This means that once an address code is placed on the address bus, this same address code is applied to both chips so that the same location in each chip is accessed at the same time.

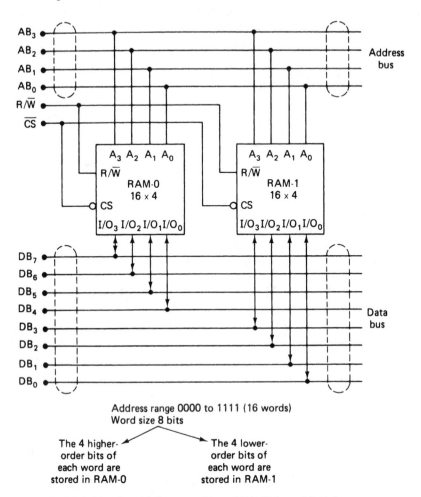

Address range 0000 to 1111 (16 words)
Word size 8 bits

The 4 higher-order bits of each word are stored in RAM-0

The 4 lower-order bits of each word are stored in RAM-1

FIGURE 3.26 Combining two 16 × 4 RAMS for a 16 × 8 memory.

Once the address is selected, we can read or write at this address under control of the common R/$\overline{\text{W}}$ and $\overline{\text{CS}}$ line. To read, R/$\overline{\text{W}}$ must be HIGH and $\overline{\text{CS}}$ must be LOW. This causes the RAM I/O lines to act as *outputs*. RAM-0 places its selected 4-bit word on the upper four data bus lines and RAM-1 places its selected 4-bit word on the lower four data bus lines. The data bus then contains the full selected 8-bit word, which can now be transmitted to some other device (typically the CPU).

To write, R/$\overline{\text{W}}$ = 0 and $\overline{\text{CS}}$ = 0 causes the RAM I/O lines to act as *inputs*. The 8-bit word to be written is placed on the data bus from some external device (such as the CPU). The upper 4 bits will be written into the selected location of RAM-0 and the lower 4 bits will be written into RAM-1.

In essence, the combination of the two RAM chips acts like a single 16×8 memory chip. We would refer to this combination as a 16×8 memory module.

The same basic idea for expanding word size will work for many different situations. Read the following example and draw a rough diagram for what the system will look like before looking at the solution.

EXAMPLE 3.9

Show how to construct a 1024×8 memory module from static RAM ICs that have a capacity of $1K \times 1$ with a common input/output pin.

Solution   The circuit is shown in Fig. 3.27, where eight RAM chips are used. Each RAM stores one of the bits of each of the one thousand twenty-four 8-bit words. Note that all of the R/$\overline{\text{W}}$ and CS inputs are wired together. Also note that the 10-line address bus is connected to the address inputs of each chip. When combined in this way, the eight chips act like a $1K \times 8$ memory module.

Expanding Capacity

Suppose we need a memory that can store thirty-two 4-bit words and all we have are the 16×4 chips. By combining two 16×4 chips as shown in Fig. 3.28, we can produce the desired memory. Once again, examine this diagram and see what you can determine from it before reading on.

Each RAM is used to store sixteen 4-bit words. The data I/O pins of each RAM are connected to a common four-line data bus. Only one of the RAM chips can be selected (enabled) at one time, so that there will be no bus contention problems. This is ensured by driving the respective $\overline{\text{CS}}$ inputs from different logic signals.

Because the total capacity of this memory module is 32×4, there have to be 32 different addresses. This requires *five* address bus lines. The upper address line AB_4 is used to select one RAM or the other (via the $\overline{\text{CS}}$ inputs) as the one that will be read from or written into. The other four address lines AB_0–AB_3 are used to select the one memory location out of 16 from the selected RAM chip.

To illustrate, when $AB_4 = 0$, the $\overline{\text{CS}}$ of RAM-0 enables this chip for READ or WRITE. Then, any address location in RAM-0 can be accessed by AB_3–AB_0. The latter four address lines can range from 0000 to 1111 to select the desired location. Thus, the range of addresses representing locations in RAM-0 are

$$AB_4AB_3AB_2AB_1AB_0 = 00000 \text{ to } 01111$$

Note that when $AB_4 = 0$, the $\overline{\text{CS}}$ of RAM-1 is HIGH, so that its I/O lines are disabled and cannot communicate (give or take data) with the data bus.

It should be clear that when $AB_4 = 1$, the roles of RAM-0 and RAM-1 are reversed. RAM-1 is now enabled, and the AB_3–AB_0 lines select one of its locations. Thus, the range of addresses located in RAM-1 is

$$AB_4AB_3AB_2AB_1AB_0 = 10000 \text{ to } 11111$$

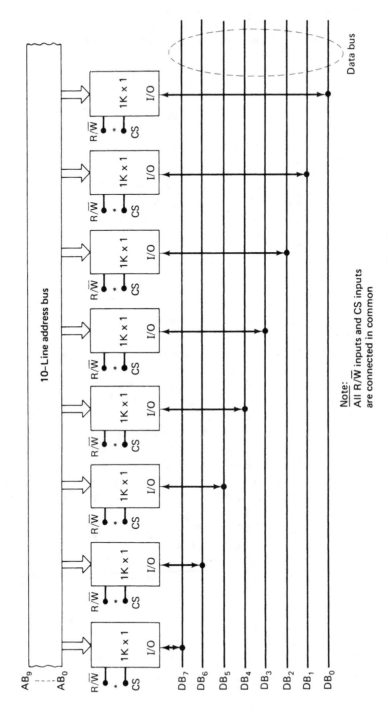

FIGURE 3.27   Eight 1K × 1 chips arranged as a 1K × 8 memory.

118

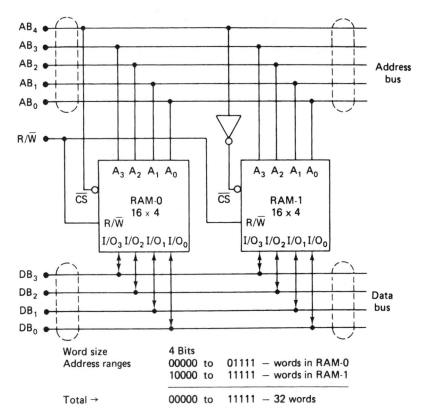

Word size   4 Bits
Address ranges   00000 to   01111 — words in RAM-0
                    10000 to   11111 — words in RAM-1

Total →   00000 to   11111 — 32 words

FIGURE 3.28   Combining two 16 × 4 chips for a 32 × 4 memory.

EXAMPLE 3.10

It is desired to combine several 2K × 8 PROMs to produce a total capacity of 8K × 8. How many PROM chips are needed? How many address bus lines are required?

Solutions   Four PROM chips are required, with each one storing 2K of the 8K words. Since 8K = 8 × 1024 = 8192 = 2^{13}, thirteen address lines are needed.

The configuration for the memory of Example 3.10 is similar to the 32 × 4 memory of Figure 3.28. However, it is slightly more complex, because it requires a decoder circuit for generating the $\overline{CS}$ input signals. The complete diagram for this 8192 × 8 memory is shown in Fig. 3.29.

Since the total capacity is 8192 words, 13 address bus lines are required. The two highest-order lines, AB_{11} and AB_{12}, are used to select *one* of the PROM chips; the other eleven address bus lines go to each PROM to select the desired location within the selected PROM. The PROM selection is accomplished by feeding AB_{11} and AB_{12} into the 74LS138 decoder. The four possible combinations are decoded to generate active-LOW signals, which are applied to the $\overline{CS}$ inputs. For example, when $AB_{11} = AB_{12} = 0$, the 0 output of the decoder goes LOW (all others are HIGH) and enables PROM-0. This causes the PROM-0 outputs to generate the data word internally stored at the address determined by AB_0 through AB_{10}. All other PROMs are disabled, so there is no bus contention.

While $AB_{12} = AB_{11} = 0$, the values of AB_{10} through AB_0 can range from all 0s to all 1s. Thus, PROM-0 will respond to the following range of 13-bit addresses:

$$AB_{12} - AB_0 = 0000000000000 \text{ to } 0011111111111$$

For convenience, these addresses can be more easily expressed in hexadecimal code to give a range of 0000 to 07FF.

Similarly, when $AB_{12} = 0$ and $AB_{11} = 1$, the decoder selects PROM-1, which then responds by outputting the data word it has internally stored at the address AB_{10} through AB_0. Thus, PROM-1 responds to the following range of addresses:

$$0100000000000 \text{ to } 0111111111111 \text{ (binary)}$$

or

$$0800 \text{ to } 0FFF \text{ (hex)}$$

You should verify the PROM-2 and PROM-3 address ranges given in the figure.

Clearly, address lines AB_{12} and AB_{11} are used to select one of the four PROM chips, while AB_{10} through AB_0 select the word stored in the selected PROM.

EXAMPLE 3.11

What size decoder would be needed to expand the memory of Fig. 3.29 to 32K $\times$ 8? Describe what address lines are used.

Solution   A 32K capacity will require 16 PROM chips. To select one of the 16 PROMs will require a 4-line-to-16-line decoder. Four address lines (AB_{14}, AB_{13}, AB_{12}, AB_{11}) will be connected as inputs to this decoder. The address lines AB_{10} to AB_0 are connected to the address inputs of each of the 16 PROMs. Thus, a total of 15 address lines are used. This agrees with the fact that $2^{15} = 32,768 = 32K$.

Combining DRAM Chips

DRAM ICs usually come with word sizes of 1 or 4 bits, so it is necessary to combine several of them to form larger word-size modules. Figure 3.30 shows how to combine eight Intel 21256 DRAM chips to form a 256K $\times$ 8 module. Each 21256 chip has a 256K $\times$ 1 capacity.

There are several important points to note. First, since 256K $= 2^{18}$, the 21256 chip has *nine* address inputs; remember, DRAMs use multiplexed address inputs. The address multiplexer takes the 18-line CPU address bus and changes it to a 9-line address bus for the DRAM chips. Second, the $\overline{RAS}$, $\overline{CAS}$, and $\overline{WE}$ inputs of all eight chips are connected together so that all chips are activated simultaneously for each memory operation. Finally, recall that the 21256 has on-chip refresh control circuitry, so there is no need for an external DRAM controller.

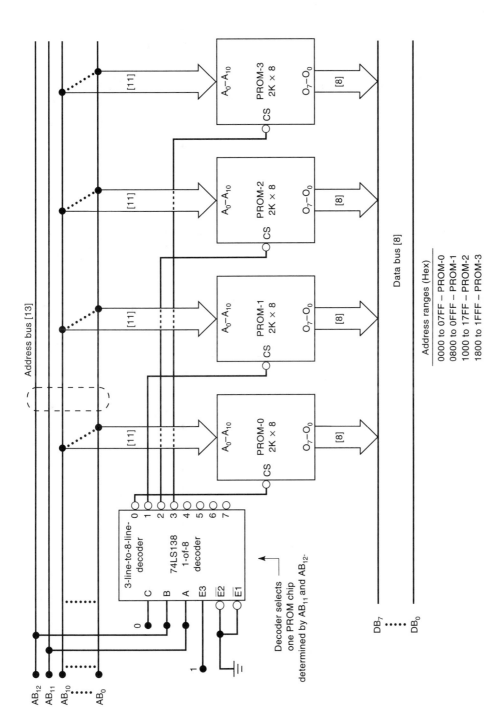

FIGURE 3.29 Four 2K × 8 PROMs arranged to form a total capacity of 8K × 8.

121

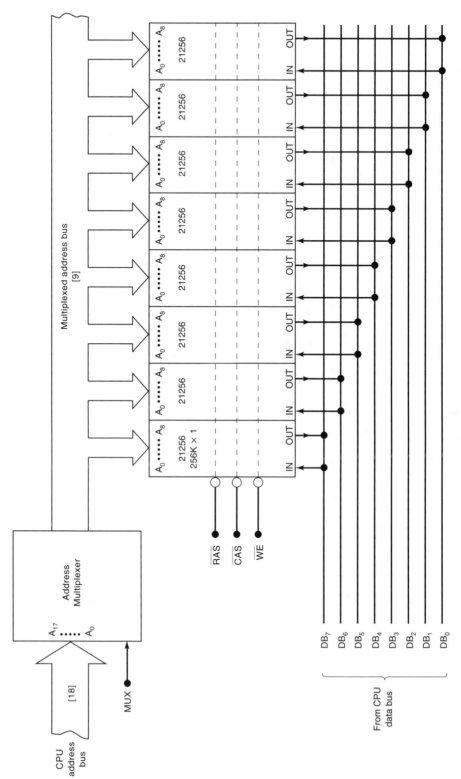

FIGURE 3.30 Eight 256K × 1 DRAM chips combined to form a 256K × 8 memory module.

GLOSSARY

Access Time (t_{ACC}) Speed specification of a memory device. It is the time from the initiation of a READ cycle to when memory data outputs are valid.

Address Number that uniquely specifies a location in memory where instructions or data are stored.

Auxiliary Memory That part of a computer's memory that is separate from the computer's internal working memory. Generally has high density and high capacity, such as a magnetic disk.

Byte A special term used for an 8-bit word.

Capacity Amount of storage space in a memory as number of bits or number of words.

Column Address Strobe ($\overline{CAS}$) Signal used to latch the column address into a DRAM.

Cycle Time The amount of time required for the memory to perform a READ or WRITE operation and then return to its original state ready for the next command.

Density See Capacity.

Downloading The process of transferring data/program from a computer's memory to another memory.

Dynamic RAM (DRAM) Memory devices that store binary data by charging the gate capacitances of MOS transistors and therefore need to be refreshed periodically so as not to lose the charge when present.

Electrically Erasable PROM (EEPROM) Semiconductor ROM memory device with which the user can erase and reprogram individual memory locations by the application of appropriate voltage levels and pulse durations.

Erasable Programmable ROM (EPROM) Semiconductor ROM memory device with which the user can completely erase and reprogram the contents of memory as many times as desired. Erasure occurs by application of UV light and clears the entire memory chip of information.

Firmware Microcomputer programs stored in ROM.

Flash Memory Nonvolatile memory IC that has the high-speed access and in-circuit erasability of EEPROMs but with higher densities and lower cost.

Fusible Link A thin fuse link present on each programmable cell of a PROM which can be selectively fused (blown) to produce the desired stored memory data.

Giga A term used to specify the capacity of a memory. "1 giga" refers to a memory with a capacity of $2^{30} = 1,073,741,824$.

Internal Memory High-speed portion of a computer's memory that holds the program and data the computer is currently working on. Also called *main memory* or *working memory*.

Main Memory See Internal Memory.

Mask-Programmed ROM Semiconductor ROM memory device that requires the manufacturer to load the information into the ROM using a photographic negative (mask) technique.

Mass Storage Storage of large amounts of data. Not part of a computer's internal memory.

Meg A term used to specify the capacity of a memory. "1 meg" refers to a memory with a capacity of $2^{10} = 1,048,576$.

Memory Cell A device or electrical circuit used to store a single bit (0 or 1).

Nibble A 4-bit binary number.

Nonvolatile Memory devices that retain stored information for an indefinite length of time and do not need electrical power to do so.

Programmable ROM (PROM) Semiconductor ROM memory device that can be programmed once by the user after purchase.

Random Access Memory (RAM) Any memory device that can go directly to an address without having to sequence through other locations. RAM is also generally used to describe a memory device that can be easily read from or written into.

READ Cycle Time (t_{RC}) Total time required between two successive READ operations.

READ-Only Memories (ROMs) Semiconductor memory devices designed primarily for having data read from them.

READ Operation Process of getting a word from memory and sending it to some other place where it can be used.

READ/WRITE Memory (RWM) Any memory that can be read from or written into with equal ease.

Refresh Counter Counter that keeps track of row addresses during a DRAM refresh operation.

Refreshing Process of recharging the cells of a dynamic memory.

Row Address Strobe ($\overline{RAS}$) Signal used to latch the row address into a DRAM chip.

Sequential Access Memory (SAM) A type of memory in which the access time is not constant but varies depending on the address location.

Static RAM Semiconductor RAM memory device that consists essentially of FF registers and the necessary circuitry for decoding. Information will remain valid as long as power is on.

Volatile Memory devices that lose all stored information when power is removed.

Word Basic unit of information or data used in a computer.

WRITE Cycle Time (t_{WC}) Total amount of time required for writing a data word into a memory location.

WRITE Operation Process of getting a word placed into a specific memory location or external device.

QUESTIONS AND PROBLEMS

Sections 3.1–3.3

1. Define the following terms:
   (a) Memory cell (b) Memory word (c) Address (d) Byte (e) Access time
2. A certain memory has a capacity of 8K × 16. How many bits are in each word? How many words are being stored? How many memory cells does this memory contain?
3. Explain the difference between the READ (fetch) and WRITE (store) operations.
4. True or false: A volatile memory will lose its stored data when electrical power is interrupted.
5. Explain the difference between SAM and RAM.
6. Explain the difference between RWM and ROM.
7. True or false: A dynamic memory will hold its data as long as electrical power is applied.
8. A certain memory has a capacity of 4M × 32. How many words does it store? What is the number of bits per word? How many memory cells does it contain?

9. How many different addresses are required by the memory of Problem 8?

10. What is the capacity of a memory that has 16 address inputs, 4 data inputs, and 4 data outputs?

11. True or false: All ROMs are nonvolatile.

12. Describe the procedure for reading from ROM.

13. Refer to Fig. 3.4. Determine the data outputs for each of the following input conditions:
    (a) $[A] = 1011; \overline{CS} = 1$ **(b)** $[A] = 0111; \overline{CS} = 0$

Sections 3.4–3.8

14. What address inputs are required if we want to read the data from register 9 in Fig. 3.5?

15. Refer to Fig. 3.5.
    (a) What register is enabled by input address 1011?
    (b) What input address code selects register 4?

16. Describe the function of the row select decoder, column select decoder, and output buffers in the ROM architecture (Fig. 3.5).

17. True or false: An MROM can be programmed by the user.

18. A certain ROM has a capacity of 16K × 4 and an internal structure like that shown in Fig. 3.5.
    (a) How many registers are in the array?
    (b) How many bits are there per register?
    (c) What size decoders does it require?

19. Refer to Fig. 3.7 and determine the data output levels when $A_1A_0 = 11$ and $\overline{EN} = 1$.

20. Change the MROM of Fig. 3.7 so that the following words are stored from top to bottom: 1011, 0100, 1010, 1110.

21. How does a PROM differ from an MROM? Can it be erased and reprogrammed?

22. True or false: PROMs are available in both bipolar and MOS versions.

23. How is an EPROM erased?

24. True or false: There is no way to erase only a portion of an EPROM's memory.

25. What are the advantages of an EEPROM over an EPROM?

26. What is the main advantage of flash memory over EPROMs?

27. What is the main advantage of flash memory over EEPROMs?

28. Where does the word *flash* come from?

29. What is V_{PP} needed for?

30. What is the function of the 28F256A's command register?

31. What is the purpose of an erase-verify command?

32. What is the purpose of the program-verify command?

Sections 3.9–3.11

33. Describe the input conditions needed to read a word from a specific RAM address location.

34. Why do some RAM chips have common input/output pins?

35. How many pins are required for a 16K × 8 RAM with common I/O and one CS input?

36. How does a static RAM differ from a dynamic RAM?

37. True or false: In a READ cycle, the R/$\overline{\text{W}}$ line must be HIGH.

38. True or false: In a WRITE cycle, the R/$\overline{\text{W}}$ and $\overline{\text{CS}}$ lines should not be activated until after the new address inputs have stabilized.

39. Draw the logic symbol for a 16K × 8 RAM with common I/O pins and two active-LOW chip ENABLE inputs.

40. A certain static RAM has the following timing parameters:

$$t_{RC} = 100 \text{ ns} \qquad t_{AS} = 20 \text{ ns}$$
$$t_{ACC} = 100 \text{ ns} \qquad t_{AH} = \text{not given}$$
$$t_{CO} = 70 \text{ ns} \qquad t_{W} = 40 \text{ ns}$$
$$t_{OD} = 30 \text{ ns} \qquad t_{DS} = 10 \text{ ns}$$
$$t_{WC} = 100 \text{ ns} \qquad t_{DH} = 20 \text{ ns}$$

(a) How long after the address lines stabilize will valid data appear at the outputs during a READ cycle?

(b) How long will output data remain valid after $\overline{\text{CS}}$ returns HIGH?

(c) How many READ operations can be performed per second?

(d) How long should R/$\overline{\text{W}}$ and $\overline{\text{CS}}$ be kept HIGH after the new address stabilizes?

(e) What is the minimum time that input data have to remain valid for a reliable WRITE operation to occur?

(f) How long must the address inputs remain stable after R/$\overline{\text{W}}$ and $\overline{\text{CS}}$ return HIGH?

(g) How many WRITE operations can be performed per second?

Sections 3.12–3.14

41. For how long can a dynamic RAM cell retain data?

42. What are the advantages of dynamic RAM over static RAM?

43. What are the disadvantages of dynamic RAM?

44. Why do DRAMs use address multiplexing?

45. What are the functions of the $\overline{RAS}$ and $\overline{CAS}$ inputs?

46. What is the function of the *MUX* signal in a DRAM system?

47. Draw the logic diagram for a 256K × 1 DRAM with an active-LOW chip select input.

48. What is the function performed by a DRAM's external refresh circuitry?

49. Describe $\overline{RAS}$-only refresh and $\overline{CAS}$-before-$\overline{RAS}$ refresh.

Sections 3.15–3.16

50. The MCM6209C is a 64K × 4 static RAM chip. How many of these are needed to form a 1M × 4 module?

51. How many are needed for a 64K × 16 module? How many for a 256K × 16 memory system?

52. True or false: When memory chips are combined to form a module with a larger word size or capacity, the CS inputs of each chip are **always** connected together.

53. True or false: When memory chips are combined for a larger capacity, each chip is connected to the same data bus lines.

54. Refer to the ROM chip represented in Fig. 3.31. Show how to combine two of these chips to produce a 2K × 8 memory module. The circuit should use no other logic devices.

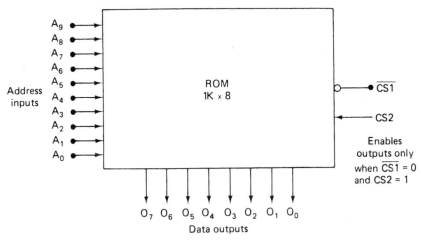

FIGURE 3.31

55. Show how to combine two MCM6206C RAM chips (Figure 3.15B) to produce a 32K × 16 module.

56. Describe how to modify the circuit of Figure 3.29 so that it has a total capacity of 16K × 8. Use the same type of PROM chips.

57. Examine the memory circuit of Fig. 3.32.
  (a) Determine the total capacity and word size.
  (b) Note that there are more address bus lines than are necessary to select one of the memory locations. This is not an unusual situation, especially in small computer systems where the actual amount of memory circuitry is much less than the maximum which the computer address bus can handle. Which RAMs will put data on the data bus when R/$\overline{\text{W}}$ = 1 and the address bus is at 00010110?
  (c) Determine the range of addresses stored in the RAM-0/RAM-1 combination. Repeat for the RAM-2/RAM-3 combination.

58. Draw the complete diagram for a 256K × 8 memory that uses RAM chips with the following specifications: 64K × 4 capacity, common input/output line, and two active-LOW chip-select inputs. [*Hint:* The circuit can be designed using only two inverters (plus memory chips).]

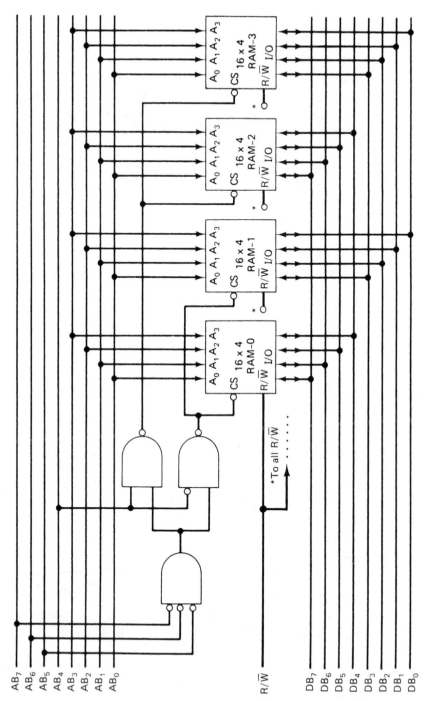

FIGURE 3.32

128

4

Introduction to Computers

OBJECTIVES

Upon completion of this chapter, you will be able to:

- Describe the function and operation of each one of the five basic elements of any computer organization.
- Understand the basic differences among the microprocessor, microcomputer, and microcontroller.
- Describe the different types of instruction words used by an 8-bit microcomputer.
- Understand the need for and the usefulness of the *prebyte* when using some of the MC68HC11 MPU instructions.
- Understand the operational role of the different types of buses and their signals in a microprocessor.
- Cite the major functions performed by a microprocessor.
- Analyze the fetch and execute cycles during the execution of a machine-language program.
- Describe the sequence of events that occur during the READ and WRITE cycles during the execution of a program.
- Cite the differences between a JUMP instruction and a BRANCH instruction.
- Describe the differences among hardware, software, and firmware.
- Describe the differences between a one-line assembler and a full-blown assembler.
- Understand the advantages and disadvantages of machine language, assembly language, and high-level languages.
- Cite the differences between interpreters and compilers.
- Use flowcharts to represent logical program sequences.

INTRODUCTION

Large-scale integration (LSI), *very-large-scale integration* (VLSI), and *ultra-large-scale integration* (ULSI) technologies can put tens of thousands of transistors on a single chip. This has made it possible to fabricate the entire *brain* of a computer as a single integrated circuit called a *microprocessor*. The addition of a relatively small number of other chips produces a complete *microcomputer*.

From the first digital computers of the 1940s to today's powerful full-size computers and revolutionary microcomputers, very little change has occurred in the basic principles of operation. Although the technology has come a long way from the time when a computer filled a gymnasium and was considered too costly for most applications, our modern computers still work with 1s and 0s using the same basic logic operations as their predecessors. In this chapter we present many of the concepts, principles, and operations that are common to all types of computers. Of course, since our main objective is to learn about microcomputers, the presentation will emphasize this category of computers.

▶ 4.1 WHAT CAN COMPUTERS DO?

For the most part, human beings can do whatever computers can do, but computers can do it with much greater speed and accuracy. This is in spite of the fact that computers perform all their calculations and operations one step at a time. For example, a human being can take a list of 10 numbers and find their sum all in one operation by listing the numbers one over the other and adding them column by column. A computer, on the other hand, can add numbers only two at a time, so adding this same list of numbers will take nine actual addition steps. Of course, the fact that the computer requires less than a microsecond per step makes up for this apparent inefficiency.

A computer is faster and more accurate than people, but unlike most people it has to be given a complete set of instructions that tell it *exactly* what to do at each step of its operation. This set of instructions, called a *program,* is prepared by one or more persons for each job the computer is to do. These programs are placed in the computer's memory unit in binary-coded form, with each instruction having a unique code. The computer takes these instruction codes from memory *one at a time* and performs the operation called for by the code. Much more will be said on this later.

Computers have found their way into many application areas that were once not feasible, and the rapid increase in the number and variety of computer applications has made them a significant part of our lives. In the following sections we present examples from some of the major areas of applications.

Internet

The *internet* would not be possible if it weren't for computers. It is an expansive network of many different types of computers connecting people and resources around the world. The internet is often referred to as the *information superhighway* and it is accessible to anyone with a computer and a modem. These computer networks have grown throughout the years in number, capacity, and degree of sophistication. Today it is possible for anyone with a relatively inexpensive home computer to have access to a vast number of resources and services provided by these computer networks. For example, we can exchange electronic mail with people throughout the world; conduct research on any subject matter from automobile purchases to the latest surgical procedures; and have complete access to files that contain text information, graphics, sound, and video.

The internet will continue to grow in sophistication and expand in capacity for years to come, and undoubtedly, computers will continue to play a vital role in its growth.

Business

A typical business task is the processing of paychecks for employees who work at an hourly rate. In a noncomputerized payroll system servicing a large company (say, 1000 employees), a substantial amount of paperwork and energy is expended in meeting the pay schedule. Calculations must be made concerning items like regular and overtime hours worked, wage rate, gross earnings, federal and state taxes, Social Security, union dues, insurance deductions, and net earnings. Summaries must also be made on items such as earnings to date, taxes to date, Social Security accumulation, vacation, and sick leave. Each of the calculations would have to be performed manually (calculator) for each employee, consuming a large amount of time and energy.

By contrast, a computer payroll system requires much less time and effort, is less prone to error, and provides a better record-keeping system. In such a system a master file is generated for each employee, containing all the necessary data (wage rate, tax exemptions, and so forth). The master files of all employees, representing a massive amount of data, are stored on magnetic disk or tape and updated each payroll cycle. The computer is programmed to read the data from the master files, combine it with data for the pay period in question, and make all the necessary calculations. Some of the advantages of the computerized system are:

1. Payroll calculation time is shortened.
2. Accumulated earnings can be generated automatically.
3. Accurate payroll documents are prepared automatically.
4. Clerical effort is greatly reduced.
5. One master employee file is used to prepare all reports.
6. Data are readily available for budgeting control and cost analysis.

Science and Engineering

Scientists and engineers use mathematics as a language that defines the operation of physical systems. In many cases, the mathematical relationships are extremely complex and must be evaluated for many different values of the system variables. A computer can evaluate these complex mathematical expressions at high speeds. In addition, it can perform repeated calculations using different sets of data, tabulate the results, and determine which sets of values produced the best results. In many cases, the computer can save an engineer hours, even days, of tedious calculations, thereby providing more time for creative work.

Process Control

Time is not a critical factor when a computer is used to process business data or do engineering calculations in the sense that the results are not required immediately (within a few milliseconds or seconds). Computers are often used in applications where the results of their calculations are required immediately to be used in controlling a process. These are called *real-time* applications.

An example of a real-time application can be found in industrial process control, which is used in industries such as paper mills, oil refineries, chemical plants, and many others. A non-computer-controlled system might involve one or more technicians located in a central control room. Instruments are used to monitor the various process parameters and send signals back to the control console, which displays pertinent readings on analog or digital meters. The technician records these readings, interprets them, and decides on what corrective actions, if any, are necessary. Corrections are made using various controls on the control console.

If the same system were under computer control, the measuring instruments would send their signals to the computer, which processes them and responds with appropriate control signals to be sent back to the process. Some advantages of the computer-controlled process are:

1. It reacts much faster and with greater precision to variations in the measured process parameters. Thus, serious conditions in the process can be detected and corrected much more quickly than can be done with human intervention.
2. Certain economic savings can be realized because the computer can be programmed to keep the process operating at maximum efficiency in the use of materials and energy.
3. Continuous records can be kept of the process parameter variations, thereby enabling certain trends to be detected prior to the occurrence of an actual problem. These records can be kept in much less space, because magnetic tape would replace a bulky paper-filing system.

Education

The use of computers in education is usually called *computer-assisted instruction* (CAI). The key here is that the computer *assists* in the educational process by providing the teacher with a versatile and relatively inexpensive tool. Students are generally "turned on" by a computer's interactive capability and its visual stimuli (graphics, color, motion) and will spend many more hours learning from a computer than they would reading textbooks or workbooks.

Of course, the success of computers in this area is highly dependent on the availability of programs for the various subjects. Numerous programs are available, ranging from elementary-school subjects, such as reading, spelling, and arithmetic, to adult courses in foreign languages and computer programming. Teachers can also develop their own programs for instruction or testing by using easy-to-learn computer languages developed just for those purposes.

The fact that computers have become a common everyday item in peoples' lives has not gone unnoticed by universities and colleges throughout the world. By taking advantage of the internet, these institutions of higher education have begun to offer many different types of courses on a variety of subjects. A college or university can offer a lecture several times a day, seven days a week, to thousands of students around the state, the country, and indeed the world. At the other end, the student receiving this lecture through the internet can videotape it and then watch it at his/her own convenience as many times as it may take in order to understand the lesson. The student can then use the internet to do the research needed for his/her homework. Clearly, both the university and the student benefit from this new and evolving technology.

Personal computers and computer networks will undoubtedly continue to get more sophisticated, easier to use, and more affordable. In time, we can expect to see these systems playing an increasingly prominent role in the delivery of educational information from teaching institutions.

▶ 4.2 HOW DO COMPUTERS THINK?

Computers do not think! The computer *programmer* provides a *program* of instructions and data that specifies every detail of what to do, what to do it to, and when to do it. The computer is simply a high-speed machine that can manipulate data, do calculations, and make decisions, all under the control of the program. If the programmer makes a mistake in the program or puts in the wrong data, the computer will produce wrong results. A popular saying in the computer field is "garbage in gives you garbage out."

Perhaps a better question to ask at this point is: How does a computer go about executing a program of instructions? Typically, this question is answered by showing a diagram of a computer's architecture (arrangement of its various elements) and then going through the step-by-step process that the computer follows in executing the program. We will do this—but not yet. First, we will look at a somewhat farfetched analogy that contains many of the concepts involved in a computer operation.

Secret Agent 89

Secret Agent 89 is trying to find out how many days before a certain world leader is to be overthrown. His contact tells him that this information is located in a series of post office boxes. In order to ensure that no one else gets the information, it is spread through 10 boxes. His contact gives him the 10 keys along with the following instructions:

1. The information in each box is written in code.
2. Open box 1 first and execute the instruction located there.
3. Continue through the rest of the boxes in sequence unless instructed to do otherwise.
4. One of the boxes will emit a deadly poisonous gas.

Agent 89 takes the 10 keys and proceeds to the post office, code book in hand.

Figure 4.1 shows the contents of the 10 post office boxes after having been decoded. Assume that you are Agent 89; begin at box 1 and go through the sequence of operations to find the number of days before the overthrow attempt. Of course, it should not be as

① Add the number stored in box **⑨** to your secret agent code number.	**②** Divide the previous result by the number stored in box **⑩**.
③ Subtract the number stored in box **⑧**	**④** If the previous result is not equal to 30, go to box **⑦**. Otherwise continue to next box.
⑤ Subtract 13 from the previous result.	**⑥** HALT. You now have the answer
⑦ Deadly poisonous gas (too bad)	**⑧** 20
⑨ 11	**⑩** 2

FIGURE 4.1   Ten post office boxes with coded message for Agent 89.

much work for you as it was for Agent 89, because you do not have to decode the messages. The answer is given in the next paragraph.

If you have proceeded correctly, you should have ended up at box 6, with an answer of 17. If you made a mistake, you might have opened box 7, in which case you are no longer with us. As you went through the sequence of operations, you essentially duplicated the types of operations and encountered many of the concepts that are part of a computer. We will now discuss these operations and concepts in the context of the secret agent analogy and see how they are related to actual computers.

In case you have not already guessed, the post office boxes are like the *memory* in a computer, where *instructions* and *data* are stored. Post office boxes 1 through 6 contain instructions to be executed by the secret agent, and boxes 8 through 10 contain the data called for by the instructions. (The contents of box 7, to our knowledge, have no counterpart in computers.) The numbers on each box are like the *addresses* of the locations in memory.

Three different classes of instructions are present in boxes 1 through 6. Boxes 1, 2, 3, and 5 are instructions that call for *arithmetic operations.* Box 4 contains a *decision-making* instruction, called a *conditional jump* or *conditional branch.* This instruction calls for the agent (or computer) to decide whether to jump to address 7 or to continue to address 5, depending on the result of the previous arithmetic operation. Box 6 contains a simple control instruction that requires no data and refers to no other address (box number). This *halt* instruction tells the agent that the problem is finished (program is completed) and to go no further.

Each of the arithmetic and conditional jump instructions consists of two parts—an *operation* and an *address*. For example, the first part of the first instruction specifies the operation of addition. The second part gives the address (box 9) of the data to be used in the addition. These data are usually called the *operand* and their address is called the *operand address*. The instruction in box 5 is a special case in which there is no operand address specified. Instead, the operand (data) to be used in the subtraction operation is included as part of the instruction.

A computer, like the secret agent, decodes and then executes the instructions stored in memory *sequentially*, beginning with the first location. The instructions are executed in order unless some type of *branch* instruction (such as box 4) causes the operation to branch or jump to a new address location to obtain the next instruction. Once the branching occurs, instructions are executed sequentially beginning at the new address.

This is about as much information as we can extract from the secret agent analogy. Each of the concepts we encountered will be encountered again in subsequent material. It is hoped that the analogy has furnished insights that should prove useful as we begin a thorough study of computers.

▶ 4.3 HOW MANY KINDS OF COMPUTERS ARE THERE?

As stated in the introduction to this chapter, all computers operate basically in the same way. Even so, there are several factors that make computers different from each other. These factors are *physical size, cost, speed,* and *word size.*

Physical size and cost are self-explanatory. Speed refers to the rate at which a computer can execute instructions. A computer's word size refers to the number of bits contained in the primary unit of data that the computer can process and store. For example, a computer with a 16-bit word size is capable of handling data words of 16 bits, and its memory can store 16-bit words. This computer would be characterized as a 16-bit computer.

When these factors are used to compare computers, we can generally classify them into three categories: *microcomputers, minicomputers,* and *mainframes (maxicomputers).* Our interest in this text is on the newest class of computers—microcomputers.

Microcomputers

This newest member of the computer family is also the smallest and least expensive. Its small size is a result of the LSI, VLSI, and ULSI technologies described earlier. They generally fall into the price range $100 to $10,000. The lower end of this range typically includes *personal computers* that are designed for the hobbyist or for domestic use. The more expensive microcomputers are designed for business and scientific applications.

A typical microcomputer can execute millions of instructions per second. Although this is very fast in human terms, it is slower than some minicomputers and most mainframes. Microcomputers normally handle word sizes of 8, 16, 32, and 64 bits.

A typical microcomputer system may consist of a keyboard, a video display, 16 megabytes of internal RAM for program and data storage, external mass memory such as a 1.44 MB 3.5″ floppy disk drive, a 3.8-GB internal hard disk drive, a 12X IDE CD-ROM (635 MB/disk max.), and an 8-MB video card.

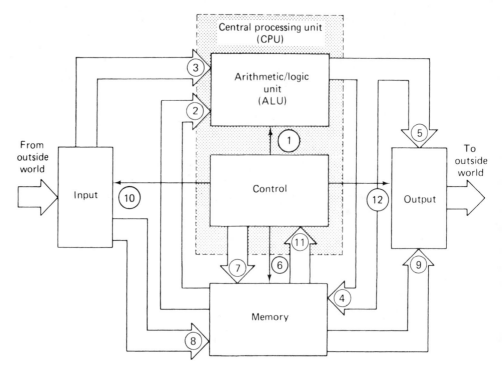

FIGURE 4.2   General computer system diagram.

▶ 4.4 BASIC COMPUTER STRUCTURE

Despite the differences in performance among the various types of computers, every computer contains five basic units: the *memory unit, arithmetic/logic unit (ALU), input unit, output unit,* and *control unit.* Figure 4.2 is a block diagram representing a general computer system showing the interconnection of the various units. Note that the control unit is in the center of the diagram because it acts as the "brains" of the computer, directing the operation of all the other units. The arrows in this diagram indicate the direction in which data or control signals are flowing. The larger arrows indicate a group of parallel lines representing a data word, an instruction, or an address; the smaller arrows represent control signals, which are usually only one or a few signal lines. The circled numbers next to each arrow will be referred to in the following descriptions of each unit.

Memory Unit

The memory unit stores groups of bits (words) that represent instructions that the computer is to execute (that is, a program), and data that are to be operated on by the program. The memory also serves as temporary storage of the results of operations performed by the ALU (arrow in Fig. 4.2). The memory unit's operation is controlled by the control unit, which signals for either a READ or a WRITE operation (arrow 6) and provides the appropriate memory address (arrow 7). Data that are to be written into memory can come from the ALU or the input unit (arrow 8), again under the control of the control unit. Data that are read from memory can be sent to the ALU (arrow 2) or the output unit (arrow 9).

As stated ion Chapter 3, a computer has both internal memory and external mass memory. Internal memory is relatively low-capacity, high-speed memory that stores programs and data that the computer is currently executing (that is, short-term storage). Semiconductor RAM and ROM are commonly used for internal memory. External memory is high-capacity, relatively low-speed memory that is used to store programs and data when they are not being used by the computer (that is, long-term storage). Magnetic tape and disk are the most common types of external mass memory.

Arithmetic/Logic Unit

The ALU performs arithmetic and logic operations on data. The control unit sends signals to the ALU that determine which operation is to be performed on the data (arrow, Fig. 4.2). The control unit also determines the source of the data as the memory unit (arrow 2) or the input unit (arrow 3). The results of the operations can be sent to memory for storage (arrow 4) or to the output unit (arrow 5).

Recall from our discussion in Chapter 2 that the *accumulator* is a register that participates in most of the operations performed by the ALU, and it receives the results of most ALU operations. This idea is reviewed in Fig. 4.3. As we progress further, we will find that the accumulator has other functions in addition to those associated with the ALU.

Input Unit

The input unit consists of devices that allow data and information from the outside world to be entered into the computer's internal memory or ALU (arrows 3 and 8 in Fig. 4.2). These devices are often referred to as *peripherals* because they are physically separated from the electronics that make up the "brain" of the computer. Some typical input peripherals are keyboards, video display terminals (VDTs), modems, CD ROM, magnetic disk drives, and analog-to-digital converters (ADCs). Most personal computers come equipped with only a keyboard as an input device; other input peripherals have to be purchased at extra cost.

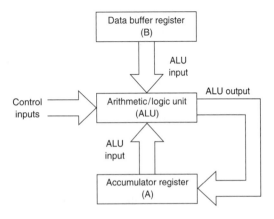

FIGURE 4.3   The accumulator is normally part of the ALU operation.

It is not unusual to consider magnetic tape and disk drive units to be both input peripherals and memory devices. One of their major functions is to store data and programs that will be inputted to the computer's internal memory upon commands from the control unit.

Output Unit

The output unit consists of peripheral devices that transfer data and information from the internal memory or ALU to the outside world (arrows 5 and 9, Fig. 4.2). Typical output peripherals include LED displays, printers, VDTs, video monitors, modems, and digital-to-analog converters (DACs). Note that the VDT can serve as both an input and an output peripheral.

Magnetic tape and disk memory units can also be considered output peripherals; data and programs from internal memory are often outputted to one of these external memory devices for long-term storage.

When a keyboard input device is combined with a visual output device, such as a printer or video monitor, the combination is commonly called a *terminal*. The keyboard/video display combination is called a *video display terminal* (VDT). A microcomputer usually has only a single terminal, whereas most mainframes and many minicomputers have several terminals, each of which can act as input to or output from the computer.

Control Unit

The function of the control unit should now be obvious. It directs the operation of all the other parts of the computer by providing timing and control signals. It is like the orchestra conductor who is responsible for keeping each of the instruments in proper synchronization. The control unit contains logic and timing circuits that generate the signals needed to execute each instruction in a program.

The control unit *fetches* an instruction from memory by sending an address (arrow 7, Fig. 4.2) and a READ command (arrow 6) to the memory unit. The instruction word comes from memory into the control unit (arrow 11). This instruction word, which is in binary code, is then *decoded* by logic circuits in the control unit to determine which operation is to be executed. Once this is determined, the control unit generates the signals needed to actually *execute* the operation.

Thus, we can say that the control unit's function is to *fetch, decode,* and *execute* the instructions that are in memory (that is, the program). As we shall soon see, the control unit will perform these same steps over and over as long as the computer is operating.

Central Processing Unit (CPU)

The ALU and control unit are usually combined into a single unit called the *central processing unit* (CPU), indicated in Fig. 4.2. The CPU is truly the "brains" of the computer because it combines the circuitry that generates all the control signals needed to execute an instruction with the circuitry that actually performs the operations called for by the instruction.

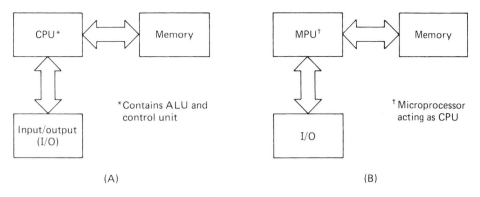

FIGURE 4.4   (A) Simplified computer diagram; (B) microcomputer diagram.

Simplified Computer System Diagram

Now that we know the function of the five basic units of a computer system, we can combine some of the units to produce a more simplified diagram to represent a computer. Figure 4.4A shows how a computer can be represented as three major blocks. The CPU block replaces the ALU and control unit. The input/output block (I/O) combines the input and output units.

Microcomputer

In a microcomputer, the CPU is often on a single IC called a *microprocessor,* and the terms CPU and microprocessor are synonymous. It is common in the computer field to refer to the microprocessor as the MPU (microprocessor unit). We will use MPU from now on. Figure 4.4B shows the simplified diagram of a microcomputer configuration.

With all this new terminology, it might be helpful at this point to summarize the important facts:

1. The CPU is the combination of the ALU and control unit of *any* computer.
2. When the CPU is a single IC, it is called a microprocessor and is referred to as the MPU.
3. When the MPU is connected to memory and I/O, the arrangement becomes a microcomputer.

▶ 4.5 MICROPROCESSORS

The MPU contains the circuitry needed to perform the functions of a CPU; many different MPUs are produced by many different IC manufacturers. Although they all perform the same essential functions, each MPU has unique characteristics that make it different from other MPUs. The major differences appear in the word size, the number and types of instructions that can be performed, the types of external control signals available, and the amount of memory that can be addressed.

The wide variety of MPUs makes it difficult to attempt to cover even a few of them in an introductory text. For this reason, in most of the work to follow, we will use one type of MPU as representative of the most popular 8-bit units currently in use. The MPU that we will use is the Motorola MC68HC11, which is one of the most powerful and prominent 8-bit microprocessors currently being used.

The MC68HC11 is actually a single-chip **microcontroller** unit (MCU) that contains an MPU, memory, and I/O circuitry. This chip can perform control operations without the need for any external circuitry *(in the single-chip mode)*. For now our interest is mainly in the MPU portion of the MC68HC11 microcontroller, so we will be referring to the 68HC11 MPU extensively throughout the text. Later, we will describe and apply the complete 68HC11 microcontroller.

You will be learning a great deal about the detailed operation of the 68HC11 MPU, how it is combined with memory and I/O devices to produce a 68HC11 MPU-based microcomputer, and how to program it to perform various operations. Although we will not say a great deal about any other MPU, most of what you learn about the 68HC11 can be applied to any other MPU or microcomputer you may encounter.

▶ 4.6 COMPUTER WORDS

The preceding description of how the various units of a computer system interact was somewhat oversimplified. To describe these interactions on a more detailed level, we must first discuss the several types of information that are continually being transferred and manipulated within the computer.

As stated earlier, the fundamental unit of information in a computer is the *word.* Although a word is made up of several bits, the computer treats each word as a single unit and stores each word in a specific memory location. The word size for the majority of microprocessors is 8 bits or 1 *byte,* but 16-bit and 32-bit MPUs are becoming increasingly prevalent. The 68HC11 is an 8-bit MPU, so our discussion will deal with computer words that are 8 bits (one byte) wide.

Words stored in a computer's memory unit can represent several types of information: (1) binary numerical data; (2) coded data; (3) instruction codes; and (4) addresses that are part of an instruction. We will examine each of these in the following sections.

▶ 4.7 BINARY DATA WORDS

These are words that simply represent a numerical quantity in the binary number system. For example, a certain location in the memory of an 8-bit (single-byte) microcomputer might contain the word 01110011, representing the desired process temperature in Fahrenheit degrees. This binary number 01110011 is equivalent to 115_{10}.

Here is an example of a 16-bit data word:

$$1010000101001001$$

which is equivalent to $41,289_{10}$.

Obviously, a wider range of numerical data can be represented with a larger word size. With an 8-bit word size, the largest data word (11111111_2) is equivalent to $2^8 - 1 = 255_{10}$. With a 16-bit word size, the largest data word is equivalent to $2^{16} - 1 = 65,535_{10}$. With 32 bits (four bytes) we can represent numbers greater than 4 billion.

Signed Data Words

A computer would not be too useful if it could handle only positive numbers. For this reason, most computers use the signed 2's-complement system discussed in Chapter 1. Recall that the most significant bit (MSB) is used as the *sign* bit (0 is positive and 1 is negative). Here is how the values +9 and −9 would be represented in an 8-bit computer:

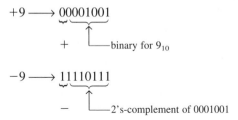

Here, of course, only 7 bits are reserved for the magnitude of the number. Thus, in the signed 2's-complement system, we can represent numbers only from -128_{10} to $+127_{10}$. Similarly, with 16-bit words, we can have a range from $-32,768_{10}$ to $+32,767_{10}$.

Combining Data Words

Often, a computer needs to process data that extend beyond the range possible with a single word. In such cases, the data can be represented by two or more words that can be stored in consecutive memory locations. For example, a 68HC11-based microcomputer can handle 8-bit data words. However, a 16-bit number such as 1010101100101001 can be stored in two consecutive memory locations as shown below.

Memory address	Contents		
C000	10101011	⟵	8 high-order bits of 16-bit number
C001	00101001	⟵	8 low-order bits of 16-bit number

Here the 8 higher-order bits of the 16-bit number are stored at memory address C000. This is called the *high-order byte.* Similarly, the 8 lower-order bits of the 16-bit number *(low-order byte)* are stored at memory address C001. The two bytes combined make up the complete 16-bit number. The 68HC11MPU would have to process the 16-bit number in two steps, one byte at a time.

Octal and Hexadecimal Data Representation

For purposes of convenience in writing and displaying data words, they can be represented in either octal or hexadecimal codes. For example, the number $+116_{10}$ can be represented in a single byte as 01110100_2. Its hex and octal representations are

$$01110100_2 = 74_{16}$$

$$01110100_2 = 164_8$$

It is important to realize that the use of hex or octal representations is solely for convenience of the computer user; the computer memory still stores the binary numbers (0s and 1s), and these are what the computer processes.

▶ 4.8 CODED DATA WORDS

Data processed by a computer do not have to be pure binary numbers. One of the other common data forms uses the BCD code (Chapter 1), where each group of 4 bits can represent a single decimal digit. Thus, an 8-bit word can represent two decimal digits, a 16-bit word can represent four decimal digits, and so on. Many computers can perform arithmetic operations on BCD-coded numbers as part of their normal instruction repertoire; others, especially some microcomputers, require special effort on the part of the programmer in order to do BCD arithmetic.

Data words are not restricted to representing only numbers. They are often used to represent alphabetic characters and other special characters or symbols using codes such as the 7-bit ASCII code (Chapter 1). The ASCII code is used by all minicomputer and microcomputer manufacturers. Although the basic ASCII code uses 7 bits, an extra parity bit (Chapter 1) is added to each code word, producing a one-byte ASCII code. The example below shows how a message might be stored in a sequence of memory locations using ASCII code with an *even* parity bit. The contents of each location are also given in hex code. Use Table 1.2 to determine the message. Note that the leftmost bit is the parity bit and the first character is stored in location $012A_{16}$.

Address location	Binary	Hex
012A	11001001	C9
012B	10111101	BD
012C	01010110	56
012D	10101111	AF
012E	11010010	D
	ASCII	

The decoded message is the familiar electrical Ohm's law, $I = V/R$.

The one-byte ASCII code is particularly suited to computers with an 8-bit word size. However, computers with other word sizes still use one-byte ASCII. For example, a 16-bit computer can pack two bytes into one memory word so that each word represents two characters. This is illustrated below, where the characters I and = are stored in one 16-bit word.

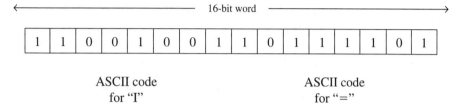

ASCII code
for "I"

ASCII code
for "="

On the other hand, a 4-bit microcomputer would have to use two consecutive memory locations to represent one byte of ASCII.

Interpretation of Data Words

Suppose you are told that a particular data word in a microcomputer's memory is 01010110. This word can be interpreted in several ways. It could be the binary representation of 86_{10}, it could be the BCD representation of 56_{10}, or it could be the ASCII code for the character V. How should this data word be interpreted? It is up to the programmer, since he or she is the one who places the data in memory together with instructions that make up the program. The programmer knows what type of data word is being used and must make sure that the program of instructions executed by the computer interprets the data properly.

▶ 4.9 INSTRUCTION WORDS

A program consists of a sequence of binary-coded instructions that the CPU must fetch from memory, decode, and execute. For most computers, the instruction words that make up a program will convey two types of information: the *operation* to be performed, and the *address* of the *operand* (data) that is to be operated on. Computers with a relatively large word size can convey all of this in a single word, while microcomputers generally require more than one word. Before we see how instructions are formatted in an 8-bit microcomputer, we will look at the instruction word format for a computer with a large word size.

Figure 4.5 shows an example of an instruction word for a hypothetical 20-bit computer. The 20 bits are divided into two parts. The first part (bits 16–19) contains the *operation code* (or *op code*). The 4-bit op code indicates the operation that the CPU is being instructed to perform. Each of the possible op codes represents a different operation, such as addition or subtraction. The second part (bits 0–15) is the *operand address,* which is the address of a location in memory where data (the operand) will be taken from or sent to depending on the operation being performed.

With 4 bits used for the op code, there are $2^4 = 16$ different possible op codes, with each one indicating a different instruction. This means that a computer using this

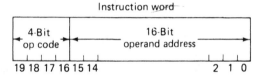

FIGURE 4.5   Typical instruction
word format.

instruction-word format is limited to 16 different possible instructions that it can perform. A more versatile computer would have a greater number of instructions and would therefore require more bits in its op code. In any case, each instruction that a computer can perform has a specific op code that the computer (control unit) must interpret (decode).

The instruction word of Fig. 4.5 has 16 bits reserved for the operand address code. With 16 bits, there are $2^{16} = 65,536$ different possible addresses. Thus, this instruction word can specify 16 different instructions and 65,536 operand addresses. As an example, a 20-bit instruction word might be

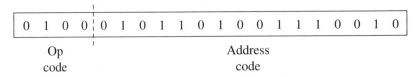

| 0 | 1 | 0 | 0 | 0 | 1 | 0 | 1 | 1 | 0 | 1 | 0 | 0 | 1 | 1 | 1 | 0 | 0 | 1 | 0 |

Op code   Address code

The op code 0100 represents one of 16 possible operations; let us assume that it is the code for *addition* (ADD). The address code is 0101101001110010 or, more conveniently, 5A72 in hexadecimal. In fact, this complete instruction word can be expressed in hexadecimal as

$$4 \quad 5 \quad A \quad 7 \quad 2$$

Op code Address

This complete instruction word, then, tells the computer to do the following:

Fetch the data word stored in address location 5A72, send it to the ALU, and *add* it to the number in the accumulator register. The sum will then be stored in the accumulator (the previous contents of the accumulator are lost).

Microcomputer Instruction Format

It should be made clear at this time that the 68HC11 MPU has *two accumulators,* among other important internal registers that will be introduced and discussed at the proper time. The two accumulators that are used by the 68HC11 MPU are called accumulator A and accumulator B. We will be using accumulator A almost exclusively as we introduce the various types of the 68HC11 MPU instructions. There is no operational difference between instructions that use accumulator A and instructions that use accumulator B, except for the obvious choice of accumulator registers.

An 8-bit MPU like the 68HC11 cannot provide the op code and operand address in a single 8-bit word. With a one-byte word size, there are three basic instruction formats: single-byte, two-byte, and three-byte. These are illustrated in Fig. 4.6.

The **single-byte instruction** contains only an 8-bit op code; there is no operand address specified. Because there is no operand address, a single-byte instruction is used for operations that do not have to access the data portion of memory. An example would be the instruction *Arithmetic Shift Left* (ASLA), which instructs the 68HC11 to shift the content of accumulator A left one bit. Because accumulator A is a register that is part of the MPU, there is no need to specify an operand address. Incidentally, the 68HC11 MPU uses op

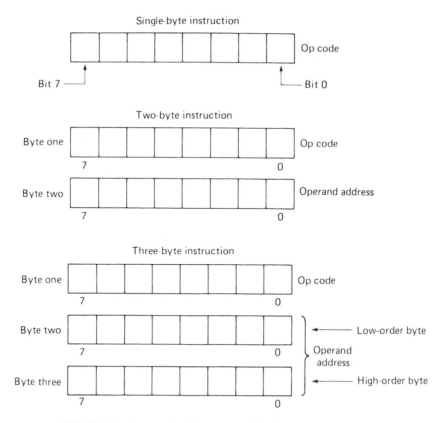

Single-byte instruction

Bit 7 ———| |——— Bit 0

Op code

Two-byte instruction

Byte one — 7 ... 0 — Op code

Byte two — 7 ... 0 — Operand address

Three-byte instruction

Byte one — 7 ... 0 — Op code

Byte two — 7 ... 0 — Low-order byte

Byte three — 7 ... 0 — High-order byte

Operand address

FIGURE 4.6   Instruction formats used in 8-bit microcomputers.

code 00101000_2 (or 48_{16}) to represent the ASLA operation. Other microprocessors would use a different op code to represent the operation. In general, different MPUs have different sets of op codes because of differences in how their control circuitry was designed.

The first byte of the **two-byte instruction** shown in Fig. 4.6 is an op code, and the second byte is an 8-bit address code that specifies the operand address. These two bytes are always stored in memory in this order. This is illustrated on the next page.

The left-hand column lists the address location in memory where each byte of each instruction is stored. The second and third columns give the actual words stored at each memory location in binary and hex. The right-hand column describes the meaning of each memory word.

The byte stored at address C000 is the op code part of the first instruction; it is the 68HC11 op code for a *load accumulator A* (LDAA) instruction. The byte stored at C001 is the operand address part of the first instruction. This complete two-byte instruction tells the MPU to do the following:

Take the data currently stored in memory address 15 and load it into accumulator A. The contents of address 15 remain unchanged.

Memory address (Hex)	Memory word Binary	Hex	Description
C000	10010110	96	Op code for LDAA
C001	00010101	15	Address containing data to be loaded in accumulator A
C002	10010111	97	Op code for STAA
C003	00101010	2A	Address where contents of accumulator A will be stored

The byte stored at address C002 is the op code for the second instruction; it is the op code for a *store accumulator A* (STAA) instruction. The byte stored at C003 is the operand address part of the second instruction. This complete two-byte instruction tells the MPU to:

Take the contents of accumulator A and store it in memory address 2A.
The contents of accumulator A remain unchanged.

There are other two-byte instructions where the second byte is *not* an operand address. As you will see soon, the *second byte* of a two-byte instruction can also be a byte of *data,* or a *branch offset.* These two types of two-byte instructions will be addressed at the appropriate time in the text.

If we refer to the **three-byte instruction** of Fig. 4.6, we see that again the first byte is the op code. The second and third bytes form a 16-bit operand address. An example of a three-byte instruction is shown below.

Memory address (Hex)	Memory word Binary	Hex	Description
C000	10111011	BB	Op code for ADDA
C001	11100000	EO	High-order byte of operand address
C002	11110110	F6	Low-order byte of operand address

The instruction tells the MPU to do the following:

Take the data stored in memory address E0F6, add it to the current contents of accumulator A, and place the result into accumulator A.

It should be clear that the three-byte instruction is essentially the same as the two-byte instruction except that a longer address code is used. Many MPUs, like the 68HC11, permit either an 8-bit (single-byte) or 16-bit (two-byte) operand address. In reality, as we shall see, the 68HC11 always uses a 16-bit address, even for two-byte instructions. It does this by automatically appending a high-order byte of 00_{16} to the single-byte address. For example, the operand address 35 would actually become 0035_{16}.

The single-byte, two-byte, and three-byte instruction formats that we have just discussed always begin with an op code byte; these formats are used by most 8-bit MPUs. However, in the 68HC11 MPU there are several instructions that deviate from the previous discussion. For example, all of the instructions that use the *Y register* (another internal MPU register) will have a specific *prebyte* which precedes the op code byte. This prebyte indicates that the instruction uses the internal Y register of the MPU. Therefore, in the particular case of the MC68HC11 MPU, **some** instructions will have a two-byte op code: a prebyte and the actual op code for the instruction that is to be executed (more about this in Example 4.1).

Basic Program Execution

A program consists of instructions that tell the computer exactly what to do step by step. For an 8-bit microcomputer, the program will consist of single, two-, or three-byte instructions stored in memory in an orderly manner. The program can be stored in RAM if it is to be modified or replaced later, or it can be stored in some type of ROM if it is to remain relatively permanent.

The MPU will fetch (READ), decode, and execute the instructions from memory one at a time beginning at some prescribed starting address. Because an 8-bit microcomputer often uses more than one memory word per instruction, the MPU may actually perform more than one fetch operation before it can execute an instruction. This is illustrated in Fig. 4.7.

The MPU *always* starts by fetching the op code byte and then decoding the op code to determine what to do next. It is this op code that tells the MPU whether or not it has to fetch an operand address before it can execute the instruction, and whether the operand address requires one or two fetch operations. The 68HC11 MPU continually repeats the series of steps shown in Fig. 4.7 until power is removed from the chip.

It should be pointed out that the time required for the MPU to fetch and execute an instruction will vary depending on the type of instruction. This is not only because of the

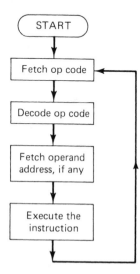

FIGURE 4.7 The series of steps followed by the MPU in executing a stored program of instructions.

differences in the operand address, but also because of the different sequence of events that can take place during the execution phase. This will become more apparent as we provide more details on each instruction.

EXAMPLE 4.1

The 68HC11 can handle 8-bit words and 16-bit addresses.
(a) From what you know thus far about the 68HC11 MPU, what would you say is the maximum number of different instructions that this MPU can execute?
(b) What is the maximum capacity of internal memory that can communicate with the MPU?

Solution
(a) With an 8-bit op code there are $2^8 = 256$ possible op codes, each of which can represent a different instruction. Thus, at first glance, one would think that any MPU that can handle only 8-bit words could not possibly have any more than 256 different instructions. The designers of the 68HC11, however, found a need to have instructions in excess of 256. Hence, the need for the previously mentioned "prebyte." The designers of the 68HC11 decided to reserve a few special codes (18_{16}, $1A_{16}$, and CD_{16}). Any of these special codes when followed by another byte means that a particular instruction uses two bytes as its op code. Thus, the integration of the prebyte allowed the designers of the 68HC11 MPU to come up with an 8-bit MPU that actually recognizes 308 different instructions.
(b) A 16-bit address code can specify $2^{16} = 65,536$ different memory locations. The maximum memory capacity would thus be $65,536 \times 8$, or $64K \times 8$.

EXAMPLE 4.2

How many fetch operations does the MPU have to perform as it executes an instruction to ADD the data from memory location A2FF to the accumulator?

Solution   Four fetch operations are required: one to fetch the op code, two more to fetch the operand address (A2FF), and a fourth one to fetch the data that are to be added to the accumulator during the execution phase.

▶ 4.10 THE 68HC11 MPU—A SIMPLIFIED VERSION

Now that we have discussed the basic steps that an MPU follows as it executes a program of instructions, we are prepared to take a more detailed look at the MPU. The microprocessor is a very complex device that contains a great deal of logic circuitry, numerous registers with various functions, and numerous signal lines that connect it to the other elements in the microcomputer. In other words, it can be overwhelming and even intimidating to start out by considering a full-blown microprocessor.

Our approach here will be to introduce a simplified version of the 68HC11 MPU by omitting some of its more advanced elements, and retaining only what is necessary to describe how an MPU executes a stored program. The omitted portions will be added later as they are needed. Note that only one of the accumulators is shown.

The simplified diagram of the 68HC11 MPU is shown in Fig. 4.8. We will first describe the function of each of the elements in the diagram, then we will describe how they

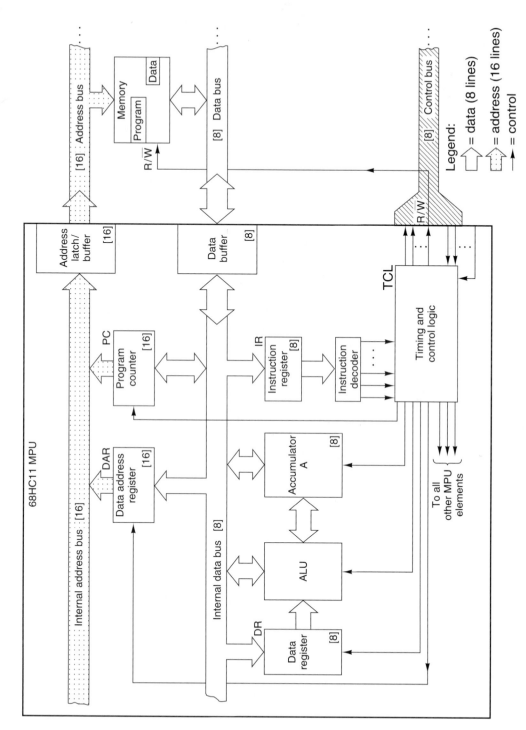

FIGURE 4.8   Simplified diagram of 68HC11 MPU.

149

interact during the execution of a program. This "stripped-down" version of the 68HC11 MPU contains the basic elements that are common to almost all MPUs.

The MPU depicted in Fig 4.8 is the portion enclosed by heavy black lines, and it is shown connected to the memory unit. For simplicity, we have not shown any I/O block in this diagram. We will assume that the program and data are already in memory, and we will not be concerned with how they got there until later in our study. This will allow us to concentrate on the MPU and memory.

Buses

There are three buses external to the MPU and two buses within the MPU. The external address and data buses are extensions of the same buses inside the MPU, so there are really only three different buses: *address, data,* and *control.* The numbers in brackets in Fig. 4.8 indicate how many signal lines make up each bus.

The *address bus* is a 16-line bus. It carries the 16-bit address code from the MPU to the memory unit to select the memory location which the MPU is accessing for a READ or WRITE operation. The address bus is a *unidirectional* bus, because information flows in only one direction.

The *data bus* is an eight-line *bidirectional* bus over which 8-bit words can be sent from the MPU to memory (that is, a WRITE operation) or from the memory to the MPU (a READ operation). Although it is called the "data" bus, the information carried on this bus will not always be data; it will often be instruction codes (op code, operand address) that are being fetched by the MPU.

The *control bus* is a grouping of all the timing and control signals needed to synchronize the operations of the MPU with the other units of the microcomputer. Some of the control lines are outputs from the MPU, and others are inputs to the MPU from I/O devices (not shown in Fig. 4.8). Most 8-bit MPUs, like the 68HC11, will have an 8-bit data bus and 16-bit address bus. However, a wide variation exists among the various types of MPUs as to the number and type of signals included on the control bus. For now, we will only need to consider the READ/WRITE signal ($R/\overline{W}$), which is generated by the MPU's timing and control section. All MPUs have this control signal or its equivalent.

MPU Registers

Recall that the MPU contains the ALU and control portions of a microcomputer. It also contains several registers that are used to store various kinds of information needed by the MPU as it performs its functions. In other words, these registers serve as dedicated memory locations *inside* the MPU chip.

Each register shown in Fig. 4.8 is indicated by its full name and its abbreviation, and by a number in brackets specifying the size of the register in bits. We will use these abbreviations in the discussions that follow.

Note that most of the registers are connected to the internal data bus so that information can be transferred between these registers and the memory unit over the data bus.

The Program Counter (PC)

This register normally functions as a 16-bit counter that controls the sequence in which the instructions are fetched from memory. At any given instant, the contents of the PC indicate the address in memory from which the next byte of instruction code is to be fetched.

Whenever the MPU is to fetch a byte of instruction code, control signals from the timing and control block will place the contents of the PC onto the internal address bus, and latch them into the address latch/buffer that drives the external address bus. This presents the memory unit with a 16-bit address code equivalent to the count in the PC. The PC count is then incremented to prepare for the next instruction FETCH operation.

Data Address Register (DAR)

The PC provides an instruction code address to the memory unit during an instruction FETCH operation. The DAR provides an operand address to the memory unit when the MPU has to access memory during the execution phase of an instruction. For example, during the execution of a store accumulator A instruction (STAA), the DAR will hold the operand address corresponding to the memory location where the contents of accumulator A are to be stored. Signals from the timing and control block will place the contents of the DAR onto the internal address bus and latch them into the address latch/buffer.

Thus, we can say that the PC always holds instruction addresses that refer to the program portion of memory, and the DAR always holds data (operand) addresses that refer to the data portion on memory.

The Instruction Register (IR) and the Timing and Control Logic (TCL)

To fetch an op code from program memory, the MPU's control circuitry generates signals that do the following: (1) place the contents of the PC on the address bus; (2) set $R/\overline{W} = 1$ for a READ operation; and (3) take the resulting memory word from the data bus and load it into the instruction register (IR). Thus, at the completion of an op code fetch, the IR holds the op code.

The IR holds the op code while the instruction decoder circuit decodes it and signals the timing and control logic (TCL) to generate the proper sequence of control signals to complete the execution of the indicated instruction. This sequence of control signals is controlled by program instructions stored in the TCL (Fig. 4.8). These instructions are often referred to as a *microprogram*. A microprogram is built into the MPU and controls how the MPU executes a machine language instruction; it cannot be modified by the user. A microprogram is not to be confused with the user-supplied program that is stored in memory *outside* the MPU.

The Accumulator (A) and Data Register (DR)

These two registers hold the operands that the ALU operates on during the execution phase of an instruction. The operands are loaded into these registers from memory. The results of an ALU operation are then transferred to the accumulator. Note that both the accumulator and the DR can receive data from memory over the data bus, but only the accumulator can send data to memory. Recall that the 68HC11 MPU has two accumulators (accumulator A and accumulator B); however, only one of them (accumulator A) is used for the following discussion.

▶ 4.11 EXECUTING A PROGRAM

We are now ready to observe how the various 68HC11 MPU registers and circuits work together to execute an actual program. At this point, we are interested primarily in how the microcomputer operates. Thus, we will use a very simple program that adds two 8-bit binary numbers.

Before we look at this sample program, we must know what instructions are available for use in the program. Every microprocessor has a list of instructions that it is designed to perform; this is called its *instruction set*. The 68HC11 has over 300 different instructions in its instruction set, but we will be using only a few of them for now. These are listed in Table 4.1.

The first column in Table 4.1 gives the name of the operation performed by each instruction. The second column gives the *mnemonic* (pronounced "nemonic") for each instruction. A mnemonic is usually a three- or four-letter abbreviation or memory aid that is

TABLE 4.1   Some 68HC11 Instructions

Operation	Mnemonic	Op code	Description
Load Accumulator A	LDAA	B6	Accumulator A is loaded with data from the memory location with the address given by the two bytes following the op code (i.e., a two-byte operand address).
Store Accumulator A	STAA	B7	The contents of accumulator A are stored in memory location with address given in two-byte operand address.
Add to Accumulator A	ADDA	BB	The data in the memory location specified by the two-byte operand address are added to the accumulator A. The result is left in the accumulator A.
Subtract from Accumulator A	SUBA	B0	Same as the ADDA, except data are subtracted from accumulator A.
Halt	WAI	3E	WAI stands for Wait. This instruction can be used to halt execution of a program. However, it is not the only one that can be used for this purpose (more about this later).
Jump	JMP	7E	Load PC with the two-byte operand address, and take the next instruction from this new address (similar to GOTO statement in BASIC).
Branch if Equal to Zero	BEQ	27	If the last operation performed by the CPU produced a result of zero, add the byte that follows the op code (*offset*) to the PC, and take the next instruction from this new address. Otherwise, fetch the next op code in sequence (similar to IF-THEN statement in BASIC).

used extensively to represent the instruction. The third column in Table 4.1 gives the hexadecimal op code for each instruction. The last column gives a description of exactly what operation is performed by each instruction.

Sample Program

Below is a short program that uses some of the instructions from Table 4.1. The first column gives the addresses in memory where the program is stored, and the second column gives the contents of each memory location. Both of these are given in hex for convenience, but remember that they actually exist in binary within the computer circuits. Once again, we will assume that this program is already in memory, and for now we will not be concerned as to how it was placed there.

Memory address (Hex)	Memory word (Hex)	Mnemonic	Description
C000	B6	LDAA	; LOAD accumulator A
C001	C1		; ⎰ Address of
C002	00		; ⎱ operand X
C003	BB	ADDA	; ADD Y to contents of accumulator A
C004	C1		; ⎰ Address of
C005	01		; ⎱ operand Y
C006	B7	STAA	; STORE the contents of accumulator A
C007	C1		; ⎰ Address where the contents of
C008	02		; ⎱ accumulator A will be stored
C009	3E	WAI	; Halt execution of the program

The function of this program is to add two 8-bit numbers (X and Y) that are stored in data memory locations C100 and C101, respectively. The sum is then stored in address C102.

Program Execution

To begin executing the program, the PC has to be set to the address of the first instruction. In our sample program, the starting address is C000. We will assume that the timing and control logic (TCL) has already set **[PC]** = C000, and we will not be concerned with how it does this until later.

As you read through the following step-by-step description, you may have to refer back to the program listing and the MPU diagram in Fig. 4.8 for clarification or review.

1. *Fetch op code* for LDAA. The TCL places **[PC]** = C000 onto the address bus so that the memory receives this address code. The TCL also sets R/$\overline{\text{W}}$ = 1 for a READ operation. The memory responds by placing the word B6 from address C000 onto the data bus. The TCL causes this word to be loaded into the IR. This step can be stated symbolically as **[M]** → **[IR]**, and is illustrated in Fig. 4.9.

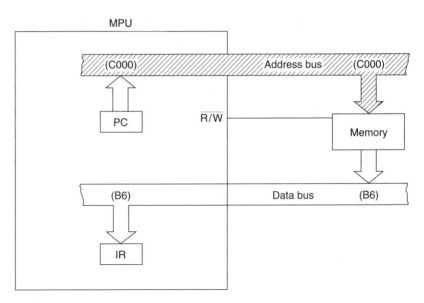

FIGURE 4.9   MPU fetching op code from address C000.

2. *Increment the PC.* The program counter is incremented so that **[PC]** = C001. Symbolically, **[PC] + 1** → **[PC]**. This gets the PC ready for the next fetch operation.

3. *Decode op code.* The instruction decoder (Fig. 4.8) decodes the op code (B6) and signals the TCL to begin generating the sequence of control signals needed to continue fetching and executing the LDAA instruction. The TCL executes the microprogram steps for the op code B6.

4. *Fetch operand address* (high-order byte). The TCL places **[PC]** = C001 on the address bus and sets $R/\overline{W}$ = 1. The memory responds by placing the word C1 on the data bus. This word is loaded into the high-order byte of the DAR. Remember that the DAR holds 16 bits (two bytes). This step can be symbolized as **[M]** → **[DAR_high]**.

5. *Increment* **[PC]** *to C002.*

6. *Fetch operand address* (low-order byte). The TCL places **[PC]** = C002 on the address bus and sets $R/\overline{W}$ = 1. The memory responds by placing the word 00 on the data bus, and the TCL loads it into the low-order byte of the DAR. This step can be symbolized as **[M]** → **[DAR_low]**. The DAR now holds the operand address C100.

7. *Increment* **[PC]** *to C003.*

8. *Execute LDAA.* The operand address from the DAR is placed on the address bus and $R/\overline{W}$ is set HIGH. The memory responds by placing the data from address C100 onto the data bus; this is the operand X. The TCL causes these data to be loaded into accumulator A. This operation can be symbolized as **[M]** → **[A]**, as illustrated in Fig. 4.10.

9. *Fetch op code* for ADDA. The TCL places **[PC]** = C003 on the address bus and sets $R/\overline{W}$ = 1. Memory places the word BB on the data bus, and the TCL loads this word into the IR. Symbolically, **[M]** → **[IR]**.

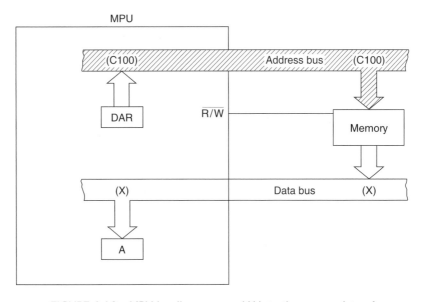

FIGURE 4.10   MPU loading operand X into the accumulator A.

10. *Increment* **[PC]** to C004.

11. *Decode op code.* The instruction decoder signals the TCL to begin generating the sequence of control signals needed for execution of the ADDA instruction.

12. *Fetch operand address* (high-order byte). The address C004 from the PC is placed on the address bus and R/$\overline{\text{W}}$ is set HIGH. The memory then places the word C1 on the data bus to be loaded into the high-order byte of the DAR. Symbolically [**M**] → [**DAR**$_{\text{high}}$].

13. *Increment* **[PC]** to C005.

14. *Fetch operand address* (low-order byte). The address C005 from the PC is placed on the address bus and R/$\overline{\text{W}}$ is set HIGH. The memory then places the word 01 on the data bus to be loaded into the low-order byte of the DAR. Symbolically, [**M**] → [**DAR**$_{\text{low}}$]. At this point the DAR holds the operand address C101.

15. *Increment* **[PC]** to C006.

16. *Execute ADDA.* The operand address from the DAR is placed on the address bus and R/$\overline{\text{W}}$ is set HIGH. Memory places the data word from memory location C101 on the data bus; this is the operand Y. The TCL then loads these data into the data register (DR) and commands the ALU to add it to accumulator A (which holds operand X). The result is placed in accumulator A. Symbolically, [**M**] + [**A**] → [**A**].

17. *Fetch op code* for STAA. [**PC**] = C006 is placed on the address bus and R/$\overline{\text{W}}$ is set HIGH. Memory then places the word B7 on the data bus, and it is loaded into the IR.

18. *Increment* **[PC]** to C007.

19. *Decode op code.* TCL begins steps to execute STAA.

20. *Fetch operand address* (high-order byte) from memory location given by [**PC**] = C007, and place it in the high-order byte of the DAR.

21. *Increment* **[PC]** to C008.

22. *Fetch operand address* (low-order byte) from address C008 and place it in the low-order byte of the DAR. The DAR now holds the operand address C102.

23. *Increment* **[PC]** to C009.

24. *Execute STAA.* The operand address C102 from the DAR is placed on the address bus. The TCL then places the contents of accumulator A on the data bus and clears R/$\overline{W}$ to 0 so that **[A]** gets written into memory location C102. Symbolically, **[A]** → **[M]**.

25. *Fetch next op code* from address given by **[PC]** = C009, and load it into the IR.

26. *Increment* **[PC]** to C00A

27. *Decode op code.* TCL recognizes the WAI instruction.

28. *Execute WAI*.* The MPU stops all further MPU operations.

It may be necessary to review the foregoing steps several times to fully understand how the MPU operates. Although we used a simplified version of the 68HC11 MPU and a relatively simple example program, the operation is exactly as described.

▶ 4.12 JUMP AND BRANCH INSTRUCTIONS

We will not describe the complete instruction set of the 68HC11 MPU until Chapter 7. However, there are two more types of instructions that we will discuss here because of the way in which they alter the sequence of instructions that the 68HC11 executes. You may want to review the JMP and BEQ instructions in Table 4.1 before reading further.

The JMP Instruction

The sample program that was analyzed in the preceding section can be described as a *straight-line* program. It is so called because the MPU fetches the instructions from memory, starting at address C000, and continues in sequence. This is accomplished by incrementing the PC after each fetch operation.

Although straight-line programs are easy to write and understand, they are limited to relatively simple programming tasks. Most programs use a technique called *looping.* Looping allows the MPU to break out of the normal straight-line sequence, and jump or branch to a different area of program memory to continue executing instructions.

The JMP instruction causes the MPU to "jump" to a specified memory address (other than the next one in sequence) for its next instruction. If you are familiar with programming in the BASIC language, you will find that the JMP instruction is like the GOTO statement in BASIC.

---

*The WAI instruction will halt the execution of the program. However, this instruction will also cause some other changes within the 68HC11 MPU. Later in Chapter 8, we will discuss the full implications of using the WAI instruction to halt execution of a program. We will also show other ways of halting execution of a program in upcoming chapters.

The JMP instruction is illustrated below.

Memory address (Hex)	Memory word (Hex)	Mnemonic	Description
C100	48	ASLA	; SHIFT [A] left one bit
C101	7E	JMP	; JUMP to C15F for the next instruction
C102	C1		; ⎡ Address of ⎤
C103	5F		; ⎣ next instruction ⎦
C104	—		
C105	—		
• •	•		
• •	•		
• •	•		
C15F	B7	STAA	; STORE [A] in memory location C300
C160	C3		; ⎡ Address of location where the ⎤
C161	00		; ⎣ contents of [A] will be stored ⎦

This is a section of a program stored in memory. Let us assume that the MPU has been executing this program. Let us further assume that it has just completed execution of the ASLA instruction at C100. Its next step is to fetch the op code for the JMP instruction at C101. Once the MPU determines that it is a JMP instruction, it knows that a two-byte address follows the op code. It fetches this address (C15F) in two steps. It then replaces the current contents of the PC (C104) with C15F. With PC now holding the address C15F, the MPU will fetch its next op code from this address. In other words, instead of fetching and executing the instruction at C104, the MPU jumps over addresses C104 through C15E and goes to C15F.

As this example shows, the JMP instruction is a three-byte instruction. The op code byte is followed by the two-byte *jump address* that tells the MPU where to jump.

The BEQ (Branch if Equal to Zero) Instruction

When the MPU encounters a JMP op code in a program, it *always* alters its execution sequence by jumping to the new address given by the two bytes that follow the op code. There is another powerful class of instructions that can be used to alter the execution sequence. These are called *conditional branch* instructions because they will alter the execution sequence only when specific conditions are met. The 68HC11 MPU has many different conditional branch instructions; for now we will only look at the BEQ instruction as a representative example.

The BEQ instruction, and all conditional branch instructions, are two-byte instructions. The first byte is, of course, the op code. The second byte is a signed binary number called the *relative address offset* or simply *offset*. The offset is used to determine the address to which the MPU will branch for its next instruction. The offset is *not* an address, but is a number that must be added to the program counter to form a new address. This is illustrated in the short program sequence below.

Memory address (Hex)	Memory word (Hex)	Mnemonic	Description
C200	B0	SUBA	; Subtract the contents of address C29B
C201	C2		; from accumulator A
C202	9B		; Leave result in accumulator A
C203	27	BEQ	; If result of last operation is Zero, branch
C204	14		; to C219. If not, go to C205. { Offset = 14 }
C205	??	?	
• •	•		
• •	•		
• •	•		
C219	B7	STAA	; STORE [A] in address C127
C21A	C1		
C21B	27		

Let us assume that the MPU has just finished executing the SUBA instruction at C200–C202 and accumulator A holds the result. The MPU then fetches the op code at C203. When the MPU sees that it is a BEQ instruction, it fetches the offset byte at C204. Then it has to *make a decision* based on the result of the last operation.

If the SUBA operation produced a result of exactly zero (that is $00_{16} = 00000000_2$), the MPU will add the offset byte to the current contents of the PC. With [PC] = C205 after fetching the offset byte, then

$$\begin{array}{rll} [PC] & = & C205 \\ + \quad \text{offset} & = & 14 \\ \hline \text{new } [PC] & = & C219 \end{array}$$

Because the new contents of the PC are C219, the MPU will *branch* to address C219 for its next instruction, and will continue from there.

If the result of the SUBA operation had *not* been equal to zero, the MPU would *not* add the offset to [PC]. Instead, it would take its next instruction in sequence from address C205 (that is, it would not branch).

This example shows that the BEQ instruction will cause the MPU to branch from C205 to C219 on the condition that the result of the last operation is zero. Otherwise, the MPU continues in normal sequence. Those who are familiar with the BASIC language should see that the BEQ instruction is very similar to the IF-THEN statement in BASIC.

Although this example showed how the MPU can branch forward (to a higher address), branch instructions can also cause the MPU to branch backward (to a lower address). In Chapter 7 we show how this is done.

▶ 4.13 HARDWARE, SOFTWARE, AND FIRMWARE

A computer system contains hardware, software, and firmware. The *hardware* refers to the electronic, mechanical, and magnetic devices that physically make up the computer. The amount of hardware varies widely from small microcomputers to large mainframes, but one thing is the same for all computers: The hardware is useless without a program or programs in memory.

Software refers to the programs that direct all the activities of the computer system from start-up to shutdown. All software falls into one of two categories: *applications software* or *systems software.* Applications software is used for specific tasks, such as performing statistical analyses, controlling industrial processes, and producing video games.

Systems software is more general than applications software. It supports all applications software by directing the basic functions of the computer. For example, systems software controls the initialization process that the computer follows when it is turned on. Another example is the systems software that allows us to enter programs in a language such as BASIC.

All software has to reside in the computer's internal memory unit when it is to be executed. Typically, the software is loaded into internal memory from external memory, such as tape or disk. When a program is in ROM, it is often referred to as *firmware,* because it is always there. A familiar example of firmware is the video game ROM cartridge.

▶ 4.14 PROGRAMMING LANGUAGES— MACHINE LANGUAGE

Programming involves writing a program in some code or language that the computer can interpret and execute. There are many different programming languages in use today; they range from the use of 0s and 1s all the way up to the use of English-language statements. Each type of language has its advantages and shortcomings relative to the other types, as we shall see. Regardless of what type of language the programmer uses to write a program, however, the program must eventually be translated to the *only* language any computer understands—the language of 0s and 1s, which is referred to as *machine language.* The computer performs specific operations in response to specific binary patterns (op codes) that form its instruction set. These binary patterns represent the actual language the machine (computer) understands and works with.

Manufacturers define the *machine language* their computers understand and the set of instructions represented. In general, any two different computers will have different machine languages. For example, Motorola's 68HC11 microprocessor uses the code 10111011_2 for its addition instruction, whereas Intel's 8085 uses the code 10000110_2. This means that a machine language program written for one microcomputer will generally not work on any other microcomputer. There are exceptions to this, when one microprocessor is an improved or enhanced version of another.

The *object* of any programming task is to place the machine language codes for a particular sequence of instructions into the computer's memory. For this reason, the machine language program stored in memory is also referred to as the *object program.* When a programmer actually writes a program on paper in machine language, it will consist of sequences of 0s and 1s. For example, below is a short object program for adding two numbers using the 68HC11 machine language:

```
10110110
11000011
00000000
10111011
11100000
11111111
10110111
11000100
10101010
```

Clearly, the function of this program is far from obvious to anyone except the person who wrote it or perhaps someone who has all the 68HC11 codes memorized. Even the person who wrote it would have a hard time recognizing it after not having seen it for a while.

Writing programs directly in binary machine language has several disadvantages. First, it is very difficult to write all but the simplest programs without making an error, because after a while the strings of 0s and 1s all begin to look alike. Similarly, errors are difficult to detect; a misplaced 0 or 1 can easily get lost among hundreds or thousands of bits. Furthermore, the process of entering a machine language program into the computer's memory can be extremely tedious and prone to error. Each byte is entered via eight binary switches on the computer's front panel. This means, for example, that a program of 100 bytes, not very long by most standards, will require 800 different switch settings.

Hex Machine Language

Machine language programming can be made more readable by using octal or hexadecimal code. We will use hex code (as we did earlier) because it is standard in the microcomputer field. The programmer writes the program using hex codes to represent the op codes, operand addresses, and data. The program shown above would appear as follows:

```
B6
C3
00
BB
E0
FF
B7
C4
AA
```

Writing a program in hex is certainly simpler and less prone to error than binary because each entry requires only two digits instead of eight. In addition, an error in any of the digits would be easier to detect.

A hex program is entered into the computer's memory from a hex keyboard, which serves as an input device. Of course, the hex program has to be converted to a binary object program before it is stored in memory. There is usually a program in ROM called a *keyboard monitor program* that the computer executes as you punch in a program on the hex keyboard. The monitor program detects which hex keys you are pressing, converts them to binary, and stores them in memory.

Programming in hex, although an improvement over binary, is still far from convenient. Furthermore, a hex program is still difficult to read or understand unless you have all the hex op codes memorized—hardly a reasonable requirement.

▶ 4.15 ASSEMBLY LANGUAGE

Machine language programming (binary or hex) is the lowest level of programming. It is so called because the programmer is communicating with the computer at the computer's basic level. Many of the difficulties of communicating at this level can be overcome by using the next-higher-level language: *assembly language.*

Instead of using binary or hex representations for instruction codes, assembly language uses mnemonics like those we used in our earlier examples. Mnemonics are easily committed to memory because with a few exceptions, it is easy to tell what operations they represent. Every microprocessor manufacturer provides a list of mnemonics that can be used with its MPU. Below is a 68HC11 assembly language version of the hex program for adding two numbers. An assembly language program is also referred to as a *source* program, because it will later be converted to a machine language *object* program.

Assembly Language Source Program

Memory address	Instruction mnemonic	Comments
C200	LDAA $D0FF	; Get first data word
C203	ADDA $D500	; Add second data word
C206	STAA $D700	; Store sum in memory

Each line in this assembly language listing contains one *complete* instruction. Remember that each instruction may be one, two, or three bytes of code. The "memory address" column gives only the address of the op code byte for each instruction. For example, the op code for the LDAA instruction will be stored in C200, and the operand address in C201 and C202. The op code for ADDA will be stored in C203, and so on.

The "mnemonics" column gives the mnemonic and operand address for each instruction. Note that the address is preceded by a $; this is used to indicate that the address is in hex. Thus, LDAA $D0FF is the assembly language representation for "load accumulator A from hex address D0FF." Similarly, STAA $D700 means "store accumulator A in hex address D700."

The "comments" column is often included in an assembly language listing to make it clear what the program is doing. Even without these comments, the mnemonics make it fairly easy to follow the program logic.

Assembling the Program

An assembly language source program is easier to write and easier to follow than a machine language program, but it eventually has to be converted to machine language before it can be placed in memory and executed. This conversion process is called *assembling* the source program.

One method for doing this is called *hand assembly*. Hand assembly simply means taking each line of the assembly language source program, looking up the codes for each mnemonic, and replacing the line of assembly language with object (machine) code. For example, to hand-assemble the first instruction of the program above, you would have to look up the op code for LDAA.

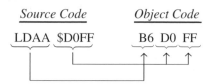

In this case, the source code assembles into three bytes of hex object code. Each line of the assembly language program has to be converted in the same manner. It is this object code, of course, that has to be entered into the program memory.

In a typical procedure, a programmer writes an assembly language program, goes over it, and modifies and corrects it as needed. When the programmer is satisfied that the program will do the job, the hand-assembly process is performed, and the hex object program is entered into memory.

Clearly, hand assembly is a rote process that can be tedious, inefficient, time consuming, and subject to careless errors especially when the program is a long one. Hence, it is a method that is rarely used by today's programmers.

Assemblers

The process of assembling (converting) an assembly language source program into a machine language object program can be done by the computer itself. To do this, the computer must have a special program called an *assembler* stored in its memory. The assembler program can be in ROM (that is, a resident assembler), or it can be loaded into RAM from disk. The size of the assembler program may vary, depending on the number of features and capabilities that it has. Assemblers can be divided basically into two different types; *full-blown assemblers* and *one-line assemblers*. Full-blown assemblers are more refined than one-line assemblers and consequently have become the assembler of choice of most programmers.

Generally, a full-blown assembler takes a *source code file* and produces both an *object code file* and a *list file*. The object code file contains the machine code needed by the microcomputer to execute the program. The list file is a text file that shows (1) source code instructions and their respective translation into hex; and (2) any error messages that were found. Microcomputers typically use a small one-line assembler, which basically duplicates the hand-assembly process previously described in converting one line of assembly language into machine code. There are many complex assemblers available in the market that have special features and capabilities that can make assembly language programming more efficient. However, our discussion focuses on the one-line assembler since it is the type of assembler that is used most often by microcomputers. The assembly process typically follows these steps:

1. The one-line assembler program is loaded into the computer's internal RAM (unless it is already in ROM).

2. The programmer loads the assembly language source program into the computer's RAM, either from the keyboard or an external memory unit (i.e., disk). For example, the source program above would be stored in memory just as shown, using ASCII code for the characters.

3. The computer is then commanded to execute the one-line assembler program.

4. The computer executes the one-line assembler program, which converts source code instructions such as LDAA $D0FF into object code that it places into RAM.

5. Once the entire source code instructions have been converted into a complete object program and placed into RAM, the object program then can be stored on disk for later use, so that the assembly process does not have to be repeated.

6. The object program can now be executed since it is in executable machine language form.

Disadvantages of Assembly Language

Assembly language is certainly a big improvement over machine language, especially if your computer has an assembler program. Programming in assembly language, however, is still quite a challenge because it requires detailed knowledge of the microcomputer being used. It requires knowledge of (1) the registers and instruction set of the MPU; (2) the address modes that the MPU uses to address memory and I/O devices; and many other details.

Another disadvantage of assembly language programs is that they are not *portable;* that is, an assembly language program written for one type of MPU will generally not run on another MPU.

▶ 4.16 HIGH-LEVEL LANGUAGES

Although assembly language is much more convenient than machine language, it still requires that the programmer be very familiar with the computer's internal structure and its complete set of instruction mnemonics. In addition, the programmer has to write an instruction for each step the computer has to perform. For example, to add two numbers, the programmer has to tell the computer to fetch the first number, place it in the accumulator, fetch the second number, add it to the accumulator, and store the result in a memory location. This step-by-step process can become quite laborious for complex programs. In fact, to become an accomplished machine or assembly language programmer, it takes a great deal of practice and a great deal of time.

To overcome these difficulties, a number of high-level languages have been developed. Some of the more common ones are BASIC, FORTRAN, PASCAL, and C. These *high-level* languages make it possible to communicate with a computer using English-language words and mathematical symbols without the need for detailed knowledge of the computer's internal architecture or instruction set. Furthermore, with high-level languages, one statement can contain many steps, corresponding to many machine language instructions. To illustrate, the following is a statement written in a language called BASIC:

LET RESULT = A + B

It should be obvious, even to a nonprogrammer, that this simple instruction statement represents a program for adding two numbers. It should also be obvious that this program is much easier to write and understand than its machine language and assembly language counterparts.

The main purpose of any high-level language is to relieve the computer user from having to worry about the details of machine or assembly language programming. Instead, the programmer can concentrate on solving the problem at hand using the straightforward commands and rules of the high-level languages. Another advantage of high-level languages is that the same program can be run on two computers with different machine languages, assuming that both computers *understand* the particular high-level language being used. For example, a program written in PASCAL for a microcomputer that uses a 68HC11 MPU would also work on a microcomputer that has an 80486 MPU, provided that each computer has some means for *translating* the PASCAL language statements into its own machine language codes.

Interpreters and Compilers

How does a computer translate a high-level language such as BASIC? Just as the use of assembly language required a special *assembler program,* the use of a high-level language requires a special program. This special program can be classified as either an *interpreter program* or as a *compiler program.* Both are much larger programs than assemblers and require much more memory space.

Interpreters and compilers differ in the process used for translating high-level language. An interpreter takes each high-level instruction or command statement (for example, LET RESULT = A + B) and causes the computer to go through the steps required to execute the operation. It does *not* convert each statement into machine language codes to be placed in memory; that is, it does not create an object program. A compiler, on the other hand, translates each statement into the sequence of machine language codes required to execute the operation. It creates an object program in memory, which must then be run to perform the programmed task. Stated another way, a compiler translates the *complete* high-level program into an object program that is placed in memory for later execution, while an interpreter translates small chunks of the program and executes them as it goes along without creating an object program.

High-level languages do have some drawbacks that make them unsuitable for some applications. They usually produce programs that run slower and use more memory than machine or assembly language programs. One reason is that these high-level languages perform according to prescribed rules that cannot take advantage of all the idiosyncrasies and subtleties of a particular computer. A programmer using machine or assembly language can often take advantage of his or her intimate knowledge of the computer to produce a more efficient program. Another reason is that the interpreter or compiler translation process takes a certain amount of time. Interpreters are particularly slow with typical program execution times that are ten to fifty times longer than a machine language version.

Furthermore, high-level languages are not generally well suited to the large class of microprocessor applications that deal with controlling external devices or processes. These applications involve sending data and control information to output devices and receiving data and status information from input devices. Very often the control and status information is a few binary digits (bits) that have specific hardware-related meanings. High-level languages are generally designed to process decimal numbers, and they are much less efficient than assembly language at handling bits.

In some applications, the slower execution time of high-level language programs is a major drawback. Applications such as machine control, process control, and communications require the MPU to execute a program as fast as possible. These are called *real-time* applications because the program is controlling a process or an event that is occurring while the program is being executed. Machine and assembly language are better suited than high-level languages for real-time applications because of their faster execution.

We will use assembly language throughout this book since we will deal predominantly with real-time control applications.

▶ 4.17 FLOWCHARTS

A flowchart is a graphical representation showing the logical sequence that a program follows. Flowcharts are especially helpful in representing complex programs. We will use them for even the simple programs that we encounter in the following sections because they will help us to understand what the program is doing. The symbols used in programming flowcharts are shown in Fig. 4.11. Although these symbols are somewhat standard, there may be some variations.

Input/Output

The *input/output* block is used to represent operations involving the MPU reading data from an input device or writing data to an output device. For example, this symbol is used when the MPU is outputting data to a display device.

Processing

The *processing* block is used to represent any operations that the MPU performs on data (other than I/O operations). Examples of operations that would be included in a processing block include arithmetic operations, logic operations, shifting, and data movement.

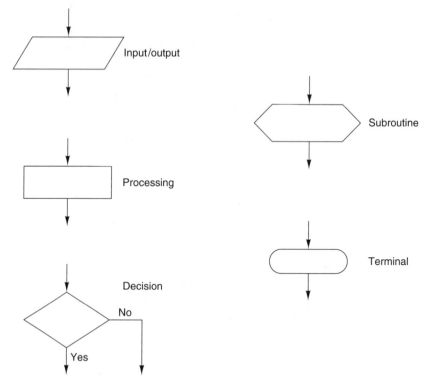

FIGURE 4.11   Flowchart symbols.

Decision

The diamond-shaped *decision* blocks are used whenever the MPU has to make a decision. The most common situation of this type occurs when the MPU executes conditional branch instructions. The decision block has two output arrows that indicate the two possible paths that the MPU can take.

Subroutine

This block is used whenever the MPU is instructed to jump or branch to a *subroutine*. A subroutine is a sequence of instructions that performs a special task that the MPU may need to do several times during the execution of a major program. We will have more to say about subroutines later.

Termination

The *termination* symbol is used to represent terminal points in a program or subroutine. Words such as START, BEGIN, END, STOP, and RETURN are used within these termination blocks.

EXAMPLE 4.3

Draw a flowchart for a program to add 7 data bytes coming from an input device (i.e., sensor) and then store the result in memory.

Solution

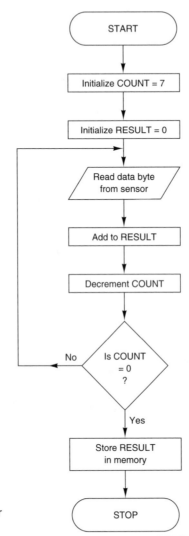

FIGURE 4.12 Flowchart for problem of Example 4.3.

GLOSSARY

Accumulator   A register used as both an input to the ALU and an output from the ALU.

Address Bus   Lines that carry the address code from the MPU to the memory unit.

Arithmetic/Logic Unit (ALU)   That part of a computer that performs arithmetic and logic operations on data during program execution.

Assembler   A program that allows the computer to convert assembly language to machine language.

Assembly   The process of converting an assembly language source program into a machine language object program.

Assembly Language   A programming language that allows the use of mnemonics in place of binary or hex machine language instructions.

Byte   An 8-bit word. Many microprocessors have a word size of one byte.

Central Processing Unit (CPU)   Combination of control unit and ALU.

Compiler   A program that translates a complete high-level language program to a machine language object program.

Conditional Branch Instruction   This causes the MPU to branch to an address other than the next one in sequence for its next instruction *provided that a specific condition is met.*

Control Bus   Grouping of all timing and control signals external to the MPU.

Control Unit   That part of a computer that directs the operation of all other computer units by providing timing and control signals.

Data Address Register (DAR)   MPU register that holds the operand address during instruction execution.

Data Bus   Bidirectional lines that carry data between the MPU and memory.

Data Register (DR)   MPU register that holds one of the operands during an ALU operation.

Firmware   Programs and data stored in ROM.

Flowchart   A graphical representation showing the logical sequence that a program follows.

Full-Blown Assembler   Program that converts a source code program into an object code program and a list file.

Hardware   The electronic, mechanical, and magnetic components that make up a computer.

High-Level Languages   Programming languages that use English-language words and mathematical symbols, and require no detailed knowledge of the computer.

Input Unit   Consists of devices that allow data and information to enter the computer's internal memory or ALU from the outside world

Instruction   The binary code that tells the CPU what operation is to be performed, and where to find the data to be operated on.

Instruction Register (IR)   MPU register that holds op code.

Internet   An extensive network of many different types of computers connecting people and resources around the world.

Interpreter   A program that translates a high-level language program to machine language one statement at a time and executes it. It does not produce an object program for later use.

JUMP (unconditional)   An instruction that causes the MPU to jump unconditionally to an address other than the next one in sequence for its next instruction.

List File   A text file that is generated by a "full-blown" assembler and that shows the source code instructions and any error messages that might have been detected during the assembly process.

Machine Language   The language of 0s and 1s. The only language that the computer's circuitry understands. The lowest level programming language.

Memory Unit   That part of a computer that stores programs and data.

Microcomputer   A relatively small, inexpensive computer based on a microprocessor chip.

Microcontroller (MCU)   Single-chip IC that contains an MPU, memory, and I/O circuitry.

Microprocessor (*also* MPU)   An LSI chip that performs the functions of a CPU.

Microprogram   Program instructions stored in the MPU that direct the sequence of control signals that are sent to the various MPU circuits to execute the particular machine language instructions.

Mnemonic   A three- or four-letter abbreviation for a computer instruction.

Object Code File   A machine language program that is the result of the assembly process performed by an assembler. This object code file (or object program) can now be executed since it is in executable machine language form.

Object Program   The machine language program that is derived from either an assembly language or a high-level language source program.

Offset   A byte that follows the op code for a conditional branch instruction such as BEQ. The offset is added to the PC to determine the address to which the MPU will branch.

One-Line Assembler   Assembler program that converts one line of source code (i.e., LDAA $C1FF) at a time into machine language.

Operand   Data that are operated on by the computer as it executes a program.

Operand Address   Address in memory where an operand is currently stored or is to be stored.

Operation Code (Op Code)   The part of an instruction that tells the computer what operation to perform.

Output Unit   Consists of peripheral devices that transfer data and information from internal memory or ALU to the outside world.

Prebyte   First byte of a two-byte op code. For example, in the 68HC11 MPU all of the instructions that use the Y register will have a specific prebyte that precedes the op code byte.

Program   Complete sequence of instructions that direct a computer to perform a specific task or solve a problem.

Program Counter (PC)   MPU register that keeps track of instruction addresses during program execution.

Programmer   One who designs or writes a program.

Real-Time   Refers to applications where the results of a computer's operations on data are required immediately for controlling an external device or process.

Relative Address Offset   See Offset.

Single-Byte Instruction   MPU instruction that contains only the op code.

Software   The programs that direct all the activities of the computer.

Source Code File   See Source Program.

Source Program   A program written in assembly language.

Three-Byte Instruction   MPU instruction where the first byte is the op code and both the second and third bytes make up the operand address.

Two-Byte Instruction   MPU instruction where the first byte is the op code and the second byte could be (1) the low-order byte of an operand address; (2) data; or (3) an offset.

Word   Fundamental unit of information in a computer.

QUESTIONS AND PROBLEMS

Sections 4.1–4.5

1. List some of the application areas where computers are used.
2. What are the advantages of using a computer in real-time process control?
3. Name the three categories of computers. Which one is the most recent development?
4. How many more times powerful is a 64-bit mainframe that executes 5 million instructions per second than a 16-bit microcomputer that executes 1 million instructions per second?
5. Name the five basic units of a computer.
6. Indicate the computer unit being referred to in each of the following statements.
   (a) Programs and data are stored here.
   (b) A keyboard is part of this unit.
   (c) Arithmetic operations are done here.
   (d) A video monitor is part of this unit.
   (e) Places programs and data into internal memory.
   (f) Directs the operation of all the units.
   (g) Fetches and decodes instructions.
7. Which two computer units make up the CPU?
8. Define CPU, microprocessor, microcomputer, and MPU.
9. Describe the *basic* differences between an MPU and a microcontroller.

Sections 4.6–4.8

10. A certain computer has a word size that can accommodate four bytes. How many bits are in this word size?
11. The contents of two consecutive memory locations in a certain computer are shown in the following table. All values are in hexadecimal.

Memory address	Contents
0350	B8
0351	24

    (a) If the two data words represent the two halves of a large binary number, what is the *decimal* value of that number? Assume that the high-order byte is in address 0350.
    (b) If the two data words are in ASCII code with an *even*-parity bit (MSB), what do the words represent?
12. How does an 8-bit microcomputer store 24-bit words?

13. Show how the ASCII-coded message "HELLO" would be stored in the memory of an 8-bit microcomputer.

Section 4.9

14. A certain 24-bit computer has the following instruction word format:

Op code	Operand address
8 bits	16 bits

   (a) How many different instructions can this instruction word specify?
   (b) How many different memory addresses can it specify?
   (c) What internal memory capacity would this computer require to operate at full capacity?

15. What portion of an instruction tells the MPU what operation to perform? What portion tells the MPU where data are to be taken from or sent to during the instruction execution?

16. Explain the different kinds of information carried by single-byte, two-byte, and three-byte instructions.

17. Why is a prebyte used by the 68HC11 MPU as part of its instruction set, while some other 8-bit MPUs do not have a need for it?

18. What three operations does the MPU perform repetitively as it executes any program?

19. Describe the operations being performed when each of the following instructions is executed: LDAA, STAA, and ADDA.

20. What tells the MPU whether or not it is supposed to fetch an operand address as part of an instruction?

21. How many accumulator registers does the 68HC11 MPU have?

Section 4.10

22. Name the three buses that are part of a typical microcomputer. Which bus is unidirectional?

23. The R/$\overline{\text{W}}$ signal generated by the MPU is part of the _____ bus.

24. Which MPU register holds the op code while it is being decoded?

25. Which MPU register provides the address from which the next instruction byte is to be fetched?

26. Which MPU registers hold the operands that are inputs to the ALU?

27. Where is the result of the ALU operation placed?

28. Which MPU register provides the operand address to the memory unit during an instruction execution?

29. What is the basic function of a microprogram?

30. During an LDAA instruction, data are taken from _____ and transferred to _____ .

31. During a STAA instruction, data are taken from _____ and transferred to _____ .

32. During the execution of an ADDA instruction, the ALU adds the contents of _____ to the operand fetched from _____ , and places the result in _____ .

33. True or false: The MPU always increments the PC after each op code fetch.

34. (a) Give the step-by-step description of how the 68HC11 MPU fetches, decodes, and executes the instruction below. Assume that initially **[PC]** = C800 and **[A]** = 05. Also assume that the content of memory location C457 is 03 (that is, **[C457]** = 03).

Memory address	Memory word
C800	BB
C801	C4
C802	57

(b) At the completion of this instruction, **[PC]** = _____ , **[A]** = _____ , and **[C457]** = _____ .

35. (a) Add an instruction to follow the instruction of Problem 34 so that the MPU stores the result in address C457.
(b) Repeat Problem 34(b).
(c) What would happen if address C457 were a ROM location?

36. Examine the following 68HC11 MPU program and answer the following questions:

Memory address	Memory word
E237	B6
E238	F6
E239	07
E23A	B0
E23B	F6
E23C	07
E23D	3E

(a) During the execution of this program, how many times does the address F607 appear on the address bus?

(b) How many times does the MPU perform a memory READ operation? A WRITE operation?

(c) How many times is a new word loaded into the IR?

(d) How many times is a new word loaded into the DR?

(e) How many times is a new word loaded into accumulator A?

(f) What are the final contents of accumulator A?

Section 4.12

37. Modify the program of Problem 36 so that following the SUBA instruction the MPU jumps to address 57EC for its next instruction.

38. What is a relative address offset?

39. Explain how a conditional branch instruction such as BEQ differs from an unconditional jump instruction (JMP).

40. Study the following 68HC11 MPU program and answer the questions:

Memory address	Memory word
C300	B6
C301	C3
C302	50
C303	B0
C304	C3
C305	51
C306	27
C307	03
C308	B7
C309	C3
C30A	52
C30B	3E
C30C	??

Assume that the following operands are initially stored in data memory: **[C350]** = 08; **[C351]** = 06; **[C352]** = FF.

(a) What will be **[A]** and **[C352]** at the completion of the program?

(b) Assume that **[C351]** = 08 initially and repeat Part (a).

41. A certain program has a BEQ instruction at address 07A2. What offset should be used to cause branching to 07BC?

Sections 4.13–4.17

42. Explain the difference between software and firmware.

43. What is the only language that a computer's circuitry understands?

44. What are the disadvantages of programming in binary machine language?

45. What type of programming language uses alphabetic abbreviations for each type of instruction?

46. What are the advantages of programming in assembly language as compared to machine language?

47. What function does a "full-blown" assembler program perform?

48. Describe the basic difference between a "one-line assembler" and a "full-blown assembler."

49. Which of the following types of programming languages requires a familiarity with the computer's internal architecture?
(a) Machine language (b) Assembly language (c) High-level languages

50. What are the advantages of high-level languages compared to machine and assembly languages?

51. What are the disadvantages of high-level languages?

52. Explain the difference between an *interpreter* and a *compiler*.

53. The following program is written in 68HC11 assembly language. Convert it to its machine language object program (that is, perform a hand assembly).

Memory address	Mnemonic		Comments
0000	LDAA	$C2ED	; Get data
0003	SUBA	$C35A	; Subtract data
0006	BEQ	$005B	; If [A] = 0, branch to 005B
0008	STAA	$C298	; Store if [A] ≠ 0
000B	JMP	$0035	; Jump to new address

54. Draw the five standard flowchart symbols and describe the type of operation each represents.

55. Draw the flowchart for the program of Problem 40.

5

Microcomputer Structure and Operation

OBJECTIVES

Upon completion of this chapter, you will be able to:

- Identify the basic elements of a microcomputer, a microprocessor, and a microcontroller.
- Understand the basic functions performed by the address bus, data bus, control bus, and clock signals.
- Understand the functions of the 68HC11's Ports B and C when it is operating in the normal expanded mode.
- Describe the response of the 68HC11 MPU due to a RESET pulse.
- Understand the function of the system E-clock and the internal PH2 clock during program execution.
- Describe the READ and WRITE cycles of the 68HC11 MPU when it's operating in the normal expanded mode.
- Describe how the address bus and the data bus on the 68HC11 MPU are time-multiplexed.
- Analyze the bus activity during a program execution by the 68HC11 MPU in the normal expanded mode.
- Understand and use a memory map.
- Cite the difference between the terms "page" and "4K page."
- Understand the required latching circuitry needed to multiplex Port C's signals.
- Design the necessary logic circuitry to decode a specific range of addresses for RAM, ROM, and I/O.
- Understand the usefulness of partial decoding.
- Select and use the appropriate circuits in order to buffer MPU buses.
- Cite the differences between a memory-mapped and an isolated I/O-based system.
- Apply existing digital systems troubleshooting techniques to troubleshoot memory systems.

INTRODUCTION

In Chapter 4 we described how a microcomputer fetches and executes a stored program. Our objective there was to look at the many operations that take place under the control of any microprocessor. That description purposely omitted the details on electrical connections, signals, and timing in order to keep the presentation uncluttered. In this chapter we start to add some of the details that are necessary for a solid understanding of microcomputer operation. We will use the "stripped-down" version of the 68HC11 MPU in its *normal expanded mode* (i.e., MPU inputs MODA = 1, and MODB = 1) because it is still adequate for our purposes. The "extras" will be added in Chapter 6.

▶ 5.1 MICROCOMPUTER ELEMENTS

It is important to review the distinction between the microcomputer (μC) and the microprocessor (μP*). The μC contains several elements, as illustrated in Fig. 5.1. The main element is the μP, which is typically a single LSI chip containing the Control unit and ALU portions of the μC. Most single-chip μPs are NMOS, CMOS, or HCMOS devices because of their high packing densities. HCMOS is a recent industry development that employs a new design technique that substantially increases the operating speed of CMOS technology while keeping its low power and high noise immunity characteristics (e.g., the 68HC11 has a nominal bus speed of 2 MHz). Bipolar devices (TTL, ECL) have much lower packing densities than MOS devices, so that bipolar μPs are generally formed by combining several chips to produce the desired word size.

The memory unit in Fig. 5.1 shows both RAM and ROM devices, typical of most μCs. The RAM section consists of one or more RAM chips arranged to provide the desired capacity. The RAM section is used to store programs and data that can change during the operation of the computer. It can also be used for storage of intermediate and final results during program execution.

The ROM section consists of one or more LSI chips to store instructions and data that do not change. For example, it might store a program that causes the μC to continually monitor a keyboard, or it might store a table of ASCII codes needed for outputting information to a printer unit.

The input and output sections contain the interface circuits needed to allow the I/O devices to properly communicate with the rest of the computer. In some cases, these interface circuits are LSI chips designed by μP manufacturers to interface their μPs to a variety of I/O devices. In other cases, the interface circuits may be as simple as a buffer register.

The microprocessor, then, is generally a single LSI chip (and maybe several support chips) that incorporates the functions of a control unit (fetching, interpreting, and executing instructions) and an arithmetic/logic unit, but lacks the memory and I/O interface circuitry needed to make a complete computer. The microcomputer is thus a microprocessor chip supported by appropriate memory devices and I/O chips.

---

*We will use the abbreviation "μP" for microprocessor whenever we are talking about it as a device; we will use MPU when we are talking about its operation in a microcomputer.

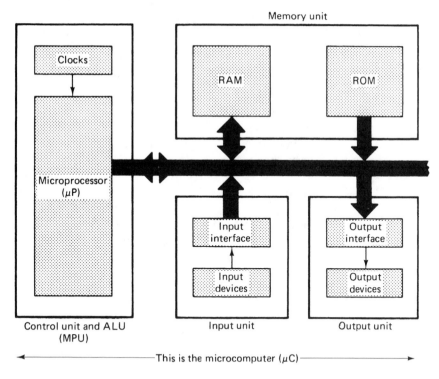

FIGURE 5.1   Basic elements of a µC.

These definitions are not as clear-cut as they may seem. LSI technology is constantly developing new devices that tend to incorporate more and more functions on one chip. For example, there are already available from Motorola several devices called *microcontrollers* (all of the 68HC11 IC family), which contain an MPU, a nominal amount of RAM, ROM, EEPROM, Timer, A/D converter, and I/O circuitry, all on a single chip. These single-chip microcontrollers contain all the elements needed to function as a complete µC, although they sometimes require additional memory and I/O support chips to expand their capabilities.

▶ 5.2 WHY µPs AND µCs?

When the first single-chip µPs were introduced several years ago, it was difficult to foresee the tremendous impact these devices would have on the creation of new products. But designers have rapidly become aware of the capabilities and versatility of these devices. Microprocessors are being utilized in new products in place of *discrete logic;* discrete logic refers to conventional logic designs using flip-flops, gates, counters, registers, and other medium-scale integration (MSI) functions. For instance, a traffic-light controller that previously required 200 TTL chips can now be built with only a few ICs using a µP-based system costing less than $20.

These are several fundamental reasons for the superiority of μP-based designs over discrete logic designs:

1. Fewer IC packages, printed circuit boards, and connectors, thereby reducing assembly costs.

2. Greater reliability, owing to the decreased number of IC interconnections.

3. Lower power requirements, making power supply design easier.

4. Simpler system testing, evaluation, and redesign. Because μP-based equipment operates under the control of a program in memory (usually ROM), its operation is easily modified by simply changing the program (replacing or reprogramming the ROM). It is easier to change the *firmware* in such a system than to change the wiring in a discrete logic system.

5. Because product features can be added to μP-based equipment simply by changing the firmware, manufacturers are increasing the capabilities and value of their products. For example, makers of μP-controlled cash registers are adding automatic tax computation by putting extra steps into the program stored in ROM; if the tax rate changes, the ROM can be replaced or reprogrammed to allow for the change.

Despite these advantages, μPs and μCs cannot compete with discrete logic in areas where high speed is required. Even those μPs that utilize high-speed bipolar technology or high-density CMOS (HCMOS) are at a speed disadvantage because of the sequential nature of programmed computer control. Microcomputers perform operations one at a time in anywhere from 30 ns to 20 μs per operation; in discrete logic systems many operations can be performed in parallel (simultaneously). Of course, μPs can be utilized in those portions of high-speed systems that do not require the utmost in speed.

Typical Applications

In a typical application a μC receives *input* information or data, executes a sequence of instructions which somehow operates on or *processes* this input information, and then provides *output* information or data. The input and output operations, of course, involve interfacing with the outside world, while the processing function is done inside the μC under the control of a program stored in memory (RAM or ROM).

For example, in a μC-controlled engine status display system for an automobile (Fig. 5.2A), the *input* information consists of engine parameters such as temperature, oil pressure, and fuel consumption rate. Each of these physical quantities is converted to an electrical quantity by some type of transducer. The electrical quantities are then converted into a digital form to be inputted to the μC. The μC then *processes* the input data (puts them into the correct format to be displayed) and then *outputs* the formatted data to the display panel.

Another example is a μC-controlled electric oven (Fig. 5.2B). Here *input* information is entered by the user via a keyboard to tell the μC the desired cooking temperature and cooking time. The μC responds to this input information by executing a program that generates an *output* signal to control the oven burners for the desired temperature and time duration. During this control process, the oven temperature is transduced to electrical and then digital form and serves as another μC *input*. The temperature input allows the μC to

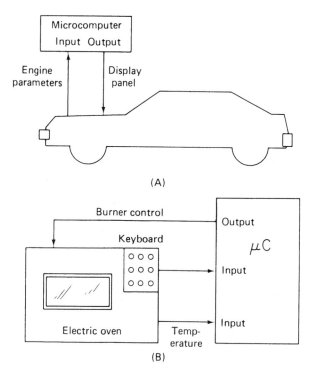

(A)

(B)

FIGURE 5.2   Examples of μC applications.

compare the actual oven temperature with the desired temperature for proper control of the burners.

▶ 5.3 MICROCOMPUTER ARCHITECTURE

The architecture of a computer refers to the way in which all of the elements are interconnected. The architecture of most 8-bit microcomputers is similar to the one shown in Fig. 5.3, which is built around the 68HC11 MPU. For the following discussion let us assume that the 68HC11 MPU is operating in its *normal expanded mode;* that is, inputs MODA and MODB are tied HIGH as shown (more about these modes later in the chapter). The normal expanded mode allows external memory and I/O devices to be added to the 68HC11 MPU. The diagram of Fig. 5.3 shows how the basic elements of the μC are connected together using the three buses described in Chapter 4. Although this diagram may appear somewhat complex, it still does not show all the electrical interconnections. We will add these details gradually after discussing the overall operation. We start by reviewing the bus system.

The three buses carry all the information and signals involved in the μC operation. The MPU is continually involved in sending (WRITING) or receiving (READING) data or information to or from a memory or I/O device. it is important to understand that all information transfers are referenced to the MPU, so that a WRITE operation always means

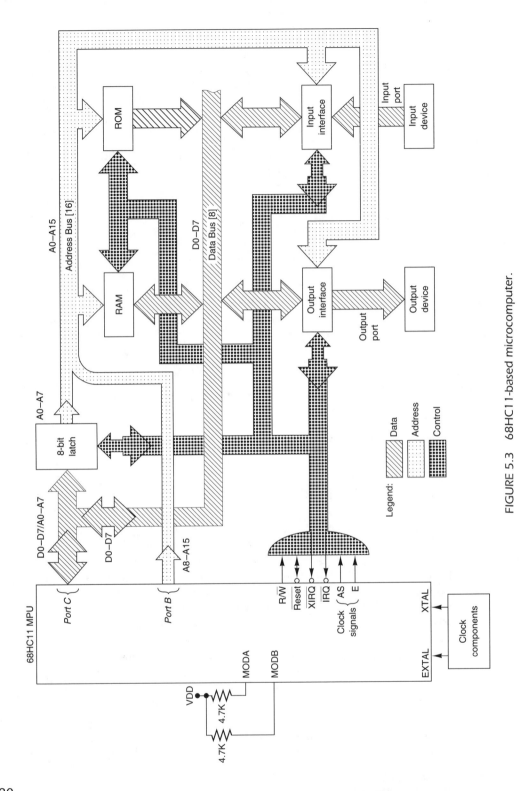

FIGURE 5.3 68HC11-based microcomputer.

that the MPU is sending information to another device; similarly, a READ operation always means the MPU is receiving information.

Ports B and C

Before we take a look at the various buses, we must first talk about the concept of *ports*. A port is a set of pins on the chip through which digital information is transmitted both to and from the MPU. The 68HC11 has five different ports designated as Ports A, B, C, D, and E, respectively. For now we are interested only in Ports B and C. The other ports will be described as we need them.

When operating in the normal expanded mode (MODA = MODB = 1) the 68HC11 MPU uses Port B as an output port for outputting the high-order address byte, $A_8–A_{15}$, to the address bus. In this mode, Port C is used to perform two different tasks at different times depending on the states of the E-clock and address strobe (AS) signals which are two of the control bus signals. At certain times Port C will function as an output port through which the MPU outputs the low-order byte, $A_0–A_7$, of the address. At other times Port C will function as an input/output (bidirectional) port through which data, $D_0–D_7$, moves in and out of the MPU. Port C is said to be *time-multiplexed* because at different times it will carry address signals $A_0–A_7$ or data signals $D_0–D_7$. Because of this time-multiplexing characteristic of Port C, an 8-bit latch has to be used whenever we interface memory or I/O devices to the 68HC11 MPU. The function of the 8-bit latch in Fig. 5.3 is to store the low-order byte of the address at the proper time and make it available for future use. Once the low-order byte of the address is latched, the MPU can use Port C for the data byte.

Address Bus

The address bus consists of 16 MPU outputs representing a 16-bit address that originates in the MPU and is sent to all the memory and I/O devices. Recall that the MPU alone can place logic levels onto the address bus. The 16-bit address allows 65,536 possible addresses, each of which can correspond to a RAM or ROM location, or to an I/O device. For example, address $C0A9_{16}$ might be a RAM or a ROM location, or it might be an 8-bit buffer register that is part of the interface circuit for an input device.

Whenever the MPU wants to communicate with (that is, READ from or WRITE to) a certain memory location or I/O device, the MPU must place the appropriate address code at its address pins, $A_0–A_{15}$, onto the address bus. First, the low-order byte ($A_0–A_7$) of the address at Port C is latched into the 8-bit latch at the proper time during the E-clock. The address bits coming from the 8-bit latch ($A_0–A_7$) and Port B ($A_8–A_{15}$) are then *decoded* to select the desired memory or I/O device. This decoding process usually requires decoder circuits that are not shown on the diagram of Fig. 5.3; this detail will be added later.

Data Bus

This bidirectional bus is used to transmit 8-bit words between the MPU and any memory or I/O device. The MPU's eight data pins from Port C ($D_0–D_7$ in Fig. 5.3) can act as inputs to the MPU or outputs from the MPU depending on whether it is performing a READ or a WRITE operation. Again, recall that in the case of the 68HC11 MPU, data bus signals

D_0–D_7 are time-multiplexed with the low-order byte of the address. When the 68HC11 MPU places data on the data bus (D_0–D_7) via Port C, the low-order byte of the address has already been stored at the outputs of the 8-bit latch.

During a READ operation, pins D_0–D_7 of Port C act as inputs that receive data that have been placed on the data bus by the memory or I/O device selected by the address code on the address bus. During a WRITE operation the MPU's data pins from Port C act as outputs that place data onto the data bus; these data are then accepted by the selected memory or I/O device.

Control Bus

This is the set of MPU input and output signals that synchronize the operation of the MPU with the other μC elements. The diagram of Fig. 5.3 shows only those 68HC11 control signals that are most often used in typical microcomputer systems; the more specialized control signals will be introduced in Chapter 6. Some of the control signals are MPU outputs (for example, R/$\overline{\text{W}}$, E, AS), some are inputs (for example, $\overline{\text{XIRQ}}$, $\overline{\text{IRQ}}$), and some are bidirectional such as $\overline{\text{RESET}}$.

Read/Write (R/$\overline{\text{W}}$)   The MPU generates this logic signal to tell the other μC elements the direction that data will be transmitted over the data bus. For a READ operation R/$\overline{\text{W}}$ = 1, and for a WRITE operation, R/$\overline{\text{W}}$ = 0. This allows the memory and I/O devices to respond properly whether the MPU is sending data or expecting to receive data.

Address Strobe (AS)   In the normal expanded mode this MPU output is used to enable an external 8-bit address latch (Fig. 5.3). The low-order byte of the address is allowed through the 8-bit latch while the address strobe signal (AS) is HIGH, and the stable address information is then latched by the 8-bit latch when signal AS is LOW.

$\overline{\text{RESET}}$ This control signal is significantly different on the 68HC11 MPU from the $\overline{\text{RESET}}$ signal on most other MPUs where it is strictly an *input* signal from an external source that initiates all of the MPU's internal circuits. For the 68HC11 the $\overline{\text{RESET}}$ signal can function as either an input or output. In other words, the logic level on the $\overline{\text{RESET}}$ pin of the MPU can be controlled either by the MPU's internal circuitry, or by an applied external source. In either case, $\overline{\text{RESET}}$ is a normally HIGH signal that is driven LOW to initiate a *reset sequence* that initializes the MPU's internal circuitry and any external devices connected to the $\overline{\text{RESET}}$ signal to their starting states. One of the many operations that take place during this reset sequence is the loading of the Program Counter (PC) with the address of the first instruction to be executed. Once $\overline{\text{RESET}}$ is returned HIGH, the 68HC11 will begin fetching and executing instructions from memory beginning at that address.

Another important function that is controlled by the $\overline{\text{RESET}}$ signal is the capturing of the logic levels present at the MPU's MODA and MODB input pins. At the instant when the $\overline{\text{RESET}}$ signal returns HIGH the levels at MODA and MODB are read and latched into a special internal MPU register. These logic levels determine which of four possible operating modes the 68HC11 will assume (normal expanded, normal single-chip, special bootstrap, or special test). Once established, the mode of operation cannot change until another $\overline{\text{RESET}}$ pulse occurs. In the diagram of Fig. 5.3, we have MODA = MODB = 1 which selects the **normal expanded mode** which is the mode we will be using extensively. The other modes will be described later.

At this point there is no need to present the details on the different ways $\overline{RESET}$ signals can be activated. For now, we will just consider it to be a signal that controls the startup of the MPU and the whole microcomputer system.

Interrupt Requests ($\overline{XIRQ}$ and $\overline{IRQ}$) These are active-LOW input signals to the MPU that come from one or more I/O devices. An I/O device will activate $\overline{XIRQ}$ or $\overline{IRQ}$ whenever it wants to get the MPU's attention, usually for the purpose of transferring data. We will have much more to say about interrupts when we look at the MPU in more detail in Chapter 6, and when we talk extensively about I/O modes in Chapter 8.

Clock Signals

The 68HC11 MPU uses a single system clock signal called the *E-clock*. The E-clock signal is generated on the 68HC11 chip and is used both internally and externally. The frequency of this signal is determined by the external clock components connected to the EXTAL and XTAL input pins on the chip; the components include a quartz crystal and a resistor/capacitor combination. Figure 5.4 shows the two possible clock arrangements recommended by Motorola to be used by the 68HC11 MPU. The circuit of Fig. 5.4(A) is used when high-frequency operation is desired (greater than 1 MHz), and the circuit of Fig. 5.4(B) is used for low-frequency operation (less than 1 MHz). The frequency applied to pins EXTAL and XTAL is always four times higher than the MPU's *system clock* or E-clock. For example, in a typical 68HC11 MPU-based µC system, for maximum clock frequency operation, an 8 MHz quartz crystal is used. Thus, the frequency of the E-clock is 2 MHz. There are other timing signals that are used strictly internal to the 68HC11 and consequently, we the users do not have access to them. One of these signals is called the *PH2* (phase 2) clock. Although we do *not* have access to this signal it is important that at least we are aware of its existence. This will help us explain some of the timing sequences performed by the MPU during the execution of a program.

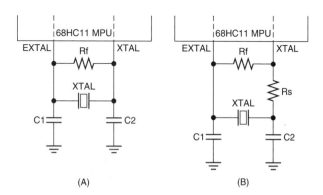

FIGURE 5.4   (A) High-frequency crystal connections; (B) low-frequency crystal connections.

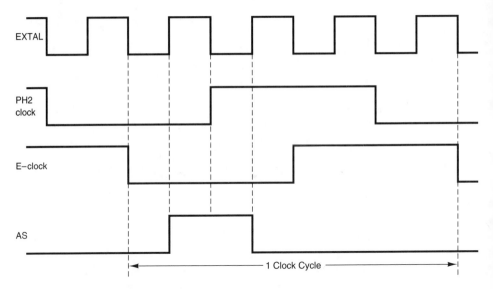

FIGURE 5.5   Timing relationships for the 68HC11 MPU clocks and AS signal
in the expanded mode.

The clock signals shown in Fig. 5.5 synchronize every action that occurs internal and external to the 68HC11 MPU while operating in normal expanded mode. For example, the MPU increments the program counter on the positive-going edge of PH2, and latches data from the data bus into accumulator A on the negative-going edge of the E-clock. While the E-clock is LOW, signal AS (address strobe) goes HIGH and it is during this time that address information is placed on the address bus via Ports B and C. In general, PH2 is used exclusively for internal MPU operations, whereas E and AS are used for both internal and external operations.

The PH2 clock signal has the same frequency as the system E-clock; however, the E-clock lags 90° behind the internal PH2 clock. The falling edge of E is considered to be the start of an MPU clock cycle. Thus, one MPU clock cycle starts on the falling edge of one E-clock and ends on the falling edge of the next. Note that the rising edge of PH2 does not occur until after the falling edge of E, and vice versa. In other words, the PH2 and E clocks are nonoverlapping.

I/O Interfacing

The μC diagram of Fig. 5.3 shows one input device and one output device connected to the bus system. In practice, there can be several I/O devices connected to the MPU. The MPU can communicate with the I/O devices over the data bus in much the same way as it can with RAM and ROM. Often, however, the I/O devices cannot be connected directly to the data bus, but must be connected to it through an interface circuit as shown. The interface circuit is used whenever the I/O device uses voltage levels, timing, or data format other than those used by the MPU.

For example, a typical input device is the keyboard of a video display terminal (VDT) that *serially* transmits ASCII-coded data representing the operator's key actuations. The μC data bus, however, accepts only 8 bits of parallel data. Thus, an interface circuit is used to convert the serial input data to parallel data for the data bus.

I/O Ports

The point where the input device connects to its interface circuit in Fig. 5.3 is called an *input port*. Similarly, the point where the output device is connected to its interface circuit is called an *output port*. Most μCs have several I/O ports, each designed to accept a particular type of I/O device. Some examples are parallel printer ports, serial ports, and general-purpose user ports.

▶ 5.4 READ AND WRITE TIMING

The MPU is continually performing READ and WRITE operations as it executes a program. The MPU performs a READ operation whenever it does any of the following:

1. Fetches the op code portion of an instruction from program memory (RAM or ROM).
2. Fetches the operand address portion of an instruction from program memory.
3. Fetches data from memory or an input device during the execution phase of an instruction (for example, LDAA, ADDA, SUBA).

The MPU performs a WRITE operation whenever it does one of the following:

1. Transfers data from an internal MPU register (such as accumulator A) to a RAM location for storage; for example, an STAA instruction.
2. Transfers data from an internal MPU register to an output device.

Because of the number of instruction FETCH operations that the MPU must perform during a program execution, the number of READ operations is usually much greater than the number of WRITE operations.

READ Operation Timing

We are now ready to examine the timing relationships among the various bus signals as the 68HC11 MPU of Fig. 5.3 performs a READ operation. Everything is referenced to PH2 clock, E-clock, and the AS signal, as illustrated in the timing diagram of Fig. 5.6. This timing diagram shows the activity on the R/$\overline{\text{W}}$ and AS control lines, and Ports B and C for one MPU clock cycle during which the MPU performs a READ operation. Recall that Port B carries the high-order byte of the address bus, and Port C at different times will carry either the low-order address byte or bidirectional data. There are five critical time points corresponding to five signal edges.

1. **Point 1** is the rising edge of the AS (Address Strobe) pulse. We will assume that R/$\overline{\text{W}}$ = 0 prior to the occurrence of this clock transition. Also prior to this point, there will be half of the "old address" (A_8–A_{15}) at Port B (that is, the address placed there by the

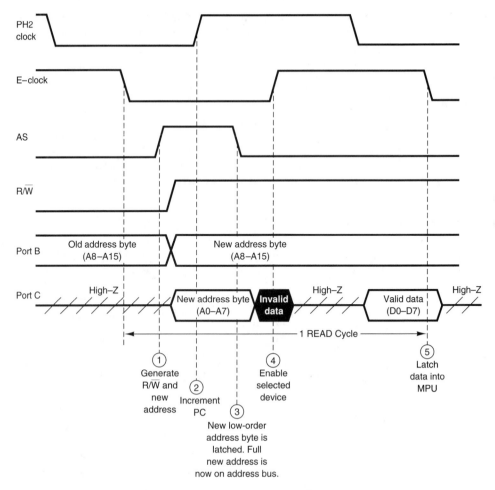

FIGURE 5.6   68HC11 MPU bus activity during a READ cycle in the expanded mode.

MPU during the preceding clock cycle). The data bus (Port C) will be in the high-impedance (high-Z) or "floating" state because no device tied to the data bus will be enabled until the second half of the READ cycle. This high-Z state is represented by a hash-marked line.

When the rising edge of the AS signal occurs, the MPU responds by making R/$\overline{\text{W}}$ = 1 to signal a READ operation, and by outputting a new address: A_0–A_7 on Port C and A_8–A_{15} on Port B. Note that the diagram of Fig. 5.6 shows that each of these changes is slightly delayed from point 1 due to propagation delays in the MPU internal circuitry. Also note that the address bus waveforms (Ports B and C) show both possible transitions (1 → 0 and 0 → 1) because some of the 16 address lines will be changing in one direction and some will be changing in the other.

2. None of the bus signals changes at **point 2,** which is the rising edge of PH2 clock. However, the MPU uses this clock edge to increment the PC internal to the MPU.

3. **Point 3** is the falling edge of the AS signal. At this time, the low-order byte of the address coming from Port C is latched in the external 8-bit latch (Fig. 5.3). The full new address (that is, the low-order byte that is now present and stable at the output of the 8-bit latch and the high-order byte from Port B) is on the address bus and selects the memory or I/O device from which the MPU is to READ. Shortly after the falling edge of the AS signal, the MPU removes the low-order byte of the address previously present on Port C; thus, Port C begins to change and eventually becomes *invalid data* as shown by the shaded area in Fig. 5.6.

4. **Point 4** is the rising edge of the E-clock. When the E-clock goes HIGH, *only* the selected memory or I/O device will be enabled, and it will begin to place its data onto the data bus so that some data lines go HIGH and some go LOW. All the unselected memory and I/O devices will not affect the data bus because their outputs will be in the high-Z state. At this point, Port C goes to the high-Z state and becomes an input port ready to transfer valid data from the data bus into the MPU. The data on the data bus change from the high-Z state to valid data some time after point 4, depending on the internal delays of the enabled memory or I/O device.

5. On the falling edge of the E-clock (**point 5**), the MPU takes the data from the data bus (Port C) and latches them into one of its internal registers, such as the IR or accumulator A. Clearly, for proper data transfer to occur, the memory or I/O device must be capable of putting valid data onto the data bus prior to the falling edge of the E-clock. Thus, it is important that these devices have an operating speed that is compatible with the MPU E-clock frequency.

   After the E-clock returns LOW, the selected memory or I/O device is disabled and the data bus returns to its high-Z state.

EXAMPLE 5.1

A certain type of PROM has a specified maximum output ENABLE delay time of 500 ns. Can it be used with the 68HC11 MPU operating with a 2-MHz E-clock?

Solution No. With a 2-MHz E-clock, the duration of the second half of the E-clock will be around 250 ns. The falling edge of the E-clock will occur well before the PROM's data outputs have stabilized on the data bus.

WRITE Operation Timing

Figure 5.7 shows the bus activity for one MPU E-clock cycle during which the MPU performs a WRITE operation. Once again the five critical times correspond to the 5 signal edges.

1. We will assume that $R/\overline{W} = 1$ prior to the rising edge of the AS signal. The data bus (Port C) will be floating (high-Z) because no device will be enabled until the second half of the E-clock. When the rising edge of the AS signal occurs, the MPU makes $R/\overline{W} = 0$ to signal a WRITE operation. It also places a new address on the address bus (Ports B and C). This new address selects the memory or I/O device to which the MPU is to WRITE.

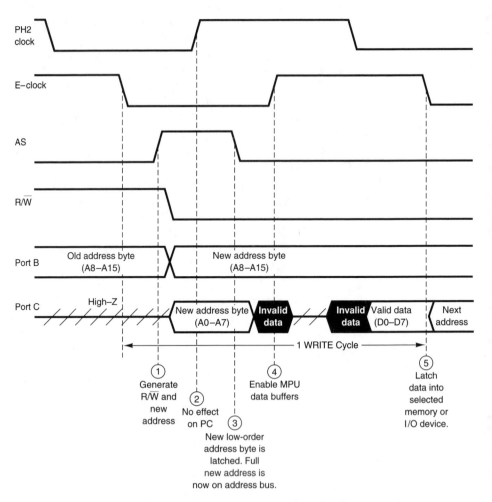

FIGURE 5.7 68HC11 MPU bus activity during a WRITE cycle in the expanded mode.

2. The rising edge of the PH2 clock is *not* used to increment the PC as it was during the READ cycle because the PC is not used during a WRITE operation. Recall from Chapter 4 that the DAR is used to supply the memory address during a WRITE operation (for example, STAA).

3. When the falling-edge of the AS signal occurs (point 3), the low-order byte of the operand address coming from Port C is latched in the external 8-bit latch (Fig. 5.3), the same way it was during the READ operation. The full new address which is now on the address bus selects the memory or I/O device to which the MPU is to WRITE. Shortly after the falling edge of the AS signal, Port C will change to invalid data.

4. When the rising edge of the E-clock occurs (point 4), the MPU's data bus output buffers will be enabled, and data from one of its internal registers will be placed on the data bus (Port C). The output buffers of all memory and I/O devices will be held in the high-Z

state because this is a WRITE operation. The MPU data on the data bus will become valid a short time (typically 100 ns) after point 4.

5. On the falling edge of the E-clock, the data on the data bus (Port C) will be latched into the selected memory or I/O device. After the E-clock returns LOW, the MPU will output the *next address* at Ports B and C for the next READ operation. Note that after a WRITE operation the next address is already available in the PC. This address was determined during the *previous* READ operation.

Summary

The activities that occur on the various transitions of the critical signals (i.e., PH2, E, AS, and R/$\overline{\text{W}}$) are summarized below:

1. On the rising of the AS signal, the MPU places a new address on its Port B and C outputs and establishes the correct R/$\overline{\text{W}}$ level.
2. When appropriate, the MPU increments **[PC]** on the rising edge of PH2.
3. On the falling edge of the AS signal, the low-order byte of the new address is externally latched.
4. The rising edge of the E-clock is used to enable the data outputs of *one* of the devices tied to the data bus. During a READ operation, it will be the selected memory or I/O device; during a WRITE operation, it will be the MPU.
5. On the falling edge of the E-clock, the data on the data bus are latched into the appropriate device. During a READ operation, it will be one of the MPU internal registers; during a WRITE operation, it will be the selected memory or I/O device.

▶ 5.5 BUS ACTIVITY DURING PROGRAM EXECUTION

Now that you are familiar with the 68HC11's signal timing during the READ and WRITE operations in the normal expanded mode, we will study the bus signal activity during the execution of a program. We do not intend to show the bus activity for a wide variety of the 68HC11 MPU instructions; instead we will use a small segment of a program to illustrate the basic ideas. The 68HC11 manufacturer's literature (M68HC11 Reference Manual) can be consulted for a complete description of the bus activity for each instruction.

The program segment that we will use is shown on page 190. It begins at address C300 and consists of an ADDA instruction followed by an STAA instruction. Note the use of assembly language mnemonics for each instruction. The ADDA $D75C is the instruction for adding the contents of memory location D75C to accumulator A. The op code (BB) is stored at address C300, followed by the operand address (D75C) stored at C301 and C302. Recall that the $ is used to indicate that the address is in hex. Similarly, STAA $D250 is the instruction for storing the contents of accumulator A in memory location D250.

This program segment requires eight MPU clock cycles for its complete execution. These are numbered one through eight in Fig. 5.8. For each of these cycles, the diagram shows the information that appears on the address bus (Ports B and C), data bus (Port C), and R/$\overline{\text{W}}$ line. For convenience, the address and data bus values are given in hex.

Memory address	Memory word	Mnemonic	Description
C300	BB	ADDA $D75C	; Add data from address D75C to
C301	D7		; accumulator A and place result in
C302	5C		; accumulator A
C303	B7	STAA $D250	; Store the contents of accumulator A
C304	D2		; in address D250
C305	50		
C306	??	????	; Next op code

We will assume that the 68HC11 MPU has been executing instructions and is ready to fetch the next op code at C300 ([**PC**] = C300). We will also assume that memory location D75C is storing the data word 2A, and that [**A**] = 12. In the cycle-by-cycle description that follows, we will divide each clock cycle into five steps (a,b,c,d,e) corresponding to the five signal edges (Figs. 5.6 and 5.7).

Cycle 1

(a) On the rising edge of the AS signal, the MPU places [**PC**] = C300 onto the address bus (Ports B and C), and sets R/$\overline{W}$ = 1 for a READ operation.

(b) The MPU increments [**PC**] to C301 on the rising edge of the PH2 clock. This does not affect the address bus because the C300 has been latched into the MPU's internal address bus latch that drives the address bus (Fig. 4.8).

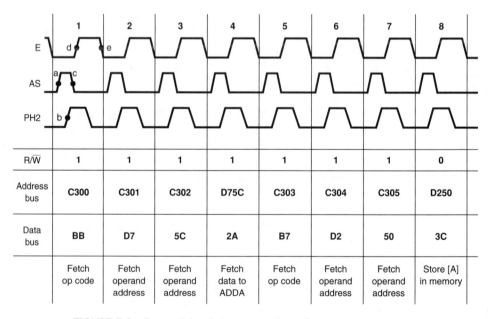

FIGURE 5.8 Bus activity during execution of a program segment.

(c) On the falling edge of the AS signal, the low-order byte of the address, 00, is latched from Port C into the external 8-bit latch (Fig. 5.3) which it will hold on the address bus. The address bus is now C300.

(d) Memory location C300 is enabled on the rising edge of the E-clock, and it places its data word, BB, onto the data bus (Port C).

(e) On the falling edge of the E-clock, the MPU takes this data word and latches it into its instruction register (IR) because it is an op code. Once the data are in the IR, the op code is decoded and the MPU finds out that this is an ADDA instruction. Thus, it knows that it has to fetch the operand address.

Cycle 2

(a) $[PC]$ = C301 is placed on the address bus, and $R/\overline{W}$ = 1 for a FETCH operation.

(b) $[PC]$ is incremented to C302.

(c) The low-order byte of the address, 01, is latched from Port C into the external 8-bit latch. The address bus is now C301.

(d) Memory location C301 is enabled and it places its data word, D7, onto the data bus.

(e) The MPU takes this data word and latches it into the high-order byte of the data address register (DAR). Recall that the DAR holds the operand address which will be needed during the execution phase of an instruction.

Cycle 3

(a) $[PC]$ = C302 is placed on the address bus, and $R/\overline{W}$ = 1 for a FETCH operation.

(b) $[PC]$ is incremented to C303.

(c) The low-order byte of the address, 02, is latched from Port C into the external 8-bit latch. The address bus is now C302.

(d) Memory location C302 is enabled and it places its data word, 5C, onto the data bus.

(e) The MPU takes this data word into the low-order byte of the (DAR). Thus, $[DAR]$ = D75C.

Cycle 4

(a) The MPU places $[DAR]$ = D75C onto the address bus, and sets $R/\overline{W}$ = 1 in order to fetch the operand from memory.

(b) Because the PC is not used in this cycle, it is not incremented. It was previously incremented to C303 in preparation for the next op code fetch.

(c) The low-order byte of the operand address, 5C, is latched from Port C into the external 8-bit latch. The address bus is now D75C.

(d) Memory location D75C is enabled, and it places its data word, 2A, onto the data bus.

(e) The MPU latches this data word into the data register (DR), which feeds the ALU (see Fig. 4.8). The ALU adds it to the current data, 12, in accumulator A to produce a sum, 3C. This sum is then placed in accumulator A.

Cycle 5

    (a) The **[PC]** = C303 is placed onto the address bus, and R/$\overline{\text{W}}$ = 1 for an op code fetch.

    (b) **[PC]** is incremented to C304.

    (c) The low-order byte of the address, 03, is latched from Port C into the external 8-bit latch. The address is now C303.

    (d) Memory location C303 is enabled, and it puts its data word, B7, onto the data bus.

    (e) The MPU latches this data word into the IR, decodes it, and recognizes it as an STAA operation, so it knows it has to fetch an operand address.

Cycle 6

    (a) **[PC]** = C304 is placed on the address bus, and R/$\overline{\text{W}}$ = 1 for a FETCH operation.

    (b) **[PC]** is incremented to C305.

    (c) The low-order byte of the address, 04, is latched from Port C into the external 8-bit latch. The address bus is now C304.

    (d) Memory location C304 is enabled, and it puts its data word, D2, onto the data bus.

    (e) The MPU latches this data word into the high-order byte of the DAR.

Cycle 7

    (a) **[PC]** = C305 is placed on the address bus, and R/$\overline{\text{W}}$ = 1.

    (b) **[PC]** is incremented to C306.

    (c) The low-order byte of the address, 05, is latched from Port C into the external 8-bit latch. The address bus is now C305.

    (d) Memory location C305 is enabled, and it places its data word, 50, onto the data bus.

    (e) The MPU latches this data word into the low-order byte of the DAR, so that **[DAR]** = D250. This is the address where **[A]** is to be stored.

Cycle 8

    (a) MPU places **[DAR]** = D250 onto the address bus and makes R/$\overline{\text{W}}$ = 0 for a WRITE operation since **[A]** is to be stored in memory.

    (b) Nothing takes place on the rising edge of the PH2 clock.

    (c) The low-order byte of the operand address, 50, is latched from Port C into the external 8-bit latch. The address bus is now D250.

    (d) The MPU's output data buffers are enabled, and **[A]** = 3C is placed onto the data bus.

    (e) This data word is written into the selected memory location, D250, to complete the STAA $D250 operation.

This cycle-by-cycle operation continues as the MPU continues executing instructions. At this point, you should have a pretty good understanding of the types of signal activity that occur as the 68HC11 MPU executes a program in the normal expanded mode.

▶ 5.6 MPU ADDRESS SPACE ALLOCATION

When the MPU performs a READ or WRITE operation, it must first place an address on the address bus to select one and only one memory location or I/O device. The 68HC11, like most 8-bit MPUs, has a 16-bit address bus that can specify any of 64K = 65,536 different addresses. In hex, these addresses range from 0000 to FFFF. This address range is called the microcomputer's *address space.* The microcomputer designer has to allocate this address space among RAM, ROM, and I/O devices that are part of the system (i.e., tied to the various buses). The manner in which the total address space is apportioned among these devices depends on many factors which we will not be concerned with for now. Figure 5.9 is an example of how the address space might be allocated for a small 68HC11-based system operating in the normal expanded mode. Recall that in this mode, external memory and I/O can be connected to the MPU as in Fig. 5.3.

Memory Map

The diagram in Fig. 5.9 is called a *memory map,* even though it includes I/O addresses as well as RAM and ROM. Note that the highest address, FFFF, is at the top of the map, and the lowest address, 0000, at the bottom. We will often refer to address 0000 as the bottom of the address space, and FFFF as the top of the address space. In this example, the bottom of the address space, 0000 to 03FF, has been allocated to RAM. This means there are 1024_{10} words (1K) stored in RAM. The top of the address space, F800 to FFFF, has been assigned to ROM; thus, there are 2048 words (2K) stored in ROM. The memory map shows that a total of 256 addresses, A000 to A0FF, are reserved for I/O devices. As we shall see, this does not necessarily mean that there will be 256 different I/O devices. The remaining part of the address space is not assigned to any device. In other words, addresses 0400–9FFF and A100–F7FF are not currently being used. Of course, these unused addresses are available for future memory or I/O expansion.

On-Chip Memory and I/O

The address allocation task is more complicated for the 68HC11 MPU than for other MPUs that are not part of a microcontroller chip. Recall that the 68HC11 microcontroller (MCU) is an IC that contains not only a 68HC11 MPU, but also a certain amount of memory and I/O connected to the MPU *internal to the chip.* This allows the 68HC11 MCU to function as a controller in the single-chip mode without the need for any externally connected memory or I/O. This means that a portion of the 64K address space will be taken up by the on-chip RAM, ROM, EEPROM, and I/O. The amount of address space used by the on-chip memory and I/O will vary depending on which version of the 68HC11 family of MCUs is being used. Table 5.1 is a partial list of the 68HC11 family members. Each of these versions contains the same 68HC11 MPU (i.e., accumulators, IR, DAR, PC, etc.) that we have been using thus far, but has different amounts of RAM, ROM, and EEPROM. We will use the 68HC11A8 version in all our subsequent discussions and applications in this book because it is the version upon which the other versions are built and is the one most widely used in design applications.

TABLE 5.1

Part number	EPROM	ROM	EEPROM	RAM	CONFIG[2]	Comments
MC68HC11A8	—	8K	512	256	$0F	Family Built Around This Device
MC68HC11A1	—	—	512	256	$0D	'A8 with ROM Disabled
MC68HC11A0	—	—	—	256	$0C	'A8 with ROM and EEPROM Disabled
MC68HC11A2	—	—	2K[1]	256	$FF	No ROM Part for Expanded Systems
MC68HC811A8	—	—	8K+512	256	$0F	EEPROM Emulator for 'A8
MC68HC11E9	—	12K	512	512	$0F	Four Input Capture/Bigger RAM/12K ROM
MC68HC11E1	—	—	512	512	$0D	'E9 with ROM Disabled
MC68HC11E0	—	—	—	512	$0C	'E9 with ROM and EEPROM Disabled
MC68HC11E2	—	—	2K[1]	256	$FF	Like 'A2 with 'E9 Timer
MC68HC11D3	—	4K	—	192	N/A	Low-Cost 40-pin Version
MC68HC711D3	4K	—	—	192	N/A	One-Time-Programmable Version of 'D3
MC68HC11F1	—	—	512[1]	1K	$FF	High-Performance, Nonmultiplexed 68-pin

1. The EEPROM is relocatable to the top of any 4K memory page. Relocation is done with the upper four bits of the CONFIG register.
2. CONFIG register values in this table reflect the value programmed prior to shipment from Motorola. (Redrawn courtesy of Motorola Inc.).

As the table shows, the 68HC11A8 MCU has 8K bytes of ROM, 512 bytes of EEPROM, and 256 bytes of RAM. It also has 64 bytes allocated to I/O registers. All of these will have assigned addresses in the available 64K address space. The ROM and EEPROM will have fixed address assignments; the RAM and I/O address assignments can be varied through the bits of a special MPU register, CONFIG. In any case, the presence of these on-chip devices must be taken into account when we want to operate the 68HC11 in its expanded mode; that is, connect external memory and I/O to its buses. We need to know what address space the on-chip devices are occupying so that we avoid assigning the same addresses to external memory or I/O. We also need to know if and how the on-chip devices can be disabled or reallocated to a different area of the memory map. For now, though, we will not concern ourselves with these considerations because our main purpose in the following sections is to focus on the method for interfacing memory and I/O devices to an MPU over the various buses so that the MPU can communicate with them using the appropriate device addresses. We will assume, then, that the address assignments we use in the upcoming illustrations do not conflict with the 68HC11A8 on-chip memory and I/O address assignments.

EXAMPLE 5.2 _____

Show how the number of RAM addresses is determined for the memory map of Fig. 5.9.

Solution There are at least two ways to do this. The first method involves converting the first and last addresses to decimal. The RAM hex addresses range from 0000 to 03FF, where $0000_{16} = 0_{10}$ and $03FF_{16} = 1023_{10}$. Thus, there are 1024 addresses.

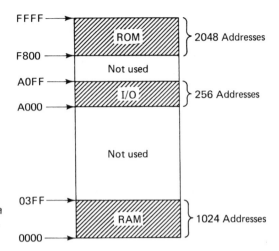

FIGURE 5.9 Memory map for a small 68HC11-based microcomputer (expanded mode).

The second method requires converting the first and last addresses to binary as shown below.

$$\begin{array}{ccccccccccccccccc}
& A_{15} & A_{14} & A_{13} & A_{12} & A_{11} & A_{10} & A_9 & A_8 & A_7 & A_6 & A_5 & A_4 & A_3 & A_2 & A_1 & A_0 \\
0000_{16} = & 0 & 0 & 0 & 0 & 0 & 0 & 0 & 0 & 0 & 0 & 0 & 0 & 0 & 0 & 0 & 0 \\
03FF_{16} = & 0 & 0 & 0 & 0 & 0 & 0 & 1 & 1 & 1 & 1 & 1 & 1 & 1 & 1 & 1 & 1
\end{array}$$

Note that the 6 most significant bits remain at 0, while the other 10 bits cover the complete range from all 0s to all 1s. Thus, there are $2^{10} = 1024$ different addresses.

You should be able to use either of these methods to determine the number of addresses allocated to ROM and I/O in Fig. 5.8.

Memory Pages

The 65,536 addresses can be divided into 256 blocks of 256 addresses, where each block is called a *page*. Figure 5.10 shows how the address space is organized into pages. Each page consists of all hex addresses beginning with the same two digits. For example, page 00 includes all 256 hex addresses in the range 0000 to 00FF. Similarly, page 6A includes hex addresses 6A00 to 6AFF.

Using page organization, we can think of each address as consisting of a page number and a word number. To illustrate, consider the address 1E66:

$$\underbrace{1 \quad E}_{\text{page number}} \quad \underbrace{6 \quad 6}_{\text{word number}}$$

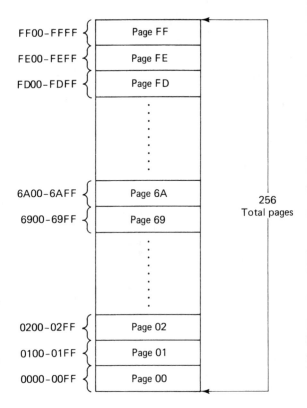

FF00–FFFF	Page FF
FE00–FEFF	Page FE
FD00–FDFF	Page FD
	. . . .
6A00–6AFF	Page 6A
6900–69FF	Page 69
	. . . .
0200–02FF	Page 02
0100–01FF	Page 01
0000–00FF	Page 00

256 Total pages

FIGURE 5.10   64K address space organized into 256 pages of 256 addresses.

The two most significant digits are the page number, and the least significant digits specify the word number on that page.

EXAMPLE 5.3 ───

Determine how many pages are allocated for RAM in the memory map of Fig. 5.9, and use this number to calculate the total number of RAM addresses. Repeat for ROM and I/O.

Solution   RAM occupies addresses 0000 to 03FF; this includes pages 00, 01, 02, and 03, for a total of four pages. Since each page is 256 addresses, the total number of RAM addresses is $4 \times 256 = 1024$.

ROM occupies pages F8, F9, FA, FB, FC, FD, FE, and FF, for a total of eight pages and $8 \times 256 = 2048$ addresses.

I/O uses all addresses on page A0, for a total of 256 addresses.

EXAMPLE 5.4 ───

A certain microcomputer has 4096 RAM locations starting at address 0000. How many pages of memory are allocated to RAM? Determine the complete RAM address range.

Solution $4096/256 = 16$ pages. The pages are 00, 01, 02, 03, . . . 0C, 0D, 0E, 0F. The complete address range is 0000 to 0FFF.

EXAMPLE 5.5

A certain program stored in ROM occupies all of page FD. What addresses does the program occupy?

Solution   FD00 to FDFF.

4K Pages

By using the first two hex digits of the 4-digit address as the page number, we end up with 256 pages containing 256 addresses each. Often it is helpful to partition the 64K address space into larger blocks of addresses. One way is to use only the first hex digit to define the

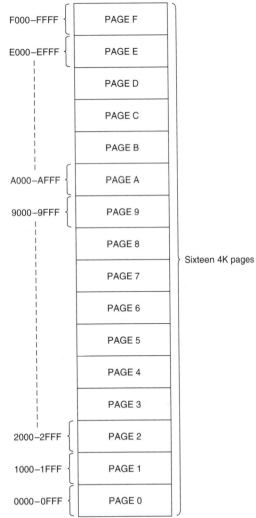

F000–FFFF	PAGE F
E000–EFFF	PAGE E
	PAGE D
	PAGE C
	PAGE B
A000–AFFF	PAGE A
9000–9FFF	PAGE 9
	PAGE 8
	PAGE 7
	PAGE 6
	PAGE 5
	PAGE 4
	PAGE 3
2000–2FFF	PAGE 2
1000–1FFF	PAGE 1
0000–0FFF	PAGE 0

Sixteen 4K pages

FIGURE 5.11   64K address space organized into sixteen 4K pages.

page number. For example, page 1 will have addresses from 1000 to 1FFF; page 2 will have addresses from 2000 to 2FFF, and so on. Each page will contain 4096 (4K) addresses, so we call these *4K* pages. Fig. 5.11 illustrates how the 64K address space is divided into sixteen 4K pages. We will have occasion to refer to 4K pages when we talk about address allocation. Whenever we use the term "4K page," it refers to the organization of Fig. 5.11; whenever we use the term "page," it means the organization of Fig. 5.10. The following examples illustrate.

EXAMPLE 5.6

How many pages of memory are contained in a 4K page?

Solution   A 4K page is 4096 addresses; a page is 256 addresses. Thus, one 4K page contains $4096/256 = 16$ pages.

EXAMPLE 5.7

(a) On what page is address A567? (b) On what 4K page is address A567?

Solution   (a) The first two digits determine the page number. Therefore, address A567 is one of the 256 addresses on page A5.
(b) The first digit determines the 4K page. Therefore, address A567 is on the 4K page that begins at address A000.

▶ 5.7 MEMORY MODULES

The amount of RAM and ROM that is part of a microcomputer will vary widely depending on the computer's intended application and its price range. General-purpose personal computers, such as the Apple Macintosh, IBM PC, etc., will typically contain 64 MB or more of RAM and over 64K of ROM. Smaller microcomputers and microcontrollers, such as the M68HC11 Evaluation Board (EVB), are intended for machine-language control applications and will typically have 8K of RAM and 8K of ROM. Of course, most microcomputers allow for possible memory expansion.

The ROM portion of a microcomputer's memory generally consists of ROM, EPROM, and EEPROM chips that store 8-bit words (bytes). The situation is different with RAM because RAM chips come in word sizes of 1, 4, and 8 bits. The designer may use RAM chips that store 8-bit words, or may combine several RAM chips to produce a module that has an 8-bit word size. Chapter 3 reviewed how this is done. In the following examples of memory address decoding we will utilize 8-bit RAM modules, and we will not be concerned with whether each module is a single RAM chip or a combination of RAM chips.

▶ 5.8 ADDRESS DECODING

Once the μC designer has decided on what arrangement of memory modules to use to produce the desired storage capacity, the next step is to design the address decoding circuitry. This circuitry takes the address that the MPU places on the address bus and converts it to the chip select signals that are required by each memory module or I/O device. One and only one of these chip select signals will be activated for each possible address.

Figure 5.12 shows the general idea of address decoding. A number of the address lines coming from the MPU are connected as inputs to the address decoder. The decoder responds by activating one of its outputs, which then selects (enables) one of the memory modules. In general, the higher-order address lines are used for this purpose, and the number that are used depends on the number of memory modules. For example, if there are four memory modules, address lines A_{15} and A_{14} can be used as inputs to a 1-of-4 decoder.

The lower-order address lines coming from the MPU are connected to the address inputs of the memory modules. These address lines are decoded by the decoding circuitry on the memory chips to select the one memory location to be accessed for a READ or WRITE operation. The number of address lines used for this purpose depends on the capacity of the modules. For example, if the modules are 4K $\times$ 8, they require 12 address inputs because $4096 = 2^{12}$. Thus, address lines A_0–A_{11} have to be connected to the RAM modules.

Summarizing the address decoding process, the higher-order address lines are decoded to select one memory module, and the lower-order address lines are used to select the desired memory word from that module.

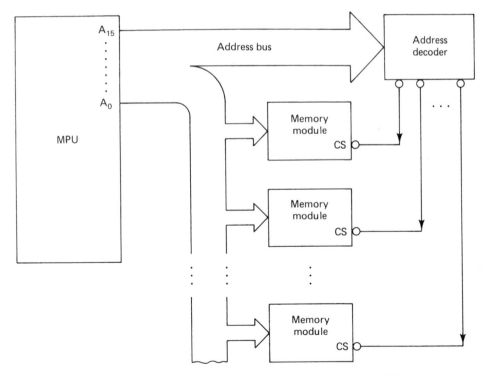

FIGURE 5.12 Typical address decoding arrangement. (Note: R/$\overline{W}$ and data bus are not shown.)

▶ 5.9 COMPLETE MICROCOMPUTER DECODING EXAMPLE

We will now describe the complete address decoding logic for a 68HC11-based micro-computer that has the memory map given in Fig. 5.13. It should be pointed out that several possible ways exist to implement the decoding logic for a given memory map because many different decoder chips are available. The implementations we have chosen to present are representative of those commonly used by microcomputer designers.

The memory map of Fig. 5.13 shows that the bottom 4K page of the address space is allocated to RAM. This is done in almost all 68HC11-based systems because the 68HC11 instruction set provides the programmer with efficient ways of storing *variable* data in page 00 of memory. For the programmer to take advantage of this, page 00 has to be RAM. The top four 4K pages of address space are allocated to ROM. Again, this is characteristic of the 68HC11 systems because the 68HC11 requires that some important information has to be stored *permanently* at addresses FFFC to FFFF.

The map shows that addresses 8000 to 8FFF are allocated for I/O devices. The choice of I/O addresses is usually based on a variety of considerations, such as simplifying decoding logic, leaving room for RAM and ROM expansion, and many others. We will say more about this when we look at the detailed decoding logic.

RAM Decoding Logic

The RAM is to occupy addresses 0000 to 0FFF, a total of 4096 addresses. Thus, the system uses a RAM capacity of 4K × 8. We will use four 1K × 8 RAM modules shown connected to the MPU buses in Fig. 5.14. Remember that each module may actually consist of several RAM chips.

Examine Fig. 5.14 and note the following points:

1. The 68HC11A8 MPU has inputs MODA = MODB = 1 which will place the MPU in the normal expanded mode. Remember that this mode allows us to connect external memory and I/O to the MPU using Ports B and C for the address and data buses.

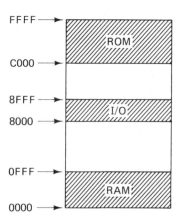

FIGURE 5.13   Memory map for a 68HC11-based μC.

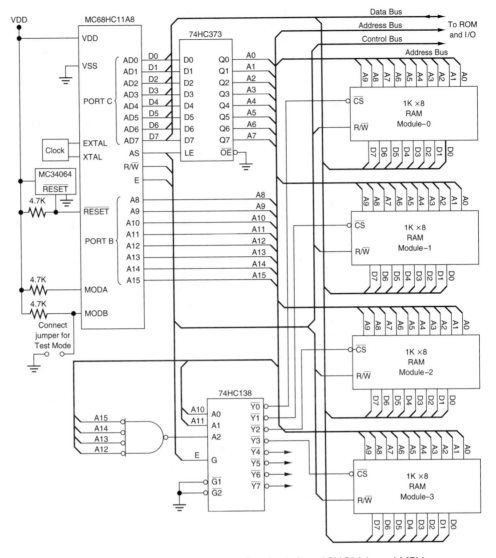

FIGURE 5.14   Typical RAM decoding logic in a 68HC11-based MPU.

2. Each RAM module has its data I/O lines connected to the data bus (Port C), but only the selected module will place data onto this bus.

3. The MPU's R/W̄ line is connected to each module. Only the selected module will respond to this control signal.

4. The 74HC373 transparent latch will be enabled when control signal AS goes HIGH, and it will latch the low-order byte of the address (A_0–A_7) coming from Port C of the MPU when AS signal goes LOW. The address will be stable by this time (see Figs. 5.6 and 5.7).

5. The 74HC138 1-of-8 decoder generates the CHIP SELECT signals $\overline{Y0}$, $\overline{Y1}$, $\overline{Y2}$, and $\overline{Y3}$, which enable the 1K modules 0, 1, 2, and 3, respectively. These signals select a

specific RAM module in response to the decoder inputs, which are derived from higher-order address lines A_{10}–A_{15} and the E-clock signal.

6. Each module has its address inputs connected to the MPU address bus lines A_0–A_9. These address lines controlled by the MPU select the specific word within the selected module.

Each module stores 1024 8-bit words. We can determine the addresses of the data words stored in a particular module by determining the conditions that activate its CHIP SELECT input ($\overline{CS}$). To illustrate, module-3 will be selected whenever $\overline{Y3}$ is LOW. $\overline{Y3}$ will be LOW only when the decoder's input code is $A_2 = 0$, $A_1 = 1$, $A_0 = 1$, *and* when its ENABLE G input is HIGH. The decoder's A_2 input will be LOW only when the OR gate inputs, A_{15}, A_{14}, A_{13}, and A_{12}, are LOW. The A_1 input will be HIGH when A_{11} is HIGH and the A_0 input will be HIGH when A_{10} is HIGH. Putting this all together, module-3 will be enabled when the following address is placed on the address bus:

A_{15} A_{14} A_{13} A_{12} A_{11} A_{10} A_9 A_8 A_7 A_6 A_5 A_4 A_3 A_2 A_1 A_0

  0   0   0   0   1   1   X   X   X   X   X   X   X   X   X → Selects module-3

The Xs under A_9–A_0 indicate "don't cares" because these address lines are not used by the decoder to select module-3. A_9–A_0 can be any combination ranging from 0000000000 to 1111111111, depending on which word in module-3 is being accessed. Thus, the complete range of addresses for module-3 is determined by first using all 0s, and then all 1s for the Xs.

A_{15} A_{14} A_{13} A_{12} A_{11} A_{10} A_9 A_8 A_7 A_6 A_5 A_4 A_3 A_2 A_1 A_0

  0   0   0   0   1   1   0   0   0   0   0   0   0   0   0 → $0C00_{16}$

  0   0   0   0   1   1   1   1   1   1   1   1   1   1   1 → $0FFF_{16}$

Finally, this gives us 0C00 to 0FFF as the range of hex addresses stored in module-3. When the MPU places any address in this range onto the address bus, module-3 will be enabled for either a READ or a WRITE, depending on the state of $R/\overline{W}$.

A similar analysis can be used to determine the address ranges for each of the other RAM modules. The results are:

Module-0: 0000-03FF

Module-1: 0400-07FF

Module-2: 0800-0BFF

Module-3: 0C00-0FFF

E-clock Signal

The decoder's active-HIGH ENABLE input G is driven by the E-clock. This ensures that the decoder will be enabled only during the E-clock portion (E = 1) when a stable address is on the address bus. This will prevent glitches from appearing at the decoder outputs during the address line transitions that occur when the E = 0. These glitches, if allowed to occur, could enable a RAM at the wrong time and cause incorrect information to be written

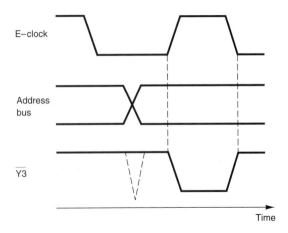

FIGURE 5.15 RAM decoder outputs are enabled only during E-clock equals 1.

into it. Figure 5.15 shows the timing for the $\overline{Y3}$ signal during a READ or WRITE operation from any address in the range 0C00 to 0FFF. Note that $\overline{Y3}$ does not go LOW until the positive half of the E-clock occurs, even though the MPU places the address for module-3 on the address bus during the AS signal. The broken line on $\overline{Y3}$ shows where a glitch might occur if the decoder were enabled while the address lines are changing.

EXAMPLE 5.8

What will happen to the RAM modules for addresses higher than 0FFF?

Solution For addresses greater than 0FFF, one or more of the A_{15}–A_{12} address lines will be HIGH. This will produce a HIGH at the A_2 input of the decoder. With $A_2 = 1$, decoder outputs $\overline{Y0}$–$\overline{Y3}$ cannot be LOW. Thus, none of the RAM modules will be enabled. This, of course, is what we want because the higher addresses are to be used for ROM and I/O.

Partial Decoding

The decoding scheme in Fig. 5.14 uses all the address bus lines to select a memory location. This technique, sometimes referred to as *full decoding,* is applicable to systems where every address is being used (or will eventually be used) for RAM, ROM, or I/O. This situation is not the case in small general-purpose μCs and dedicated μCs. For μCs that do not plan to use all the address space, a designer can use a *partial decoding* scheme to minimize the decoding circuitry. Partial decoding does not use all the address lines.

We could have used partial decoding for the μC in Fig. 5.14 because its memory map (Fig. 5.13) indicates that not all the address space is being used. For example, the four-input OR gate can be eliminated and replaced by a direct connection from A_{15} to the decoder, as shown in Fig. 5.16. With this change, address lines A_{14}, A_{13}, and A_{12} are not used, and therefore have no effect on the decoder. The conditions needed to generate a LOW at $\overline{K3}$ to select RAM module-3 now become

A_{15}	A_{14}	A_{13}	A_{12}	A_{11}	A_{10}	A_9	A_8	A_7	A_6	A_5	A_4	A_3	A_2	A_1	A_0	
0	X	X	X	1	1	X	X	X	X	X	X	X	X	X	X	-Selects module-3

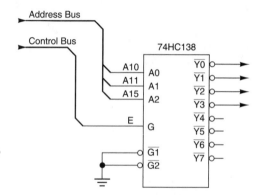

FIGURE 5.16 Modification to Figure 5.14 to achieve partial decoding.

A_{14}, A_{13}, and A_{12} are now don't cares, so that each one can be at either logic level. Thus, there are $2^3 = 8$ possible sets of conditions that can be used on these address lines. For each one, there will be a different address range as A_9–A_0 are varied. For example, with $A_{14}A_{13}A_{12} = 000$, the range will be 0C00 to 0FFF; with $A_{14}A_{13}A_{12} = 001$, the range will be 1C00 to 1FFF; and so on, until with $A_{14}A_{13}A_{12} = 111$, the range will be 7C00 to 7FFF. The MPU can use any of these address ranges to access module-3 because none of them overlap with the addresses that are allocated to ROM or I/O.

As this illustration has shown (Fig. 5.16), partial decoding reduces the decoding logic but produces more than one possible address range for accessing the same device. This is no problem, as long as none of these ranges include addresses that have been assigned to other memory or I/O devices.

EXAMPLE 5.9

Can A_{14} be used instead of A_{15} in Fig. 5.16?

Solution   No, because this would cause module-3 to be selected by addresses in the range 8C00 to 8CFF. This range has been allocated to I/O.

ROM Decoding Logic

We are now ready to add the ROM to our microcomputer. Referring back to the memory map in Fig. 5.13, we see that ROM is to occupy addresses C000 to FFFF. This is a total of 16,384 8-bit words. Thus, we need a ROM capacity of 16K $\times$ 8. We will use four 2732 EPROMs, each having a 4K $\times$ 8 capacity. Figure 5.17 shows them connected to the MPU buses. We will assume that the address, data, and control lines come from Fig. 5.14.

Examine Fig. 5.17 and note the following points:

1. Each ROM has its data outputs connected to the MPU data bus, but only the enabled ROM will place its data onto the data bus.
2. Each ROM has two active-LOW control inputs: chip ENABLE ($\overline{CE}$) and OUTPUT ENABLE ($\overline{OE}$). The $\overline{CE}$ input is used to activate the chip; when $\overline{CE}$ is HIGH, the ROM is in a "power-down" mode, where it draws very little power from the 5V supply

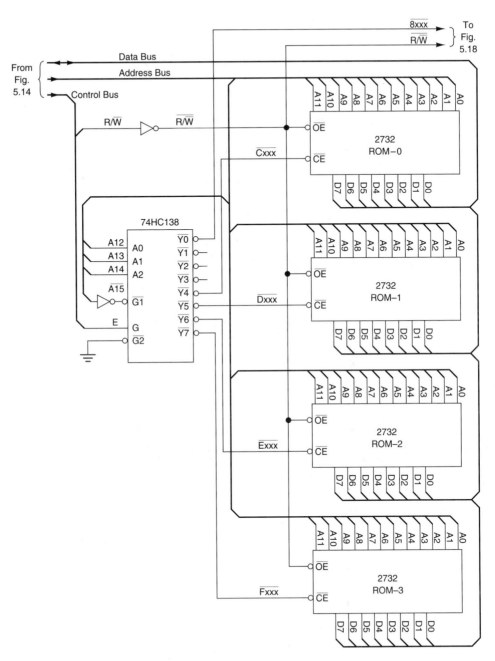

FIGURE 5.17   Typical ROM decoding logic.

line; when $\overline{\text{CE}}$ is LOW, the ROM is "powered up" and it will respond to the address inputs and the $\overline{\text{OE}}$ input. With $\overline{\text{CE}} = 0$, the $\overline{\text{OE}}$ has to be LOW to enable the ROM output buffers. Thus, both $\overline{\text{CE}}$ and $\overline{\text{OE}}$ have to be LOW to obtain output data from the ROM.

3. The MPU's R/$\overline{\text{W}}$ line is inverted and connected to the $\overline{\text{OE}}$ input of each ROM. During an MPU READ operation, the HIGH at R/$\overline{\text{W}}$ will activate the $\overline{\text{OE}}$ of that ROM whose $\overline{\text{CE}}$ is also LOW.

4. The 74HC138 decoder generates the $\overline{\text{CE}}$ signals. These signals are labeled $\overline{\text{Cxxx}}$, $\overline{\text{Dxxx}}$, $\overline{\text{Exxx}}$, and $\overline{\text{Fxxx}}$ to indicate the address ranges being selected. For instance, the $\overline{\text{Cxxx}}$ signal selects the ROM with address range C000 to CFFF. The decoder derives these signals from address lines A_{15}–A_{12} and the E-clock signal. Address line A_{15} is inverted in order to satisfy the active-LOW requirement of input $\overline{\text{G1}}$ of the decoder.

5. The address inputs to each ROM come from address bus lines A_0–A_{11}. These address lines select the specific data word within the selected ROM.

Each ROM stores 4096 8-bit words. We can determine the address range of each ROM by determining the conditions that activate its $\overline{\text{CE}}$ input. To illustrate, let us look at ROM-2. It will be enabled when decoder output $\overline{\text{Exxx}}$ goes LOW; that is, $\overline{\text{Y6}} = 0$. This will occur only when the following decoder input conditions are met:

$$A_{15} = 1, A_{14} = 1, A_{13} = 1, A_{12} = 0, \text{ and E-clock} = 1$$

The latter condition is used for the same reason stated earlier. Thus, ROM-2 will be enabled when the MPU address is

$$A_{15} \ A_{14} \ A_{13} \ A_{12} \ A_{11} \ A_{10} \ A_9 \ A_8 \ A_7 \ A_6 \ A_5 \ A_4 \ A_3 \ A_2 \ A_1 \ A_0$$

$$1 \quad 1 \quad 1 \quad 0 \quad X \quad X \quad X \quad X \quad X \quad X \quad X \quad X \quad X \quad X \quad X \quad X \quad \rightarrow (\overline{\text{Exxx}}_{16})$$

Once again, the Xs indicate "don't cares" because address lines A_{11}–A_0 are not used by the decoder to enable ROM-2. A_{11}–A_0 are used by ROM-2 to select the specific address location within the ROM. The complete range of hex addresses for ROM-2 is therefore E000 to EFFF.

A similar analysis can be used to determine the address ranges for each ROM. The results are:

ROM-0: C000–CFFF

ROM-1: D000–DFFF

ROM-2: E000–EFFF

ROM-3: F000–FFFF

EXAMPLE 5.10

Can another ROM be connected to the circuit in Fig. 5.17 with its $\overline{\text{CE}}$ input connected to the decoder's $\overline{\text{Y0}}$ output?

Solution No, this decoder output is $\overline{\text{8xxx}}$ and it responds to addresses in the range 8000 to 8FFF. This address range has already been allocated to I/O and cannot be used for ROM (see memory map, Fig. 5.13).

EXAMPLE 5.11

A ROM cannot be written into. Describe what happens when the MPU, through some programming error, executes the instruction: STAA $D776.

Solution When the MPU places the address D776 onto the address bus, decoder output $\overline{\text{Dxxx}}$ will go LOW to select ROM-1. However, because a store operation is being performed, R/$\overline{\text{W}}$ will be LOW. This places a HIGH at all ROM $\overline{\text{OE}}$ inputs to disable all of the ROM outputs. Thus, ROM-1 cannot put its data onto the data bus to conflict with the data being placed there by the MPU.

   Of course, the MPU data will not be stored in any device because address D776 will not select any RAM or I/O device.

I/O Decoding Logic

The last portion of decoding circuitry is used to select an input or output device to participate in data transfer with the MPU. The memory map for our μC (Fig. 5.13) shows one 4K page of addresses (8000 to 8FFF) allocated for I/O devices. This is a range of 4096 addresses, but it does not mean that the μC will have that many I/O devices tied to its data bus. In fact, most μCs will typically have three to six I/O devices, although some may have only two, the absolute minimum if the μC is to communicate with the outside world. Assigning such a wide range of addresses to I/O is commonly done so that partial decoding can be used to minimize decoding logic. Of course, this wastes a lot of address space, so it would not be done where RAM or ROM capacities are to be maximized.

   For our example μC, we have chosen to use two simple I/O devices called *ports*. We will save the more complex devices until later chapters. Figure 5.18 shows the decoding logic for interfacing one input port and one output port to the μC buses. Study this diagram and note the following:

1. The input port consists of a 74HC244 IC, which contains eight tri-state buffers. The buffer outputs are connected to the μC data bus. The buffer inputs serve as the actual input port through which external data can be applied. The buffer outputs are enabled when the chip's two $\overline{\text{OE}}$ inputs are driven LOW; this allows the external data onto the data bus so that the MPU can read them.

2. The output port consists of a 74HC377 IC, which contains eight edge-triggered D flip-flops with a common INPUT ENABLE ($\overline{\text{IE}}$) and a common clock input (CLK). The eight flip-flops form an 8-bit output register. The D inputs are connected to the μC data bus so that data from the bus can be latched into the register whenever a positive-going transition occurs at CLK while $\overline{\text{IE}}$ = 0. The Q outputs serve as the actual output port through which data from the MPU can be sent to the external world.

3. The decoding logic consists of two NAND gates and three inverters. The inputs to this logic come from signals generated in the RAM and ROM decoding logic (Figs. 5.14 and 5.17). The $\overline{\text{8xxx}}$ and R/$\overline{\text{W}}$ signals come from Fig. 5.17; E-clock and R/$\overline{\text{W}}$ come from Fig. 5.14. The only address bus line used in the I/O decoding logic is A_2. This line selects either the input or output port.

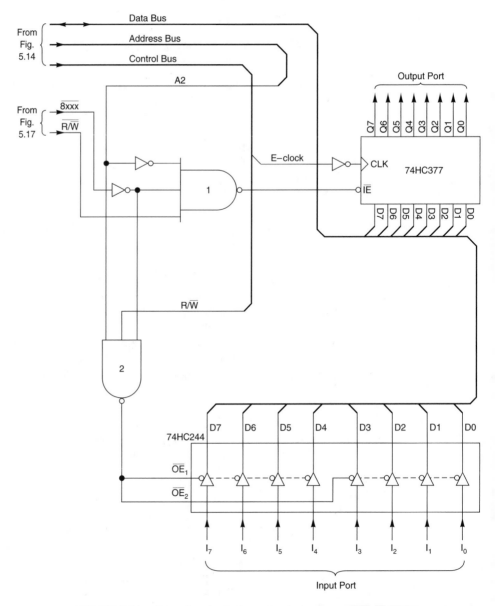

FIGURE 5.18   Decoding logic for a simple input and output port.

MPU Reading from the Input Port

When the MPU wants to read data from the input port, it has to generate the appropriate logic levels to place a LOW at the output of NAND-2. This requires HIGHS at each
of the NAND-2 inputs so that we have (1) $R/\overline{W} = 1$, which, of course, indicates a READ
operation; (2) $\overline{8xxx} = 0$, which means that the levels on the four higher-order address lines
are 1, 0, 0, and 0, respectively; and (3) $A_2 = 1$.

Thus, the MPU will read data from the input port whenever it performs a READ operation on any address of the form

$$A_{15} \ A_{14} \ A_{13} \ A_{12} \ A_{11} \ A_{10} \ A_9 \ A_8 \ A_7 \ A_6 \ A_5 \ A_4 \ A_3 \ A_2 \ A_1 \ A_0$$

$$1 \quad 0 \quad 0 \quad 0 \quad X \quad X \quad X \quad X \quad X \quad X \quad X \quad X \quad X \quad 1 \quad X \quad X$$

Clearly, since so many of the address lines are don't cares, there are many different hex addresses that will select the input port. For simplicity, we will set each X equal to 0. This produces the address $1000\ 0000\ 0000\ 0100_2 = 8004_{16}$, which we will designate as the input port address.

EXAMPLE 5.12

What assembly language instruction will cause the data present at the input port to be transferred to accumulator A?

Solution   LDAA $8004, which assembles into the three-byte machine language code: B6, 80, 04. Recall that B6 is the op code for the LDAA operation, and 8004 is the operand address.

MPU Writing to the Output Port

For the MPU to write data into the output register, two conditions have to be met: The output of NAND-1 has to be LOW, and the E-clock signal has to make a negative-going transition. Recall that during a WRITE operation, the MPU data to be written will be valid on the data bus when the E-clock goes from HIGH to LOW. A LOW output from NAND-1 will occur only when each input is HIGH, so we have (1) $R/\overline{W} = 0$ for WRITE operation; (2) $\overline{8xxx} = 0$; and (3) $A_2 = 0$.

Thus, the MPU can send data to the output port by performing a WRITE operation to any address of the form

$$A_{15} \ A_{14} \ A_{13} \ A_{12} \ A_{11} \ A_{10} \ A_9 \ A_8 \ A_7 \ A_6 \ A_5 \ A_4 \ A_3 \ A_2 \ A_1 \ A_0$$

$$1 \quad 0 \quad 0 \quad 0 \quad X \quad X \quad X \quad X \quad X \quad X \quad X \quad X \quad X \quad 0 \quad X \quad X$$

Once again, for simplicity we will set each X equal to 0. This gives us an address $1000\ 0000\ 0000\ 0000_2 = 8000_{16}$, which we will designate as the output port address.

When the MPU writes data into the output port register, the data will remain at the output port until the MPU writes a different data word into the register.

EXAMPLE 5.13

What assembly language instruction will cause data from accumulator A to appear at the output port?

Solution   STAA $8000, which assembles into the three-byte machine language code: B7, 80, 00. Recall that B7 is the op code for STAA, and 8000 is the operand address.

▶ 5.10 BUFFERING THE MPU BUSES

The combined circuitry from Figs. 5.14, 5.17, and 5.18 essentially makes up our complete μC. The 68HC11 MPU, RAM, and ROM are LSI chips that are generally manufactured using some MOS technology. The decoders, gates, inverters, tri-state buffers, and output register are all HCMOS devices to minimize power requirements and loading.

If you look at these three circuit diagrams, you will notice that the MPU's address, data, and control lines are all driving several loads. For example, address line A_{15} drives an OR gate input and an inverter input. Address line A_2 drives four RAM modules, four ROM chips, an inverter, and a NAND gate. Each data bus line is connected to four RAM modules, four ROM modules, an input port, and an output port. The R/$\overline{W}$ control signal is connected to four RAM modules, an inverter, and a NAND gate.

Generally, an 8-bit MPU is a MOS device; its bus lines do not have much output current capability and, typically, cannot drive more than one standard TTL load without logic level deterioration, and cannot drive the bus capacitances without significant signal distortion. These bus capacitances are present because of the many devices tied to each bus line; each device typically contributes 5 to 10 pF. In most well-designed systems, the MPU's buses will be *buffered* from the rest of the circuitry using devices that are variously called *buffers, line drivers,* or *bus drivers*. This is illustrated in Fig. 5.19.

Figure 5.19A shows the MPU address and control lines connected to noninverting buffers. The buffer outputs typically have enough current capability to drive 5 or 10 TTL loads. The buffers can also drive the capacitive load that appears on those address bus lines that are connected to several RAM and ROM chips. The 74LS244 chip is commonly used for this purpose; it contains eight buffers per chip. These buffers are tri-state and are usually connected so that they are permanently enabled.

Because the buffer outputs have exactly the same logic levels as the inputs, the outputs are often labeled the same as the inputs except for the addition of the letter *B*. For example, the output of the A_0 buffer is labeled BA_0 and is referred to as the *buffered* A_0 signal.

The MPU data bus lines are also usually buffered. There is an important difference, however, in that the data lines are bidirectional and therefore require a more complex buffering arrangement. Fig. 5.19B shows how a data line can be buffered using two tri-state buffers. The R/$\overline{W}$ signal controls which buffer is enabled. During an MPU WRITE operation, the LOW at R/$\overline{W}$ enables buffer 1 to allow data from D_7 to appear on the data bus. For a READ operation, the HIGH at R/$\overline{W}$ enables buffer 2 to allow data from the data bus into the MPU. Note that only one buffer is activated at one time. The same arrangement is used for each data line.

Several ICs are available, such as the 74LS242, that contain pairs of buffers connected in the arrangements shown in Fig. 5.19B. These ICs are typically called *bidirectional buffers* or *transceivers*.

In the case of the 68HC11 MPU, however, we can take advantage of the high-speed CMOS (HCMOS) technology used in its fabrication process. A typical HCMOS device has an input current requirement of 1 μA. According to the 68HC11 data sheet, any of its outputs in the HIGH state can supply a current of 0.8 mA. Thus, an output pin on the 68HC11 MPU can drive 800 HCMOS inputs without exceeding that output's *fan-out*. Fan-out simply indicates the maximum number of inputs that the output of a digital circuit can drive reliably without being loaded down.

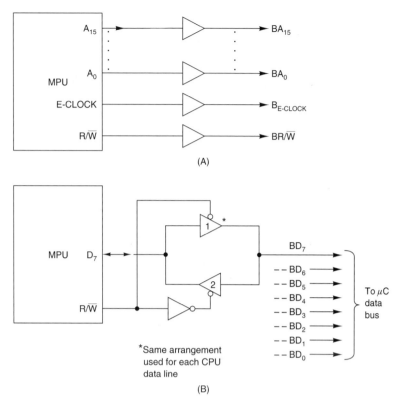

FIGURE 5.19 (A) Buffered address line; (B) bidirectional buffers for MPU data lines.

The HCMOS logic family offers the user a wide selection of digital circuits. For example, most of the logic circuits that are found in the 74TTL logic family are also available in the 74HC logic family. Consequently, we can design a 68HC11-based microcomputer using only HCMOS ICs, thereby minimizing the inherent loading limitations and signal level deterioration that occur when two different logic families are interfaced. Nevertheless, it is not uncommon to encounter design situations where bus loading is a concern even though the HCMOS MPU might be driving only HCMOS loads, especially capacitive loading which can distort signal quality. In such cases, HCMOS buffers such as 74HC244 or 74HC242 can be used in the same manner as previously described in order to reduce the loading problems.

▶ 5.11 MEMORY-MAPPED AND ISOLATED I/O

Many microprocessors, like the 68HC11, communicate with I/O devices and memory in exactly the same way; that is, the I/O devices are addressed just like memory, and the MPU uses the R/$\overline{\text{W}}$ signal to determine the direction of data transfer. The I/O devices and memory share the memory map, with some addresses reserved for I/O and others for memory.

The same instructions are used by the MPU to read or write data to I/O devices as to RAM and ROM. In other words, the MPU makes no distinction between memory and I/O. This method for handling I/O is called *memory-mapped I/O*.

As mentioned earlier, the two basic methods by which the MPU can communicate with I/O devices are *memory-mapped I/O* and *isolated I/O*. The discussions thus far have concentrated on memory-mapped I/O, where the I/O devices are treated just like memory locations; that is, they have addresses just like memory, and the MPU uses the $R/\overline{W}$ control signal to control the direction of data transfer. The same instructions are used by the MPU to communicate with I/O devices as with RAM and ROM. In other words, for memory-mapped I/O the CPU makes no distinction between memory and I/O devices.

Some microprocessors, such as the 8080/8085 and Z-80, are designed to use *isolated I/O* techniques where the MPU treats memory and I/O devices separately, using different control signals for each. Figure 5.20 shows how the 8085 microprocessor performs isolated I/O. The 8085 uses *three* control signals to specify which operation is being performed. The signal $\overline{RD}$ is driven LOW by the MPU for any READ operation from memory or I/O. The $\overline{WR}$ line is driven LOW by the MPU for any WRITE operation from memory or I/O. The MPU uses the $IO/\overline{M}$ line to specify whether memory or I/O is being communicated with; a HIGH specifies I/O, a LOW specifies memory.

The table in Fig. 5.20 shows the logic levels that the MPU places on these lines for each of the four possible operations. Note that only address lines A_0–A_7 are used for I/O.

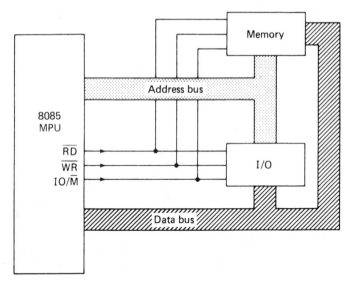

Operation	$\overline{RD}$	$\overline{WR}$	$IO/\overline{M}$	Address
Read memory	0	1	0	A_0 - A_{15}
Write memory	1	0	0	A_0 - A_{15}
Read I/O	0	1	1	A_0 - A_7
Write I/O	1	0	1	A_0 - A_7

FIGURE 5.20   Isolated I/O as implemented using the 8085 µP.

This means that the MPU can communicate with $2^8 = 256$ I/O devices. For example, when the MPU wants to read from an input device, it generates $\overline{RD} = 0$, $\overline{WR} = 1$, $IO/\overline{M} = 1$, and places an 8-bit *device* address on the address bus. The memory devices will not respond to the address bus, since $IO/\overline{M} = 1$.

Because the $IO/\overline{M}$ line distinguishes between memory and I/O, the memory can use all the 65,536 addresses that are possible with 16 address lines. This is an advantage of isolated I/O over memory-mapped I/O. A disadvantage of isolated I/O is that special program instructions are required to perform I/O operations. The two most common are IN and OUT instructions. Memory-mapped I/O uses the same instructions for I/O and memory and does not require special instructions. In addition, memory-mapped I/O has the advantage of being able to use the same wide variety of instructions for I/O that are available for memory, thereby providing more programming flexibility.

▶ 5.12 TROUBLESHOOTING CASE STUDY

Each RAM and ROM IC that is part of a computer's internal or external memory typically contains thousands of memory cells. A single faulty memory cell can cause a complete system failure (commonly known as a "system crash") or, at least, unreliable system operation. The testing and troubleshooting of memory systems involves the use of techniques and equipment that are not often used on other parts of the digital system. Because memory consists of thousands of identical circuits acting as storage locations, any tests of its operation must involve checking to see exactly which locations are working and which are not. The problem typically can be traced to a bad memory IC; a bad decoder IC; logic gate, or signal buffer; or a problem in the circuit connections (i.e., shorts or open connections).

Generally, testing a RAM involves writing a known pattern of 1s and 0s to each memory location and reading them back to verify that the location has stored the pattern properly. The method used to test the memory in the troubleshooting case study is called the *checkerboard pattern*. It is so-called because this test writes and reads patterns of alternating 1s and 0s (i.e. 10101010 and 01010101) into each RAM location. The checkerboard pattern performs two different tests. First, it determines whether or not the RAM is storing the proper pattern of 1s and 0s. Second, it determines whether or not there are any shorts between adjacent data lines.

Let's consider the following scenario: A technician is testing the external RAM decoding logic circuitry of Figure 5.14. All of the integrated circuits on the printed circuit board are inserted into IC sockets and she knows that this printed circuit board was working properly before it failed.

In order to test the circuitry the technician runs a RAM-TEST program that is stored in ROM (read only memory). The RAM-TEST program tests the RAM by going through the following sequence:

It writes or stores AA_{16} in each RAM location.
It reads back the contents of each memory location in RAM and displays it on a video terminal.
It writes or stores 55_{16} in each RAM location.
It reads back the contents of each memory location in RAM and displays it on a video terminal.

By observing the data displayed on the video terminal, the technician concludes that the RAM-TEST program writes data AA_{16} to all memory cells and reads data AA_{16} from all memory cells properly. However, after the program writes data 55_{16} to each of the four RAM modules, it reads back 55_{16} only from RAM modules 0, 1, and 2. All of the memory locations in RAM module-3 read back 54_{16}. Table 5.2 shows *data written to memory vs. data read from memory* for all the address locations in the four RAM modules.

TABLE 5.2

Address (hex)	Data written to memory	Data read from memory
0000 ↓ 0FFF	$10101010_2 = AA_{16}$ " $10101010_2 = AA_{16}$	$10101010_2 = AA_{16}$ " $10101010_2 = AA_{16}$
/////////////////////	/////////////////////////////	/////////////////////////////
0000 ↓ 03FF	$01010101_2 = 55_{16}$ " $01010101_2 = 55_{16}$	$01010101_2 = 55_{16}$ " $01010101_2 = 55_{16}$
0400 ↓ 07FF	$01010101_2 = 55_{16}$ " $01010101_2 = 55_{16}$	$01010101_2 = 55_{16}$ " $01010101_2 = 55_{16}$
0800 ↓ 0BFF	$01010101_2 = 55_{16}$ " $01010101_2 = 55_{16}$	$01010101_2 = 55_{16}$ " $01010101_2 = 55_{16}$
0C00 ↓ 0FFF	$0101010\mathbf{1}_2 = 55_{16}$ " $0101010\mathbf{1}_2 = 55_{16}$	$0101010\mathbf{0}_2 = \mathbf{54}_{16}$ " $0101010\mathbf{0}_2 = \mathbf{54}_{16}$

Clearly, something has failed or malfunctioned in this memory circuit. When RAM is tested with data AA_{16} there is no apparent problem. However, after data 55_{16} is written into RAM module-3 the data read back from RAM module-3 is always 54_{16}. By observing the contents of Table 5.2 carefully we can see that the least significant bit of the data is the only bit that differs between what is supposed to be the correct data (data written to memory) and what turns out to be the wrong data (data read from memory). Furthermore, it appears that the least significant bit of the data being read from module-3 is always a logic LOW. Obviously, any fault that would cause a LOW on the data bus line D_0 at the time when RAM module-3 is being read would produce the observed results.

The following is a list of some *possible* causes for this circuit malfunction:

1. D_0 of the RAM module-3 is externally shorted to ground.

2. D_0 of the RAM module-3 is internally shorted to ground.

3. D_0 of the RAM module-3 is externally open.

4. D_0 of the RAM module-3 is internally open.

5. Internal fault in RAM module-3.

Let us use the troubleshooting tools previously discussed in Chapter 2 in order to find out which of the above possible causes we might have. We will now describe how each of the causes could be proved or disproved.

D_0 of the RAM Module-3 is Externally Shorted to Ground We can find this short by using an ohmmeter and by performing a continuity check between D_0 of RAM module-3 and ground. We can also use the logic pulser and current tracer to find out the exact location of this short. Although this fault would perhaps seem to be a possible cause for the RAM malfunction it is not a probable one; if D_0 of RAM module-3 were externally grounded then common data bus line D_0 and address bus line AD_0 would also be grounded. Note that the common data bus line D_0 is connected to all RAM, ROM, I/O, and the MC68HC11 MCU. Therefore, if data bus line D_0 was permanently grounded, we can assume that the RAM-TEST program could not have run properly. In fact, if data bus line D_0 was permanently grounded there is a good chance that the 68HC11 MCU would have not been able to function at all. Therefore, we can safely rule out this as a cause for the malfunction.

D_0 of the RAM Module-3 is Internally Shorted to Ground We can rule out this fault for the same reason given in the previous explanation, since the circuit would not behave differently whether D_0 of the RAM module-3 were internally or externally shorted to ground.

D_0 of the RAM Module-3 is Externally/Internally Open This would cause D_0 to float. A floating signal in a circuit that belongs to **H**igh-Speed **C**MOS logic family (68**HC**11) assumes an unpredictable logic state. It can assume a logic HIGH or a logic LOW, or something in between. This is the reason why some 68HC11-based circuits have all eight data bus lines pulled up to +5V through pull-up resistors. This prevents the possibility of a data line assuming an indeterminate logic level. Since there are no pull-up resistors on the data bus lines in our circuit, it is possible that we could have obtained the results shown on Table 5.2. Although this is a possibility, it is however not probable. The chances are pretty remote that a floating D_0 of RAM module-3 would *always* assume a logic LOW.

Internal Fault in RAM Module-3 Memory ICs sometimes develop internal faults; that is, something inside the chip that prevents writing or reading of data properly. These faults do not manifest themselves unless and until the memory module is selected and enabled. In other words, such faults will not produce a permanent LOW or permanent HIGH on the data pin, but can produce an incorrect logic level to be written into or read from the memory module when it is selected and enabled. This is the most likely cause of the problem in our circuit. Some internal malfunction is causing D_0 of RAM module-3 to always produce a LOW level when this module is being read. This can be verified by removing and replacing the suspected IC. This is easy to do in this particular example because the RAM chips are inserted into IC sockets. If the RAM chips were soldered directly into the printed circuit board we would have to unsolder the RAM IC carefully so as not to burn either the metal traces on the printed circuit board or the printed circuit board itself. This requires some degree of skill and experience in printed circuit board repair on the part of the technician.

GLOSSARY

Address Bus Unidirectional bus from the MPU used to select the memory or I/O device with which the MPU wants to communicate. For the 68HC11 MPU, this is a 16-line bus.

Address Space   The range of addresses that are available in a µC.

Address Strobe (AS)   When the 68HC11 MPU is operating in the normal expanded mode, this output signal is used to enable an external 8-bit address latch.

Checkerboard Pattern   Pattern of 1s and 0s that is sometimes used to test RAM systems for proper operation. This pattern also allows the detection of shorts between adjacent memory data cells.

Control Bus   A bus carrying signals that are used to synchronize the operation of the various µC elements.

Data Bus   Bidirectional bus over which data flow between the MPU and memory and I/O devices. For the 68HC11 MPU, this is an 8-line bus.

Discrete Logic   Conventional logic designs utilizing flip-flops, gates, counters, registers, and other medium-scale-integration (MSI) functions.

E-Clock   This is the system clock of a 68HC11 MPU-based microcomputer. The E-clock frequency is always four times smaller than that of the externally generated EXTAL clock.

Full Decoding   Address decoding schemes that use all address bus lines.

HCMOS   High-density CMOS logic family.

I/O Port   Where an I/O device connects to an interface circuit that is connected to the computer data bus.

Interrupt Request ($\overline{\text{IRQ}}$ or $\overline{\text{XIRQ}}$)   68HC11 MPU control inputs used when an I/O device wants to get the MPU's attention.

Isolated I/O   Technique whereby the MPU uses a different set of control signals for communicating with I/O than it does for memory.

Memory Map   A diagram showing how the address space is allocated among RAM, ROM, and I/O.

Memory Module   A combination of memory chips arranged to store 8-bit words.

Memory Page   A block of 256 consecutive addresses. In a 16-bit address system, each page consists of all addresses beginning with the same two hex digits.

Memory-Mapped I/O   Technique by which the MPU does not distinguish between memory and I/O devices.

Microcontroller   An IC that contains an MPU, a nominal amount of RAM, ROM, and I/O circuitry.

MODA/MODB inputs   MPU inputs whose logic levels determine the mode of operation for the 68HC11 MPU.

Normal Expanded Mode   One of four modes of operation of the 68HC11 MPU. In this mode, the 68HC11's Port B is used to output the low-order address byte. Port C is used to multiplex the high-order address byte and data, depending on the states of the E-clock and address strobe (AS) signals.

Partial Decoding   Address decoding schemes that do not use all of the address bus lines.

PH2 Clock   This is a clock that is used strictly for internal operations of the 68HC11 MPU. The PH2 (phase-two) clock has the same frequency as the system E-clock; however the E-clock lags 90° behind the internal PH2 clock.

Port   A set of pins on a chip through which digital information is transmitted both to and from the MPU.

Read Operation   Data are transferred into the MPU from memory or an input device.

READ/WRITE ($R/\overline{W}$)   An MPU control output signal that tells external devices the direction of data flow.

RESET   An MPU control signal that initializes the internal MPU circuits.

Time-Multiplexed   Port C of the 68HC11 MPU is said to be time-multiplexed because in the normal expanded mode it carries different sets of information at different times.

WRITE Operation   Data are transferred from the MPU to memory or an output device.

QUESTIONS AND PROBLEMS

Sections 5.1–5.2

1. Describe the difference between a microprocessor and a microcomputer.
2. **(a)** List the major elements of a microcomputer.
   (b) Describe the difference between a microcomputer and a microcontroller.
3. Which of the following is *not* an advantage that a μP-based system has over discrete logic?
   (a) Generally easier to design.
   (b) Can operate at higher speeds.
   (c) Is more flexible—can be modified more easily.
   (d) Uses fewer chips.

Section 5.3

4. Assume that the 68HC11 MPU is being used in the normal expanded mode. For each of the following statements, indicate which 68HC11 MPU bus or buses are being described.
   (a) A unidirectional bus.
   (b) Carries signals used to synchronize data transfer operations.
   (c) The MPU uses this bus to select a specific memory location for data transfer.
   (d) During a WRITE operation, this bus carries data from the MPU.
   (e) The number of lines on this bus determines the maximum memory capacity.
   (f) The number of lines on this bus determines the memory word size.
   (g) The $R/\overline{W}$ signal is part of this bus.
   (h) This bus is a combination of the signals coming from Port B and an external 8-bit latch.
   (i) Port C is said to be time-multiplexed because at different times it will carry different signals from these buses.
5. Describe the function of the following control bus signals: $R/\overline{W}$, AS, $\overline{RESET}$, $\overline{IRQ}$, E-clock, and PH2 clock.
6. What is the difference between the E-clock and the PH2 clock?
7. What is an I/O port?

Sections 5.4–5.5

8. Which of the following is a READ operation, and which is a WRITE operation?
   (a) The op code portion of an instruction is transferred from memory into the instruction register, IR.

(b) The contents of accumulator A are transferred to RAM.

(c) The low-order byte of the operand address is transferred from memory into the data address register, DAR.

9. How many READ operations does the MPU perform when it fetches and executes the following instruction: LDAA $4F87? How many WRITE operations?

10. Refer to section 4.12 and repeat Question 9 for each of the following instructions:
(a) STAA $4F87   **(b)** JMP $0321   **(c)** BEQ $9800

11. Assume that a 68HC11 MPU is being used in the normal expanded mode. List the events that occur coincident with the following signal edges during a READ cycle:
(a) Positive-going transition of the AS signal.
(b) Positive-going transition of the PH2 clock.
(c) Negative-going transition of the AS signal.
(d) Positive-going transition of the E-clock signal.
(e) Negative-going transition of the E-clock signal.

12. Repeat Problem 11 for a WRITE operation.

13. A certain 68HC11 MPU is using a 2-MHz E-clock with pulse duration of 250 ns. How much time will a memory device have to respond during a READ operation?

14. Explain why the 68HC11 MPU does not increment the **[PC]** on the rising edge of *every* PH2 clock?

15. Change the first instruction to LDAA $D75C and modify the bus activity shown in Fig. 5.8.

Sections 5.6–5.7

16. A certain microcomputer allocates addresses 0000 to 7FFF to RAM, 8800 to 8FFF to I/O, and C800 to FFFF to ROM.
(a) Draw the memory map for this μC.
(b) Determine the total RAM capacity.
(c) Determine the total ROM capacity.
(d) How many different I/O devices can this μC accommodate?

17. **(a)** How many "pages" are allocated to RAM for the μC described in Problem 16? How many pages for ROM? For I/O?
(b) How many "4K pages" are allocated to RAM for the μC described in Problem 16? How many for ROM?

18. A certain microcomputer has 16,384 ROM locations starting at address C000. How many pages does this represent? How many 4K pages? What is the complete range of ROM addresses?

19. How much on-chip memory is there in the 68HC11E9 MCU? In the 68HC11A8 MCU?

20. What is the address of word 5A on page 37?

21. On what 4K page is address 375A?

22. True or false: RAM chips are usually combined to form a RAM-module that has an 8-bit word size.

Sections 5.8–5.9

23. Modify the RAM decoding logic of Fig. 5.14 as shown in Fig. 5.21. Then determine the address range for each RAM module.

24. Explain why the E-clock signal is used to enable the decoder in Fig. 5.14.

25. Explain the difference between full and partial decoding. What is the advantage of partial decoding, and when can it be used?

26. Assume that the partial decoding modification of Fig. 5.16 is used in Fig. 5.14.
    (a) Determine the eight different address ranges that can access module-1.
    (b) Explain why each of the following instructions, when executed by the MPU, will produce the same result: ADDA \$0352, ADDA \$7352, ADDA \$5352.

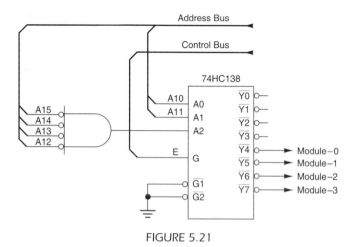

FIGURE 5.21

27. Show how the ROM capacity in Fig. 5.17 can easily be expanded to 28K.

28. A technician tests the ROM circuitry of Fig. 5.17 by having the MPU read data from the various ROMs. The results show that (1) data read from addresses C000 to CFFF and F000 to FFFF are correct; (2) data read from D000 to DFFF correspond to data that are supposed to be at E000 to EFFF; and (3) data read from E000 to EFFF correspond to data that are supposed to be at D000 to DFFF. Which of the following circuit faults could produce these erroneous results?
    (a) The connection to the A_1 input of the decoder is open.
    (b) Connections to decoder inputs A_0 and A_1 have been reversed.
    (c) Connections to the $\overline{CE}$ inputs of ROM-1 and ROM-2 have been reversed.

29. The circuit of Fig. 5.17 uses 2732 EPROMs, each of which is organized as 4K × 8. Modify the circuit so that it uses 2716 EPROMs, each of which is organized as 2K × 8. The total ROM address space is still to be C000 to FFFF.

30. Figure 5.22 shows the decoding circuitry for a hypothetical μC. It uses three 4K × 8 ROMs and two 1K × 8 RAMs. Determine the total address range for RAM and the total address range for ROM.

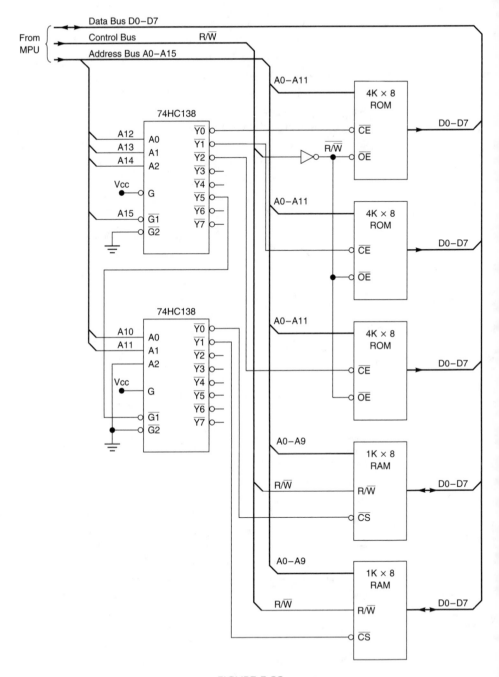

FIGURE 5.22

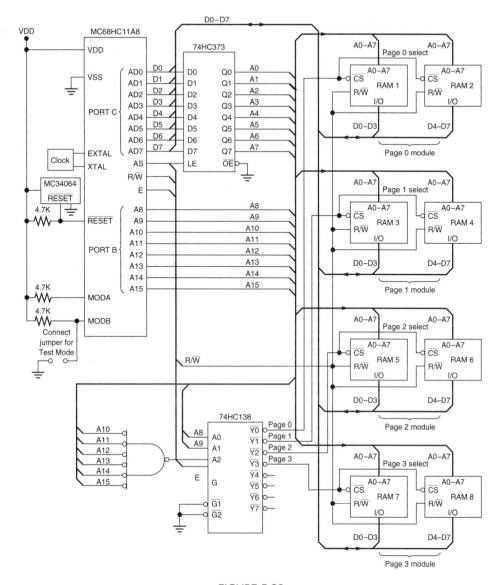

FIGURE 5.23

31. Figure 5.23 is the RAM decoding logic for a page-organized 68HC11-based μC.
  (a) What is the capacity of each RAM chip?
  (b) What is the capacity of each RAM module?
  (c) Determine the address range for each RAM module.

32. Modify the logic of Fig. 5.23 to include four more pages of RAM (pages 04-07). (*Hint:* It requires more modification than simply using the other four decoder outputs.)

33. Modify the I/O decoding logic of Fig. 5.18 to include two input ports and two output ports. The addresses must stay within the range 8000 to 8FFF.

Sections 5.10–5.11

34. Why is it often necessary to buffer the address, data, and control signals in a μC?

35. How many HCMOS inputs can an output of a 68HC11 MPU drive without exceeding the output's fan-out?

36. Describe the main differences between memory-mapped I/O and isolated I/O, and list their relative advantages and disadvantages.

Section 5.12

37. Refer to the RAM decoding logic circuit of Figure 5.14. Assume that all of the ICs are inserted into IC sockets. A technician builds and tests the prototype circuit of Figure 5.14 by using the checkerboard pattern method. After analyzing the results he concludes that he cannot access any of the RAM modules. That is, addresses ranging from 0000_{16} through $0FFF_{16}$ do not cause any RAM data to be placed on the data bus.

(a) Determine *four* different possible causes for the malfunction.

(b) Determine which of the following troubleshooting tools could have been used to isolate each of the four possible faults

Ohmmeter

Logic probe

Combination of logic probe and current tracer

Logic analyzer

(c) How would the operation of this RAM memory circuit be affected if output $\overline{Y3}$ of the 74HC138 decoder were to be stuck on the LOW state? Assume that the other decoder outputs are functioning properly.

6

The Microprocessor: Heart of the Microcomputer

OBJECTIVES

Upon completion of this chapter, you will be able to:

- Understand the block diagram of the 68HC11 MPU.
- Describe functions of the various control bus signals used by the 68HC11 MPU.
- Name the four ways the 68HC11 MPU can be reset.
- Explain how the reset address vectors work.
- Understand and recount the function of the instruction register (IR), the data address register (DAR), and the accumulator registers (ACCA, ACCB).
- Cite the differences between a general-purpose register and an index register.
- Comprehend the usefulness of the condition code register and the significance of each of its flags.
- Specify the function of the stack and the stack pointer register.
- Describe the 68HC11 programming model.
- Understand and explain the arithmetic/logic unit of the MPU.
- Describe the two major directions in which microprocessors have evolved since their introduction in 1971.

INTRODUCTION

Although they vary in their architecture, all microcomputers and microcontrollers have one element in common—the microprocessor chip that we have been referring to as the MPU. As we know, the MPU functions as the central processing unit of the μC. In essence, the MPU is the heart of the μC because its capabilities determine the capabilities of the μC. Its speed determines the maximum speed of the μC; its address and data pins determine the μC's memory capacity and word size; and its control pins determine the type of I/O interfacing that must be used.

The MPU performs a large number of functions, including, but not limited to:

1. Providing timing and control signals for all elements of the μC
2. Fetching instructions and data from memory
3. Transferring data to and from I/O devices
4. Decoding instructions
5. Performing arithmetic and logic operations called for by instructions
6. Responding to I/O-generated control signals such as RESET and INTERRUPT

The MPU contains all the logic circuitry for performing these functions, but it should be kept in mind that a great deal of the MPU's internal logic is not externally accessible. For example, we cannot apply an external signal to the MPU chip to increment the program counter (PC). Instead, the MPU elements are *software-accessible.* This means that we can affect the internal MPU circuitry only by the *program* we put into memory for the MPU to execute. This is what makes the MPU so versatile and flexible—when we want to change the MPU's operation, we simply change the program (for example, by changing the ROMs that store the program). This is generally easier than rewiring hardware.

In this chapter we expand the simplified version of the 68HC11 MPU to include most of its internal elements and external control signals. Our study of the more complete 68HC11 MPU will purposely include some repetition of material discussed in the preceding chapters; this is necessary to produce a smooth blending of the new material with the old.

▶ 6.1 68HC11 MPU—MORE COMPLETE VERSION

Figure 6.1 is a block diagram for the internal structure of the 68HC11 MPU. If we compare this diagram to the simplified version used in our previous discussions, we find the following differences:

1. There are *five* 16-bit registers connected to the 68HC11's internal address bus. An index register X, an index register Y, and a stack pointer register (SP) have been added to the PC and DAR. Each of these registers is shown consisting of two 8-bit halves. For example, PC_H is the high-order byte and PC_L is the low-order byte of the PC.
2. There are *two* 8-bit accumulators, ACCA and ACCB, connected to the ALU and the internal data bus. Accumulators A and B can be used as individual 8-bit registers or as a single 16-bit register called a *doubled accumulator* (ACCD). Note that the 68HC11 MPU has **only** two accumulators (ACCA and ACCB). However, when ACCD is used it is actually the *concatenation* or joining of accumulators A and B.
3. There is an 8-bit condition code register (CCR) connected to the ALU.
4. All control bus signals used by the 68HC11 in the expanded mode are shown. Also shown is a clock generator block representing the external circuitry needed to generate the system E-clock required by the 68HC11 MPU.

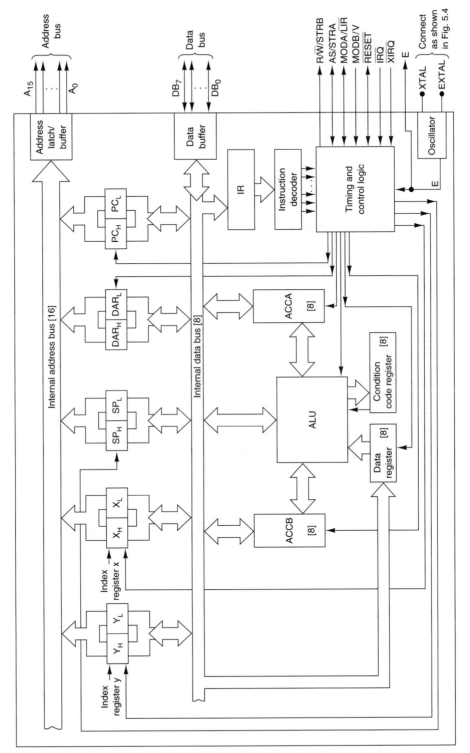

FIGURE 6.1   Block diagram of the 68HC11 MPU.

225

The following sections describe the function of each of the 68HC11's internal elements and external control signals of Fig. 6.1. The discussion will divide the MPU into three sections: timing and control, registers, and the ALU.

▶ 6.2 TIMING AND CONTROL SECTION

We will not discuss the timing and control section of the MPU in too much detail for two reasons. First, it is the one area on the MPU chip over which we have very little control. Second, we do not have to know the detailed structure of the timing and control section to develop useful programs for the MPU.

The major function of this MPU section is to fetch and decode instructions from program memory and then generate the necessary control signals required by the ALU and register section for executing these instructions. The operation of fetching and decoding instructions together with control-signal generation was discussed in Chapter 4 and therefore need not be described any further.

Control Bus Signals

The timing and control section also generates *external* signals that are sent to other μC elements as part of the system's control bus. We used two of the control bus signals, R/$\overline{\text{W}}$ and AS, in our description of the expanded-mode operation of the 68HC11 MPU in Chapter 5. In addition to generating output signals for the control bus, the MPU control section also responds to control bus input signals that are sent from other μC elements to the MPU chip. The $\overline{\text{RESET}}$ and $\overline{\text{IRQ}}$ (Interrupt Request) are examples of control signals that are inputs to the MPU.

Each MPU has its own unique set of input and output control signals that are described in detail in manufacturers' operation manuals. We will define the control signals utilized by the 68HC11 MPU.

AS Signal　This output signal is called the address strobe and is used by the 68HC11 MPU when it is operating in the normal expanded mode. The low-order byte of the address is allowed through an external 8-bit latch while the AS signal is HIGH, and the stable address information is then latched by the 8-bit latch when AS signal is LOW. When the 68HC11 MPU is operating in the single-chip mode this line becomes an input signal called Strobe A (STRA). STRA can be used as an edge-detecting interrupt input. We will not be using the STRA signal in this textbook. You may refer to Section 5.3 for more details on the AS signal.

E-Clock　The 68HC11 MPU uses a single system clock signal called the *E-clock*. The E-clock signal is generated on the 68HC11 chip and is used both internally and externally. The frequency of this signal is determined by the external clock components connected to the EXTAL and XTAL input pins on the chip (see Fig. 5.4). The frequency applied to pins EXTAL and XTAL is always four times higher than the MPU's *system clock* or E-clock. The E-clock synchronizes every action that occurs internal and external to the 68HC11 MPU. You may refer to Section 5.3 to review details on the E-clock signal as well as other timing signals that are not part of the control bus.

RESET Most 8-bit MPUs use this input to get the MPU started upon power-up, or restarted any time thereafter. However, the 68HC11 MPU can be reset four different ways: *external* reset, *power-on* reset (POR), *computer operating properly* (COP) reset, and *clock monitor* reset. During an *external* reset this input is pulsed LOW, and the 68HC11 responds by initializing its internal circuits. As part of this initialization process the 68HC11 MPU loads the contents of memory locations FFFE and FFFF into the program counter (PC). This action places a 16-bit address in the PC to tell the MPU where to go to fetch its first instruction in response to the $\overline{\text{RESET}}$ signal.

The contents of memory locations FFFE and FFFF combine to make a 16-bit address that points to the location of the first instruction to be fetched by the MPU. This address is called the *reset address vector* and is always stored in ROM because it has to be there when power is first applied. The procedure that we have just described for an external reset is the same for a power-on reset. The difference is that the external reset is initiated by the application of a negative-going pulse to the $\overline{\text{RESET}}$ pin, while a power-on reset is internally generated when internal circuitry detects a positive-going transition on the V_{DD} line, thereby initiating a power-on reset by driving the $\overline{\text{RESET}}$ pin LOW. In either case, the contents of memory locations FFFE and FFFF (reset address vector) are loaded into the program counter (PC).

To illustrate, suppose that ROM locations FFFE and FFFF contain 2A and C6, respectively. When the 68HC11 MPU senses an externally activated $\overline{\text{RESET}}$ pin, it automatically does the following:

1. Fetches the contents of ROM address FFFE and loads it into PC_H.
2. Fetches the contents of ROM address FFFF and loads it into PC_L so that **[PC]** is now 2AC6. This is shown symbolically in Fig. 6.2.
3. Begins fetching and executing instructions at address 2AC6.

For proper operation, the pulse at the $\overline{\text{RESET}}$ pin must have a minimum pulse duration. In all four cases of 68HC11 resets, the $\overline{\text{RESET}}$ pin has to be held LOW for at least four E-clock cycles in order for the MPU to stabilize.

It is important to understand that the reset address vector stored in ROM locations FFFE, FFFF directs the MPU to the first instruction to be executed. Generally, this first instruction will be part of a sequence of instructions that the MPU executes to initialize the system. The instructions that make up this initialization sequence will be different depending on the type of system and its application. It will be different for a

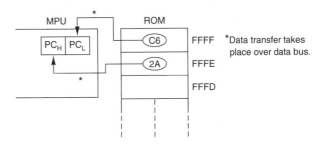

FIGURE 6.2 When reset condition occurs, PC is loaded with new address (Reset Address Vector) from ROM locations FFFE, FFFF.

general-purpose microcomputer than for a dedicated-application microcomputer or a microcontroller. Some of the common functions performed at initialization are

1. Initialize MPU registers (e.g., CCR, Stack Pointer)
2. Initialize I/O device control registers
3. Perform test on system RAM
4. Check status of I/O devices
5. Send messages to output devices (e.g., video display, LEDs, printer) to inform operator of system status or to prompt for input commands

The **computer operating properly reset** (COP reset) was designed to monitor and detect software errors. For instance, a COP failure occurs when the MPU gets "hung up" for an unusual period of time. This may prevent the MPU from executing certain portions of a program within the expected time. Another possibility for a COP failure is a situation where the running program stays in an endless loop awaiting for some signal from an external sensor. The way COP reset is accomplished is by using the 68HC11 internal *watchdog* timer. This timer runs continuously during normal operation of the system and must be continuously reset by appropriate instructions in software before it times out. If for whatever reason the timer does not get reset, a COP failure condition occurs, thereby causing a COP reset. Once a COP reset occurs the program counter (PC) gets loaded with the COP reset vector from ROM locations FFFA and FFFB respectively. The MPU will then fetch the next instruction to be executed from this new address.

The **clock monitor reset** is designed to oversee the E-clock frequency. Should the E-clock frequency drop below 10 KHz, a clock monitor reset is triggered. Once this condition occurs, the program counter (PC) is loaded with the clock monitor reset vector from ROM locations FFFC and FFFD, respectively. The MPU will then fetch and execute its next instruction from this new address.

EXAMPLE 6.1 _____

After a COP reset occurs in a 68HC11 MPU-based system operating in the expanded mode, the MPU is to fetch the first instruction to be executed from memory location $C2AB. What must be done for this to occur?

Solution   In order for the 68HC11 MPU to fetch and execute the first instruction from memory location $C2AB, the COP reset vector must send the MPU to that location. The first thing the MPU does after a COP reset is detected is to fetch the 16-bit address from ROM locations FFFA and FFFB and load it into the program counter (PC). Therefore, ROM locations FFFA and FFFB must hold the data C2 and AB, respectively.

$R/\overline{W}$ This MPU output control signal informs the external devices (memory, I/O) as to whether a READ ($R/\overline{W}$ = 1) or WRITE ($R/\overline{W}$) = 0) operation is being performed. This line in the 68HC11 MPU assumes two different roles depending on which mode of operation is being used. When the 68HC11 MPU is in the expanded mode this line is called the $R/\overline{W}$ line. When the 68HC11 MPU is operating in the single-chip mode it is called strobe

B (STRB) and it can be used as a handshake signal. We will not be using the STRB signal in this textbook.

Load Instruction Register ($\overline{\text{LIR}}$) This output signal is available for debugging purposes when the 68HC11 MPU is operating in the expanded mode. The $\overline{\text{LIR}}$ signal goes LOW during the first cycle of each instruction. This output signal can be used to trigger external testing equipment such as a logic analyzer or oscilloscope to determine the beginning of each new instruction. However, during a reset condition the $\overline{\text{LIR}}$ *output* pin becomes the MODA *input* pin. As previously described, the logic levels present at the mode select inputs (MODA, MODB) during reset will determine the 68HC11 MPU operating mode.

Interrupt Request ($\overline{\text{IRQ}}$) This MPU input is used by I/O devices to *interrupt* the execution of the current program and cause the MPU to load the $\overline{\text{IRQ}}$ interrupt vector located in ROM locations FFF2 and FFF3 into the program counter (PC) and as a result jump to a special program called the $\overline{\text{IRQ}}$ *interrupt service routine*. When a signal from an I/O device drives $\overline{\text{IRQ}}$ LOW, the MPU executes this special program, which normally involves servicing the interrupting device. When this execution is complete, the MPU resumes execution of the program it had been working on when it was interrupted. The $\overline{\text{IRQ}}$ input can be disabled at any time under program control so that the MPU will not respond when $\overline{\text{IRQ}} = 0$.

Nonmaskable Interrupt Request ($\overline{\text{XIRQ}}$) This is another MPU interrupt input but it differs from $\overline{\text{IRQ}}$ in that once enabled its effect cannot be disabled. Immediately after any reset operation, the $\overline{\text{XIRQ}}$ input is disabled in order to allow the 68HC11 MPU-based system to establish initial conditions. After these initial conditions have been established, then the 68HC11 MPU can be software programmed to interrupt when $\overline{\text{XIRQ}} = 0$. Once this procedure is complete and the $\overline{\text{XIRQ}}$ input is enabled it can never be disabled again. The $\overline{\text{XIRQ}}$ interrupt, like $\overline{\text{IRQ}}$, is used by I/O devices to *interrupt* the MPU's execution of the current program and cause the 68HC11 MPU to load the program counter (PC) with the $\overline{\text{XIRQ}}$ interrupt vector located in ROM locations FFF4 and FFF5, respectively. Once the program counter is loaded with the $\overline{\text{XIRQ}}$ interrupt vector, the MPU jumps to a special program called the $\overline{\text{XIRQ}}$ *interrupt service routine* and services the interrupt. We will have much more to say about the 68HC11's interrupt operation in Chapter 8.

▶ 6.3 REGISTER SECTION

The most common operation that takes place inside the MPU is the transfer of binary information from one register to another. The number and types of registers that an MPU contains are key parts of its architecture and have a major effect on programming effort required in a given application. The register structure of different MPUs varies considerably from manufacturer to manufacturer. However, the basic functions performed by the various registers are essentially the same in all MPUs. They are used to store data, addresses, instruction codes, and information on the status of various MPU operations. Some are used as counters that can be controlled by software (program instructions) to keep track of things such as the number of times a particular sequence of instructions has been executed, or the sequential memory locations from which data are to be taken. We will describe the 68HC11 MPU registers (see Fig. 6.1), their functions, and how they can be affected by software. It should be stated that the latter item is an extremely important one from the programmer's viewpoint; this will become increasingly apparent as we get further into programming and applications.

Instruction Register (IR)

The function of the *instruction register* (IR) has already been discussed. When the MPU fetches an instruction word from memory, it sends it to the IR. It is stored there while the instruction decoding circuitry determines which instruction is to be executed. The IR is automatically used by the MPU during each instruction cycle, and the programmer never has a need to access this register. The size of the IR is the same as the word size. Because the 68HC11 is an 8-bit MPU, the IR is 8 bits wide.

Program Counter (PC)

The *program counter* (PC) has also been discussed previously. The PC always contains the address in memory of the next instruction code that the MPU is to fetch. When the MPU's $\overline{\text{RES}}$ input is activated, the PC is set to the address of the first instruction to be executed. The MPU places the contents of the PC on the address bus and fetches the first byte of the instruction from that memory location. (Recall that for 8-bit MPUs, one byte is used for the op code and the following one or two bytes for the operand address.) The MPU automatically increments the PC after each use and in this way executes the stored program sequentially unless the program contains an instruction that alters the sequence (such as a JMP instruction).

The size of the PC depends on the number of address bits the MPU can handle. The 68HC11 MPU uses 16-bit addresses; therefore, its PC is 16 bits. However, the PC is divided into two smaller registers, PC_H and PC_L, each of which holds one-half of an address. This is illustrated in Fig. 6.1. PC_H holds the 8 high-order bits of the 16-bit address, and PC_L holds the 8 low-order bits. The reason for using PC_H and PC_L is that, as we will see later, it is often necessary to store the contents of PC in memory. Because the memory stores 8-bit words, the 16-bit PC must be broken into two halves and stored in two successive memory locations.

The programmer has no *direct* access to the PC. That is, there are no direct instructions to load the PC from memory or to store the PC contents in memory. However, there are many instructions that cause the PC to take on a value other than its normal sequential value. JMP (*unconditional* jump) is an example of an instruction that changes the PC so that the MPU executes instructions out of their normal sequential order.

Data Address Register (DAR)

The *data address register* (DAR) is sometimes called a *memory address register* or an *address latching register*. It is used to hold the address of data that the MPU is reading from or writing into memory. For example, when executing an ADD instruction, the MPU places the operand address portion of the ADD instruction into the DAR. The contents of the DAR are then placed on the address bus so that the MPU can fetch the data that is to be added to accumulator A or accumulator B.

Accumulator

The *accumulator* is a register that takes part in most of the operations performed by the ALU. It is also the register in which the results are placed after most ALU operations. In many ALU instructions, the accumulator is the source of one of the operands and the destination of the result.

In addition to its use in ALU instructions, the accumulator has other uses; for instance, it can be used as a storage register for data that are being sent to an output device or as a receiving register for data that are being read from an input device. The 68HC11 MPU has two 8-bit accumulators, A and B (ACCA, ACCB), which speeds up program execution by allowing two operands to remain in the MPU. Since addition and subtraction instructions can be performed involving both accumulators, the process is faster because no extra clock cycles are required to fetch the second operand from some memory location. The instruction op codes specify which accumulator is to be used; for example, if the contents of a memory location is to be *loaded into accumulator A* (LDAA), the op code $B6_{16}$ would be specified. However, if we wanted to load the contents of that same memory location into accumulator B (LDAB), the op code would be $F6_{16}$.

As stated earlier, sometimes ACCA and ACCB are combined into a 16-bit accumulator D (ACCD).

General-Purpose Registers

Although the 68HC11 MPU has no specific *general-purpose register,* the accumulators can perform the functions of a general-purpose register in many programming situations. General-purpose registers are used for many of the temporary storage functions required inside the MPU. They can be used to store data that are used frequently during a program, thereby speeding up program execution since the MPU does not have to perform a memory READ operation each time the data are needed.

There are normally several instructions which the programmer can use to access a general-purpose register (GP). The most common are

1. Load GP from memory: $[M] \rightarrow [GP]$
2. Store GP in memory: $[GP] \rightarrow [M]$
3. Transfer contents of one GP register to another GP register: $[GP_1] \rightarrow [GP_2]$
4. Increment GP by 1: $[GP + 1] \rightarrow [GP]$
5. Decrement GP by 1: $[GP - 1] \rightarrow [GP]$

The last two instructions are extremely useful to a programmer. They allow the GP to be used as an up or down counter to keep track of the number of times a particular operation or sequence of operations is executed. This is illustrated in Fig. 6.3, which shows a *flowchart* of a portion of a program. A flowchart, as described in Section 4.17, is essentially a block diagram showing the sequence of major steps in a program. It is used to document the logical operation of a program such that any programmer can look at it and determine what the program is doing. The programmer usually lays out the flowchart prior to actually writing the program; this is especially helpful in complex programs containing many branches.

The flowchart in Fig. 6.3 represents a small portion of a larger program flowchart. It shows how **GP** is used as a down counter to keep track of the number of times the instruction sequence in block 2 is executed. At the start of the program **GP** is loaded from memory with value COUNT (block 1). COUNT represents the number of times the programmer wants the sequence in block 2 to be executed. After executing block 2, the contents of **GP** is decremented (block 3). The program then moves to block 4, which is called a *decision* block. A decision block is always drawn in the shape of a diamond. In this block, the new contents of the **GP** is examined to see if it is exactly zero. If **[GP]** ≠ 0, the program will branch back to block 2 to execute the sequence there. If **[GP]** = 0, the program will go on to block 5. This can be accomplished with a branch instruction such as Branch If Not Equal to Zero (BNE).

It should be clear that the program will execute blocks 2, 3, and 4 for a number of times equal to COUNT, at which time **[GP]** will have been decremented to 0, causing the program to go to block 5. For the 68HC11 MPU, either ACCA or ACCB could have been used as **GP** in this example. As pointed out in the diagram, the portion of the program that gets executed several times is called a *program loop*. Program loops are very common in

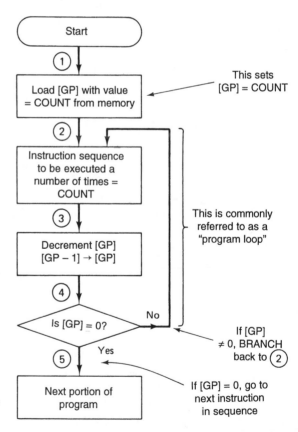

FIGURE 6.3   Flowchart that illustrates the use of a general-purpose register as a counter.

all but the simplest programs. In fact, many programs use more than one MPU register as counters to produce a loop within a loop. More will be said on this in our work on µC programming.

Index Register

The 68HC11 MPU has two 16-bit index registers: index register X and index register Y. An *index register,* like a general-purpose register, can be used for general MPU storage functions and as a counter. In addition, it has a special function that is of great use in a program where tables or arrays of data must be handled. In this function, the index register takes part in determining the addresses of data the MPU is accessing. This operation is called *index addressing* and is a special form of addressing available to the programmer. There are several different forms of indexed addressing that are used by different types of MPUs. We will describe one of the most common forms here and show how it can be valuable in certain types of programming operations used by the 68HC11.

The basic idea of indexed addressing is that the *actual* or *effective* operand address called for by an instruction is the sum of the *offset* portion of the instruction plus the *contents* of the index register, X or Y in the case of the 68HC11 MPU. To illustrate, let us assume that index register X holds the *base* address $C450_{16}$. Let us also assume that the 68HC11 MPU is executing a Load Accumulator A instruction using indexed addressing. The symbolic code for this instruction would be LDAA IND, X. The IND stands for index addressing and represents the offset value to be added to [**X**]. For the 68HC11 MPU, the offset is always a single byte. This instruction is illustrated below:

Address	Instruction code	Mnemonic	Description
C000	A6	LDAA $04, X	; Load accumulator A from address [**X**] + 04.
C001	04		; Offset byte.

To execute this instruction, the 68HC11 MPU fetches the op code A6 from memory location C000. It determines that an LDAA IND, X operation is to be performed in which a data word is to be loaded into accumulator A. The effective address of the data word is determined by taking the 8-bit offset portion of this instruction from memory location C001 and *adding* to it the contents of index register X. Thus,

$$\text{effective address} = \text{offset} + [\mathbf{X}]$$

$$= 04 + C450$$

$$= C454$$

This effective address C454, then, is the address from which the 68HC11 MPU reads the data word to be placed into accumulator A. The operation described above can also be accomplished by using index register [**Y**]. Let us assume that the [**Y**] register holds the base address $C450_{16}$. The code would look somewhat different because the instruction involves register [Y]. Recall from Section 4.9 that the 68HC11 MPU uses a prebyte any time an instruction uses the Y register. Hence, the instruction would look as follows:

Address	Instruction code	Mnemonic	Description
C000	18	LDAA $04, Y	; Load accumulator A from
C001	A6		; address [Y] + 04.
C002	04		; Offset byte.

In this case the instruction starts out with the prebyte 18, which indicates that the next byte is the op code of an instruction that uses the [Y] index register. This prebyte will precede *all* 68HC11 MPU instructions that involve the [Y] index register.

Whether we use the [X] register or the [Y] register the effective address of the data word is determined the same way. The only difference is that now the 8-bit offset portion of this instruction is the *third* byte of the instruction and in this case is taken from memory location C002. Thus,

$$\text{effective address} = \text{offset} + [Y]$$

$$= 04 + C450$$

$$= C454$$

As this example has shown, the actual address from which data are to be taken depends on the current contents of index register X or index register Y. If the contents of X or Y are changed and this instruction is repeated, a new data address would be used. This characteristic makes indexed addressing extremely useful in handling tables of data stored in memory. This is illustrated in the following example.

EXAMPLE 6.2

A table of seven data words is stored in memory locations 2061 through 2067. Draw the flowchart for a program that will add these seven data words and store the sum in memory location address 2068. Use indexed addressing.

Solution   The required flowchart is shown in Fig 6.4. Examine it closely and note the following important points:

1. Accumulators A and B are cleared to zero before any ADD operation occurs.
2. Index register [X] is initially loaded with the number 2067.
3. Accumulator B is initially loaded with 07, which is the number of memory locations to be added. ACCB is being used to count down the number of times that blocks 5–8 are executed.
4. The instructions in blocks 5–8 are executed a total of *seven* times before ACCB is decremented to 00 and the program goes to block 9 to store the final sum in memory location 2068.

5. The ADD operation (block 5) is executed using data from a different address each time, starting with 2067 and ending with 2061. In this way, the complete table of data has been added to accumulator A.

This example only begins to illustrate the usefulness of indexed addressing. Without indexed addressing, the flowchart for adding the seven data words would require drawing the ADD operation block seven times with a different memory address each time. The comparison becomes even more dramatic if a larger number of data words are to be added. For

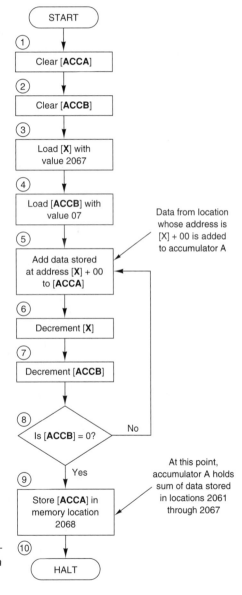

FIGURE 6.4 Flowchart of a short program that uses indexed addressing to add seven numbers stored in sequential memory locations.

instance, to add 50 data words the flowchart of Fig. 6.4 would remain basically the same except that the initial value of ACCB would be changed to $32_{16} = 50_{10}$. The flowchart of Fig. 6.4 can also be drawn using the index Y register instead of the index X register; the end result would be exactly the same. A detailed description of index addressing appears in Chapter 7.

Condition Code Register (CCR)

Also often referred to as a *status register* or *process status register,* the *condition code register* consists of individual bits with different meanings assigned by the MPU manufacturer. These bits are called *flags,* and each flag is used to indicate the status of a particular MPU condition. The logic value of some of the flags can be examined under program control to determine what sequence of instructions to follow. We will define and describe the 8 bits that constitute the condition code register for the 68HC11 MPU.

b_7	b_6	b_5	b_4	b_3	b_2	b_1	b_0
S	X	H	I	N	Z	V	C

C: The *Carry* flag reflects the carry status of arithmetic operations such as addition and subtraction. For example, if the 68HC11 MPU is performing an addition instruction where it adds two 8-bit data words, the value of the carry out of the MSB position becomes the value of the Carry flag.

   The C flag bit also takes part in various shift and rotate instructions, and can be set or cleared using the program instructions SEC and CLC, respectively. These attributes are discussed more fully in Chapter 7.

V: The *Overflow* flag is used to indicate overflow whenever signed numbers are being added or subtracted. Recall that for signed numbers, the MSB (bit 7) is used as a sign bit with 0 = positive and 1 = negative. This leaves 7 bits to represent the magnitude of a number, giving a range from -128_{10} to $+127_{10}$ that can be represented in 8 bits. The overflow flag is automatically set HIGH whenever an arithmetic operation produces a result outside this range.

   The V flag can be cleared or set by the programmer using the CLV or SEV instructions, respectively.

Z: The *Zero* flag is automatically set to 1 whenever any arithmetic, data transfer, or data manipulation operation produces a zero result. Z is automatically cleared to 0 for any other result; that is, a nonzero result.

N: The *Negative* flag is used to indicate the sign of the result of any arithmetic, data manipulation, or data transfer operation. In fact, the N flag is *always* equal to the sign bit of the result; that is, bit 7 for 8-bit operations and bit 15 for 16-bit operations.

I: The *Interrupt Mask* flag is used to indicate whether the effects of the 68HC11's Interrupt Request pin ($\overline{\text{IRQ}}$) have been disabled. When I = 1, the effect of $\overline{\text{IRQ}}$ is disabled; when I = 0, the $\overline{\text{IRQ}}$ input can be used to interrupt the microprocessor.

   The I flag can be set or cleared by the programmer using SEI and CLI instructions. It is also set or cleared automatically by the MPU at various times. This is discussed in Chapter 8.

H: The *Half-Carry* flag is changed only by addition instructions. H = 1 when the addition produces a carry out of bit position 3 and into bit position 4. This indicates that if these data represent the addition of BCD digits, the sum has produced an illegal BCD code, and therefore, needs to be corrected. Therefore, whenever the programmer is performing addition using BCD data, he or she must follow the addition instruction with a Decimal Adjust Accumulator A (DAA) instruction. This instruction tells the 68HC11 MPU to check the H and C flags to determine the proper correction factor to be added to the result. The DAA operation will adjust the contents of ACCA and the C bit to represent the correct binary-coded decimal sum and the correct state of the Carry flag. Note that in the 68HC11 MPU the DAA instruction is used only with accumulator A, and consequently accumulator A must hold the result of the BCD addition.

X: The *X Interrupt Mask* flag is used to indicate whether the effects of the 68HC11's Nonmaskable Interrupt Request pin ($\overline{\text{XIRQ}}$) have been enabled. When X = 1, the effect of $\overline{\text{XIRQ}}$ is disabled; when X = 0, the $\overline{\text{XIRQ}}$ input can be used to interrupt the microprocessor. The X flag is somewhat similar to the I flag. However, the X flag cannot be as easily set or cleared as the I flag. For example, there is no instruction that can change the condition of the X flag from zero to one. When the 68HC11 MPU is first turned on or after any reset condition, the X flag gets set automatically. For a short time after a reset occurs, some initial conditioning of internal circuitry of the MPU takes place. Only then may the X flag be cleared with a *Transfer Accumulator A to the Condition Code Register* (TAP) instruction, thereby enabling the $\overline{\text{XIRQ}}$ input pin. Once the X flag is enabled (X = 0) it can never again be disabled by the programmer, hence the name nonmaskable interrupt. The reasons why the $\overline{\text{XIRQ}}$ works this way will be further discussed in Chapter 8.

S: The *Stop Disable* flag is used to prevent the STOP instruction from being executed. The STOP instruction, once executed, causes the oscillator and all of the 68HC11 MCU clocks to stop. This instruction is used when a drastic reduction in power consumption is desired. Clearly, the execution of this instruction at the wrong time can be disastrous. That is why the execution of this instruction is dependent on the condition of the S bit. The S bit is set during reset and at this time the STOP instruction, should it be executed by mistake, is treated as if it is a *No Operation* (NOP) instruction. The NOP instruction causes only the program counter to be incremented and no other MPU registers are affected. The programmer can either set or clear the S flag with a TAP instruction.

Conditional Branching

An example of the most common use of flags involves *conditional branch* instructions. The 68HC11 MPU instruction set contains several conditional branch instructions that can change the sequence of instructions to be executed depending on the flag values. The Branch If Equal to Zero (BEQ) instruction is a prime example. When the MPU executes the BEQ instruction, it examines the value of the Zero flag. If the Zero flag is LOW, indicating that the previous instruction produced a *nonzero* result, the next instruction to be executed will be taken in normal sequence. If the Zero flag is HIGH, indicating a *zero* result, the program will branch to a new address for its next instruction. The new address is calculated by adding the *offset,* which is part of the branch instruction, to the contents of the program counter (PC). The 68HC11 MPU will continue in sequence from this new location. Other examples are Branch If Carry Clear (BCC) and Branch If Carry Set (BCS), both of which examine the Carry flag. There are more than twenty such instructions in the 68HC11 MPU instruction set. We will introduce all of these conditional branch instructions and show the details of their operation in the next chapter.

Stack Pointer Register

Before defining the function of the stack pointer register, we must define the *stack.* The stack is a portion of RAM reserved for the temporary storage and retrieval of information, typically the contents of the MPU's internal registers. This area of memory is called a stack because it operates as follows:

1. Each time a word is to be stored in this area of RAM, it is placed in an address location that is one less than the address of the previous word stored on the stack. To help illustrate this, refer to Fig. 6.5. Let us assume that we have four words that we want to store on the stack. Word A, the first word, will be stored at address 0165. Word B, the second word, will be stored at address 0164. Similarly, word C goes into address 0163 and word D into 0162.

2. Words stored on the stack are read from the stack in the opposite order from that in which they were placed on the stack. Referring to Fig. 6.5, this means that word D must be read first, then word C, word B, and finally word A.

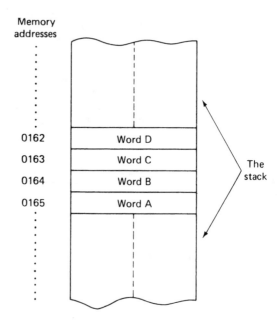

FIGURE 6.5   Words are removed from the stack in the opposite order (D, C, B, A) from that in which they were placed on the stack (A, B, C, D).

3. Once a word is read from the stack, its location on the stack is available for storage.

The operation of the stack can be likened to the manner in which we stack plates in a cupboard. Each time we add a plate to the stack, we place it on top of the stack; each time we remove a plate from the stack, we take it from the top of the stack. The last plate placed on the stack is the first plate removed from the stack. In fact, this type of stack is often referred to as a *last-in, first-out* (LIFO) stack.

This brings us to the *stack pointer register* (SP). This register acts as a special memory address register used only for the stack portion of RAM. Whenever a word is to be stored on the stack, it is stored at the address contained in the SP. Similarly, whenever a word is to be read from the stack, it is read from the address specified by the SP. The contents of the SP are initialized by the programmer at the beginning of the program. Thereafter, the SP is automatically decremented *after* a word is stored on the stack and incremented *before* a word is read from the stack. (The incrementing and decrementing are done automatically by the MPU controls section.)

The operation of the SP is illustrated in Fig. 6.6. Let us assume that the most recent stack operation stored a word in location 0164. After the operation, the SP was decremented to 0163 to indicate that location 0163 is the next location available on the stack.* This is symbolized in Fig. 6.6 by the SP pointing to location 0163. If the next stack operation is a store, a word will be stored in 0163 and the SP will be decremented to 0162. Another store operation will place a word in 0162 and decrement the SP to 0161. Now, let us assume that a stack READ operation is to be performed. The stack pointer is pointing to

---

*The 68HC11 SP always points to the next available storage location on the stack.

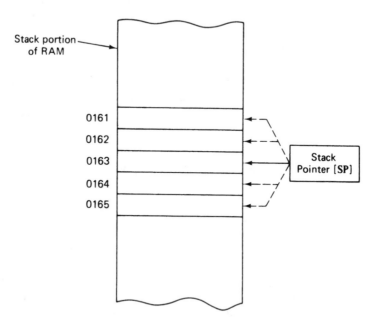

FIGURE 6.6 The stack pointer register always points to the next available location on the stack.

0161 and is automatically incremented to 0162 and the word stored there is read by the MPU. Similarly, subsequent READ operations would increment the SP to 0163, 0164, 0165, and so on.

Several situations exist in which the stack portion of memory is used. As we shall see later, the MPU *automatically* saves return addresses and other critical information on the stack during subroutine calls and interrupts. The programmer can also store data and information on the stack at any time by using special instructions. For example, the contents of the accumulator can be stored on the stack using an instruction of the type

PSHA   *Push* accumulator A on the stack

This instruction stores **[ACCA]** at the stack location indicated by the SP and then decrements the SP.

The opposite operation can be performed using an instruction such as

PULA   *pull* accumulator A off the stack

This instruction causes the SP to be incremented, and then loads accumulator A from the stack location indicated by the SP. These push and pull instructions are useful because the programmer does not have to specify a memory address. The address is, of course, specified by the SP.

The MPU takes care of incrementing and decrementing the SP, so the programmer really does not have to worry about that aspect of the operation. The programmer, however, must take care to initialize the SP and ensure that the SP never points to locations outside the RAM area reserved for the stack; otherwise, a stack storage operation might write over a word in the program or data area of RAM. For the 68HC11 MPU the SP register is 16 bits long, allowing the programmer the freedom to place the stack anywhere in RAM. The stack is located by the programmer initializing the SP register. This is done by loading the address where the stack is to be located into the SP register using an LDS (Load Stack Pointer) instruction. In addition, the programmer must be sure to take words off the stack in the reverse order in which they were placed on the stack. In Chapter 7 we will see how the stack and stack pointer are used by the programmer.

68HC11 MPU Programming Model

An MPU is often represented by its *programming model,* which shows only those internal registers that the programmer can directly control via the MPU's instruction set. Figure 6.7 shows the 68HC11 programming model consisting of two 8-bit accumulators (ACCA and ACCB), a 16-bit double accumulator D (ACCD) which is really just the combination of ACCA and ACCB, 16-bit X and Y index registers, a 16-bit stack pointer, a 16-bit program counter, and an 8-bit condition code register.

A programming model is valuable because it shows the registers that the programmer has to work with when he or she writes programs for the MPU. It is particularly useful for comparing different microprocessors.

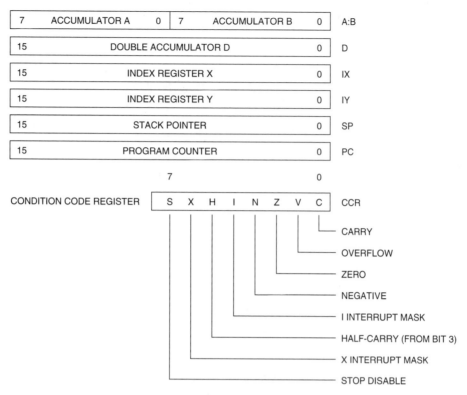

| 7 | ACCUMULATOR A | 0 | 7 | ACCUMULATOR B | 0 | A:B |

| 15 | DOUBLE ACCUMULATOR D | 0 | D |

| 15 | INDEX REGISTER X | 0 | IX |

| 15 | INDEX REGISTER Y | 0 | IY |

| 15 | STACK POINTER | 0 | SP |

| 15 | PROGRAM COUNTER | 0 | PC |

7   0

CONDITION CODE REGISTER | S | X | H | I | N | Z | V | C | CCR

- CARRY
- OVERFLOW
- ZERO
- NEGATIVE
- I INTERRUPT MASK
- HALF-CARRY (FROM BIT 3)
- X INTERRUPT MASK
- STOP DISABLE

FIGURE 6.7 M68HC11 programmer's model.

▶ 6.4 ARITHMETIC/LOGIC UNIT

Most modern MPUs have arithmetic/logic units (ALUs) that are capable of performing a wide variety of arithmetic and logic operations. These operations can involve two operands, such as accumulator A and a data word from memory, or accumulator A and another MPU internal register. Some of the operations involve only a single operand, such as accumulator B, a register, or a word from memory.

A simplified diagram of the 68HC11 ALU is shown in Fig. 6.8. The ALU block represents all the logic circuitry used to perform arithmetic, logic, and manipulation operations on the operand inputs. Two 8-bit operands (operands 1 and 2) are shown as inputs to the ALU, although frequently only one operand is used. Also shown as an input to the ALU is the Carry flag, C, from the MPU condition code register (CCR). The reason for this will be explained later. The functions the ALU will perform are determined by the control signal inputs from the MPU control section.

The ALU produces two sets of outputs. One set is an 8-bit output representing the results of the operation performed on the operands. The other is a set of condition signals that are sent to the MPU condition code register to set or clear various flag bits. For example, if the result of an ALU operation is exactly zero, a signal is sent to the Z flag in the CCR to

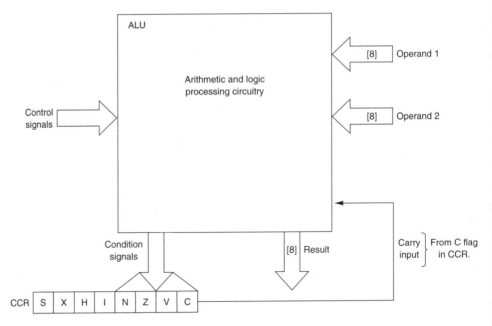

FIGURE 6.8   Simplified diagram of the 68HC11's ALU.

set it to the HIGH state. If the result of the ALU operation produces a carry into the ninth bit position, a signal is sent to set the C flag in the CCR. Other signals from the ALU will set or clear the N and V flags.

The operand inputs 1 and 2 can come from several sources. When two operands are to be operated on by the ALU, one of the operands always comes from accumulator A or B, and the other operand often comes from a data word fetched from memory that is stored in a data buffer register within the MPU (see Fig. 6.1). In some operations the second operand can be the contents of the other accumulator. The result of the ALU operation performed on the two operands is normally sent to the accumulator. If the two operands are ACCA and ACCB, the result is always sent to ACCA. Several of the 68HC11 instructions use the double accumulator D as a 16-bit operand along with a 16-bit operand from memory (two successive bytes) as inputs to the ALU to be arithmetically combined.

When only one operand is to be operated on by the ALU, the operand can be the contents of accumulator A, accumulator B, an index register, or a memory data word. The result of the ALU operation is then sent back to the source of the operand. When the single operand is a memory word, the result is sent to a data buffer register, from where the MPU writes it back into the memory location of the original operand.

Single-Operand Operations

We will now describe some of the ALU operations performed on a single operand.

1. **CLEAR.** All bits of the operand are cleared to 0. If the operand comes from accumulator A, for example, we can symbolically represent this operation as $0 \longrightarrow$ **[ACCA]**.

2. **COMPLEMENT (or Invert).** All bits are changed to their opposite logic level. If the operand comes from accumulator A, for example, this operation is represented as $[\overline{ACCA}] \longrightarrow [ACCA]$. If the operand comes from memory, this operation is represented as $[\overline{M}] \longrightarrow [M]$. The 68HC11 MPU has instructions that can complement (1's-complement) the contents of either accumulator or the contents of any memory location. In all cases the original operand is replaced by its complement.

3. **NEGATE.** This instruction replaces the operand with its 2's-complement value. This is accomplished by subtracting the operand from 00_{16}. For example, if accumulator A is loaded with 01_{16} and then the negate instruction NEGA is executed, the result will be $00_{16} - 01_{16} = FF_{16}$, which of course is the negative of 01_{16}. Assuming that accumulator A is being negated, this instruction can be symbolically represented as $0 - [ACCA] \longrightarrow [ACCA]$. The 68HC11 MPU has instructions that can negate (2's-complement) either one of the accumulators (NEGA, NEGB) or the operand of any memory location.

4. **INCREMENT.** The operand is increased by 1. For example, if the operand is 11010011, it will have 00000001 added to it in the ALU to produce a result of 11010100. This instruction is very useful when the program is using one of the MPU registers as a counter. Symbolically, this is represented as $[ACCA + 1] \longrightarrow [ACCA]$. The 68HC11 MPU has increment instructions that use the 8-bit accumulators A and B (INCA, INCB), the 16-bit index registers X and Y (INX, INY), and the 16-bit stack pointer (INS).

5. **DECREMENT.** The operand is decreased by 1. In other words, the number 00000001 is subtracted from the operand. This instruction is useful in programs where a register is used to count down from an initial value, as was done in our earlier examples of general-purpose and index registers (Figs. 6.3 and 6.4). Symbolically, the operation is represented as $[ACCA - 1] \longrightarrow [ACCA]$. The 68HC11 MPU has decrement instructions that use the 8-bit accumulators A and B (DECA, DECB), the 16-bit index registers X and Y (DEX, DEY), and the 16-bit stack pointer (DES).

6. **EXCHANGE.** This instruction is not available on all MPUs; however, the 68HC11 MPU has two instructions (XGDX, XGDY) that allow us to exchange the contents of the double accumulator D (ACCD) with the contents of either one of the index registers. Assuming that we are using the X register, symbolically the operation would be represented as $[X] \longleftrightarrow [ACCD]$. This instruction is very useful when 16-bit arithmetic operations are to be performed on an index register. These 68HC11 MPU instructions, like some others that we have not yet talked about, do not affect any of the flags in the condition code register.

7. **SHIFT.** The bits of the operand are shifted to the left or to the right one place, the empty bit is made 0, and the bit shifted out gets shifted into the Carry flag bit, C, of the condition code register. This process is illustrated below for an Arithmetic Shift Left (ASL) operation.

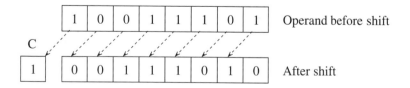

Note that a 0 is shifted into the rightmost bit. Also, note that the original leftmost bit is shifted out and is shifted into the Carry flag bit, C, of the condition code register. Another illustration is shown below for a Logic Shift Right (LSR) operation.

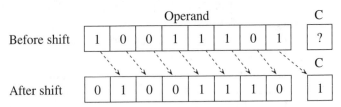

Note that a 0 is shifted into the leftmost bit and also note that the original rightmost bit is shifted into C (the original value of C is lost).

These types of operations are used by the programmer to test the value of a specific bit in an operand. This is done by shifting the operand the required number of times until the bit value is in the C flag. A Conditional Branch instruction is then used to test the C flag to determine what instruction to execute next. The 68HC11 MPU allows the operation referred to as Arithmetic Shift Right (ASR). The ASR operation shifts each bit to the right and moves the LSB into the Carry flag bit. The MSB, however, is shifted to the right and also retained in the MSB position. This method of shifting, when using a 2's-complement number, preserves the sign of the operand allowing the equivalent of dividing the operand by 2. This process is illustrated below for an Arithmetic Shift Right (ASR) operation.

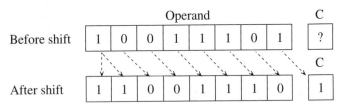

8. **ROTATE.** This is a modified SHIFT operation in which the C flag becomes part of a circulating shift register along with the operand; that is, the value shifted out of the operand is shifted into C and the previous value of C is shifted into the empty bit of the operand. This is illustrated below for a ROTATE-RIGHT (ROR) operation.

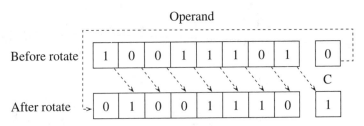

Note that the original C bit is shifted into the leftmost bit of the operand and that the rightmost bit of the operand is shifted into C. A ROTATE-LEFT (ROL) operates in the same manner except in the opposite direction.

Two-Operand ALU Operations

The circuitry in the ALU performs the *add* and *subtract* operations in the binary number system and always treats the two operands as 8-bit binary numbers. This is true even when the program calls for BCD arithmetic, the only difference being the extra steps needed to correct the BCD result by use of the Decimal Adjust Accumulator A (DAA) instruction following the add accumulator A instruction (ADDA). You should be aware that the DAA instruction works only with accumulator A, since it assumes that the result of the previous sum is in accumulator A.

With an 8-bit data word, decimal numbers from 0 to 255 can be represented in binary code, assuming that all 8 bits are used for the numerical value. However, if the programmer wishes to use both positive and negative numbers, the MSB of each data word is used as the *sign* bit. The other 7 bits of each data word represent the magnitude; for positive numbers the magnitude is in true binary form, while for negative numbers the magnitude is in 2's-complement form.

The beauty of this method for representing signed numbers is that it requires no special operations by the ALU. The circuitry in the ALU will perform addition and subtraction on the two operands in the same manner regardless of whether the operands are unsigned 8-bit data words or 7-bit data words plus a sign bit. As was shown in Chapter 1, the sign bit participates in the add and subtract operations just like the rest of the bits. What this means is that the MPU really does not know or care whether the data it is processing are signed or unsigned. Only the programmer is concerned about the distinction, and he or she must at all times know the format of the data being used in the program.

As an aid to the programmer, almost all MPUs transfer the value of bit 7 of the ALU result to a flag bit in the condition code register. For the 68HC11 MPU, it is the Negative flag, N. N will be set to 1 if the ALU result has a 1 in bit 7 and will be cleared to 0 if bit 7 is a 0. The program can then test to see whether the result was positive or negative by performing a Conditional Branch instruction based on the Sign flag. For example, a Branch-if-minus instruction (BMI) will cause the 68HC11 MPU to examine the N flag in the condition code register to determine what sequence of instructions to follow next. We will now discuss some of the ALU operations performed on two operands.

1. **ADD.** The ALU produces the binary sum of two operands. Typically, one of the operands comes from one of the accumulators, the other from memory, and the result is sent to the accumulator. Symbolically, this operation is **[ACCX] + [M] $\longrightarrow$ [ACCX]**, where ACCX can be either ACCA or ACCB. Since the 68HC11 MPU has two accumulators (ACCA, ACCB), the two operands to be added can also come from each accumulator. The result is then sent to accumulator A as symbolically represented here: **[ACCA] + [ACCB] $\longrightarrow$ [ACCA]**. The advantage of this operation is that no cycles are used to fetch data from memory for this addition. If the addition of the two operands produces a carry out of the MSB position, the Carry flag, C, in the condition code register is set to 1. Otherwise, C is cleared to 0. In other words, C serves as the ninth bit of the result.

2. **SUBTRACT.** The ALU subtracts one operand (obtained from memory) from the second operand (one of the accumulators) and places the result in the accumulator.

Symbolically, this is **[ACCX]** − **[M]** ⟶ **[ACCX]**. Using the 2's-complement method of subtraction (Chapter 1), the operand from memory is 2's-complemented and then added to the operand from the accumulator. Also, accumulator B can be subtracted from accumulator A as shown symbolically **[ACCA]** − **[ACCB]** ⟶ **[ACCA]**. Once again, the Carry bit generated by this operation is stored in the C flag.

3. **MULTIPLY.** The 68HC11 MPU instruction multiplies the 8-bit unsigned binary number in accumulator A by the 8-bit unsigned binary number in accumulator B and places the product in the double accumulator D. This instruction is not available in most 8-bit MPUs. However, all 8-bit MPUs can perform multiplications of two operands through a series of shifting and adding operations. This sequence of instructions which the programmer develops for performing such complex arithmetic operations is called a subroutine. A multiplication subroutine for obtaining the product of two 8-bit numbers might consist of as many as 20 or 30 instruction steps, requiring 200 μs to execute. The 68HC11 MPU can execute this single-byte multiplication instruction (MUL) in about 5 μs. Symbolically, this operation can be shown as **[ACCA]** × **[ACCB]** ⟶ **[ACCD]**.

4. **INTEGER DIVIDE.** This 68HC11 MPU instruction divides an unsigned 16-bit operand in the double accumulator D by a 16-bit operand in the index register X. The resulting quotient is placed in the index register X and the remainder is placed in the double accumulator D. As with the multiplication instruction, the divide instruction is not available in most 8-bit MPUs. By using a similar subroutine technique as that mentioned for the multiplication, 8-bit MPUs can divide one operand by another by performing a series of shifting and subtracting operations. The 68HC11 MPU can execute this single-byte divide instruction (IDIV) in about 20 μs. Symbolically, this operation can be shown as **[ACCD]** / **[X]** ⟶ **[X]** ; r ⟶ **[ACCD]**.

5. **COMPARE.** This operation is the same as subtraction except that the result is not placed in the accumulator. Symbolically, this is **[ACCX]** − **[M]** or **[ACCA]** − **[ACCB]**. The subtraction is performed solely as a means for determining which operand is larger without affecting the contents of the accumulator. Depending on whether the result is positive, negative, or zero, various condition flags will be affected. The programmer can then use Conditional Branch instructions to test these flags. The 68HC11 MPU also has instructions that will allow us to compare either one of the 16-bit index registers (CPX, CPY) or the double accumulator D (CPD) with any 16-bit number stored in two consecutive memory locations.

6. **LOGICAL AND.** The corresponding bits of the two operands are ANDed and the result is placed in the accumulator. Symbolically, this is written **[ACCX]** · **[M]** ⟶ **[ACCX]**. One of the operands is always one of the accumulators and the other comes from memory. Consequently, the 68HC11 MPU has just two instructions (ANDA, ANDB) that we can use to logically AND two operands. As an example, let us assume that **[ACCA]** = 10110101 and **[M]** = 01100001. The ANDA operation is performed as follows:

bit → numbers	7	6	5	4	3	2	1	0	
	1	0	1	1	0	1	0	1	Original contents of ACCA

0	1	1	0	0	0	0	1

Operand from memory

0	0	1	0	0	0	0	1

Result of AND that is sent to ACCA

Note that each bit of the result is obtained by ANDing the corresponding bits of the operands. For example, bit 7 of the result is $1 \cdot 0 = 0$. Similarly, bit 5 of each operand is a 1, so bit 5 of the result is $1 \cdot 1 = 1$.

7. **LOGICAL OR (Inclusive-OR).** The corresponding bits of the two operands are ORed and the result is placed in the accumulator. Symbolically, this is shown as **[ACCX] OR [M]** $\longrightarrow$ **[ACCX]**. A plus sign (+) can be used in place of OR, but it might cause confusion with the binary addition operation. As with the AND instructions, the 68HC11 MPU has only two OR instructions (ORAA, ORAB) that we can use to logically OR two operands. Using the same two operands used in the illustration of the AND operation above, the result of the OR (sometimes called *inclusive-OR*) operation will be 11110101.

8. **EXCLUSIVE-OR.** The corresponding bits of the two operands are EX-ORed and the result is placed in the accumulator. Symbolically, this is **[ACCX]** $\oplus$ **[M]** $\longrightarrow$ **[ACCX]**. Using the same two operands used in prior illustrations, the result of the EX-OR operation will be 11010100. Once again, as with the AND and OR instructions the 68HC11 MPU has only two EX-OR instructions (EORA, EORB) that we can use to logically EX-OR two operands. The logic AND, OR, and EX-OR operations are very useful to a programmer. We examine some of their uses in Chapter 7.

This list of arithmetic/logic operations includes the uncommon multiplication and division instructions that are available in the 68HC11 MPU, but does not include the more complex operations of square roots, trigonometric operations, logarithms, and so on. These operations are not explicitly performed by most currently available 8-bit MPUs because of the extra circuitry they would require. To perform such operations, the programmer can instruct the MPU to execute subroutines consisting of appropriate series of simple arithmetic operations much like the ones mentioned for the multiplication and division operations. This method, however, may take too long to execute and may not be a viable option. If a long execution time is undesirable, it is possible to use an external LSI chip containing a high-speed multiplier or divider. Such LSI multipliers and dividers are available with execution times in nanoseconds, and can be connected to the MPU as I/O devices. Also, there are arithmetic processor chips, which can be interfaced to an MPU to perform most of the operations available on a scientific calculator. These chips are fairly expensive and are used only when many high-speed computations are required. Another alternative to slow subroutines is to use a ROM as a storage table which can store such data as multiplication tables, trigonometric tables, and logarithmic tables.

▶ 6.5 MICROPROCESSORS—CATEGORIZED BY ALU SIZE

The most common way to categorize microprocessors is by the number of bits in the data words that their ALU operates on at one time. For example, if an MPU has an ALU that can perform arithmetic/logic operations on 8-bit operands, then it is referred to as an 8-bit MPU. Similarly, a 16-bit MPU would have an ALU that is capable of operating on 16-bit operands. Recall that the 68HC11 MCU (microcontroller unit) chip contains a built-in MPU. That built-in MPU, as we have seen above, can perform operations on 8-bit operands and 16-bit operands. Technically, however, it is an 8-bit processor because its ALU performs its 16-bit operations eight bits at a time. Thus, the 68HC11 MPU is classified as an 8-bit MPU.

The bit size of the MPU is an important factor in determining the speed at which an MPU can perform tasks that require many computations or the processing of large amounts of data. An MPU that can handle data words with a greater number of bits will generally execute such tasks more efficiently. For instance, a 16-bit MPU can process data words of 16 bits in one operation rather than in two consecutive 8-bit operations. In general, we can say that MPUs with a larger word size are better at performing complex scientific/ engineering calculations—what we often call "number crunching."

▶ 6.6 MICROPROCESSORS—TWO DIRECTIONS

The first commercially available microprocessor was the Intel 4004, a 4-bit device produced in 1971. For the past 28 years, as designers have discovered more and more applications for microprocessors, the microprocessor manufacturers have responded by developing devices with the features, enhancements, and performance improvements needed to meet these needs. Over this period, microprocessors have evolved in two principal directions.

General-Purpose MPUs

One major direction of MPU development was geared toward providing the central processing function for general-purpose microcomputers. General-purpose MPU chips have given microcomputers most, if not all, of the computer capabilities of minicomputers. In 1974, Intel Corporation came out with the 8080 microprocessor, the first powerful, general-purpose 8-bit MPU. Motorola followed soon after with the MC6800, another general-purpose 8-bit MPU. These two devices dominated the scene for several years along with MOS Technology's 6502—used as the CPU in the Apple II computers—and the Zilog Z80—the CPU in Radio Shack's TRS-80 computers.

Both Intel and Motorola made improvements over these early MPUs: Intel produced the 8085, an enhanced 8080, and Motorola developed the 6802, an improved 6800. Motorola also came out with the 6809, a high-performance general-purpose MPU with many more op codes and addressing modes than the 6800/6802. The 6809 also has a few 16-bit instructions, but is still considered an 8-bit processor.

In the late '70s Intel introduced the 8086, a full-blown 16-bit MPU developed for use in general-purpose microcomputers. Its arithmetic logic unit, internal registers, and most of its instructions work with 16-bit words. The 8086 has a 16-bit data bus and a 20-bit address bus. The 20-bit address allows the 8086 to access $2^{20} = 1,048,576 = 1$ Meg memory locations. Motorola followed on the heels of the 8086 by introducing its first entry into the 16-bit race: the MC68000. Like the 8086, the 68000 works directly with 16-bit words, can address over a million bytes of memory, and executes instructions much more rapidly than any 8-bit MPU. These 16-bit MPUs also have the capability of performing multiplication and division operations in a single instruction; most 8-bit MPUs (the 68HC11 is an exception) require a lengthy, time-consuming sequence of instructions to multiply or divide numbers.

The evolution of general-purpose MPUs has continued with the development of 32-bit processors such as the Intel 80386 and 80486—used in IBM PCs and clones—and the 68020 and 68030—used in the Apple Macintosh microcomputers. These 32-bit MPUs work with gigabytes (10^9 bytes) or terabytes (10^{12} bytes) of memory.

All of these general-purpose MPUs are designed to be used in conjunction with other ICs in order to produce a complete functioning microcomputer. They require external memory and I/O interface chips that will work together with the MPU to provide all of the necessary elements of a computer.

Single-Chip Devices: Microcomputers and Microcontrollers

This is the second major direction of microprocessor development. These are single ICs that contain all of the essential elements of a computer: input, output, memory, and CPU (control unit and ALU). Any chip that has all of these elements, regardless to what degree, can be referred to as a *single-chip microcomputer*. The earliest device in this category was introduced in 1978 by Intel: the 8048 contains an 8-bit MPU, RAM, ROM, and some parallel I/O ports all in one 40-pin package. Intel has some current single-chip devices: notably, the 8051 and 80C196. Motorola has the 6801 and 68HC11 devices in this category. The 8051 and 6801 are comparable 8-bit devices that contain programmable counters and an asynchronous serial I/O port (UART) in addition to a CPU, RAM, ROM, and parallel I/O ports. The 68HC11 as we have seen is an 8-bit device that contains all of this plus a built-in A/D conversion capability and EEPROM, as well as a synchronous serial communications port. The 80C196 is a 16-bit single-chip device. Intel has also developed a family of 32-bit devices: the 80960 family. Motorola has a 32-bit device as well, the MC68332.

Most of these single-chip microcomputers have been designed for use as *dedicated* or *embedded controllers*. They are not meant to be used as general-purpose computers. Rather, they are meant to be used in a particular *control* function in which they help monitor and control a machine, a piece of equipment, or a process. For this reason, they are more commonly referred to as *microcontrollers (MCUs)*. MCUs are employed in a wide variety of control applications to sense and control external events. A partial list of these applications is shown here:

Appliance control	Automatic teller machines
Microwave ovens	Photocopiers
Washing machines	Automobile ignition systems
Sewing machines	Anti-lock brakes
Metal-working machines (e.g., lathes)	Medical instrumentation
VCRs	

Microcontrollers, like the 68HC11 we are using in this text, are designed to provide programmed computer control with a minimum of external circuitry. The programs stored in the chip's on-board ROM completely determine how the equipment or process will be controlled by the microcontroller. To change how the equipment or process is to be controlled, the designer may simply have to change only the stored program of instructions.

A Microcontroller Is a Microcomputer

The 68HC11 is classified as a microcontroller, but it has all of the elements of any microcomputer (or computer for that matter). In addition, it has an expanded mode that allows it to be connected to external memory and I/O if needed. In fact, if we wanted to, we could use the 68HC11 as part of a general-purpose microcomputer. As such, everything we are presenting by using the 68HC11 as the focus of our attention is applicable to almost any other microprocessor or microcomputer. The important things we are attempting to teach are ideas, concepts, principles, and techniques. The 68HC11 is the vehicle we have chosen to help demonstrate all of these. Hopefully, everything learned here can be applied and extended to whatever microprocessor, microcomputer, or microcontroller you will encounter.

GLOSSARY

Clock Monitor Reset   A special 68HC11 reset that occurs when the E-clock frequency drops below 10 KHz.

Computer Operating Properly (COP) Reset   A 68HC11 reset that goes active when the MPU gets "hung up" for an unusual period of time.

Condition Code Register (CCR)   Register whose individual bits (flags) have different meanings assigned by the MPU manufacturer concerning the status of a particular MPU condition.

Conditional Branching   Process by which an MPU makes a decision of "yes" or "no." This decision is determined by, and is dependent on, the logic condition of a particular flag in the condition code register.

Decision Block   Diamond-shaped block used in a flowchart to indicate a branching instruction.

Decrement   To reduce the contents of a register, being used as a counter, by one, unless otherwise specified.

Double Accumulator D   A 16-bit register in the 68HC11 MPU that is formed by linking accumulators A and B together.

Embedded Controller   See Microcontroller.

Execution Speed   Speed at which an MPU executes instructions. It is measured by multiplying the clock cycle time by the number of clock cycles required to execute an instruction.

Flag   A single binary bit used to indicate the status of a particular MPU condition.

Flowchart   Block diagram showing the sequence of major steps in a program such that any programmer can determine what the program is doing.

General-Purpose Register   One of a specific number of software-accessible registers in an MPU that can be used for temporary storage or for any other general-purpose function.

Increment   To increase the contents of a register, being used as a counter, by one, unless otherwise specified.

Index Addressing   Addressing scheme in which the actual operand address called for by an instruction is the sum of the 16-bit address stored in the index register plus the offset byte specified in the instruction.

Index Register   Used to generate the effective address of an operand in indexed addressing situations. Effective address = [index register] + offset portion of the instruction. The 68HC11 MPU has two index registers: X and Y.

Interrupt Request ($\overline{\text{IRQ}}$)   MPU input signal driven by external devices to interrupt the normal sequential flow of program execution and cause the MPU to attend to some specific need of the interrupting device.

Interrupt Service Routine   A program that has been written by the user and is stored in either ROM or RAM. This program is specially written to service a particular interrupting device and is executed every time that an interrupt occurs starting at the address pointed to by an interrupt vector.

Load Instruction Register (LIR)   A 68HC11 MPU output signal that indicates the beginning of each instruction and that can be used to trigger external testing equipment.

Microcontroller (MCU)   Single-chip microcomputer designed to be used in a particular control function in which it helps to monitor and control a process.

Nonmaskable Interrupt ($\overline{\text{XIRQ}}$)   An MPU input signal similar to $\overline{\text{IRQ}}$ except that this input cannot be software disabled.

Programming Model   Picture depicting the internal MPU registers that a programmer can directly control via the MPU's instruction set.

$\overline{\text{RESET}}$ MPU input signal used by an MPU to initialize internal circuits during power-on or when required by an externally generated user signal. The 68HC11 MPU, in particular, can also be reset when a Computer Operating Properly (COP) condition occurs, or when the internal clock monitor circuitry is triggered.

Single-Chip Microcomputer   Any single chip that contains an input device, an output device, memory, and a CPU (control unit and ALU).

Stack   Portion of RAM reserved for temporary storage and retrieval of information, typically the contents of the MPU's internal registers during an interrupt.

Stack Pointer Register   Special memory address register used only for the stack portion of RAM.

Vector   A 16-bit address that is stored in ROM and always points to the location of the first executable instruction of a special program in memory.

Watchdog Timer   Internal 68HC11 MPU timer that runs continuously and is used by the Computer Operating Properly reset circuitry in order to determine whether or not a COP reset ought to occur.

QUESTIONS AND PROBLEMS

Sections 6.1–6.3

1. List all of the 16-bit registers internal to the 68HC11 MPU.
2. In the 68HC11 MPU, what is the difference between accumulator B and the double accumulator D?
3. Name the signals that make up the 68HC11 MPU control bus.
4. What are the clock requirements of the 68HC11 MPU, and how can they be generated?
5. **(a)** What function does the *external* $\overline{\text{RESET}}$ signal serve on the 68HC11 MPU?
   (b) List all the possible ways the 68HC11 MPU can be reset.

(c) What determines where the MPU goes for its first instruction following an external reset?

(d) Repeat for a COP reset.

6. While operating in the expanded mode, what does MODA/$\overline{\text{LIR}}$ = 0 imply on the 68HC11 MPU?

7. Describe the function of the AS output signal on the 68HC11 MPU. Repeat for the STRA input signal.

8. (a) Explain the difference between the interrupt signals $\overline{\text{IRQ}}$ and $\overline{\text{XIRQ}}$ of the 68HC11 MPU.

(b) List the interrupt vectors on the 68HC11 MPU. What function do they serve?

9. The Instruction Register (IR)

(a) Stores flags

(b) Holds instruction addresses

(c) Is used in special address modes

(d) Stores op codes

10. The Program Counter (PC)

(a) Holds operand addresses   (b) Holds instruction addresses

(c) Holds data addresses   (d) Holds op codes

11. The Data Address Register (DAR)

(a) Holds instruction addresses   (b) Holds operand addresses

(c) Holds flags   (d) Holds op codes

12. Which register partakes in many of the operations performed by the ALU?

(a) Program counter   (b) Instruction register

(c) Data address register   (d) Accumulator

13. Which of the following are not typical uses of the MPU's general-purpose registers?

(a) Sometimes used as index registers   (b) Holds address of next available location on the stack

(c) Temporary storage   (d) Counters

14. Assume that [**X**] = 02A0. A program contains the following instruction:

Address	Instruction code	Mnemonic	Description
C400	A6	LDAA $40, X	; Load accumulator A indexed by X.
C401	40		; Offset byte.

From what memory address will the accumulator be loaded? How would the above program change if we used the load accumulator A indexed by Y instruction?

15. During conditional branch instructions, the contents of which register are examined to determine the next sequence of instructions to be performed.

(a) Index register   (b) Data address register

(c) Condition code register   (d) Instruction register

16. What information does the Overflow flag (V) of the condition code register indicate following the addition of signed numbers?

17. What information does the I flag of the condition code register impart?

18. Once enabled, explain how the X flag of the condition code register can be disabled.

19. List the eight 68HC11 MPU flags. Which one indicates whether the result of an operation was exactly zero? Which one indicates the sign of the result? Which one is used to drastically decrease the overall power consumption of the 68HC11 MPU? Which one is used by the Decimal Adjust Accumulator A (DAA) instruction in order to determine the proper correction factor to be added to the result of a BCD addition?

20. The stack
  (a) Is an area of ROM used for the retrieval of information, typically tables and codes
  (b) Is an area of RAM used for the temporary storage and retrieval of information, typically the MPU's internal registers
  (c) Is an area of RAM used for the storage of a program to be executed at some future time
  (d) Is an area of ROM used for controlling I/O interfacing

21. Last-in, first-out describes the operation of
  (a) RAM   **(b)** ROM   **(c)** Stack   **(d)** ALU

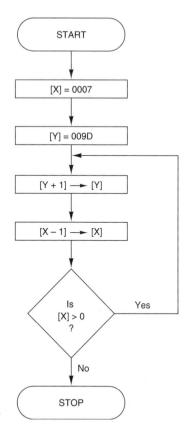

FIGURE 6.9

22. Refer to the flowchart in Fig. 6.9. Determine the values of X and Y at the end of the program.

23. Which register stores the address of the next location to be used in a special section of memory reserved for temporary storage during operations such as subroutine calls and interrupt servicing?
(a) Condition code register   (b) Data address register
(c) Program counter register   (d) Stack pointer register

24. The stack pointer is incremented and decremented
(a) By the programmer in his or her main program
(b) By the MPU each time data are placed on or taken off the stack
(c) By external logic circuits each time a READ operation is performed
(d) By external logic circuits each time a WRITE operation is performed

25. A table of 50 data words is stored in memory locations $C100_{16}$ to $C131_{16}$. Draw a flowchart for a program that will take these data words and move them to memory locations $C200_{16}$ to $C231_{16}$. (*Hint:* Use indexed addressing.)

26. Assume that $[SP] = 01FF_{16}$. If *three* PSHA instructions are followed by *two* PULA instructions, what will be the new $[SP]$?

27. Sketch the 68HC11 MPU programming model.

Section 6.4

28. When the ALU in the 68HC11 MPU performs an arithmetic or logic operation between two operands, where does the result usually end up? Repeat for single-operand operations.

29. Which one of the following is an ALU single-operand instruction?
(a) ADD   (b) COMPARE
(c) AND   (d) NEGATE

30. Which one of the following is an ALU two-operand instruction?
(a) INCREMENT   (b) SHIFT
(c) ROTATE   (d) COMPARE

31. What is the difference between a SHIFT operation and a ROTATE operation?

32. How does a COMPARE operation differ from a SUBTRACT operation?

33. What are some of the ways that the more complex arithmetic operations such as multiplication and division can be performed in some MPU systems? How does the 68HC11 MPU perform these arithmetic operations?

34. What role does the double accumulator D in the 68HC11 MPU play during the execution of a multiplication instruction? Repeat for the division instruction.

Sections 6.5–6.6

35. How are microprocessors categorized?

36. Generally, state the basic difference between an 8-bit MPU and a 16-bit MPU.

37. Give several examples of general-purpose MPUs.

38. What are the basic elements needed to have a single-chip microcomputer?

39. What is an embedded controller?

40. True or False:

    (a) All microcomputers are microcontrollers.

    (b) All microcontrollers are microcomputers.

7

Programming the 68HC11 MPU

OBJECTIVES

Upon completion of this chapter, you will be able to:

- Fully understand all of the flags within the condition code register of the 68HC11 MPU.
- Use and understand all of the 68HC11's instruction modes.
- Use the complete 68HC11 MPU instruction set.
- Understand the different instruction classifications of the 68HC11 MPU instruction set.
- Understand the need for and the usefulness of subroutines.
- Use programmed time-delay loops.
- Cite some of the basic components of the timer system in the 68HC11 MPU and understand their operation.
- Analyze and understand the detailed operation of the arithmetic/logic unit of the MPU.
- Cite and use the various steps in the software development process.

INTRODUCTION

There are basically two things that you can do with a microprocessor: You can interface it to other devices, such as memory and I/O devices, and you can program it. Both of these activities are necessary in any meaningful application of a microprocessor or a microcontroller such as the 68HC11 MPU. We introduced the basic ideas of interfacing in Chapter 5, and we will build on this in Chapters 8 and 9. In this chapter we concentrate on programming the 68HC11 MPU in machine language with elements of assembly language.

The 68HC11 MPU has 108 different types of instructions. Although we will describe most of these in this chapter, we concentrate on those that are most commonly used by novice programmers. As we discussed earlier, each microprocessor has a unique machine and assembly language. It might seem that learning how to program the 68HC11 MPU, or any other microprocessor, would be useful only if one is to be using that specific microprocessor a great deal. Fortunately, the types of instructions and programming techniques that are used with the 8-bit 68HC11 MPU are similar to those used by all 8-bit microprocessors. Thus, once you become proficient at programming the fairly sophisticated 68HC11 MPU, it should be relatively easy to learn how to program other 8-bit MPUs as well as 16- and 32-bit MPUs.

In this chapter and in subsequent chapters we will be indicating the op codes for each instruction we use. These 68HC11 op codes are listed in Appendix A along with other details on each 68HC11 instruction. You might want to check where an op code comes from each time a new one is presented.

The material in this chapter should serve as a good introduction to microprocessor programming, but it is not intended to teach you how to become a proficient assembly language programmer. This requires much more than one chapter in a textbook. More important, it requires that you analyze programs written by good programmers, write programs of your own, and run them on a computer. This chapter will prepare you to continue this learning process.

▶ 7.1 68HC11 MPU PROGRAMMING MODEL

In Chapter 6 we presented the programming model for the 68HC11 MPU. It is repeated in Fig. 7.1. Recall that it contains only those internal MPU registers that are of concern to the programmer: (1) the two 8-bit accumulators, ACCA and ACCB; (2) the 16-bit double accumulator, ACCD; (3) the two 16-bit index registers, X and Y; (4) the 16-bit stack pointer register, SP; (5) the 16-bit program counter, PC; and (6) the 8-bit condition code register, CCR.

The Condition Code Register (Flags)

Each 68HC11 MPU register has been described in previous chapters, but the condition code register (CCR) requires some elaboration. Recall that this register contains 8 bits. These 8 bits are called *flags,* and they are used by the MPU to monitor different conditions that exist during the execution of a program. The programmer can use conditional branch instructions to check the logic state of these flags to determine whether to branch or to continue in sequence. We will examine the function of each flag.

Zero Flag (Z)

Whenever the MPU executes an instruction that transfers a byte of data or performs an arithmetic, logic, or shift operation, it will automatically set or clear the Z flag according to whether or not the result of the operation is zero (00_{16} or 0000_{16}).

When the result is zero, the MPU sets Z = 1.
When the result is not zero, the MPU clears Z = 0.

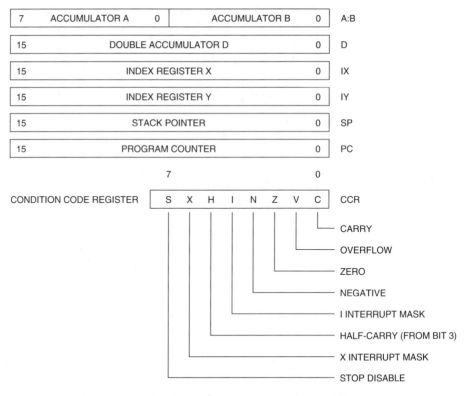

FIGURE 7.1   68HC11 programmer's model.

Any instruction that processes data or transfers data between registers or between a register and memory will affect the Z flag. The MPU sets or clears the Z flag so that it can keep track of the "zero-ness" of the last operation it performed. Here are some examples of operations that will cause the MPU to set Z = 1.

1. Subtraction of an operand from ACCA, producing a result of 00000000_2.
2. Loading ACCB with a data byte from memory that is equal to 00000000_2.
3. Decrementing the contents of the X register such that $[X] = 0000_{16}$.
4. Incrementing the contents of the Y register such that $[Y] = 0000_{16}$.
5. Clearing the contents of accumulator A, accumulator B, or any memory location such that the final result in any of these registers becomes 00000000_2.

Of course, if any of these operations produced a nonzero result, the MPU would make Z = 0.

Negative Flag (N)

The MPU sets or clears this flag to indicate the *sign* of the result of any operation that transfers or processes data. In other words, N is always equal to the sign bit (MSB) of the result.

It is important to understand that the MPU will make N the same as the MSB of the result even when the program is not using signed numbers. The MPU does not know whether the data represent unsigned numbers, signed numbers, or nonnumerical information; the programmer has to keep track of those things.

To illustrate the N flag, let us suppose that the 68HC11 MPU has just executed an addition instruction and places the result in ACCA. If this result is 01100111, the MPU will make N = 0 since bit 7 (the MSB) is 0. If this result is 11000110, the MPU will make N = 1 since bit 7 is 1. Likewise, if the 68HC11 MPU executes an addition instruction and places the result 7362_{16} (0111001101100010_2) in a 16-bit register such as the X, Y, or ACCD, the MPU will make N = 0 since bit 15 (the MSB) is 0. If this result is $F362_{16}$ (1111001101100010_2), the MPU will make N = 1 since bit 15 is 1.

Carry Flag (C)

This flag is a multipurpose flag that the MPU can use in several different ways. It is used to indicate a carry out of the MSB position when two 8-bit numbers or two 16-bit numbers are added. This is illustrated below for two different cases.

$$
\begin{array}{cl}
& 10101000 \longleftarrow \text{original contents of ACCA} \\
+ & \underline{01010110} \longleftarrow \text{operand (from memory)} \\
& 11111110 \longleftarrow \text{result to be stored in ACCA}
\end{array}
$$

↑——————————— **no carry**

Here the addition operation produces no carry from the MSB position. Thus, the MPU will clear the C flag to 0.

$$
\begin{array}{cl}
& 10101000 \longleftarrow \text{original contents of ACCA} \\
+ & \underline{01100110} \longleftarrow \text{operand (from memory)} \\
1 & 00001110 \longleftarrow \text{result to be stored in ACCA}
\end{array}
$$

↑——————————— **carry**

Here the addition produces a carry of 1; this causes the MPU to set the C flag.

The C flag is also used to keep track of "borrows" when a subtract operation is performed on unsigned binary numbers. For example, when a binary number is subtracted from a smaller binary number, the MSB will have to "borrow" a 1 to complete the subtraction. When this happens, the MPU will set C = 1 to indicate that a borrow has occurred. If a subtraction operation does not require a borrow, the MPU will clear C = 0.

The C flag also takes part in the various shift and rotate instructions that were described in Chapter 6. We will discuss these in more detail later.

The 68HC11 MPU has specific single-byte instructions that can be used by the programmer to set or clear the C flag at any time. The SEC instruction (op code OD), when executed, will set C to 1. The CLC instruction (op code OC), when executed, will clear C to 0. There are no corresponding instructions for the Z or N flags.

Any 8-bit MPU will have a C flag that is affected by additions and subtractions in the manner which we have just described. However, the 68HC11 MPU also uses the C flag during its multiply (MUL) instruction and its divide (IDIV, FDIV) instructions. We will elaborate on the multiplication and division instructions later in this chapter.

Overflow Flag (V)

The V flag is used to indicate *overflow* when *signed* numbers are added or subtracted by the MPU. Recall that for signed numbers, the MSB is the sign bit with $0 = $ positive and $1 = $ negative. This leaves only 7 bits for the magnitude, with 2's-complement used for negative values. With a sign bit and 7 magnitude bits, the numbers that can be represented will range from -128_{10} to $+127_{10}$. The MPU will automatically set $V = 1$ when an addition or subtraction operation produces a result that falls outside the range. An example of an overflow situation follows:

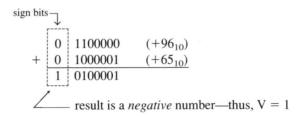

result is a *negative* number—thus, $V = 1$

Here the addition of two positive numbers produces a result that has a 1 in the sign bit position. This would seem to indicate that the result is negative. This, of course, is impossible, and it has been caused by overflow from the addition of the magnitude bits into the sign bit position. The MPU, upon sensing this overflow, will set $V = 1$. If no overflow had occurred, the MPU would clear $V = 0$.

Overflow can also occur when subtraction is performed between two numbers with opposite signs. Again, the MPU's internal logic can sense the overflow condition and will set or clear V accordingly.

The V flag should not be confused with the C flag. V is used for signed arithmetic operations and indicates an overflow of the 7-bit magnitude capacity. C is used for unsigned operations and indicates an overflow of the 8-bit magnitude capacity.

The 68HC11 MPU has two instructions, SEV and CLV, that the programmer can use to set and clear the V flag, respectively. The 68HC11 MPU also has a number of other instructions that indirectly affect the condition of the V flag. We will point these out as we encounter them in subsequent discussions.

Interrupt Mask Flag (I)

This flag can be set or cleared by using the SEI or CLI instructions, respectively. The function of this flag will be described by our detailed treatment of interrupts in Chapter 8.

Nonmaskable Interrupt Flag (X)

This flag can only be cleared by two *software* instructions, TAP (transfer from ACCA to CCR) and RTI (return from interrupt). The X flag can only be set by two *hardware* conditions, system reset and the detection of an $\overline{\text{XIRQ}}$ signal. The function of this flag will also be described when we discuss interrupts in Chapter 8.

Half-Carry Flag (H)

The H flag indicates whether or not a carry is produced from bit position 3 to bit position 4 during the addition of two 8-bit binary numbers. The MPU will use this flag whenever the 8-bit binary numbers represent BCD digits. We will say more about this later in the chapter.

There are no specific instructions for clearing or setting the H flag.

Stop Disable Flag (S)

The Stop Disable flag when set to 1 will prevent the STOP instruction from being executed. The STOP instruction causes the oscillator and all of the 68HC11 MCU clocks to stop. The S flag is automatically set during reset and must be cleared in order for the STOP instruction to be executed. Otherwise, the STOP instruction will be treated as a NOP (No operation) instruction. The programmer can either set or clear the S flag with a TAP instruction.

Summary of Flags

The condition code register (CCR) in the 68HC11 MPU contains eight flags that indicate specific conditions that occur as the MPU executes a program. Each of these flags conveys information to the MPU or to the programmer. By using a series of conditional branch instructions that are part of the 68HC11 MPU instruction set, the programmer can test the values of some of these flags to determine what sequence of instructions to follow next. This represents the basis for all of the "decision-making" capabilities of any computer.

▶ 7.2 68HC11 MPU ADDRESS MODES

Instructions can be classified according to how the operand address portion of the instruction is specified. In our earlier discussions of the 68HC11 MPU programming, we used primarily two types of instructions. One type consisted of an op code byte followed by a two-byte operand address. The other type consisted only of an op code, since no operand address was required.

The 68HC11 MPU actually has seven different *address modes;* that is, ways that the operand address portion of an instruction can be specified. As we shall see, none of the 108 different types of the 68HC11 MPU instructions utilizes all of the available address modes. For example, the ADD instruction can use only five different address modes. The following paragraphs will describe each address mode. Each of the modes (except the inherent mode) results in the MPU generating a 16-bit effective address which it places on the address bus during the execution portion of an instruction cycle.

Extended Addressing

This address mode uses a two-byte operand address following the op code. The format for *extended addressing* is

Byte 1	Op code
Byte 2	ADH
Byte 3	ADL

Two-byte operand address

where ADH is the high-order address byte and ADL is the low-order address byte.
An example of an instruction that uses extended addressing is shown below.

	Instruction code	*Assembly language*
Op code $\longrightarrow$	B6	LDAA $2E17
Operand	2E	
address	17	

This instruction will cause the MPU to take the data from address location 2E17 and load them into accumulator A. The op code B6 tells the MPU that it has to fetch the next two bytes to determine the operand address.

The assembly language equivalent for this instruction is LDAA $2E17. The mnemonic LDAA indicates that the operation to be performed is "load accumulator A"; the $2E17 specifies the hex address of the memory location or input device from which data are to be taken to be loaded into accumulator A.

EXAMPLE 7.1

Describe the operation performed by the instruction below.

Instruction code	*Assembly language*
FB	ADDB $0253
02	
53	

Solution This instruction will cause the MPU to take data from address 0253 and add them to the contents of accumulator B. The op code FB tells the MPU what operation to perform (ADDB) and what address mode to use.

EXAMPLE 7.2

Describe the operation performed by the instruction below.

Instruction code	Assembly language
18	STY $C107
FF	
C1	
07	

Solution This instruction involves the Y index register, hence the need for the prebyte 18. Recall that some 68HC11 MPU instructions require a two-byte op code; the prebyte followed by the op code. For this particular instruction (STY) the prebyte is 18 and the op code is FF. Thus, the instruction STY $C107 will cause the MPU to store the most significant byte of the Y index register in memory location C107 and the least significant byte of the Y index register in memory location C108, respectively. Recall that both index registers X and Y are 16-bit registers, and each memory location holds one byte. Consequently, it requires two consecutive memory locations to store the entire contents of register Y.

Direct Addressing

Instructions that use extended addressing typically require three bytes and take four cycles to execute; one to fetch the op code, two to fetch the operand address, and one to perform the operation on the operand. Of course, instructions that have a prebyte associated with them will always require one extra cycle to execute as compared to those instructions that do not have a prebyte.

Direct addressing requires only two bytes and typically takes only three clock cycles to execute.

The format for direct addressing is shown below.

Byte 1 | Op code |
Byte 2 | ADL | ⟵── low-order address byte;
high-order byte (ADH) is always 00_{16}.

The first byte is the op code. The second byte is ADL, the low-order address byte. There is no high-order byte. The high-order address byte is automatically understood to be $00000000_2 = 00_{16}$. An example that uses direct addressing is given below.

	Instruction code	Assembly language
Op code ⟶	96	LDAA $50
ADL ⟶	50	

This instruction will cause the MPU to take data from address location 0050 and load them into accumulator A. The assembly language equivalent is LDAA $50. It could also be written as LDAA $0050.

When the MPU interprets the op code, 96, it knows that direct addressing is being used (recall that B6 was the op code for LDAA using extended addressing). Then it fetches ADL = 50 and automatically adds the ADH = 00 to form the complete operand address 0050.

EXAMPLE 7.3

Describe the operation performed by the 68HC11 MPU instruction below.

Instruction code	Assembly language
DB	ADDB $9C
9C	

Solution   This instruction will cause the MPU to take data from address 009C and add them to accumulator B. The op code DB tells the MPU what operation to perform (ADDB) and what address mode to use.

It is clear that the direct address mode always produces an operand address that is on page zero since the first byte is 00. For this reason, this address mode is often called *page-zero addressing.*

Since it requires fewer instruction bytes and has a shorter execution time than extended addressing, programmers will use direct addressing whenever possible. Typically, addresses on page zero are used for the storage of data and operands used by the program, and the program will move data in and out of this area of memory. This means that addresses 00xx on the memory map will have to be RAM addresses.

Immediate Addressing

There are many situations where the data that are to be loaded into an MPU register or operated on in the ALU are a known, fixed value. For example, there might be a step in a program where you want to load accumulator A with the value 24_{16}, or where you want to add 02_{16} to the current contents of accumulator B. For situations such as these, it is not necessary to specify an operand address; instead, the operand itself is specified immediately following the op code. This is called *immediate addressing,* and the format is shown below.

$$
\begin{array}{l}
\text{Byte 1} \quad \boxed{\text{Op code}} \\
\text{Byte 2} \quad \boxed{\text{Operand}} \quad \longleftarrow \text{operand to be operated on}
\end{array}
$$

The first byte is again the op code. The second byte is *not* an operand address; it is the operand that the MPU will operate on when it executes the instruction.

Here is an example of an instruction using immediate addressing:

	Instruction code	Assembly language
Op code $\longrightarrow$	86	LDAA #$24
Operand $\longrightarrow$	24	

This instruction will cause the MPU to load accumulator A with the data word 24. The 24 is not an operand address, but is the operand itself. The address of this operand is the address *immediately* following the op code; hence the name "immediate addressing."

The assembly language representation for this instruction is LDAA #$24. The # symbol is used to indicate immediate addressing; the value that follows the # symbol is always data. The $ symbol is still used to indicate that the data are in hex.

EXAMPLE 7.4

What operation will the 68HC11 MPU perform for the instruction below?

	Instruction code	Assembly language
Op code $\longrightarrow$	CE	LDX #$03A7
16-bit	03	
data	A7	

Solution This instruction uses the immediate addressing mode as indicated by the # symbol. Since X is a 16-bit register, the data to be loaded into X are specified by the two bytes immediately following the op code. Thus, this three-byte instruction will load index register X with data 03A7.

EXAMPLE 7.5 _____

Describe the sequence of operations performed by the instruction sequence below.

Address	Instruction code	Assembly language
C200	D6	LDAB $65
C201	65	
C202	CB	ADDB #$02
C203	02	
C204	F7	STAB $DF00
C205	DF	
C206	00	

Solution   The first instruction uses direct addressing to load data from address $0065 into accumulator B. Remember that the data address is understood to be on page 00 (i.e., ADH = 00).

The second instruction uses immediate addressing (note the # symbol) to add the data 02 to accumulator B.

The third instruction uses extended addressing to store the new contents of accumulator B into memory address $DF00.

Inherent Addressing

Inherent addressing is used by instructions that do not need to access memory or I/O addresses, and for which the operand is obvious from the instruction mnemonic. For example, the instruction to "clear accumulator A" has the mnemonic CLRA and the op code 4F. When the 68HC11 MPU sees this op code, it knows that the operand is the contents of accumulator A. It then proceeds to make $[\textbf{ACCA}] = \textbf{00}_{16}$.

Another example is the instruction to "increment the X register." The mnemonic is INX and the op code is 08. This op code tells the MPU that the operand is the contents of the X register. The MPU then increments X (adds 1 to it).

All the instructions that set or clear flags in the condition code register use inherent addressing. For example, the instruction for "setting the C flag" has the mnemonic SEC and op code OD. This op code tells the MPU that the operand is the contents of the CCR, and the MPU proceeds to set bit 0 (the C flag) of this register.

EXAMPLE 7.6 _____

Determine the contents of the 68HC11 MPU internal Y register and the state of the Z flag at the completion of the instruction sequence below.

Address	Instruction code	Assembly language
C200	18	LDY #$FFFE
C201	CE	
C202	FF	
C203	FE	
C204	18	INY
C205	08	
C206	18	INY
C207	08	

Solution   All three instructions in the sequence use the Y index register. In the case of the 68HC11 MPU, these instructions require prebyte 18. Hence, instructions LDY #$FFFE (18, CE) and INY (18, 08) each has a two-byte op code. The LDY #$FFFE instruction uses immediate addressing to load [**Y**] with the 16-bit data $FFFE_{16} = 1111\ 1111\ 1111\ 1110_2$. The first INY instruction will increment [**Y**] to FFFF. The second INY instruction will cause [**Y**] to recycle to 0000_{16}. This last operation will cause Z to be set to 1.

Indexed Addressing

This address mode was introduced in Chapter 6 during our discussion of the index registers X and Y. It is a very powerful address mode that makes it easy to handle tables or blocks of data in memory. In Chapter 6 we saw how it was used to simplify the addition of a long list of 8-bit numbers. Later we will demonstrate more applications of this extremely important address mode.

The format for indexed addressing is shown below.

Byte 1 ⟶ | Op code |
Byte 2 ⟶ | Offset | ⟵—This is added to [**X**] or [**Y**] to get the operand address.

When indexed addressing is used for the 68HC11 MPU, it is always a two-byte instruction (except for those instructions that use a prebyte and a few unique Branch instructions that will be discussed later). The first byte as always is the op code. The second byte is called the *offset,* and it is an *unsigned* 8-bit number. This offset is added to the current contents of the index register X (or Y) to obtain the effective operand address. In other words,

$$\text{operand address} = [\mathbf{X}] + \text{offset}$$

or

$$\text{operand address} = [\mathbf{Y}] + \text{offset}$$

In this mode, the operand address is not given to the MPU explicitly; instead, the MPU has to compute the operand address by adding the offset byte to X or Y. For example, if the offset byte is $2A_{16}$ and the current contents of X is $C000_{16}$, the operand address is C000 + 2A = C02A.

An example of indexed addressing is given below.

	Instruction code	Assembly language	Comment
Op code $\longrightarrow$	A6	LDAA $2A, X	; Effective address = [X] + 2A
Offset $\longrightarrow$	2A		

This instruction will cause the MPU to add 2A to [X] to obtain the operand address. The MPU will then load the data from this address into accumulator A.

The assembly language representation for this instruction is LDAA $2A, X. This is interpreted as follows: "load accumulator A with the data from address location given by adding 2A to the X register."

EXAMPLE 7.7

Describe the operations performed by the instruction sequence below.

Instruction code	Assembly language
CE	LDX #$E000
E0	
00	
18	LDY #$E200
CE	
E2	
00	
AB	ADDA $32,X
32	
18	ADDB $50,Y
EB	
50	
A7	STAA $00,X
00	
18	STAB $00,Y
E7	
00	

Solution

(a) The first instruction uses immediate addressing to load register X with the value E000.
(b) The second instruction uses immediate addressing to load register Y with the value E200.
(c) The third instruction uses indexed addressing to add data to accumulator A. The data are taken from address E000 + 32 = E032 ([X] + 32).

(d) The fourth instruction uses indexed addressing to add data to accumulator B. The data are taken from address E200 + 50 = E250 ([**Y**] + 50). Note the prebyte 18.

(e) The fifth instruction uses indexed addressing to store the contents of ACCA in address E000 + 00 = E000 ([**X**] + 00).

(f) The sixth instruction uses indexed addressing to store the contents of ACCB in address E200 + 00 = E200 ([**Y**] + 00). Again, note the prebyte 18.

Relative Addressing

In our brief introduction to machine language in Chapter 4, we talked about *conditional branch* instructions which use the relative address mode. We saw how conditional branch instructions, when the correct condition is met, can alter the sequence of instructions that the MPU will execute. As stated then, this class of instructions is what gives any computer its important "decision-making" capability. In the case of the 68HC11 MPU, these branch instructions can be divided into four different classifications: unconditional, simple conditional, signed conditional, and unsigned conditional. Since relative addressing, conditional, and unconditional branch instructions are so important, we devote a complete section to these topics later in the chapter.

▶ 7.3 THE 68HC11 MPU INSTRUCTION SET

The total number of possible op codes available to the 68HC11 MPU is in the thousands, but only 308 are actually used to represent different operations that the MPU can perform. The instruction set of the 68HC11 MPU contains 108 different types of instructions. The difference between the number of different op codes and the number of different *types* of instructions occurs because many of the different types of instructions can use more than one address mode.

For example, one of the most common types of instructions is LDAA (load accumulator A from memory). The 68HC11 MPU can execute an LDAA operation using any of five address modes: immediate, direct, extended, indexed X, and indexed Y. Each of these will have a different op code. Some of the instruction types, such as CLC (clear the C flag), use only one address mode, inherent.

A complete list of the 108 different types of 68HC11 MPU instructions is given in Table 7.1. Each type is indicated by its assembly language mnemonic and a brief description of the operation. Some of these descriptions are not extensive enough to describe the instructions completely; we elaborate on each instruction type in detail in the following sections.

Some instruction descriptions in Table 7.1 are followed by an *a* to indicate that they can be performed on either ACCA or ACCB. For example, the load accumulator instruction LDA can be LDAA or LDAB for loading ACCA or ACCB, respectively. Similarly, the ADD instruction can be ADDA or ADDB. Other instruction types are denoted by *b* to indicate that they can be performed on data that are either in the accumulator or in memory. For example, the logical shift right operation, LSR, can be performed on data from ACCA, ACCB, ACCD, or memory.

You should slowly scan this table and become familiar with the types of instructions available in the 68HC11 MPU language. You will notice that there is no explicit HALT in-

TABLE 7.1   68HC11 MPU Instruction Types

Mnemonic	Description	Mnemonic	Description
ABA	Add contents of accumulator B to accumulator A	**CMP**	Compare[b]
		COM	Complement[b]
ABX	Add contents of accumulator B to index register X	**CPD**	Compare double accumulator
		CPX	Compare index register X with memory
ABY	Add contents of accumulator B to index register Y	**CPY**	Compare index register Y with memory
		DAA	Decimal adjust accumulator A
ADC	Add operand and C flag to accumulator[a]	**DEC**	Decrement[b]
ADD	Add operand without carry to accumulator[a]	**DES**	Decrement stack pointer
ADDD	Add the contents of two consecutive memory locations to the contents of accumulator D	**DEX**	Decrement index register X
		DEY	Decrement index register Y
		EOR	Exclusive-OR with memory[a]
AND	Logically AND operand with accumulator[a]	**FDIV**	Fractional divide
ASL	Arithmetic shift left[b]	**IDIV**	Integer divide
ASLD	Arithmetic shift left double accumulator	**INC**	Increment[b]
ASR	Arithmetic shift right[b]	**INS**	Increment stack pointer
BCC	Branch if C flag is cleared (C = 0)	**INX**	Increment index register X
BCLR	Clear bit(s) in memory	**INY**	Increment index register Y
BCS	Branch if C flag is set (C = 1)	**JMP**	Unconditional jump
BEQ	Branch if result equals zero (Z = 1)	**JSR**	Jump to subroutine
BGE	Branch if result greater than or equal to zero	**LDA**	Load accumulator from memory[a]
		LDD	Load double accumulator from memory
BGT	Branch if result greater than zero	**LDS**	Load stack pointer from memory
BHI	Branch if higher	**LDX**	Load index register X
BHS	Branch if higher or the same	**LDY**	Load index register Y
BIT	Bit test[a]	**LSL**	Logical shift left[b]
BLE	Branch if result less than or equal to zero	**LSLD**	Logical shift left double accumulator
BLO	Branch if lower	**LSR**	Logical shift right[b]
BLS	Branch if lower or the same	**LSRD**	Logical shift right double accumulator
BLT	Branch if result less than zero	**MUL**	Multiply unsigned numbers
BMI	Branch if minus (N = 1)	**NEG**	Negate (2's-complement) operand[b]
BNE	Branch if result not equal to zero (Z = 0)	**NOP**	No operation
BPL	Branch if plus (N = 0)	**ORA**	Logically OR operand with accumulator[a]
BRA	Branch always	**PSH**	Push data onto stack[a]
BRCLR	Branch if bit(s) clear	**PSHX**	Push index register X onto stack
BRN	Branch never	**PSHY**	Push index register Y onto stack
BRSET	Branch if bit(s) set	**PUL**	Pull data from stack[a]
BSET	Set bit(s) in memory	**PULX**	Pull index register X from stack
BSR	Branch to subroutine	**PULY**	Pull index register Y from stack
BVC	Branch if overflow flag clear (V = 0)	**ROL**	Rotate operand left[b]
BVS	Branch if overflow flag set (V = 1)	**ROR**	Rotate operand right[b]
CBA	Compare accumulator A with accumulator B	**RTI**	Return from interrupt
		RTS	Return from subroutine
CLC	Clear C flag	**SBA**	Subtract accumulator B from accumulator A
CLI	Clear I flag		
CLR	Clear[b]	**SBC**	Subtract memory from accumulator with carry[a]
CLV	Clear V flag		

TABLE 7.1   68HC11 MPU Instruction Types—cont'd

Mnemonic	Description	Mnemonic	Description
SEC	Set carry C flag	**TEST**	Test operation (Test Mode Only)
SEI	Set I flag	**TPA**	Transfer from condition code register to accumulator A
SEV	Set V flag		
STA	Store accumulator in memory[a]	**TST**	Test contents of accumulator or memory[b]
STD	Store double accumulator in memory	**TSX**	Transfer from stack pointer to index register X
STOP	Stop processing		
STS	Store stack pointer in memory	**TSY**	Transfer from stack pointer to index register Y
STX	Store index register X in memory		
STY	Store index register Y in memory	**TXS**	Transfer from index register X to stack pointer
SUB	Subtract memory from accumulator[a]		
SUBD	Subtract memory from double accumulator	**TYS**	Transfer from index register Y to stack pointer
SWI	Software interrupt		
TAB	Transfer from accumulator A to accumulator B	**WAI**	Wait for interrupt (halt)
		XGDX	Exchange double accumulator and index register X
TAP	Transfer from accumulator A to condition code register		
		XGDY	Exchange double accumulator and index register Y
TBA	Transfer from accumulator B to accumulator A		

[a]*Instruction operates on either accumulator*
[b]*Instruction operates on either accumulator or memory*

struction. In most applications, the "wait for interrupt" instruction, WAI, can serve to halt the MPU after it has completed execution of the program instructions. The MPU will stop fetching op codes from memory and will wait for an interrupt that has not been masked or for a reset signal.

▶ 7.4 INSTRUCTION DESCRIPTIONS

A description of each of the 68HC11 MPU instructions is provided in Appendix A. Rather than having the instruction descriptions spread throughout the chapter, we have placed them at the end of the book so that they can be referred to easily. In this section we present some examples to show how to obtain different kinds of information from the Appendix. Before we do this, however, you should read the introductory comments in the Appendix and briefly scan the descriptions to see the format that is being used.

Each of the following examples refers to the Appendix.

EXAMPLE 7.8

Find the op codes for the assembly language instructions ADDA #$34, ADDB #$34.

Solution   Look for the mnemonic ADD. The table below the description of this mnemonic gives information for both the ADDA and ADDB instructions. The ADDA and ADDB instructions each have five possible address modes. We are interested in the *imme-*

diate mode because of the # in the assembly language instructions. From the table entry for the IMMediate address mode, we find that the op code for ADDA (IMM) is 8B. Thus, the instruction ADDA #$34 will assemble into the two bytes, 8B 34.

Similarly, we find that the op code for ADDB (IMM) is CB. Thus, ADDB #$34 assembles into the two bytes, CB 34.

EXAMPLE 7.9

Convert LDX $A433 and LDY $A433 into machine language code.

Solution   These instructions use the *extended* mode to load data into the X and Y registers. Look for mnemonic LDX and find the table entry for the EXTended address mode. The op code for LDX (EXT) is specified as FE. Thus, LDX $A433 is assembled into FE A4 33.

Likewise, look for mnemonic LDY and find the table entry for the EXTended address mode. The op code for LDY (EXT) is specified as 18 FE. The LDY instruction is one of those 68HC11 MPU instructions that takes two bytes to express: a prebyte, 18, and the op code, FE. Thus, LDY $A433 is assembled into four bytes, 18 FE A4 33.

EXAMPLE 7.10

Assemble STAB $67 into machine code.

Solution   This instruction uses the *direct* address mode since only two hex digits are specified as the operand address (i.e., the operand address is actually $0067). Look for mnemonic STA and find the table entry for STAB (DIR). The op code is given as D7. Thus, STAB $67 assembles into D7 67.

EXAMPLE 7.11

The 68HC11 MPU can perform certain operations on data that are in memory as well as data that are in either accumulator A or accumulator B. One of these operations is the *clear* operation, which clears all bits to 0 (i.e., replaces the memory or accumulator data with 00_{16}). Look at Appendix A for the mnemonic CLR. This is the mnemonic for the instruction that clears the contents of a memory location. Now look for the mnemonics CLRA/CLRB. These are the mnemonics for clearing ACCA and ACCB, respectively. Whenever there is an operand that can be performed on either memory data or accumulator data, the mnemonics will have separate entries in the Appendix.

Assemble the following instructions into machine code: CLR $03FF, and CLRA.

Solution   The op code for CLR (EXTended) is given as 7F. Thus, CLR $03FF assembles into 7F 03 FF. The op code for CLRA (INHerent) is 4F. Thus, CLRA assembles into 4F. Note that CLRA (INH) is a single-byte instruction.

EXAMPLE 7.12

Compare the time required for the 68HC11 MPU to increment ACCA with the time required to increment the Y register.

Solution Look for the mnemonic INCA/INCB, which is the mnemonic for incrementing ACCA or ACCB. The associated table below the description of this mnemonic shows that *two* clock cycles are required to execute the INCA instruction. Now look for the mnemonic INY, which is the mnemonic for incrementing the contents of the index register Y. The table indicates that *four* clock cycles are required to execute this instruction. More cycles are required to increment Y than to increment accumulator A. This is because (1) index Y register is a 16-bit register that has to be incremented in two steps by the MPU's 8-bit arithmetic circuitry; and (2) the INY instruction has a prebyte associated with it, which makes it a two-byte instruction instead of the single-byte instruction INCA.

EXAMPLE 7.13

Which flags in the MPU's condition code register (CCR) are affected by the execution of the instruction LDAA #$A5?

Solution Look for the mnemonic LDA and find the table entry for LDAA (IMM). The table shows that the N and Z flags will be affected by the data that are being loaded into accumulator A; this is indicated by the $\updownarrow$ under the N and Z columns in the table. In this case, the data are $A5_{16} = 10100101_2$. Since the data are not equal to zero, the Z flag will be cleared to 0. The N flag will be set to 1 because the sign bit (MSB) of the data is a 1.

    The table also shows that the V flag will be cleared to 0 whenever this instruction is executed, regardless of the data.

EXAMPLE 7.14

Repeat for LDX #$00A5.

Solution Look for the mnemonic LDX and find the table entry for LDX (IMM). As in the previous example, the table shows that the N and Z flags will be affected by the data that are being loaded into the 16-bit register X; again, this is indicated by the $\updownarrow$ under the N and Z columns in the table. In this case, the data are $00A5_{16} = 0000000010100101_2$. Since these data are also not equal to zero, the Z flag will be cleared to 0. In contrast to the previous example, the N flag will be cleared to 0 because the sign bit (MSB) of the data is a 0.

    The table also shows that the V flag behaves the same way as in the previous example; it's always cleared to 0.

▶ 7.5 PROGRAM LISTING FORMAT

The following sections of this chapter contain many programming examples to illustrate the 68HC11 MPU instruction set. The program listings use the format shown in the example program below.

Address	Label	Instruction code	Mnemonic	Comments
C100	START	86	LDAA #$D6	; Load ACCA with data
C101		D6		
C102		B7	STAA $C200	; Store data in C200
C103		C2		
C104		00		
C105	END	3E	WAI	; Halt execution

The first column lists the hexadecimal memory addresses where the program bytes are stored. The second column is used to give labels or names to some of these address locations. For example, location C100 is given the label START to indicate that it is the first address in the program, and address C105 is given the label END to indicate that it is the last instruction in the program. For our purposes here, the labels are not a necessary part of the program, but are just a convenient way to refer to certain steps in a program or certain data storage locations. If we were writing programs that were to be assembled by a full-blown assembler, these labels would actually be part of the program, and they could be used in place of actual numerical addresses. The *AS11 assembler,* provided free of charge by Motorola to users of the 68HC11 MPU, is an example of a full-blown assembler.

The third column gives the hexadecimal instruction codes. These codes represent the actual binary patterns that are stored in the program memory (i.e., it is the machine language object program).

The fourth column gives the assembly language mnemonic together with the operand address or operand (immediate mode). The fifth column includes explanatory comments that will help you to follow the program. These comments are not only a help to someone who is reading someone else's program, but they also allow the programmer to keep track of the program logic during the writing of the program. Comments always begin with a semicolon (;).

▶ 7.6 INSTRUCTION CLASSIFICATIONS

It is difficult to group the 68HC11 MPU instructions, or any microprocessor's for that matter, into distinct classifications because some instructions will fit into more than one category, and some specialized instructions defy classification. Nonetheless, we briefly describe some of the broad instruction classifications. Keep in mind that our choice of 68HC11 MPU instruction categories is not unique, and probably would not meet with unanimous agreement. We are doing it simply as a way to have a convenient hook on which to hang each instruction.

Condition Code Register Instructions

This group of instructions contains those used to set and clear some of the flags in the CCR.

Register-Memory Transfers

This group of instructions contains those in which data are transferred from an MPU register to memory (i.e., store operation) or from memory to an MPU register (i.e., load operation). Of course, these data transfers can also take place between an MPU register and input/output devices. There are no data transfer instructions that directly transfer data from one memory location to another.

Register-Register Transfer

Instructions that involve the transfer of data from one MPU register to another fall into this category.

Arithmetic Instructions

This category includes all addition, subtraction, multiplication, and division instructions.

Logic Instructions

This category includes all logic operations between two operands, one of which is the contents of an accumulator.

Shift and Rotate Instructions

This group of instructions includes those that shift data left or right.

Data Altering Instructions

This category contains instructions that perform operations on a single operand (e.g., CLRA, CLRB).

Data Test Instructions

This group includes instructions that perform some type of test on a data byte or on certain bits of a data byte (e.g., TSTA).

Jump and Branch Instructions

This category contains instructions that cause the MPU to change its execution sequence.

Subroutine Instructions

These instructions deal with the use of subroutines.

Interrupt Handling Instructions

These instructions are used to handle the MPU's response to interrupts from I/O devices.

▶ 7.7 CCR INSTRUCTIONS

There are six instructions that the programmer can use to set or clear the V, C, and I flags and there is one special instruction that the programmer can use to clear the X flag and/or to set or clear the S flag.

Function	Mnemonic	Op code
Clear C flag	CLC	0C
Clear I flag	CLI	0E
Clear V flag	CLV	0A
Set C flag	SEC	0D
Set I flag	SEI	0F
Set V flag	SEV	0B
Transfer [ACCA] to [CCR]	TAP	06

The CLV and SEV instructions are not used as often as the other six. The CLI, SEI, and TAP instructions are used to control the MPU's response to certain types of interrupts ($\overline{\text{IRQ}}$ and $\overline{\text{XIRQ}}$) and to set or clear the S flag. We describe the functions of the I and X flags in our discussion of interrupts in Chapter 8.

▶ 7.8 REGISTER-TO-MEMORY TRANSFER INSTRUCTIONS

The 68HC11 MPU can execute twelve different instructions that transfer data between one of its registers and a memory location (or I/O device). The LDAA, LDAB, LDD, LDS, LDX, and LDY instructions are used to *load* data from memory (or an input device) into accumulator A, accumulator B, double accumulator, stack pointer register SP, index register X, and index register Y, respectively. The STAA, STAB, STD, STS, STX, and STY instructions are used to respectively *store* the contents of accumulator A, accumulator B, double accumulator, stack pointer register SP, index register X, and index register Y into a memory location (or output device). Each of these instructions can use several address modes. Refer to Appendix A for the available address modes, op codes, and other information pertaining to each of these instructions.

The PSHA, PSHB, PSHX, and PSHY instructions are used to push the contents of ACCA, ACCB, X, and Y onto the stack at the address specified by the stack pointer register (SP). The PULA, PULB, PULX, and PULY instructions will pull data off the top of the stack and load them into ACCA, ACCB, X, and Y, respectively.

EXAMPLE 7.15 _____

Study the short program below and determine the contents of ACCA, ACCB, ACCD, and the N and Z flags at the completion of the program.

Address	Label	Instruction code	Mnemonic	Comments
C300	START	86	LDAA #$D7	; Load ACCA with data
C301		D7		
C302		97	STAA $27	; Store ACCA in memory
C303		27		
C304		D6	LDAB $27	; Load ACCB from memory
C305		27		
C306	END	3E	WAI	; Halt execution

Solution   The first instruction, LDAA #$D7, uses the immediate address mode to load the data D7 into ACCA. The second instruction, STAA $27, uses the direct address mode to store ACCA into memory location 0027_{16}.

The third instruction loads ACCB with the data from address 0027. The last instruction, WAI, essentially halts the MPU. The following table summarizes the status of the pertinent MPU registers, flags, and memory locations after the execution of each instruction.

Instruction	Status after execution
LDAA #$D7	$[\mathbf{ACCA}] = D7_{16} = 11010111_2$: N = 1, Z = 0
STAA $27	$[\mathbf{\$0027}] = D7_{16} = 11010111_2$: N = 1, Z = 0
LDAB $27	$[\mathbf{ACCB}] = D7_{16} = 11010111_2$: N = 1, Z = 0: $[\mathbf{ACCD}] = D7D7$
WAI	No changes

EXAMPLE 7.16 _____

The program below stores the contents of ACCA and ACCB onto the stack, and then later restores them into ACCA and ACCB. Determine the addresses on the stack where the contents of ACCA and ACCB were stored and explain how the stack pointer [SP] is incremented and decremented during the execution of the program.

Address	Label	Instruction code	Mnemonic	Comments
C300	START	8E	LDS #$01FF	; Load SP
C301		01		
C302		FF		
C303		36	PSHA	; Push ACCA onto the stack
C304		37	PSHB	; Push ACCB onto the stack
:		:	:	:
C310		33	PULB	; Pull ACCB from the stack
C311		32	PULA	; Pull ACCA from the stack
C312	END	3E	WAI	; Halt execution

Solution The LDS #$01FF instruction uses the immediate address mode to load the stack pointer (SP) with 01FF. Recall that the SP is a 16-bit register, so that two successive bytes have to be specified after the op code. The PSHA instruction pushes [ACCA] into the memory location specified by [SP] = 01FF and then automatically decrements [SP] to 01FE. The PSHB instruction pushes [ACCB] into the memory location specified by [SP] = 01FE and then automatically decrements [SP] to 01FD. Thus, at this time, ACCA is stored in location 01FF and ACCB in location 01FE. Sometime later a PULB instruction is executed which automatically increments the [SP] from 01FD back to 01FE and then transfers the contents of memory location 01FE back into ACCB. Next, a PULA instruction is executed which again automatically increments the [SP] back to 01FF and then transfers the contents of memory location 01FF back into ACCA. Finally, the WAI instruction is executed which halts the MPU from executing any more instructions.

▶ 7.9 REGISTER-TO-REGISTER TRANSFER INSTRUCTIONS

The 68HC11 MPU has ten different instructions that transfer data between its various registers.

Function	Mnemonic	Op code
Transfer [ACCA] to [ACCB]	TAB	16
Transfer [ACCA] to [CCR]	TAP	06
Transfer [ACCB] to [ACCA]	TBA	17
Transfer [CCR] to [ACCA]	TPA	07
Transfer [SP] to [X]	TSX	30
Transfer [SP] to [Y]	TSY	18 30
Transfer [X] to [SP]	TXS	35
Transfer [Y] to [SP]	TYS	18 35
Exchange [D] with [X]	XGDX	8 F
Exchange [D] with [Y]	XGDY	18 8F

The first four instructions transfer a single byte of data, the next four instructions transfer two bytes of data, and the last two instructions exchange 16 bits of data between two registers. With the exception of the exchange instructions, the data in the *source* register are transferred to the *destination* register while being retained in the source register. In the case of the last two instructions (XGDX and XGDY), the 16 bits of data are simply exchanged between the two 16-bit registers involved.

The TSX, TXS, TSY, and TYS instructions are not as straightforward as the other transfer instructions. Refer to Appendix A for a complete description of these operations.

EXAMPLE 7.17

Use the appropriate transfer instruction to write a more efficient version of the program in Example 7.15.

Solution   The program of Example 7.15 was used to load a data byte into ACCA and then transfer it to ACCB. This can be accomplished with only three instructions, as shown below.

Address	Label	Instruction code	Mnemonic	Comments
C300	START	86	LDAA #$D7	; Load ACCA with data
C301		D7		
C302		16	TAB	; Transfer data to ACCB
C303	END	3E	WAI	; Halt execution

EXAMPLE 7.18

Write a 68HC11 MPU program that will take the data word from the top of the stack and load it into ACCA *without* affecting the contents of the SP.

Solution   The normal way to take data off the stack and load them into ACCA is to use a PULA instruction. The PULA operation will increment SP before it pulls data. This is done because the SP would have been decremented when the data were pushed onto the stack.

One way to accomplish the stated operation is shown in the program below.

Address	Label	Instruction code	Mnemonic	Comments
C200	START	30	TSX	; Transfer [SP] to [X]
C201		A6	LDAA $00,X	; Load ACCA from the address
C202		00		; specified by [X]
C203	END	3E	WAI	; Halt execution

To analyze this program, let's assume that [SP] = C36B. The SP is pointing at address C36B, which is the *next* available location on the stack; address C36C is the top of the stack, where the last data were pushed on the stack. This is illustrated below.

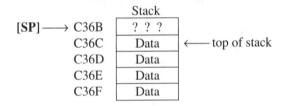

The TSX instruction transfers [SP] to [X] and then increments [X]. At the end of this instruction, then, [X] = C36B + 1 = C36C. The LDAA $00, X instruction uses the indexed address mode to load ACCA from the address given by [X], because the offset is 00. Since [X] = C36C, data will be taken from this address and loaded into ACCA. Thus, data have been taken from the top of the stack ($C36C) without affecting the SP.

▶ 7.10 ARITHMETIC INSTRUCTIONS

Unlike the 68HC11 MPU, most 8-bit MPUs have arithmetic instructions that are limited to addition and subtraction. Although this might appear to be a severe limitation, it really is not. The other arithmetic operations (multiplication, division, square roots, trigonometric functions, etc.) can be performed by sequences of instructions called subroutines that use addition and subtraction together with other instructions. Programmers have developed subroutines for all the common arithmetic operations, and these subroutines can be placed in memory and used over and over. We will say much more about subroutines later.

The 68HC11 MPU has thirteen different types of arithmetic instructions. Each of these performs an arithmetic operation on two operands. For six of these instruction types (ADD, ADDD, ADC, SUB, SUBD, and SBC) one of the operands comes from memory and the other from one of the accumulators. For three of these instruction types (ABA, SBA, MUL) one of the operands comes from accumulator A and the other from accumulator B. For two of these instruction types (ABX and ABY) one of the operands comes from accumulator B and the other from either one of the index registers, X or Y. And, for two of these instruction types (IDIV and FDIV), one of the operands comes from the double accumulator and the other from index register X.

ABA—Add Accumulator B to Accumulator A

This instruction, as described in Appendix A, adds the contents of ACCB to ACCA and places the result in ACCA. The result will affect the H, N, Z, V, and C flags.

Recall that the ALU does not know whether the two operands are signed or unsigned numbers; only the programmer knows that. The ALU adds the two 8-bit numbers as if they were unsigned numbers.

To illustrate, let's assume that [ACCA] = 01000101_2 = 69_{10} and [ACCB] = 00110010_2 = 50_{10}. The ALU will add these two numbers as shown below.

$$01000101_2 = 69_{10} \longleftarrow [\textbf{ACCA}]$$
$$+ \quad 00110010_2 = 50_{10} \longleftarrow [\textbf{ACCB}]$$
$$\overline{01110111_2} = 119_{10} \longrightarrow \text{result placed in } [\textbf{ACCA}]$$

no carry ⟍↑

The addition does not produce a carry from bit 7 (MSB) position. Thus, the MPU will make C = 0. The H flag is affected only by arithmetic additions of 8-bit operands. Whenever there is a carry-out from bit position 3 into bit position 4, the MPU will make H = 1. Therefore, in this example H = 0. Since the result is not exactly zero, the MPU will make Z = 0. The MPU will also make N = 0 since the N flag takes on the value of the sign bit of the result (even if signed numbers are not being used).

The overflow flag, V, will be cleared to 0 because the sign bit of the result is the same as the sign bits of the two operands. Recall that the V flag is used to indicate an overflow into the sign bit position when signed numbers are added or subtracted.

ADDA/ADDB/ADDD—Add Memory to Accumulator

The ADDA and ADDB instructions are used to add a data byte from memory to one of the accumulators (ACCA, ACCB), with the result placed in the accumulator. The ADDD instruction is used to add the two bytes of data from the double accumulator (ACCD) with two bytes of data from two consecutive memory locations specified by an operand address. The result is placed back into the double accumulator. The N, Z, V, and C flags are affected by the result. The H flag is affected by the instructions ADDA and ADDB; however, it is not affected by the ADDD instruction since it involves 16-bit operands. Each of these instructions can use several address modes as described in Appendix A.

ADCA/ADCB—Add Memory to Accumulator with Carry

These instructions are similar to the ADDA and ADDB instructions except that the C flag participates in the addition operation. For example, the ADCA instruction adds the operand from memory *and the C flag* to the contents of accumulator A. The following two cases illustrate the ADC instruction. In the first case, we will assume C = 1 prior to the ADCA operation.

$$00111010_2 \longleftarrow \text{operand from memory } [\textbf{M}]$$
$$00100101_2 \longleftarrow [\textbf{ACCA}]$$
$$+ \quad 1_2 \longleftarrow \text{C flag}$$
$$\overline{01100000_2} \longrightarrow \text{result placed in } [\textbf{ACCA}]$$

no carry; ⟍↑
therefore, C = 0

Note that the initial value of the C flag is added to the two operands. The result produces no carry-out of the bit 7 position; thus, the MPU will clear C = 0 after the addition operation.

Let's try a second example where C = 0 prior to the ADCA instruction.

$$01101001_2 \longleftarrow \text{operand from memory } [\mathbf{M}]$$
$$11100110_2 \longleftarrow [\mathbf{ACCA}]$$
$$+ \qquad 0_2 \longleftarrow \text{C flag}$$
$$1 \quad \overline{01001111_2} \longrightarrow \text{result placed in } [\mathbf{ACCA}]$$

carry; ———————↑
therefore, C = 1

In this example, the result produces a carry-out of the bit 7 position, so the MPU will set C = 1 at the completion of the addition operation.

If you are wondering why it would be necessary to add the C flag to the operands, the reason has to do with *multibyte* addition. Multibyte addition is used to add numbers that are longer than one byte. The carry generated by the addition of low-order bytes is added to the addition of the higher-order bytes. This will be illustrated in Problem 30 at the end of this chapter.

ABX/ABY—Add Accumulator B to Index Register X or Y

The ABX and ABY instructions are used to add the *unsigned* 8-bit number in ACCB to the contents of index register X or Y, with the result placed in the same index register. These instructions use the inherent address mode only and neither one of them affects any of the flags in the CCR register. The 68HC11 MPU instruction set has no equivalent instruction to add accumulator A to an index register.

SBA—Subtract Accumulator B from Accumulator A

This instruction subtracts [**ACCB**] from [**ACCA**] and places the result in ACCA. The ALU uses the 2's-complement method for subtraction; that is, it adds the 2's-complement of [**ACCB**] to [**ACCA**]. The result affects the N, Z, and V flags in the same manner as the addition operation described earlier. The C flag, however, is affected in a different way:

After a subtract operation is performed, the C flag is complemented so that it indicates the occurrence of a borrow.

When a number is subtracted from a smaller number, there will be a borrow, so the MPU will set C = 1. When a number is subtracted from a larger or equal number, there will be no borrow, so C will be cleared to zero. In other words, the C flag is set if the absolute value of ACCB is larger than the absolute value of ACCA; otherwise it is cleared. The following example will illustrate.

Assume that [**ACCA**] = $00001001_2 = 9_{10}$ and [**ACCB**] = $00000101_2 = 5_{10}$. The SBA operation is shown below.

$$00001001_2 \longleftarrow [\mathbf{ACCA}]$$
$$+ \quad 11111011_2 \longrightarrow \text{2's-complement of } [\mathbf{ACCB}]$$
$$1 \quad \overline{00000100_2} \longrightarrow \text{result placed in } [\mathbf{ACCA}]$$

carry; ———————↑
therefore, C = 0

Here, the addition of the 2's-complement of [ACCB] to [ACCA] produces a carry-out of bit 7. This will always happen when a number is subtracted from a larger or equal number. The MPU, however, will make C = 0 to indicate that no borrow has occurred. In other words, the MPU complements (inverts) the C flag to indicate the borrow status.

Now let's assume that $[ACCA] = 00000101_2 = 5_{10}$ and $[ACCB] = 00001001_2 = 9_{10}$. The SBA operation is shown below.

$$
\begin{array}{r}
00000101_2 \longleftarrow [\textbf{ACCA}] \\
+ \quad 11110111_2 \longleftarrow \text{2's-complement of } [\textbf{ACCB}] \\
\hline
11111100_2 \longrightarrow \text{result placed in } [\textbf{ACCA}]
\end{array}
$$

no carry;
therefore, C = 1

In this case, there is no carry out of bit 7. This will always happen when a number is subtracted from a smaller number. The MPU will set C = 1 to indicate that a borrow has occurred. The borrow is used in a multibyte subtraction operation (see Problem 32 at the end of this chapter).

SUBA/SUBB—Subtract Memory from Accumulator

These instructions are used to subtract a memory data word from one of the accumulators, with the result placed in the accumulator. The N, Z, V, and C flags are affected in the same way as for the SBA instruction. Each of these instructions uses several address modes as described in Appendix A.

EXAMPLE 7.19

Figure 7.2 is the flowchart for a program that performs several addition and subtraction operations. Write a program for this flowchart.

Solution   The program is shown below starting at address C200.

Address	Label	Instruction code	Mnemonic
C200	START	B6	LDAA $C000
C201		C0	
C202		00	
C203		D6	LDAB $0050
C204		50	
C205		10	SBA
C206		8B	ADDA #$3C
C207		3C	
C208		B0	SUBA $C682
C209		C6	
C20A		82	
C20B		16	TAB
C20C	END	3E	WAI

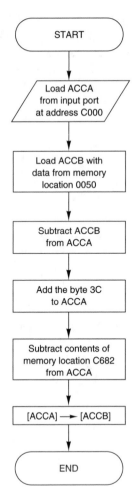

FIGURE 7.2   Flowchart for Example 7.19.

Inside the flowchart:

START

Load ACCA from input port at address C000

Load ACCB with data from memory location 0050

Subtract ACCB from ACCA

Add the byte 3C to ACCA

Subtract contents of memory location C682 from ACCA

[ACCA] → [ACCB]

END

Examine this program carefully and note how each instruction corresponds to one of the blocks in the flowchart. Also check the address modes and op codes used for each instruction.

SUBD—Subtract Memory from Double Accumulator

This instruction is used to subtract a 16-bit number stored in two consecutive memory locations from the contents of the double accumulator, with the result placed in the double accumulator. The N, Z, V, and C flags are affected in the same way as for the SUB instruction. Each of these instructions uses several address modes as described in Appendix A.

EXAMPLE 7.20

Examine the 68HC11 MPU program below and determine the value stored in memory locations 0050 and 0051, respectively, at the end of the program execution. Note the data stored in memory locations C100 to C106.

Address	Label	Instruction code	Mnemonic
C000	START	CC	LDD $C100
C001		C1	
C002		00	
C003		83	SUBD $C102
C004		C1	
C005		02	
C006		DD	STD $0050
C007		50	
C008	END	3E	WAI
: :		: :	: :
C100		00	
C101		FA	
C102		00	
C103		EA	
C105		45	
C106		AA	
: :		: :	
: :		: :	

Solution   The first instruction, LDD $C100, uses the extended mode to load the 16-bit double accumulator with two bytes of data stored in memory locations C100 and C101, respectively. Thus, the instruction LDD $C100 will load the double accumulator with $00FA_{16}$. The next instruction, SUBD $C102, will cause the MPU to subtract the 16-bit number stored in consecutive memory locations C102 and C103 ($00EA_{16}$) from [ACCD] and place the result in [ACCD]. Symbolically, [ACCD] − [M:M + 1] ⟶ [ACCD]. Hence, $00FA_{16}$ − $00EA_{16}$ ⟶ 0010_{16}. Before the program halts, instruction STD $0050 uses the direct addressing mode to store the contents of double accumulator (0010_{16}) in memory locations 0050 and 0051, respectively. In other words, instruction STD $0050 causes the MPU to store the contents of ACCA (00_{16}) in memory location 0050 and the contents of ACCB (10_{16}) in memory location 0051. Recall that the double accumulator is the concatenation of accumulator A and accumulator B.

SBCA/SBCB—Subtract Memory from Accumulator with Carry

These instructions will subtract a memory data byte *and the C flag* from one of the accumulators. To illustrate, assume that [ACCB] = 28_{16}, and the data word stored in memory location C250 is 12_{16}. Also assume that C = 1. When the MPU executes the instruction SBCB \$C250, it will subtract [C250] and the C flag from [ACCB] as shown below. All values are hexadecimal.

$$
\begin{array}{rl}
28 & \text{[ACCB]} \\
-12 & \text{[C250]} \\
\underline{-1} & \text{C flag} \\
15 & \longrightarrow \text{result placed in ACCB}
\end{array}
$$

The SBC instructions are used only when multibyte subtractions are performed, and the C flag represents the borrow generated by subtraction of lower-order bytes.

DAA—Decimal Adjust the Accumulator A

This instruction is used only after two BCD-coded operands are added and the result placed in accumulator A. The ALU adds the two operands as if they were straight binary numbers, and the binary result is placed in ACCA. The DAA instruction can then be used to convert the result in ACCA to correct BCD form. To illustrate, assume [ACCA]= 01000110 (BCD) = 46_{10}, and [ACCB] = 00100111 (BCD) = 27_{10}. Execution of the ABA instruction proceeds as follows:

$$
\begin{array}{rl}
0100\ 0110 & \text{[ACCA]} \\
+\quad 0010\ 0111 & \text{[ACCB]} \\
\hline
0110\ 1101 & \longrightarrow \text{result placed in ACCA}
\end{array}
$$

The result is not in correct BCD form. It can be converted to correct BCD by execution of a DAA instruction. The DAA instruction will correct it by adding 0110 to the [ACCA] as shown below.

$$
\begin{array}{rl}
0110\ 1101 & \text{[ACCA] after ABA instruction} \\
+\qquad 0110 & \text{[ACCB]} \\
\hline
0111\ 0110 &
\end{array}
$$

$$
\begin{array}{cc}
7 \quad 3 & \longrightarrow \text{correct BCD placed in ACCA}
\end{array}
$$

The DAA instruction can be used to follow any addition instruction that places the result in ACCA. In other words, there are three possible instruction sequences that can be used for adding operands that represent BCD-coded data; these are ABA, DAA; ADDA, DAA; and ADCA, DAA. You can consider these pairs of instructions as performing the operation of adding BCD numbers and producing BCD results.

The DAA instruction cannot be used with ACCB, and it cannot be used for BCD subtraction.

MUL—Multiply Accumulator A by Accumulator B

The MUL instruction multiplies an 8-bit unsigned binary value in accumulator A (ACCA) by the 8-bit unsigned binary value in accumulator B (ACCB) and places the 16-bit unsigned product in the double accumulator (ACCD). The C flag is set if bit 7 of the result (bit 7 of ACCB) is set. The C flag is useful whenever rounding of the most significant byte of the product is desired. If the C flag is set after the MUL instruction is executed, it means that the lower byte (ACCB) of the result is greater than 0.5 (assuming multiplication of mixed numbers). In such cases, we may choose to round the most significant byte (ACCA) of the product by executing the sequence: MUL, ADCA #$00. This program sequence will add 1 to the most significant byte of the product (ACCA) if the C flag is set due to the execution of the MUL instruction.

EXAMPLE 7.21

(a) Write a program for the 68HC11 MPU that will multiply the unsigned decimal numbers 11.625 and 15.125 in memory locations C200 and C201, respectively, and place the rounded-off result to the nearest unit in memory location C202.

(b) Explain the step-by-step execution of the program.

Solution

(a) The first step is to write the multiplicand and the multiplier as unsigned 8-bit binary numbers and then convert them to hex. (Note: you may want to refer to Chapter 1 to review how to write binary numbers with a *binary point*.)

$$11.625 = 1011.1010_2 = BA_{16}$$

$$15.125 = 1111.0010_2 = F2_{16}$$

It is important to know that the MPU will assume data BA_{16} and $F2_{16}$ to be whole integers. The computer has no idea that the data represent mixed numbers; that is, an integer part and a fractional part. Only the programmer knows that a binary point separates the two parts.

Now, let us write a program sequence needed to multiply $BA_{16} \times F2_{16}$, round off the product to the nearest unit, and then store it in memory location C202.

Memory Address	Instruction code	Mnemonic	Description
C000	B6	LDAA $C200	; [C200] ⟶ [ACCA]
C001	C2		
C002	00		
C003	F6	LDAB $C201	; [C201] ⟶ [ACCB]
C004	C2		
C005	01		
C006	3D	MUL	; [ACCA] × [ACCB] ⟶ [ACCD]
C007	89	ADCA #$00	; [ACCA] + [C] + 00 ⟶ [ACCA]
C008	00		
C009	B7	STAA $C202	; [ACCA] ⟶ [C202]
C00A	C2		
C00B	02		
C00C	3E	WAI	; Halt execution of the program.

(b)

1. The first instruction to be executed by the program above is the LDAA $C200. This instruction loads ACCA with the contents of memory location C200. Thus, at the end of the execution of this instruction, ACCA will be loaded with $1011.1010_2 = 11.625_{10}$ as illustrated below. Since at this point we don't know what the data in ACCB are, we will assign an X to each bit of ACCB.

ACCA   ACCB

1 0 1 1 . 1 0 1 0	X X X X X X X X

assumed binary point ———↑

2. The next instruction is the LDAB $C201 instruction. This instruction loads ACCB with the contents of memory location C201, which results in $[\textbf{ACCB}] = 1111.0010_2 = 15.125_{10}$.

ACCA   b7   ACCB   b0

1 0 1 1 . 1 0 1 0	1 1 1 1 . 0 0 1 0

↑——— binary points ———↑

3. The next instruction to be executed is the MUL instruction. This instruction multiplies $[\textbf{ACCA}] \times [\textbf{ACCB}]$ and places the 16-bit product in ACCD. After a MUL instruction is executed the original contents of ACCA and ACCB are replaced with the result of the multiplication. It is important to realize that, as far as the 68HC11 MPU is concerned, ACCA = $10111010_2 = 186_{10}$ and ACCB = $11110010_2 = 242_{10}$. Thus, once the MUL instruction is executed, the final result is ACCD = $1010111111010100_2 = 45,012_{10}$ which is the correct result that ends up in ACCD as shown below. Recall that ACCD is the concatenation of ACCA and ACCB, with ACCA as the high-order byte. Note that this result has to have a binary point inserted as shown because the original numbers were mixed numbers with an assumed binary point.

Since bit 7 of [**ACCB**] is a 1, the C flag will be set to a 1.

←——————— ACCD ———————→

ACCA   b7   ACCB   b0

1 0 1 01 1 1 1	1 1 0 10 1 0 0

· ←——— binary point

4. Next, instruction ADCA #$00 is executed. This instruction adds the contents of the C flag to the sum of the [**ACCA**] and data 00_{16}, symbolically, $[\textbf{ACCA}] + [\textbf{C}] + \textbf{00} \longrightarrow [\textbf{ACCA}]$. Recall that C = 1 since the result of the multiplication has bit 7 HIGH (bit 7 = 1 of ACCB). Therefore, the 68HC11 MPU will add the contents of ACCA ($10101111_2 = AF_{16} = 175_{10}$) to the contents of the C flag (1_2) and data 00_{16}, as shown below.

$$10101111_2 = 175_{10} \longleftarrow \textbf{[ACCA]}$$
$$1_2 = 1_{10} \longleftarrow \text{carry flag}$$
$$+ \quad 00000000_2 = 00_{10} \longleftarrow \text{immediate data}$$
$$\overline{10110000_2 = 176_{10}} \longleftarrow \textbf{[ACCA]}$$

It should be clear that after the ADCA #00 instruction is executed, the data in ACCA is the product of the multiplication 11.625×15.125 rounded off to the nearest unit, or 176_{10}. In this example, the user would discard the lower byte of the data in ACCB.

5. Instruction STAA $C202 stores the contents of ACCA ($10110000_2 = 176_{10}$) in memory location C202.

6. Instruction WAI halts the execution of any further instructions by the MPU.

This is one possible solution for Example 7.21. Obviously, you might have done it differently. There is no right or wrong way of writing any program, as long as the required task gets accomplished. Nevertheless, some ways are more efficient than others. As stated before in this textbook, we are not concerned with how good a programmer you'll become so much as whether or not you understand how an 8-bit MPU manipulates data and executes instructions in order to accomplish a desired task.

IDIV/FDIV—Integer Divide and Fractional Divide

The 68HC11 MPU has two different divide instructions: an integer divide (IDIV) instruction and a fractional divide (FDIV) instruction. The IDIV instruction allows the MPU to perform an *unsigned* integer divide of the 16-bit binary number in ACCD (numerator) by the 16-bit binary number in the index register X (denominator). The result of the division (quotient) is placed in the X register and the remainder is placed in ACCD. When the IDIV instruction is executed, the C flag will be set if the denominator was $0000; otherwise the C flag is cleared. The IDIV instruction will always clear the V flag. The Z flag will be set to 1 only if the quotient is $0000. The N flag is *not* affected. The following example illustrates the IDIV instruction.

EXAMPLE 7.22

Let us assume that ACCA, ACCB, and the index register X of the 68HC11 MPU have the following data: $\textbf{[ACCA]} = 01_{16}$, $\textbf{[ACCB]} = 81_{16}$, and $\textbf{[X]} = 0014_{16}$. Determine the following after the execution of an IDIV instruction:

1. The value in the accumulator A.

2. The value in the accumulator B.

3. The value in the index register X.

4. The values of the C, V, and Z flags.

Solution   The execution of the Integer Divide (IDIV) instruction will cause the 68HC11 MPU to divide the contents of the double accumulator (ACCD) by the contents of the index register X. The quotient is loaded into the index register X and the remainder is stored in the double accumulator. The C flag is set if the denominator is zero, otherwise, it is cleared. Therefore, in this example, the MPU will divide the contents of ACCD (0181_{16})

by the contents in the index register X (0014_{16}). The result of the division is 0013_{16} which will be placed in the index X register and the remainder (0005_{16}) is stored in ACCD (ACCA = 00, ACCB = 05). This problem can be easily checked by performing the same division using decimal numbers. The required hex-to-decimal conversions would yield: [**ACCD**] = 0181_{16} = 385_{10}, [**X**] = 0014_{16} = 20_{10}. Therefore, **385 ÷ 20 = 19** with a remainder of **5**. Of course, the result is 19_{10} = 13_{16}, which confirms the results obtained by the MPU. Since the denominator is $\$0014_{16}$, the C flag is cleared. The V flag is always cleared after this instruction is executed. The Z flag will be 0 since the quotient is not $\$0000$.

The FDIV instruction differs from the IDIV instruction in that the numerator, [**ACCD**], is assumed to be less than the denominator, [**X**]. Consequently, a quotient less than one (fractional result) occurs. The quotient is placed in the index register X and the remainder is placed in the double accumulator. The V flag is set if the original contents of the index register X are less than, or equal to, the contents of ACCD. The Z, C, and N flags are affected the same as for the IDIV instruction.

The following example illustrates the FDIV instruction.

EXAMPLE 7.23 ——————————————————————————————————

Let us assume that ACCA, ACCB, and the index register X of the 68HC11 MPU have the following data: [**ACCA**] = 00_{16}, [**ACCB**] = $0C_{16}$, and [**X**] = 0010_{16}. What are the final results in [**X**], [**ACCD**], and the C, V, and Z flags after an FDIV instruction is executed?

Solution   The execution of the Fractional Integer Divide (FDIV) instruction will cause the 68HC11 MPU to divide [**ACCD**] = $000C_{16}$ by the contents of the index register X = 0010_{16}. The result of the division is loaded into the index register X = $C000_{16}$ and the remainder is stored in ACCD = 0000_{16}. The C, V, and Z flags are all cleared. This problem can be checked by performing the same division using the equivalent decimal numbers. The hex-to-decimal conversions are as follows: [**ACCD**] = $000C_{16}$ = 12_{10}, [**X**] = 0010_{16} = 16_{10}. Therefore, **12 ÷ 16 = 0.75** with a remainder of 0. Of course, the result in X = $.1100\ 0000\ 0000\ 0000_2$ = $C000_{16}$ = 0.75_{10}, which confirms the results obtained by the MPU.

▶ 7.11 LOGICAL INSTRUCTIONS

This group of instructions takes the contents of the accumulator and an operand from memory, performs a bit-by-bit logic operation on them, and stores the results in the accumulator. There are three such logic instructions available on the 68HC11 MPU.

AND—performs the logical AND operation
ORA—performs the logical OR operation
EOR—performs the logical EX-OR operation

These three operations are illustrated below for the same accumulator and operand values:

7	6	5	4	3	2	1	0	
1	0	1	0	1	0	1	0	[ACCA]

1	1	0	1	0	0	1	1	**Operand**

1	0	0	0	0	0	1	0	**AND result**

1	1	1	1	1	0	1	1	**ORA result**

0	1	1	1	1	0	0	1	**EOR result**

It is important to realize that these logic operations work on each bit position separately and independently from the others. For example, bit 7 of the accumulator is ANDed with bit 7 of the operand to produce bit 7 of the result; likewise, bit 6 of the accumulator is ANDed with bit 6 of the operand to produce bit 6 of the result, and so on for the other bits.

Affected Flags   These logical instructions will affect the N, Z, and V flags. If the result is 00000000, the Z flag will be set; otherwise, it will be cleared. If the result has a 1 in bit 7, the N flag will be set, otherwise, the N flag will be cleared. The execution of any of these logical operations will always cause the V flag to be cleared.

AND Masking

The most common use of the AND instruction is to selectively *clear* specific bits of a data word while not affecting the other bits. This can be done by ANDing the data word with another word, called a *mask,* which the programmer chooses to select which bits he wants to clear. This is illustrated as follows:

D_7	D_6	D_5	D_4	D_3	D_2	D_1	D_0	Data word

0	1	1	1	1	0	1	1	Mask for clearing bits 2 and 7

0	D_6	D_5	D_4	D_3	0	D_1	D_0	Result of ANDing

Here the bits of the data word, D7 through D0, can be any pattern of 1s and 0s. The mask word has 1s in each bit position except bits 7 and 2. The result of ANDing the data word with the mask word shows that bits 7 and 2 are 0 while the other bits are the same as the data word. This is because of the properties of the AND operation—anything ANDed with 0 is 0, and anything ANDed with 1 is unchanged.

Thus, the overall effect of the operation is to clear bits 2 and 7 of the data word without affecting the other bits. Clearly, any of the data bits can be cleared by putting a 0 in the appropriate position of the mask word. This process is often referred to as *AND masking*.

This masking technique is also often used to isolate the value of a single bit of a data word. The data word might be a status word read from an input device, and a particular bit of the status word could be used to tell the microprocessor what sequence of instructions to follow. This is illustrated as follows:

D_7	D_6	D_5	D_4	D_3	D_2	D_1	D_0	Status word from input device

0	0	0	1	0	0	0	0	Mask for isolating D_4

0	0	0	D_4	0	0	0	0	Result of ANDing

The mask has a 1 only in the bit 4 position, so the result of the AND operation has 0s in all bit positions except bit 4, which will equal D_4. If D_4 is 0, the result will be all 0s, so the Z flag is set to 1. If D_4 is 1, the Z flag will be cleared to 0. Thus, by testing the Z flag, the program can determine the D_4 status and alter its instruction sequence accordingly. This testing is done using conditional branch instructions, which we will be discussing shortly.

ORA Masking

The ORA instruction can be used to selectively *set* specific bits of a data word while not affecting the other bits. This is done by using a mask word that has 1s only in those bit positions that are to be set. This is illustrated as follows:

D_7	D_6	D_5	D_4	D_3	D_2	D_1	D_0	Data word

0	1	1	1	0	0	0	0	Mask for setting bits 4, 5, 6

D_7	1	1	1	D_3	D_2	D_1	D_0	Result of ORing

Here the mask word has 1s in bit positions 4, 5, and 6. The result of ORing the mask with the data word produces a word with 1s in these positions regardless of the values of D_6, D_5, and D_4. The other data word bits are unaffected. This is due to the properties of the OR operation—anything ORed with 1 is 1, and anything ORed with 0 is unchanged. This process of selective bit setting is called *OR masking*.

EOR—Selective Inversion

The EOR instruction is often used to selectively *invert* specific bits of a data word while not affecting the other bits. This is illustrated as follows:

D_7	D_6	D_5	D_4	D_3	D_2	D_1	D_0	Data word

0	0	1	0	0	0	0	0	EOR mask for inverting D_5

D_7	D_6	$\bar{D}_5$	D_4	D_3	D_2	D_1	D_0	Result of EOR operation

The result shows that D_5 has been inverted, as the result of the 1 in the mask word, while the other bits of the data word are unchanged. This is a result of the following EX-OR truth table:

Data bit (D)	Mask bit (M)	Result $= D \oplus M$
0	0	0
1	0	1
0	1	1
1	1	0

Whenever the mask bit is a 1, the result is the inverse of the data bit; whenever the mask bit is a 0, the result is the same as the data bit.

One common application of the EOR operation occurs when the microcomputer reads a data word from an input device that places *inverted* data on the microcomputer data bus. This could be taken care of by the addition of tri-state inverters between the device outputs and the data bus. A less costly solution is to read the data into the microcomputer and then use an EOR instruction to invert the *complete* data word. This is easily accomplished using the following instruction sequence:

Instruction code	Mnemonic	Comments
B6	LDAA $F700	; Load data from input device
F7		; at address F700
00		
88	EORA #$FF	; Invert the contents of
FF		; accumulator A

The mask word FF (hex) $= 11111111_2$ is used to invert each bit of the accumulator.

EXAMPLE 7.24 _____

Assume that $[ACCA] = 37_{16}$ and $[ACCB] = A2_{16}$. For each of the following instructions, determine the result and the values of the N and Z flags:

(a) ANDA #$E3   (b) ORAA #$C8   (c) EORB #$A2

Solution

(a) The instruction ANDs the data word E3 with $[ACCA] = 37_{16}$ to produce $[ACCA] = 23_{16} = 00100011_2$. The Z flag will be 0 since the result is not zero; the N flag will be 0 since bit 7 of the result is 0.

(b) The instruction ORs the data word C8 with $[ACCA] = 37_{16}$ to produce $[ACCA] = FF_{16} = 11111111_2$. The Z flag is 0 and the N flag is 1.

(c) The instruction EX-ORs the data word A2 with $[ACCA] = A2_{16}$ to produce $[ACCB] = 00_{16}$. The Z flag is set to 1 since the result is zero; the N flag is 0.

EXAMPLE 7.25

Write an instruction sequence that takes a data byte from memory location C6A5, clears its LSB, sets its MSB, and returns it to memory without affecting any other bits.

Solution The required instruction sequence has to (1) load the data from memory into one of the accumulators; (2) AND-mask the accumulator with 11111110 to clear the LSB; (3) OR-mask the accumulator with 10000000 to set the MSB; and (4) store the result in memory.

Address	Label	Instruction code	Mnemonic	Comments
C100	START	F6	LDAB $C6A5	; Load data into ACCB
C101		C6		
C102		A5		
C103		C4	ANDB #$FE	; AND-mask to clear
C104		FE		; LSB
C105		CA	ORAB #$80	; OR-mask to set MSB
C106		80		
C107		F7	STAB $C6A5	; Restore data to
C108		C6		; memory
C109		A5		
C10A	END	3E	WAI	; Halt

▶ 7.12 SHIFT AND ROTATE INSTRUCTIONS

The 68HC11 MPU can perform nine different shift operations on an 8-bit operand. However, some of the operations are identical (ASL=LSL and ASLD=LSLD); that is, they perform the same function, have the same op code, but share a different mnemonic. The following are all the shift and rotate 68HC11 MPU instructions:

ASL—Arithmetic shift left *(same as LSL)*

ASR—Arithmetic shift right (with bit 7 unchanged)

LSL—Logical shift left *(same as ASL)*

LSR—Logical shift right

ASLD—Arithmetic shift left double accumulator *(same as LSLD)*

LSLD—Logic shift left double accumulator *(same as ASLD)*

LSRD—Logical shift right double accumulator

ROL—Rotate left

ROR—Rotate right

Six of the operations can be performed on ACCA, ACCB, or the contents of a memory location, while three of the operations can be performed on the double accumulator. For example, there are three rotate left instructions: ROL, ROLA, and ROLB. Thus, altogether the 68HC11 MPU has 17 different shift/rotate instructions. Each of them is described in Appendix A. You should refer to these descriptions as you go through the following illustrative examples.

EXAMPLE 7.26 _____

Assume that $[ACCA] = B6_{16}$, $[ACCB] = 6A_{16}$, $[C250] = 37_{16}$, and C = 1. For each of the following instructions, determine the operand and C flag after the instruction is executed.

(a) ASL $C250   **(b)** ASRA   **(c)** LSLD   **(d)** LSRA

(e) ROL $C250   **(f)** RORB

Solution

(a) ASL $C250 operates on the contents of memory location C250. The operation proceeds as follows:

```
C          D7  D6  D5  D4  D3  D2  D1  D0
┌───┐      ┌───┬───┬───┬───┬───┬───┬───┬───┐
│ 1 │ ←─── │ 0 │ 0 │ 1 │ 1 │ 0 │ 1 │ 1 │ 1 │ ←── 0    [C250] before shift
└───┘      └───┴───┴───┴───┴───┴───┴───┴───┘

┌───┐      ┌───┬───┬───┬───┬───┬───┬───┬───┐
│ 0 │      │ 0 │ 1 │ 1 │ 0 │ 1 │ 1 │ 1 │ 0 │         [C250] after shift
└───┘      └───┴───┴───┴───┴───┴───┴───┴───┘
```

Observe that each bit of the operand is shifted left, with bit 7 shifting into the C flag and a 0 shifting into bit 0. Thus, $[C250] = 01101110 = 6E_{16}$ and C = 0 after the shift left operation.

In executing this instruction, the MPU loads the memory operand into the ALU, performs the shift operation on the operand, and then stores the result back into memory.

(b) ASRA operates on the contents of ACCA. The operation proceeds as follows:

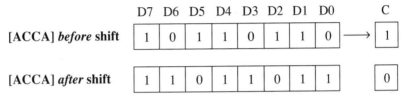

Note that each bit of the operand is shifted right. Bit 0 shifts into the C flag and bit 7 is left unchanged. Thus, $[ACCA] = 11011011 = DB_{16}$ and C = 0 after the operation.

(c) LSLD operates on the contents of the double accumulator. The operation proceeds as follows:

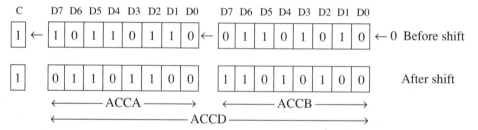

Observe that each bit of the operand is shifted left, with bit 7 of ACCA shifting into the C flag, bit 7 of ACCB shifting into bit 0 of ACCA, and a 0 shifting into bit 0 of ACCB. Thus, $[\text{ACCD}] = 0110110011010100 = 6\text{CD4}_{16}$ and $C = 1$ after the shift left operation.

(d) LSRA operates on $[\text{ACCA}]$. The operation proceeds as follows:

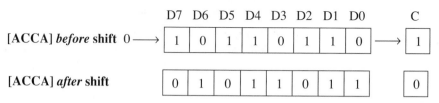

Observe that each bit is shifted right. Bit 0 is shifted into the C flag and a 0 is shifted into bit 7. Thus $[\text{ACCA}] = 01011011 = 5\text{B}_{16}$ and $C = 0$ after the operation.

(e) ROL $C250 operates on $[\text{C250}]$.

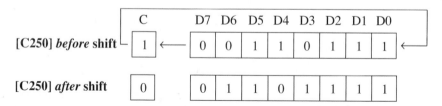

Observe that each bit is shifted left, with the C flag rotated into bit 0 and bit 7 shifted into the C flag. Thus $[\text{C250}] = 01101111 = 6\text{F}_{16}$ and $C = 0$ after the rotate operation.

(f) RORB operates on $[\text{ACCB}]$.

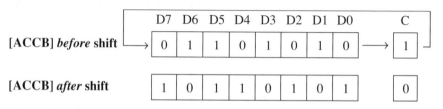

Each bit is shifted right, with the C flag rotated into bit 7 and bit 0 shifted into the C flag. Thus, $[\text{ACCB}] = 10110101 = \text{B5}_{16}$ and $C = 0$ after the rotate operation.

Application: BCD-to-ASCII Conversion

Computers often transmit data to an output device to be printed or displayed. Some common output devices are teletypewriters, printers, and video terminals. These devices typically require the data to be in ASCII-coded form. Thus, if the computer wants to send a character (number, letter, symbol, and so forth) to a printer to be printed, it has to transmit the correct ASCII code for that character to the printer.

Let us consider a typical application in which BCD-coded data from the computer's memory are to be transmitted to an ASCII printer. Each byte of memory data consists of two BCD-coded decimal digits. For example, the decimal number 64 is stored as 01100100, the BCD code for 64_{10}. When two decimal digits are represented by one memory word, it is often referred to as *packed BCD* (that is, the BCD codes for two digits are packed into one data word).

The table that follows shows that the 8-bit ASCII code for any decimal digit has 0011 in the four MSB positions followed by the digit's BCD code.

Decimal digit	ASCII
0	0011 0000
1	0011 0001
2	0011 0010
3	0011 0011
4	0011 0100
5	0011 0101
6	0011 0110
7	0011 0111
8	0011 1000
9	0011 1001

The computer has to unpack the packed BCD and convert the BCD code for each digit to its 8-bit ASCII code for transmission to the printer. For example, if the packed BCD word is 01100100 = 64_{10}, the computer has to generate 00110110 (ASCII for "6") and 00110100 (ASCII for "4") to transmit to the printer. Figure 7.3 is a flowchart for a program that will perform this operation. We will go through it step by step using the packed BCD word 01100100.

1. Load ACCA with the packed BCD word.

$$[ACCA] = \textbf{01100100}$$

2. Perform *four* right shifts on [ACCA], with 0s shifted in from the left. This can be done using four successive LSRA instructions. The result is

$$[ACCA] = \textbf{00000110}$$

The BCD code 6, the MSD of the decimal number, is now in the proper position for the ASCII code.

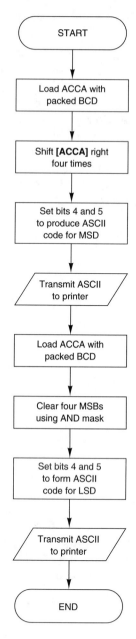

FIGURE 7.3 Flowchart for converting packed BCD to ASCII.

3. **[ACCA]** is ORed with 00110000 to set bits 4 and 5. The result is

$$[ACCA] = 00110110$$

which is the ASCII code for 6.

4. The MPU transmits **[ACCA]** to the printer output port by performing a STAA operation.

5. The packed BCD word is again loaded into ACCA:

$$[ACCA] = 01100100$$

6. [ACCA] is ANDed with 00001111 to clear the four MSBs to produce

$$[ACCA] = 00000100$$

7. [ACCA] is ORed with 00110000 to produce

$$[ACCA] = 00110100$$

which is the ASCII code for 4.

8. The MPU transmits [ACCA] to the printer output port.

▶ 7.13 DATA-ALTERING INSTRUCTIONS

In addition to shift and rotate operations, the 68HC11 MPU can perform five other operations on a single operand. Most of these operations can be performed on a memory byte and on the contents of one of the accumulators. Two of the operations can be performed on the X index register, the Y index register, and the stack pointer.

The Complement Operation (COM)

This operation will take the 1's-complement of a data byte [i.e., it complements (inverts) each bit]. The three types of complement instruction are:

COM— complement memory byte
COMA—complement [ACCA]
COMB—complement [ACCB]

The COM instruction uses both the extended and indexed address modes, while the COMA and COMB instructions use the inherent addressing mode.

EXAMPLE 7.27 ───

Determining [ACCA] after the following instruction sequence is executed: LDAA #$37, COMA.

Solution   LDAA #$37 produces $[ACCA] = 00110111_2$. The COMA instruction inverts each bit to produce $[ACCA] = 11001000_2 = C8_{16}$.

The Negate Operation (NEG)

This operation is really the 2's-complement operation. It is called a *negate* operation because when dealing with signed numbers, the 2's-complement operation converts a positive number to negative, and vice versa.

The three types of negate instruction are:

NEG—2's-complement memory data
NEGA—2's-complement [ACCA]
NEGB—2's-complement [ACCB]

The NEG instruction can use the extended and indexed address modes, while the NEGA and NEGB instructions use the inherent addressing mode.

EXAMPLE 7.28

The 68HC11 MPU does not have a single instruction that will subtract [ACCA] from [ACCB]. Write an instruction sequence that will subtract [ACCA] from [ACCB] and place the result in ACCB.

Solution

Instruction code	Mnemonic	Comments
40	NEGA	; 2's-complement [ACCA]
1B	ABA	; Add it to [ACCB]
16	TAB	; Transfer to ACCB

The first two instructions perform the subtraction operation by adding the 2's-complement of ACCA to ACCB. Since the ABA instruction leaves the result in ACCA, the TAB instruction is needed to transfer the result to ACCB.

The Clear Operation (CLR)

This operation simply clears each bit of the operand to 0. The three types of clear instruction are:

CLR—clear memory byte
CLRA—clear [ACCA]
CLRB—clear [ACCB]

The CLR instruction can use the extended and indexed address modes, while the CLRA and CLRB instructions use the inherent addressing mode.

These instructions are often used to clear a memory location or an accumulator to zero before using it as a *counter*. In programming, a counter is used to keep track of the number of times some operation or event occurs, such as the number of times a program loop has been executed.

The Clear Bit(s) Operation (BCLR)

The BCLR operation clears selected bit(s) of the data in the specified memory location and adjusts the N and Z flags accordingly. The BCLR instruction uses the direct and indexed address modes. Assume that $[X] = 1000$ and $[1050] = F2$ and consider the following sequence:

Address	Instruction code	Mnemonic
C100	1D	BCLR $50,X, $80
C101	50	
C102	80	

In this example we use the BCLR instruction in the indexed X address mode. Therefore, the effective address of the operand is determined by adding the offset byte ($50) to the contents of the index X register ($1000). The result is an effective operand address of 1050. Thus, the BCLR instruction will clear those data bit(s) in the operand that correspond to 1s in the mask byte. Since the mask byte is 80 (10000000_2), bit 7 of the data in memory location 1050 will be cleared. The other bits will be unaffected. Thus, the result is $[1050] = 72_{16} = 01110010_2$.

The Set Bit(s) Operation (BSET)

The BSET operation sets selected bit(s) of the data in the specified memory location and adjusts the N and Z flags accordingly. Like the BCLR instruction, the BSET instruction can use the direct and indexed address modes. Assume that $[0050] = AA$ and consider the following sequence:

Address	Instruction code	Mnemonic
C100	14	BSET $50 $55
C101	50	
C102	55	

The BSET instruction above uses the direct address mode. This instruction will set the data bits in memory location 0050 specified by the mask byte, 55. Since mask byte $55_{16} = 01010101_2$, bits 0, 2, 4, and 6 will be set. The other bits will be unaffected. Thus, the result is $[0050] = FF_{16} = 11111111_2$.

The Increment Operation (INC)

This operation adds 1 to an operand. There are three types of increment instructions that operate on an 8-bit operand. They are:

INC—increment memory data
INCA—increment [ACCA]
INCB—increment [ACCB]

The INC instruction can use the extended and indexed address modes, while the INCA and INCB instructions use the inherent addressing mode.

There are three increment instructions that operate on the 16-bit registers X, Y, and SP.

INX—increment index register X
INY—increment index register Y
INS—increment stack pointer register

The INX, INY, and INS instructions all use the inherent addressing mode.

Increment instructions are often used to increment a memory location or register that is being used as a counter.

EXAMPLE 7.29

Assume that the data byte FE is stored in address C250. Determine **[C250]** after the execution of two successive INC $C250 instructions.

Solution   The first INC $C250 will add 1 to FE to produce FF. The second INC $C250 will add 1 to FF to produce 00. The MPU will ignore any carry produced by an increment instruction (see Appendix A).

The Decrement Operation (DEC)

This operation subtracts 1 from an operand. There are three types of decrement instructions that operate on an 8-bit operand. They are:

DEC—decrement memory data
DECA—decrement [ACCA]
DECB—decrement [ACCB]

The DEC instruction can use the extended and indexed address modes, while the DECA and DECB instructions use the inherent addressing mode.

There are three decrement instructions that operate on the 16-bit registers X, Y, and SP.

DEX—decrement index register X
DEY—decrement index register Y
DES—decrement stack pointer register

The DEX, DEY, and DES instructions all use the inherent addressing mode.

Decrement instructions are often used to decrement a memory location or register that is being used as a down counter.

EXAMPLE 7.30

Determine [**ACCB**] after execution of the following instruction sequence: CLRB, DECB.

Solution   The CLRB instruction produces [**ACCB**] = 00000000_2. The DECB instruction then subtracts 1 from [**ACCB**]. It does this by adding the 2's-complement of 00000001_2 as shown below.

$$
\begin{array}{ll}
00000000 & \longleftarrow [\textbf{ACCB}] \\
+\ 11111111 & \longleftarrow \text{2's-complement of } 00000001 \\
\hline
11111111 = FF_{16} & \longleftarrow \text{result in ACCB}
\end{array}
$$

Note that this subtraction operation would normally produce a borrow, and the MPU would make C = 1. For decrement instructions, however, the MPU ignores the borrows, and it does not change the C flag.

EXAMPLE 7.31

A certain program is monitoring an input port to check the status of a certain bit. It uses the INX instruction to count the number of times that this bit is a 1. Each time the program checks the input port and finds that the bit is a 1, it will execute INX. If [**X**] is 0000_{16} at the start of the program and $01A3_{16}$ at the end of the program, how many times was the input bit a 1?

Solution $01A3_{16} = 1 \times 16^2 + 10 \times 16^1 + 3 \times 16^0$
$= 256 + 160 + 3 = 419$

Thus, X will have been incremented 419 times during execution of the program.

▶ 7.14 JUMP INSTRUCTIONS

In Chapter 4 we described the unconditional jump instruction, JMP, and showed how it caused the MPU to jump to a different memory location for its next instruction rather than continuing in sequence.

EXAMPLE 7.32

Examine the instruction sequence below. Determine [**ACCA**] when the MPU halts.

Address	Instruction code	Mnemonic
C100	86	LDAA #$6A
C101	6A	
C102	7E	JMP $C150

Address	Instruction code	Mnemonic
C103	C1	
C104	50	
C105	4A	DECA
C106	3E	WAI
: :		
: :		
C150	4C	INCA
C151	43	COMA
C152	3E	WAI

Solution   The LDAA #$6A produces [ACCA] = 6A. The JMP $C150 instruction will cause the MPU to jump to address C150 for its next instruction instead of continuing on to C105. In other words, the MPU "jumps over" addresses C105–C14F. At C150 the MPU executes the INCA instruction to produce [ACCA] = $6A_{16} + 1_{16} = 6B_{16} = 01101011$. It then continues on to C151, where it complements [ACCA] to produce [ACCA] = $10010100 = 94_{16}$. Finally, the MPU halts at C152.

The JMP instruction in this example used the extended address mode. The 68HC11 MPU also allows the use of the indexed address mode. For example, the instruction JMP $25, X will cause the MPU to take its next instruction from the address obtained by adding 25_{16} to [X].

▶ 7.15 CONDITIONAL BRANCHING

Conditional branch instructions are used to allow the MPU to alter its execution sequence only if a specific condition is met. This class of instructions gives the computer its "decision-making" ability. Conditional branch instructions operate as follows:

1. The MPU fetches the op code and determines what condition is to be checked.
2. The MPU checks the specified condition. Some examples of conditions that it can check are: (a) Is the result equal to zero (that is, is $Z = 1$)? (b) Is the result negative (that is, is $N = 1$)? (c) Is the C flag HIGH?
3. If the specified condition is met, the contents of the PC are changed to a new address. This causes the MPU to branch to the new address for its next instruction.
4. If the condition is not met, the MPU takes its next instruction in sequence.

The partial flowchart in Fig. 7.4 illustrates this operation. Note the diamond-shaped block that is used for all conditional branch instructions. In this illustration, the MPU is checking for the "result equal to zero" condition by checking for $Z = 1$ in the CCR. If $Z = 1$, the operation branches to a new location and continues executing instructions from that point. If $Z = 0$, the operation "falls through" the decision block and continues in normal sequence.

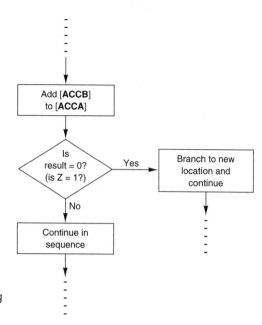

FIGURE 7.4 Flowchart illustrating conditional branch operation.

Relative Addressing

In Chapter 4 we introduced the conditional branch instructions and the relative address mode. Recall that conditional branch instructions consist of an op code followed by an offset byte. The offset byte is a *signed* binary number that is added to the PC to obtain the new address whenever branching is to occur.

Consider the following instruction sequence:

Address	Label	Instruction code	Mnemonic	Comments
0250	START	1B	ABA	; Add accumulators
0251		27	BEQ $027D	; Branch to 027D if
0252		2A		; result is zero
0253		97	STAA $7A	; Otherwise, store
0254		7A		; result in 007A

The BEQ instruction of 0251 consists of an op code, 27, followed by an offset byte, 2A. This BEQ instruction causes the MPU to check for a zero result by checking for Z = 1. If the result is *not* zero, the MPU will continue on to 0253 to fetch its next instruction. If the result *is* zero, the MPU will branch forward to 027D for its next instruction, and will continue from there. The MPU determines this new address by adding the offset byte to the current contents of the PC.

$$\begin{array}{ll} \text{Current } [\textbf{PC}] & 0253 \\ \text{Offset} & +\ \underline{002A} \\ \text{New } [\textbf{PC}] & 027D \end{array}$$

Note that the current $[\textbf{PC}]$ is the address of the op code that follows the BEQ instruction; that is, the address the MPU would go to if branching did not occur.

Offset Range

The offset byte is a signed binary number. When its MSB is 0, the offset is a positive value ranging from $00000000_2 = 00_{16} = 0_{10}$ to $01111111_2 = 7F_{16} = +127_{10}$. A positive offset, when added to the PC, can cause forward branching by as much as $7F_{16} = 127_{10}$ addresses. When its MSB is 1, the offset is a negative value ranging from $11111111_2 = FF_{16} = -1_{10}$ to $10000000_2 = 80_{16} = -128_{10}$. A negative offset, when added to the PC, can cause backward branching by as much as $80_{16} = -128_{10}$ addresses. Thus, the available branching range is -128 to $+127$.

In the preceding example, the offset of 2A was a positive offset because $2A_{16} = 00101010_2 = +42_{10}$. Suppose that the offset had been $7F_{16}$. The new address would then become

$$\begin{array}{ll} \text{Current } [\textbf{PC}] & 0253 \\ \text{Offset} & +\ \underline{007F} \\ \text{New } [\textbf{PC}] & 02D2 \end{array}$$

In this case, the MPU will branch forward to address 02D2. This represents the maximum possible branch forward.

Now let us consider an offset of $FD_{16} = 11111101_2 = -3_{10}$. When the offset is negative, the MPU adds it to the PC as follows:

$$\begin{array}{ll} \text{Current } [\textbf{PC}] & 0253 \\ \text{Offset} & +\underline{FFFD} \\ \text{New } [\textbf{PC}] & \not{1}\ 0250 \end{array}$$

ignore carry ⟶

Note that the MPU actually adds FFFD to the current $[\textbf{PC}]$. This is because the addition is a 16-bit addition, and FFFD is the 16-bit representation for -3. Also note that the carry is ignored. The result indicates that the MPU will branch backward three addresses to 0250.

We can summarize the procedure for determining the new address when branching is to occur:

1. *Positive offset.* Add the offset to the current $[\textbf{PC}]$, which **is** the address of the op code that immediately follows the offset byte.
2. *Negative offset.* Attach "FF" to the offset byte and add it to the current $[\textbf{PC}]$. Ignore the carry.

EXAMPLE 7.33 _____

In the following instruction sequence, the BCC instruction will cause the MPU to branch to address 580E if the preceding shift operation produces $C = 0$. Verify this.

Address	Label	Instruction code	Mnemonic	Comments
57A0	START	48	ASLA	; Shift [ACCA] left
57A1		24	BCC $580E	; Branch to 580E if
57A2		6B		; result C = 0
57A3		3E	WAI	; Halt if C = 1

Solution

$$
\begin{array}{lr}
\text{Current } [\mathbf{PC}] & 57A3 \\
\text{Offset} & +\ \underline{006B} \\
\text{New } [\mathbf{PC}] & 580E
\end{array}
$$

EXAMPLE 7.34

Change the instruction code at 57A2 to 94 and determine the branching address.

Solution   The offset is negative since $94_{16} = 10010100_2 = -108_{10}$

$$
\begin{array}{lr}
\text{Current } [\mathbf{PC}] & 57A3 \\
\text{Offset} & +\ \underline{FF94} \\
\text{New } [\mathbf{PC}] & \text{1} \ 5737
\end{array}
$$

The MPU will branch to 5737 for its next instruction.

Calculating the Offset

We have seen how to use the offset part of a conditional branch instruction to calculate the address to which the MPU will branch. This is useful when one is analyzing someone else's machine language program, especially when it is not accompanied by a flowchart or descriptive comments. Of course, the machine language programmer has to calculate the value of each offset to be included with each branch instruction in a program. Calculation of the offset value proceeds as follows:

1. For a *branch forward,* subtract the current [**PC**] from the new [**PC**]. If the result is less than or equal to $7F_{16} = 127_{10}$, the result is the desired offset. If the result is larger than 7F, the branch instruction cannot produce branching to the new address. In other words, the new address is *out of range.*

2. For a *branch backward,* subtract the [**PC**] from the current [**PC**]. The result is the number of addresses to be branched and has to be less than or equal to $80_{16} = 128_{10}$. If it is, the result is 2's-complemented to produce the desired negative offset. If it isn't, the new address is out of range.

EXAMPLE 7.35

Consider the instruction sequence below. Calculate the value of the offset byte portion of the BEQ instruction.

Address	Label	Instruction code	Mnemonic	Comments
0370	START	10	SBA	; Subtract accumulators
0371		27	BEQ $039C	; Branch to 039C if
0372		??		; result is zero
0373		97	STAA $50	; Otherwise, store
0374		50		; [ACCA]
0375		3E	WAI	; Halt

Solution   After the MPU fetches the BEQ op code and offset, the [PC] is 0373; this is the current [PC]. The new [PC] is 039C, so a forward branching is to occur. The required offset is obtained by subtracting as follows:

$$
\begin{array}{lr}
\text{New [PC]} & 039C \\
\text{Current [PC]} & -\ 0373 \\
\hline
\text{Offset} & 0029
\end{array}
$$

Thus, the byte of address 0372 has to be 29.

EXAMPLE 7.36 _____

Recalculate the offset if the BEQ is to branch to 031D.

Solution   Since this is a backward branch, the new [PC] = 031D is to be subtracted from the current [PC] = 0373.

$$
\begin{array}{lr}
\text{Current [PC]} & 0373 \\
\text{New [PC]} & -\ 031D \\
\hline
\text{Offset} & 0056
\end{array}
$$

This result has to be 2's-complemented to obtain the negative offset. Thus, the required offset byte is AA.

EXAMPLE 7.37 _____

Repeat Example 7.36 if BEQ is to branch to 02A3.

Solution

$$
\begin{array}{lr}
\text{Current [PC]} & 0373 \\
\text{New [PC]} & -\ 02A3 \\
\hline
\text{Offset} & 00D0
\end{array}
$$

Since the difference is greater than 80_{16}, the new [PC] is out of range. Thus, no offset value will work.

Branching Out of Range

In Example 7.37 the BEQ instruction could not be used because it required an offset that is too large. For situations such as this, the programmer can combine a branch instruction and a JMP instruction to produce the desired result. The branch instruction to be used is the one that checks for the opposite condition; that is, a branch if not equal zero, BNE. To illustrate, the program of Example 7.35 may be modified as shown below.

Address	Label	Instruction code	Mnemonic	Comments
0370	START	10	SBA	; Subtract accumulators
0371		26	BNE $0376	; Branch to 0376 if
0372		03		; result is not zero
0373		7E	JMP $02A3	; Otherwise, jump to
0374		02		; address 02A3
0375		A3		
0376		97	STAA $50	; Store result
0377		50		
0378	END	3E	WAI	; Halt

The BNE instruction will branch forward to 0376 when the result of the subtract operation is *not* equal to zero. If the result is equal to zero, the MPU will not take the branch; instead, it will fall through to the JMP instruction at 0373. Then it will execute the jump back to address 02A3 and continue from there.

The overall operation, then, is that the MPU will jump to address 02A3 whenever the subtraction produces a zero result, or will continue on to 0376 when the subtraction produces a nonzero result. It should be clear that this is the desired operation.

This technique can be used whenever it is necessary to have the MPU branch to an address that is outside the range of a conditional branch instruction.

▶ 7.16 68HC11 CONDITIONAL BRANCH INSTRUCTIONS

Table 7.2 is a listing of the 68HC11's conditional branch instructions. Each one will cause the MPU to branch when a specific condition exists. The necessary conditions for each branch instruction are also given in Table 7.2 and are described further in Appendix A.

TABLE 7.2   68HC11 MPU Conditional Branch Instructions

Mnemonic	Condition for Branching
BCC	Carry flag is cleared (C = 0)
BCS	Carry flag is set (C = 1)
BEQ	Result equal to zero (Z = 1)

TABLE 7.2   68HC11 MPU Conditional
Branch Instructions—cont'd

Mnemonic	Condition for branching
BGE	Result greater than or equal to zero (signed)
BGT	Result greater than zero (signed)
BHI	[**ACCX**] higher than operand (unsigned)
BHS	[**ACCX**] higher or same as operand (unsigned)
BLE	Result less than or equal to zero (signed)
BLO	[**ACCX**] lower than operand (unsigned)
BLS	[**ACCX**] lower or same as operand (unsigned)
BLT	Result less than zero (signed)
BMI	Result is minus (N = 1)
BNE	Result not equal to zero (Z = 0)
BPL	Result is plus (N = 0)
BVC	Overflow flag is cleared (V = 0)
BVS	Overflow flag is set (V = 1)

The 68HC11 MPU has three other branch instructions that differ from those in Table 7.2 in that they produce *unconditional* branching; that is, the MPU will *always* branch to the new address determined by the offset byte. The unconditional branch instructions are

Mnemonic	Condition for branching
BRA	Branch always
BRN	Branch never
BSR	Branch to subroutine

The BRA instruction operates like the unconditional jump, JMP, in that it always directs the MPU to a new address for its next instruction. BRA, however, uses relative addressing, so the new address is limited by the size of the offset byte. Conversely, BRN (branch never) causes the MPU to ignore the offset and proceed to the next instruction in the sequence. The BRN instruction is useful in debugging when we need to bypass a branch instruction without having to change the offset byte. The BSR instruction is used to direct the MPU to a subroutine; we will describe its operation in our discussion on subroutines.

We will now look at some typical programming examples that use conditional branch instructions. For each example, you should verify that the offset bytes are correct.

EXAMPLE 7.38

Write an instruction sequence starting at address 0225 that examines the data from an input port at address C700 and causes a branch to address 024C only if the LSB of the data is HIGH.

Address	Label	Instruction code	Mnemonic	Comments
0225	START	B6	LDAA $C700	; Load ACCA from
0226		C7		; input port
0227		00		
0228		44	LSRA	; Shift LSB into C flag
0229		25	BCS $024C	; Branch to 024C if
022A		21		; C flag is HIGH
022B				; Otherwise, continue
: :		: :	: :	; in sequence

Solution   The first instruction loads ACCA with the data from the input port. The LSRA instruction shifts the LSB of ACCA into the C flag. The BCS instruction then checks for C = 1 to determine if branching should occur.

EXAMPLE 7.39

Modify the program of Example 7.38 so that it branches to 0200 when the MSB of the input port is HIGH.

Address	Label	Instruction code	Mnemonic	Comments
0225	START	B6	LDAA $C700	; Load ACCA from
0226		C7		; input port
0227		00		
0228		2B	BMI $0200	; Branch to 0200 if
0229		D6		: MSB = 1
022A		: :	: :	: :
: :		: :	: :	: :

Solution   Here it is not necessary to perform a shift operation because the MSB is the sign bit. When the LDAA instruction is executed, the N flag will take on the value of the MSB of the data. The BMI instruction then checks the N flag and branches if it is HIGH.

EXAMPLE 7.40

Assume that both accumulators are holding *unsigned* data. Write an instruction sequence that starts at address 5C00 and branches to 5C6F if [ACCA] is larger than [ACCB]; otherwise, the program halts.

Address	Label	Instruction code	Mnemonic	Comments
5C00	START	10	SBA	; Subtract accumulators
5C01		22	BHI $5C6F	; Branch to 5C6F if
5C02		6C		; [ACCA] > [ACCB]
5C03	END	20	BRA $5C03	; Halt
		FE		

Solution The SBA instruction subtracts [ACCB] from [ACCA] and leaves the result in ACCA. The BHI instruction checks to see if the *unsigned* number in ACCA was higher than the one in ACCB. If this condition is met, the MPU branches to 5C6F. If the unsigned number in ACCA is not larger than the one in ACCB, the MPU will fall through and execute the instruction at address 5C03. Up until now, we have always used the WAI instruction to halt execution of a program. Another way to halt execution of a program is to use the unconditional branch instruction, BRA. When the op code 20 is followed by the offset byte FE, the 68HC11 MPU will branch backward to the address of the op code for the BRA instruction. Thus, an endless loop is created by continuous execution of the BRA instruction.

EXAMPLE 7.41

How would you change the preceding program if the accumulators are holding *signed* numbers?

Solution Change BHI to BGT. The BGT instruction will check to see if the result of the subtraction of the *signed* numbers is greater than zero.

EXAMPLE 7.42

In Example 7.21 we illustrated how the 68HC11 MPU uses the MUL instruction to multiply two unsigned binary numbers. However, as previously stated, not all 8-bit MPUs have this powerful instruction. If the MUL instruction is not available on a particular 8-bit MPU, a sequence of programming instructions can be written in order to have the MPU multiply two 8-bit numbers.

Figure 7.5 is a flowchart for a program that multiplies two unsigned 8-bit numbers, DATA1 and DATA2, that are stored in memory. The multiplication is accomplished through the process of repeated addition. For example, assume that DATA1 = 2 and DATA2 = 4. The product 2 × 4 can be obtained by adding 2 four times. In other words, the value of DATA2 is the number of times that we add the value of DATA1.

In the flowchart, ACCA is initially cleared and ACCB is loaded with DATA2. The loop in the flowchart represents the repeated execution of the addition of DATA1 to [ACCA]. After each addition, [ACCB] is decremented and checked for a zero result. When it is finally decremented to zero, the required number of addition operations will have been performed, and the final result is in ACCA.

Write the program for this flowchart starting at address 0260. Assume that DATA1 and DATA2 are in memory locations 0080 and 0081, respectively, and that the result is to be stored in 0082.

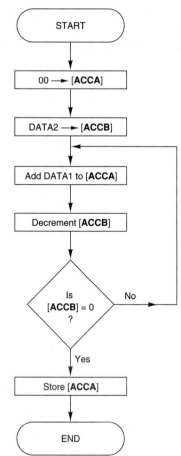

FIGURE 7.5 Flowchart of "repeated addition" multiplication program of Example 7.42.

Solution

Address	Label	Instruction code	Mnemonic	Comments
0260	START	4F	CLRA	; Clear ACCA to 00
0261		D6	LDAB $81	; Load ACCB with DATA2
0262		81		
0263	LOOP	9B	ADDA $80	; Add DATA1 to ACCA
0264		80		
0265		5A	DECB	; Decrement [ACCB]
0266		26	BNE $0263	; if not zero, branch back
0267		FB		; to LOOP
0268		97	STAA $82	; Multiplication done,
0269		82		; store result
026A	END	3E	WAI	; Halt

In this program ACCB is being used as a *down counter* that counts down from an initial value equal to DATA2. The BNE instruction is used to check for [ACCB] ≠ 00 after each decrement operation to determine when the required number of additions have taken place.

EXAMPLE 7.43 _____

Assume that the status of an I/O device whose address is C525 is being monitored by the 68HC11 MPU. Starting at address C600, write a program sequence that causes the MPU to branch to address location C625 only if the data byte from the I/O device has bits 0, 2, and 4 all clear; otherwise, it continues to check the status of the I/O device.

Solution

Address	Label	Instruction code	Mnemonic	Comments
C600	START	B6	LDAA $C525	; Read the I/O device
C601		C5		
C602		25		
C603		84	ANDA #$15	; Clear bits 1, 3, 5, 6,
C604		15		; and 7
C605		27	BEQ $C625	; If bits 0, 2, and 4 are
C606		1E		; zero, branch to C625
C607		7E	JMP $C600	; Check I/O device again
C608		C6		
C609		00		

The LDAA $C525 instruction loads ACCA with the status data of the I/O device. The ANDA #$15 instruction clears all the bits in [ACCA] except bits 0, 2, and 4. If bits 0, 2, and 4 were all zero when the I/O device was read, then at this time [ACCA] = 00. Thus, when the BEQ $C625 instruction is executed the MPU branches to address location C625 for the next instruction. If, however, bits 0, 2, and 4 are not all zero when the MPU reads the I/O device, then the MPU executes the next instruction at C607 which tells it to jump back to C600 to check the I/O device once again.

Bit-Manipulation Branch Instructions

The 68HC11 MPU has two conditional branch instructions that are much different than the two-byte branch instructions we have been using up to now. These special conditional branch instructions are:

Mnemonic	Condition for branching
BRCLR	Specific bits of operand are clear (0)
BRSET	Specific bits of operand are set (1)

These instructions require more than two bytes because they must specify an operand address and a mask byte in addition to the offset byte. The operand address can be specified using direct addressing or one of the indexed addressing modes. Below is an example of the assembly language format for a BRCLR instruction using direct addressing.

$$\text{BRCLR} \quad \$50 \quad \$F0 \quad \$C25F$$

operation   operand   mask byte   branch to
address   address

In executing this instruction, the MPU will fetch the operand byte from the operand address (in this case, $0050). Then it will AND that operand with the mask byte ($F0). If the resulting byte is all zeros, the MPU will branch to address $C25F for its next instruction; otherwise it will continue in sequence. In other words, branching will occur if the operand has 0s in the same bit positions in which there are 1s in the mask byte.

The above instruction assembles into four bytes of machine language code as shown in the following listing:

Address	Instruction code	Mnemonic	Comments
C200	13	BRCLR $50 $F0 $C25F	; Branch to $C25F if the
C201	50		; 4 MSBs of data word at
C202	F0		; $0050 are zeros
C203	5B		
C204	86	LDAA #$1F	; Otherwise, come here to
C205	1F		; continue in sequence
C206	: :	: :	
: :	: :		

The first byte at C200 is the op code (13) for BRCLR (DIR); the second byte is the operand address (50); the third byte is the mask byte (F0); and the fourth byte is the relative offset for the branch operation.

The BRSET instruction operates in the same way as BRCLR except it complements the operand byte before ANDing with the mask byte. In this way, branching will occur only if there are 1s in the original operand in the same bit positions as the 1s in the mask byte.

EXAMPLE 7.44

Modify the program of Example 7.43 so that it uses the branch clear (BRCLR) instruction and the X indexed addressing.

One possible way:

Address	Label	Instruction code	Mnemonic	Comments
C600	START	CE	LDX #$C500	; Load index register X
C601		C5		; with the data C500
C602		00		
C603		1F	BRCLR $25,X $15 $C625	; Branch to address C625,
C604		25		; if bits 0, 2, and 4 of
C605		15		; [C525] are cleared
C606		1E		
C607		7E	JMP $C603	; Check the I/O device
C608		C6		; again
C609	END	03		

The LDX instruction loads the X register with C500. The next instruction, BRCLR, is a four-byte instruction that uses indexed addressing to specify the operand address. The first byte is the op code. The second byte is the offset address byte. In this example, the positive offset address byte, 25, is added to the contents of the X register which results in the effective address C525. Bits 0, 2, and 4 of the data in this address will be checked for zeros. The third byte, $15, is the mask byte (00010101) that will determine whether or not bits 0, 2, and 4 are all cleared. Finally, the fourth byte is the *relative offset* byte (1E) that will be added to the present contents of the PC (C607) to produce the address (C625) to which the MPU will branch if the branching conditions are met.

▶ 7.17 COMPARE INSTRUCTIONS

This class of instructions performs the subtraction operation on two operands, but does not place the result in any register. The result is used only to affect the flags in the CCR. These flags can then be checked using the appropriate conditional branch instruction to determine the relative values of the operands (i.e., A = B, A < B, or A > B).

CBA—Compare Accumulators

This instruction subtracts [ACCB] from [ACCA], *but does not* place the result in [ACCA]. The result is used only to affect the N, C, V, and Z flags.

EXAMPLE 7.45

Assume that both accumulators are holding *unsigned* data. Write an instruction sequence that starts at address 5C00 and branches to 5C6F if [ACCA] is smaller than [ACCB]; otherwise, the program halts. The contents of both accumulators are to be unchanged.

Solution

Address	Label	Instruction code	Mnemonic	Comments
5C00	START	11	CBA	; Compare accumulators
5C01		25	BLO $5C6F	; Branch to 5C6F if
5C02		6C		; [ACCA] < [ACCB]
5C03	END	3E	WAI	; Otherwise, halt

The CBA instruction subtracts [ACCB] from [ACCA] but does not put the result in ACCA; the contents of both accumulators are unchanged. The BLO instruction checks to see if the C flag is a 1 since this would indicate that [ACCA] < [ACCB]. If this condition is met, the program branches to 5C6F. Compare this program with Example 7.40.

CMPA/CMPB—Compare Accumulator with Memory

These instructions will subtract the contents of the specified memory location from the specified accumulator, but the result is not placed in the accumulator. The result is used to affect the N, Z, V, and C flags.

By using CMP instructions, the program can compare the contents of an accumulator with a data word from memory or an input device without changing the accumulator contents. The following examples will illustrate how CMP and branch instructions can be combined to alter the instruction execution sequence in accordance with the relative values of two operands.

EXAMPLE 7.46 _____

Write an instruction sequence that continually checks the data at an input port until it is greater than $+35_{10} = 23_{16}$, after which it stores the data in memory location 0922 and halts. The input port has address FC00, and the data are signed binary.

Solution   The flowchart for this sequence is shown in Fig. 7.6. Note how the decision block checks for [ACCA] $\leq 23_{16}$ and, if true, branches back to reload the input port. If [ACCA] > 23, the program falls through the decision block and stores the result. The program is given below. Study it carefully.

Address	Label	Instruction code	Mnemonic	Comments
0200	START	B6	LDAA $FC00	; Load input port data
0201		FC		; into ACCA
0202		00		

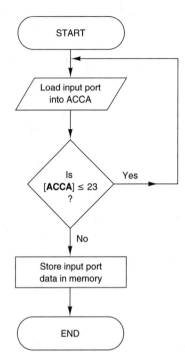

FIGURE 7.6

Address	Label	Instruction code	Mnemonic	Comments
0203		81	CMPA #$23	; Compare [ACCA] to
0204		23		; $35_{10} = 23_{16}$
0205		2F	BLE $0200	; If [ACCA] $\leq 23_{16}$, go
0206		F9		; back and do it again
0207		B7	STAA $0922	; If [ACCA] > 23, store
0208		09		; value in memory
0209		22		
020A	END	3E	WAI	; Halt

Note how the CMPA and BLE instructions perform the operation represented by the decision block. BLE is used because the data are signed binary. Also note that the CMPA instruction does not change [ACCA], so ACCA still holds the input port data when the STAA instruction is executed.

EXAMPLE 7.47 ───

A keyboard is interfaced to a microcomputer input port such that, at any time, the data at the input port are the ASCII code for the key that is currently down. When no key is down, the data word is FF. An instruction sequence is to be written to do the following:

(a) Read the keyboard data.

(b) If no key is down, repeat (a).

(c) If RETURN key is down, halt the program.

(d) If any other key is down, go back to (a) and read the keyboard again. Figure 7.7 is the flowchart for this operation. The keyboard data are loaded into ACCB. The first decision block then checks for data = FF. If true, this means that none of the keys are down, so the program branches back to reload the keyboard data into ACCB. Otherwise, the program falls through this decision block to the second decision block. There it checks for keyboard data ≠ 0D, the ASCII code for the RETURN key. If true, it branches back to reload. Otherwise, the program falls through the halts.

Write the program for this flowchart starting at address 0400. The input port address is C090.

Solution

Address	Label	Instruction code	Mnemonic	Comments
0400	START	F6	LDAB $C090	; Load keyboard data
0401		C0		; into ACCB
0402		90		
0403		C1	CMPB #$FF	; Compare with FF
0404		FF		
0405		27	BEQ $0400	; If = , branch back to
0406		F9		; reload keyboard data
0407		C1	CMPB #$0D	; Compare with 0D, the ASCII
0408		0D		; code for RETURN key
0409		26	BNE $0400	; If ≠, branch back to
040A		F5		; reload keyboard data
040B	END	3E	WAI	; Otherwise, halt

Analyze the program carefully and note how it corresponds to the flowchart. Especially note how the compare and branch instructions are used to implement the decision blocks.

CPX/CPY/CPD—Compare X, Y, or Double Accumulator with Memory

These instructions operate like CMPA and CMPB except that they compare two 16-bit numbers since X, Y, and ACCD are 16-bit registers. For example, suppose that you want the program to branch to address 0450 only if [**X**] = 205E. This can be accomplished using the instruction sequence CPX #$205E, BEQ $0450.

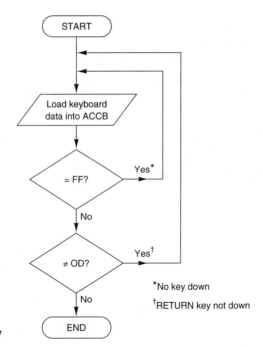

START

Load keyboard
data into ACCB

= FF?   Yes*

No

≠ OD?   Yes†

No

*No key down

†RETURN key not down

END

FIGURE 7.7

▶ 7.18 BIT AND TST INSTRUCTIONS

These are special data testing instructions that can check one or more bits of an operand without affecting the operand.

BITA/BITB—Bit Test

This instruction performs the bit-by-bit AND operation of the specified data byte with the specified accumulator, but does not place the result in the accumulator. The result is used only to affect the N and Z flags.

This allows you to use AND masking to isolate one or more bits of an accumulator without affecting the contents of the accumulator. For example, consider the following instruction sequence:

Address	Label	Instruction code	Mnemonic	Comments
1200	START	85	BITA #$08	; Isolate bit 3 of ACCA
1201		08		
1202		27	BEQ $12C0	; If 0, branch to 12C0
1203		BD		
1204		85	BITA #$04	; Isolate bit 2 of ACCA
1205		04		
1206		26	BNE $12D0	; If 1, branch to 12D0
1207		CA		
1208	END	3E	WAI	; Halt

The first instruction will AND [**ACCA**] with 00001000_2 to produce a result that will be 00000000_2 only if bit 3 of [**ACCA**] is 0. Thus, the second instruction will branch to address 12C0 only if bit 3 is 0. Similarly, the third and fourth instructions will check bit 2 of [**ACCA**] and branch to 12D0 only if it is 1. Note that [**ACCA**] is not changed by the first BITA instruction, so that the second BITA instruction operates on the same data. The BITB instruction operates the same way as the BITA instruction, except that it uses accumulator B.

TST—Test Contents of Memory

This instruction examines the data in the specified memory location and adjusts the N and Z flags accordingly. Consider the following instruction sequence:

Address	Label	Instruction code	Mnemonic	Comments
0900	START	7D	TST $F700	; Test data at address
0901		F7		; F700
0902		00		
0903		27	BEQ $09F0	; If zero, branch to 09F0
0904		EB		
0905		2B	BMI $09EA	; If negative, branch to
0906		E3		; 09EA
0907	END	3E	WAI	; Halt

The TST instruction examines the data at address F700 (memory or input port) and makes N the same as the MSB of the data, and makes Z = 1 only if the data are zero. The BEQ instruction will produce branching only if the data are zero (Z = 1). The BMI instruction will produce branching only if the data are negative (N = 1).

TSTA/TSTB—Test Contents of Accumulator

These instructions perform the TST operation on the data in the specified accumulator.

EXAMPLE 7.48

Assume that [**ACCB**] = 27_{16} and determine what the following instruction sequence does.

```
TSTB
BMI    $0880
BNE    $0890
WAI
```

Solution $27_{16} = 00100111_2$, so TSTB will make N = 0 and Z = 0. Therefore, the BMI instruction will not produce branching, but the BNE instruction will produce branching to 0890.

▶ 7.19 SUBROUTINES

Programs will often require that a specific function be performed at various times during the program execution. For instance, a program might be outputting ASCII-coded data to a printer at several points in a program. Another example would be the need to perform the multiplication of two operands several times during a program's execution. The sequences of instructions needed to perform these functions could be written into the program at each point where they are needed. This would be acceptable when the sequences are relatively short (two or three instructions) and the number of repetitions is not too great (two or three times). When this is not the case, the programmer can treat the sequences as *subroutines*.

A subroutine is a sequence of instructions that performs a specific task. It is written once and is stored in a specific area of memory. Then, whenever the main program wants

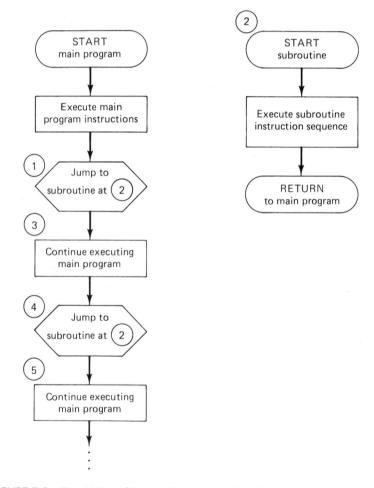

FIGURE 7.8   *Illustration of how a jump to a subroutine can occur at any point in the main program; at the end of the subroutine, the operation always returns to the main program.*

to perform that task, the MPU jumps to the address of the subroutine, executes the subroutine, and returns to the main program.

The flowchart in Fig. 7.8 illustrates how a subroutine is used in a program. There are actually two flowcharts. The one on the left is the main program that the MPU will normally be executing; the other is the subroutine that the MPU will jump to several times during the execution of the main program.

Here we see that the MPU jumps to the subroutine at two different points in the main program. Block 1 instructs the MPU to jump to block 2 to execute the subroutine. At the end of the subroutine, the MPU is directed to return to the main program to continue execution at block 3. At block 4, the MPU is again directed to jump to the subroutine. After executing the subroutine the second time, the MPU is directed to return back to the main program to continue execution at block 5.

The use of the subroutine can be repeated as many times as needed during the main program, and it is a much more efficient use of program memory space than the alternative of repeating the subroutine instruction sequence each time it is needed.

A jump to a subroutine is often referred to as a *subroutine call*. For example, in Fig. 7.8 the main program "calls the subroutine" at two different times. The terms *subroutine jump* and *subroutine call* are used interchangeably.

JSR and RTS Instructions

These instructions control how the MPU jumps to and returns from a subroutine. The jump-to-subroutine instruction, JSR, directs the MPU to the address of the subroutine. The return-from-subroutine instruction, RTS, directs the MPU back to the main program. The operation of these instructions is illustrated by the simple example shown below. The main program, MAIN, begins at address location C100 and continues to C107. The subroutine, SHIFT, resides at addresses C160–C164.

Address	Label	Instruction code	Mnemonic	Comments
C100	MAIN	96	LDAA $A6	; Load ACCA with data
C101		A6		
C102		BD	JSR $C160	; Jump to SHIFT subroutine
C103		C1		; at C160
C104		60		
C105		97	STAA $A7	; Continue main program and
C106		A7		; store ACCA
C107	END	3E	WAI	; Halt
: :		: :	: :	:
: :		: :	: :	:
C160	SHIFT	44	LSRA	; Shift [ACCA] right four
C161		44	LSRA	; times
C162		44	LSRA	
C163		44	LSRA	
C164	RETURN	39	RTS	; Return to main program

When the MPU executes the JSR instruction at C102, it fetches the subroutine address, C160, and loads it into the program counter, but only after pushing the current $[PC]$ = C105 onto the stack. Note that the current $[PC]$ is the address of the op code of the instruction following the JSR instruction. This address, C105, is the address in the main program to which the MPU will return after it executes the subroutine. Thus, we can call it the *return address*. If we assume that $[SP]$ = 01FF prior to the JSR operation, then the stack data will look like this after the JSR:

Stack address	Data	
01FE	C1	; Return
01FF	05	; address

After loading the subroutine address into the PC, the MPU begins executing the subroutine at C160. When the MPU executes the RTS instruction at C164, it will pull the data above off the stack and place them back into the PC; that is, it loads the return address into the PC. The MPU will then continue execution of the main program at C105.

To summarize: When the MPU executes a JSR, it saves the return address on the stack, jumps to the subroutine address, and executes the subroutine. At the end of the subroutine, the RTS instruction causes the MPU to take the return address off the stack, place it back in the PC, and continue execution of the main program.

EXAMPLE 7.49

What would happen if the JSR instruction in the program above were changed to a JMP instruction?

Solution   When the MPU executes JMP $C160, it will load C160 into the PC, but it will not save the return address on the stack. It will then execute the subroutine. When it executes RTS, it will take two data bytes off the stack and place them into the PC. Unfortunately, these two bytes will not be the return address but will be something unpredictable. This will cause the MPU to go to an unpredictable address for its next instruction and will result in unpredictable and somewhat random operation. In other words, the program is said to "crash."

This analysis shows that a JMP instruction should not be used to access a subroutine.

BSR—Branch to Subroutine

The JSR instruction can use either the extended or indexed address mode. The BSR instruction uses the relative address mode to branch to a subroutine. Otherwise, the two instructions operate the same. Of course, the BSR is limited to branching to subroutines that are within the offset range -128_{10} to $+127_{10}$.

Saving MPU Registers During Subroutine Calls

When a main program jumps to a subroutine, it may be necessary to store the current contents of some of the MPU registers if their values are critical and would be destroyed by instructions in the subroutine. This can be accomplished by saving the registers on the stack prior to calling the subroutine, and by restoring them after returning from the subroutine. This is illustrated below for saving [ACCA], [ACCB], and [X].

Address	Instruction code	Mnemonic	Comments
0200	36	PSHA	; Save [ACCA]
0201	37	PSHB	; Save [ACCB]
0202	3C	PSHX	; Save [X]
0203	BD	JSR $1F36	; Call subroutine at 1F36
0204	1F		
0205	36		
0206	38	PULX	; Restore [X]
0207	33	PULB	; Restore [ACCB]
0208	32	PULA	; Restore [ACCA]
0209	: :	: :	
: :	: :	: :	

The current contents of ACCA, ACCB, and X are pushed onto the stack just prior to the subroutine call so that the execution of the subroutine will not cause their values to be lost. When the subroutine returns control back to the main program, [X], [ACCB], and [ACCA] are pulled off the stack so that these registers are restored to their previous values.

Nesting Subroutines

A subroutine can contain a JSR instruction; in other words, a subroutine can jump to another subroutine. This is sometimes referred to as *nesting* subroutines. In complex programs it is not unusual to see several levels of nesting, where one subroutine jumps to another, which jumps to another, and so on. As with a single subroutine jump, the stack is used to keep track of the return addresses so that each RTS instruction will send the MPU back to where it was prior to the subroutine jump.

▶ 7.20 INTERRUPT HANDLING INSTRUCTIONS

There are four instructions that the programmer can use to handle external interrupts:

CLI—Clear Interrupt Mask flag, I
SEI—Set Interrupt Mask flag, I
TAP—Transfer from ACCA to CCR
RTI—Return from Interrupt

We will postpone a discussion of these instructions until Chapter 8, after we describe the 68HC11 interrupt operation.

▶ 7.21 APPLICATIONS USING INDEXED ADDRESSING

The indexed addressing mode is extremely useful in programming applications that involve blocks or tables of data. In this section, we will examine some of these applications.

Movement of Data Blocks

One operation that occurs quite often is the movement of blocks of data from one area of memory to another. To illustrate, let us pose a typical problem with the help of Fig. 7.9A. Here we see a group of six data bytes stored in memory locations 0270 through 0275. Call this block 1. We want to transfer these bytes into memory locations 03A3 through 03A8, which we will call block 2. This operation can be programmed in a straightforward manner by simply repeating the following sequence *six* times (once per data byte):

Instruction code	Mnemonic	Comments
B6	LDAA $0270	; Load Data 0
02		; Address in block 1
70		
B7	STAA $03A3	; Store Data 0
03		; Address in block 2
A3		
: :	: :	(Repeat with different block 1 and block 2 addresses)

This would require 36 bytes of program codes. Clearly, this method would become prohibitive as the *size* of the data blocks increased.

A more efficient method using indexed addressing is flowcharted in Fig. 7.9B. The 16-bit X and Y registers are used as the index registers for addressing and also as loop counters to keep track of the number of bytes of data being moved. Note that [**X**] is initially set to point to the *source* address of Data 0 in *block 1*, while [**Y**] is initially set to point to the *destination* address of Data 0 in *block 2*. Both index registers are incremented following the transfer of each byte from block 1 to block 2. After each byte transfer from block 1 to block 2, [**X**] is incremented and its contents are compared to the number 0276. After the *sixth* byte transfer, [**X**] will have been incremented from 0275 to 0276. At this point, the execution of the CPX instruction causes the Z flag to be 1, since the result is $0000. Therefore, the BNE instruction will not result in a branch (recall that the BNE instruction causes a branch only if Z = 0). Consequently, the program will stop looping and no further transfers will take place.

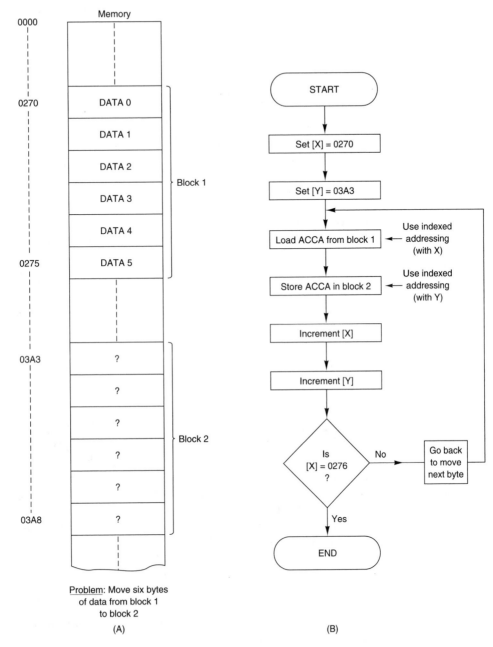

FIGURE 7.9 Indexed addressing can be used in moving blocks of data from one area of memory to another.

The sequence of instruction codes for this process follows. Study it carefully before proceeding.

Address	Label	Instruction code	Mnemonic	Comments
C125	START	CE	LDX #$0270	; Initialize [X] to point to
C126		02		; source address of Data 0 in
C127		70		; block 1
C128		18	LDY #$03A3	; Initialize [Y] to point to
C129		CE		; destination address of Data 0
C12A		03		; in block 1
C12B		A3		
C12C	LOOP	A6	LDAA $00,X	; Load ACCA with the contents
C12D		00		; of memory location [X] + 00
C12E		18	STAA $00,Y	; Store ACCA in memory
C12F		A7		; location [Y] + 00
C130		00		
C131		08	INX	; Increment [X]
C132		18	INY	; Increment [Y]
C133		08		
C134		8C	CPX #$0276	; Compare [X] with the number
C135		02		; 0276
C136		76		
C137		26	BNE $C12C	; If [X] ≠ 0276, return to LOOP
C138		F3		
C139	END	3E	WAI	; Halt

The instructions from address C12C (LOOP) to C137 will be repeated six times until [X] and [Y] are incremented to 0276 and 03A9, respectively. [X] is initially set to 0270, so that the first time the LDAA instruction is executed, 00 is added to the base address, 0270, to obtain the effective address 0270. Likewise, [Y] is initially set to 03A3, so that the first time the STAA instruction is executed, 00 is added to the base address, 03A3, to obtain the effective address 03A3. This results in the transfer of Data 0 to its corresponding location in block 2. The second time through the loop, [X] will be 0271 and Data 1 will be moved to memory location 03A4 in block 2 pointed to by [Y]. This continues until the sixth time through the loop, when [X] = 0275 and [Y] = 03A8 produces the transfer of Data 5. The subsequent INX and INY instructions result in [X] = 0276 and [Y] = 03A9, which terminates the looping process and causes the program to continue on to C139 for the next instruction.

This method requires only 20 program bytes as compared to 36 using the straightforward approach. Furthermore, this same sequence of 20 bytes can be used to move any block of data regardless of its size to any place in memory simply by changing the initial contents for [X], [Y], and the operand of the CPX instruction. For example, let us assume that we wanted to move 64 bytes of data from block 1 starting at address C300 to block 2 starting at address D400. The X and Y registers would have to be initialized to C300 and

D400, respectively, and the operand for the CPX instruction would have to be changed to C340. Note that $64_{10} = 40_{16}$; hence, C300 + 40 = C340.

Tables

The use of memory *tables* can significantly speed up microcomputer operations, such as code conversions, complex arithmetic calculations, message generation, and control output generation. Tables are simply lists of related data that are stored in sequential memory locations. The data in these tables usually are constant for a given application and are typically stored in ROM or loaded into RAM from a tape or disk storage unit.

The principal advantage of a table is that it eliminates the need to perform any calculations in order to produce an answer. An answer is obtained simply by finding the correct address in the table and reading the contents of that location. Proper use of a table requires setting up the data in the table and establishing a means for accessing any entry in the table. We will look at a typical application that lends itself to the use of tables.

Figure 7.10A shows part of a 68HC11 MPU-based process control system. A 4-bit HCMOS input port is used to transfer process information into the MPU. This information is obtained from process-monitoring circuits such as limit switches, over-temperature sensors, level detectors, and so on, whose outputs have been converted to proper logic levels. The tri-state HCMOS input port buffers are enabled by the decoding logic when any page D9 address is placed on the system address bus.

An 8-bit HCMOS output port register is used to latch control outputs from the MPU data bus and transmit them to various process control circuits, such as solenoid-controlled valves, relays, and triacs. Data are latched into the output register when any page DD address is placed on the address bus.

The MPU periodically reads data from the input port to determine the status of the process-monitoring circuits. With four inputs there are 16 possible input status codes, so the MPU must determine which code is present and then load the appropriate control outputs into the output port register. The most efficient way to do this is to store the various output control words in a table and use the input code to access the table. Figure 7.10B shows the 16 output control words stored in ROM table at address EE00 through EE0F. The least significant hex digit of each address corresponds to the input code. For example, an input code of $1001_2 = 9_{16}$ corresponds to address EE09 and an output control word of 10000111.

The following instruction sequence is used to read the input port, find the correct table entry, and transmit the output control word. It uses an input port address of D900 and an output port address of DD00.

Address	Label	Instruction code	Mnemonic	Comments
C226	START	86	LDAA #$EE	; Initialize ACCA with ROM page
C227		EE		
C228		F6	LDAB $D900	; Load input port data into ACCB
C229		D9		

Address	Label	Instruction code	Mnemonic	Comments
C22A		00		
C22B		C4	ANDB #$0F	; Clear four MSBs of ACCB
C22C		0F		
C22D		8F	XGDX	; Transfer ROM address to [X]
C22E		A6	LDAA $00,X	; Fetch output control word
C22F		00		
C230		B7	STAA $DD00	; Write control word into
C231		DD		; output port
C232		00		

Let us follow through this sequence step by step assuming that the input data are 1011_2.

Step 1. Accumulator A is loaded with the ROM page address, EE.

$$[ACCA] = 1\ 1\ 1\ 0\ 1\ 1\ 1\ 0$$

Step 2. Accumulator B is loaded from the input port and its contents become

$$[ACCB] = X\ X\ X\ X\ \underbrace{1\ 0\ 1\ 1}_{\text{Input code}}$$

Note the 4 MSBs of ACCB are unknown since the input port supplies only the 4 LSBs.

Step 3. The ANDB instruction is used to clear the four MSBs of accumulator B without affecting the other bits. This results in

$$[ACCB] = 0\ 0\ 0\ 0\ \underbrace{1\ 0\ 1\ 1}_{\text{Input code}}$$

Step 4. $[ACCD] \longrightarrow [X]$, so now $[X] = 1110\ 1110\ 0000\ 1011_2 = EEOB_{16}$.

Step 5. The LDAA $00,X instruction now enters the control word table at address EEOB + 00 = EEOB and loads ACCA with 00101101.

Step 6. This control word is written into the output register.

▶ 7.22 THE NO-OPERATION (NOP) AND STOP INSTRUCTIONS

The NOP Instruction

This is a single-byte instruction with op code = 01. When the MPU executes a no-operation (NOP) instruction, it performs no useful operation except for incrementing the PC to prepare for the next op code fetch. Although it may appear that there is no reason

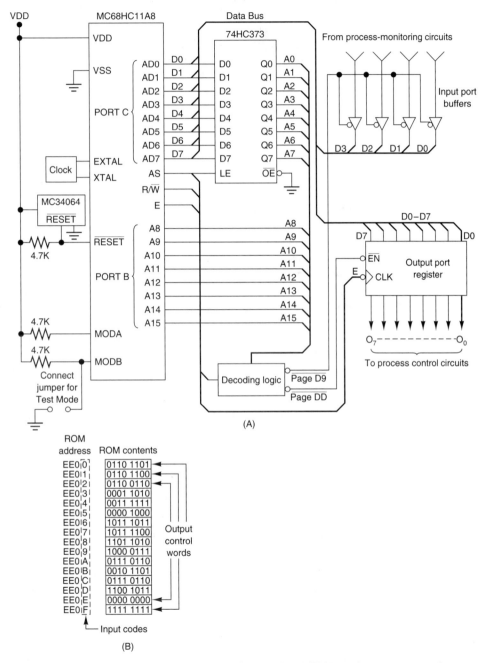

(A)

ROM address	ROM contents	
EE0'0'	0110 1101	
EE0'1'	0110 1100	
EE0'2'	0110 0110	
EE0'3'	0001 1010	
EE0'4'	0011 1111	
EE0'5'	0000 1000	
EE0'6'	1011 1011	
EE0'7'	1011 1100	Output
EE0'8'	1101 1010	control
EE0'9'	1000 0111	words
EE0'A'	0111 0110	
EE0'B'	0010 1101	
EE0'C'	0111 0110	
EE0'D'	1100 1011	
EE0'E'	0000 0000	
EE0'F'	1111 1111	

└── Input codes

(B)

FIGURE 7.10   (A) Partial diagram of a 68HC11 MPU-based process control system; (B) a table of output control words stored in ROM.

ever to use a NOP instruction, a few programming situations arise where NOPs can be useful. The three most common applications of this instruction are:

1. To replace program codes that are no longer needed during the development of a machine language program. During this process, the program is stored in RAM, where it can be easily modified. If the programmer decides that a particular instruction is not needed, he or she can replace the unneeded instruction codes with NOPs. The NOPs will not affect any of the registers or memory locations. After the program has been developed and is working satisfactorily, the programmer can rewrite it without the NOPs.

2. To leave spaces in a program for possible insertion of program codes during program development. During the initial writing of a program, a programmer can sometimes anticipate that he or she may later want to insert one or more instructions at various points in the program. NOPs can be placed at appropriate points in the initial program to allow for this.

3. To achieve a time delay. The MPU will execute a NOP instruction in two clock cycles. The programmer can insert the required number of NOPs for the desired time delay. This becomes impractical for delays of more than several clock cycles, and other methods have to be used.

The STOP Instruction

The STOP instruction, when executed, causes the oscillator and all of the 68HC11 MCU clocks to stop. This instruction is used when the user wants to place the system in a minimum-power standby mode in which all MPU registers and I/O pins remain unaffected. The execution of the STOP instruction is controlled by the stop disable flag, S, in the CCR. If the stop disable flag has been set to 1, the STOP instruction is prevented from being executed by the MPU and the MPU will treat it as a NOP (No operation) instruction. The NOP instruction causes only the program counter to be incremented, and no other MPU registers are affected. The S flag is automatically set during a reset or an interrupt, and it must be cleared in order for the STOP instruction to be executed. The programmer can either set or clear the S flag with a TAP instruction.

▶ 7.23 PROGRAM-CONTROLLED TIMING INTERVALS (DELAYS)

When a program is being used to control and/or respond to peripheral input/output devices, it is often necessary to insert time delays in the program with specific durations. Here are some situations where programmed time delays are needed.

1. The logic signals from certain input devices take time to stabilize; mechanical switches with their inherent "switch bounce" are prime examples. Suppose that a program is instructing the MPU to read data from an input port in order to detect a switch transition. The program will have to incorporate a time delay between successive readings so that the switch bounce will not be detected and interpreted as a switch transition.

2. A program can be used to generate pulses at an output port with specific pulse durations to control the ON and OFF times of devices, such as motors, displays, and so on.

3. When the MPU is interfaced to serial I/O devices such as a video display terminal (VDT) or a serial printer, it may have to generate and/or respond to logic level changes that occur at specific time intervals. For example, some VDTs transmit and receive serial data at the rate of 38400 bits per second.

Programmed Time Delays

There are several methods of generating software time delays. All 8-bit MPUs can produce a time delay in a program by inserting a sequence of instructions that the MPU executes in an amount of time equal to the desired delay. The instruction sequence has no other function but to use up time. However, some single-chip microcomputers and microcontrollers (MCUs), and the 68HC11 MCU in particular, can also produce software time delays by using an internal 16-bit *timer counter register,* called TCNT. This special counter is an integral part of the *main timer system* of the 68HC11 MCU. By using this free-running counter the 68HC11 MPU can produce time delays using many fewer instructions. However, for the following discussions and examples of time delays, if we ignore the existence of the TCNT register, then the 68HC11 MPU behaves like most 8-bit MPUs that do not have special built-in timers. In Section 7.25 we will demonstrate an alternative way of producing time delays by using the timer system of the 68HC11 MPU.

EXAMPLE 7.50 _____

A certain 68HC11 MPU is operating from a 2-MHz clock. Determine the total time required for the execution of the following instruction sequence.

PSHA
NOP
NOP
NOP
PULA

Solution   The execution times of each instruction can be found in Appendix A. The PSHA instruction takes three clock cycles, each of the NOP instructions takes two clock cycles, and the PULA instruction takes 4 clock cycles. Thus, the total execution time is $3 + 2 + 2 + 2 + 4 = 13$ clock cycles. Since one E-clock cycle is equivalent to 500 ns $\left[\dfrac{1}{2 \text{ MHz}} \right]$, the total execution time is 13×500 ns $= 6.5$ µs.

_____

This example uses a straight sequence of instructions whose only purpose is to produce a time delay. This method is limited to relatively short delays because each instruction contributes only a few microseconds; for instance, a delay of 1 ms would require 1000 NOP instructions. A time-delay loop is a more efficient method for achieving delays greater than 30 or 40 clock cycles.

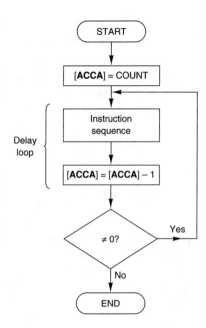

FIGURE 7.11   Flowchart of a typical time-delay loop.

Time-Delay Loops

A simple time-delay loop works as follows:

1. Load a register with an initial value.
2. Execute an instruction sequence for time delay.
3. Decrement the register.
4. If register is not zero, repeat steps 2 and 3.

The register is used as a down counter whose initial value determines how many times the timing loop is executed.

The flowchart in Fig. 7.11 illustrates a time-delay loop that uses ACCA as the counter. The first block shows that ACCA is loaded with a value called COUNT. The value of COUNT can range up to 255_{10}, and controls the number of times that the delay loop will be executed. The delay loop consists of three blocks, one of which is an instruction sequence that is chosen to produce the desired delay.

EXAMPLE 7.51

The program below uses COUNT = 40 and a single NOP instruction in the delay loop. Calculate the total execution time. Assume a 2-MHz clock.

Address	Label	Instruction code	Mnemonic	Comments
C350	START	86	(2) LDAA # $40	: Load ACCA with
C351		40		; COUNT = 40_{16} = 64_{10}

Address	Label	Instruction code	Mnemonic	Comments
C352	LOOP	01	(2) NOP	; Delay two cycles
C353		4A	(2) DECA	; Decrement ACCA
C354		26	(3) BNE $C352	; If not zero, branch back to
C355		FC		; LOOP
C356	CONT	??	? ?	; Continue on to next portion of
		??	? ?	; program

Solution   The number in parentheses preceding each instruction mnemonic indicates the number of clock cycles to execute that instruction. The LDAA instruction is executed only once. The NOP, DECA, and BNE instructions are executed 64 times (COUNT = 40_{16} = 64_{10}). Thus, the total execution time is

$$2 + 64 \times (2 + 2 + 3) = 450 \text{ clock cycles}$$

(Note that 1 cycle of the E-clock (2-MHz) is equal to 500 ns.)

Therefore, 450 clock cycles $\times$ 500 ns = **225 μs.**

The foregoing example showed that the total delay time is calculated by adding the execution times of those instructions that are external to the loop to the execution times of those inside the loop multiplied by COUNT. That is,

$$\textbf{total delay} = \mathbf{T_E + (COUNT \times T_L)}$$

Where T_E is the time delay external to the loop and T_L is the time delay inside the loop. In the example, T_E = 2 cycles, T_L = 7 cycles, and COUNT = 64 to produce a total delay of 450 clock cycles. Note that it is more convenient to express all the execution times as a number of cycles, and then convert the final result to actual units of time.

EXAMPLE 7.52

Change the value of COUNT in the program of Example 7.51 to produce a delay of approximately 0.5 ms.

Solution   Since 0.5 ms = 500 μs, and 1 clock cycle is 500 ns = 0.5 μs, the desired delay is 500 μs/0.5 μs = 1000 clock cycles. Thus, we have

$$1000 = T_E + (COUNT \times T_L)$$
$$= 2 + (COUNT \times 7)$$

or

$$COUNT = 142.57$$

The nearest integer value is COUNT = 143_{10} = $8F_{16}$. Using COUNT = $8F_{16}$, the actual total delay will be

$$2 + (143 \times 7) = 1003 \text{ cycles} = \textbf{501.5 μs.}$$

EXAMPLE 7.53

Change the program to produce an approximate delay of 2.0 ms.

Solution This delay is too great to be achieved by simply increasing COUNT. With COUNT $= FF_{16} = 255_{10}$, the delay will be only

$$2 + (255 \times 7) = 1787 \text{ cycles} = \textbf{893.5 } \boldsymbol{\mu}\textbf{s}.$$

We can increase the total delay by increasing the delay within the loop (T_L) by either adding an appropriate number of NOP instructions, or by changing the 8-bit register ACCA to the 16-bit register X, or Y. Let us consider the first option.

To achieve the 2.0 ms delay, we want 2 ms/0.5 μs = 4000 cycles delay

$$4000 = 2 + (\text{COUNT} \times T_L)$$

or

$$\text{COUNT} \times T_L = 3998$$

If we choose COUNT $= 234_{10}$, then

$$T_L = 3998 \text{ cycles}/234 \approx 17$$

Thus, we can add *five* NOPs (i.e., 10 clock cycles) to the loop to achieve $T_L = 17$. The exact delay will be

$$2 + (234 \times 17) = 3980 \text{ cycles} = \textbf{1.99 ms}$$

The revised program is shown below. Note the six NOPs and the new value of COUNT loaded in ACCA.

Address	Label	Instruction code	Mnemonic	Comments
C350	START	86	(2) LDAA #$EA	; Load ACCA with
C351		EA		; COUNT $= EA_{16} = 234_{10}$
C352	LOOP	01	(2) NOP	; Delay two cycles
C353		01	(2) NOP	; Delay two cycles
C354		01	(2) NOP	; Delay two cycles
C355		01	(2) NOP	; Delay two cycles
C356		01	(2) NOP	; Delay two cycles
C357		01	(2) NOP	; Delay two cycles
C358		4A	(2) DECA	; Decrement ACCA
C359		26	(3) BNE $C352	; If not zero, branch back to
C35A		F7		; LOOP
C35B	CONT	??	? ?	; Continue

A more efficient way of solving this problem is to load the COUNT value in either one of the 16-bit index registers, X or Y, instead of the 8-bit ACCA. This increases the maximum COUNT number from 255_{10} to $65,535_{10}$. Note that some 8-bit MPUs may not have 16-bit general-purpose registers that the programmer can use, and clearly this alternative way of solving this problem would not be possible. The following sequence is one possible way of modifying the program of Example 7.51 to generate a delay of 2 ms using the 68HC11 MPU.

Address	Label	Instruction code	Mnemonic	Comments
C350	START	CE	*(3)* LDX #$01F3	; Load X with COUNT = $01F3_{16}$
C351		01		; = 499_{10}
C352		F3		
C353	LOOP	01	*(2)* NOP	; Delay two cycles
C354		09	*(3)* DEX	; Decrement X
C355		26	*(3)* BNE $C352	; If not zero, branch back to
C356		FC		; LOOP
C357	CONT	??	? ?	; Continue

Study the program above and note the following changes:

1. The time delay external to the loop, $T_E = 3$ cycles or 1.5 μs.

2. The time delay inside the loop, $T_L = 8$ cycles (2 + 3 + 3) or 4 μs.

Thus, since 2.0 ms ≈ 4000 cycles, we want

$$4000 = T_E + (COUNT \times T_L)$$

$$= 3 + (COUNT \times 8)$$

or

$$COUNT = 499.625$$

The nearest integer value is COUNT $500_{10} = 01F4_{16}$. Using COUNT = $01F4_{16}$, the actual total delay will be

$$3 + (500 \times 8) = 4003 \text{ cycles} = \textbf{2.001 ms}$$

Loop Within a Loop

In this last example one of the alternatives was to increase the total delay by adding more instructions to the delay loop. This method becomes inefficient for longer delays where many instructions would have to be included inside the delay loop. A better solution for longer delays would be to use a *loop within a loop*. This is flowcharted in Fig. 7.12.

Here both accumulators are used as loop counters. ACCB is used as the inner loop counter and ACCA as the outer loop counter. The outer loop, blocks 2–6, will be executed a number of times equal to COUNT1. The inner loop, blocks 3 and 4, will be executed a number of times equal to COUNT2 × COUNT1. Thus, long delays can be achieved by using large values for COUNT1 and COUNT2.

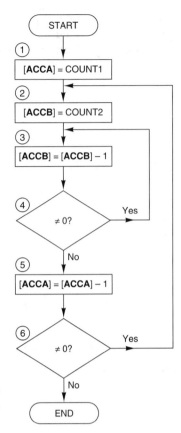

FIGURE 7.12 Flowchart of delay loop within delay loop for achieving longer total delay time.

▶ 7.24 TIME-DELAY SUBROUTINES

When a programming application requires the generation of many timing intervals, it is more efficient to use time-delay subroutines than it is to insert a time-delay sequence each time it is needed. The flowchart in Fig. 7.13 is a time-delay subroutine that produces an approximate delay of 1 ms × [X]. For example, if [X] = 0005 prior to the start of this subroutine, the delay will be 5 ms; if [X] = 0008, the delay will be 8 ms. The main program has to load X with the desired value prior to jumping to this subroutine. The subroutine uses X as the outer loop counter and Y as the inner loop counter.

The listing for this subroutine is given in the following table:

Delay Subroutine (1 ms × [X])

Address	Label	Instruction code	Mnemonic	Comments
C800	START	18	*(4)* LDY #$011C	; [Y] = 011C$_{16}$ = 284$_{10}$
C801		CE		
C802		01		

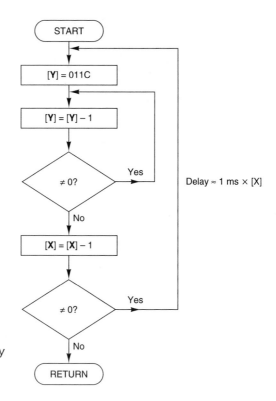

FIGURE 7.13 Flowchart of delay subroutine with delay = 1 ms × **[X]**.

Delay Subroutine (1 ms × [X])

Address	Label	Instruction code	Mnemonic	Comments
C803		1C		
C804	LOOP	18	*(4)* DEY	; Decrement **[Y]**
C805		09		
C806		26	*(3)* BNE $C804	; If not zero, branch to LOOP
C807		FB		
C808		09	*(3)* DEX	; Decrement **[X]**
C809		26	*(3)* BNE $C800	; back to START
C80A		F6		
C80B	RETURN	39	*(5)* RTS	; Return to main program

The exact calculation of the delay produced by this subroutine will be left as an end-of-chapter exercise.

Using the Delay Subroutine

To illustrate the use of this subroutine, we will assume that the MPU is interfaced to an output port register. Fig. 7.14A shows a simplified diagram. Some or all of the register outputs, $Q_7 - Q_0$, are used to control external devices. Let us assume that only Q_7 and Q_6 are currently being used and we want the MPU to do the following:

1. Initially clear all register outputs.
2. Set $Q_7 = 1$ for 5 s, then clear it back to 0.
3. Wait for 0.7 s.
4. Set $Q_6 = 1$ for 2.3 s, then clear it back to 0.

The timing diagram is shown in Fig. 7.14B.

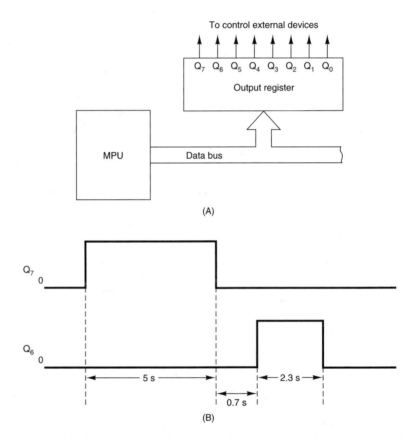

(A)

(B)

FIGURE 7.14   (A) MPU controlling external device timing via an output register; (B) typical timing for control outputs.

This operation can be accomplished by a program that uses the foregoing delay subroutine at address C800. The program has to generate three separate timing intervals: 5 s, 0.7 s, and 2.3 s. The assembly language program is given below. It assumes that the output port is 8000_{16}.

Mnemonic	Comments
CLR $8000	; Clear all register outputs
LDAB #$80	; [ACCB] = 80_{16} = 10000000_2
STAB $8000	; Set $Q_7 = 1$
LDX #$1388	; [X] = 1388_{16} = 5000_{10} for 5 s delay
JSR $C800	; Call delay subroutine
CLR $8000	; Clear Q_7 back to 0
LDX #$02BC	; [X] = $02BC_{16}$ = 700_{10} for 0.7 s delay
JSR $C800	; Call delay subroutine
LDAB #$40	; [ACCB] = 40_{16} = 01000000_2
STAB $8000	; Make $Q_6 = 1$
LDX #$08FC	; [X] = $08FC_{16}$ = 2300_{10} or 2.3 s delay
JSR $C800	; Call delay subroutine
CLR $8000	; Clear Q_6 back to 0
WAI	; Halt

Study the program carefully and verify that it will generate the timing waveforms in Fig. 7.14B. Note how ACCB is used to set and clear the appropriate bits of the output register. Also note how the various timing intervals are obtained by loading X with the value equal to the desired number of milliseconds before jumping to the subroutine at C800.

EXAMPLE 7.54

Write a program segment to generate 5 cycles of a 50-Hz square wave at the Q_0 output in Fig. 7.14. Assume that the contents of the Y register must retain its current value after the segment is executed.

Solution The Q_0 output will have to change states every 10 ms since the period of a 50-Hz signal is 20 ms. The program segment below will produce the desired waveform. It uses the output register as a counter, and it toggles the Q_0 bit every 10 ms by using an INC instruction. ACCB is used to keep track of the total number of *half-cycles* generated.

Also, note how [Y] is saved on the stack at the start of the program segment. This is necessary because the delay subroutine at C800 uses the Y register and will, therefore, lose whatever is in Y prior to the subroutine call. The [Y] is restored to its original value by the PULY instruction at the end of the segment.

Address	Label	Instruction code	Mnemonic	Comments
C300	START	18	PSHY	; Save [Y] on the stack
C301		3C		
C302	START	7F	CLR $8000	; Clear all output bits to 0
C303		80		
C304		00		

Address	Label	Instruction code	Mnemonic	Comments
C305		C6	LDAB #$0A	; [ACCB] = 10_{10} half-cycles
C306		0A		
C307	TOGGLE	7C	INC $8000	; Increment output register
C308		80		; to toggle Q_0
C309		00		
C30A		CE	LDX #$000A	; [X] = 10 ms delay
C30B		00		
C30C		0A		
C30D		BD	JSR $C800	; Jump to delay subroutine
C30E		C8		
C30F		00		
C310		5A	DECB	; Decrement [ACCB]
C311		26	BNE $C307	; If ≠ 0, branch back to TOGGLE
C312		F4		
C313		18	PULY	; Restore [Y]
C314		38		

▶ 7.25 THE TIMER SYSTEM OF THE 68HC11 MCU

The *timer system* is a complex but useful component of the overall 68HC11 MCU. Discussion of this system in detail would go beyond the scope of this book and would not add to the basic understanding of microprocessors and microcomputers. Furthermore, the commercially available *68HC11 Reference Manual* from Motorola discusses all of the intricate and unique internal systems of the 68HC11 MCU. Therefore, we will introduce the timer system and/or any of its components whenever appropriate, and then only to the extent that is necessary to show the difference in performance between a typical 8-bit MPU and the 68HC11.

A 16-bit timer counter register (TCNT) is the principal internal component of the main timer system of the 68HC11 MCU. The TCNT* counter starts automatically from a count of $0000 as the MPU comes out of a reset condition, and then is incremented continuously at a clock rate derived from the E-clock. When TCNT reaches its maximum count of $FFFF, it recycles back to $0000 and resumes counting. It is important to understand that TCNT is continually counting as the MPU executes a program of instructions. The programmer can insert instructions in the program that can read the contents of TCNT to determine the count at that point in time. This can be done using any instruction that will read a *double-byte* into the MPU (i.e., LDD, LDX, or LDY) from address $100E, since the TCNT register is located at addresses $100E and $100F in the 68HC11A8 memory map as illustrated below.

---

*A complete list of the 68HC11 MCU built-in control registers can be found in Appendix C.

TCNT

7	6	5	4	3	2	1	0	
Bit 15	Bit 14	Bit 13	Bit 12	Bit 11	Bit 10	Bit 9	Bit 8	($100E)

Bit 7	Bit 6	Bit 5	Bit 4	Bit 3	Bit 2	Bit 1	Bit 0	($100F)

The rate at which the TCNT counter is clocked, or incremented, is determined by the states of the timer prescaler select bits, PR0 and PR1. These two bits are part of another MCU built-in register called TMSK2* (Timer MaSK 2), which resides at address location $1024. The following illustration shows the position of the control bits, PR0 and PR1, as well as four other control bits not relevant to this discussion, TOI, RTII, PAVOI, and PAII.

TMSK2 ($1024)

	7	6	5	4	3	2	1	0
	TOI	RTII	PAVOI	PAII	0	0	**PR1**	**PR0**
At Reset:	0	0	0	0	0	0	0	0

PR0 and PR1 select the factor by which the E-clock frequently will be divided. The resultant clock is the signal used to increment the 16-bit TCNT counter. PR0 and PR1 can be changed to cause a division of the E-clock by a factor of 1, 4, 8, or 16, as indicated by Table 7.3. The only way the prescale rate can be changed is by writing the appropriate word to the TMSK2 register within the first 64 bus cycles after reset. Since bits PR1 and PR0 can only be changed during a small window of time after a reset occurs, they are often referred to as *time-protected bits*.

To illustrate, assume that a crystal frequency of 8 MHz is used, so the E-clock, which is the 68HC11 main bus clock, will be at 2 MHz. If PR1 = 1 and PR0 = 0, a

TABLE 7.3   Crystal Frequency vs. PR1, PR0 Values

PR1	PR0	Prescale Factor	Crystal Frequency		
			2^{23} Hz	8 MHz	4 MHz
			One Count (resolution)/Overflow (Range)		
0	0	1	477 ns/31.25 ms	500 ns/32.77 ms	1μs/65.54 ms
0	1	4	191 μs/125 ms	2 μs/131.1 ms	4 μs/262.1 ms
1	0	8	3.81 μs/250 ms	4 μs/262.1 ms	8 μs/524.3 ms
1	1	16	7.63 μs/0.5 s	8 μs/524.3 ms	16 μs/1.049 s
			2.1 MHz	2 MHz	1 MHz
			Bus Frequency (E-Clock)		

prescaler factor of 8 is selected as shown in Table 7.1. The table also indicates that for this scale factor and an E-clock of 2 MHz, the counter will be incremented once every 4 μs, and will reach its maximum range (overflow) in 262.1 ms.

When the free-running TCNT counter cycles from $FFFF to $0000, the timer over-flow flag (TOF) is set in the 8-bit TFLG2* (timer flag 2) register. The TFLG2 register resides at address location $1025. The TCNT counter counts continuously even if the TOF flag is not cleared. However, by properly monitoring the TOF flag in the TFLG2 register, the programmer can keep track of the number of times the TCNT counter cycles. This can be useful in determining time delays since we know how long it takes for the TCNT count from $0000 to $FFFF (i.e., 32.77 ms when the E-clock = 2 MHz and PR0 = PR1 = 0).

TFLG2   ($1025)

	7	6	5	4	3	2	1	0
At	TOF	RTIF	PAVOF	PAIF	0	0	0	0
Reset:	0	0	0	0	0	0	0	0

Each of the four flag bits in TFLG2 are set to 1 by a specific condition in the timer system. TOF is the only flag we are concerned with for now. Any of these flags can be cleared to 0 by writing a 1 to the corresponding bit position. In other words, any MPU instruction that writes 10000000 into address $1025 will clear the TOF bit; *all other bits will be unaffected.* For example, the following instruction sequence will clear TOF:

        LDAA #$80   ; load ACCA with 10000000$_2$
        STAA $1025   ; write [ACCA] into TFLG2 to
                         ; clear TOF (timer overflow flag)

EXAMPLE 7.55

Let us suppose that we want to use the main timer system of a 68HC11 MPU, oper-ating with an E-clock of 2 MHz, to run a speed-test-cycle on a certain motor. Further-more, let us assume that the 68HC11 MPU is being used in its expanded mode and that PR0 and PR1 control bits in the TMSK2 register are cleared. The address for the output port that is used to control the motor is C700. If bit 7 of the output port is HIGH, the motor turns ON. If bit 7 of the output port is LOW, the motor turns OFF. Write a subroutine starting at address C200 that will perform the speed-test-cycle on the motor as follows:

1. Turn ON the motor.
2. Wait 30 seconds to allow the motor to reach maximum speed.
3. Run the motor at maximum speed for 5 minutes.
4. Turn OFF the motor.
5. Wait 1 minute to allow the motor to come to a complete stop.
6. Return to the main program.

---

*A complete set of the 68HC11 MCU built-in central registers can be found in Appendix C.

Solution

Motor Subroutine

Address	Label	Code	Mnemonic	Comments
C200	MTRSUB	18 CE 00 00	LDY #$0000	; [Y] = 0000 for delay subroutine
C204		86 80	LDAA #$80	; [ACCA] = 80_{16} = 1000000_2
C206		B7 C7 00	STAA $C700	; Turn ON motor
C209		CE 22 57	LDX #$2257	; [X] = 2257_{16} = $10,071_{10}$
C20C		FF C4 00	STX $C400	; [X] $\longrightarrow$ [C400]
C20F		BD C3 00	JSR $C300	; Jump to delay subroutine
C212		7F C7 00	CLR $C700	; Turn OFF the motor
C215		18 CE 00 00	LDY #$0000	; [Y] = 0000 for delay subroutine
C219		CE 07 27	LDX #$0727	; [X] = 0727_{16} = $1,831_{10}$
C21C		FF C4 00	STX $C400	; [X] $\longrightarrow$ [C400]
C21F		BD C3 00	JSR $C300	; Jump to delay subroutine
C222		39	RTS	; Return to main program

⋮ ⋮

⋮ ⋮

Delay subroutine

Address	Label	Code	Mnemonic	Comments
C300	BGNSUB	C6 80	LDAB #$80	; [ACCB] = 80_{16}
C302		F7 10 25	STAB $1025	; TOF flag = 0 in TFLG2
C305	COUNT	F6 10 25	LDAB $1025	; Read TOF flag
C308		2A FB	BPL $C305	; If TOF = 0, branch to COUNT
C30A		18 08	INY	; [Y] = # of times TCNT cycled
C30C		18 BC C4 00	CPY $C400	; Compare [Y] with 5.5 minutes
C310		26 FE	BNE $C300	; If [Y] ≠ DELAY, go to BGNSUB
C312		39	RTS	; Return to MOTOR SUBROUTINE

Before we proceed in explaining the step-by-step description of the above subroutines, we want to point out the fact that in these subroutines we are showing all the data required to express an instruction on one line. This is often done in order to make the length of the program listing shorter and make it easier to follow its flow.

As you read through the following step-by-step description, you may want to refer to Appendix A for clarification or review of certain instructions.

1. **Address C200:** Register Y is cleared in order to be used as a counter by the DELAY SUBROUTINE.
2. **Address C204:** ACCA is loaded with data $80 to make bit 7 = 1.
3. **Address C206:** The motor is turned ON by sending the contents of ACCA to the output port at address C700.
4. **Address C209:** [X] is initialized with the data 2257_{16} = 10071_{10}. The decimal value 10071 represents the number of times that the TCNT counter must cycle to produce a

time delay of 5.5 minutes. Note that with PR0 = PR1 = 0 and E-clock at 2 MHz Table 7.1 shows that it takes 32.77 ms for the TCNT counter to cycle once. Therefore, 10071×32.77 ms ≈ 5.5 minutes. We need a delay of 5.5 min. because the motor needs 30 s to reach maximum speed and then it must remain at the speed for 5 minutes.

5. **Address C20C:** [X] is stored in memory location C400 to be used by the DELAY SUBROUTINE later.

6. **Address C20F:** The program jumps to the subroutine starting at address C300. The return address $C212 is automatically stored on the stack.

7. **Address C300:** [ACCB] = 80_{16}. This will make bit 7 of ACCB HIGH.

8. **Address C302:** The data in ACCB are loaded in the TFLG2 register. This will clear the TOF flag in register TFLG2. Recall that this flag, TOF, is set every time the TCNT counter cycles through $FFFF.

9. **Address C305:** Register TFLG2 is read in order to determine whether or not the TOF flag is set.

10. **Address C308:** If the TOF flag is not set, the program branches back to COUNT and will read the condition of the TOF flag again. If the TOF flag is set, the program will fall through and execute the next instruction in the sequence.

11. **Address C30A:** Register Y is incremented every time the TOF flag is set. Recall that the TOF flag is set every time the TCNT counter cycles.

12. **Address C30C:** [Y] is compared with [C400] in order to determine if [Y] has reached the count of 2257_{16} (5.5-minute delay).

13. **Address C310:** If [Y] $\neq$ 2257, then the program branches to the beginning of the subroutine (BGNSUB) and the process repeats itself until [Y] = 2257. When [Y] = 2257, the program executes the next instruction in the sequence at $C312.

14. **Address C312:** A 5.5-minute delay has been accomplished and now the program returns from the DELAY subroutine to the MOTOR subroutine at $C212.

15. **Address C212:** The output port is cleared in order to make its bit 7 = 0. This will turn OFF the motor.

16. **Address C215:** Register Y is cleared in order to be used as a counter by the DELAY SUBROUTINE.

17. **Address C219:** [X] is initialized with the data $0727_{16} = 1831_{10}$. The decimal value 1831 represents the number of times that the TCNT counter must cycle to produce a time delay of 1 minute. Again, recall that it takes 32.77 ms for the TCNT counter to cycle once. Therefore, 1831×32.77 ms ≈ 1 minute. We need a delay of 1 min. in order for the motor to come to a complete stop.

18. **Address C21C:** [X] is stored in memory location C400 to be used by the DELAY SUBROUTINE later.

19. **Address C21F:** The program jumps to the subroutine starting at address C300. The DELAY subroutine is executed in the same manner as it was for the 5.5-minute delay. The difference now is that the delay will be approximately 1 minute, after which control is returned to the MOTOR subroutine at $C222.

20. **Address C222:** The program returns from the MOTOR subroutine to the main program.

This program used nested subroutines. Clearly, it could have been written in many different ways, using different instructions. The intent was to show how the programmer can take advantage of the 68HC11 built-in TCNT counter and its associated registers to produce a time delay.

It should be noted that the above program in all likelihood will *not* produce time delays of exactly 5.5 minutes and 1 minute, respectively. There are two reasons that might contribute to these errors. First, when we jump to the DELAY subroutine and clear the TOF flag, we don't know at which count the TCNT counter is. For example, let us assume that the TCNT counter is at count FFFA when we clear the TOF flag in the DELAY subroutine. This means that five E-clock cycles later the TOF flag would be set. In our program, that would cause the Y register to increment for the first time about 32.76 ms (32.77 ms − 2.5 µs) prematurely. The second source for an error is the fact that the TCNT counter is always counting, even when the 68HC11 MPU is executing instructions. Consequently, from the time the TOF flag is read until it's read again, the TCNT counter is incremented three times during the BPL instruction. This may cause the TCNT counter to cycle and therefore induce a minuscule error into the count. In either case, however, the errors are of no significance since we are dealing with time delays that are in the minute range and we are dealing with an application where an error of a few milliseconds would not significantly affect the outcome of the motor test.

▶ 7.26 THE SOFTWARE DEVELOPMENT PROCESS

We have examined the instruction set of the 68HC11 MPU, have seen some of the more common programming techniques, and have written some relatively short programs. In practice, the actual writing of the program codes is a small portion of the software development process. If this were a text on microcomputer programming, we would now describe the details of the complete process by which a program is developed. For our purposes here, however, we briefly describe this process to show the many steps needed to produce a program that will work in a given application.

Although programmers usually develop their own style and methodology, the general sequence of software development consists of the following steps:

Problem Definition

The programmer has to determine the subtasks that the microprocessor must perform in order to accomplish the overall tasks. For example, what is necessary for the MPU to control an industrial process, run a series of tests on a printed circuit board, or handle communications between a central computer and a remote terminal?

Problem definition requires the determination of the number, types, and characteristics of the system inputs and outputs. The programmer has to ask questions such as the following:

1. What signals will the computer receive? What are the characteristics of these signals?
2. Are these inputs generated by human beings, or by electronic circuitry?
3. What should be done if there are errors in these input signals?

4. What output signals must the computer produce? What are the desired characteristics of these outputs?

Because many microprocessor applications involve human interaction, the programmer must also consider such questions as:

1. How is the operator to enter data or control information?
2. What errors is the operator most likely to make?
3. What kind of output displays would be the most valuable to the operator?
4. Is the system easy for the operator to use?

The programmer not only has to determine how the MPU is to process the input data to produce the desired output data but also has to be concerned with memory and timing constraints. For example, in some applications it may be more important to process the data as fast as possible regardless of how much memory is required. This might dictate the use of memory data tables instead of time-consuming calculations to produce the desired outputs. Other applications may require a conservation of memory in order to keep hardware costs down.

Program Design (Flowcharting)

After defining the problem, the programmer will generally break the problem down into small tasks and will determine the sequence in which these tasks will be performed. The development of a flowchart is a valuable tool in this step of the process. It not only helps the programmer to see the logic that the program must follow but also aids in determining the feasibility of using subroutines for repetitive tasks.

It is important during this program design phase that the programmer resist the temptation to start writing instruction codes. The program design should be completely formulated before the program is actually written. This is similar to finalizing a block diagram for an electronic circuit before drawing a detailed circuit diagram.

Program Coding

Once the flowchart has been designed, the programmer can convert it into instruction codes. Coding is the writing of the program in a form that the computer can directly understand or can translate. If the program is written in assembly language or in a high-level language like BASIC or Pascal, it must be translated into a machine language program before the computer can execute it. Recall that an assembly language source program is converted into a machine language object program by another program called an *assembler*. The assembler already resides in the computer's memory; it may be in ROM, or it may have been loaded from disk memory into RAM. Also recall that a high-level language program is converted to machine language by an interpreter or compiler program.

Testing and Debugging

This is probably the most time-consuming phase of the software development process. All but the simplest programs will contain one or more errors in *syntax* or *logic*. A syntax error occurs when the programmer failed to follow one of the rules of the programming language being used. An example would be a missing colon (:) between BASIC statements on the same line. Another would be a missing $ in front of a hex value in an assembly language instruction. Syntax errors are usually easy to find and fix because most compilers, interpreters, and assemblers will detect and print out syntax errors.

Logic errors are errors in the program design; that is, the program does not violate any syntax rules, but the program does not perform as intended. This is like a circuit that is connected correctly but does not produce the intended operation because the design is faulty. An example of a logic error would be the programmer neglecting to load the contents of an MPU register before jumping to a time-delay subroutine that uses the value in that register. These errors are somewhat harder to detect than syntax errors because the computer has no way of knowing what the programmer intends the program to do.

Several debugging tools are available for tracking down errors in program logic. One of the most common is called *single stepping* or *tracing*. In this mode the MPU will execute a single instruction each time the operator actuates a single-step or trace key. In other words, the MPU stops after each instruction and waits for the next single-step or trace command. This allows the operator to examine the contents of any MPU register, memory location, or the status of any input/output port at the completion of each instruction before going on to the next. The operator can step slowly through a program, checking for program errors as he or she proceeds. Motorola makes system evaluation boards that are commercially available, such as the EVB board that allows the user to test and debug software to be used in 68HC11-based applications. These evaluation boards are examples of development systems that have all of the needed debugging techniques, such as the single-step or trace modes and the capacity to allow insertion of breakpoints, just to mention a few. In the particular case of the EVB board, every time the operator invokes the trace or single-step mode the system, after executing the next instruction in the sequence, displays on the CRT screen the contents of all the pertinent registers of the 68HC11 MPU. With such development systems one can test and improve the system's design before it is implemented in its final form.

The single-step mode does have certain drawbacks. It is very slow. It may take several days to single-step through a program that the MPU normally executes in 1 s. Furthermore, it cannot be used to check out programs that are generating time delays for input or output operations, because the single-step mode slows down the timing considerably. Thus, this mode should be used only for debugging short instruction sequences that do not use any time delays.

Another debugging technique uses *breakpoints*. A breakpoint is a place in a program where the MPU will automatically suspend execution and branch to a special *breakpoint routine* that is usually part of the system monitor program in ROM. The breakpoint routine is an instruction sequence that typically does the following:

1. Stores the current values of the MPU registers in RAM where they can be examined by the operator, or outputs them to a video display or printer for easy examination. The latter operation is called a *register dump*.
2. Waits for the operator to *clear the breakpoint* and send the MPU back to continue execution of the main program.

When the breakpoint technique is used, the MPU executes the program at the normal clock rate until it reaches a breakpoint. Thus, the programmer can allow the MPU to execute a segment of the program at full speed until a breakpoint is reached, after which the contents of the MPU registers and any memory locations can be examined to see if the program segment functioned correctly.

The 68HC11 MPU has a special instruction called *software interrupt,* SWI, that can act as a breakpoint. SWI is a single-byte instruction with op code = 3F. The programmer can insert this op code at any point in the program where a breakpoint is desired. SWI actually causes the MPU to respond in the same manner as it does to interrupt signals from external devices. This MPU response to interrupts will be discussed in detail in Chapter 8.

A much different type of debugging tool is the *logic analyzer,* which is an instrument similar to an oscilloscope. It can be used to capture and display the logic levels present on all of the microcomputer's buses for a specified number of clock cycles. It can typically display the information in the form of timing diagrams or as binary or hex tables. Logic analyzers are particularly useful in detecting glitches, incorrect signal sequences, incorrect timing, and incorrect program sequencing. Although it is a very useful debugging tool, the logic analyzer's high cost ($3,000 to $20,000) precludes its widespread use.

Program Documentation

This final step in the software development process is the one that is most often slighted. *Documentation* includes several forms of descriptive material that allow program users to understand the operation and logic. It also allows the program designer to maintain a library of material that can make future programming tasks easier. The most common forms of documentation include flowcharts, source and object program listings, descriptive comments, memory maps, and circuit diagrams where applicable.

GLOSSARY*

AND Masking   Using the AND operation to clear specific bits of a data word while not affecting the others.

Breakpoint   A place in a program where the MPU will suspend execution and branch to a special routine that allows the operator to examine the MPU registers.

Carry Flag (C)   A multipurpose flag used in arithmetic and shift operations.

Condition Code Register (CCR)   68HC11 MPU register that holds the eight bits (flags) that monitor the various conditions that exist during program execution.

Debugging   See Program Debugging.

Direct Addressing   The byte following the op code specifies the page zero operand address. See Zero-Page Addressing.

EVB Board   A Motorola development system board that allows the user to test and debug software to be used in a 68HC11-based application.

Extended Addressing   The two bytes following the op code specify the operand address.

---

*Refer to Appendix A for all instruction definitions.

Half-Carry Flag (H)   An MPU flag used to indicate whether or not a carry is produced from bit 3 to bit position 4 during the addition of two 8-bit binary numbers.

Immediate Addressing   The byte following the op code is the operand.

Indexed Addressing   The operand address is obtained by adding the offset byte that follows the op code to the contents of an index register.

Inherent Addressing   Single-byte instructions that do not require an operand address.

Interrupt Mask Flag   An MPU flag used to control MPU response to interrupts.

Multibyte Arithmetic   Addition or subtraction of numbers larger than one byte.

Negative Flag (N)   An MPU flag that indicates the status of the sign bit (MSB) of the result.

Nesting Subroutines   The main program jumps to a subroutine that contains a jump to a subroutine, and so on.

Nonmaskable Interrupt Flag (X)   An MPU flag used to control MPU response to nonmaskable interrupts.

Offset   See Relative Offset.

OR Masking   Using the OR operation to set specific bits of a data word while not affecting the others.

Overflow Flag (V)   An MPU flag used to indicate overflow of 7-bit capacity when signed numbers are added or subtracted.

Packed BCD   The BCD codes for two decimal digits are packed into one data byte.

PR0/PR1   Control bit in the TMSK2 register. The combination of both PR0 and PR1 select the factor by which the E-clock will be divided. The resultant clock is the signal that will clock the TCNT counter.

Program Debugging   Procedures for checking a program for logic and syntax errors.

Relative Addressing   Used in conditional branch instructions to determine the branching address by adding the offset to the **[PC]**.

Relative Offset   The second byte of a simple conditional branch instruction or the fourth byte of a bit manipulation branch instruction. It is a signed number that is added to **[PC]** whenever branching is to occur.

Single Stepping   A debugging procedure whereby the MPU executes an instruction and stops until it receives a command to continue to the next instruction. This allows the operator to examine register and memory contents after each instruction.

Software Interrupt   A special 68HC11 MPU instruction that can act as a breakpoint during software testing.

Stop Disable Flag (S)   An MPU flag that is used to suspend the operation of all MPU clocks.

Subroutine   Sequence of instructions that performs a specific task. Whenever the main program wants to perform the task, the MPU jumps to the subroutine, executes it, and returns to the main program.

Tables   Lists of related data that are stored in sequential memory locations.

TCNT Counter   Special counter that is an integral part of the main timer system of the 68HC11 MCU.

TFLG2 Register   Built-in timer flag register that contains four flags used by various functions within the 68HC11 MCU.

Time-Delay Loop   Sequence of instructions specifically used to provide time delay. The sequence is repeated as many times as necessary to produce the required delay.

Time-Protected Bits   Special MCU register bits that can be changed only during a small window of time after an initial system reset.

TOF (Timer Overflow Flag)   A TFLG2 register flag that gets set whenever the TCNT counter cycles from $FFFF to $0000.

TMSK2 Timer   Built-in 8-bit register whose control bits are used by various system functions within the 68HC11 MCU.

Trace Mode   See Single Stepping.

Zero Flag (Z)   An MPU flag indicating whether the last operation produced data of 00.

Zero-Page Addressing   Two-byte instruction where the second byte specifies the low-order byte of the operand address; the high-order byte is always 00. See Direct Addressing.

QUESTIONS AND PROBLEMS

Section 7.1

1. Draw the 68HC11 MPU programming model. Show all registers and indicate the size of each.
2. Identify the 68HC11 MPU flag being described in each statement.
   (a) Is involved with maskable interrupts
   (b) Is made LOW when result is not zero
   (c) Indicates the sign of the result
   (d) Is affected by both arithmetic and shift operations
   (e) Indicates overflow when signed numbers are added
   (f) Indicates overflow when unsigned numbers are added
   (g) Indicates overflow from bit 3 to bit position 4 during the addition of two 8-bit binary numbers
   (h) Is made LOW in order to stop all MPU clocks
3. Which 68HC11 MPU flags can be set or cleared by specific program instructions?

Section 7.2

4. Each of the following is an assembly language instruction that will load data into accumulator A. For each, indicate where the data comes from. Assume that $[X] = 0200_{16}$.
   (a) LDAA #$2D   (b) LDAA $7C   (c) LDAA $57BB
   (d) LDAA $3F,X
5. Explain the difference between the direct address mode and the extended address mode.
6. Which 68HC11 address mode always uses two bytes following the op code?
7. Which address mode requires no bytes following the op code?
8. Which address mode might require one byte or two bytes following the op code?
9. Study the following instruction sequence. What will **[ACCA]**, **[ACCB]**, and **[ACCD]** be at the end of the sequence?

Address	Instruction code	Mnemonic
0350	CE	LDX #$8F00
0351	8F	
0352	00	
0353	DF	STX $FE
0354	FE	
0355	96	LDAA $FE
0356	FE	
0357	D6	LDAB $FF
0358	FF	

10. Which address mode is used in conditional branch instructions?

11. Which address mode involves the use of the X and Y registers?

Sections 7.3–7.4

12. Why are there 308 different op codes if the 68HC11 instruction set contains only 108 different types of instructions?

13. How many different types of 68HC11 instructions can operate on either the accumulator or memory?

14. Use Appendix A to find the op codes for each of the following assembly language instructions:
    (a) ADDA #$20   (b) ADDB $20   (c) CLV   (d) SUBA $20,Y
    (e) LDS #$01FF   (f) NEGB   (g) NEG $0A44   (h) DEX
    (i) TBA   (j) COM $50,X   (k) COMB   (l) CPX $45,Y   (m) MUL

15. Convert each of the instructions of Problem 14 to its machine language codes.

16. Which of the instructions of Problem 14 will have no effect on the C flag? Which ones will never affect the Z flag?

17. Determine which of the instructions of Problem 14 have the longest execution times.

Sections 7.5–7.6

18. List and briefly describe the 11 different classifications of 68HC11 instructions.

19. List the five columns that exist in a typical listing of an assembly language program.

Sections 7.7–7.9

20. Refer to the program of Problem 9. Indicate the status of the pertinent MPU registers, flags, and memory locations after the execution of each instruction as was done in Example 7.15.

21. Modify the program in Example 7.16 so that [ACCA] is stored in location 0285 and [ACCB] is stored in location 0286.

22. Refer to the program of Example 7.16. Replace the PULB and PULA instructions with a single PULX instruction. What overall operation does this program now perform?

23. Examine the following instruction sequence. At what memory address will **[ACCB]** be stored?

LDX #$0987
TXS
PSHB

24. Why are there no instructions for transferring **[X]** to **[ACCA]** or **[ACCB]**?

Section 7.10

25. Write an instruction sequence that subtracts the data at memory location 0350 from the sum of **[ACCA]** and **[ACCB]** and leaves the result in ACCB.

26. Write an instruction sequence that adds **[ACCB]** and **[ACCA]**, subtracts the result from the data at memory location 0350, and leaves the result at address 0350. Assume that the original **[ACCB]** does not have to be preserved.

27. Repeat Problem 26 but preserve the original **[ACCB]**.

28. Determine **[ACCA]** and the status of the N, Z, V, and C flags after the MPU performs the ABA instruction on the following hex data.
   (a) **[ACCA]** = 32; **[ACCB]** = 4A
   (b) **[ACCA]** = 6B; **[ACCB]** = 95
   (c) **[ACCA]** = 75; **[ACCB]** = 3C
   (d) **[ACCA]** = F5; **[ACCB]** = 86
   (e) **[ACCA]** = A7; **[ACCB]** = A7

29. Repeat Problem 28 using the SBA instruction.

30. *Multibyte addition.* Suppose that we want to add two 16-bit numbers, DATA1 and DATA2, and store the result, SUM, in memory using the following data addresses:

Address	Contents	
0050	DATA1 (H)	High-order byte of DATA1
0051	DATA1 (L)	Low-order byte of DATA1
0052	DATA2 (H)	High-order byte of DATA2
0053	DATA2 (L)	Low-order byte of DATA2
0054	SUM (H)	High-order byte of SUM
0055	SUM (L)	Low-order byte of SUM

The flowchart of Fig. 7.15 shows how the 68HC11 MPU can perform this multibyte addition.
   (a) Write the program for this flowchart starting at address 0400 and using the data addresses specified above. Especially note the difference between the addition operation performed in blocks 2 and 5.

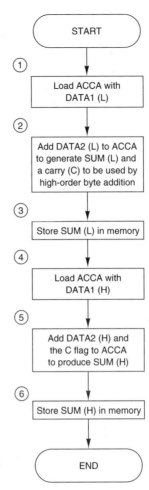

FIGURE 7.15 Flowchart for multi-byte addition (Problem 30).

START

① Load ACCA with DATA1 (L)

② Add DATA2 (L) to ACCA to generate SUM (L) and a carry (C) to be used by high-order byte addition

③ Store SUM (L) in memory

④ Load ACCA with DATA1 (H)

⑤ Add DATA2 (H) and the C flag to ACCA to produce SUM (H)

⑥ Store SUM (H) in memory

END

(b) Test your program using the following set of data:

$DATA1 = 0100010100001010_2 = 450A_{16}$
$DATA2 = 0010000001111111_2 = 207F_{16}$

(c) Repeat for

$DATA1 = 0000001011111111_2 = 02FF_{16}$
$DATA2 = 0000000000000011_2 = 0003_{16}$

31. Show how the flowchart and program of Problem 30 can be modified to perform the addition of two 24-bit numbers.

32. *Multibyte subtraction.* The flowchart of Fig. 7.15 can be readily modified to represent the subtraction of two 16-bit numbers (i.e., DATA1 minus DATA2) by changing block 2 to a subtract operation (SUBA) and block 5 to a subtract-with-carry operation (SBCA).
   (a) Write the program for this revised flowchart.
   (b) Test your program for the sets of data given in Problem 30.

33. Write a program to solve Problem 30 in a more efficient way by using instructions that employ double accumulator D. Repeat for Problem 32.

34. Memory locations C080 and C081 each contain a two-digit decimal number encoded as BCD data. Write a program to add the two decimal numbers and store the decimal result in memory location C082.

35. Write a program that will multiply the data byte in memory location C300 by the byte in memory location C400 and place the product in memory locations C500 and C501.

36. Write a program that will use the IDIV instruction to divide the data byte in memory location C300 by the byte in memory location C400 and place the result in memory locations C500 and C501.

37. Assume that [**ACCD**] = 00F5 and [**X**] = 000F. After an IDIV instruction, determine the contents of ACCA, ACCB, and X, respectively.

Section 7.11

38. Assume that memory location 007F holds a data byte = 37_{16}, [**ACCA**] = C8, and [**ACCB**] = FE. For each of the following instructions, determine the resultant content of ACCA and the status of the N and Z flags.
    (a) ANDA $7F   (b) ANDA #$03   (c) ORAB $7F   (d) ORAB #$01
    (e) EORA #$E5   (f) EORA $7F

39. Write an instruction sequence that takes a data word from an input port at address B800 and *clears* bits 6 and 7 of the word without affecting the other bits.

40. Repeat Problem 39 but *set* bits 6 and 7 without affecting the other bits.

41. The 68HC11 MPU is to take a data word from an input port at address B800 and process it such that a result of zero is produced *only* if the data word is exactly 01100011. Show how this can be done first using a subtract instruction, then using an EOR instruction.

42. Write an instruction sequence that takes an input data word, clears the four MSBs, and inverts the four LSBs. For example, if the data word is 10110110, the result should be 00001001.

Section 7.12

43. Assume that [**Y**] = 0600, [**ACCA**] = A9, [**ACCB**] = 7A, [**0670**] = 73, and C = 0. For each of the following instructions, determine the operand and C flag after the instruction is executed.
    (a) ASL $0670   (b) ASRB   (c) LSRB   (d) ROL $70,Y   (e) RORA
    (f) LSRD

44. What is *packed* BCD?

45. Write the program for the BCD-to-ASCII conversion flowchart of Fig. 7.3. Assume that the packed BCD is in memory location 09DC and the printer output port is at address 7C00.

46. The data that an MPU receives from an input port are often in ASCII code. These data might be coming from an ASCII-coded keyboard, a remote video terminal, or an instrument like a digital voltmeter (DVM). The MPU must often convert these data to BCD before they can be processed.

The MPU can be programmed to convert the ASCII-coded decimal digits to packed BCD. For example, assume that memory locations 0050 and 0051 contain 00111001 and 00110101, respectively; these are the ASCII codes for the digits 9 and 5, respectively. These data bytes are to be converted to 10010101, which is the packed BCD representation of 95_{10}.

(a) Draw the flowchart for a program that will perform this conversion. That is, it will take the two ASCII-coded digits from addresses 0050 and 0051 and will produce the packed BCD equivalent. Assume that address 0050 contains the most significant digit.

(b) Write the program from the flowchart.

Sections 7.13–7.14

47. Assume the following contents of the 68HC11 MPU registers: [ACCA] = 6C, [ACCB] = 00, [X] = 3CFF, [SP] = 05A3. If memory location [3D00] = FF, determine the register and memory data after each of the following instructions is executed.

(a) COMA   (b) NEGB   (c) INX   (d) DEX   (e) CLRB

(f) NEGA   (g) BCLR $01,X $55   (h) DECB

48. The 68HC11 has no single instruction that will complement (invert) the contents of the X register. Write an instruction sequence that will perform this operation.

49. Write an instruction sequence that will 2's-complement the contents of the X register.

50. Refer to the program of Example 7.32. Change the instruction at C152 to JMP $C105. Determine [ACCA] when the MPU finishes execution of this revised program.

51. True or False: A JMP instruction will always alter the instruction execution sequence.

52. True or False: A JMP instruction can send the MPU to any memory address for its next instruction.

Section 7.15

53. Describe the steps the MPU follows in executing a conditional branch instruction.

54. Describe two major differences between a JMP instruction and a conditional branch instruction.

55. A certain program has the op code for a BEQ instruction located at address C450. What is the highest address to which the MPU can branch? What is the lowest address to which it can branch?

56. In the program below, branching will occur if the LSB of [**ACCB**] is a 1. Determine the branching address.

Address	Label	Instruction code	Mnemonic	Comments
C640	START	54	LSRB	; Shift [**ACCB**] right
C641		25	BCS $????	; Branch of ???? if
C642		57		; C = 1
C643	END	3E	WAI	; Otherwise, halt

57. Repeat Problem 56 for the following different offset values at address C642:
   (a) D4   **(b)** 77   **(c)** FD   **(d)** 05

58. Refer to the program of Problem 56. Determine the offset value needed to produce branching to each of the following addresses:
   (a) C69D   **(b)** C600   **(c)** C633   **(d)** C6C2   **(e)** C700

59. Revise the program of Problem 56 so that the MPU will go to address C700 if the LSB of [**ACCB**] is 1.

Section 7.16

60. The flowchart in Fig. 7.16 is for a program that reads the data from an input port at address 0900. If the input data have 0s in bit positions 3 and 5, the program then

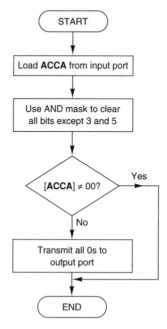

FIGURE 7.16

transmits all 0s to an output port at address 0A00. Otherwise, the program halts. Study the flowchart and note how AND masking is used to isolate bits 3 and 5. Write the program for this flowchart starting at address C200.

61. Modify the program of Problem 60 so that it will transmit all 0s to the output port only if the input data have 1s in bit positions 4 and 6. (*Hint:* One way this can be done is to use the OR masking followed by a complement operation.)

62. Assume that both accumulators are holding *unsigned* data. Write a program that starts at address 7000 and loads FF into memory address C800 only if the number in ACCA is less than or the same as that in ACCB. Otherwise, it loads 00 into address C800. Draw the flowchart.

63. Repeat Problem 62 assuming that the accumulators hold *signed* data.

64. The multiplication program of Example 7.42 does not check for overflow of ACCA's 8-bit capacity. Modify the program so that if the result of any of the repeated addition operations exceeds FF, the program will store FF in address 0083.

65. State the major differences between the BHI instruction and the BGT instruction.

66. Starting at memory location C500, write *one* line of assembly language that will cause the 68HC11 MPU to:
    (a) branch to memory location C53A if bits 0, 2, 4, and 6 of the data word at $0035 are zeros.
    (b) branch to memory location C53A if bits 1, 3, 5, and 7 of the data word at $00F5 are ones.

Section 7.17

67. How do compare instructions differ from subtract instructions?

68. Assume that both accumulators are holding unsigned data. Write an instruction sequence that starts at address 0300 and branches to 0277 if [**ACCA**] is smaller than [**ACCB**]; otherwise, the program branches to 0333.

69. Write an instruction sequence starting at address 0500 which does the following:
    (a) Loads [**ACCB**] with ASCII data from an input port at address F600.
    (b) If the data are the ASCII code for the character "N," the program is to branch to address 0530.
    (c) If the data are the ASCII code for the character "Y," the program is to branch to address 0550.
    (d) Otherwise, the program is to go back and reload ACCB from the input port.

70. Consider the following instruction sequence. Determine where the program will branch to for each of the following values of unsigned data in memory location 0050.
    (a) 95   (b) B7   (c) E1

Address	Label	Instruction code	Mnemonic
C600	START	96	LDAA $50
C601		50	
C602		43	COMA
C603		81	CMPA #$48
C604		48	
C605		22	BHI $????
C606		D6	
C607		27	BEQ ????
C608		55	
C609		20	BRA $????
C60A		6B	

71. A DVM is monitoring the output voltage from a temperature transducer. The DVM sends 8 bits of BCD-coded data to the 68HC11 MPU. These BCD data range from 00 through 99 and represent the temperature in degrees Celsius. The MPU has been reading these data periodically and storing them in memory locations 0F00–0FFF.

Figure 7.17 is the flowchart for a program that scans all these memory locations, counts the number of times that the temperature exceeded 85 degrees, and stores the final count in address 00A0. Study the flowchart and do the following:
(a) Describe the function of the X register.
(b) Describe the function of ACCB.
(c) Write the program. Pay particular attention to the two decision blocks. Each one represents a compare instruction followed by a conditional branch instruction.

72. Write a program sequence that starts at C100 and will compare two 16-bit numbers, VALU1 and VALU2, stored in memory locations C500 through C503, respectively. If VALU1 = VALU2, the program branches to C150. If VALU1 is greater than VALU2, the program branches to C160. Otherwise the program branches to C170.

Section 7.18

73. How does the BITA instruction differ from the ANDA instruction?
74. Assume that $[ACCB] = 55_{16}$ and determine what the following instruction sequence will do.

BITB #$0A
BEQ $0C60
BITB #$40
BNE $0C80
BRA 0C40

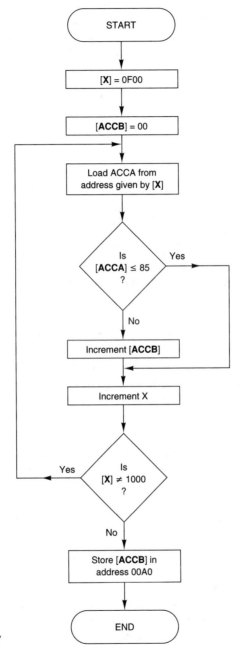

FIGURE 7.17

75. Repeat Problem 74 for [**ACCB**] = 4F. Repeat for [**ACCB**] = 3C.

76. Assume [**ACCA**] = 7F and determine what the following instruction sequence will do.

INCA
TSTA
BEQ $05C0
BPL $05FF
BRA $05D0

77. Repeat Problem 76 for [**ACCA**] = FF. Repeat for [**ACCA**] = 5F.

Section 7.19

78. Explain how a JSR instruction operates differently from a JMP instruction.

79. How does the MPU find its way back to the correct place in the main program when it executes an RTS instruction?

80. Refer to the example program in Section 7.19. Suppose that the instruction at address C160 is changed from LSRA to PSHA. Now, when the 68HC11 MPU executes the RTS instruction, the MPU will not get back to the correct point in the main program. Explain what happens.

81. Refer to the example in Section 7.19.
   (a) Show how the JSR instruction can be replaced by a BSR instruction with appropriate offset.
   (b) Could this have been done if the subroutine had been at address C200?

82. Explain what is meant by nesting subroutines.

Section 7.21

83. In the example of Fig. 7.9, we moved six bytes of data from one area of memory to another. Write a sequence of instructions that will move a block of 100 bytes which are stored in locations 0005 through 0068 to a new area of memory, C450 through C4B3.

84. What hardware and software changes would have to be made for the configuration of Fig. 7.10 if *six* inputs are used?

85. Write a program that uses indexed addressing to accomplish the following: Sequentially reads data from memory addresses 03D8 to 03FF and sends it to an output port (address C800).

86. Consider the following program. Address F700 is an input port that is driven by a set of eight logic signal inputs; address F800 is an output port with eight logic signal outputs. The program is designed to (1) read the input data; (2) compare it to a set of data words stored in ROM; (3) transmit the input data to the output port *only if* the input data matched one of the ROM data.

Address	Label	Instruction code	Mnemonic
C300	START	B6 F7 00	LDAA $F700
C303		CE 08 00	LDX #$0800
C306		A1 00	CMPA 00,X
C308		27 09	BEQ $C313
C30A		08	INX
C30B		8C 08 1F	CPX #$081F
C30E		26 F6	BNE $0306
C310		7E C3 00	JMP $C300
C313		B7 F8 00	STAA $F800
C316		7E C3 00	JMP $C300

Study the program and answer the following questions:
- **(a)** How many different possible output data words are there?
- **(b)** What is the range of ROM addresses that stores the data?
- **(c)** What happens if the input data do not match any ROM data?

87. Modify the program of Problem 86 so that it compares the input data with ROM data addresses C9E0 to CA55.

Sections 7.22–7.24

Assume a 2-MHz MPU E-clock for each of the following problems.

88. State the three most common applications for the NOP instruction.

89. When the S bit in the condition code register (CCR) is set, what function does the STOP instruction perform? What function does the STOP instruction perform when the S bit in the CCR is cleared?

90. Refer to the program of Example 7.46. Assume that the input port data word is 35_{16} and calculate the total execution time for this program.

91. Repeat Problem 90, but this time assume that the MPU has to read the input port *eight* times before it finds a value $>23_{16}$.

92. Refer to the program of Example 7.47. Assume that the operator is pressing the RETURN key, and calculate the total execution time for this program.

93. Refer to the program of Example 7.53.
- **(a)** Use COUNT = FA and determine how many NOPs have to be used in the delay loop to produce a total delay time of approximately 5 ms.
- **(b)** Use either the X or Y register instead of ACCA and change the value of COUNT to produce a delay of approximately 4 ms. Do not add NOPs to original program.

94. Calculate the exact delay for the delay subroutine of Section 7.24 for $[X] = 01$. Repeat for $[X] = 05$.

95. Refer to the example of Section 7.24 as it relates to Fig. 7.14. Change the program so that:

1. $Q_7 = 1$ for 7 s, then clear it back to 0.
2. Wait 1 s.
3. Set $Q_6 = 1$ for 3.7 s

96. Assume that a time-delay subroutine with delay = 0.1 ms × [**X**] is stored at address C800. Write a program that will generate the output port waveforms shown in Fig. 7.18A. The port address is 8000.

97. Repeat Problem 96 for the waveforms of Fig. 7.18B.

98. The following program uses a delay subroutine at C800 to generate waveforms at each of the eight port outputs (address $8000). The subroutine produces a delay of 1 ms × [**X**]. Analyze the program and determine the frequencies of each output.

Address	Label	Instruction code	Mnemonic
C300	START	7F 80 00	CLR $8000
C303		CE 00 03	LDX #$0003
C306		BD C8 00	JSR $C800
C309		7C 80 00	INC $8000
C30C		CE 00 02	LDX #$0002
C30F		BD C8 00	JSR $C800
C312		7C 80 00	INC $8000
C315		20 EC	BRA $C303

99. Refer to the program of Example 7.54. Rewrite the program sequence so that a 25% Duty Cycle waveform is generated at Q_0.

Section 7.25

100. (a) What is the highest decimal count that the 68HC11 MCU built-in TCNT counter can reach?

(b) Show how the TCNT counter can be reset to a count of $0000.

(c) Give three examples of how the contents of the TCNT counter can be read.

101. Assume that the crystal frequency of a 68HC11 MCU is 8 MHz and determine the following:

(a) How long will it take for the TCNT counter to recycle if the TMSK2 register has flags PR0 = 1 and PR1 = 0? If PR0 = PR1 = 1?

(b) What causes the TOF flag in the TFLG2 register to get set?

(c) Show a program sequence that would clear only flags TOF and PAOVF in the TFLG2 register.

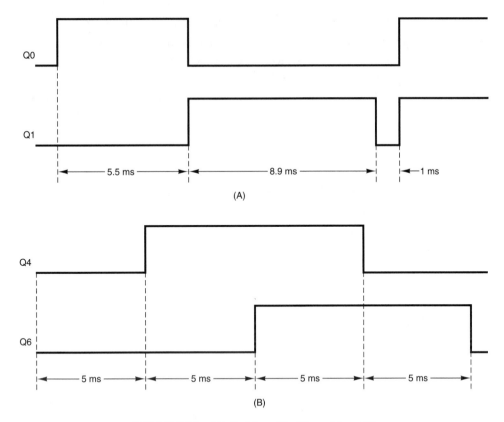

FIGURE 7.18   (A) Problem 96; (B) problem 97

102. A certain 68HC11 MCU-based system uses an 8 MHz crystal frequency. Within the first 64 bus cycles after a reset of the 68HC11 MCU the following sequence of instructions are executed:

LDAA #$03
STAA $1024

Refer to the program sequence used in Example 7.55 and determine the new speed-test-cycle times for the motor under test.

103. Repeat Problem 102 if a crystal with a frequency of 4 MHz is being used.

Section 7.26

104. Briefly describe the five steps in the development of a program.

105. What steps should the programmer perform before the actual writing of program codes?

106. Describe the difference between errors in syntax and errors in logic.

107. Describe the drawbacks of the single-step or trace mode.

108. Describe how breakpoints can be used for debugging.

109. What can a typical logic analyzer do?

110. What is an EVB board?

111. What basically happens when an SWI instruction is executed by the 68HC11 MPU?

8

Input/Output Modes

OBJECTIVES

Upon completion of this chapter, you will be able to:

- Understand the basic terms used to describe I/O data transmission.
- Cite the various I/O transfer alternatives.
- Understand the difference between MPU-initiated and device-initiated I/O transfers.
- Interface an A/D converter to an MPU.
- Understand how to use port E of the 68HC11 MCU to perform A/D conversions using the 68HC11 MCU built-in A/D converter.
- Cite the advantages and disadvantages of conditional I/O transfers.
- Use and understand Interrupts and their operational requirements.
- Understand the possible consequences of interrupting an Interrupt Service Routine (ISR).
- Understand the need for the different types of interrupts available in the 68HC11 MCU.
- Interface multiple devices to an MPU in order to achieve multiple interrupts.
- Understand the different types of functions performed by port A of the 68HC11 MCU.
- Have a basic understanding of the concept and the requirements of Direct Memory Access.

INTRODUCTION

In most μC applications, the MPU must communicate with a variety of I/O devices. The information that passes between the MPU and these peripheral devices can be classified as either *data* or *control*. Data are typically numeric or alphanumeric information encoded in some suitable binary code, such as straight binary, BCD, or ASCII. Control information is usually one of several types: commands from the MPU, requests for service from I/O devices, control codes from the MPU, or status codes from I/O devices. In all but the simplest μC systems, the transmission of this information between the MPU and I/O devices is a critical part of the system design. In this chapter we discuss the various methods of I/O transfer used in μC systems. In Chapter 9 we deal with interfacing between the MPU and I/O devices.

▶ 8.1 SOME BASIC TERMS

The discussion of I/O always involves the transmission of *data* from one device to another. Various terms are used to distinguish between the device that is sending the data and the device that is receiving the data. At various times in the subsequent sections, we will use the terms *sender, transmitter,* and *source* to refer to the device sending data, and the terms *receiver* and *destination* to refer to the device receiving data.

It is important to understand that both the "sender" and "receiver" of *data* will at various times send *control* information to each other. For example, when the MPU is ready to send data to an output device, it might first send a control signal (DAV) to inform the output device that there are *data available* for it (see Fig. 8.1). The output device, upon receiving the DAV signal from the MPU, can accept the data and then send a control signal (DACK) back to the MPU to inform the MPU that it has *accepted* the data. This process of exchanging control signals during data transfer is commonly referred to as *handshaking,* a term we will use often in the discussions that follow. As we shall see, some types of I/O transfer do not use handshaking; in these cases, the data sender transmits the data to the receiver without sending a DAV signal.

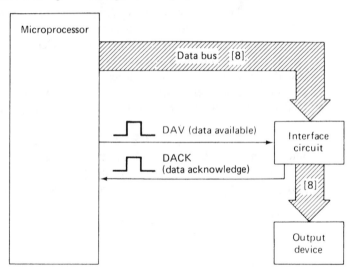

FIGURE 8.1   *Handshaking between the MPU and an output device.*

▶ 8.2 SOME EXAMPLES OF I/O

Before we get into the details of I/O transfer we will briefly describe two common I/O cases to give a better perspective of the types of situations that occur in μC systems.

Process/Instrument Control

In applications where an MPU is used to control an instrument, a piece of equipment, or a process, the program that is to be executed is permanently stored in ROM. When the instrument or process is turned on, a signal is generated and activates the $\overline{RESET}$ input of the MPU. $\overline{RESET}$ (described in Chapter 6), once activated, directs the MPU to take the first instruction from a startup program that is stored in an area of ROM memory. Upon activation of the external (or power-on) $\overline{RESET}$ input, the 68HC11 MPU automatically reads the contents of two specific address locations, FFFE and FFFF. The two bytes obtained from these locations are sent to the program counter as the 16-bit address where the first instruction is stored. These two bytes are called the reset vector since they tell the 68HC11 MPU where to get the first instruction after $\overline{RESET}$ occurs. The reset vector can specify any 16-bit address as the starting address of the program; however, this program is generally stored in a ROM area of memory.

As the MPU executes the program stored in ROM, it will be called upon to receive data inputs from devices that are monitoring some physical process variable (e.g., temperature, speed, displacement, flow rate, and so forth). It takes these data and operates on them according to the program of instructions. Based on the results of these operations, the MPU sends data or control signals to the process through appropriate output devices, such as relays, digital-to-analog converters, and readouts.

In many process or instrument control applications, there is no human intervention once the operation is initiated. The MPU operates automatically and continuously under the control of the program stored in ROM. The operation of the MPU is changed by changing ROMs so that a different sequence of instructions is executed. For example, in the particular case of the 68HC11A8 MCU, this program could be stored in the 8K built-in ROM.

Keyboard Entry/Display

Many situations arise where an MPU must communicate with a human operator. An obvious example is where the MPU is part of a µC that is being used as a general-purpose computing machine. This is the principal use of personal computers by computer hobbyists. Another example is the µP-controlled electronic scale used in supermarkets, where the operator supplies price information to the MPU, which then transmits the total cost of the purchase to the operator. Clearly, these and similar applications require an efficient and convenient means for the operator and MPU to communicate. A very common technique uses a *keyboard* for an operator-controlled *input* device and hexadecimal or decimal LED displays as MPU-controlled *output devices.*

In these applications, a ROM stores a keyboard monitor program that the MPU executes upon activation of the $\overline{RESET}$ input. The keyboard and its interface circuitry will have a specific address (or addresses) assigned to it based on the system memory map as described in Chapter 5. The keyboard monitor program causes the MPU to read the keyboard continually to look for key actuations, and when one is sensed, the MPU reads the keyboard data and determines which key has been actuated. The MPU then executes instructions depending on which key was actuated.

In a general-purpose µC, the operator can send various types of information from the keyboard. For example, the operator can punch in a program using a hexadecimal-encoded keyboard. As he or she keys in the hex codes for each instruction, the MPU, under the control of the *monitor* program, reads the codes from the keyboard and places them in RAM. The area of RAM where the operator's program is to be stored is also keyed in by the operator. When the complete program has been placed in RAM, the operator then directs the MPU to execute the program by punching in the starting address and a specific control key (for example, RUN or GO).

When the μC finishes executing the operator's program, it can be returned to its keyboard monitoring mode by applying a $\overline{\text{RESET}}$ signal to the MPU chip. This is often done with a Reset key that is part of the keyboard. The μC is then ready to accept new information from the operator.

Of course, as the μC executes the operator's program, it must transmit information and results to the operator in some manner. LED displays provide a convenient means for the μC to do this. Again, the displays and their associated circuitry will have a particular address (or addresses) assigned to them based on the system memory map, and the program must contain instructions that access these addresses and therefore cause the MPU to write data into the displays. The displays are also often used as part of the keyboard monitor program to display the keys being actuated so that the operator can see what has been punched in.

These two examples should begin to give you an idea of the types of communication that can take place between the MPU and I/O devices. As we go further in this chapter, you will learn more of the details on the interfacing required for not only these two situations but many others as well.

▶ 8.3 INPUT/OUTPUT ALTERNATIVES

There are several different ways in which I/O transfers can be initiated and controlled. For example, the transfer of data between an MPU and I/O device can be initiated either by the MPU or by the device. Once the I/O transfer has been initiated, it can be carried out under the control of the MPU or, in some cases, under the control of the I/O device. The basic alternatives are presented in Fig. 8.2.

When the MPU initiates an I/O transfer, it always does so under program control whereby it is called on to execute one or more instructions that transfer data between an MPU register (for example, accumulator) and the peripheral device. This MPU-initiated transfer can take place *unconditionally,* where the I/O device must *always* be ready for communication, or it can take place *conditionally* only when the I/O device is ready for communication. Conditional transfer always requires some form of handshaking between the MPU and the device prior to the actual transfer of data.

There are two types of device-initiated I/O transfer, both of which require an exchange of control signals between the device and the MPU. An *interrupt transfer* involves the I/O device sending a signal to one of the 68HC11 MPU's interrupt inputs ($\overline{\text{XIRQ}}$, $\overline{\text{IRQ}}$) to inform the MPU that the device is ready for data transfer. The MPU, in response, will interrupt the execution of the program it is currently working on and will jump to a new program called the *interrupt service routine,* which contains instructions for transferring data to or from the interrupting device. A *direct memory access* (DMA) transfer is the other device-initiated transfer, and it is the only type of data transfer that is *not* under MPU (program) control. The data transfer takes place under the control of special interface circuits called *DMA controllers* such as the 6844. Direct memory access is so called because data are transferred between I/O devices and RAM directly, without involving the MPU.

We will now investigate these various I/O transfer alternatives in more detail.

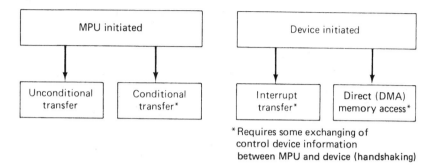

FIGURE 8.2   Basic I/O transfer alternatives.

▶ 8.4 MPU-INITIATED—UNCONDITIONAL I/O TRANSFER

This type of data transfer is used only in situations where an output device is always ready to accept data from the MPU or an input device always has data ready for the MPU. In such cases, there is no need for any exchange of control signals between the MPU and the I/O device. The MPU simply executes instructions that cause it to write data into the output device or to read data from the input device. We will look at two specific examples that illustrate how this form of transfer takes place.

MPU Transmitting Data to LED Displays

The MPU can send an 8-bit data word to be displayed on some type of readout. One possible method is shown in Fig. 8.3, where eight *light-emitting diodes* (LEDs) are used to display a single byte of data transmitted from the MPU. The open-collector inverters and the LEDs have been added to the High-Speed CMOS output port described in Chapter 5 (Fig. 5.18), to provide the operator a visual indication of the data written to this output port. Recall from our discussion in Section 5.9 that the MPU can send data to the output port by performing a WRITE operation to address 8000_{16}. When the MPU writes data into the output port register, the data will appear at the Q outputs of the FFs that comprise this register.

The contents of any one of the 8-bit MPU's *internal* registers can be displayed in this same manner provided there is an appropriate instruction in the MPU's instruction set. For example, the 68HC11's ACCA can be displayed by utilizing the assembly language instruction STAA $8000, which assembles into the three-byte machine language code: B7, 80, 00.

Often, the use of single LEDs to display MPU data in binary form is not as desirable as displaying it in hexadecimal form. Special LED displays are available that contain the LED hexadecimal display and the decoder/driver circuitry in a single device.

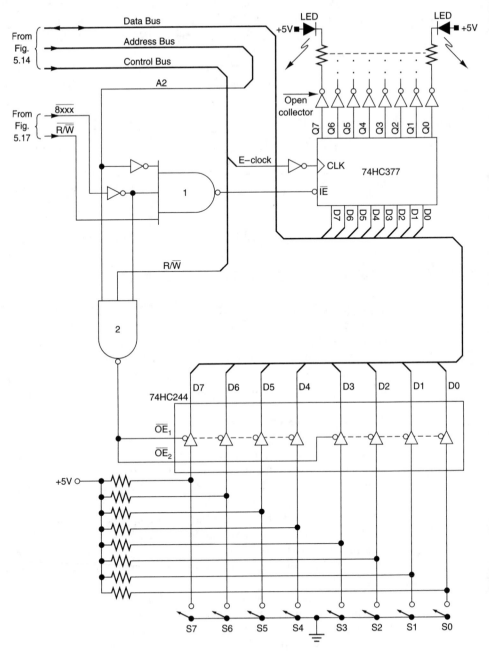

FIGURE 8.3   Switches and LEDs connected as I/O devices for entering and displaying single-byte data.

Simple Input Port

As another example of MPU-initiated, unconditional transfer, we will consider a simple input port used to enter an 8-bit data word into the MPU. For purposes of illustration, we will assume that the data word is coming from a set of eight switches. These switches might be located on a μC's front panel to allow the operator to manually set the data word to be read by the MPU. They could also be switches that are part of some physical process that the MPU is controlling. As part of its control program, the MPU may have to examine the status of these various switches to decide what control action to take. In either case, the switch-to-MPU interface would be similar to that shown in Fig. 8.3.

In Fig. 8.3 we can see that the switches and their associated pull-up resistors have been added to the tri-state buffers of the input port described in Chapter 5 (Fig. 5.18). The MPU can acquire switch data at any time by performing a READ operation from address $8004. This operation can be performed, for example, by the assembly language instruction LDAA $8004, which assembles into the three-byte machine language code: B6, 80, 04. This instruction will cause the MPU to read the value of the switch inputs and load them into ACCA, with S_7 loaded into accumulator's MSB (bit 7) and S_0 into the LSB (bit 0). For example, if switches S_7, S_6, S_2, and S_1 are closed and the others are open, ACCA will be loaded with the number 00111001_2.

Once the switch data have been loaded into ACCA, they can be used for many different purposes. In some cases the switch data represent a numerical value on which the program will perform operations. At other times the switches may represent some type of code that the program has to examine to determine what instruction sequence to perform next. To illustrate, consider a typical situation where the MPU must be programmed to do the following:

1. Read the switch data.
2. Examine the status of S_5.
3. If $S_5 = 0$, continue to execute the main program sequence of instructions.
4. If $S_5 = 1$, store the contents of the switch register in memory location 0800_{16} before continuing with the main program sequence of instructions.

The program flowchart for implementing this sequence of operations is shown in Fig. 8.4. Let us follow through this flowchart for the case where the switch inputs are $S_7 S_6 S_5 S_4 S_3 S_2 S_1 S_0 = 10101001$.

In block 1, these data are read into the MPU and stored in accumulator A (that is, LDAA $8004). Thus, [ACCA] becomes

A7	A6	A5	A4	A3	A2	A1	A0
1	0	1	0	1	0	0	1

↑——— status of S_5

Note that the status of S_5 is now stored in bit A_5.

Block 2 transfers the contents of ACCA to ACCB, leaving the contents of ACCA unaffected. Blocks 3 and 4 each contain a shift ACCA left instruction so that the contents of ACCA are shifted two places to the left. The ACCA contents become

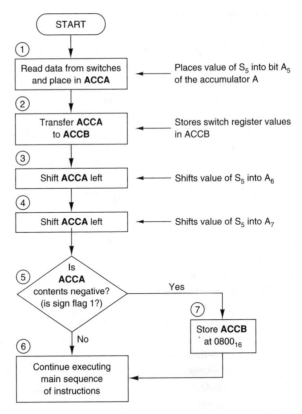

FIGURE 8.4   Flowchart for program that examines status of switch S_5 to determine which instruction sequence to follow.

A7	A6	A5	A4	A3	A2	A1	A0
1	0	1	0	0	1	0	0

↑——— status of S_5

The value of S_5 has been shifted into A_7. Recall that the MPU can interpret A_7 as a sign bit. This is done in block 5, where a conditional branch instruction examines the sign bit. If $A_7 = 0$, the MPU continues to execute the main program sequence of instructions. If $A_7 = 1$, the program branches to block 7 to execute the instruction that stores the contents of the switch register into memory location 0800_{16}. This is accomplished by storing the contents of ACCB in memory location 0800_{16}.

In summary, the program flowcharted in Fig. 8.5 loads ACCA with the switch data, transfers the contents of ACCA to ACCB, shifts ACCA left the number of times needed to bring the desired switch value into the sign-bit position, and tests this sign bit to determine what instructions to execute next. There are other methods that can be used to isolate and examine a single bit of a data word. In Chapter 7 BIT and BRSET instructions could be used for this purpose.

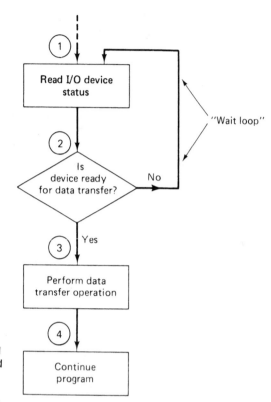

FIGURE 8.5. Flowchart showing typical sequence of steps involved in a conditional (polled) I/O data transfer.

▶ 8.5 MPU-INITIATED—CONDITIONAL (POLLED) I/O TRANSFER

In this type of I/O transfer, the MPU must determine whether the peripheral device is ready for communication before the actual data transfer takes place under program control. Normally, this is a three-step process whereby the MPU must read *status* information from the peripheral device, test this status to see if the device is ready, and then perform the data transfer when the device is ready. This type of I/O is often called *polled* I/O because the device has to be polled continually to see if it is ready. The sequence of steps is shown in the flowchart of Fig. 8.5. Study it carefully.

As the flowchart shows, the MPU keeps executing blocks 1 and 2 until the I/O device indicates that it is ready for data transfer. This loop is called a *wait loop* because the MPU operation stays in this loop while it waits for the I/O device to get ready. When the device is ready, the operation proceeds to block 3, where the MPU performs the data-transfer operation with the device. After the data transfer is completed, the MPU continues with the rest of the program.

This type of I/O transfer requires some handshaking between the MPU and the I/O device. The control signals required for this handshaking will depend on the device. In order to show how analog-to-digital conversions can be accomplished by using any 8-bit MPU, we will go through a complete example using the 68HC11 MPU and an

analog-to-digital (A/D) converter as an external input device. First, however, we will describe the type of A/D converter that will be used.

Tri-State Output A/D Converter

For process control applications, many types of transducers are available that will change
a physical quantity, such as temperature or light intensity, into a linearly proportional voltage. This voltage is an analog quantity that can have any value within a given range, such
as 0 to 10 V. To interface this analog voltage to a digital controller requires that the voltage be converted to its digital representation by an A/D converter. Figure 8.6 shows one
type of A/D converter, which is easily interfaced to a μP system.

This type of converter changes the analog voltage input V_A to an 8-bit digital output
($D_7 - D_0$), which can be either a straight binary or a BCD representation of the input. The
conversion process is initiated by a pulse applied to the A/D converter's START input.
The complete conversion process will take an amount of time that depends on the A/D
conversion method which the particular converter uses. This time, called *conversion time*,
t_c, can be as high as 100 μs for some A/D converters. During this t_c interval, as the conversion process is taking place, the A/D converter's EOC output will go LOW. The EOC output returns HIGH when the conversion is complete.

The digital output lines $D_7 - D_0$ come from tri-state latches that are part of the converter. A HIGH on the ENABLE input will enable these outputs so that the digital representation of V_A is present on these lines. A LOW on the ENABLE input puts these output
lines in their high-Z state. In most situations, the ENABLE input will be pulsed HIGH only
after the EOC output has indicated that the conversion is complete. If the ENABLE input
is made HIGH during the t_c interval, the output lines will indicate the results of the previous A/D conversion.

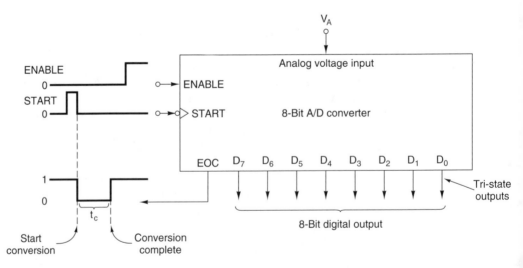

FIGURE 8.6 Typical A/D converter used in μP-based process control systems.

Interfacing the A/D Converter to the MPU

In a typical application, the input to the A/D converter is an analog voltage, V_A, generated by a process transducer and its associated circuitry. The digital output of the converter is loaded into the MPU upon command. The MPU then processes this digital value according to its stored program and generates appropriate control outputs to the process. The operation requires several communications between the MPU and the A/D converter, as outlined below:

1. The MPU issues a START pulse to the A/D converter to tell it to convert the current value of V_A to its digital equivalent.
2. The MPU then continually reads and tests the status of the converter's EOC output until it returns HIGH, indicating that the conversion is complete.
3. The MPU then reads the A/D output into one of its internal registers.

Clearly, this sequence requires *three* different control signals from the MPU to the A/D converter—one for START, one to transfer the EOC (End-of-Conversion) output into the MPU to be tested, and one to transfer the A/D digital output into the 68HC11 MPU. One means for implementing this operation is shown in Fig. 8.7. Study it carefully before reading on.

The AD outputs $D_7 - D_0$ are connected to the data bus so that they can be transferred into the MPU when NOR gate 1 produces a HIGH at the ENABLE input. The EOC output is connected to the top data bus line (D_7) through a tri-state buffer. Thus, the EOC output can be transferred into the MPU when the buffer is enabled by a HIGH from NOR gate 3. The START input to the A/D converter comes from NOR gate 2, which will provide a pulse when the MPU generates the proper address code.

We have chosen to use the $\overline{80xx}$ SELECT line for the A/D converter. However, we will also need to use two of the lower-order address lines, A_0 and A_1, to allow us to select which of the three NOR gates will be activated. Let us look at each NOR gate more closely.

NOR Gate 1   It has inputs A_0, A_1, $\overline{R/W}$, and $\overline{80xx}$, and its output will go HIGH only when these inputs are all LOW. This condition occurs when the MPU performs a READ operation from address 8000 (A_1 and A_0 are both 0). This enables the outputs of the A/D converter so that they will be transferred into the MPU over the data bus. The assembly language instruction LDAA $8000 will accomplish the loading of data from the A/D converter into the MPU.

NOR Gate 2   It has inputs $\overline{A_0}$, $\overline{R/W}$, and $\overline{80xx}$, and its output will go HIGH whenever the MPU performs a READ from address F901 ($A_0 = 1$). This READ operation, however, is a *dummy READ* because nothing is being placed on the data bus. It is used simply as a means for generating the 8001 address code to produce a positive pulse out of NOR gate 2 to start the A/D conversion. The assembly language instruction LDAA $8001 will accomplish generating the START pulse for the A/D converter.

Recall that the situation where no device is placing data on the data bus is called *floating* the data bus. For most MPUs, when the data bus is floating during a READ operation, an ambiguous data word will be read into the MPU's internal register. This is no problem here since the MPU is not going to use the ambiguous word anyway.

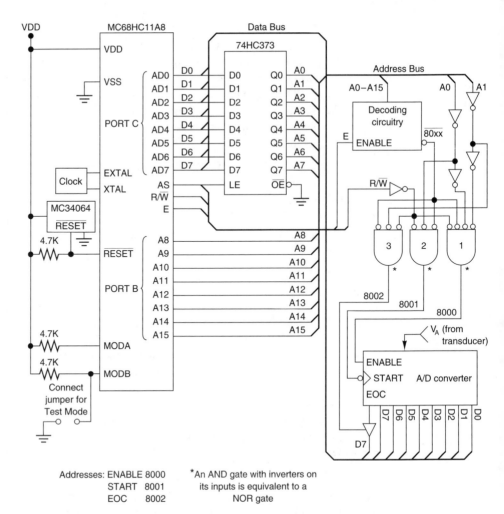

Addresses: ENABLE 8000 *An AND gate with inverters on
START 8001   its inputs is equivalent to a
EOC 8002   NOR gate

FIGURE 8.7   Interfacing an A/D converter to a 68HC11 MPU using conditional (polled) I/O transfer.

NOR Gate 3   It has inputs $\overline{A_1}$, $\overline{R/\overline{W}}$, and $\overline{80xx}$ and its output will go HIGH whenever the MPU performs a READ from address 8002. This places the BUSY output onto data bus line D_7 for transfer into the MPU. Note that the other seven data bus lines will be floating. This again is no problem, because the MPU is interested only in the status of the EOC output. The assembly language instruction LDAA $8002 will load the EOC output into ACCA (that is, [ACCA] = D_7xxxxxxx).

Now we are ready to look at how the MPU must be programmed in order to execute the transfer of data from the A/D converter. Figure 8.8 shows the program flowchart. Examine it carefully before reading on.

When the MPU gets to a point in its program where it requires data from the A/D converter, it begins by sending a START pulse (block 1). It does this by executing a dummy instruction to read address 8001.

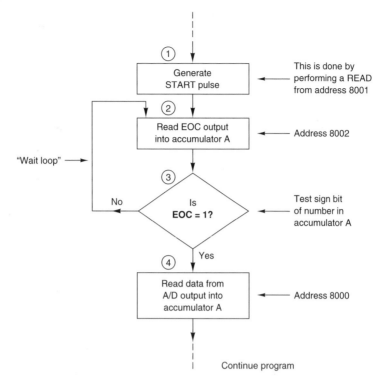

① Generate START pulse ← This is done by performing a READ from address 8001

② Read EOC output into accumulator A ← Address 8002

"Wait loop" →

③ Is EOC = 1? ← Test sign bit of number in accumulator A

No

Yes

④ Read data from A/D output into accumulator A ← Address 8000

Continue program

FIGURE 8.8   Flowchart showing steps taken by MPU to obtain data from A/D converter.

The MPU then proceeds to continuously read the EOC output and test to determine if it is a 1 (blocks 2 and 3). It repeats this process as many times as necessary until the EOC output goes HIGH. Since the EOC bit is connected to data bus line D_7, it will be loaded into bit 7 of accumulator A, the sign-bit position. Thus, it can be tested using a conditional branch instruction such as Branch If Plus (BPL), which examines the N flag and, if it is a 0, will branch back to block 2. If the N flag is 1 (indicating EOC = 1), the program will continue to block 4. Here the MPU executes an instruction to transfer the A/D outputs into accumulator A.

Generally in a program concerning the acquisition of data from an A/D converter, there will be many times when it will be necessary to get new data. This is a perfect time for a subroutine because it will save the programmer from having to rewrite the code sequence each time it is needed. By setting up this sequence of instructions as a subroutine, the programmer can simply jump to it using a JSR instruction any time a new data acquisition is necessary.

The program sequence contained on page 000 can be used to acquire data at any point in the user's program as long as it is accessed as a subroutine. Because this sequence of instructions uses ACCA, the original contents of ACCA and the contents of the CCR (condition code register) may need to be saved; this is done by placing them on the stack at the beginning of the subroutine and removing and replacing them in reverse order at the end of the subroutine.

Address	Label	Instruction code	Mnemonic	Comments
0C00	START	36	PSHA	; Push **[ACCA]** on the stack
0C01		07	TPA	; Transfer **[CCR]** → **[ACCA]**
0C02		36	PSHA	; Place **[CCR]** on the stack
0C03		B6	LDAA $8001	; Generate START pulse
0C04		80		
0C05		01		
0C06	CHEOC	B6	LDAA $8002	; Check EOC bit
0C07		80		
0C08		02		
0C09		2A	BPL $0C06	; Branch back to CHEOC if 0
0C0A		FB		; otherwise, get data
0C0B	GTDATA	B6	LDAA $8000	; Load A/D output into ACCA
0C0C		80		
0C0D		00		
0C0E		97	STAA $0050	; Store A/D output in memory
0C0F		50		; for later use
0C10		32	PULA	; Restore **[CCR]**
0C11		06	TAP	; from stack
0C12		32	PULA	; Restore **[ACCA]**
0C13	END	39	RTS	; Return from subroutine

Disadvantage of Conditional I/O Transfer

The preceding example should point out the major drawback of conditional or polled I/O transfer—the MPU has to *wait* for the I/O device. In some cases, especially for slow I/O devices, the MPU will waste a lot of its time reading and testing the status of the I/O device. If there is nothing else for the MPU to do while the I/O device is getting ready, it does not matter. However, in many applications, the MPU can be doing other tasks while it is waiting, such as processing data or communicating with other I/O devices (keep in mind that a typical MPU can execute an instruction in a few microseconds). In a later part of this chapter we will see how this can be accomplished using the interrupt mode of I/O transfer.

▶ 8.6 THE 68HC11 MCU BLOCK DIAGRAM

In Chapter 5 we stated that the 68HC11 microcontroller chip has five ports—A, B, C, D, and E—that are used to get information into and out of the 68HC11 MPU. Thus far, we have used only ports B and C. We will be looking at port E in the next section, port A a little later in the chapter, and port D in Chapter 9. This is a good time to present the block diagram of the *complete* 68HC11 MPU shown in Fig. 8.9; it is also repeated in Appendix B for easy reference.

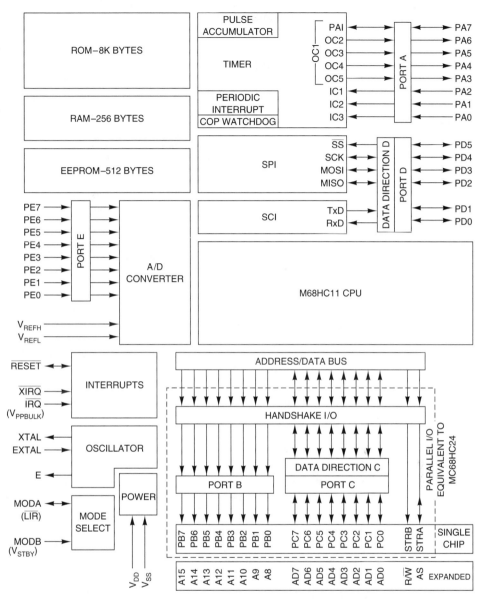

FIGURE 8.9 The 68HC11 MCU block diagram. (Copyright of Motorola, Used by Permission)

Figure 8.9 shows all of the major elements and the five ports that make up the 68HC11 microcontroller chip. This is a functional block diagram, so there is very little detail as to how the various blocks are interconnected. However, the diagram does show how the major blocks are related to the pins of the MPU (i.e., the signals at the pins).

We are already familiar with some of the blocks. The MPU block is located in the approximate center of the diagram. The upper left-hand corner has the on-chip RAM,

ROM, and EEPROM memory that is connected to communicate with the MPU. The Mode Select logic in the lower left-hand corner is used to select the single-chip or expanded mode of operation; we have been exclusively using the expanded mode thus far. The clock oscillator block which generates the E-clock and other timing signals used on the chip is located just above the Mode Select block. Right above that is the Interrupt Logic block which processes the interrupt and reset signals. The lower right-hand portion of the diagram shows ports B and C with their two possible functions. In the single-chip mode, they function as standard parallel ports: port B as an output port, and port C as an input/output port. In the expanded mode, they function as the data address lines from the MPU.

The top center of the diagram shows the timer system block, one of whose functions was covered in Chapter 7's discussion of time delays. To the right of this block is the multifunction port A which interacts with the timer system block for some of its operations. Right below port A is port D, a 6-bit bidirectional port used for *serial* communication with the MPU.

To the left of the MPU is the on-chip A/D converter system. Port E is an input port shown feeding into the A/D block. As we shall see, port E can function as an *analog* input port into the A/D block, or as a standard *digital* input port into the MPU.

▶ 8.7 PORT E OF THE 68HC11 MCU—A/D CONVERTER

Port E of the 68HC11 MCU has a dual function. It can be used as a general-purpose 8-bit *input* port or it can be used in conjunction with the 68HC11A8 MCU built-in 8-bit successive approximation analog-to-digital (A/D) converter. When port E is used as a general-purpose input port, its memory address is $100A. For example, the user may read the contents of port E by simply executing the instruction LDAA $100A. This instruction will load the logic levels present at the input pins of port E into ACCA. However, when port E is used as part of the A/D converter system of the 68HC11 MCU, it allows the user to perform A/D conversions without the need for an external A/D converter. Clearly, this is a much more practical and simpler way of performing A/D conversions, since it eliminates the special interfacing circuitry that is always needed whenever an input device has to be interfaced to an MPU.

The A/D system of the 68HC11 MCU is made up of port E, the A/D converter, the option control register (OPTION), and the A/D control/status register (ADCTL). The latter two registers are not shown on the 68HC11 block diagram. The following is a condensed description of the function and the inherent characteristics of the A/D system. A more detailed description of Port E and the A/D system can be found in the *Motorola M68HC11 Reference Manual.*

The OPTION Control Register

The OPTION* register is a special 68HC11 MPU 8-bit register that resides in the memory map at address location $1039. One of its functions is to control whether port E will operate as a general-purpose input port or become an integral part of the built-in A/D converter.

---

*A complete list of the 68HC11 MCU built-in control registers can be found in Appendix C.

7	6	5	4	3	2	1	0	
ADPU	CSEL	IRQE	DLY	CME	0	CR1	CR0	OPTION $1039

At reset   0   0   0   1   0   0   0   0

The A/D system of the 68HC11 MPU uses bits 6 (CSEL) and 7 (ADPU) of the OPTION control register to control certain aspects of the A/D conversion process. If control bit ADPU (A/D Power-Up) of the OPTION control register is cleared, then port E is an 8-bit input port whose contents will be available by reading the port E register at address $100A. However, if bit ADPU is set, then the A/D system is operative, and the port E register is inactive. In this mode, the inputs at port E become *analog* inputs; in other words, there are eight different analog input channels, PEO–PE7. The ADPU bit is always cleared when the MCU is coming out of a reset condition. When the ADPU is set by a software instruction, a small delay should be used to allow the A/D converter's charge pump and comparator circuits to stabilize before an A/D conversion is initiated.

The CSEL (Clock SELect) bit of the OPTION register is used to select an on-chip RC oscillator when the E-clock is running too slow. CSEL should be cleared whenever E-clock is at or above 2 MHz. CSEL should be set whenever E-clock is below 750 KHz. Neither ADPU nor CSEL are time-protected bits, and consequently they can be set or cleared by the user at any time by writing to address $1039.

The Analog-to-Digital Control/Status Register (ADCTL)

The ADCTL* register resides at address $1030 and is part of the A/D conversion system of the 68HC11 MPU. ADCTL is both a control register and a status register. All bits in this register can be read from or written into with the exception of bit 7 (CCF) and bit 6. The CCF (Conversions Complete Flag) is a status bit and it can only be read. Bit 6 is a nonfunctional bit and it is always zero. During a reset condition, bits 6 and 7 will always be cleared, while bits 0–5 are unaffected (U).

7	6	5	4	3	2	1	0	
CCF	0	SCAN	MULT	CD	CC	CB	CA	ADCTL $1030

At reset   0   0   U   U   U   U   U   U

An A/D conversion sequence is initiated every time a WRITE operation to register ADCTL at address $1030 is executed. As Fig. 8.10 shows, once this WRITE operation takes place, the A/D converter executes four consecutive conversions on four analog input channels (i.e., port E inputs). This sequence of four conversions *always* occurs even when only a single analog input channel is being used; in such a case, four consecutive conversions are performed on the same analog input.

It can be seen from Fig. 8.10 that each conversion takes 32 E-clock cycles so that the total conversion time for all four conversions is 128 cycles. With an E-clock of 2 MHz, this translates into 64 μs. After each individual conversion of an analog channel, the 8-bit result is stored in a result register. The four respective results are stored in the four A/D Result registers, ADR1, ADR2, ADR3, and ADR4, at memory addresses $1031, $1032, $1033,

---

*A complete list of the 68HC11 MCU built-in control registers can be found in Appendix C.

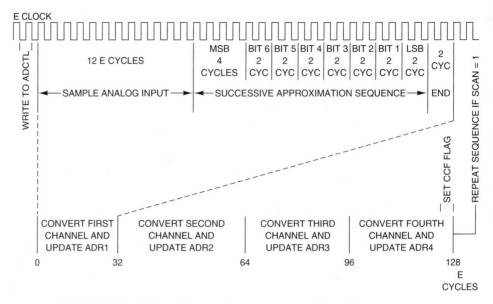

FIGURE 8.10   Timing diagram for a sequence of four A/D conversions.
(Copyright of Motorola, Used by Permission)

and $1034, respectively. These 8-bit registers are READ-ONLY registers; they cannot be written into by any software instruction.

Whenever an A/D conversion sequence is initiated by a WRITE operation into AD-CTL, the Conversions Complete Flag (CCF) is automatically cleared. This bit will remain at 0 until all four conversions are complete, at which point it will be set as indicated in Figure 8.10. The MPU can be programmed to poll the CCF bit to determine if the A/D conversion process has been completed and the results have been placed in ADR1–ADR4.

The SCAN (Continuous Scan Control) bit in the ADCTL register is used to control whether the signals at the input channels of port E are continuously scanned or they are scanned only once before the conversion is terminated. If the SCAN bit is cleared, the A/D system of the 68HC11 MCU will (1) perform the four requested A/D conversions, one at a time; (2) consecutively store the results into the four respective A/D result registers, ADR1–ADR4; and (3) set the CCF bit in the ADTCL register before it terminates the conversion process. On the other hand, if the SCAN bit is set, the A/D system will (1) perform the four requested A/D conversions, one at a time; (2) consecutively store the results into the four respective A/D result registers, ADR1–ADR4; and (3) repeat the process by rewriting the old conversion values stored in the result registers ADR1–ADR4 with the new conversion values.

The MULT (MULTiple-Channel/Single-Channel) control bit and the four channel select bits (CD, CC, CB, CA) in the ADTCL register determine which port E analog channels will have an A/D conversion performed on them. There are two modes: the *single-channel* mode and the *multiple-channel* mode. When the software writes a 0 into the MULT bit, the single-channel mode is selected. In this mode, the A/D system will perform the four consecutive conversions on the analog signal present at the one input channel of port E specified by the channel select bits. In the single-channel mode, the software must

TABLE 8.1   A/D Channel Assignments

CD	CC	CB	CA	Channel signal	Result in ADRx if MULT = 1
0	0	0	0	PE0	ADR1
0	0	0	1	PE1	ADR2
0	0	1	0	PE2	ADR3
0	0	1	1	PE3	ADR4
0	1	0	0	PE4*	ADR1
0	1	0	1	PE5*	ADR2
0	1	1	0	PE6*	ADR3
0	1	1	1	PE7*	ADR4
1	0	0	0	Reserved	ADR1
1	0	0	1	Reserved	ADR2
1	0	1	0	Reserved	ADR3
1	0	1	1	Reserved	ADR4
1	1	0	0	V_H**	ADR1
1	1	0	1	V_L**	ADR2
1	1	1	0	1/2 V_H**	ADR3
1	1	1	1	Reserved**	ADR4

(Copyright of Motorola, used by permission).
*Not available in 48-pin package versions.
**These channels intended for factory testing.

also write into the channel select bits of ADTCL to select the port E channel according to the A/D channel assignment table shown in Table 8.1. The table shows all 16 possible combinations of the CD–CA bits. However, in reality only the first eight are used; the next four combinations are reserved for future revisions of the 68HC11 chip, and the bottom four are used only for factory testing.

To illustrate, let's assume that the software writes the data word 00000011 into ADTCL. Since MULT = 0, this selects the single-channel mode. With CD–CA = 0011, this selects PE3 as the single port E input channel whose analog signal will be converted to a digital result. Actually, the A/D system will perform four consecutive conversions on PE3 and store the four results in ADR1–ADR4, respectively. If the signal at PE3 does not change significantly during the 128 E-clock cycles it takes to perform the conversions, the four results will be approximately the same.

When software writes a 1 in the MULT bit, the multiple-channel mode is selected. In this mode, the A/D system will perform the four consecutive conversions on four different channels that are part of a group of four selected by the CD and CC bits of ADTCL. In this mode, CB and CA have no effect. Looking at Table 8.1, CD–CC = 00 selects PE0–PE3 as the group of four channels to be converted. CD–CC = 01 selects PE4–PE7. The other combinations of CD–CC are not normally used.

To illustrate, if the software writes the data word 000100xx into ADTCL, the multiple-channel mode is selected since MULT = 1. Since CD–CC = 00, the PE0–PE3 channels are selected for conversion, and the results will be placed in ADR1–ADR4, respectively.

EXAMPLE 8.1

Let us assume that we want to use the A/D system of the 68HC11 MCU to perform A/D conversions on signals present at pins PE0–PE3 of port E. The A/D conversions should use the 68HC11 MCU 2 MHz E-clock.

(a) Write a program sequence that will (1) activate the A/D system and condition register ADTCL for the single-channel conversion of input PE2; (2) perform the conversion once and then stop the conversion process; and (3) store the results of the conversion of channel PE2 in memory location C200.

(b) How long will the complete conversion process take, and where can the results of the A/D conversion be found?

(c) Change the appropriate instruction in the program of step (a) so that *continuous* multiple-channel conversions of inputs PE0–PE3 occur.

Solution

(a) One possible solution is as follows:

Address	Label	Instruction code	Mnemonic		Comments
C000	START	18	LDY #$1000		; Condition Y register to point
C001		CE			; to the OPTION and ADCTL
C002		10			; registers
C003		00			
C004		18	BSET $39,Y	$80	; Set bit ADPU in OPTION
C005		1E			; register to power-up A/D
C006		39			; system
C007		80			
C008		18	BCLR $39,Y	$40	; Clear bit CSEL in OPTION
C009		1D			; register in order for the A/D
C00A		39			; system to use the E-clock
C00B		40			;
C00C		C6	LDAB #$02		; [ACCB] = 02
C00D		02			
C00E		18	STAB 30,Y		; Select channel PE2 and clear
C00F		E7			; SCAN and MULT bits of the
C010		30			; ADCTL register. Start
					; conversion process
C011	CHECKF	B6	LDAA $1030		; Read status register ADCTL
C012		10			; to see if conversion is done
C013		30			
C014		2A	BPL $C011		; If CCF = 0, conversion is in
C015		FB			; progress, go to CHECKF to check
					; again
C016		B6	LDAA $1033		; If CCF = 1, read the result of
C017		10			; the A/D conversion from the
C018		33			; ADR3 register

Address	Label	Instruction code	Mnemonic	Comments
C019		B7	STAA $C200	; Store the result of the A/D
C01A		C2		; conversion of channel PE2 in
C01B		00		; memory address C200
C01C		3E	WAI	; Halt

(b) The results of the four conversions will be stored in the four consecutive ADR registers (ADR1–ADR3). Each of the values stored in the ADR registers took about 16 μs to acquire. Consequently, from the time the conversion process started until the CCF flag was set, it took about 64 μs.

(c) The control bits SCAN and MULT in the ADCTL register must be changed. Recall that the SCAN bit controls whether or not the conversion process is done once (SCAN = 0), or is continuously performed (SCAN = 1). The MULT bit controls whether or not the conversion is performed on a single input channel (MULT = 0), or on each channel of a group of four channels (MULT = 1). Therefore, the A/D system will perform sequential and continuous conversions on channels PE0–PE3 if both the SCAN and MULT bits are set. Consequently, the instruction sequence must be modified in the above program as follows:

Address	Label	Instruction code	Mnemonic	Comments
: :		: :	: :	
C00C		C6	LDAB #$32	; [ACCB] = 32
C00D		32		
: :		: :	: :	

Limits on the A/D Converter Input Voltage Levels

Let us assume that port E of the 68HC11 MCU has been conditioned to function as the input channels of the A/D converter. Perhaps the first consideration to be made when using the A/D converter in the 68HC11 MCU is the establishment of the permissible range of voltages of the input analog signal. The difference between the input reference voltages V_{REFH} and V_{REFL} applied to the 68HC11 MCU (see Fig. 8.9, left side) is the range of analog voltages that can be converted by the A/D converter. For proper operation of the A/D converter the reference input voltages V_{REFH} and V_{REFL} should not be higher than 6 V or lower than 0 V, respectively. The difference between these two reference voltages should be at least 2.5 V. This difference is important since it affects the *resolution* or *step-size* of the A/D converter. The resolution or step-size of an A/D converter is always equal to the weight of the LSB of the resulting conversion value. Obviously, the smaller the resolution of the A/D converter, the closer the digital result represents the converted analog signal.

EXAMPLE 8.2

Let us assume that a certain 68HC11 MCU has inputs $V_{REFH} = 4$ V, $V_{REFL} = 0$ V, and that an input voltage of 3.701 V at channel PE2 is to be converted by the A/D converter using the program of Example 8.1(a).

(a) What is the range of the A/D converter?

(b) What is the resolution of the A/D converter?

(c) What data is stored in memory location C200 at the end of the conversion?

Solution

(a) The range of the A/D converter is simply the difference between V_{REFH} and V_{REFL} voltages, or 4 V.

(b) The resolution $= \dfrac{V_{REFH} - V_{REFL}}{2^n - 1} = \dfrac{4 \text{ V}}{255} = 15.69$ mV.

Where $(2^n - 1)$ represents the maximum binary number that can be outputted by the 8-bit A/D converter. Thus, 15.69 mV represents the resolution of the A/D converter.

(c) The contents of the A/D converter after the conversion has been terminated will be 3.701 V/15.69 mV $\approx 236_{10} = EC_{16}$. Therefore, memory location C200 will be loaded with EC_{16}.

▶ ## 8.8 DEVICE-INITIATED I/O TRANSFER—INTERRUPTS

This type of I/O transfer makes more efficient use of the computer's time because the MPU will not have to check repeatedly to see if the device is ready for transfer. Instead, the MPU is free to do other tasks, and when the I/O device is ready, it will send a signal to one of the MPU's interrupt inputs. This will cause the MPU to suspend execution of the program it is currently working on and to perform a special *interrupt service routine*. This service routine typically contains the instructions for transferring data to or from the interrupting device. When the MPU completes execution of the interrupt service routine, it returns to the program it was executing at the time the interrupt occurred. This process is illustrated in Fig. 8.11.

Here we have a portion of the memory map for a typical situation. Memory locations $C000_{16}$–$C3FF_{16}$ (pages C0–C3) contain the *main program* of instructions which the MPU must execute. An interrupt service routine (ISR) is stored in locations C500–C510. During normal operation the MPU is executing the main program. Let us suppose that while it is in the process of executing a single-byte instruction at address C250, an I/O device sends an interrupt signal to the MPU (see point 1, Fig. 8.11). The MPU will ignore this interrupt signal until it has finished executing the instruction at C250. When it completes that instruction, it senses the presence of the interrupt signal. Then, the MPU branches to address C500 (point 2) and begins executing the instructions in interrupt service routine (ISR). It continues executing the instructions in the ISR until it reaches address C510. This address will contain an instruction telling the MPU to return to the main program where it left off when it was interrupted. This return from interrupt (RTI) instruction will cause the MPU to return to address C251 in the main program and continue from there (point 3).

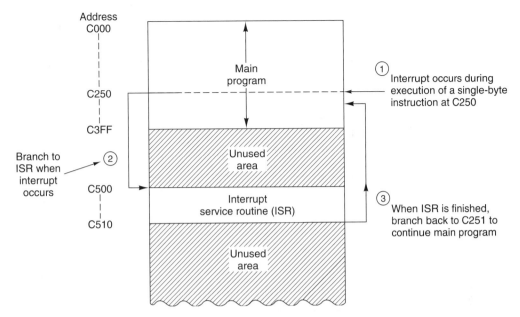

FIGURE 8.11   Example of how an interrupt causes a change in the execution of a program.

Interrupt Considerations

The interrupt process we have just described eliminates the need for the MPU to waste its time continually checking to see if an I/O device is ready for communication. Interrupt operation is extremely useful in applications where the MPU must interface with several I/O devices whose needs for servicing are *asynchronous*—that is, they might occur at any time and so cannot be handled through programmed unconditional I/O transfer. Although the interrupt process appears fairly straightforward, a little thought will raise several important questions about its operation. We will now consider these questions to see how MPU manufacturers have dealt with them.

▶ 8.9 RETURN ADDRESS

After executing the ISR, how does the MPU know what address in the main program it should branch back to? This is a sensible question, since an interrupt can occur at any time and there is no way of predicting what instruction the MPU will be processing when the interrupt occurs. This problem is taken care of *automatically* within the MPU by temporarily storing the current contents of the program counter (PC) before branching to the ISR. The 68HC11 MPU will store the PC on the *stack* together with the contents of the index X register, index Y register, ACCA, ACCB, and CCR. Figure 8.12 shows how the contents of these registers are placed on the stack portion of memory. When the return from interrupt (RTI) instruction is executed at the end of the ISR, the MPU *automatically* pulls the information off the stack in the reverse order, restoring the MPU registers to the exact contents

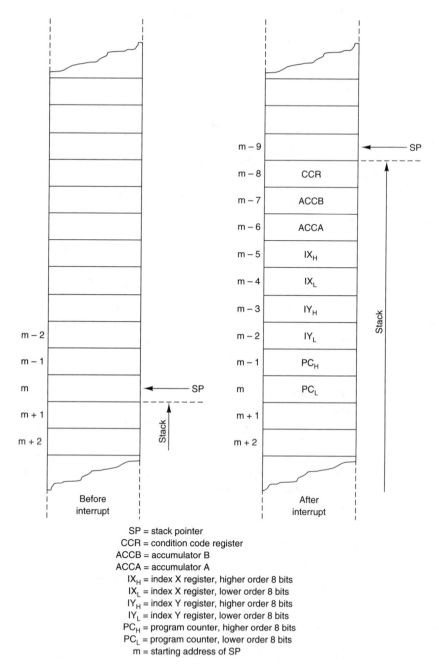

		m − 9		← SP
		m − 8	CCR	
		m − 7	ACCB	
		m − 6	ACCA	
		m − 5	IX$_H$	
		m − 4	IX$_L$	
		m − 3	IY$_H$	
m − 2		m − 2	IY$_L$	
m − 1		m − 1	PC$_H$	
m	← SP	m	PC$_L$	
m + 1		m + 1		
m + 2		m + 2		

Before interrupt

After interrupt

SP = stack pointer
CCR = condition code register
ACCB = accumulator B
ACCA = accumulator A
IX$_H$ = index X register, higher order 8 bits
IX$_L$ = index X register, lower order 8 bits
IY$_H$ = index Y register, higher order 8 bits
IY$_L$ = index Y register, lower order 8 bits
PC$_H$ = program counter, higher order 8 bits
PC$_L$ = program counter, lower order 8 bits
m = starting address of SP

FIGURE 8.12   Saving register contents of the 68HC11 MPU on the stack after an interrupt.

they had prior to the execution of the ISR. The 68HC11 stack operates on a last-in, first-out (LIFO) basis.

To illustrate, for the example of Fig. 8.11 the PC is at C250 when the interrupt occurs. As stated before, the MPU finishes executing the single-byte instruction at C250, which includes incrementing the PC to C251. This value, C251, is the return address which the MPU stores in two successive locations on the stack (remember that the PC is 16 bits, and each memory location stores 8 bits). The 68HC11 MPU then places the contents of IY_L, IY_H, IX_L, IX_H, ACCA, ACCB, and CCR onto successive stack locations. Then, when the MPU executes the RTI instruction, it replaces the contents of the registers by pulling them off in the reverse order that they were placed on the stack. The last information pulled from the stack is the return address (C251), which is transferred into the PC so that the MPU takes its next instruction from C251 in the main program memory.

▶ 8.10 DISABLING THE INTERRUPT

What happens when an I/O device interrupts the MPU while it is executing a portion of a program that requires continuous processing? This might happen, for example, when the MPU is in a *timing loop* or when the MPU is communicating with another I/O device. In situations like these, the occurrence of an interrupt could have undesirable results. For this reason, all microprocessors have some provision for disabling the interrupt operation under program control. This is usually done by designating a flip-flop in the MPU as the *Interrupt Mask flag, I,* and having instructions that the programmer can use to set or clear this flag. This flag is included as part of the 68HC11 MPU CCR register.

When a signal occurs at the 68HC11's $\overline{\text{IRQ}}$ input, the MPU will ignore it if the Interrupt Mask flag, I, has been set to 1 by a previous program instruction, or if I is still in the 1 state it comes up in after an MPU reset operation. If I has been cleared to 0 by a previous program instruction, the MPU will respond to the interrupt input in the normal manner. Thus, the programmer has the capability of disabling (masking) or enabling the effects of the $\overline{\text{IRQ}}$ interrupt input during any portion of a program. The easiest way to do it is through the use of the Set Interrupt Mask (SEI) and Clear Interrupt Mask (CLI) instructions, which can be inserted anywhere in a program.

Because its effect can be masked (disabled) at any time by setting I, the $\overline{\text{IRQ}}$ input is called a *maskable interrupt request* input.

The program below illustrates how the SEI and CLI instructions can be used to disable the effects of an interrupt signal at $\overline{\text{IRQ}}$ during the execution of a critical time delay sequence. The MPU will not respond to the interrupt until after I has been cleared by CLI.

Address	Instruction code	Mnemonic	Comments
C100	0F	SEI	; Disable interrupt
C101	86	LDAA #$C0	; Load ACCA with count
C102	C0		
C103	4A	DECA	; Decrement ACCA
C104	26	BNE $C103	; Branch back if ACCA ≠ 0

Address	Instruction code	Mnemonic	Comments
C105	FD		
C106	0E	CLI	; Enable interrupt
C107	: :	: :	; Continue

▶ 8.11 TYPES OF INTERRUPT INPUTS

How many different types of interrupt inputs does an MPU usually have? The 68HC11 MPU has two types of interrupt inputs: *maskable* and *nonmaskable*. A *maskable* interrupt is the type of interrupt we discussed above and whose occurrence is ignored by the MPU when the Interrupt Mask flag (I) is set in the CCR. The operation of a *nonmaskable* interrupt is independent of the status of the I flag. The nonmaskable interrupt is a type of interrupt whose occurrence is ignored by the 68HC11 MPU when the Interrupt Mask flag (X) in the CCR is set. However, during normal operation of the MPU, *once the X flag is cleared, the user can never set it (mask it) again,* so the 68HC11 MPU will thereafter always respond to a *nonmaskable* interrupt. In other words, if the X flag is 0 the effects of a *nonmaskable* interrupt input *cannot* be disabled by the programmer.

The single nonmaskable interrupt, $\overline{XIRQ}$, in the 68HC11 MPU is always an active-LOW input. If the X bit in the CCR is cleared, then a LOW level signal at the $\overline{XIRQ}$ input will interrupt the MPU. If the X bit is set, then the MPU will not respond to the $\overline{XIRQ}$ input of the MPU. The $\overline{XIRQ}$ input has priority over the $\overline{IRQ}$ input; that is, if flags I = X = 0, and both of these inputs were activated simultaneously, the MPU would respond to the $\overline{XIRQ}$ first.

Unlike for the I flag, there are no instructions that will directly clear or set the X flag in the CCR. The TAP instruction is often used to clear the X flag. The program below shows how the nonmaskable interrupt flag, X, in the CCR can be cleared so that the 68HC11 MPU will respond to a $\overline{XIRQ}$ interrupt. The MPU will not respond to the $\overline{XIRQ}$ interrupt input until after the TAP instruction is executed. Once X has been cleared, it cannot be set by software. In other words, any attempt to set X using a TAP instruction will have no effect on X; it will stay at 0.

Address	Instruction code	Mnemonic	Comments
C100	07	TPA	; [CCR] → [ACCA]
C101	86	ANDA #$BF	; Clear bit 6 of [ACCA]
C102	BF		
C103	06	TAP	; Restore [CCR] with X = 0
C104	: :	: :	; Continue

Both the maskable and nonmaskable interrupt flags (I and X) are automatically set when the MPU undergoes a reset condition. This is done in order to keep any interrupt signals from being acknowledged unless, and until, the 68HC11 MPU system has been initialized. For example, part of this initialization would be the loading of the stack pointer (SP) so that it points to the address in RAM where the stack is to be located.

Active Signal Conditions   As mentioned above, the nonmaskable $\overline{XIRQ}$ input is a level-sensitive input that is activated by a LOW logic level. The maskable $\overline{IRQ}$ input can be programmed to be level-sensitive or edge-sensitive. This is done by controlling the IRQE bit (bit 5) of the OPTION control register.

7	6	5	4	3	2	1	0	
ADPU	CSEL	**IRQE**	DLY	CME	0	CR1	CR0	**OPTION** $1039

At Reset   0   0   0   1   0   0   0   0

After an MPU reset condition, the IRQE bit is 0. This programs the $\overline{IRQ}$ input to be an active-LOW, level-sensitive input. This means that the occurrence of a LOW level at $\overline{IRQ}$ will interrupt the MPU, and a constant LOW will continually interrupt the MPU (provided that I = 0). The user can program the $\overline{IRQ}$ input to be edge-sensitive so that it responds only to a *negative-going transition*. This is done by making the IRQE a 1 by having the MPU execute an instruction that writes the appropriate word into address $1039. When it is edge-sensitive, $\overline{IRQ}$ will interrupt the MPU only when $\overline{IRQ}$ makes a HIGH-to-LOW transition (if I = 0); a constant LOW at $\overline{IRQ}$ will have no effect.

Unlike the OPTION register bits ADPU and CSEL that were discussed earlier in this chapter, IRQE is a time-protected control bit. Consequently, the programming of this bit must be done within the first 64 E-clock cycles after a reset. This short time window of 64 cycles in which certain control bits can be changed is a special feature of the 68HC11 that prevents the accidental changing of these time-protected bits while the MPU is operating in its normal mode.

Figure 8.13 shows the 68HC11's two main interrupt inputs. Here $\overline{IRQ}$ is assumed to be programmed for edge-sensitive activation (IRQE bit is a 1). Like the 68HC11, most MPUs will have both level-sensitive and edge-sensitive interrupt inputs.

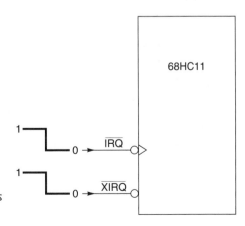

FIGURE 8.13   The 68HC11 has two interrupt inputs.

IRQ Versus $\overline{\text{XIRQ}}$ The principal differences between the $\overline{\text{IRQ}}$ and $\overline{\text{XIRQ}}$ inputs are summarized as follows:

1. The MPU can ignore the $\overline{\text{IRQ}}$ input if the I flag is a 1; it can ignore $\overline{\text{XIRQ}}$ if the X flag is a 1. However, the I flag can be set and cleared at any time by software. The X flag can be cleared only once, then it remains at 0.
2. The $\overline{\text{IRQ}}$ can be programmed as a level-sensitive or edge-sensitive input via the IRQE bit in the OPTION register. $\overline{\text{XIRQ}}$ is always level-sensitive.
3. The $\overline{\text{XIRQ}}$ input has priority over the $\overline{\text{IRQ}}$ input. When they are activated simultaneously (while X = I = 0), the MPU will respond to $\overline{\text{XIRQ}}$ first.

Power Failure Interrupt

A major use of an MPU's nonmaskable interrupt input is in a power-failure shutdown routine. Here a special circuit detects whenever the system power supply voltage drops below a certain level and generates a signal to the nonmaskable interrupt input. The MPU then immediately branches to the ISR, which contains instructions for storing the contents of the MPU's internal registers and important RAM locations in a special area of EEPROM memory or RAM that can operate from battery power (such as a CMOS RAM). This process requires only a few microseconds and can be completed before the power supply voltage drops low enough to destroy the contents of these registers.

Handshaking in the Interrupt Process

Use of the maskable interrupt, $\overline{\text{IRQ}}$, often requires some handshaking between the MPU and the device that generates the $\overline{\text{IRQ}}$ signal. We will illustrate this for the A/D converter interface that was discussed in Section 8.5. Let us assume that the IRQE bit in the OPTION register of the 68HC11 MPU is in its default configuration (IREQ = 0) and therefore, the MPU will respond to a LOW-level signal at the $\overline{\text{IRQ}}$ input. Figure 8.14 shows the necessary modifications of the circuit of Fig. 8.7 for operation using the interrupt method. First, note that the EOC output is not connected to the data bus since the MPU is not going to read its value to determine when the A/D converter has data ready. Instead, the positive-going transition of the EOC signal will clock the JK FF, causing the MPU's $\overline{\text{IRQ}}$ input to go LOW when the A/D converter has finished its conversion and has new data for the MPU.

If the MPU's interrupt mask flag, I, is LOW when $\overline{\text{IRQ}}$ goes LOW, the MPU will respond to the interrupt input in the manner previously outlined. If the MPU's I flag is HIGH when $\overline{\text{IRQ}}$ goes LOW, the MPU will ignore the interrupt input and will continue executing the instructions in its current program until a CLI instruction clears I to 0. Then, the MPU will respond to the $\overline{\text{IRQ}}$ input (assuming that it is still LOW) and will go through the normal interrupt sequence.

As the 68HC11 MPU recognizes the interrupt and branches to the interrupt service routine (ISR), it *automatically* sets the I flag to 1. This is done to ensure that the MPU will not respond to this same interrupt input again. For this example, the ISR will contain the instruction that reads the A/D output into ACCA. It may also contain instructions for processing these data. The last instruction in the ISR will be a ReTurn from Interrupt (RTI) instruction, which returns the MPU to the program it was previously executing.

Upon executing the RTI instruction, the original values of the CCR will be pulled off the stack and restored, thereby making I = 0. With I = 0, the MPU could end up responding to the same $\overline{IRQ}$ = 0 signal again unless some type of precautionary measures are taken. Clearly, then, it is necessary to set the $\overline{IRQ}$ input back to 1 prior to the RTI instruction or the MPU will respond to the same interrupt when it returns to the main program. This can be done by having an instruction somewhere in the ISR to send a LOW pulse to clear the JK FF and set $\overline{IRQ}$ = 1. For our example, we are using OR gate 3, which can be driven LOW by the execution of a dummy READ instruction from address 8002. The complete ISR for servicing the A/D converter of Fig. 8.14 is shown on page 000.

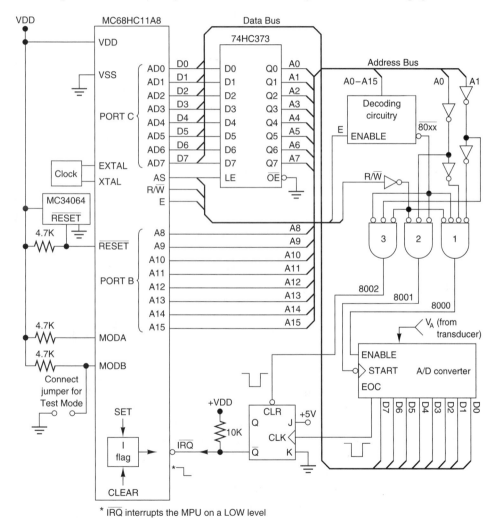

FIGURE 8.14 Interfacing the A/D converter to the 68HC11 MPU using the maskable interrupt, $\overline{IRQ}$.

Address	Label	Instruction code	Mnemonic	Comments
C500	ISR	B6	LDAA $8002	; Dummy READ to clear FF and
C501		80		; make $\overline{\text{IRQ}}$ HIGH
C502		02		
C503		B6	LDAA $8000	; Load A/D data into ACCA
C504		80		
C505		00		
C506		97	STAA $60	; Store A/D data in memory
C507		60		
C508	RETURN	3B	RTI	; Return to main program

The first instruction generates the pulse at OR gate 3 to set $\overline{\text{IRQ}}$ back to HIGH. The second instruction loads the A/D output data into ACCA. The third instruction stores these data in memory for later use. Finally, the RTI instruction sends the MPU back to the main program, where it was when it was interrupted by the A/D converter. Because $\overline{\text{IRQ}}$ is now HIGH, the MPU cannot be interrupted until after it commands the A/D converter to perform another conversion.

▶ 8.12 ADDRESS OF AN ISR—INTERRUPT VECTORS

When an interrupt occurs, how does the MPU know what address it should branch to for the ISR? The answer to this will vary from one MPU to the next and can best be determined by reading the manufacturer's literature. We will, however, describe the methods used by the 68HC11 MPU.

The reader may recall from our earlier discussion of the $\overline{\text{RESET}}$ operation that the 68HC11 MPU obtains a 16-bit reset vector from two fixed locations in memory (usually ROM). This reset vector is the address where the MPU will find the first instruction of the program it is to execute after it responds to the $\overline{\text{RESET}}$ input. When an interrupt occurs, the MPU obtains a 16-bit *interrupt vector* from two fixed locations in memory. This interrupt vector is then loaded into the program counter as the address where the MPU will go for the first instruction of the ISR.

To illustrate, Fig. 8.15 shows how the last fourteen bytes of ROM are used to store some of the various address vectors for the 68HC11 MPU. Note that the 68HC11 has over twenty different vectors that are stored in ROM and that are used by different systems of the 68HC11 MPU; not all are discussed in this textbook. When the $\overline{\text{RESET}}$ input is externally activated (a LOW for the 68HC11 MPU), the MPU automatically takes the contents of ROM locations FFFE and FFFF and loads them into the program counter. For the example in Fig. 8.15, the $\overline{\text{RESET}}$ vector is C000, so the MPU begins executing instructions starting at that address. When the $\overline{\text{IRQ}}$ input is activated and the MPU recognizes it (I = 0), the MPU automatically transfers the contents of locations FFF2 and FFF3 into the PC after having automatically saved the current contents of the PC and the other registers on the stack. For this example, the $\overline{\text{IRQ}}$ vector in Fig. 8.15 is C150, so the MPU begins executing the ISR at address C150. Similarly, when a $\overline{\text{XIRQ}}$ occurs, the $\overline{\text{XIRQ}}$ vector stored in loca-

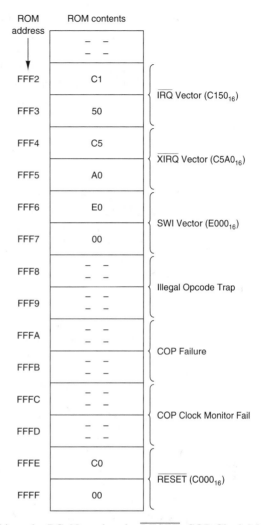

FIGURE 8.15 Partial memory map of reset and interrupt vectors for a 68HC11 MPU.

ROM address	ROM contents	
	– – – –	
FFF2	C1	$\overline{\text{IRQ}}$ Vector (C150$_{16}$)
FFF3	50	
FFF4	C5	$\overline{\text{XIRQ}}$ Vector (C5A0$_{16}$)
FFF5	A0	
FFF6	E0	SWI Vector (E000$_{16}$)
FFF7	00	
FFF8	– – – –	Illegal Opcode Trap
FFF9	– – – –	
FFFA	– – – –	COP Failure
FFFB	– – – –	
FFFC	– – – –	COP Clock Monitor Fail
FFFD	– – – –	
FFFE	C0	$\overline{\text{RESET}}$ (C000$_{16}$)
FFFF	00	

tions FFF4 and FFF5 will be loaded into the PC. Note that the $\overline{\text{RESET}}$, COP Clock Monitor Fail, COP Failure, Illegal Opcode Trap, SWI, $\overline{\text{XIRQ}}$, and $\overline{\text{IRQ}}$ vectors are different and each therefore points to a different interrupt service routine.

Normally, once a system has been developed and its design finalized, the address that indicates where the ISR starts is permanently stored in the interrupt vector locations. In a development system, such as the EVB board, the ISRs can be placed any place in RAM since the interrupt vectors will always point to an address in RAM where the user will store the address of the first ISR instruction to be executed.

Software Interrupt

The SWI vector is utilized by the 68HC11 MPU during the execution of a *software interrupt*. The 68HC11 instruction set includes an instruction (SWI) that forces the MPU to respond the same as it does to an externally generated interrupt. This software interrupt capability is extremely useful in helping to debug programs. When the MPU executes the SWI instruction, it automatically stores all MPU registers on the stack (PC, Y, X, ACCA, ACCB, and CCR) and it sets the I flag in the CCR. Then it transfers the contents of locations FFF6 and FFF7 into the PC. For our example, the SWI vector is E000, so that the MPU will then go to address E000 to execute the ISR stored there. The SWI instruction is not maskable by either the I or the X bit in the CCR, so the MPU will always branch to the ISR once it executes the SWI instruction.

▶ 8.13 INTERRUPTING AN ISR

Can an interrupt service routine be interrupted? Assume the MPU has been interrupted by a signal at $\overline{\text{IRQ}}$ and is in the process of executing the ISR for the interrupting device. It cannot be interrupted by another signal at the maskable interrupt input, $\overline{\text{IRQ}}$, as long as the Interrupt Mask flag, I, is 1, which is usually the case. However, if I is 0, the ISR can be interrupted by the $\overline{\text{IRQ}}$ input. Of course, if the MPU has a nonmaskable interrupt input, like the 68HC11's $\overline{\text{XIRQ}}$, the MPU can be interrupted while it is executing the ISR by a signal on this input, regardless of the state of the I flag (assuming X = 0).

To illustrate the sequence of events that occurs when an ISR is interrupted, we will use the example depicted in Fig. 8.16. Here we have a 68HC11 MPU operating in the expanded mode, which has separate I/O devices connected to its $\overline{\text{IRQ}}$ and $\overline{\text{XIRQ}}$ interrupt inputs. (Both $\overline{\text{IRQ}}$ and $\overline{\text{XIRQ}}$ respond to a LOW level signal.) Also shown is the memory map that will be used for the illustration. The main program occupies address space from C000 to C100. The ISR for device 1 is located in addresses C150–C160, and the ISR for device 2 is located in addresses C5A0–C5B0. Locations FFF2–FFFF contain the address vectors described earlier (Fig. 8.15).

Let us suppose that device 1 sends a LOW signal to $\overline{\text{IRQ}}$ while the MPU is executing a single-byte instruction at C036 in the main program. When the MPU finishes executing this instruction, it recognizes the interrupt (assume that I = 0) and will fetch the $\overline{\text{IRQ}}$ vector from locations FFF2 and FFF3. This address vector, C150, is placed in the program counter after the previous contents of the PC (which were C037) have been stored on the stack along with index registers, Y and X, ACCA, ACCB, and CCR (which had bit I = 0). Then, the 68HC11 MPU will automatically make I = 1 so that it does not get interrupted by another $\overline{\text{IRQ}}$ signal. The MPU then begins executing the ISR for device 1 at C150.

Now let's suppose further that the X flag in the CCR is 0 and that device 2 sends a LOW signal to $\overline{\text{XIRQ}}$ while the MPU is executing a single-byte instruction at C154. Regardless of the status of I, the 68HC11 MPU will recognize this interrupt as soon as it finishes this instruction and will fetch the $\overline{\text{XIRQ}}$ vector from locations FFF4 and FFF5. This address vector, C5A0, is placed in the PC after the previous contents (C155) and the contents of the other 68HC11 MPU registers have been placed on the stack, including the CCR (which had X = 0). Then, the MPU automatically sets both the I (which was already set) and X flags in order to prevent any interrupt while servicing an $\overline{\text{XIRQ}}$ interrupt. The MPU now begins to execute the ISR for device 2 at C5A0.

The last instruction of this ISR is a ReTurn from Interrupt (RTI), which tells the MPU to branch back to where it was when the $\overline{\text{XIRQ}}$ occurred. To accomplish this the MPU reads the top nine bytes from the stack and places them in their respective registers.

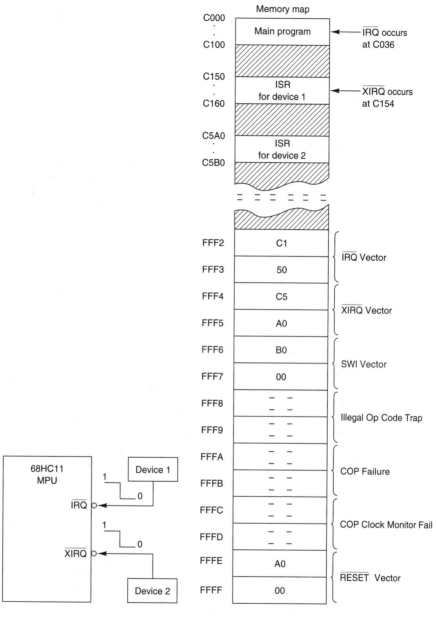

FIGURE 8.16   Interrupting an ISR.

The last two bytes are placed in the PC. This will set **[PC]** = C155 so that the MPU can now return to executing the ISR for device 1. The last instruction of this ISR is also an RTI, which tells the MPU to branch back to where it was when the $\overline{\text{IRQ}}$ occurred. The MPU again removes the top nine bytes from the stack and loads them into their respective registers. The last two bytes are placed into the PC so that **[PC]** = C037.

With [PC] = C037, the MPU returns to the main program and continues executing instructions from that point. This example not only illustrates the interrupt process, but also shows the usefulness of the stack in ensuring that everything returns to normal after each ISR has been executed.

▶ 8.14 MULTIPLE INTERRUPTS

If an MPU has only one or two interrupt input pins, how can it service a greater number of I/O devices? In the simplified version of the 68HC11-based circuit of Fig. 8.17, we see how several I/O devices can share a common interrupt input line to the MPU. The interface circuitry for each device generates an active-HIGH interrupt output which is passed through an open-collector inverter and tied to the $\overline{IRQ}$ input of the MPU. The outputs of the interface circuitry also drive tri-state buffers that are tied to the MPU data bus. A HIGH from any one of the interface circuits will drive the $\overline{IRQ}$ input LOW and interrupt the MPU. In this way, any number of different I/O devices can interrupt the MPU. When the MPU recognizes that an interrupt has occurred, it must somehow determine *which* device has generated the interrupt signal so that it will know what ISR to execute to service that device.

The simplest method of handling multiple interrupts is the polled interrupt method. Polled interrupt methods are slow but generally require very little external hardware. When an interrupt occurs, the MPU goes to a general ISR, where it executes a sequence of programmed instructions to determine the source of the interrupt. This is commonly done by having the MPU poll the status of each interrupt source, one at a time (as was done in our previous example of conditional I/O transfer from an A/D converter) until it finds the device that is ready for I/O transfer. Depending on which device it turns out to be, the program will cause the MPU to branch to the proper service routine for that device.

Even with the polled interrupt method there needs to be some provision for handling *simultaneous interrupts* from two or more devices. Usually, a *priority* system is set up where each device is assigned a different priority. When two devices interrupt the MPU at the same time, the MPU will service the higher-priority device first and then the lower-priority device. With polled interrupts, a priority system is easily established by the order in which the program polls the various devices. For the situation shown in the simplified 68HC11 MPU circuit of Fig. 8.17, when an interrupt occurs, the MPU can branch to a general ISR that polls the status of each device sequentially. Polling the status can be accomplished by having the MPU perform an LDAA operation from D900 to load the status of the interface outputs into the MPU's accumulator A. Once the status information is in ACCA, a SHIFT LEFT operation can be performed to place the most significant bit into the carry position. If this bit is 1 (indicating that the first device was actually trying to interrupt the MPU) the Carry flag will be set in the MPU condition code register (CCR). A conditional branch instruction such as Branch if Carry Set (BCS) can be used to direct the MPU to the proper location to begin executing the ISR for I/O device 1. If the Carry flag had not been set, the program would continue by performing another left shift operation. If the Carry flag is set this time, the BCS instruction would direct the MPU to a different location to begin executing the ISR instructions for I/O device 2. This process would continue until all devices had been tested and, if necessary, serviced. The order in which the I/O devices are connected to the data bus generates the priority in which these devices get

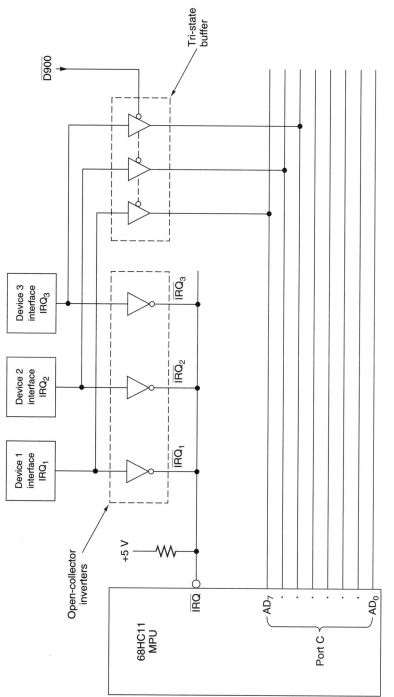

FIGURE 8.17 Multiple I/O devices connected to a common interrupt line.

serviced. The device that gets connected to data bus line AD_7 is the device that has the highest priority since its status will be shifted into the Carry position and tested first. Other programming techniques, such as bit masking, can be used to set up the priority scheme. If at some later time the need arises to change the present priority scheme, a simple software alteration that changes the masking pattern accomplishes this task. This allows the programmer great flexibility in handling I/O operations without the concerns of having to make hardware changes.

Polling Device Status Registers

In microprocessor-based systems, it is common to have many I/O devices connected to the MPU through fairly complex interface circuits. One of the functions of these interface circuits is to send an interrupt signal to the MPU when the I/O device wants the MPU's attention (e.g., when it has data ready for the MPU). These interfaces typically contain a device status register which, among other things, has a bit or flag that indicates whether or not the interface circuit has generated the MPU interrupt. When two or more I/O interfaces are connected to the same MPU interrupt input pin, the MPU can determine which interface generated the interrupt signal by polling the individual device status registers and checking the appropriate flags. A priority scheme is established by the order in which the MPU, as it executes the ISR, polls the various device status registers.

Preprocessing an Interrupt

The 68HC11 MPU instruction set includes an instruction that is referred to as the WAIt for Interrupt (WAI). When this instruction is executed the MPU *prepares* for an interrupt by placing the contents of the program counter (PC), index registers (Y) and (X), ACCA, ACCB, and CCR onto the stack. While in the wait state, the MPU continuously executes read bus cycles to the address on the stack where the CCR was stored. In other words, while in the wait state, nothing happens, or the MPU is simply "spinning its wheels" waiting for some interrupt to occur. The MPU will remain in this state until an $\overline{IRQ}$ or $\overline{XIRQ}$ input occurs. When the MPU leaves its wait state, it sets the I bit (and the X bit, if the interrupt was a $\overline{XIRQ}$) before the interrupt vector is fetched. Since its register contents have already been saved on the stack, the MPU will be directly vectored to the proper ISR address. This procedure saves approximately 12 cycles and therefore shortens the MPU response time once an interrupt occurs. The WAI instruction can also be used when a mode of reduced power-consumption operation of the MPU is desired until an interrupt occurs.

As stated in Chapter 7, the WAI is often used as a halt instruction since the MPU stops executing instructions.

Summary of Complete Interrupt Sequence

The steps that the MPU follows while servicing the *maskable* interrupt, $\overline{IRQ}$, are summarized in Fig. 8.18. Each of these steps is performed automatically by the 68HC11 MPU and does not require special instructions from the program. Of course, the programmer has to write the ISR and make sure that it is at the correct address location specified by the interrupt vector.

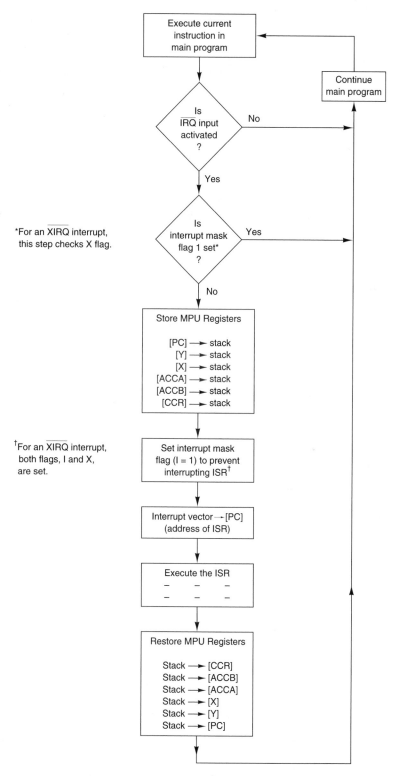

FIGURE 8.18 Steps that the 68HC11 MPU follows to service the maskable interrupt $\overline{IRQ}$.

Note that the MPU checks the $\overline{\text{IRQ}}$ input each time it completes the execution of an instruction in the main program to see if it is being activated by an interrupting device. Also note that the stack is being used to save the return address (PC), index registers (Y) and (X), ACCA, ACCB, and CCR.

The MPU follows these same steps for the nonmaskable interrupt ($\overline{\text{XIRQ}}$) except that (1) the X-interrupt mask flag is checked instead of the I-interrupt mask flag and (2) the interrupt mask flags, I and X, are both set by the MPU to prevent interrupting the ISR.

▶ 8.15 PORT A OF THE 68HC11 MCU

Refer to the 68HC11 MCU block diagram of Fig. 8.9 or Appendix B for the following discussion. The 68HC11 MCU has a few more special built-in interrupt features that are associated with port A, and which are not normally available in 8-bit MPUs. Port A, whose location in the memory map is $1000, is an 8-bit port. It includes three input-only pins (PA0, PA1, PA2), four output-only pins (PA3, PA4, PA5, PA6), and one programmable I/O pin (PA7). The three input pins, PA0, PA1, and PA2, can be used as general-purpose input pins or they can be used in conjunction with one of three *Timer Input Capture registers* (TIC1–TIC3) in the 68HC11 MCU. The following is an introduction to the Input-Capture functions of the 68HC11 MCU and how they interrelate with port A.

Input-Capture Registers

The three **Timer Input Capture Registers*** TIC1, TIC2, and TIC3 are all 16-bit registers and they are associated with pins PA2, PA1, and PA0, respectively.

PA2 Capture

7	6	5	4	3	2	1	0	TIC1
Bit 15	-	-	-	-	-	-	Bit 8	$1010
Bit 7	-	-	-	-	-	-	Bit 0	$1011

PA1 Capture

7	6	5	4	3	2	1	0	TIC2
Bit 15	-	-	-	-	-	-	Bit 8	$1012
Bit 7	-	-	-	-	-	-	Bit 0	$1013

PA0 Capture

7	6	5	4	3	2	1	0	TIC3
Bit 15	-	-	-	-	-	-	Bit 8	$1014
Bit 7	-	-	-	-	-	-	Bit 0	$1015

---

*A complete list of the 68HC11 MCU built-in control registers can be found in Appendix C.

When an edge (transition) occurs on one of the input pins (PA2–PA0) the present value in the 16-bit timer counter register, TCNT (described in Chapter 7), is copied into the appropriate timer input capture register. The edge that triggers the input-capture is determined by three pairs of *edge bits* in the Timer ConTroL register 2 (TCTL2).

TCTL2 ($1021)

7	6	5	4	3	2	1	0
0	0	EDG1B	EDG1A	EDG2B	EDG2A	EDG3B	EDG3A

At Reset: 0   0   0   0   0   0   0   0

The TCTL2* register, whose place in the memory map is $1021, can be written to by the user at any time, in order to program the edge(s) the input-capture-functions of the 68HC11 MCU will react to. Table 8.2 shows the various logic combinations of the edge bits and how they will affect the capture.

EXAMPLE 8.3

(a) Write an instruction sequence that will program the TCTL2 register to capture the time of a rising edge on pin PA2.

(b) Write a program sequence that will program the TCTL2 register to allow pins PA0–PA2 to be used as general-purpose input port pins.

(c) Assume that the programming of TCTL2 has been done according to step (a). Explain what happens when a positive-going transition occurs at input pin PA2.

Solution

(a) PA2 pin of the 68HC11 MPU is connected to the Input Capture register 1 (TIC1). Edge bits EDG1B and EDG1A in the TCTL2 register control the type of edge detection that the input capture register, TIC1, will recognize. Table 8.2 shows that EDG1B = 0 and EDG1A = 1 in order for the capture to occur on the rising edge of the PA2 input. Therefore, one possibility for the program sequence is

```
LDAB    #$10
STAB    $1021
```

TABLE 8.2

EDGxB	EDGxA	Configuration
0	0	Capture disabled
0	1	Capture on rising edges only
1	0	Capture on falling edges only
1	1	Capture on any edge (rising or falling)

x = 1, 2, or 3

---

*A complete list of the 68HC11 MCU built-in control registers can be found in Appendix C.

(b) In order for input pins PA0–PA2 to be used as general-purpose input port pins, we must disable the input capture function. Table 8.2 shows that if EDGxB and EDGxA bits are cleared, the capture function is disabled. Therefore, the following sequence will clear all the EDGxB and EDGxA bits in the TCTL2 register.

```
LDAB    #$00
STAB    $1021
```

(c) Upon detection of the positive-going transition at the input pin PA2, a time capture of the event will be recorded. That is, the current value from the 16-bit timer counter, TCNT, will be transferred into the 16-bit input capture register, TIC1.

The Input Capture Flags and the Input Capture Interrupts

When the signal edge specified by the edge-bits in register TCTL2 is detected, an *input capture* occurs at one of the three input capture registers TIC1, TIC2, or TIC3. Consequently, the corresponding Input Capture status Flag IC1F, IC2F, or IC3F is automatically set in the 68HC11 MCU built-in main Timer FLaG register 1 (TFLG1).* *These status bit(s) can be cleared by writing the appropriate word with 1s in the corresponding data bit(s) that we want to clear.* The memory address of register TFLG1 is $1023.

TFLG1 ($1023)

	7	6	5	4	3	2	1	0
	OC1F	OC2F	OC3F	OC4F	OC5F	IC1F	IC2F	IC3F
At Reset:	0	0	0	0	0	0	0	0

These input capture status flags can be read by the user at any time to determine whether or not a capture has occurred. If a certain flag is found to be set, the user may want to execute a certain program sequence that will utilize the time-of-the-capture value stored in the appropriate input capture register. In other words, the user may want to utilize the TFLG1 register in a conditional or polled I/O operation.

However, in some applications, there might be a need for the user to execute a certain program sequence as soon as a capture is made. In other words, a device-initiated I/O transfer or an interrupt-driven operation may be desired. Such applications are controlled by the bits IC1I-IC3I in the main Timer interrupt MaSK register 1 (TMSK1) of the 68HC11 MCU.*

TMSK1 ($1022)

	7	6	5	4	3	2	1	0
	OC1I	OC2I	OC3I	OC4I	OC5I	IC1I	IC2I	IC3I
At Reset:	0	0	0	0	0	0	0	0

If an Input Capture Interrupt Enable (ICxI) control bit is clear, the corresponding input-capture interrupt is *disabled* and the input-capture is operating in a conditional or polled

---

*A complete list of the 68HC11 MCU built-in control registers can be found in Appendix C.

TABLE 8.3

Time input capture register	Port A pin #	68HC11 MCU interrupt vector addresses
TIC1	PA2	FFEE, FFEF
TIC2	PA1	FFEC, FFED
TIC3	PA0	FFEA, FFEB

mode. If the IC×I is set, an automatic interrupt is generated whenever the corresponding IC×F is set by an input capture. The input-capture interrupts are *internally* generated by the 68HC11 MCU. Like any other interrupt, once activated and recognized, the 68HC11 MPU will load the PC with the appropriate interrupt vector and begin execution of the corresponding interrupt service routine (ISR). However, in this case, before leaving the ISR the programmer must make provisions for the clearing of the appropriate IC×F flag by writing to the TFLG1 register in the manner described earlier. Since there are three Input Capture registers (TIC1–TIC3) and three corresponding Input Capture Interrupt enables (IC1I–IC3I) in the 68HC11 MCU, there must also be three different Input Capture register Interrupt vectors. Table 8.3 shows the Interrupt vector addresses where the different vectors are to be stored.

EXAMPLE 8.4

The input capture feature of the 68HC11 MCU is often used to determine the period of an unknown signal or the duration of a pulse. Write a program sequence that will use the input-capture feature of the 68HC11 MCU to measure the period (in E-clock cycles) of an input waveform at pin PA2 and store it in memory locations C500 and C501, respectively. Use the conditional or polled I/O mode. Assume that the timer system has been programmed to count E-clock cycles.

Solution   One possibility.

Address	Label	Instruction code	Mnemonic	Comments
C100	START	CE 10 00	LDX #$1000	; Initialize the X register
C103		18 CE C5 00	LDY #$C500	; Initialize the Y register
C107		86 10	LDAA #$10	; Set EDGE bits in TCTL2 for
C109		A7 21	STAA 21,X	; capture on rising edges
C10B		BD C2 00	JSR $C200	; Jump to SUB1 to check IC1F
C10E		EC 10	LDD $10,X	; Save first capture
C110		18 ED 00	STD $00,Y	; in **[C500]** and **[C501]**
C113		BD C2 00	JSR $C200	; Jump to SUB1 for second rising edge
C116		EC 10	LDD $10, X	; Read second capture
C118		B3 C5 00	SUBD $C500	; Calculate the period
C11B		18 ED 00	STD $00,Y	; Store period in **[C500]** and **[C501]**
C11E	HALT	20 FE	BRA $C11E	; Halt program execution

Address	Label	Instruction code	Mnemonic	Comments
		Subroutine to clear and check the IC1F flag in the TFLG1 register		
C200	SUB1	86 04	LDAA #$04	; Clear flag IC1F in TFLG1
C202		A7 23	STAA $23,X	; register
C204	CHKFLG	1F 23 04 FC	BRCLR $23,X $04 $C204	; Detecting a rising edge
C208		39	RTS	; Return from subroutine

Study the above program carefully and note the following:

Address C100   The X register is initialized for later use.

Address C103   The Y register is initialized for later use.

Address C107/9   Edge bits EDG1B and EDG1A in the TCTL2 register are programmed for capture on rising edges of pin PA2.

Address C10B   Program jumps to the SUB1 subroutine to check IC1F for occurrence of first rising edge.

Address C10E/10   Save the contents of input capture register TIC1 ($1010–$1011) in memory locations C500 and C501. These contents represent the time-capture of the first rising edge of the input signal; that is, the 16-bit value in TCNT register at capture.

Address C113   Program jumps to the SUB1 subroutine to check for next rising edge.

Address C116   Load the contents of input capture register TIC1 in the double accumulator. This value represents the time-capture of the *second* rising edge of the input signal.

Address C118   The time of the first capture is subtracted from the time of the second capture in order to determine the period in E-clock cycles of the unknown input frequency.

Address C11B   The result is stored in memory locations C500 and C501, respectively. This value represents the period of the input waveform in E-clock cycles. To find the actual period we must multiply the number of E-clock cycles by the period of the E-clock.

Address C11E   The program halts.

Address C200/2   The IC1F flag in the TFLG register is cleared.

Address C204/8   This BRCLR instruction monitors the status of the IC1F flag. If the IC1F flag is cleared, the program is in a loop that continually checks for a change in the status of the IC1F flag. Once the IC1F flag is set, the program falls through the returns to the main program. When the IC1F flag is set, it indicates that a rising edge at the input capture register TIC1 has been detected.

TCNT Overflow

Note that the input capture feature of the 68HC11 MCU makes use of the 16-bit timer, TCNT. Recall that the TCNT counter is continuously incremented and that an overflow flag, TOF, in the TFLG2 register is set when TCNT cycles. When an input capture occurs, the present count in the TCNT timer is automatically transferred into the appropriate input capture register. In Example 8.4, if the period of the input waveform is longer than

65,536 E-clock cycles, then an overflow of the TCNT timer will occur and consequently the result from the execution of the instruction at memory address C11B may not be representative of the period of the input waveform. If the timer overflows once during the detection of the consecutive rising edges of the waveform, the above program will still work. For example, let us assume that the first rising edge is detected when the TCNT = $000F. The instructions at memory address locations C10E–C110 will store this value in $C500 and $C501, respectively. If the period is 65,530 E-clock cycles, the input capture register, TIC1, will capture the value $0009 when the second rising edge is detected. Clearly, this represents a situation where the TCNT timer overflowed once. The 16-bit subtraction executed by the instruction at memory location C118 would have stored a final result of FFFA ($0009–000F) in memory locations C500 and C501, respectively. This is the correct result, since the unsigned hexadecimal number FFFA represents 65,530 E-clock cycles. Hence, if we assume that a 2-MHz E-clock is being used, the period of the input waveform would be $65,530 \times 500$ ns ≈ 32.65 μs. However, if more than one overflow of the TCNT timer occurs during an input capture, then the program must be modified to keep track of the number of times the TOF flag is set during an input capture.

EXAMPLE 8.5

The program of Example 8.4 is somewhat inefficient. Suppose that due to some operational malfunction one of the rising edges of the input waveform is never detected. The program would be forever stuck in a loop waiting for a rising edge to occur. Modify the program sequence written for Example 8.4 to use the input capture interrupt capabilities of the 68HC11 MCU. In other words, change the program so that the MPU can be doing something else while waiting for a rising edge of the input waveform to be detected. Assume that the interrupt vector address for the input capture register 1 (FFEE, FFEF) is loaded with data, C2 and 00, respectively. That is, the interrupt vector for this interrupt is C200.

Solution   One possibility.

Main Program

Address	Label	Instruction code	Mnemonic	Comments
C100	START	CE 10 00	LDX #$1000	; Initialize the X register
C103		18 CE C5 00	LDY #$C500	; Initialize the Y register
C107		7F C4 00	CLR $C400	; Clear memory location C400
C10A		86 10	LDAA #$10	; Set EDGE bits in TCTL2 for
C10C		A7 21	STAA $21,X	; capture on rising edges
C10E		BE C0 00	LDS $C000	; Initialize the stack pointer
C111		1C 22 04	BSET $22,X $04	; Enable IC1I interrupt
C114		1D 23 FB	BCLR $23,X $FB	; Clear IC1F flag
C117		0E	CLI	; Enable interrupts
C118		:	:	; *Continue with other tasks*
:		:	:	; :

Address	Label	Instruction code	Mnemonic	Comments
			ISR1 (For first rising edge)	
C200	ISR1	B6 C4 00	LDAA $C400	; Check to see if ISR1 has
C203		26 1B	BNE $C220	; been already executed
				; If yes, branch to ISR2
C205		EC 10	LDD $10,X	; Save first capture
C207		18 ED 00	STD $00,Y	; in **[C500]** and **[C501]**
C20A		1D 23 FB	BCLR $23,X $FB	; Clear IC1F flag
C20D		7C C4 00	INC $C400	; Condition **[C400]** for ISR2
C210	RET1	3B	RTI	; Return from interrupt
			ISR2 (For second rising edge)	
C220	ISR2	EC 10	LDD $10,X	; Save second capture
C222		B3 C5 00	SUBD $C500	; Calculate the period
C225		18 ED 00	STD $00,Y	; Store the waveform's period
C228		1D 23 FB	BCLR $23,X $FB	; Clear IC1F flag
C22B		7F C4 00	CLR $C400	; Condition **[C400]** for ISR1
C22E	RET2	38	RTI	; Return from interrupt

Study the above program carefully and note the following:

Address C100 Register X is initialized.

Address C103 Register Y is initialized.

Address C107 Memory location C400 is cleared. This memory location will be used as a counter to determine which of the two ISRs (ISR1 or ISR2) will be executed.

Address C10A/C Register TCTL2 is conditioned for input capture on rising edges.

Address C10E Stack pointer is initialized to point to an area in RAM.

Address C111 Input capture interrupt bit, IC1I, in the TMSK1 register is set. This allows the 68HC11 MCU to automatically generate an interrupt when an edge is detected. When this happens, the IC1F flag is set in the TFLG1 register.

Address C114 The IC1F flag in the TFLG1 register is cleared and, therefore, it is conditioned for the first rising edge detection. Recall that in order to clear a bit(s) in either the TFLG1 or TFLG2 register of the 68HC11 MCU, a 1 must be written to the bit position that we want to clear. Since we want to clear only bit 2 of the TFLG1 register, the masking byte of the BCLR instruction must be $FB. *(Normally, this would write 0s into all bits except bit 2, and a 1 into bit 2. However, because of the idiosyncrasy of TFLG1, this operation will actually clear bit 2 and leave the other bits unaffected. Refer to Section 7.25.)*

Address C117 The I flag in the CCR must be cleared in order for *any* of the nonmaskable 68HC11 MPU interrupts to be recognized.

Address C118 The MPU can now go on to execute instructions for other tasks.

The first time a rising edge is detected at pin PA2, the 68HC11 MCU generates an internal interrupt. At this time, all the data present in all of the MPU internal registers are saved on the stack and the PC is loaded with address C200 (the vector stored in FFEE, FFEF) which is the address of the first instruction in the ISR1.

Address C200/3   The contents of memory location C400 are checked. If **[C400]** = 00 it means that this is the first rising edge detection and ISR1 is executed. If **[C400]** = 01, it means that this is the second edge detection and ISR2 at address $C220 will be executed.

Address C205/7   The time of the first capture is saved and stored in memory locations C500 and C501.

Address C20A   Clear the input capture flag IC1F to prepare for next rising edge.

Address C20D   The contents of memory location C400 are incremented so that **[C400]** = 01. Consequently, on the next detection of a rising edge, **[C400]** will be checked by the instruction at $C200–$C203 and ISR2 at $C220 will be executed.

Address C210   Return to the main program and continue.

Eventually, the second edge will be detected and the MCU will again generate an internal interrupt. The MPU will again go to ISR1 since the vector stored in FFEE, FFEF is still C200. However, the program instructions at the beginning of ISR1 (C200 and C203) will determine that [C400] ≠ 00 and automatically send the 68HC11 MPU to C220 which is the address of the first instruction in the ISR2.

Address C220/5   The time of the second capture is saved and subtracted from the time of the first capture. The resulting period (in E-clock cycles) is stored in memory locations C500 and C501.

Address C228/B   System is ready to measure the period of the next input waveform at pin PA2.

Address C22E   Return to the main program.

The Output Compare Registers

You may want to refer to the 68HC11 MCU block diagram of Fig. 8.9 for the following discussion of the Output Compare functions. The 68HC11 MCU has five 16-bit *Timer Output Compare* registers, TOC1 through TOC5, which are shown below, along with their respective memory address.*

7	6	5	4	3	2	1	0	**TOC1**
Bit 15	-	-	-	-	-	-	Bit 8	**$1016**
Bit 7	-	-	-	-	-	-	Bit 0	**$1017**

---

*A complete list of the 68HC11 MCU built-in control registers can be found in Appendix C.

7	6	5	4	3	2	1	0	TOC2
Bit 15	-	-	-	-	-	-	Bit 8	$1018
Bit 7	-	-	-	-	-	-	Bit 0	$1019

7	6	5	4	3	2	1	0	TOC3
Bit 15	-	-	-	-	-	-	Bit 8	$101A
Bit 7	-	-	-	-	-	-	Bit 0	$101B

7	6	5	4	3	2	1	0	TOC4
Bit 15	-	-	-	-	-	-	Bit 8	$101C
Bit 7	-	-	-	-	-	-	Bit 0	$101D

7	6	5	4	3	2	1	0	TOC5
Bit 15	-	-	-	-	-	-	Bit 8	$101E
Bit 7	-	-	-	-	-	-	Bit 0	$101F

The Output Compare registers (TOC1–TOC5) are associated with port A pins PA7–PA3, respectively. Port A pins PA6–PA3 are output pins *only,* while PA7 is an I/O pin. The Output Compare registers (TOC2–TOC5) control Port A pins PA6–PA3, respectively. The 8-bit TCTL1* register, whose address in the memory map is $1020, uses a pair of control bits (OMx, OLx) to control the action of each of the corresponding output compare functions.

TCTL1 ($1020)

7	6	5	4	3	2	1	0
OM2	OL2	OM3	OL3	OM4	OL4	OM5	OL5

At Reset: 0 0 0 0 0 0 0 0

If both OMx and OLx bits are clear, then the corresponding pin of port A functions as an output port. In other words, the Timer Output Compare register associated with the corresponding port A pin is disabled, so that pin will operate as a general-purpose output pin. The last three possible combinations of OMx and OLx of Table 8.4 are simply used to control whether the corresponding port A pin will toggle, clear, or set after a successful compare operation.

Each of the Output Compare registers can be programmed to signal the 68HC11 MCU of a certain event that might have occurred at a specific time. Again, the previously introduced timer TCNT plays a vital role in the operation of the Output Compare registers. Each of the five Output Compare registers has an associated 16-bit comparator. During

---

*A complete list of the 68HC11 MCU built-in control registers can be found in Appendix C.

TABLE 8.4

OMx	OLx	Configuration
0	0	OCx does not affect pin (OC1 still may)
0	1	Toggle OCx pin on successful compare
1	0	Clear OCx pin on successful compare
1	1	Set OCx pin on successful compare

x = 2, 3, 4, or 5

Output Compare operations, the contents of the free-running timer TCNT are compared with the contents of each 16-bit Output Compare register. When the contents of the timer TCNT are equal to the contents of one of the Compare registers, the corresponding Output Compare register flag in the TFLG1 register is set. Note that the Timer interrupt MaSK register 1 (TMSK1) and Timer FLaG register 1 (TFLG1) are used by both the Input Capture and the Output Compare functions of the 68HC11 MCU.*

TFLG1 ($1023)

7	6	5	4	3	2	1	0
OC1F	**OC2F**	**OC3F**	**OC4F**	**OC5F**	**IC1F**	**IC2F**	**IC3F**

At Reset: 0   0   0   0   0   0   0   0

The Output Compare Flags (OC1F–OC5F) in the TFLG1 register operate basically the same way as the previously discussed Input Capture Flags (IC1F–IC3F) during the Input Capture operations. For example, let us assume that the present count in the timer TCNT matches the contents of the Timer Output Compare register 5 (TOC5). When this happens, the Output Compare Flag (OC5F) in the TFLG1 register is set. If the Output Compare Interrupt enable bit 5 (OC5I) in register TMSK is cleared, then the TFLG1 register can be used in a conditional or polled I/O operation.* By reading [**TFLG1**] and then masking the appropriate bit, we can determine the status of a specific Output Compare Flag. If the Output Compare Interrupt enable bit 5 (OC5I) is set, then an automatic internal interrupt is generated as soon as the OC5F flag is set. Recall that *all of the status bit(s) in the TFLG1 register can be cleared by writing the appropriate word with 1s in the corresponding data bit(s) that we want to clear*. Note that, when the 68HC11 MCU is first turned on, the contents of the TFLG1 register are 00_{16}. However, 32.77 ms later (assuming a 2 MHz E-clock) the flags OC1F–OC5F in the TFLG1 register become set. This is because the Timer TCNT cycles every 32.77 ms and during that time five output compares will take place, thereby setting all five Output Compare Flags.

TMSK1 ($1022)

7	6	5	4	3	2	1	0
OC1I	**OC2I**	**OC3I**	**OC4I**	**OC5I**	**IC1I**	**IC2I**	**IC3I**

At Reset: 0   0   0   0   0   0   0   0

---

*A complete list of the 68HC11 MCU built-in control registers can be found in Appendix C.

TABLE 8.5

Timer output compare register	Port A pin #	68HC11 MPU interrupt vector addresses
TOC1	PA7	FFE8, FFE9
TOC2	PA6	FFE6, FFE7
TOC3	PA5	FFE4, FFE5
TOC4	PA4	FFE2, FFE3
TOC5	PA3	FFE0, FFE1

When the automatic internal interrupt is generated, the 68HC11 MPU will load the PC with the appropriate Output Compare Interrupt vector (assuming I=0) and begin execution of the corresponding Interrupt Service Routine (ISR). Before leaving this ISR the programmer must make provisions for the clearing of the appropriate OCxF flag by writing to the TFLG1 register with a 1 in the corresponding data bit position. There are five Timer Output Compare registers (TOC1–TOC5) and five corresponding Output Compare Interrupt enables (OC1I–OC5I) in the 68HC11 MCU. Consequently, there are five different Output Compare register Interrupt vectors. Table 8.5 shows the five different Output Compare register Interrupt vector addresses where the different vectors are to be stored.

EXAMPLE 8.6

Let us assume that the 68HC11 MPU is executing a Main program sequence. Sometime during the execution of the program we want to cause a delay of 25 ms using the Output Compare function of the 68HC11 MCU. At the completion of this delay we want to generate an internal interrupt so that a squarewave with a frequency of about 1 kHz is produced at port A pin, PA5. The program sequence for the generation of the 1 kHz squarewave should start at $C500. Starting at memory address $C200, write the program sequence that will accomplish this task. Assume that the interrupt vector for the timer Output Compare Register 3 (FFE4, FFE5) is loaded with data, C5 and 00, respectively.

Solution   One possibility.

Main Program

Address	Label	Instruction code	Mnemonic	Comments
:	:	:	:	
C200	START	CE 10 00	LDX #$1000	; Initialize the X register to ; be used by the index X ; register instructions.
C203		FC 10 0E	LDD $100E	; Load 16-bit Timer TCNT ; register into ACCD
C206	DELAY	C3 C3 50	ADDD #$C350	; Add $C350_{16}$ counts to the ; contents of ACCD ($C350_{16} =$; 25 ms).

Main Program (continued)

Address	Label	Instruction code	Mnemonic	Comments
C209		FD 10 1A	STD $101A	; Store [ACCD] in [TOC3]
C20C		1D 23 DF	BCLR $23,X $DF	; Clear flag OC3F in TFLG1 ; register at $1023.
C20F		1C 22 20	BSET $22,X $20	; Enable Interrupt enable ; control bit OC3I in TMSK1 ; at $1022
C212		0E	CLI	; Enable maskable interrupts.
C213		:	:	; *Continue main program*
:		:	:	; *tasks*

ISR
(for generating a 1 kHz squarewave)

Address	Label	Instruction code	Mnemonic	Comments
C500	ISR	86 01	LDAA #$10	; Clear control bit OM3 and ; set control bit OL3 in
C502		A7 20	STAA $20,X	; register TCTL1 at $1020 for ; toggle operation of PA5.
C504	CLRFLG	1D 23 DF	BCLR $23,X $DF	; Clear flag OC3F in TFLG1 ; register at $1023
C507	CHKFLG	1F 23 01 FC	BRCLR $23,X #01 $C507	; Check flag OC3F. When flag ; OC3F = 1, PA5 toggles.
C50B		EC 0E	LDD $1A,X	; Read the contents of TOC3 ; into [ACCD].
C50D		C3 03 E8	ADDD #$03E8	; Add 500 μs ($03E8_{16}$) to the ; contents of ACCD.
C510		ED 1A	STD $1A,X	; Store [ACCD] into register ; TOC3 at $101A.
C512		20 F0	BRA $C504	; Repeat one-half cycle again.

Study the program above and follow the step-by-step explanation of each of its instructions.

Address C200   The index X register is initialized to $1000 for all the index X instructions that will follow in the program.

Address C203   The contents of the 16-bit TCNT register are loaded into double accumulator D.

Address C206/9   To the unknown contents of the TCNT register we add the hex number C350 and store the result in the Output Compare register TOC3. If we assume that the system is operating with a 2-MHz E-clock and a prescale factor of 1, then the value C350 ($50,000_{10}$) represents an addition of 25 ms (50,000 × 500 ns) worth of counts. Therefore, at this time, the contents of the TCNT register are unknown, and the hex value in the TOC3 register is equal to the unknown value of the TCNT register plus 25 ms worth of E-clock counts.

Address C20C   This Bit Clear instruction clears the OC3F flag in the TFLG1 register. The next time this flag is set will be when the contents of the TCNT register are equal to the contents of the TOC3 register. This, of course, will be later, after a 25 ms delay.

Address C20F   This Bit Set instruction sets the OC3I control bit in the TMSK1 register. This will allow an automatic interrupt to be generated as soon as the OC3F flag gets set in the TFLG1 register. Again, this will occur after the 25 ms delay.

Address C212   The CLI instruction is needed since the 68HC11 MCU will not recognize any type of maskable interrupts unless the I flag in the Condition Code register is clear.

Address C213   The MPU can now go on to execute instructions for other tasks.

Address C500/2   Eventually, the contents of the TCNT and TOC3 registers will be equal and the 25 ms delay has been accomplished. At that time, OC3F gets set and, since OC3I = 1, an output compare interrupt is generated, and the PC will be loaded with the address vector C500. This will take us into the ISR where a frequency of about 1 kHz has to be generated at pin PA5 of Port A. The first instruction in the ISR will program bits OM3 and OL3 in the TCTL1 register. The TCTL1 register controls how the output compare pins will behave upon a successful compare. Bits OM3 and OL3 are programmed for toggle operation. In other words, when a successful Output Compare occurs, PA5 will toggle (see Table 8.4).

Address C504   This Bit Clear instruction initializes the OC3F flag in the TFLG1 register by clearing it. The OC3F flag will eventually be set when **[TCNT]** = **[TOC3]**. Note that at this time, we do not know when that will happen, since the contents of neither TCNT nor TOC3 are known.

Address C507   This BRCLR instruction keeps checking to see if the OC3F flag gets set, which will happen as soon as **[TCNT]** = **[TOC3]**. As long as the OC3F flag is clear, the BRCLR instruction will keep on branching back to CHKFLG. Eventually the contents of the two registers are equal and a successful Output Compare will occur and pin PA3 will toggle.

Address C50B   When the OC3F flag sets, the program will fall through to the instruction at address C50B. At this address, the double accumulator D is loaded with the present and unknown contents of the TOC3 register.

Address C50D/10   The double accumulator D is used to add the hex number 03E8 to the unknown contents of the TOC3 register. The value 03E8 (1000_{10}) represents 500 µs (1000 $\times$ 500 ns) worth of E-clock counts. The new contents of ACCD are stored in register TOC3. Hence, a successful Output Compare will occur when **[TCNT]** = **[TOC3]**, which will be 500 µs later. Note that the addition of 500 µs worth of E-clock counts represents half the period of a 1 kHz squarewave.

Address C512   The program branches back to CLRFLG in order to get ready for the next successful Output Compare. This process repeats itself, resulting in a toggling waveform at PA3 with a frequency of about 1 kHz.

Summary

We have seen how port A and the system timer in the 68HC11 MCU are used to provide the Input Capture and Output Compare functions, and we saw examples of how these functions can be used in applications. There are more functions and many more applications that are available using port A which will not be presented here. For a more detailed and more in-depth description of all of the port A features, refer to the *M68HC11 Reference Manual*.

The preceding functions and examples were presented to illustrate how interrupts that are generated internal to the MCU operate in much the same way as interrupts generated by external I/O devices. Like the external interrupts ($\overline{\text{IRQ}}$ and $\overline{\text{XIRQ}}$), the internal interrupts have their own vectors, and like $\overline{\text{IRQ}}$, they can be masked by the I bit in the CCR. The different internal interrupts can also be disabled (masked) by individual interrupt enable bits such as those in the Timer Mask Interrupt Register, TMSK1.

▶ 8.16 DIRECT MEMORY ACCESS (DMA) I/O TRANSFER

Up to now we have considered how data is transferred between the I/O devices and the MPU. There are many situations where a large amount of data needs to be transferred between an I/O device and the microcomputer's memory (usually RAM) in the shortest possible time. One example is the transfer of hundreds of thousands of bits of data from RAM to a high-resolution graphic CRT to maintain the video image. The rate of data transfer required can typically be 200,000 bytes per second, or one byte every 5 μs. Another common situation is the transfer of large blocks of data between a disk drive and the computer's RAM, such as when a program is loaded from disk into the computer's working memory for execution by the MPU, or when a data file is loaded from disk into RAM so it can be processed by the currently running program.

For situations such as these where large blocks of data are to be transferred between RAM and peripheral (I/O) devices, there are two basic ways the transfer can be accomplished: *programmed transfer* and *direct memory access (DMA) transfer*.

Programmed Transfer In this method, the transfer of data is done under program control; that is, the MPU executes a sequence of instructions that carries out the transfer between RAM and I/O by first taking the data into the MPU. Typically, the MPU executes an instruction to read a word from RAM and load it into the accumulator (e.g., LDAA instruction). Then it executes an instruction to write the accumulator contents into an output device (e.g., STAA). Clearly, in this method, the data does not flow directly from memory to the peripheral device because it must first pass through the MPU. This is shown symbolically in Fig. 8.19A. The same idea holds true for programmed transfer from an input device to RAM. The data actually flows from input device to the MPU and then to RAM.

Using programmed transfer in a typical MPU system, the transfer of a single data word between RAM and a peripheral device would take 5–10 μs. A lot of this time is taken up by the MPU having to fetch the instructions telling it what to do, and the need to take the data into an MPU register before it is sent to its ultimate destination. If the data could be transferred *directly* between the peripheral device and memory, it could be done a lot faster. This brings us to an alternative to programmed transfer.

Direct Memory Access (DMA) This method allows data to flow from an input device to RAM, or from RAM to an output device *without* going through the MPU, thereby providing a substantial increase in data transfer rate over programmed transfer; using DMA, a single word of data is transferred in typically 1 μs.

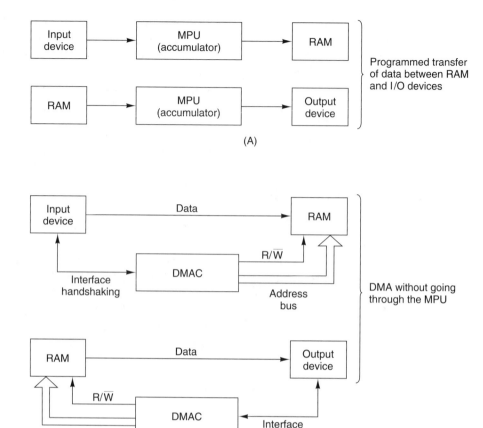

FIGURE 8.19   (A) Programmed transfer; (B) direct memory access transfer.

This idea is shown symbolically in Fig. 8.19B. Note that data flows directly between RAM and the peripheral device. This data transfer does not take place under the control of the MPU. Rather, it is controlled by a device called a *direct memory access controller (DMAC)*. The DMAC is a relatively complex IC chip that is capable of taking over control of the MPU's address bus and control bus in order to carry out the data transfer. As Fig. 8.19B shows, the DMAC can supply the RAM with the address and R/$\overline{W}$ signals needed to perform the data transfer. The DMAC also exchanges handshake signals with the I/O device during the DMA process. The MPU is noticeably absent from this symbolic diagram because it does not take part in the actual data transfer process. However, the MPU does oversee the entire operation by virtue of the fact that—under program control—it communicates with the DMAC to set up the parameters of the data transfer. The MPU communicates with the DMAC over the system buses just like any other I/O device.

It is not our intention here to describe the operation of a DMAC in detail, but a brief description of its main functions will be helpful in understanding the general idea of how DMA transfer works. The following information is based on the

Motorola 6844 DMAC chip which was developed for use with Motorola's 6800 family of MPUs.

Setup DMA Parameters   Let's assume that a program is to be loaded from the hard disk drive into RAM so that the program can be executed by the MPU. To begin the DMA process, the MPU—under program control—will write into several registers that are part of the DMAC. First, it will write a 16-bit number into the DMAC's *Address Register* to tell the DMAC the starting address in RAM where the data coming from the disk drive is to be stored. Next, the MPU will write a 16-bit number into the DMAC's *Byte Count Register* to tell the DMAC the total number of bytes to be transferred during the DMA transfer. The MPU then will write into one or more DMAC control registers to give the DMAC information including what mode of DMA transfer to use, which I/O device is involved, and whether or not to interrupt the MPU when the transfer is completed. Once the DMAC has been set up, it is ready to operate independent from the MPU. The DMAC is now ready for a DMA transfer, and it waits for the disk drive to let it know when it has data available to transfer to RAM.

Setup Disk Controller   After setting up the DMAC, the MPU, under program control, will write into several registers that are part of the Disk Controller Circuit—the circuit that interfaces the disk drive to the computer buses. The MPU will tell the Disk Controller—among other things—where on the disk to find the data (i.e., which side, which track and sector) and the number of bytes of data that are to be read from the disk. The MPU then sets a bit in the Disk Controller to initiate the read operation from the disk.

The Actual DMA Transfer   Once the Disk Controller has data ready to be transferred, it will send the DMAC a DMA Transfer Request signal. The DMAC responds by sending a DMA Request signal to the MPU's HALT input.* The MPU completes the execution of whatever instruction it is working on, and then responds to this signal at its HALT input by placing its address, data, and $R/\overline{W}$ lines in the high-Z state; in other words, it floats its buses and stops fetching and executing instructions. The MPU also sends a handshake signal such as Bus Available (BA) to the DMAC to let the DMAC know that the MPU has halted and it can now take control of the system buses and begin the DMA transfer.

The DMAC responds to the BA signal by sending a signal to the Disk Controller enabling it to put its data on the system data bus. The DMAC also places the contents of its Address Register on the address bus (recall, it was loaded with the RAM starting address by the MPU) and generates $R/\overline{W} = 0$ for a memory write operation. This will cause the data from the Disk Controller—which is on now the data bus—to be written into RAM. After this first transfer of data from the Disk Controller to RAM, the DMAC decrements its Byte Count Register and increments its Address Register. This new address is placed on the address bus and the next data byte from the Disk Controller is placed on the data bus and subsequently written into RAM by a $R/\overline{W} = 0$ signal from the DMAC.

This process continues until the Byte Count Register reaches zero, at which point all of the data has been transferred directly from the Disk Controller to RAM. The DMAC then releases the signal at the MPU's HALT input, and the MPU regains control of the sys-

---

*The MC68HC11A8 MPU, unlike other MPUs, does not have a HALT input or its equivalent since it is not designed to have DMA capabilities.

tem buses. The DMAC also activates its $\overline{IRQ}$ output which is tied to the MPU's $\overline{IRQ}$ input. The MPU can then respond to the $\overline{IRQ}$ input by branching to an interrupt service routine in which it will determine which device has interrupted it. Once it has determined that it is the DMAC causing the interrupt (by checking a status bit in a DMA control register), the MPU will know that the transfer of data from the disk drive to RAM has been completed.

DMA Transfer Modes   In this illustration of DMA transfer, the type of transfer that was used can be classified as a *Halt Burst* mode. In this mode, the MPU is halted and it responds by tri-stating its address and data buses. The DMAC then takes over control of these buses and generates the necessary control signals to transfer a *complete* block of data. After the transfer(s) is complete, the MPU regains control of the buses and continues executing its program.

A second mode of DMA transfer is referred to as the *Halt Steal* mode. This type of DMA transfer is very similar to the Halt Burst mode except that only one byte is allowed to transfer, after which the MPU regains control over the buses. After the MPU completes the execution of the next instruction, the DMAC transfers another data byte. This process continues until the entire data block is transferred. This mode allows the MPU to tend to system operation much more quickly than the Halt Burst mode, but the data transfer rate is greatly *decreased*.

A third method is referred to as *TSC Steal* mode. When operating in this mode, rather than waiting to complete the instruction the MPU is working on, the MPU clock signal is immediately frozen while the system clock continues to run. The MPU is forced to place its buses in the tri-state condition and the DMAC controller takes control and transfers a data byte. The advantage of this mode is a predictable response time since the MPU does not complete the instruction prior to responding to the transfer request. The disadvantage is that more external hardware is needed than in the other modes of DMA transfer and the transfer must be completed in a certain amount of time or data held by the MPU will be lost since its clock has been stopped.

▶ 8.17 TROUBLESHOOTING CASE STUDY

Figure 8.3 shows switches and LEDs connected as I/O devices for entering and displaying single-byte data. A technician builds the circuit and performs a final test in order to determine whether or not the circuit is working properly. The final test encompasses running the short program shown below, while comparing the status of the LEDs against the correct pattern of 1s and 0s corresponding to the condition of the eight switches.

```
START  LDAA $8004
       STAA $8000
       BRA START
```

The first instruction in the program (LDAA $8004) loads accumulator A with the conditions of switches S_7-S_0. The second instruction (STAA $8000) sends the contents of accumulator A to register 74HC377 to be displayed on the LEDs. The third instruction causes a branch to the beginning of the program to start the procedure again. The eight LEDs should light up in a pattern that mirrors the conditions of the switches S_7-S_0.

The technician observes that the LEDs that indicate the status of switches S_7–S_4 are always correct. However, the four LEDs corresponding to switches S_3–S_0 never indicate the proper status of the switches. Furthermore, the LEDs that should indicate the conditions of switches S_3–S_0 always assume a random and unpredictable pattern of 1s and 0s.

Clearly, there are many different ways of troubleshooting a fault in a digital circuit. The first and most important thing that the technician should do is to obtain a clear and precise understanding of the circuit's normal operation. This may take some time, especially if he/she is not familiar with the circuit's operation. Schematics may have to be checked and analyzed, manuals may have to be read, and manufacturers' troubleshooting tables may have to be consulted. After the technician understands what the circuit is actually doing, compared with what it is supposed to do, the next step is to troubleshoot the circuit by ruling out the obvious and by focusing on the probable.

From our discussion thus far, we already know how the circuit of Figure 8.3 should operate. Consequently, we can focus on the probable causes for the circuit's malfunction. Let's consider each one of the following faults and determine which is the most likely one to have caused the malfunction in the circuit.

1. The open collector inverters driven by outputs Q_3–Q_0 of register 74HC377 are faulty.
2. Switches S_3–S_0 are faulty.
3. Pull-up resistors to switches S_3–S_0 are not connected to the switches, or to +5 V.
4. The data inputs of register 74HC377 are disconnected from the data bus lines D_3–D_0.
5. Tri-state buffers (74HC244) connecting switches S_3–S_0 to data bus lines D_3–D_0 are faulty.

The Open Collector Inverters Driven by Outputs Q_3–Q_0 of Register 74HC377 are Faulty   The fault in the circuit causes the four LEDs corresponding to the four least significant switches to display a random and unpredictable pattern of 1s and 0s. Therefore, it would probably be wise to suspect a *floating* fault condition of some sort somewhere in the circuit. Keep in mind that in the High-Speed CMOS logic family, floating inputs may assume an indeterminate logic state. Consequently, we can confirm or dismiss any fault with the appropriate four open collector inverters by carefully checking their operation. We can do this by simply monitoring the logic levels present at the outputs Q_3–Q_0 of the register 74HC377 by using the logic probe while the program is running. The logic levels should correspond to the conditions of switches S_3–S_0. Another way of testing these inverters would be to first stop the execution of the test program. Then, with a logic pulser, inject a pulse at the input of each of the suspected inverters while monitoring that inverter's output with a logic probe. Although this is a fault that should be considered, it is not a likely one to occur. The chances of *all* four inverters failing simultaneously are pretty slim.

Switches S_3–S_0 are Faulty   The working condition of the switches can be checked using an ohmmeter (with power off) and by performing a continuity test. Even if, for some odd reason, all four switches (S_3–S_0) failed simultaneously, the pull-up resistors on each of the switches would have caused data bus lines D_3–D_0 to be at a logic HIGH. This in turn would cause the corresponding four LEDs to light up whenever register 74HC377 is loaded with data from the switches. Clearly, this is not the case, and therefore we can eliminate this as the causing fault.

Pull-up Resistors to Switches S_3–S_0 are not Connected to the Switches, or to +5 V If all four resistors going to switches S_3–S_0 were disconnected from the +5 V source, then the inputs to the tri-state buffers (IC 74HC244) would float for each corresponding switch that was open. Consequently, this would cause the corresponding outputs of the tri-state buffers to assume an indeterminate state and thereby cause the appropriate data bus line to assume an unpredictable logic level. This problem, however, would not be evident for those switches that are closed. When the output of NAND gate 2 goes LOW, a closed switch would place a logic LOW at the corresponding tri-state buffer output. This logic LOW would cause the corresponding data bus line to be LOW and consequently cause the appropriate LED to turn off. In conclusion, this could not have been the fault since the technician stated that the four LEDs displaying the conditions of switches S_3–S_0 *never* indicated the correct status of the switches.

The Data Inputs of Register 74HC377 are Disconnected from the Data Bus Lines D_3–D_0 This causes the data inputs of register 74HC377 to be always floating. Consequently, whenever register 74HC377 is clocked, its four least significant outputs, Q_3–Q_0, will assume indeterminate logic states. This, of course, would cause the corresponding LEDs to always assume a random and unpredictable pattern of 1s and 0s, regardless of the actual conditions of switches S_3–S_0. This fault would certainly cause the observed circuit malfunction to occur. Although this would be possible, an attentive technician probably would not have forgotten to connect *all* four data input lines (D_3–D_0) to register 74HC377.

Tri-state Buffers (74HC244) Connecting Switches S_3–S_0 to Data Bus Lines D_3–D_0 are Faulty We can safely assume that the tri-state buffers from the 74HC244 IC connected to the data bus lines D_7–D_4 are working flawlessly. Therefore, we can eliminate any problem with that half of the 74HC244 IC. If a fault exists on this IC it is with the tri-state buffers connected to the data bus lines D_3–D_0. Assuming that the least significant four buffers were not working at all, when signal $\overline{OE2}$ goes LOW, these buffers would not place predictable logic levels on the data bus lines D_3–D_0. It is possible, but highly unlikely that a malfunction would occur with the 74HC244 IC that would affect only the least significant four buffers. What is more probable is the presence of an open on the connection from the output of NAND gate 2 to the Enable lines of the four least significant buffers, that is, an open on the signal $\overline{OE2}$. If the technician forgot to make that connection, then the operation of the circuit would behave as the technician originally described. A visual check or a continuity test with an ohmmeter can confirm this fault.

GLOSSARY

A/D Converter Analog-to-Digital converter. Used to convert analog signals into a digital representation (straight binary, BCD) of the analog value.

ADCTL (Analog-to-Digital Control Register) Internal 68HC11 register that is part of the built-in A/D converter system of the 68HC11 MCU. This register is both a control register and a status register.

ADPU (A/D Power-Up) A control bit in the OPTION register that is used to enable/disable the A/D system of the 68HC11 MCU.

ADRI–ADR3 Four built-in A/D result registers that are used by the A/D system to store the results of four consecutive conversions.

Byte Count Register 6844 DMAC register used to store the 16-bit value corresponding to how many data bytes are to be transferred during the DMA process.

CA–CD (Channel Select Bits) Four control bits in the ADTCL register that in conjunction with the MULT bit determine which port E analog channels will have A/D conversions performed on them.

CCF (Conversion Complete Flag) A flag bit in the ADTCL register that is set at the completion of the A/D conversion of the fourth channel. This flag can be read to determine whether an A/D conversion process has been completed and the results have been placed in the A/D result registers ADR1–ADR4.

Conditional MPU-Initiated Transfer (Polled) MPU-initiated transfer of information only when I/O device is ready for communication. This process usually involves "handshaking."

Control Commands from MPU, requests for service from I/O devices, or status codes from I/O devices.

CSEL (Clock Select) A control bit in the OPTION register that is used to select an on-chip RC oscillator when the E-clock is running too slow.

Direct Memory Access (DMA) Device-initiated transfer of information in which data are transferred directly between the I/O device and RAM memory under the control of special interface circuits called Direct Memory Access Controllers (DMACs).

Direct Memory Access Controller (DMAC) External device that takes over the address and control buses of an MPU in order to carry out the data transfer between RAM and a peripheral device.

Direct Memory Access Transfer One way of transferring large blocks of data between RAM and I/O devices. In this method, the transfer of data is done without going through the MPU.

Floating Data Bus A READ command is generated but no device places data on the data bus. This technique is used in some MPU systems to generate signals necessary for starting or terminating operation of devices.

Halt Burst A mode of DMA transfer that involves halting the MPU, taking over control of the system buses, and transferring a complete block of data.

Halt Steal A mode of DMA transfer similar to Halt Burst except that only one data byte is transferred, after which the MPU regains control of the system buses.

Handshaking Exchange of control signals during a data transfer between the MPU and I/O device.

IC×I Input Capture Interrupt enable control bit (see TMSK1).

Interrupt Service Routine Special program in memory containing instructions for transferring data to or from an interrupting I/O device.

Interrupt Transfer I/O device initiates transfer of information by sending a signal to the MPU's interrupt input.

Interrupt Vector Address of the interrupt service routine to be executed when MPU is interrupted. This address is usually in ROM and is fetched by the MPU during its response to the interrupt.

$\overline{IRQ}$ The maskable interrupt input of the 68HC11 MCU.

IRQE Bit 5 of the OPTION Control Register. This bit controls whether the maskable interrupt input of the 68HC11 MCU ($\overline{IRQ}$) will recognize a LOW logic level or a negative-going transition.

LIFO (Last-In, First-Out) LIFO describes the way data flows in and out of some types of registers. Last-in-first-out is the way data flows in and out of a stack.

Maskable Interrupt Type of interrupt procedure that allows the interrupt request to be ignored if the interrupt disable flag is set.

Masking   Method of examining or changing a single bit of a data word, utilizing the logical operations of AND, OR, and EX-OR.

MULT (Multiple Channel/Single Channel)   A control bit in the ADTCL register that in conjunction with the four channel select bits (CD, CC, CB, CA) determines which port E analog channels will have an A/D conversion performed on them.

Nonmaskable Interrupt   Type of interrupt procedure that forces the MPU to respond to the interrupt request. In the particular case of the 68HC11 MPU, the nonmaskable interrupt $\overline{XIRQ}$ is honored only if the nonmaskable interrupt disable flag (X) is 0. Once X is clear, it can never be set again until the MPU is reset. Thus, the MPU will have to respond to $\overline{XIRQ}$.

OC×F   Output Compare Flag (see TFLG1).

OPTION Control Register   Internal 68HC11 MCU register that is used to control certain functions of the built-in A/D converter system.

Program Transfer   One way of transferring large blocks of data between RAM and I/O devices. In this method, the transfer of data is done through the MPU under program control.

Reset Vector   Address location of the first instruction to be executed after the actuation of the MPU's $\overline{RESET}$ input. This address is usually stored in ROM and is fetched by the MPU as it responds to the RESET signal.

Resolution of an A/D Converter   The smallest amount by which the analog input of an A/D converter must change to produce a change in its digital output. This amount is also often referred to as the step-size.

SCAN (Continuous Scan Control)   A control bit in the ADTCL register that is used to control whether the signals at the input channels of port E are continuously scanned or whether they are scanned only once before the conversion is terminated.

Step-Size   See Resolution of an A/D Converter.

SWI   The execution of this 68HC11 MCU instruction causes a software interrupt.

TCTL1 (Timer Control Register 1)   An 8-bit built-in register used to control the action of each of the output-compare functions of the 68HC11 MCU.

TCTL2 (Timer Control Register 2)   An 8-bit built-in register used to program the edge(s) the input-capture-functions of the 68HC11 MCU will react to.

TFLG1 (Timer Flag Register 1)   An 8-bit built-in register that contains five Output Compare Flags (OC1F–OC5F) and three Input Capture Flags (IC1F–IC3F). These flags are used by the Output Compare and Input Capture functions of the 68HC11 MCU.

TIC1–TIC3   Three built-in 16-bit Timer Input Capture Registers used by the 68HC11 MCU. These registers are associated with Port A pins PA2–PA0 and are used to store the contents of the TCNT timer during a capture function.

TMSK1 (Timer Interrupt Mask Register 1)   This is an 8-bit built-in register that contains, among other control bits, the three Input Capture Interrupt Enable control bits (IC1I–IC3I) used by the Input Capture functions of the 68HC11 MCU.

TOC1–TOC5 (Timer Output Compare Registers)   Five built-in 16-bit Timer Input Capture Registers used by the 68HC11 MCU. These registers are associated with Port A pins PA7–PA3 and are used by the Output Compare functions of the 68HC11 MCU in conjunction with the TCNT timer and the TFLG1 register.

TSC (Tri-State Control) Steal   A mode of DMA transfer that involves the MPU clock signal being immediately frozen without waiting for the completion of the instruction execution.

Unconditional MPU-Initiated Transfer The MPU initiates transfer of information to an I/O device. The I/O device must always be ready for communication. This process does not usually involve "handshaking."

Vector An address that indicates the location of the first instruction to be executed by the MPU as a result of an interrupt or a reset condition.

V_{REFH} and V_{REFL} Input pins to the 68HC11 MCU that define the permissible range of voltages of the input analog signals used by the A/D system.

$\overline{XIRQ}$ The nonmaskable interrupt input of the 68HC11 MCU.

QUESTIONS AND PROBLEMS

Sections 8.1–8.5

1. When interfacing an input/output device to an MPU, the term "handshaking" refers to:
   (a) The conversion of the MPU parallel data to a serial format for the I/O device
   (b) The exchange of control signals between the MPU and I/O device
   (c) Circuitry to ensure that the voltage levels of the I/O device are compatible with the MPU
   (d) The I/O device's control of the buses when the MPU is not using them

2. Direct memory access refers to:
   (a) The ability of the MPU to read or write information in any location of memory
   (b) The ability of the MPU to read information from any location in memory in the same amount of time as any other location
   (c) Under the control of special interface circuits an I/O device can transfer information directly to or from memory without the control of the MPU
   (d) A special memory chip designed to speed up the transfer of information between the MPU and memory by having a shorter access time

3. Unconditional MPU-initiated I/O transfer does *not* involve:
   (a) The MPU executing instructions that cause it to write data into an output device
   (b) The MPU executing instructions that cause it to read data from an input device
   (c) The MPU performing READ or WRITE operations as if the I/O device were simply a location in memory
   (d) Handshaking between the MPU and the I/O device

4. When conditional (polled) MPU-initiated I/O transfer is used, data are transferred when:
   (a) The MPU has data to send to the output device
   (b) The input device has data to send to the MPU
   (c) The MPU has read and tested status information from the I/O device to determine whether the device is ready for transfer
   (d) A READ or WRITE to the I/O device is encountered in a program

5. One of the major disadvantages of using conditional (polled) MPU-initiated I/O transfer is:
   (a) Additional hardware is required in interfacing the I/O device to the MPU
   (b) The MPU might waste a lot of time reading and testing the status of the I/O device.

(c) The MPU will waste a lot of time because it will have to jump to an interrupt service routine before I/O transfer can take place.

(d) The I/O device must always be ready to send or receive data upon MPU request.

6. Write the 68HC11 program for the flowchart of Fig. 8.4.

7. Refer to Fig. 8.3. Write a 68HC11 program that will cause the LEDs to display the 2's-complement of the data present at the switches.

8. Refer to Fig. 8.3. The switches are to represent two BCD-coded decimal digits. For example, 47_{10} is represented on the switches as 01000111. Write a program that does the following:

(a) Examines the switch data

(b) If the data are a valid BCD code, the data are displayed on the LEDs

(c) If the data are not valid BCD, the LED displays are not changed

(d) Repeats from step (a)

9. Refer to Fig. 8.7. Write a program that will take 50_{10} successive new readings of V_A and store them in RAM locations starting at address 0030.

10. Refer to Fig. 8.7. V_A is the output of a temperature-to-voltage transducer that is monitoring the temperature of an oven. The voltage is given by $V_A = 20\,\mathrm{mV/°C}$. The A/D converter has a resolution of 10 mV/step. Write a program that will do the following:

(a) Continually read the value of V_A.

(b) If the temperature drops below 80°C, a HIGH is sent to bit 5 of an output port that is at address 6C00. The other bits of the output port are to be left unchanged. This HIGH at bit 5 is used to turn on the burners to heat the oven.

(c) If the temperature is greater than 85°C, a LOW is sent to bit 5 of the output port without changing the other bits. This LOW will turn off the burners and allow the oven to cool.

Sections 8.6–8.7

11. Briefly describe the basic function of each of the ports in the 68HC11 MCU.

12. What are the functions of the ADPU and CSEL control bits of the OPTION Control register?

13. After a reset condition, what control byte might be loaded in the OPTION Control register that will cause the A/D system to be operational? What if the E-clock is less than 750 kHz?

14. A certain program sequence reads the contents of the ADCTL register. The CCF flag is set. What does that mean?

15. Write a program sequence that will condition the ADCTL register for a single conversion on channel 2.

16. Assume that a certain 68HC11-based system uses an E-clock of 2 MHz. Which will take longer to perform, an A/D conversion on a single analog input channel or an A/D conversion on four analog input channels? In either case, where are the data stored at the end of the conversion process?

17. Change the program sequence of Example 8.1(a) so that the 68HC11 MCU will be operating in the multiple-channel mode and will perform the A/D conversions on the four channels PE0–PE3.

18. Refer to Example 8.1. Change the BCLR instruction at address $C008 if the clock frequency used by the A/D system was less than 750 kHz.

19. What determines the range of the A/D converter in the 68HC11 MCU?

20. What special name is given to the smallest amount by which the analog input of an A/D converter must change in order to produce a change in its digital output?

21. Refer to Example 8.2. Assume that the input voltage of 3.701 V is being monitored by the 68HC11 MCU and that it can be off by ±5%. Write a program sequence that will continually perform an A/D conversion of the input voltage at PE2. If at any time the result of the A/D conversion is not within the allowable range (3.701 V ± 5%.), the program will store the out-of-range result in memory location C200 and then halt.

Sections 8.8–8.14

22. Which of the following tells the MPU where the ISR is located?
    (a) Reset vector   (b) $\overline{IRQ}$ input   (c) Interrupt vector   (d) PC

23. Describe the function of the interrupt disable flag. Is it possible for the programmer to instruct the MPU to ignore *all* types of interrupts?

24. After executing the ISR, how does the MPU know what address to return to in the main program?

25. Explain the differences between the $\overline{IRQ}$ and $\overline{XIRQ}$ inputs.

26. During the execution of an interrupt service routine, which one of the following is *not* true?
    (a) The MPU can always be interrupted by a nonmaskable interrupt.
    (b) The MPU cannot be interrupted by a maskable interrupt if the interrupt disable flag is a logic 1.
    (c) The MPU can be interrupted by a maskable interrupt if the interrupt disable flag is a logic 0.
    (d) The MPU cannot be interrupted during the execution of an interrupt service routine.

27. Refer to Fig. 8.14. Why is the FF used to drive the $\overline{IRQ}$ input instead of simply using the EOC output?

28. What is the function of OR gate 3 in Fig. 8.14? When is it activated?

29. Assume that the IRQE bit in the OPTION register of the 68HC11 MCU is changed from 0 to 1. Modify the A/D interface of Fig. 8.14 to take advantage of the modified $\overline{IRQ}$ input.

30. Assume that the nonmaskable interrupt flag, X, is 1 prior to the execution of the following instruction sequence. Will the MPU respond to $\overline{XIRQ}$ after this sequence is executed?

    ```
    TPA
    ANDA #$BF
    TAP
    ORA #$40
    TAP
    ```

31. Why are certain bits in some of the built-in registers of the 68HC11 MCU (e.g., IRQE in the OPTION register) time-protected?

32. Let's assume that the stack pointer register (SP) of the 68HC11 MCU is loaded with C1FF. Indicate where in the memory map each of the internal registers of the 68HC11 MPU will be saved after an interrupt.

33. Why are the I and X flags in the CCR automatically set when the 68HC11 MCU undergoes a reset condition?

34. When an interrupt is recognized by the 68HC11 MCU, why is the I flag in the CCR automatically set? When is it cleared?

35. Describe the polled-interrupt method for handling multiple interrupting devices.

36. Arrange the following list of events in the order in which they occur as the 68HC11 MPU services an interrupting device.
  (a) The return address is placed on the stack.
  (b) The MPU is directed to the ISR by the interrupt vector.
  (c) The MPU returns to the main program.
  (d) The ISR is executed.
  (e) The MPU checks the interrupt mask flag.
  (f) The return address is restored into the PC.

37. Refer to the interrupt interface of Fig. 8.17. Assume that the IRQE bit in the OPTION register is in its default condition and that the $\overline{\text{IRQ}}$ vector is C150. Write an ISR that does the following:
  (a) Determines which device has generated the interrupt.
  (b) If it is device 1, the MPU branches to a subroutine at C200 to execute instructions to service this device.
  (c) If it is device 2, the MPU executes a subroutine at C220.
  (d) If it is device 3, the MPU executes a subroutine at C240.
  (e) If more than one device has generated an interrupt at the same time, device 1 is to be given top priority and device 3 has lowest priority.
  (f) After servicing the interrupting device(s), return to the main program.
  (*Note:* You do not have to write the subroutines for the various devices.)

Section 8.15

38. Which Timer Input Capture register is used during an input capture on Port A pin PA0?

39. Write an instruction sequence that will program the TCTL2 register so that:
  (a) Port A pin PA2 is used to capture the time on rising edges only.
  (b) Port A pin PA1 is used to capture the time on falling edges only.
  (c) Port A pin PA0 is used to capture the time on any edge.

40. A programmer wants to use the Input Capture function of the 68HC11 MCU. Which 68HC11 MCU built-in register will be polled in order to accomplish a polled I/O operation? Which 68HC11 MCU built-in register must be initialized if an interrupt-driven operation is desired instead?

41. Assume that the TCTL2 register is loaded with data byte $18. What will be the function of Port A pin PA0?

42. Refer to Example 8.4. Assume that [**TCNT**] = $2000 when the MPU executes the program instruction at address C10E, and that [**TCNT**] = $2190 when the MPU executes the instruction at address C116. What is the *approximate* frequency of the signal at Port A pin PA2 if the frequency of the E-clock is 2 MHz?

43. Modify the program sequence used in Example 8.5 so that the pulse width of the signal at Port A pin PA2 is determined instead of the period.

44. How many Output Compare Registers does the 68HC11 MCU have? What are they used for?

45. What is the function of bits OMx and OLx in the TCTL1 register?

46. A certain program sequence is in a loop constantly checking the status of the OC3F flag in the TFLG1 register. What must happen before the OC3F flag is found to be set?

47. Clear the OC1F, OC3F, and OC5F flags in the TFLG1 register at $1023 by writing a program sequence that:
    (a) uses the LDAA and STAA instructions.
    (b) uses the BCLR indexed Y instruction.

48. Change the program in Example 8.6 so that the delay will be 30 ms and a waveform frequency of 5 kHz is produced at Port A pin PA6.

Section 8.16

49. *True or False?*
    (a) DMA refers to a method of data transfer between MPU and RAM.
    (b) During a DMA data transfer, the MPU has no control over the system buses.
    (c) DMA data transfer is faster than programmed data transfer.
    (d) DMA requires less circuitry than does programmed data transfer.
    (e) A DMA controller (DMAC) circuit duplicates many of the functions performed by the MPU, including the ability to execute a program.
    (f) The 16-bit DMAC's Address Register tells the DMAC the starting address in RAM where the data coming from the I/O is to be stored.
    (g) An MPU has to have a HALT input (or equivalent) if DMA is to take place.

50. The 6844 can perform three different modes of DMA transfer: Halt Burst, Halt Steal, and TSC Steal. For each statement below, indicate which of these modes is being described.
    (a) The MPU regains control of the buses after the transfer of each byte.
    (b) Complete blocks of data are transferred while the MPU is halted.
    (c) The MPU clock signal is frozen immediately, without waiting for the completion of the instruction execution.

51. In DMA transfer, the MPU does not take part in the actual transfer of data between memory and I/O, but the MPU is involved in the set up and at the conclusion of the DMA transfer. Describe the MPU's various functions both before and at the end of the DMA process.

Section 8.17

52. Refer to the circuit of figure 8.3. Assume that under the control of a computer program the conditions of the switches are read and displayed by the LEDs. Explain how the operation of the circuit would be affected for each of the following faults:

(a) The common ground connection to switches S_7–S_0 is open.

(b) The connection from NAND gate 1 to the input enable $\overline{\overline{IE}}$ of the register 74HC377 is externally grounded.

53. Refer to the circuit of Figure 8.7. What circuit faults might cause the program being executed by the 68HC11 MCU to be stuck in the "Wait loop" shown in the flowchart of Figure 8.8? Explain.

9

Input/Output Interfacing

OBJECTIVES

Upon completion of this chapter, you will be able to:

- Understand some of the requirements and limitations of interfacing digital circuits.
- Describe the asynchronous serial data communication format.
- Understand and describe the operation of the Motorola 6850 UART.
- Have an understanding of the hardware and software requirements needed to interface the 6850 UART to the 68HC11 MCU.
- Understand port D of the 68HC11 MCU as it relates to the built-in Serial Communications Interface (SCI) function.
- Describe how synchronous serial data communication differs from asynchronous.
- Cite the RS-232-C Standard (logic voltage levels and handshake signals).
- Describe the basic function of a modem.
- Understand the usefulness of parallel I/O interface chips, such as the Motorola 6821 Peripheral Interface Adapter (PIA).
- Interface an ASCII keyboard to a 68HC11 MCU-based system.
- Analyze the basic operation of a Video Display Terminal (VDT) and understand how its on-screen information is controlled by digital circuitry.

INTRODUCTION

In Chapter 8 we studied the general methods by which the MPU can communicate with peripheral I/O devices. This chapter is more specific in its presentation of the details of interfacing the MPU to various types of I/O devices. It includes examples of the hardware and software needed to produce communication between the MPU and some of the most commonly used peripheral devices. Several of the examples utilize the special interface ICs that are available. By including a great deal of the interface functions on a single chip, these ICs greatly simplify the construction of a device interface.

▶ 9.1 PRACTICAL INTERFACE CONSIDERATIONS

The I/O section of a computer is the interface between the computer and the outside world. Very often the computer and the external devices operate in very different ways. The computer is a digital electronic device that operates at a specific clock frequency and uses specific voltage levels to represent 0s and 1s. The interface circuits for I/O devices must convert data output from the computer into a form that the external devices can understand, and must convert data input from external devices into a form that the computer can understand. This conversion can sometimes be a relatively complex task.

The design of interface circuitry requires the consideration of several characteristics of signals being transmitted between the computer and I/O devices. We will discuss some of these characteristics now to see how they affect the I/O interface circuitry.

Logic Levels

External devices that are digital in nature generally use two different voltage levels to represent the two logic levels. These voltage levels, however, may be different from those used by the computer. Most MPUs use TTL (Transistor Transistor Logic) nominal voltages of 0 V and +5 V to represent logic 0 and logic 1, respectively. Some I/O devices, such as certain types of computer terminals, use much different voltage levels (for example, −12 V for a 0 and +12 V for a 1). The interface circuitry used for such devices must be able to convert or *translate* from one set of logic levels to another. An example of this conversion process is shown in Fig. 9.1.

The circuit in Fig. 9.1A uses an operational amplifier comparator to translate TTL logic levels, 0 V and +5 V, into −12 V and +12 V, respectively. The TTL levels are connected to the op amp's noninverting input and compared to a +1.5-V reference level that is connected to the inverting terminal. The reason a +1.5-V reference level is used is to allow for variations in the TTL levels which can range from 0 V to +0.8 V for a logic 0 and 2.0 V to 5.0 V for a logic 1. The circuit in Fig. 9.1B converts the −12-V and +12-V logic levels back to TTL levels using cascaded transistor inverters.

Signal Drive Capabilities (Loading)

Whenever we connect an output signal line to any loads, we must be concerned with the output's drive capabilities. We cannot interconnect two devices without first ensuring that the output device can maintain its output voltage in the proper range while satisfying the load's requirements. Most of the large-scale integration (LSI) chips used in a μC belong to the NMOS, CMOS, or HCMOS logic families. This includes the MPU, MCU, RAM and ROM chips, and special interface chips, such as a DMAC or a UART (to be covered shortly). These NMOS, CMOS, and HCMOS devices have no trouble driving NMOS, CMOS, or HCMOS loads because these loads require very little input current. This is not true, however, when it comes to driving TTL loads. In a μC, TTL and CMOS devices are often used in the address decoding circuitry and in the I/O interface circuitry. Three of the most popular TTL families are the 74LSxx (low-power Schottky), 74xx (standard TTL), and 74Sxx (high-speed Schottky). The CMOS 74HCTxx (High-Speed CMOS with TTL-compatible

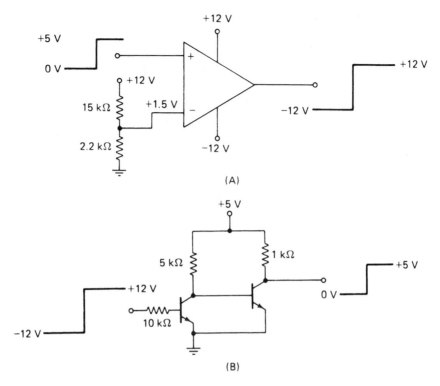

FIGURE 9.1   Circuits used to translate logic levels between two different systems.

voltages) has also become a very popular CMOS logic family because it is pin and electrically compatible with TTL. For example, a dual D-Type flip-flop chip in these four families would be designated 74LS74, 74S74, 7474, and 74HCT74, respectively.

The 74LSxx requires the least amount of input current of these three TTL families. Typically, an HCMOS output can drive ten 74LSxx inputs. In the particular case of the 68HC11 MCU any of its outputs can drive 800 HCMOS inputs. By contrast, an HCMOS output can drive only two 74xx inputs or two 74Sxx inputs. For this reason, 74LSxx devices are often used for much of a μC's external logic. However, we should mention that recent innovations in IC design have produced the 74ASxx (Advanced Schottky) and 74ALS (Advanced low-power Schottky) TTL series. The 74ASxx and 74ALSxx are becoming more prominent in applications where once the 74Sxx and 74LSxx series were the prime candidates. This is in large part due to the fact that the 74ASxx and 74ALSxx series are faster and use less power than their predecessors. If an HCMOS output has to drive more than ten loads, or if 74LSxx or 74ALSxx devices are not available, some type of buffer circuits must be used between the output and the loads. TTL inverting and noninverting buffers can provide a good interface between HCMOS outputs and TTL or other higher-power loads. These buffers can increase the current-driving capability by a factor of 10 or more.

In summary, when configuring a μC system, particular attention must be paid to the drive capabilities of the MPU and other MOS devices. The manufacturer's data sheets generally supply this information.

Driving Heavy Loads

Standard TTL buffer circuits such as the 7406 and 7407 hex* buffers can be used to drive loads requiring up to 30 V and 40 mA. Figure 9.2A shows how eight 7406 *inverting* buffers can be used to interface an MPU output port (for example, an 8-bit output register) to these loads. The 7406 has open-collector transistor outputs that can withstand up to 30 V in the OFF state and can *sink* (conduct) up to 40 mA of current in the ON state. Because

---

*"Hex" indicates six buffers on one chip.

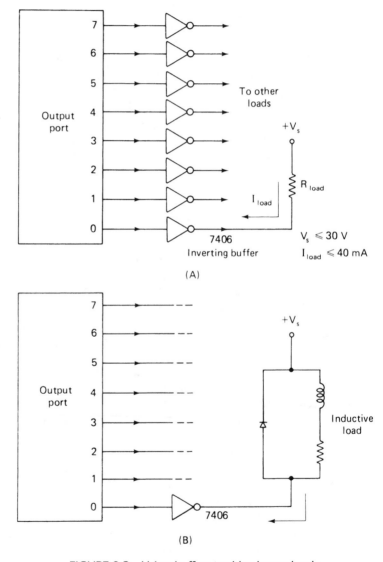

FIGURE 9.2   Using buffers to drive heavy loads.

the 7406 is an inverting buffer, a logic 0 input will turn OFF its output transistor, thereby cutting off current to the load. A logic 1 input turns ON the output transistor, providing a path to ground for the load current. The opposite logic is available using the 7407 noninverting buffer.

When used to control current to an inductive load (for example, motor, relay, or solenoid), these buffers have to be protected against the "inductive kick" that occurs when the current through the load is switched off. A diode placed across the load provides this protection by offering a path for the inductive current to decay slowly (Fig. 9.2B).

For higher-current loads, buffers are available that can handle more current. One example is the Texas Instruments 75462 dual NAND buffer chip with open collector outputs that can switch up to 300 mA of load current. For load currents greater than a few hundred milliamps, it is necessary to use a single-power transistor or a Darlington power transistor to provide both current amplification and high-current-handling capability.

Driving AC Loads

When the MPU is used to control power to an ac load operating from a 60-Hz power line, it is necessary to *isolate* the load circuit from the logic circuit output that is controlling it. In other words, a logic level from an output port must control a high-voltage, high-power device without actual electrical connections between the two devices. This is done so that the 60-Hz line voltage and its associated noise signals are not coupled back into the logic, where they could cause serious malfunctions.

The necessary isolation can be provided with either an electromagnetic relay or a solid-state relay. Some electromagnetic relays called *reed relays* are available in dual-in-line packages (DIPs) just like digital ICs. Some reed relays can be energized with 5 V and a few mA and can be easily driven from a buffer such as in Fig. 9.3. Here the relay is the inductive load, which becomes energized when the input to the 7406 is a HIGH logic level. The relay controls the set of contacts that switches ac power to the load.

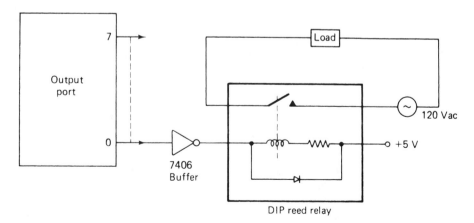

FIGURE 9.3   Reed relay used as an interface between output logic level and ac load.

A solid-state relay can also supply the necessary isolation for ac loads. Many solid-state relays use the phenomenon of *optoisolation,* where light energy is used to switch power to the load. Called *optoisolators* or *optocouplers* these devices contain an LED and a light-sensitive element, such as a photocell, photodiode, phototransistor, or light-activated SCR (LASCR), encapsulated in one package. Figure 9.4 shows several of the more common optoisolators, which are used to isolate a logic signal from a heavy load. In each case, current flows through the LED when the logic input is HIGH, causing light energy from the LED to switch power to the load. In Fig. 9.4A, a photodiode acts as the photodetector to supply current to a Darlington transistor pair. In 9.4B, the LASCR is both the photodetector and switching device. It can be used to switch ac power to the load, but it will conduct for only half of the line voltage cycle. Full-cycle ac can be applied to the load with the optoisolator in Fig. 9.4C, which employs a Triac. The cadmium sulfide (CDS) photoresistive cell becomes a low resistance when the LED conducts, allowing current to flow to the gate of the Triac during both half-cycles of the line voltage, thereby turning on the Triac.

Signal Format

The MPU handles digital, parallel data. An 8-bit MPU transmits and receives all 8 bits of data simultaneously. There are many I/O devices that do not adhere to this digital, parallel format. One class of devices uses *analog* rather than digital data. These devices require D/A and A/D converters as interfaces in order to communicate with the MPU. We saw an example of this in the preceding chapter.

Another class of I/O devices transmits and receives digital data in a *serial* format; that is, one bit at a time. These devices are often remote from the main computer with which they are communicating, so that serial transmission is less costly. Parallel transmission over long distances (that is, more than a few feet) becomes costly because of the amount of cable required, and because of the complexity of the line driver and line receiver circuits needed for transmitting and receiving pulses over long transmission lines. Printers, hard drives, modems, and video display terminals (VDTs) are examples of serial I/O devices.

In order to communicate with serial devices, the MPU's parallel data have to be converted to serial data and vice versa. There are two basic methods for performing these conversions. One is essentially a *software* conversion method that does not require any special interface chip. The other is a *hardware* approach that uses a special serial interface chip, such as the UART.

In the software method the MPU communicates with the serial device over a single line of its data bus or through a single bit of an input/output port. When the MPU is to transmit data to the device, it must execute the software that generates the serial waveform levels and time intervals. We saw how this could be done as an application of time-delay subroutines in Chapter 7. When the MPU is to receive data from a serial device, it must execute the software that continually reads the input port line and samples it at the appropriate time intervals to determine the data.

Although this method requires a minimum of external hardware, it does require a significant amount of program instructions for both the transmitting and receiving of data.

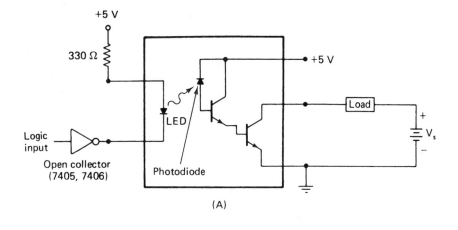

(A)

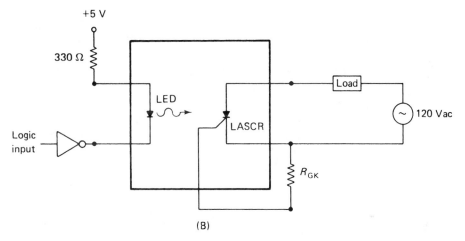

(B)

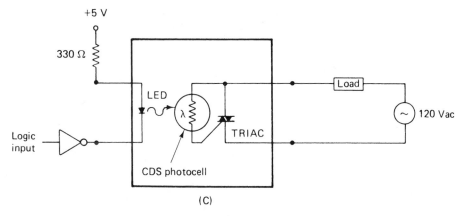

(C)

FIGURE 9.4   Three types of optoisolators.

Furthermore, with the software method, the MPU's time is occupied during the complete transmission or reception of a serial data word. With slow serial devices like a serial dot-matrix printer, the time required to receive a single ASCII-coded character could be in the milliseconds range. In many applications, this use of MPU time would be prohibitive because it may have other tasks it could be performing while the serial communication is taking place. For these reasons the hardware approach is often preferred. We will now take a detailed look at this approach.

▶ 9.2 ASYNCHRONOUS SERIAL DATA COMMUNICATION

A computer communicates with serial I/O devices using either *asynchronous* or *synchronous* communication. In asynchronous serial data communication, the transmitter can send data to the receiver at any time and there can be indeterminate time delays between one data word transmission and the next. In other words, there can be indefinite intervals when the transmitter is not transmitting data to the receiver. In addition, asynchronous communication does not require that the receiver clock be synchronized to the transmitter clock.

In synchronous communication, the transmitter is continually transmitting data to the receiver. The data words are usually sent in groups called *blocks,* and the blocks are separated by special data words called *sync characters*. These sync characters are used by the receiver to synchronize its clock signal to that of the transmitter. When the transmitter has no data to transmit, it continually transmits sync characters.

Most of the serial data communication performed by microcomputers uses asynchronous communication, so we will concentrate on this type, though we will say more about synchronous communication later.

Figure 9.5 shows the basic hardware arrangement needed for an MPU to communicate with a serial I/O device. The interface circuit performs two basic operations:

1. Takes an 8-bit parallel data word from the MPU data bus and converts it to a serial data word to be sent to the serial device

2. Takes a serial data signal from the serial device and converts it to an 8-bit parallel data word that is transferred to the MPU via the data bus

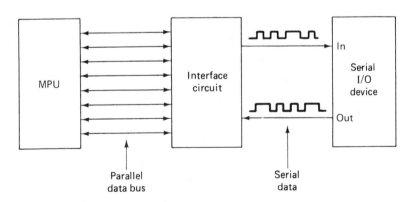

FIGURE 9.5   MPU interfaced to a serial device.

Clearly, the main function of the interface circuitry is to convert parallel data to serial data, and vice versa. Before we discuss how this can be done, we will first look at the serial data signal format.

Asynchronous Serial Signal Format

A serial data signal is divided into time intervals called *bit times* (see Fig. 9.6). During each bit time interval (T_B), the signal is either a 0 or a 1; it can change logic levels only at the start of a new bit time interval. In serial data communication, the terms *mark* and *space* are often used to represent logic 1 and 0, respectively. This terminology is a carry-over from the use of Morse code in telegraphy.

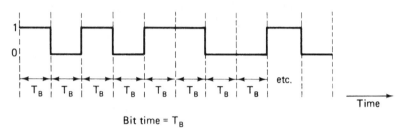

Bit time = T_B

FIGURE 9.6

When asynchronous serial data are transmitted between two devices such as an MPU and a video terminal, a standard format is used to transmit a single data word. This format (Fig. 9.7A) consists of three (or optionally, four) parts:

1. A START bit, which is always a logic 0 (that is, space).
2. Five to 8 data bits, representing the actual information being transmitted. The LSB is normally transmitted first.
3. An optional *parity* bit for error-detection capability. If the parity bit is included, either odd or even parity can be used.
4. One, 1½,* or 2 STOP bits, which are always 1s. Most frequently, there will be 2 STOP bits.

For a given system, the number of data bits, the parity-bit option, and the number of STOP bits are fixed by the design. Figure 9.7B shows an example of a serial data word that uses 7 data bits, an *even* parity bit, and 2 STOP bits. This is the format used by most terminals, where the 7 data bits are the ASCII code for the alphanumeric character being transmitted.

The complete serial data word in Fig. 9.7B begins with a START bit of 0. The signal line is assumed to be transmitting a constant HIGH level prior to the START bit. This is called *marking* or *idling*. Whenever a data word is not being transmitted, the signal line will always be *marking*. Thus, the beginning of each transmitted data word is characterized by a 1 to 0 transition when the START bit occurs. Here the START bit is followed by 7 bits of data, beginning with the LSB and ending with the MSB. Thus, the actual data being trans-

---

*One and a half STOP bits would be represented as a 1 level which lasts for 1½ bit times (i.e., 1.5 T_B).

mitted here are read as 1001011, which happens to be the ASCII code for the letter K. The data bits are followed by an *even*-parity bit; in this case it is a 0, since the 7 bits of data contain an even number of 1s. The parity bit is followed by 2 STOP bits, which are always 1s.

Asynchronous serial data transmission is often used to transmit several consecutive words from one device to another. Figure 9.8 shows the serial signal for transmitting two consecutive words. The first word is the same as that in Fig. 9.7B. After the 2 STOP bits of the first word, the START bit of the second word occurs followed by 7 data bits, a parity bit, and 2 STOP bits. The data bits of the second word are read as 1011001, which is the ASCII code for Y. When serial data words are transmitted one right after the other, the START bit of each new word immediately follows the last STOP bit of the preceding word. This represents the maximum rate of data transmission. When serial data words are not transmitted at the maximum rate, the transmitter will transmit a constant HIGH level (marking) between the STOP bits of the last word and the START bit of the next word.

The actual information that the transmitter is sending to the receiver is contained in the data bits. The data bits of each transmitted word are *framed* by the START and STOP

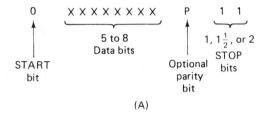

(A)

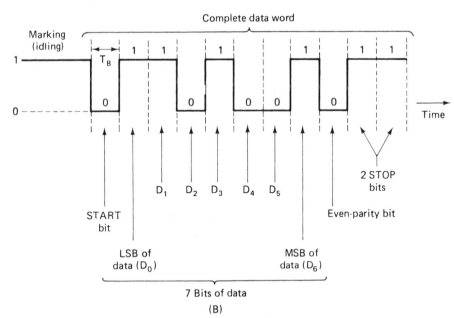

(B)

FIGURE 9.7   (A) Standard asynchronous serial data format; (B) example of a serial data word using 7 data bits, an even-parity bit, and 2 STOP bits. The data represented here are 1001011, which is the ASCII code for the letter K.

bits. The receiver uses these framing bits as a means for determining which bits are the data bits. The receiver senses the initial negative-going transition and interprets it as the START bit of the first word. It then knows that the next 7 bits of the serial signal are data bits, followed by the parity bit and STOP bits. After sensing the STOP bits, the receiver awaits the next negative-going transition, knowing that it represents the START bit of the next word. Thus, the framing bits allow the receiver to synchronize itself to the transmitter.

Baud Rate

The term *baud rate* is used to identify the rate at which the data signal is changing in a serial communications system. In general, the baud rate is given by

$$\text{Baud Rate} = \frac{1}{\text{time between transitions}} \text{ (Baud)}$$

If, for instance, the signal can change every 1 ms, the baud rate would be $\frac{1}{1 \text{ ms}} = 1000$ Baud.

    The baud rate is a measure of how frequently the serial signal may be changing, and a relative indication of the bandwidth required for a communication channel to transmit the signal faithfully. A higher baud rate means the signal is changing more rapidly and would require a greater channel bandwidth.

    In some situations, but not always, the baud rate is equivalent to the rate at which data bits are being transferred. For example, in the standard asynchronous serial data format (Fig. 9.7) a new bit is sent every bit time interval (T_B), so that data bits are being transferred at rate a given by

$$\text{Data Rate} = \frac{1}{T_B} \text{ (bits/s)}$$

If $T_B = 1$ ms, the data rate becomes 1000 bits/s. The baud rate is also 1000 because the time between signal transitions is equal to 1 ms. Thus, in this simple serial data format the baud rate and data rate are the same, although they are expressed in different units—1000 Baud versus 1000 bits/s.

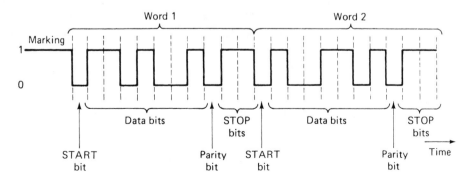

FIGURE 9.8 *Transmitted serial signal for two consecutive words.*

In more complex serial data transmission formats, a signal transition may represent 2 or more data bits. In such cases, the baud rate—the rate at which signal transitions occur—will not correspond to the data rate—the rate at which data bits are being transmitted. Common baud rates are 110, 300, 600, 1200, 2400, 4800, 9600, 14,400, and 19,200. Of course, for proper interpretation of received data, the receiver of the serial data must be operating at approximately the same baud rate as the transmitter.

EXAMPLE 9.1

A certain video display terminal is operating at a baud rate of 9600 using the standard asynchronous serial format. What is the time duration of one bit in the serial data going to and from this terminal?

Solution For this situation the baud rate and data rate are the same. Thus, since data rate = 9600 bits/s, the bit time will be 1/9600 = 104.17 μs

▶ 9.3 PARALLEL/SERIAL INTERFACE—THE UART

Now that we are familiar with the signal format used in asynchronous serial data communication, let us return to the situation of Fig. 9.5, where we found that an interface circuit is needed to convert between parallel data and serial data. Because of the extensive use of asynchronous serial transmission, several semiconductor manufacturers have developed a single-chip LSI device called a UART, or *universal asynchronous receiver transmitter*. The UART is used to implement the serial/parallel conversions required when an MPU communicates with a serial I/O device (Fig. 9.9). Although there are slight differences among various manufacturers, all UARTs have the basic elements shown: (1) a *serial* receiver (Rx), which takes a serial input and converts it to a parallel format that is stored in the receiver data register (RxDR) for eventual transmission to the MPU; (2) a *serial* transmitter (Tx), which takes a parallel data word from the transmitter data register (TxDR) and converts it to a serial format for transmission; (3) a bidirectional data bus buffer, which passes *parallel* data from the MPU to the TxDR, or from RxDR to the MPU over the system data bus; and (4) externally applied clock inputs, RxCLK and TxCLK.

When the MPU wants to transmit a data word to a serial output device, it sends the data word to the UART's transmitter data register (TxDR). Control logic in the Tx section takes this data word and frames it with a START bit, a parity bit (if used), and the desired number of STOP bits. The complete data word is then placed in a register called the *transmit* shift register (Fig. 9.10). The contents of this register are shifted right at a rate determined by the transmit data clock. This produces a serial data word (TxDATA), which is transmitted to the output device. The transmit data clock* must have a frequency equal to the desired baud rate. For example, for VDT data transmission this clock could be 9600 pulses/s, producing a baud rate of 9600 at the TxDATA output.

When a serial input device wants to send data to the MPU, it transmits a serial data word to the UART's receiver section through the RxDATA input. When control logic in the Rx section senses a HIGH-to-LOW transition on the RxDATA line, it interprets this as

---

*As we shall see, these clock frequencies are derived from TxCLK and RxCLK, respectively.

the START bit. It then shifts the remainder of the serial data word into the receiver shift register (Fig. 9.11) at a rate determined by the receiver data clock.* When the complete word is in the shift register, the data portion (D_7–D_0) is parallel-transferred to the RxDR. The MPU will eventually read the contents of the RxDR over the system data bus just like a memory location.

Clearly, for proper operation of the asynchronous serial data system of Fig. 9.9 there must be agreement between the UART and serial I/O device as to the format of the serial data; that is, baud rate, number of data bits, parity bit (odd, even, or none), and number of STOP bits. This information is usually programmed into the UART by the MPU. The UART has an internal control register, which the MPU can write into just like a memory location. The MPU's program will contain instructions that cause the MPU to send an 8-bit code to the control register over the system data bus. This code will tell the UART the characteristics of the serial data. More will be said on this when we describe the Motorola 6850 UART in detail.

---

*As we shall see, these clock frequencies are derived from TxCLK and RxCLK, respectively.

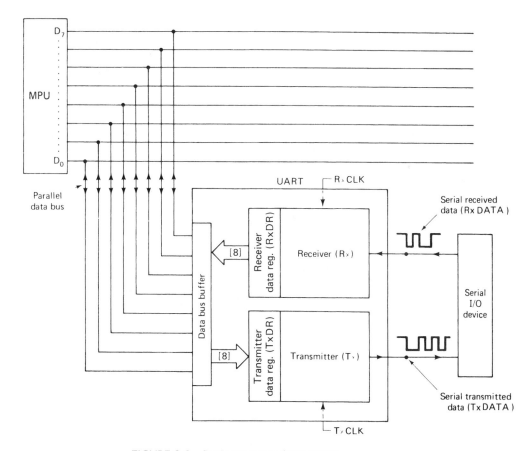

FIGURE 9.9   Basic structure for a UART.

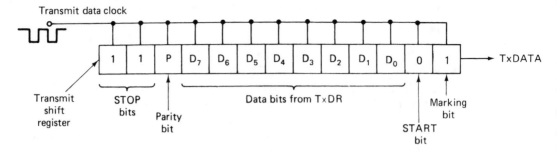

Transmit data clock

1 | 1 | P | D_7 | D_6 | D_5 | D_4 | D_3 | D_2 | D_1 | D_0 | 0 | 1 → TxDATA

Transmit shift register

STOP bits

Parity bit

Data bits from TxDR

START bit

Marking bit

FIGURE 9.10

Syncing the Receiver Section to the Serial Data

As noted earlier, the receiver initially synchronizes itself on the negative-going transition produced by the START bit. This tells the receiver that the data bits, parity bits, and STOP bits will follow. In order to facilitate its synchronization to the serial data, a UART uses an external clock that is a much higher frequency than the baud rate, usually by a factor of 16. For example, if a baud rate of 9600 is to be used, the externally applied receiver clock, RxCLK, must have a frequency of $16 \times 9600 = 153.6$ kHz. This is the actual clock frequency applied to the UART's RxCLK input pin. Since the frequency of RxCLK is 16 times the baud rate, one period of RxCLK is equal to 1/16 of 1 bit time, that is, $T_B/16$.

After it senses the first negative-going transition, the receiver waits for eight periods of RxCLK and then samples the serial input (Fig. 9.12) to see if it is still LOW. This ensures the receiver that this is a START bit and not a glitch on the serial data line. Note that

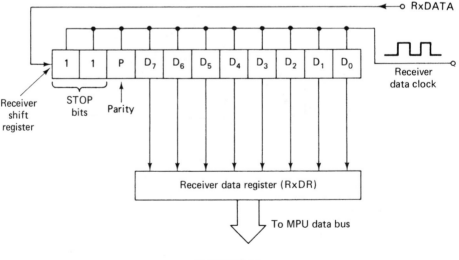

RxDATA

1 | 1 | P | D_7 | D_6 | D_5 | D_4 | D_3 | D_2 | D_1 | D_0

Receiver data clock

Receiver shift register

STOP bits

Parity

Receiver data register (RxDR)

To MPU data bus

FIGURE 9.11

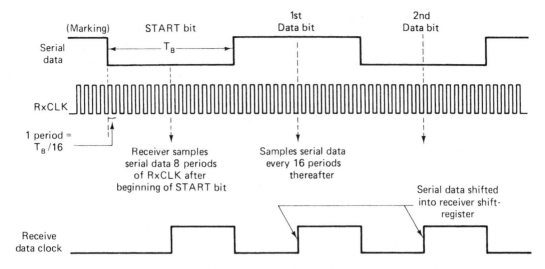

FIGURE 9.12   Receiver samples serial data using RxCLK, which has a frequency that is 16 times the baud rate.

this sample is taken at approximately* the middle of the START bit interval, since eight RxCLK pulses will occur in about ½ of 1 bit time. After sampling the START bit, the receiver samples the serial data at intervals of 16 RxCLK periods (approximately 1 bit time) providing samples that are located quite close to the middle of each bit time. Each of these samples is then shifted into the receiver shift register on the rising edge of the receive data clock, which is derived by putting RxCLK through a divide-by-16 counter (MOD-16). Note that this makes the frequency of the receive data clock equal to the baud rate.

Once the complete serial data word has been shifted into the receiver shift register, circuitry in the UART automatically checks to see that the required number of STOP bits are 1s. If any of the STOP bits is 0, a *Framing Error* flag is set. This flag is part of the UART's internal status register, which the MPU can read just like a memory location. As part of its routine for reading a received word from the UART, the MPU can read the UART's status register; if it sees that a framing error has occurred, it will take appropriate action.

The UART circuitry also checks the parity of the data portion of the received word if a parity bit has been included in the format. For example, if even parity is being used, the UART circuitry determines whether the received data (including parity bit) contains an even number of 1s. If it does not, a *Parity Error* flag is set. This flag is also part of the status register, which the MPU checks as part of its routine. If the MPU sees that a parity error has occurred, it can then take appropriate action.

As shown in Fig. 9.11, the data bits are transferred in parallel to the RxDR, which holds the data for the MPU. Once the transfer into RxDR has taken place, the receiver begins looking for the next serial data word from the serial input device and shifts it into the receiver shift register. This second word will not be transferred into the RxDR, however, until the MPU reads the previous word stored there. Thus, it is possible that a third serial

*It is approximate because RxCLK is a clock signal generated independent of the clock signal used by the device that is sending the serial data.

data word could be shifted into the receiver shift register before the second word was transferred to the RxDR, thereby effectively losing the second word. When this occurs, the UART will set an *Overrun Error* flag in its status register, which tells the MPU, upon reading the status register, that it has missed a data word. It should be realized that overrun errors can be easily avoided by ensuring that the MPU reads the data from the RxDR within the time it takes for a new serial data word to be completely shifted into the receiver. This time, of course, will depend on the baud rate being used.

▶ 9.4 MOTOROLA 6850 UART (ACIA)

We now have enough background to look closely at a specific IC UART, the MC6850, which Motorola calls an Asynchronous Communications Interface Adapter (ACIA). A thorough examination of this particular chip will illustrate the concepts and operations involved in using other UARTs and other types of interface chips. Figure 9.13 shows a block diagram of the MC6850.

In the block diagram there are six major functions, which are shown blocked off:

1. CHIP SELECT and READ/WRITE control
2. Data bus buffers
3. Transmit data register (TxDR) and transmit shift register (TSR)
4. Receive data register (RxDR) and receive shift register (RSR)
5. Status register
6. Control register

The TxDR and TSR, RxDR and RSR, and the data bus buffer were explained previously, so we will concentrate on the other functions in some detail.

CHIP SELECT and READ/WRITE Control Function

The MPU can be operating with many input/output devices. The three CHIP SELECT inputs (CS0, CS1, $\overline{CS2}$) are input lines used to address a particular UART so that the MPU can communicate with the serial I/O device that the UART is interfacing. The UART is selected when CS0 and CS1 are HIGH and $\overline{CS2}$ is LOW. Once the UART is selected, the MPU can perform one of four operations:

1. *Read the Status Register.* Information concerning the status of the UART's TxDR, RxDR, and error logic is stored in the status register. The MPU obtains this information when a read status register operation is performed.
2. *Read the RxDR.* When the UART has received a serial word from an input device, the MPU can acquire these data by performing a read RxDR operation.
3. *Write to the Control Register.* The UART's control register is an 8-bit write-only register whose contents determine such things as clock-frequency divider ratio, word size, number of stop bits, and parity. These characteristics are controlled by the MPU, which writes an 8-bit control word into the control register.

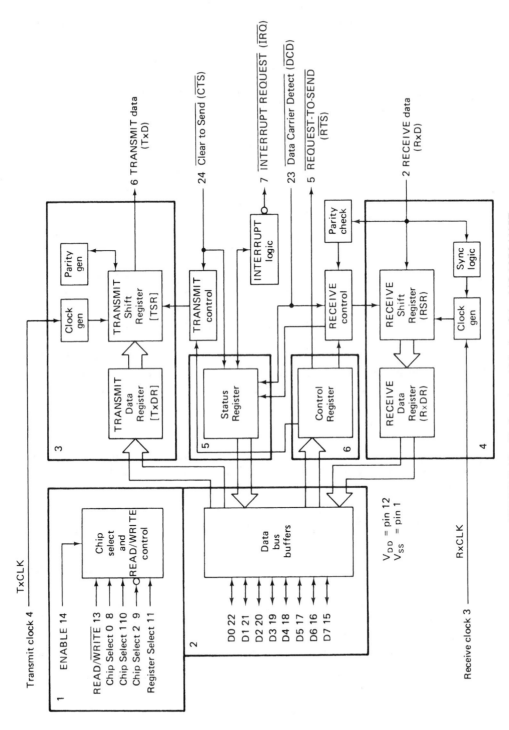

FIGURE 9.13   Six functional blocks of the MC 6850 UART.

447

4. *Write to the TxDR.* When the MPU wants to send a data word to the output device, it does so by performing a write data into TxDR operation. The UART then transmits the data serially to the device.

These four operations involve the MPU reading or writing the contents of the RxDR, TxDR, status, or control registers. The actual operation being performed at any time is determined by the levels on the CHIP SELECT, REGISTER SELECT (RS), R/$\overline{\text{W}}$, and ENABLE inputs according to the following table:

Operation	CS0	CS1	$\overline{CS2}$	RS	R/$\overline{W}$	Enable
Read Status register	1	1	0	0	1	1
Write Control register	1	1	0	0	0	1
Read RxDR	1	1	0	1	1	1
Write TxDR	1	1	0	1	0	1

For all four operations the UART chip must be selected (CS0 = CS1 = 1, $\overline{\text{CS2}}$ = 0). These inputs are normally derived from address decoding circuitry. In addition the ENABLE line must be HIGH. This input is usually connected to the E-clock signal so that all data transfers occur when E is high. Recall that this is the time when the data are stable on the data bus.

The R/$\overline{\text{W}}$ input must be driven HIGH for either of the read operations and the RS input selects which register (status or RxDR) will be read. Similarly, R/$\overline{\text{W}}$ has to be LOW for either write operation, and RS selects either the TxDR or the control register to be written into.

The Status Register

The 6850's status register is an 8-bit read-only register from which the MPU can read information concerning the status of the UART. The functions of the different bits are as follows:

Status Register

SR7	SR6	SR5	SR4	SR3	SR2	SR1	SR0
Interrupt Request (IRQ)	Parity Error (PE)	Receiver Overrun (OVRN)	Framing Error (FE)	$\overline{\text{Clear to Send}}$	$\overline{\text{Data Carrier Detect}}$	Transmit Data Register Empty (TDRE)	Receive Data Register Full (RDRF)

Modem Status (spanning SR3–SR2)

Receive Data Register Full (RDRF) This bit is automatically set HIGH when the receive shift register transfers its contents to the RxDR. This bit is cleared after the MPU reads the contents of the RxDR, indicating that the contents of RxDR are no longer current.

Transmit Data Register Empty (TDRE) This bit is set HIGH when the TxDR contents have been transferred to the transmit SHIFT register. A LOW indicates that the TxDR is still full and the MPU should not transfer another word to the UART at this time for transmission to the output device.

TABLE 9.1

CR1	CR0	Clock divide ratio
0	0	÷ 1
0	1	÷ 16
1	0	÷ 64
1	1	Master reset for UART

Data Carrier Detect ($\overline{\text{DCD}}$) and Clear to Send ($\overline{\text{CTS}}$)   Special status bits used in conjunction with modem* transmission of data. We will not consider these until our discussion of modems.

Framing Error (FE), Receiver Overrun (OVRN), and Parity Error (PE)   These bits have been discussed in the previous general discussion of UARTs. Each one indicates an error condition in the received serial data.

Interrupt Request (IRQ)   This bit always indicates the status of the UART's $\overline{\text{IRQ}}$ output line. Anytime the $\overline{\text{IRQ}}$ output is LOW, the IRQ bit of the status register will be HIGH, and vice versa. (This is useful when a number of devices are connected to the MPU's interrupt input. When interrupted, the MPU can read the UART's status register to see if the IRQ bit is 1. This will indicate that the UART's $\overline{\text{IRQ}}$ output line is 0 and the UART is the device generating the interrupt signal to the MPU.) The IRQ bit is cleared whenever the MPU performs a READ RxDR or a WRITE TxDR operation.

The Control Register

The functions of the 8 bits of this register are given below. The MPU will write the appropriate word into this register to define the characteristics of the serial data transmission.

CR7	CR6	CR5	CR4	CR3	CR2	CR1	CR0

| Receive Interrupt Enable | Transmitter Control bits | | Word length, parity, and STOP bits select | | | Clock Divide Select and Master reset | |

Clock Divide Select Bits (CR1, CR0)   Recall from Figs. 9.11 and 9.12 that there is a specific ratio between RxCLK, the clock signal applied to the UART's RxCLK input, and the receive data clock, which is used to shift the received data into the UART. This ratio can be selected as 1, 16, or 64 using the CR1, CR0 bits of the control register, as shown in Table 9.1.

It is important to realize that the receive data clock = RxCLK/clock divide ratio, and this has to equal the baud rate of the serial data. For example, if the baud rate is to be 9600

---

*A *modem* is a device used to access a computer from a remote location over telephone lines. It converts digital information to be transmitted into a series of audio tones. It also converts received audio tones into their corresponding digital codes. A modem is used on both ends of a communication link.

TABLE 9.2

CR4	CR3	CR2	Data bits	Function parity	STOP bits
0	0	0	7	Even	2
0	0	1	7	Odd	2
0	1	0	7	Even	1
0	1	1	7	Odd	1
1	0	0	8	None	2
1	0	1	8	None	1
1	1	0	8	Even	1
1	1	1	8	Odd	1

and a clock divide ratio of 16 is to be used, the frequency of RxCLK must be $9600 \times 16 = 153.6$ kHz. This is the frequency that has to be applied to the UART's RxCLK input. The same holds true for the TxCLK input.

Word Select Bits (CR4, CR3, CR2) These bits control word-length, parity and the number of STOP bits. Table 9.2 shows how these functions are determined.

Transmitter Control Bits (CR6, CR5) The most significant states for our purposes are shown in Table 9.3. $\overline{\text{RTS}}$ is a UART output signal that can be used for any purpose, but its principal function is as a modem handshake signal.

It can be set or cleared by the MPU via the UART's control register. When the transmit interrupt is enabled, the UART's $\overline{\text{IRQ}}$ output line will go LOW whenever the TDRE status bit goes HIGH, indicating that the TxDR is empty and is ready for a word from the MPU. This $\overline{\text{IRQ}}$ output can be used to interrupt the MPU whenever TDRE = 1.

Receive Interrupt Enable Bit (CR7) A HIGH on this bit enables the receive interrupt so that the UART's $\overline{\text{IRQ}}$ line will go LOW whenever the RDRF status bit goes HIGH, indicating that the UART has a data word for the MPU. The $\overline{\text{IRQ}}$ output can be used to interrupt the MPU whenever RDRF = 1.

If both transmit interrupt and receive interrupt are enabled (CR6 = 0, CR5 = 1, CR7 = 1) and $\overline{\text{IRQ}}$ is connected to the MPU's interrupt line, the MPU will read the status register as part of its interrupt service routine to determine whether TDRE = 1 or RDRF = 1 caused the interrupt. If neither interrupt is enabled or if $\overline{\text{IRQ}}$ is not connected to the MPU, the UART cannot interrupt the MPU. The MPU would then communicate with the UART using the conditional (polled) I/O technique.

TABLE 9.3

CR6	CR5	Function
0	0	$\overline{\text{RTS}}$ = 0; transmit interrupt Disabled
0	1	$\overline{\text{RTS}}$ = 0; transmit interrupt Enabled
1	0	$\overline{\text{RTS}}$ = 1; transmit interrupt Disabled

▶ 9.5 INTERFACING THE 6850 TO THE 68HC11 MPU

Figure 9.14 shows the circuit diagram for interfacing the 6850 UART to a 68HC11 MCU (configured in the expanded mode) for communication with a serial I/O device such as a Video Display Terminal (VDT). The circuit is set for both interrupt operation and conditional transfer. If interrupt operation is not going to be used, the $\overline{IRQ}$ connection can be eliminated or the MPU can disable the UART interrupts via bits CR7, CR6, and CR5 of the control register.

With the address decoding circuitry shown, the UART is assigned addresses AFxx. Any address AF00–AFFF will produce a LOW on the $\overline{CS2}$ input, thereby selecting the UART chip, since CS0 and CS1 are kept permanently HIGH. Note that the RS input is connected to the A_0 address line. Thus, by using addresses AF00 and AF01, the MPU can select the UART and control the RS input.

A 153.6 kHz clock signal is externally generated and applied to both the TxCLK and RxCLK inputs. This signal might be obtained from a crystal oscillator and frequency divider. If we assume that a UART clock ratio of 16 is being used, this 153.6 kHz clock input will produce a data transmission rate of 9600 bits/s. This is one of the standard baud rates used by VDTs. In actual practice, a frequency of 153.6 kHz $\pm$ 5% will be sufficient to guarantee reliable data transmission.

There are *four* basic operations that the MPU can perform on the UART: writing into the control register, reading the status register, writing into the TxDR, and reading the RxDR. These operations involve the MPU either writing a word into or reading a word from one of the UART registers. The three-byte instructions for each of these operations are illustrated using 68HC11 mnemonics and using accumulator A as the MPU source or destination register.

> STAA \$AF00 — write into control register
> LDAA \$AF00 — read status register
> STAA \$AF01 — write into TxDR
> LDAA \$AF01 — read RxDR

Note that address AF00 is used for both the control register and the status register. This is no problem because the R/$\overline{W}$ line determines which one is being accessed. Similarly, address AF01 is used for both the TxDR and RxDR, and the R/$\overline{W}$ line determines which of the two is selected.

MPU Transmitting

These four instructions are used whenever the MPU communicates with the serial I/O device via the UART. Let us examine the sequence of steps that the MPU must perform when it wants to transmit a single data word or a block of data to a serial output device. Refer to the flowchart shown in Fig. 9.15. Before any communication can take place, the MPU has to *initialize* the UART by sending a control word to its control register. This serves to set up the UART for the proper baud rate, number of data bits, parity, and number of STOP bits. After this is done, the MPU will execute some intermediate program of instructions. When it has some data ready to transmit, the MPU first reads the status register and checks

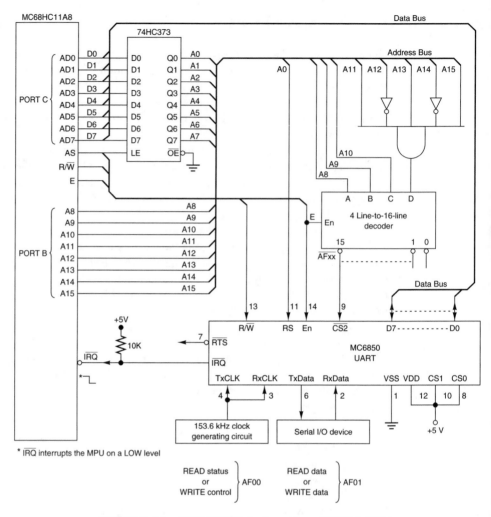

FIGURE 9.14   6850 UART interfaced to a 68HC11 MCU.

bit SR1 to see if TDRE = 1. With TDRE = 0, the UART is not ready for data and the MPU loops back to read the status register again. If TDRE = 1, the UART is ready for the next data word. The MPU then proceeds to write a data word into the TxDR to be eventually transmitted serially to the output device. This same sequence of operations is repeated until the MPU has written all its data into the output device.

MPU Receiving

Next, let us take a look at the steps involved in the MPU *receiving* data from a serial input device. For efficient use of the MPU's time, interrupt operation would be preferable. If interrupt operation is to be used for receiving data, the UART has to have its receive interrupt enabled (CR7 = 1) during the initialization process. Thereafter, whenever the UART

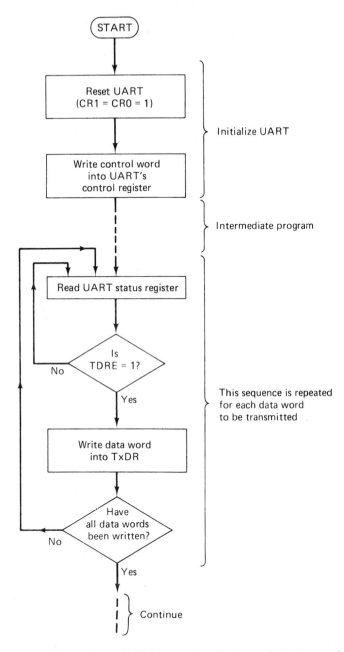

FIGURE 9.15 Flowchart of MPU operations for transmission to a serial output device.

has a data word ready (RDRF = 1), its $\overline{\text{IRQ}}$ output will go LOW, interrupting the MPU. Figure 9.16 is the flowchart for a typical interrupt service routine (ISR), which the MPU will execute in response to the UART's $\overline{\text{IRQ}}$ signal. Essentially, the MPU reads the status register and checks bits SR6, SR5, and SR4 for any error indication. If an error is indicated, the MPU branches to an error subroutine to take appropriate action. Otherwise, it reads the data from the RxDR into the accumulator. It then returns to the program it was executing prior to being interrupted. When the UART has a new data word ready, this process is repeated.

It should be pointed out here that interrupt operation is not necessary if the MPU has nothing else to do while it is waiting for data from the UART. On the other hand, interrupt operation is preferable if the MPU has other functions it can perform while waiting for data. This is especially significant when the data are coming from the input device at a very slow rate. A prime example is an MPU that is waiting for data coming in from an operator at a video terminal.

Communications Software

We have seen how the UART is interfaced to the 68HC11 MCU (Fig. 9.14) and have outlined the software needed to control the serial communications between the MPU

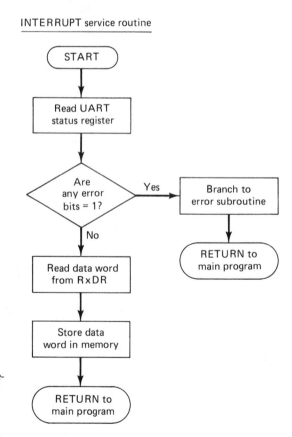

INTERRUPT service routine

FIGURE 9.16 Flowchart of MPU ISR executed in response to an interrupt signal from UART; it is assumed that the UART has been previously initialized with the Receiver Interrupt **enabled** and the Transmit Interrupt **disabled.**

and I/O device via the UART. Now we will take a more detailed look at the software. Specifically, we will examine typical examples of an *initialization routine*, a *transmission subroutine*, and a *receiver interrupt service routine*, based on the flowcharts of Figs. 9.15 and 9.16.

Initialization Routine   The instruction sequence shown below is used to initialize the UART for the desired data format, baud rate, and interrupt operation. This sequence would normally be part of the MPU's power-on initialization sequence and would be executed only once when power is first applied to the MPU.

Initialization Routine

Address	Label	Instruction code	Mnemonic	Comments
F000	INIT	86	LDAA #$03	; [ACCA] = reset code
F001		03		
F002		B7	STAA $AF00	; Write reset code to UART
F003		AF		; control register
F004		00		
F005		86	LDAA #$85	; [ACCA] = control word for UART
F006		85		
F007		B7	STAA $AF00	; Write control word to UART
F008		AF		; control register
F009		00		

EXAMPLE 9.2 _____

Describe the functions performed by this initialization sequence.

Solution   This instruction sequence performs two functions. It resets the UART and it sets up the UART control register. The reset function is accomplished by writing 1s into bits CR1 and CR0 of the control register (Table 9.1). The first two instructions perform this operation.

The third and fourth instructions write a control word into the UART control register. The control word is $85_{16} = 10000101_2$. Thus, we have

CR7	CR6	CR5	CR4	CR3	CR2	CR1	CR0
1	0	0	0	0	1	0	1

From Table 9.1 we see that CR1 = 0, CR0 = 1 specifies a divide-by-16 clock divide ratio. This tells the UART to divide the incoming TxCLK and RxCLK frequencies by 16 to determine the baud rate. If we use TxCLK = RxCLK = 153.6 kHz as in Fig. 9.14, the baud rate becomes 153.6 kHz/16 = 9600 Baud.

From Table 9.2, we see that CR4 = CR3 = 0, CR2 = 1 specifies a data format of 7 data bits followed by an odd parity bit and 2 stop bits.

Table 9.3 shows that CR6 = CR5 = 0 specifies that the $\overline{\text{RTS}}$ output will be LOW, and that the transmit interrupt function is *disabled*. Thus, the UART will not generate an interrupt signal at $\overline{\text{IRQ}}$ when the transmit data register is empty (TDRE = 1).

With CR7 = 1, the receiver interrupt function is enabled. Thus, the UART will drive $\overline{\text{IRQ}}$ LOW whenever the receiver data register is full (RDRF = 1), indicating that the UART has a data word for the MPU. The LOW at $\overline{\text{IRQ}}$ will interrupt the MPU if the MPU's I flag has been previously cleared.

Transmission Subroutine   The following subroutine can be used to send a single data word from the MPU to the UART for transmission to the serial output device. It is assumed that the data word is in ACCB. This subroutine uses the conditional I/O transfer logic of Fig. 9.15, where the MPU repetitively checks the TDRE bit of the UART's status register. Since ACCA is used by the subroutine, [ACCA] is saved on the stack at the start of the subroutine and then restored at the end. This will ensure that [ACCA] will be unchanged when the MPU returns to the main program.

Data Transmission Subroutine

Address	Label	Instruction code	Mnemonic	Comments
F100	TRANS	36	PSHA	; Save [ACCA] on stack
F101	CHKS	B6	LDAA $AF00	; Load ACCA from UART status
F102		AF		; register
F103		00		; Control register
F104		84	ANDA #$02	; Isolate TDRE by masking bit 2
F105		02		
F106		27	BEQ $F101	; If TDRE = 0, branch to CHKS and
F107		F9		; recheck
F108		F7	STAB $AF01	; If TDRE = 1, send data to
F109		AF		; UART's transmit data register
F10A		01		
F10B		32	PULA	; Restore [ACCA]
F10C	RET	39	RTS	; Return to main program

EXAMPLE 9.3

The ASCII codes 4F, 4C, 4C, 45, 48 are stored in memory locations 0051 to 0055, respectively. The characters represented by these codes spell out a five-letter word. Use the subroutine above and write a program that sends these codes to a UART for transmission to a VDT. Assume that the UART has been initialized.

What will be displayed on the VDT?

Solution   The program below uses the indexed address mode to sequentially transmit the ASCII-coded data to the UART. The data from address 0055 are transmitted first, so that the ASCII codes reach the printer in the following order: 48, 45, 4C, 4C, 4F. These codes spell out the word "HELLO."

Address	Label	Instruction code	Mnemonic	Comments
0500	START	CE	LDX #$0005	; [X] = 0005
0501		00		
0502		05		
0503	GTDATA	E6	LDAB $50, X	; Load ACCB with ASCII data from
0504		50		; [X] + 50
0505		BD	JSR $F100	; Jump to transmit subroutine
0506		F1		
0507		00		
0508		09	DEX	; Decrement [X]
0509		26	BNE $0503	; If ≠ 0, go back to GTDATA to
050A		F8		; get next data
050B	END	3E	WAI	; If = 0, transmission is complete

Receiver Interrupt Service Routine The instruction sequence shown below is the *interrupt service routine* (ISR) that the MPU will execute in response to an active $\overline{\text{IRQ}}$ signal from the UART. Recall that the UART receiver interrupt was enabled during the initialization routine.

Receiver Interrupt Service Routine[a]

Address	Label	Instruction code	Mnemonic	Comments
0F00	ISR	B6	LDAA $AF00	; Load ACCA from UART status
0F01		AF		; register
0F02		00		
0F03		84	ANDA #$70	; Mask three error status bits
0F04		70		
0F05		27	BEQ $0F0B	; If all = 0, branch to GETDAT to
0F06		04		; get data
0F07		BD	JSR $0FC0	; If not, jump to ERROR
0F08		OF		; subroutine at $0FC0 to
0F09		C0		; determine error
0F0A		3B	RTI	; Return to main program
0F0B	GETDAT	B6	LDAA $AF01	; Transfer data from UART's
0F0C		AF		; receiver data register to ACCA
0F0D		01		
0F0E		B7	STAA $C200	; Store data in memory for later
0F0F		C2		; processing
0F10		00		
0F11	RET	3B	RTI	; Return to main program

[a]This ISR follows the flowchart of Fig. 9.16. It does not contain specific instructions for saving the contents of the 68HC11 MPU's registers. Recall from our study of the 68HC11 interrupt operation that the MPU will save these on the stack automatically in response to an interrupt, and will restore them when it executes RTI.

▶ 9.6 PORT D OF THE 68HC11 MCU—SERIAL COMMUNICATIONS INTERFACE (SCI)

As shown in the block diagram of Fig. 8.9 or Appendix B, port D of the 68HC11 MCU is divided into two different sections, the Serial Peripheral Interface (SPI) and the Serial Communications Interface (SCI). We will not discuss the SPI section, however, we will focus on the operation of the SCI section since it uses the 68HC11 MCU built-in UART. This built-in UART has basically the same operational requirements as the 6850 UART introduced in previous sections. The following discussion will show how port D of the 68HC11 MCU can be used to transmit data to and receive data from an I/O device without the need of any external circuitry. The SCI is connected to the outside world via two port D pins, PD0 (RxD) and PD1 (TxD). In addition, there are eight built-in registers that are associated with the operation of the SCI. We will address the function of those bits in these eight registers that pertain only to the operation of the SCI.

7	6	5	4	3	2	1	0	
		Bit 5	Bit 4	Bit 3	Bit 2	**Bit 1**	**Bit 0**	**PORTD**

At reset   0   0   0   0   0   0   0   0   **$1008**

References   PD1/TxD PD0/RxD

7	6	5	4	3	2	1	0	
TIE	TCIE	RIE	ILIE	**TE**	**RE**	RWU	SBK	**SCCR2**

At reset   0   0   0   0   0   0   0   0   **$102D**

Port D of the 68HC11 MCU is a 6-bit bidirectional data port (PD0–PD5).* Bits 0 and 1 of PORTD register can be used as general purpose I/O port pins or they can be used in conjunction with the SCI system. If these bits are used as general-purpose I/O port pins, then the SCI system must be turned off. The SCI system is turned off by clearing the TE (Transmit Enable) and RE (Receive Enable) bits in register SCCR2 (SCI Control Register 2) at memory location $102D.* These bits are automatically cleared upon a reset condition of the 68HC11 MCU. Consequently, at reset the SCI system is automatically turned off, and port D pins PD0 and PD1 become general-purpose *input* pins. However, when the SCI system is turned on by setting bits TE and RE in the SCCR2 register, port D pin PD1 (TxD) is automatically conditioned to be an output pin. In other words, when the SCI system is turned on, port D pin PD0 (RxD) is an input pin and port D pin PD1 (TxD) is an output pin. For now, let's assume that the SCI system is disabled (TE = RE = 0) and that we want port D pins PD0 and PD1 to be general-purpose I/O pins.

7	6	5	4	3	2	1	0	
0	0	DDRD5	DDRD4	DDRD3	DDRD2	**DDRD1**	**DDRD0**	**DDRD**

At reset   0   0   0   0   0   0   0   0   **$1009**

---

*A complete list of the 68HC11 MCU built-in control registers can be found in Appendix C.

First, we must determine which direction we want data to flow through the PD0 and PD1 I/O pins. This is accomplished by writing to the bit positions DDRD0 and DDRD1 in the DDRD (Data Direction Register for port D) register at $1009.* A *zero* written into either of these bit locations will program the corresponding port D pin as an input pin. A *one* written into either of these bit locations will program the corresponding pin as an output pin.

7	6	5	4	3	2	1	0	
SPIE	SPE	DWOM	MSTR	CPOL	CPHA	SPR1	SPR0	**SPCR**

At reset   0   0   0   0   0   1   U   U   **$1028**

Bit 5 of the SPCR (SPI Control Register) register is the only bit that affects port D. If bit DWOM (port D Wire-Or Mode) is 0, port D outputs are normal. If DWOM is 1, port D outputs are in an open-drain configuration and consequently can be wire-ored (connected together). The default condition for this bit is 0.

EXAMPLE 9.4

Port D pins PD0 and PD1 are automatically programmed as input port pins upon a reset condition. Write a program sequence that will program the 68HC11 MCU port D pins PD0 and PD1 as general-purpose output port pins.

Solution   One possibility.

Address	Label	Instruction code	Mnemonic	Comments
C000	START	CE	LDX #$1000	; Load the X register with $1000
C001		10		; so that it can be used
C002		00		; by indexed X instructions
C003		1D	BCLR $2D, X $0C	; Disable the SCI by clearing
C004		2D		; the TE and RE bits in the
C005		0C		; SCCR2 register
C006		1C	BSET $09, X $03	; Make PD0 and PD1 output ports
C007		09		; by setting bits 0 and 1 in the
C008		03		; DDRD register

EXAMPLE 9.5

Assume that the 68HC11 MCU has just come out of a reset condition. Change the program sequence of Example 9.4, if the SCI system of the 68HC11 MCU is to be used for asynchronous serial data communication between the MCU and an I/O device.

---

*A complete list of the 68HC11 MCU built-in control registers can be found in Appendix C.

Solution   One possibility.

Address	Label	Instruction code	Mnemonic	Comments
C000	START	CE	LDX #$1000	; Load the X register with $1000
C001		10		; so that it can be used
C002		00		; by indexed X instructions
C003		1C	BSET $2D, X $0C	; Enable the SCI system by
C004		2D		; setting the TE and RE bits in
C005		0C		; the SCCR2 register

Other Bits in the SCCR2 Register

The SCI system can perform either interrupt or conditional I/O transfers. In interrupt I/O transfers the SCI system uses the interrupt vector (FFD6, FFD7) to point to the memory location where the first instruction of the ISR for the SCI system is located. Once in the ISR, the user can determine via a program sequence which bit in the Serial Communications Status Register (SCSR) caused the interrupt, and then take the appropriate steps to service that interrupt. The following is a summary of control bits in the SCCR2 register that can be used during an interrupt I/O data transfer by the SCI system.

TIE (Transmit Interrupt Enable)   When this bit is set, an interrupt is automatically generated whenever the TDRE bit in the SCSR register is set.

TCIE (Transmit Complete Interrupt Enable)   When this bit is set, an interrupt is automatically generated whenever the Transmit Complete bit (TC) in the SCSR register is set.

RIE (Receiver Interrupt Enable)   When this bit is set, an interrupt is automatically generated whenever the RDRF bit in register SCSR is set.

ILIE (Idle Line Interrupt Enable)   When this bit is set, an interrupt is automatically generated whenever the IDLE bit in register SCSR is set.

Serial Communications Status Register (SCSR)

7	6	5	4	3	2	1	0	
TDRE	**TC**	**RDRF**	**IDLE**	**OR**	**NF**	**FE**	**0**	SCSR

| At reset | 1 | 1 | 0 | 0 | 0 | 0 | 0 | 0 | **$102E** |

The SCSR* register has two bits that are used by the transmitter and five bits that are used by the receiver. During the transmission of a character, bits TDRE (Transmit Data Register Empty) and TC (Transmit Complete) may be affected. If the TDRE bit in the SCSR register is clear it indicates that the previous character written to the TDR

---

*A complete list of the 68HC11 MCU built-in control registers can be found in Appendix C.

(Transmit Data Register) at memory location $102F has not yet been transferred to the transmit shift register. If the TDRE bit is set, it indicates that the previous character has already been transferred out of the TDR register and into the transmit shift register, and that a new character can now be written into the TDR register. When the SCI system is transmitting characters, the TDRE bit can be read to determine whether or not the TDR register can accept a new character. The TC flag is set when no data is being transmitted and is clear when the transmitter is busy sending a character to an I/O device. Upon a RESET condition, both TDRE and TC are set to 1 to indicate that there is no transmission taking place, and that the TDR at $102F is ready for the next character.

During the receive mode of the SCI system, the RDRF (Receive Data Register Full) bit is set whenever a complete character has been received into the RDR (Receive Data Register) at location $102F. At RESET, RDRF = 0 to indicate that no character is in the RDR.

Other Bits in the SCSR

NF (Noise Flag)   This bit is set whenever the receiver circuitry has detected noise during the reception of the character currently in the RDR.

IDLE (ID1e LinE Detected Flag)   When this bit is set, it indicates that the receiver data line has become idle; that is, it is in the logic 1 state for two bit times longer than the duration of a data word.

OR (Overrun Error Flag)   When this bit is set, it indicates that a new character has been received from an input device before the previously received character has been read from the RDR.

FE (Framing Error Flag)   When this bit is set, it indicates that a framing error was detected for the received character currently in the RDR.

Serial Communications Data Register (SCDR)

7	6	5	4	3	2	1	0	SCDR $102F
R7	R6	R5	R4	R3	R2	R1	R0	**RDR (READ)**
T7	T6	T5	T4	T3	T2	T1	T0	**TDR (WRITE)**

At reset U   U   U   U   U   U   U   U

The SCDR* register at memory location $102F acts as two separate registers. When the SCDR register is read, the contents of the RDR (Receive Data Register) are accessed. When the SCDR register is written into, the TDR (Transmit Data Register) is accessed. The TDRE flag is cleared by reading the SCSR register *followed* by a write to the SCDR. Likewise, the RDRF flag is cleared by reading the SCSR register *followed* by a read of the

---

*A complete list of the 68HC11 MCU built-in control registers can be found in Appendix C.

TABLE 9.4   Baud-Rate Prescale Selects

SCP1	SCP0	Division factor	Crystal frequency				
			2^{33} Hz	8 MHz	4.9152 MHz	4 MHz	3.6864 MHz
			Highest baud rate				
0	0	1	**131.072K Baud**	125.0K Baud	**76.80K Baud**	62.50K Baud	47.60K Baud
0	1	3	43.691K Baud	41.667K Baud	25.60K Baud	20.833K Baud	**19.20K Baud**
1	0	4	**32.768K Baud**	31.250K Baud	**19.20K Baud**	15.625K Baud	14.40K Baud
1	1	13	10.082K Baud	**9600 Baud**	5.908K Baud	**4800 Baud**	4431K Baud
			2.1 MHz	2 MHz	1.2288 MHz	1 MHz	921.6 KHz
			Bus Frequency (E-clock)				

SCDR. In either case, the TDRE and/or the RDRF flags must be read as a logic 1 in order to satisfy the first step of the clearing sequence.

The SCI Baud Rate Control Register (BAUD)

7	6	5	4	3	2	1	0	
TCLR	0	SCP1	SCP0	RCKB	SCR2	SCR1	SCR0	**BAUD**
At reset 0	0	0	0	0	U	U	U	**$102B**

The BAUD* register of the 68HC11 MCU at $102B is an 8-bit register; however, only 7 bits are used. Bits TCLR and RCKB are used for test purposes and do not affect the operation of the SCI system. The SCP1 and SCP0 are called the Serial Prescaler Select bits and upon a reset condition they are automatically cleared. Table 9.4 shows how these bits are used to select a prescale factor for the SCI baud-rate generator.

The SCR2–SCR0 are the SCI Baud-Rate Select bits. These three bits are used in combination with the SCP1–SCP0 bits to specify the SCI baud rate. Upon a reset the condition of the SCR2–SCR0 bits is not affected. Table 9.5 shows the SCI baud rates that result from the various settings of bits SCR2–SCR0, and the highest baud rates from Table 9.4. Tables 9.4 and 9.5 show all the possible baud rate combinations for the various crystal frequencies. However, only the entries shown in boldface are of any practical use.

EXAMPLE 9.6

(a) A certain VDT is configured for a baud rate of 9600 and it is going to be used as an I/O device in a 68HC11 MCU-based system. Assume that the 68HC11 MCU is using a crystal

---

*A complete list of the 68HC11 MCU built-in control registers can be found in Appendix C.

TABLE 9.5   Baud-Rate Selects

| | | | | Highest baud rate (from Table 9.4) | | | | |
| | | | | 131.072K baud | 32.768K baud | 76.80K baud | 19.20K baud | 9600 baud |
SCR2	SCR1	SCR0	÷ Factor	SCI baud rate				
0	0	0	1	**131.072K Baud**	**32.768K Baud**	76.80K Baud	**19.20K Baud**	**9600 Baud**
0	0	1	2	65.536K Baud	16.384K Baud	38.40K Baud	**9600 Baud**	**4800 Baud**
0	1	0	4	**32.768K Baud**	**8192 Baud**	**19.20K Baud**	**4800 Baud**	**2400 Baud**
0	1	1	8	16.384K Baud	4096 Baud	**9600 Baud**	**2400 Baud**	**1200 Baud**
1	0	0	16	**8192 Baud**	2048 Baud	**4800 Baud**	**1200 Baud**	600 Baud
1	0	1	32	4096 Baud	1024 Baud	**2400 Baud**	600 Baud	**300 Baud**
1	1	0	64	2048 Baud	512 Baud	**1200 Baud**	**300 Baud**	150 Baud
1	1	1	128	1024 Baud	256 Baud	600 Baud	150 Baud	75 Baud

(Copyright of Motorola, Used by Permission)

frequency of 8 MHz. Write a program sequence that will program the BAUD register at $102B for a 9600-Baud rate.

(b) Repeat for a VDT that is configured for a 1200-Baud rate.

Solution

(a) One possibility.

Address	Label	Instruction code	Mnemonic	Comments
C000	BAUD	86	LDAA #$30	; Set bits SCP1 and SCP0 in BAUD
C001		30		; register for the selection of 9600 as
C002		B7	STAA $102B	; the highest baud rate (Table 9.4)
C003		10		; Clear bits SCR2–SCR0 for the baud
C004		2B		; rate selection of 9600 (Table 9.5)

Solution

(b) One possibility.

Address	Label	Instruction code	Mnemonic	Comments
C000	BAUD	86	LDAA #$33	; Set bits SCP1 and SCP0 for selection
C001		33		; of 9600 as the highest baud rate
C002		B7	STAA $102B	; (Table 9.4). Set bits SCR1–SCR0
C003		10		; and clear bit SCR2 for the baud rate
C004		2B		; selection of 1200 (Table 9.5)

Asynchronous Serial Data Communication Using the SCI System of the 68HC11 MCU

Before a two-way asynchronous serial data communication can take place between the 68HC11 MCU and an I/O device, the SCI system must first be turned on. That is, both bits TE (Transmit Enable) and RE (Receiver Enable) in the SCCR2 register must be set. The proper baud rate for the transmission also has to be established by writing the appropriate word into the BAUD register. Next, the length of each of the characters that is to be transmitted must be programmed into the SCI system. The 68HC11 MCU built-in register SCCR1 (SCI Control Register 1) at memory location $102C controls the character length that will be used during the asynchronous serial data communication.

7	6	5	4	3	2	1	0	
R8	T8	0	M	WAKE	0	0	0	SCCR1

At reset U U 0 0 0 0 0 0 **$102C**

The M (SCI character length) bit in the SCCR1 register controls the allowable character length for both the transmitter and the receiver sections of the SCI system.* If the M bit in the SCCR1 register is 0, it indicates that the character length consists of one START bit, eight DATA bits, and one STOP bit. Thus, if we count the START and STOP bits, the expected total character length is 10 bits. If the M bit in the SCCR1 register is 1, it indicates that the character length consists of one START bit, nine DATA bits, and one STOP bit, for a total character length of 11 bits. However, some I/O devices use eight DATA bits and two STOP bits in their character format. For these particular situations, the SCI system must be configured for 9-bit data characters (M = 1) and bit T8 in the SCCR1 must be set. That is, in applications where we need to transmit eight DATA bits and two STOP bits (M = 1), bit T8 must be set in order to become the extra ninth bit (STOP bit) of the TDR (Transmit Data Register). During the receiver operation, bit R8 becomes the recipient of the MSB of the received data.

EXAMPLE 9.7 ──

Assume that the ASCII codes for the message "HELLO" are stored in memory locations C500–C504 with "H" stored at C500. Write a program sequence that will transmit this message to a VDT whose baud rate is 9600 and character format is one START bit, eight DATA bits, and one STOP bit.

Solution   One possibility.

Address	Label	Instruction code	Mnemonic	Comments
C000	START	86	LDAA #$30	; Set bits SCP1 and SCP0 in BAUD
C001		30		; register for selection of 9600 as
C002		B7	STAA $102B	; the highest baud rate (Table 9.4)

───────────────
* A complete list of the 68HC11 MCU built-in control registers can be found in Appendix C.

Address	Label	Instruction code	Mnemonic	Comments
C003		10		; Clear bits SCR2–SCR0 for the baud
C004		2B		; rate selection of 9600 (Table 9.5)
C005		86	LDAA #$0C	; Turn SCI system on by setting
C006		0C		; TE = RE = 1 in SCCR2
C007		B7	STAA $102D	
C008		10		
C009		2D		
C00A		CE	LDX #$C500	; Initialize X register to be used
C00B		C5		; by indexed X instructions
C00C		00		
C00D		86	LDAA #$00	; Set character length to one
C00E		00		; START bit, eight DATA bits,
C00F		B7	STAA $102C	; and one STOP bit in SCCR1
C010		10		
C011		2C		
C012	SNDCHR	A6	LDAA $00,X	; Load ACCA with the next ASCII
C013		00		; code to be transmitted
C014		F6	LDAB $102E	; Read the SCSR register as the
C015		10		; first step in the clearing
C016		2E		; sequence of the TDRE bit
C017		B7	STAA $102F	; Send the character to be
C018		10		; transmitted into the TDR and
C019		2F		; clear TDRE
C01A		08	INX	; Increment X
C01B		8C	CPX #$C505	; Have all the characters in the
C01C		C5		; message been transmitted?
C01D		05		
C01E		27	BEQ $C028	; If complete message has been
C01F		08		; transmitted, branch to end
C020	CHTDRE	F6	LDAB $102E	; Check if TDRE = 1 to determine
C021		10		; if the TDR is ready for the next
C022		2E		; character
C023		2B	BMI $C012	; If TDRE = 1, transmit the next
C024		ED		; character
C025		7E	JMP $C020	; If TDRE ≠ 1, check TDRE again
C026		C0		
C027		20		
C028	HALT	3E	WAI	; Halt

EXAMPLE 9.8

The ASCII codes for the message "HELLO" are being sent to the SCI system by a VDT at a baud rate of 9600. These ASCII codes are to be stored in memory locations C500–C504. Assume that the character format is one START bit, eight DATA bits, and one STOP bit. Write a program sequence that will receive this message, ignore any error flags, and store it.

Solution One possibility.

Address	Label	Instruction code	Mnemonic	Comments
C100	START	86	LDAA #$30	; Set bits SCP1 and SCP0 in BAUD
C101		30		; register for selection of 9600 as
C102		B7	STAA $102B	; the highest baud rate (Table 9.4)
C103		10		; Clear bits SCR2–SCR0 for the baud
C104		2B		; rate selection of 9600 (Table 9.5)
C105		86	LDAA #$0C	; Turn SCI system on by setting
C106		0C		; TE = RE = 1
C107		B7	STAA $102D	
C108		10		
C109		2D		
C10A		CE	LDX #$C500	; Initialize X register to be used
C10B		C5		; by indexed X instructions
C10C		00		
C10D		86	LDAA #$00	; Set character length to one
C10E		00		; START bit, eight DATA bits,
C10F		B7	STAA $102C	; and one STOP bit
C110		10		
C111		2C		
C112	CHRDRF	B6	LDAA $102E	; If RDRF = 0, an ASCII code has
C113		10		; not yet been received. Continue
C114		2E		; checking the RDRF bit
C115		84	ANDA #$20	
C116		20		
C117		27	BEQ $C112	; If RDRF = 0, check again
C118		F9		
C119		B6	LDAA $102E	; Read the SCSR register as the
C11A		10		; first step in the clearing
C11B		2E		; sequence of the RDRF bit
C11C		B6	LDAA $102F	; Read the received character
C11D		10		; from the RDR and clear RDRF
C11E		2F		
C11F		A7	STAA $00,X	; Store the ASCII character in
C120		00		; the proper memory location
C121		08	INX	; Increment X
C122		8C	CPX #$C505	; Have all ASCII characters in
C123		C5		; the message been received?
C124		05		
C125		27	BEQ $C12A	; If yes, HALT
C126		03		
C127		7E	JMP $C112	; If all ASCII characters in the
C128		C1		; message have not been received,
C129		12		; check the RDRF again
C12A	HALT	3E	WAI	

This concludes the overview coverage of the 68HC11 built-in UART. The SCI discussion was used as a comparison between the operation of the built-in 68HC11 UART and that of the Motorola 6850 UART which was interfaced to the 68HC11 MCU and whose operation was discussed in Sections 9.4–9.5. For a more in-depth understanding and complete coverage of both the SCI and SPI systems of the 68HC11 MCU, consult the *M68HC11 Reference Manual* by Motorola.

▶ 9.7 SYNCHRONOUS SERIAL DATA COMMUNICATION

This is a more efficient, yet more costly, method of transferring serial data. In *synchronous serial communication,* the individual data words are transmitted continuously one after the other (i.e., a block of data) without any intervening START or STOP bits. The receiver is synchronized to the transmitter through the use of special **sync characters** that the transmitter sends before each block of data. The transmitter also continuously sends these sync characters when the communications channel is idle (no data being transmitted). The sync character is a special agreed-upon character code. When ASCII character codes are being used, the sync character code is $00010110_2 = 16_{16}$, which is given the mnemonic SYN. The receiver uses the SYN character to synchronize its internal clock with that of the transmitter. When the transmitter stops sending SYN characters and begins sending a message, the receiver automatically knows that every 8 bits received after the last SYN character is a data character. It will then shift in the 8-bit serial data (e.g., ASCII characters) following the SYN characters and convert them to parallel data that can be read by a computer.

Several message formats are used in synchronous serial communication. One of the more popular is illustrated in Fig. 9.17. It is part of the *binary synchronous communications protocol* or BISYNC, for short. This diagram shows a typical transmission sequence with time progressing from left to right. It begins with the transmitter sending SYN characters while it is idling. When the transmitter is ready to send a message (i.e., data), it will send a special character called *start-of-text* (STX) which in ASCII is 02_{16}. The STX character tells the receiver that the message characters will follow. The transmitter then sends a block of ASCII characters that represent the message. The message portion may contain 128 or 256 characters (this will vary from system to system). The transmitter sends an *end-of-text* (ETX) character to indicate the end of the message. The ASCII code for ETX is 03. Immediately following the ETX character, a *block check character* (BCC) is sent. BCC is not an ASCII code; it is a single byte that represents some complex parity information calculated from the data bytes in the message. The function of the BCC is to detect if any error has occurred in the transmission or reception of the data. The receiver can recalculate its own BCC from the data in the message, and compare it with the BCC sent by the transmitter. If they are different, the receiver can send a message to the transmitter requesting that it send its previous message over again.

After the BCC character, the transmitter can send the next portion of the message by first sending two SYN characters which the receiver can use to resynchronize its clock, followed by an STX character and the data. If the transmitter has no more data to send (i.e., the complete message has been sent), it will send continuous SYN characters.

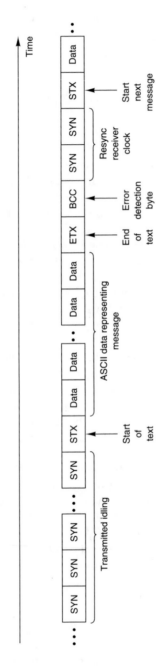

FIGURE 9.17 Typical transmission synchronous communication sequence using BISYNC format.

Synchronous communication is more efficient than asynchronous because only about 2 or 3 percent of the transmitted data is taken up by SYN characters and other special characters, compared to about 20 percent for asynchronous. However, the transmitter and receiver circuitry for synchronous operation is more complex. The Motorola MC6852 chip is a synchronous serial data adaptor that is the counterpart to the MC6850 UART chip. The MC6852 can be used to interface an MPU to an I/O device that uses synchronous serial communications.

▶ 9.8 EIA RS-232-C STANDARD

The Electronics Industry Association (EIA) has adopted several serial data communications standards. The oldest and most widely used is the RS-232-C standard. It specifies signal voltage levels and handshaking signals to be used when serial data is being sent between *data terminal equipment* (DTE) such as a computer or a terminal, and *data communication equipment* (DCE) such as a *modem* (to be introduced in the next section). For now we will consider only the RS-232-C voltage levels. The handshake signals will be described when we talk about modems.

The RS-232-C voltage levels are defined as follows:

$$\text{Logic } 1 = \text{more negative than } -3 \text{ V}$$

$$\text{Logic } 0 = \text{more positive than } +3 \text{ V}$$

Any voltage between -3 V and $+3$ V has an undefined logic level. Typically, an RS-232-C system uses nominal voltages of -12 V for a logic 1 and $+12$ V for a logic 0. Note that the more negative voltage is a logic 1. This is referred to as *negative logic*.

In a conventional microcomputer system, the standard logic voltage levels conform to the standard TTL voltage levels of 0 V and $+5$ V for a 0 and 1, respectively. These voltage levels are also used by all of the MOS and CMOS devices in the system. These TTL levels are not compatible with peripheral equipment that uses RS-232-C, and consequently some type of interface circuitry is needed to convert between TTL and RS-232-C voltages. Figure 9.18A shows two ICs designed specifically for level-conversion between TTL and RS-232-C. The Motorola MC1488 converts TTL inputs to RS-232-C outputs, and the MC1489 converts RS-232-C inputs to TTL outputs.

Although the RS-232-C standard was developed for use with computer-to-modem communication, it is often used for other situations such as computer-to-terminal communications. This is illustrated in Fig. 9.18B where the MPU is communicating with a video display terminal that uses RS-232-C serial data. The MPU is interfaced to the terminal through a UART and level-conversion ICs. When the MPU wishes to transmit a character to the terminal, the following steps occur:

1. The MPU sends parallel, TTL-level data to the UART.
2. The UART converts these to serial TTL data at its TxDATA output.
3. The serial TTL data are converted to serial RS-232-C data by the MC1488 IC and transmitted to the VDT.
4. The VDT receives the serial data, determines what character it represents, and causes that character to be printed on the screen.

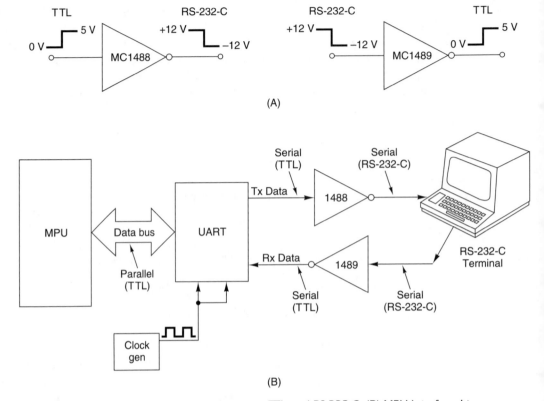

FIGURE 9.18 (A) ICs used to convert between TTL and RS-232-C; (B) MPU interfaced to an RS-232-C terminal.

When the VDT is transmitting to the MPU, the following steps occur:

1. The terminal outputs an RS-232-C serial data signal representing a character (usually the one just entered by the operator).
2. The MC1489 IC converts it to a serial TTL data signal to drive the UART's RxDATA input.
3. The UART converts the received serial signal to parallel data that can be read by the MPU over the data bus.

▶ 9.9 INTRODUCTION TO MODEMS

The term *modem* is shorthand for the cumbersome term *modulator-demodulator*. A modem is an electronic circuit that sends digital 1s and 0s over a standard telephone line as modulated sinewaves; that is, a certain characteristic of the sinewave is modulated (changed) according to the logic level being transmitted. A modem on the other end of the phone line receives the modulated signal and demodulates it; that is, converts it back to digital 1s and 0s. The frequencies of the modulated sinewaves are kept within the bandwidth of the telephone lines which is usually around 3 kHz.

There are a variety of modulation techniques used in modern modems that modulate one or more of the following sinewave characteristics: amplitude, frequency, phase. Since our purpose here is to provide only a basic introduction to the major concepts involved in computer-to-computer communications using modems, we will limit our discussion to one straightforward method that changes frequency with logic level.

Frequency Shift Keying (FSK)

In this modulation scheme, a logic 0 is represented by a sinewave at one frequency, and a logic 1 by a sinewave at a higher frequency. This is illustrated in Fig. 9.19A. Note how the frequency of the FSK waveform changes according to the state of the logic signal. A mo-

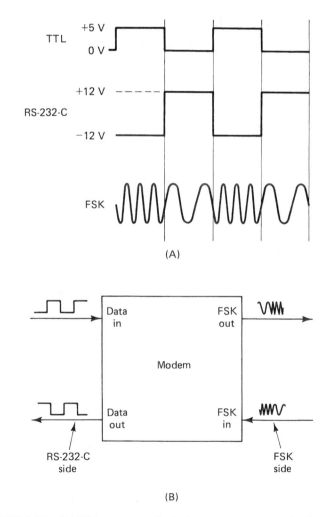

FIGURE 9.19 (A) FSK represents logic levels as sinewave of different frequencies; (B) a modem converts between RS-232-C and FSK.

dem that uses FSK is symbolized in Fig. 9.19B. The modem can be thought of as having an RS-232-C side and an FSK side. It converts an RS-232-C serial data input to an FSK output signal to be sent over the phone line. It converts an FSK input signal from the phone line to an RS-232-C serial data output.

Figure 9.20 illustrates a typical situation where a microcomputer is communicating with a remote main computer over a telephone line. The diagram in Fig. 9.20 shows that a UART and a modem are used to interface the microcomputer to the telephone lines, and, similarly, a modem and a UART are used to interface the main computer to the telephone lines. The Motorola 6860 IC is a chip that implements the FSK modulation and demodulation functions and the necessary handshake signals for serial data communications up to a baud rate of 600 bits/s. However, the 6860 cannot be connected to the phone lines directly; it requires interface circuitry that includes filters and acoustic coupling.

The diagram in Fig. 9.20 shows that there are several RS-232-C signal connections between each UART and its modem (for simplicity, the TTL/RS-232-C converters are not shown). Two of these signals, TxDATA and RxDATA, are the serial data signals. The other signals are handshake signals that control the communication between the UART and the modem. The RS-232-C standard specifies six handshake signals for use with a mo-

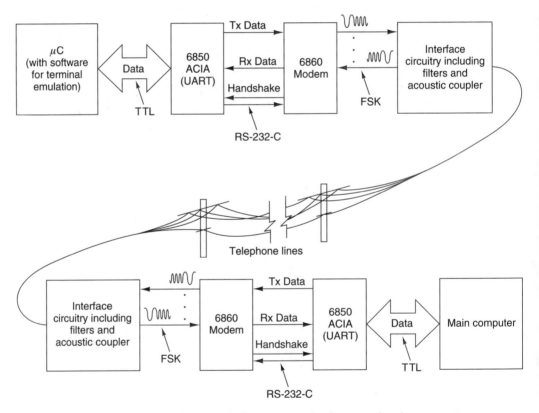

FIGURE 9.20 Modems are used to permit data communications to take place over standard telephone lines.

dem, but in many practical situations only two or three of them are actually utilized. Here are the three that are used most often.

Request to Send ($\overline{RTS}$). This active LOW signal is generated by the UART and sent to the modem. When LOW, it tells the modem that the microcomputer wants to send data over the phone lines to the remote computer. Recall that the MPU controls this UART output by writing to the UART's control register (bits CR6 and CR5).

Clear to Send ($\overline{CTS}$). This active Low signal is generated by the modem and sent to the UART in response to the $\overline{RTS}$ signal. When the modem is ready to accept data for transmission, it responds by making $\overline{CTS} = 0$. Recall that bit SR3 of the UART's status register reflects the status of the UART's $\overline{CTS}$ input line. Thus, the MPU can determine whether the modem is ready by reading the UART's status register and checking for $\overline{CTS} = 0$.

Data Carrier Detect ($\overline{DCD}$). This active LOW signal is a modem output that is asserted (activated) when the modem has detected a signal on the phone line that indicates that a remote modem has made contact with it over the phone line. The modem sends this signal to the UART's $\overline{DCD}$ input. Recall that bit SR2 of the UART reflects the status of the UART's $\overline{DCD}$ input, so the MPU can determine when its modem is connected to a remote modem by reading the UART's status register.

Originate and Answer Modems

For the system depicted in Fig. 9.20, the microcomputer can initiate the communication process by performing the necessary handshaking functions with its modem via the UART. The microcomputer then sends parallel data to the UART, which converts them to serial data and sends them to the modem. The modem converts the data to an FSK waveform and transmits it over the phone lines. The microcomputer's modem is called the *originate* modem because the microcomputer is initiating the communication. An originate modem might use the following FSK frequencies:

Mark (logic 1): 1270 Hz
Space (logic 0): 1070 Hz

The FSK waveform is received by the remote modem that is interfaced to the main computer. This modem converts the FSK signal to a serial data signal and transmits it to its UART's RxDATA input. The UART converts it to parallel data for the main computer.

If the main computer wishes to respond to the data that it has received, it can send data back over the phone lines through its UART and modem. The main computer's modem then becomes an *answer* modem, and it converts the main computer's data to the following FSK frequencies:

Mark (logic 1): 2225 Hz
Space (logic 0): 2025 Hz

Thus, the answer modem sends data back to the originate modem using a different set of frequencies than that used by the originate modem. This allows for simultaneous two-way communication over the same phone lines (that is, FSK-coded data can be transmitted in both directions at the same time). This is called a *full-duplex* mode of communication. In a *half-duplex* mode of communication, data can be transmitted in both directions, but not at the same time.

The same type of operation occurs when the main computer initiates the communication process. Its modem becomes the originate modem and uses the 1070 Hz and 1270 Hz frequencies for transmission over the phone lines. The microcomputer's modem receives these frequencies and demodulates them back to a serial data signal for its UART. If the microcomputer wishes to respond, it can send data back over the phone lines using its modem as an answer modem operating with frequencies of 2025 Hz and 2225 Hz.

Advanced Features

Most currently available modems contain a built-in MPU that controls all of the modem operations. These *smart modems* can do things like automatically dialing a specified phone number using either tone or pulse dialing, and redialing when the number is busy or not answering. A smart modem can automatically adjust its transmit circuitry to the baud rate of the modem it is communicating with. Many smart modems can be set to answer a call after a programmed number of rings. These and many more features are made possible by the built-in MPU.

We presented the FSK method of modulation as an illustration of basic modem operation. Most of the currently used modems employ more sophisticated modulation methods that permit higher data rates (56,000 bits/s) while still working within the phone line's relatively low bandwidth of 3 kHz. Many smart modems are designed to work at several different data rates and modulation methods so they can communicate with a variety of modems.

▶ 9.10 PARALLEL I/O INTERFACE CHIPS

The 6850 UART is a fairly complex peripheral interface chip that allows a parallel-data device (the MPU) to communicate with serial devices. Many peripheral devices operate with parallel data, and some common parallel devices are D/A and A/D converters, keyboards, parallel printers, and a wide variety of test and measurement instrumentation. Although these I/O devices can be connected to the MPU through the simple input and output ports we have previously discussed, IC manufacturers have developed parallel interface chips that provide capabilities beyond the basic I/O ports. Some of these capabilities include:

1. *Programmability.* The ports, and in many cases the individual bits of each port, can be configured as either input or output by the MPU. The MPU performs this function by writing to control registers on the chip.
2. *Handshaking.* Several control signal lines are made available to allow control information to be passed between the MPU and the peripheral device.
3. *Interrupt control.* This function allows the MPU to control the peripheral device's interrupt capability.
4. *Timers.* Some parallel interface chips include on-chip timers. These timers operate from the system clock (E-clock) and can be programmed by the MPU for various modes of operation.

The MC6821 Peripheral Interface Adapter (PIA)

This Motorola integrated circuit is a parallel interface chip that provides many of these features. Figure 9.21 shows a simplified block diagram of the MC6821's port structure. From this diagram we can see that the device communicates with the MPU over an 8-bit bidirectional data bus which is simply connected to the MPU's data bus. Two completely independent 8-bit bidirectional ports are available to be connected to various peripheral devices. In this very basic arrangement the MPU can send information to port A or port B by simply performing a WRITE operation to the specific port address. The MPU can also receive information from peripheral devices by way of port A or port B by performing a READ operation from the specific port address of the PIA.

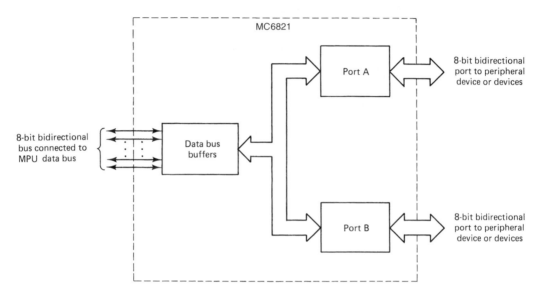

FIGURE 9.21   Simplified diagram of the 6821 parallel interface chip.

A more in-depth look at the MC 6821 is necessary to get a full grasp of the power and flexibility that this chip provides μC system designers. Figure 9.22 is a more detailed block diagram of the MC 6821. The chip can be thought of as two completely independent 8-bit I/O ports. Ports A and B contain *data direction registers* (DDRA, DDRB) which allow the programmer to specify independently each pin of both ports as either an input or an output pin. Putting a "0" in a data direction register bit causes the corresponding pin on the port to act as an input. Placing a "1" in a particular bit position of the DDR causes the corresponding pin on the port to act as an output.

The *control registers* (CRA, CRB) allow the programmer to choose certain interrupt and peripheral control capabilities. Also, the control register provides certain status information concerning interrupt activity.

The *output registers* (ORA, ORB) hold data that are to be sent to output devices until such devices are ready to accept it. Inputs CA1, CA2, CB1, and CB2 can be used as status inputs for conditional I/O transfer, or for interrupt interfacing capabilities. Under software

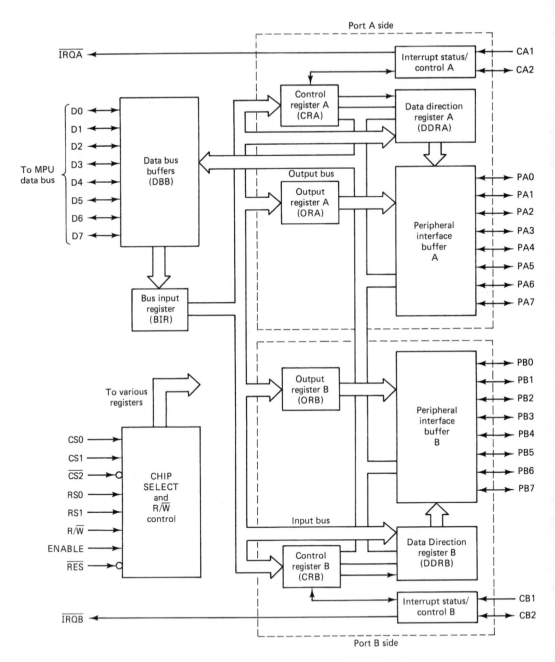

FIGURE 9.22   Block diagram of the MC 6821 PIA.

control CA2 and CB2 can be programmed, via the control register, to act as peripheral control *outputs* that can be used in various handshaking schemes. We will describe these functions in more detail later.

In dealing with this chip the MPU must be able to communicate with six different registers. In Fig. 9.22 you will notice that the CHIP SELECT and R/$\overline{\text{W}}$ control section has only two register select inputs, RS0 and RS1. This seems to indicate that the MPU can only communicate with four registers. However, one bit in each control register is used to distinguish between addressing of the data direction register and the output register. This allows the choice then of communicating with one of *six* different registers; two data direction registers, two control registers, and two output registers. The REGISTER SELECT and CHIP SELECT inputs operate in the same manner as those of the 6850 UART.

Using the 6821 for Unconditional Transfer   The 6821 can easily be used to implement the I/O formats discussed in Chapter 8. The format for MPU-initiated unconditional transfer is implemented by connecting the data bus buffers of the 6821 to the MPU data bus while port A, port B, or both are connected to I/O devices. To set up port A as an *output* port, for example, the MPU must write all 1s into data direction register A (DDRA). The port A pins are thereby set up to act as outputs, and whenever the MPU needs to send data to the output device connected to port A, it simply performs a WRITE operation to output register A (ORA). The main advantage of this type of interface chip is its programmability. If at some future point in time port A needs to be made an input port, the MPU simply writes all 0s into data direction register A. Then whenever the MPU performs a READ operation of port A, whatever logic levels are present on PA_0 through PA_7 will be placed onto the data bus to be latched into the MPU. These same ideas pertain to the port B portion of the chip.

Using the 6821 for Conditional Transfer   Microprocessor-initiated conditional transfer of data can easily be implemented using the 6821. Each control register has 2 read-only bits or flags reserved for status information. These flags are activated by inputs CA1, CA2 or CB1, CB2, respectively. The device can be programmed via the control register to respond to either positive- or negative-going transitions on these inputs. Thus, the appropriate transitions on the CA or CB inputs will set corresponding status flags in the control register. For conditional transfer, the MPU would read the contents of the control register and test these status bits before any transfer of information takes place. These status flags are cleared whenever the MPU performs a READ operation from the corresponding port or when a $\overline{\text{RESET}}$ is generated.

EXAMPLE 9.9 _____

Figure 9.23 shows how the MC6821 could be used to interface a Centronics-type parallel input printer to the 68HC11 MPU. Port B of the MC6821 is used as an output port through which ASCII codes are sent from the MPU to the parallel printer. Port A of the MC6821 is used as an I/O port for the various handshake signals needed between the MPU and the printer. Describe the steps involved in the transfer of ASCII codes from the 68HC11 MPU to the printer.

Solution
1. Pins PB0 through PB7 are programmed as *output* pins by having the MPU write all 1s into DDRB. Pin PA0 is also programmed as an output pin, while pins PA1 through PA4

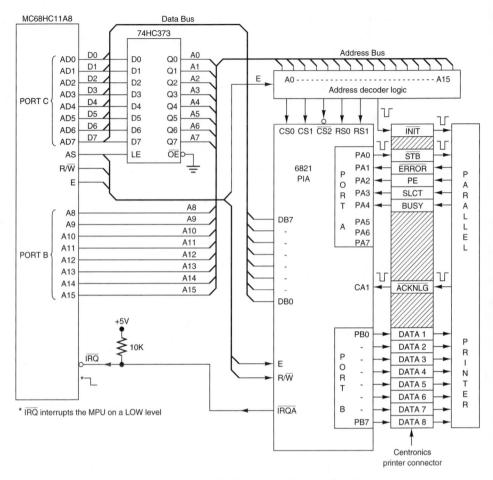

FIGURE 9.23   6821 PIA in a typical application.

are programmed as input pins. Pins PA1 through PA4 are programmed as *input* pins by having the MPU WRITE all 0s into DDRA. The programming of the port lines is usually done at the beginning of the program.

2. The $\overline{\text{INIT}}$ signal is used to initialize the printer (i.e., clear buffers, reinitialize the print-head to starting position).

3. When the MPU wishes to send an ASCII code to the printer it can check the BUSY signal by reading port A and checking PA4. If the BUSY signal is LOW it indicates that the printer is *not* busy and that it is ready to receive the next ASCII code from the MPU. The MPU will then send an ASCII code by executing a WRITE operation to ORB. The addresses used for DDRB, ORB, and the other PIA registers are determined by the address decoder logic just as they were for the 6850 UART.

4. After an ASCII code is sent to port B by the MPU, the printer receives a short negative strobe pulse ($\overline{\text{STB}}$) from the MPU to signify that the data lines (PB0–PB7) are stable and ready to be accepted by the printer.

5. While the *conditional* transfer of the ASCII code is taking place, the BUSY signal is HIGH, indicating that the printer is busy and that it cannot receive any more data from the MPU. The BUSY signal goes LOW when the printer is ready to receive another ASCII code. The BUSY signal works in conjunction with the $\overline{\text{ACKNLG}}$ (acknowledge) signal. The $\overline{\text{ACKNLG}}$ goes LOW for about 5 μs when the printer is ready to receive another ASCII code. The rising edge of the $\overline{\text{ACKNLG}}$ signal tells the MPU that it can send the next character. Some systems use the BUSY signal to do the handshake and some use the $\overline{\text{ACKNLG}}$ signal. In this example we allowed for both options.

6. In this example we are using input CA1 of the 6821 to monitor the activity of the $\overline{\text{ACKNLG}}$ signal in order to determine whether or not the printer is ready for the next ASCII code. Consequently, at the beginning of the program the MPU must also send the appropriate control word to Control Register A (CRA) for making input pin CA1 respond to a positive-going transition. Thus, when $\overline{\text{ACKNLG}}$ goes from LOW to HIGH, it will set the flag in CRA that is activated by CA1. The MPU can determine the status of this flag by reading the contents of CRA. If this flag is HIGH, the MPU then knows that the printer is ready for the next ASCII code.

Note that an $\overline{\text{INIT}}$ pulse is required for the initialization of the printer. Here it is shown being generated from the address decoder circuitry as was done in Chapter 8 (Fig. 8.7). The $\overline{\text{INIT}}$ pulse could alternatively be provided by using, for example, port A pin PA5 as an output pin, or the PIA's CA2 pin (Fig. 9.22) as an output signal. Likewise, the $\overline{\text{STB}}$ pulse that is sent by the MPU to indicate new, stable data for the printer can be generated from PA0, as shown, or by using CA2.

The following is a brief description of the remaining Centronics interface signals used in the interface circuit of Fig. 9.23:

$\overline{\text{ERROR}}$ This signal is used to signal the MPU of any printer problem (i.e., printer off-line, paper jam).

PE   This signal indicates that the printer is out of paper.

SLCT   This signal may be used to tell the MPU that the printer is turned on.

6821 Interrupt Mode   For I/O transfer using the interrupt mode, the 6821 has an active-LOW interrupt output associated with each port. These outputs, $\overline{\text{IRQA}}$ and $\overline{\text{IRQB}}$, can be tied to the MPU interrupt request input ($\overline{\text{IRQ}}$). The operation of these interrupt outputs can be enabled or disabled under program control by writing appropriate words to the control register. When the interrupt feature is utilized, an INTERRUPT output is activated (goes LOW) whenever the *Interrupt* flag in the associated control register is set.

The Interrupt flag is the same flag used as a status flag in the conditional transfer mode, and is activated (set HIGH) by appropriate transitions on the CA or CB inputs. Thus, the CA or CB inputs act as INTERRUPT inputs which can be driven by an I/O device. The following example illustrates.

EXAMPLE 9.10 ──────────────────────────────

Describe how the Centronics interface circuit of Fig. 9.23 can interrupt the 68HC11 MPU for ASCII data transfer.

Solution For interrupt operation several things must be done. First, since the printer is using port A for the handshake signals, the $\overline{\text{IRQA}}$ output is connected to the active-LOW 68HC11 MPU $\overline{\text{IRQ}}$ input. Second, the MPU must write a control word into CRA to enable $\overline{\text{IRQA}}$ and specify that a positive transition on CA1 will set the interrupt flag. Thus, when the printer is ready for a new ASCII code, the $\overline{\text{ACKNLG}}$ signal produces a positive transition on CA1 which sets the Interrupt flag in CRA. This in turn causes $\overline{\text{IRQA}}$ to go LOW to interrupt the MPU. The MPU can be programmed to respond to this interrupt by first reading port A to determine the status of the $\overline{\text{ERROR}}$ and PE signals before it sends the next ASCII code to be printed. This READ operation will automatically clear the Interrupt flag and drive $\overline{\text{IRQA}}$ back HIGH to prepare for the next interrupt sequence.

6821 Handshaking Features One of the unique features of this chip is that CA2 and CB2 can be made to function as outputs instead of inputs. By writing an appropriate word into the control register, CA2 and CB2 can operate as outputs in three different modes for handshaking purposes and peripheral control. The first mode allows CA2 or CB2 outputs to be set or cleared corresponding to the logic level written into a bit position of the control register.

The second mode used in handshaking arrangements works such that when an input device interrupts the MPU using input CA1, output CA2 is made to go HIGH. When the MPU reads port A to get the new data, output CA2 is made to go LOW, signaling the peripheral device that data have been accepted and new data can be sent. For port B operation, the CB2 output is cleared when the MPU performs a WRITE operation to port B. When the output device accepts this information, it sends a signal back, activating input CB1, which can then interrupt the MPU by use of $\overline{\text{IRQB}}$, signaling the MPU that the output device has accepted this new information. Because of this second mode, port A is more easily interfaced when used in conjunction with an input device and port B for an output device.

The third mode, referred to as a pulsed mode, causes output CA2 to generate a pulse each time the MPU reads the contents of port A, and output CB2 to generate a pulse whenever the MPU writes to port B.

As can be seen, this device is fairly sophisticated and allows great freedom to the system designer. The main advantage of this chip over handwired logic is its programmability. Under software control its basic operation can easily be changed even while the system is in full operation.

▶ 9.11 KEYBOARD INPUT DEVICES

A microprocessor is a complex LSI device that is one of the marvels of semiconductor technology. Even so, this device is rendered useless unless it has a program of instructions to execute. When used in dedicated applications such as process controllers, equipment and appliance controllers, and traffic controllers, the MPU executes fixed programs that are stored in ROM. Any operation change to be made in such applications simply requires replacing the ROM with a different ROM. On the other hand, there are numerous situations where the MPU must not only execute many different programs, but continually modify them. For these applications, the programs have to be stored in RAM. This is particularly true of general-purpose and hobbyist μCs, where the user is continually developing, testing, and running different programs. The same holds true for the development systems that engineers use to develop programs for MPU-based equipment. All the extensive testing, modifying, and debugging of these programs is done using RAM. Then the final programs are put into ROM as part of the finished product.

When RAM is to be used for program storage, there has to be some means of easily entering programs and data into memory. One of the more common techniques used in low-cost microcomputers and MPU development systems utilizes a *hexadecimal keyboard*. This keyboard contains 16 digit keys, one for each hex digit 0 through F, and several control keys. A typical hex keyboard format is shown in Fig. 9.24. In addition to the hex digit keys, this keyboard has four control keys, which determine the keyboard function being performed. For example, to read the contents of memory location 80AB, the user punches the hex keys 8-0-A-B, in that order, and then punches the EXAMINE key. This will cause the MPU to read address location 80AB and display its contents, usually on LED readouts. A new word can then be stored in this address location by punching in the two hex digits and then punching the STORE key. Punching in a four-digit hex address and then punching the GO key causes the MPU to go to that address to begin executing instructions. The RESET key is used to activate the MPU's $\overline{RESET}$ input and to reset other conditions in the system.

There are a wide variety of methods used to interface a keyboard such as this to an MPU. We will not attempt to show them all here. Instead, we will examine one of the more popular approaches, referred to as *software keyboard scanning*. This technique requires a *keyboard monitor program,* stored in ROM, that controls all the keyboard operations. The basic operation proceeds as follows:

1. Depressing the RESET key resets the MPU and causes it to begin executing the keyboard monitor program stored in ROM. This means that the monitor program must be located at the address where the MPU takes its first instruction after being reset. In the 68HC11 MPU, this is determined by the reset vector at addresses FFFE and FFFF.

2. As the MPU executes the monitor program, it continually scans the keyboard outputs until it senses that a key has been depressed, and then determines which of the keys it is.

3. If the monitor program determines that it is one of the hex-digit keys, the 4-bit code for that particular key is fetched from a KEY-CODE table stored in ROM. For example, if the "A" key has been depressed, the code 1010 will be fetched from the KEY-CODE table. This code will then usually be sent to an LED readout for display and also to a RAM location for temporary storage until it is needed.

4. If the monitor program determines that one of the control keys has been depressed, the program performs the corresponding operation. For example, if the EXAM. key is actuated, the monitor program fetches the word stored in the address location specified by the preceding *four* key actuations and sends it to LED readouts for display.

5. The monitor program continues to scan the keyboard looking for key actuations until the GO key is depressed. Upon sensing that the GO key has been actuated, the monitor program executes an unconditional jump to the address location specified by the pre-

ceding *four* key actuations. The codes for these key actuations were previously stored in RAM (step 3). This will cause the MPU to stop executing the monitor program and begin executing the program stored at the punched-in address. Since the monitor program is no longer being executed, the keyboard relinquishes control to the MPU (i.e., all subsequent key actuations are ignored). The keyboard will regain control when the user punches the RESET key (step 1).

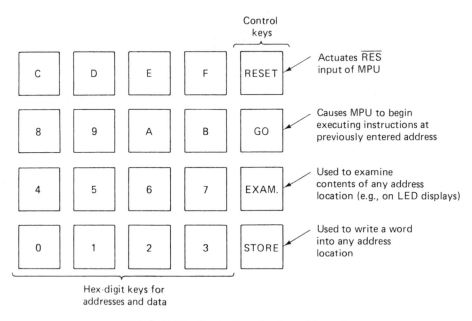

FIGURE 9.24 Typical hex keyboard format.

Interfacing the Keyboard

Implementation of a keyboard scanning technique requires some means for the MPU to read the status of each key under the control of the monitor program. The keyboard is treated as an input device with a specific address or range of addresses that the MPU uses to read the keyboard data. Figure 9.25 shows one possible scheme for interfacing the keyboard of Fig. 9.24 to a 68HC11 MPU.

In this arrangement, all of the keyswitches, except for RESET, are arranged in a matrix of four rows by five columns. Each matrix keyswitch, when actuated, will connect the output of one of the inverters 0–4 to the input of one of the tri-state buffers 0–3. For example, depressing the "C" key will connect the output of inverter 4 to point W, the input to buffer 3. Similarly, depressing the "GO" key will connect the output of inverter 0 to the input of buffer 2. With no keys depressed, the buffer inputs will be pulled up to the HIGH state by the pull-up resistors. The buffer outputs are connected to the lower four lines $(D_3–D_0)$ of the system data bus. The buffers are enabled by a HIGH level from the AND gate output.

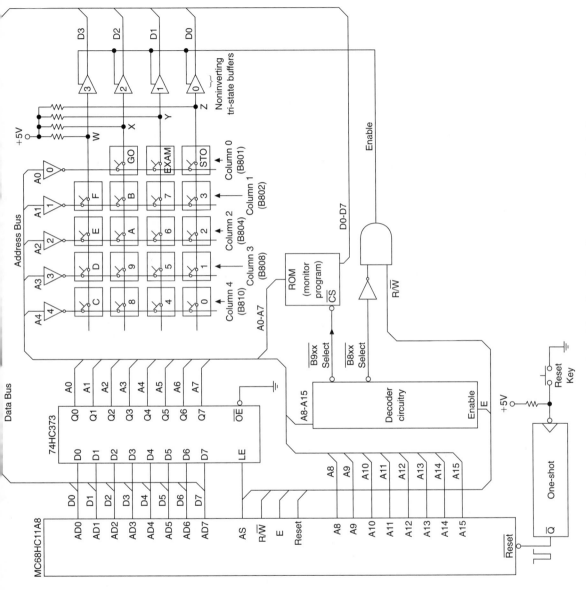

FIGURE 9.25 Hex keyboard interface for software scanning technique.

The keyboard is assigned addresses B8xx; specifically, each column of keys is assigned a different address on page B8 according to the following table:

Column	Assigned hex address
4	B810
3	B808
2	B804
1	B802
0	B801

The MPU can read the status of the keys in any column by reading from the appropriate address. For example, the MPU can read column 3 by executing the instruction LDAA $B808. During the execution of this instruction, the MPU places B808 on the address bus. This produces a LOW at the address decoder's $\overline{\text{B8xx}}$ SELECT output, which is inverted and applied to the AND gate along with R/$\overline{\text{W}}$ = 1 to produce a HIGH that enables the buffers. This allows the data at the buffer inputs to be placed on the data bus for transfer into accumulator A (ACCA).

The low-order address lines will be $08_{16} = 00001000_2$, so that only address line A_3 is HIGH. This will produce a LOW at the inverter 3 output. Inverters 0, 1, 2, and 4 will all have a HIGH output since address lines A_0, A_1, A_2, and A_4 are all LOW. This means that if any key in column 3 is down while the MPU is executing LDAA $B808, a LOW will be connected to the corresponding buffer input and then transferred into ACCA over the data bus.

For example, if the "9" key is down, the LOW from inverter 3 will pass through buffer 2 and onto the data bus. All the other buffer inputs will be HIGH, so that the levels 1011 will be applied to data bus lines $D_3D_2D_1D_0$, and loaded into ACCA. Thus, the LDAA $B808 instruction will produce [ACCA] = xxxx1011. The four MSBs are indeterminate because data bus lines $D_7D_6D_5D_4$ are floating. This is inconsequential because the MPU will only check the four lower-order bits of ACCA to see if any of them are LOW. This will tell the MPU which key in column 3, if any, is down.

EXAMPLE 9.11

Assume that the MPU is executing LDAA $B808. Determine what data will be loaded into ACCA if (a) the "1" key is down; (b) the "F" key is down; (c) no key is down.

Solution
(a) The depressed "1" key will connect the LOW from the inverter 3 output to data bus line D_0 through buffer 0. This will load xxxx1110 into ACCA.

(b) The "F" key connects inverter 1 to buffer 3, but the inverter 1 output is HIGH since A_1 is LOW. Thus, all of the buffer outputs will place HIGHs onto the data bus, and xxxx1111 will be loaded into ACCA.

(c) With no key down, all buffer outputs will be HIGH, and xxxx1111 will be loaded into ACCA.

In a similar manner, the MPU can read the status of the keys in any of the other columns by using the appropriate column address. For example, LDAA $B801 will load column 0 into ACCA, and LDAA $B802 will load column 1 into ACCA.

EXAMPLE 9.12

Assume that the MPU executes LDAA $B804, and the resulting data word in ACCA is xxxx1101. What key is down?

Solution   Address B804 will produce a LOW at the inverter 2 output so that the keys in column 2 are being checked. Since a LOW is coming from the buffer 1 onto the data bus, the "6" key must be down.

As the MPU executes the keyboard monitor program in ROM, it will continually scan the keyboard columns, reading them one at a time, until it reads a 0 into ACCA. When it finds a 0, the MPU determines which key is down and branches to the appropriate instruction sequence to respond to that key actuation. A keyboard monitor program is a fairly complex program and will vary in complexity depending on the MPU and the type of keyboard being used. Some of the practical considerations that the keyboard monitor program has to deal with include keyswitch bounce, multiple readings of the same key actuation, and actuation of a second key before release of the first key.

Keyswitch bounce occurs when a key is first depressed and rarely lasts for more than 10 ms. When this bounce occurs it can appear to the MPU that the same key has been actuated several times instead of just once. The monitor program can eliminate this problem by not servicing the keyboard more often than, say, every 20 ms. In other words, after sensing a key actuation, the monitor program will *delay* for about 20 ms before scanning the keyboard for a new key actuation. This delay is obtained by having the MPU go through a *timing loop* in the monitor program.

A typical monitor program can completely scan and service a typical hex keyboard in less than 1 ms. This means that the same key depression might be erroneously detected many times before the key is released. To avoid this, the monitor program must check to see that the actuated key has been released before it scans the keyboard for new key actuations. A somewhat related problem occurs when the user depresses a second key before the first key is released. Again, the monitor program solves this problem by checking for the release of the first key before it scans the keyboard for new key actuations. This is called a *two-key rollover* technique, and it allows the user to punch in a fast succession of key inputs without error.

This scheme of interfacing a hexadecimal keyboard can be used basically by any 8-bit MPU. However, in a 68HC11 MCU-based system, instead of an external ROM chip, the MCU built-in 8K ROM could be used to store the monitor program. In this case, the monitor program would have been developed by the user *before* ordering the 68HC11 MCU from the manufacturer. Once ordered, the ROM would be programmed at Motorola during the manufacturing of the 68HC11 MCU.

ASCII Keyboard Interface

A hex keyboard is used to communicate with a computer using only the 16 hex digits 0 through F. The next higher level of communication uses the familiar English alphabet, numerals, punctuation marks, and other commonly used symbols (e.g., %, $, #). The universal binary code used for this type of communication is the 7-bit ASCII code. With 7 bits, there are $2^7 = 128$ possible codes, representing 94 different characters and 34 different machine commands (e.g., carriage return, backspace). With 128 ASCII characters it would appear that an ASCII keyboard requires 128 key switches. Fortunately, an ASCII keyboard uses a shift key just like in a typewriter, to allow each key to have two functions. Thus, only 64 keys are needed.

ASCII keyboards are laid out similar to a conventional typewriter keyboard for easy two-hand operation. Each key is a switch that, when depressed, connects two points together in the same manner as shown for the hex keyboard. ASCII keyboards often operate into a keyboard encoder circuit which generates the 7-bit ASCII code bit pattern for the key being depressed. This bit pattern is transferred to the MPU over the data bus. Again, a KEY ACTUATION output allows either polled operation or interrupt operation to be used. ASCII keyboard encoders are more complex than hex keyboard encoders because of the greater numbers of keys and codes.* Some of the more sophisticated keyboard encoder chips also contain special *debouncing* and *two-key rollover* features.

ASCII can also be interfaced to an MPU using a software scanning technique such as that used for the hex keyboard.

Figure 9.26 illustrates another method of interfacing an ASCII keyboard to an MPU for software scanning. It uses a PIA chip to provide the row-scanning function (port B) and the column-scanning function (port A). The MPU keyboard monitor program scans a keyboard row by sending a word to port B with only a single 0 in that row position. It then reads port A and checks for a zero in any bit position to indicate a key closure. To illustrate, let's assume that port B's address is 4006 and port A's address is 4004. The MPU will check the top row of keys by executing the following instructions:

```
LDAA #$7F    ;[ACCA] = 01111111
STAA $4006   ;Make PB7 = 0
LDAB $4004   ;Load ACCB with
             ;keyboard data
```

The first two instructions place 01111111 at the port B outputs. With $PB_7 = 0$, a key down in the top row will connect this LOW to the port A input corresponding to the key column. The last instruction loads the port A levels into ACCB. For example, if the rightmost key in the top row is down, a LOW will appear at PA_0 and [**ACCB**] = 11111110. If none of the top row keys are down, [**ACCB**] = 11111111.

The MPU can scan the other rows by shifting the 0 from one port B position to another and then loading ACCB from port A. When it detects a 0 in ACCB, the MPU knows

---

*An ASCII keyboard encoder chip often contains a ROM that stores the ASCII codes of the various keyboard characters and functions.

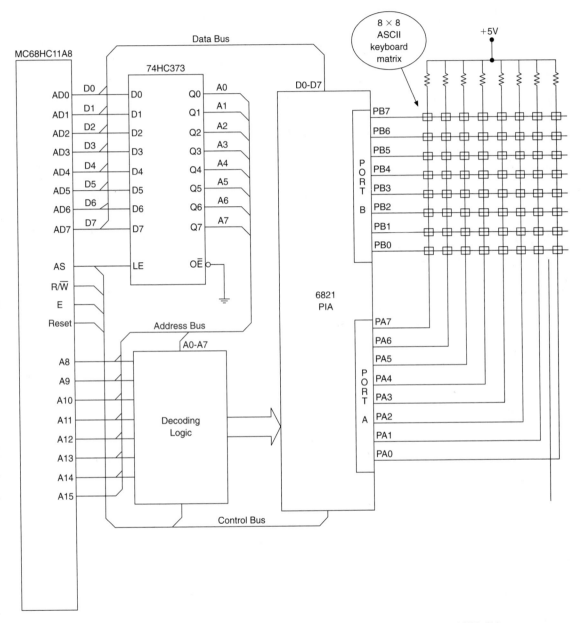

FIGURE 9.26   ASCII keyboard interfaced to the MC68HC11 through a 6821 PIA.

that a key is down, and it can proceed to determine which key is down from the position of the 0 in ACCB.

▶ 9.12 VIDEO DISPLAY TERMINALS (VDTS)

A VDT is an I/O device that allows an operator to easily and quickly enter and display large amounts of alphanumeric information on a TV monitor. A TV monitor differs from a conventional TV set in that it has a direct video input, while a TV set generally requires video information modulating a carrier. In other words, a video signal can be applied directly to a monitor, while a TV set includes circuitry that locks onto a particular carrier frequency (channel) and extracts the video information from the carrier (demodulation).

Video Display Introduction

Before we can get into the details of how to display information on a TV monitor, we need to have some idea of the basics of video display. Let us assume that we have a certain amount of memory reserved for display purposes. This memory space will store the information that we wish to display on the TV monitor. Each memory address will store one ASCII-coded character and the format chosen for display will determine the actual memory requirements. Typical formats are 16 lines of 32 characters, 16 lines of 64 characters, and 16 lines of 80 characters. If we choose the simplest format of 16 lines of 32 characters, we will need a minimum of $16 \times 32 = 512$ memory spaces to store a complete screen of information. Figure 9.27 shows a partial display. One horizontal line consists of a maximum of 32 characters, including spaces. A complete display would consist of a maximum of 16 such horizontal character lines.

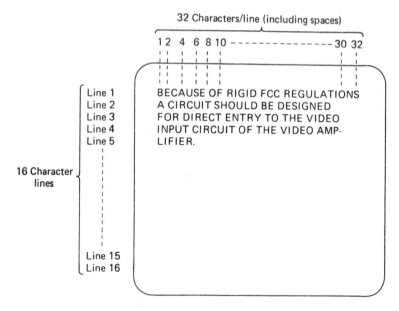

FIGURE 9.27   Partial TV display.

The display consists of digital information being sequentially read from memory and converted to the appropriate video signals to be fed into the TV. Of course, certain timing and control signals will also need to be generated. To understand how binary information stored in memory can be converted to video information, we need to discuss some basic television operation. This topic will be presented in a somewhat simplified manner so as not to detract from the more pertinent concepts.

Television Operation Introduction

We will only look at the simplest television display to be used solely for displaying alphanumeric information. The actual display (see Fig. 9.28) is made up of an electron beam being horizontally swept across the picture tube from left to right in about 53.5 μs, starting at the upper left-hand corner of the screen. The beam is then blanked and returned (retraced) back to the left side of the screen in about 10 μs. During this retrace the beam is gradually deflected downward by a small amount.* This sequence is repeated until the electron beam traverses the entire screen, ending up in the lower right-hand corner of the screen. This complete scan of the TV screen is referred to as a *frame* or *vertical sweep*. *Vertical retrace* occurs when the electron beam is blanked and returned to the upper left-hand corner of the screen. One complete vertical sweep and retrace requires 16.67 ms (a rate of 60 Hz). Because vertical retrace takes about 1.25 ms, we are left with 15.42 ms for one vertical sweep time, and since each horizontal line takes 63.5 μs, this gives a total of 15.42 ms/63.5 μs = 242 possible lines per frame. As shown in Fig. 9.28, to synchronize operation of the system we need to generate one horizontal sync pulse at the end of each horizontal line and one vertical sync pulse at the end of each frame (242 lines).

The next question we must deal with is: How can we get ASCII-coded data stored in memory to be displayed as alphanumeric characters on the TV screen? The answer to this comes in the form of an integrated circuit known as a *character generator*.

---

*In actual practice, the beam is continuously being deflected downward as it moves horizontally.

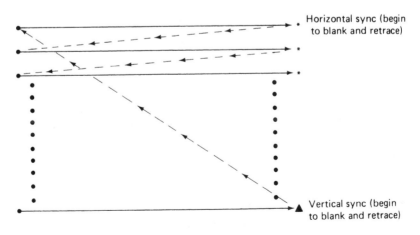

FIGURE 9.28   TV scanning.

Character Generation The data stored in each memory location correspond to a particular ASCII code. We must be able to convert this information into a form that can be used by the video section. This is accomplished by converting each ASCII code into a *dot-matrix* pattern. Typical patterns consist of a 5 × 7 matrix or a 7 × 9 matrix.

Figure 9.29A shows a 5 × 7 dot-matrix pattern for the letter E. Each solid dot can be represented by a logic 1 and each blank dot by a logic 0, as shown in Fig. 9.29B. With this format the dot-matrix equivalent of an ASCII character can be transmitted as seven serial bit patterns, one for each row of dots.

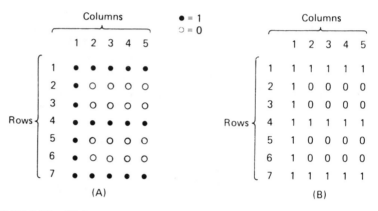

FIGURE 9.29 (A) Dot-matrix representation of the letter E; (B) logic-level representation of the letter E.

Figure 9.30 shows the 2513 character-generator integrated circuit that transmits these bit patterns. It has two sets of inputs. One set consists of the ASCII code bits that select the particular character. The 2513 generates only the upper-case characters, so that only 6 ASCII code bits are needed. The second set of inputs are row select inputs that select which row of each character's dot matrix will be present at the five output pins. For example, $R_2R_1R_0 = 001$ selects row 1, 010 selects row 2, and so

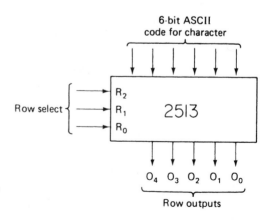

FIGURE 9.30 Model 2513 character-generator integrated circuit.

on up to row 7. For row inputs $R_2R_1R_0 = 000$, no row is selected and the five outputs will be 0. This can be used to provide vertical spacing between characters in a complete system.

To output the complete dot matrix of a character, we must sequence through all seven rows. Each row pattern appears at the character-generator outputs. These outputs are in a parallel format, and to be able to display this information on a television system, it must be converted to a serial signal. As a row of information is made available at the output of the 2513, it is transferred to a shift register and shifted out serially. As the electron beam is sweeping horizontally across the TV screen, the 1s and 0s contained in the row of information being shifted out are used to turn the electron beam on and off. In this fashion the TV would have to complete seven horizontal scans to display the full character. Figure 9.31 shows the arrangement of the 2513 and the use of a shift register to shift out the row information serially.

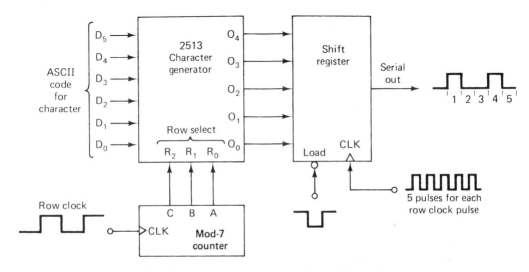

FIGURE 9.31   Parallel-to-serial conversion of row information.

Complete Display System   A block diagram for the complete system operation is given in Fig. 9.32. The overall system can be broken down into several segments, described below.

1. *Memory:* a total of 512 RAM memory spaces. Each memory location stores the ASCII code for one character. We can visualize this memory space arranged as 16 lines of 32 characters per line.

2. *Character Counter (CC):* a MOD-32 counter used to select one character out of the 32 possible per character line using address lines A_4 through A_0.

3. *Character Line Counter (CLC):* a MOD-16 counter used to select one character line out of the 16 possible using address lines A_8 through A_5. The combined function of the CC and CLC counters is to determine what character position on the TV screen is being written onto at a given point in time. As the CLC is sequenced, it selects which character line of 16 is written on the screen. As the CC is sequenced, it selects which character of the 32 in a given character line is written onto the screen.

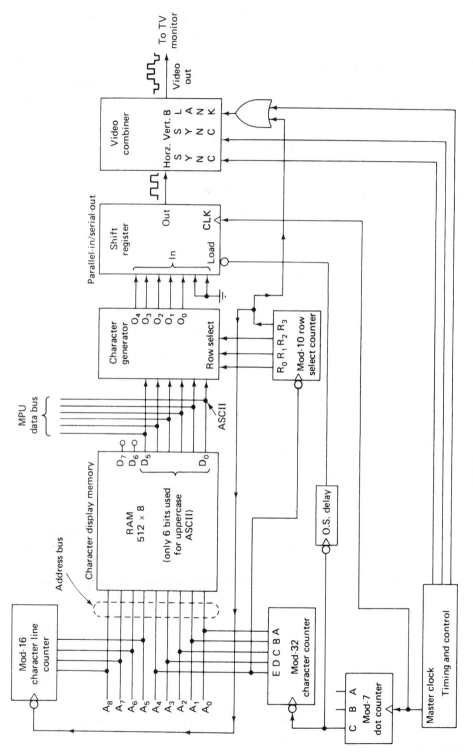

FIGURE 9.32 Complete display system.

4. *ROW Select Counter (RSC):* a MOD-10 counter used to select a particular row of the selected character. Count 0 selects row 0 of the character matrix; this puts 0s at outputs O_4 through O_0 of the character generator. These 0s produce a black level (blank) on the screen and provide a row of spacing above the character. Counts 8 and 9 generate a signal that is fed to the video combiner and used to produce two more rows of blanking. Therefore, between character lines we have a total of three blank lines for spacing.

5. *Shift Register:* a 7-bit register used to convert the 5-bit parallel output of the character generator to a 7-bit serial output. The two LSBs of the shift register are always loaded as LOWS and used to provide two blanking spaces for horizontal character spacing.

6. *Dot Counter:* a MOD-7 counter used to keep track of which dot of a character matrix row is being shifted out. It is also used to increment the character counter and generate a load pulse for the shift register.

7. *O.S. Delay:* a one-shot used to provide a delay so that when the dot counter is reset and a new memory address selected, enough time is provided for the new data out of memory and the outputs of the character generator to become stable before loading the shift register.

8. *Timing and Control:* circuitry that might consist of such things as crystal-controlled oscillators, counters, gates, phase-locked loops, or special function-integrated circuits used to generate the master clock signal, horizontal sync, vertical sync, and blanking signals.

9. *Video Combiner:* discrete circuitry used to combine the data information from the shift register and the timing and control information into one signal with proper voltage levels. This signal is then fed to the TV monitor and provides the display.

Final Words on Video Display

You might now ask how the information contained in RAM initially gets there. With proper interfacing and control, the address bus and data bus can be tied into the µC system such that the MPU can read from or write into the display memory like any other memory location in the system. A keyboard can be interfaced to the MPU such that information can be entered into the MPU and then echoed (transferred) to the display memory. This allows for great flexibility in software control of the system.

To enter data into the system, we need to know where the character we want to enter will be placed on the display. This is taken care of by adding another feature to our basic display, called a *cursor*. The cursor is usually a blinking box, underline, or overline that shows the user where a new character will be placed on the display. Figure 9.33 shows the cursor on the screen, indicating that the next piece of information to be entered will be next to the H in the second line.

Generally, the keyboard will allow one to change the position of the cursor by moving it to the right or left (backspace) one space at a time and one line up or down at a time. With these four controls we can easily locate the cursor anywhere on the display and insert new information.

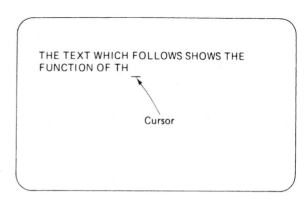

THE TEXT WHICH FOLLOWS SHOWS THE
FUNCTION OF TH

Cursor

FIGURE 9.33   Adding a cursor
to the display.

Video and graphics displays have become increasingly sophisticated and complex. With the improvements in LSI and VLSI techniques, many of the functions described above have been incorporated into integrated circuits. Motorola manufactures a number of chips that deal with video display applications. The MC6845 is an example of a complex, yet versatile CRT Controller (CRTC). It was specially designed by Motorola to be used in MPU-based controllers for monochrome or color CRT applications. It combines in one IC the ROM character generator, the shift register, the cursor control logic, 512K bytes of address space for use in graphics systems, all the video timing signals needed for the CRT operation, and many other functions. It can be programmed using software to operate with almost any alphanumerical screen format (e.g., 80 × 24, 72 × 64, 132 × 20). In conclusion, the MC6845 is an all-inclusive 40-pin IC that meets all of the operational requirements needed to interface an MPU to a CRT.

▶ SECTION 9.13 TROUBLESHOOTING CASE STUDY

Refer to the circuit of Figure 9.25 and review its operation by reading Section 9.11 in your textbook.

A technician is testing the circuit of Figure 9.25 and finds that the hexadecimal keyboard is unresponsive. In other words, when a key on the hexadecimal keyboard is depressed the microcomputer does not respond to the key actuation. No data can be entered via the keyboard—the computer is spinning its wheels and getting no place. The technician knows from reading the operating manual that the *keyboard scan program* in ROM (monitor program) starts at address $B900_{16}$, and it is the first program in the ROM that gets executed after the Reset key is actuated. According to the operating manual the following is *part* of the hexadecimal keyboard scan program:

Address	Label	Mnemonic
B900	CLMN4	LDAA $B810
B903		CMPA #FF
B905		BEQ CLMN3
B907		JSR $B9C0

Address	Label	Mnemonic
B90A	CLMN3	LDAA $B808
B90D		CMPA #FF
B90F		BEQ CLMN2
B911		JSR $B9C0
B914	CLMN2	LDAA $B804
B917		CMPA #FF
B919		BEQ CLMN1
B91B		JSR $B9C0
B91E	CLMN1	LDAA $B802
B921		CMPA #FF
B923		BEQ CLMN0
B925		JSR $B9C0
B928	CLMN0	LDAA $B801
B92B		CMPA #FF
B92D		BEQ CLMN4
B92F		JSR $B9C0
B932	REPEATSCAN	BRA CLMN4

The technician decides to use the logic analyzer to look at the activity on the signals A_4–A_0 and D_3–D_0. Clearly, the combination of the address signals A_4–A_0 and data signals D_3–D_0 allows the program monitor to determine the condition of the keyswitches. He monitors these addresses and data lines by connecting channels Ch_0–Ch_{24} of the logic analyzer to the address bus lines A_0–A_{15} and the data bus lines D_0–D_7, respectively. He sets up the logic analyzer to trigger on the negative-going transition of the $\overline{RESET}$ pulse and on *Word Recognizer* $B900_{16}$. He also uses the E-clock as the *external clock* of the logic analyzer. After pressing the Reset key he observes the following sequence of events:

1. Instruction LDAA $B810 is executed and accumulator A is loaded with the FF_{16}.
2. Instruction LDAA $B808 is executed and accumulator A is loaded with the FF_{16}.
3. Instruction LDAA $B804 is executed and accumulator A is loaded with the FF_{16}.
4. The program executes the JSR B9C0 instruction. However, the logic analyzer shows that the program is stuck in a waiting loop in the subroutine that continually executes a LDAA $B804 instruction.

Let us analyze the results recorded by the logic analyzer and try to deduce from them the cause for the malfunction in the circuit of Figure 9.25.

Instruction LDAA $B810 is Executed and Accumulator A is Loaded with the FF_{16}   This shows the 68HC11 MCU reading the status of column 4. Since accumulator A gets loaded with FF_{16}, we can conclude that no key in column 4 (keys C, 8, 4, or 0) has been depressed.

Instruction LDAA $B808 is Executed and Accumulator A is Loaded with the FF_{16} This shows the 68HC11 MCU reading the status of column 3. Since accumulator A gets loaded with FF_{16}, we can conclude that no key in column 3 (keys D, 9, 5, or 1) has been depressed.

Instruction LDAA \$B804 is Executed and Accumulator A is Loaded with the FB_{16}
This shows the 68HC11 MCU reading the status of column 3. Since accumulator A gets loaded with $FB_{16} = 11111011_2$ we can conclude that the output of Inverter 2 is shorted to the input of tri-state buffer 2. Therefore, we can assume that the "A" key in that column was, or is actuated. The monitor program will now proceed to *service* that key. Again, we cannot stress enough the complexity of a keyboard monitor program. Although keyboard monitor programs differ in complexity depending on the type of keyboard and computer being used, certain tasks are common to all keyboard monitor programs. For example, all keyboard monitor programs must check for keyswitch bounce, multiple readings of the same key actuation, actuation of a second key before release of the first key, etc. In the program that we are using in this troubleshooting case study, all of these tasks would be accomplished once the computer leaves the main program in order to execute the subroutine at address location $B9C0_{16}$.

The Program Executes the JSR B9C0 Instruction. However, the Logic Analyzer Shows that the Program is Stuck in a Waiting Loop that Continually Executes a LDAA \$B804 Instruction   Since the monitor program detected a "key down" it must then service that key. It does that by jumping to a subroutine starting at location $B9C0_{16}$. From the previous discussion, we know that several things must be done once the monitor program jumps to the subroutine at $B9C0_{16}$. We know that in our particular example, the program detected the "A" key and that it jumped to the subroutine at $B9C0_{16}$ in order to service that key. However, it appears that the program never finishes servicing the "A" key. It gets stuck in a *waiting loop* in the subroutine program, executing endlessly a LDAA \$B804 instruction. Then, the obvious question is—what is the program waiting for? Since the monitor program keeps executing a LDAA \$B804 instruction, we can conclude that it is rechecking the status of the "A" key. Remember that the program, among other things, will check to see when the key being serviced is released. The program will not check for another key actuation unless and until the previous one has been released. Clearly, if the "A" key were permanently stuck in the *down* position it would by default make the connection between the output on inverter 2 and the input of tri-state buffer 2. If this occurred, the program would go into an endless loop reading the status of the "A" key and waiting for it to be released before proceeding to check the next column. This of course, would keep the microprocessor busy spinning its wheels in an endless loop. This fault can be easily confirmed by first turning off the power to the circuit. Then, with the aid of an ohmmeter, the technician can perform a continuity test between the output of inverter 2 and the input of tri-state buffer 2.

GLOSSARY

Asynchronous Serial Communication   Method of serial data communication in which a START bit is used to synchronize the receiver to the transmitter.

Baud Rate   The rate at which the data signal is changing in a serial communication system:

$$\text{Baud Rate} = \frac{1}{\text{time between transitions}} \text{ (Baud)}$$

Binary Synchronous Communications Protocol (BISYNC)   Type of message format used by synchronous serial communication.

Bit Time   Period of time allotted to 1 data bit in a serial transmission system

Block Check Character (BCC)   Special data byte used in synchronous data communication that represents some complex parity information calculated from the data bytes in the message.

Centronics   Type of interface used to connect an MPU to a parallel I/O device.

Character Generator   Special IC that will accept an ASCII-coded word for input and produce a dot-matrix pattern of that character.

Cursor   Special symbol used in a video system to indicate the position where the next character will be placed on the screen.

Data Direction Register for Port D (DDRD)   A 68HC11 MCU built-in 6-bit bidirectional register used by the serial communications interface system. This register allows the user to program port pins PD0 through PD5 as input or output pins.

Data Rate   In some situations the data rate is equivalent to the baud rate. However, in more complex serial transmission formats, a signal transition may represent 2 or more data bits. In such cases, the data rate will be different from the baud rate.

$$\text{Data Rate} = \frac{1}{1 \text{ Bit Time}} \text{ (bits/s)}$$

End-of-text (ETX)   Special character code used in synchronous data communication.

FSK   Using two different sinewave frequencies to represent digital logic levels.

Full Duplex   Data in serial transmission scheme can be transmitted in both directions simultaneously.

Idling   See Marking.

Marking   Whenever there is no serial data word being transmitted in an asynchronous serial transmission system, the signal line is kept at a logic 1 level.

Modem   Device used to transmit or receive digital information using standard telephone lines. Fre-quency-shift keying is used in this scheme and the device is used to modulate and demodulate the signals.

Monitor Program   Program stored in ROM utilized to scan a keyboard upon application of a reset signal.

Optocoupler   See Optoisolator.

Optoisolator   Solid-state device that can be used to electrically isolate the load from the control signal source. Light energy is used to turn power on and off to a load.

Parity Bit   Extra bit attached to a code group to make the number of 1s conform to a predetermined form (odd or even). This is used in error-detection schemes in transmission of data.

RS-232-C Standard   A serial data communication standard that specifies signal voltage levels and handshake signals.

SCI Baud Rate Control Register (BAUD)   A 68HC11 MCU built-in 7-bit control register. Two of the bits in this register (TCLR, RCKB) are used for test purposes only. The other five bits are used to select the proper baud rate of the asynchronous serial data communication between the MCU and an I/O device.

SCI Control Register 1 (SCCR1)   A 68HC11 MCU built-in 4-bit control register used to establish the character length for both the transmitter and the receiver sections of the SCI system.

SCI Control Register 2 (SCCR2)   A 68HC11 MCU built-in 8-bit register used by the serial communications interface system. Bits RE and TE in this register can be conditioned to turn on or off either the transmitter or the receiver sections of the built-in UART.

SCI Data Register (SCDR)   A 68HC11 MCU built-in data register that functions as a double 8-bit register. When data is read from it, the RDR (Receive Data Register) is accessed. When data is written into it, the TDR (Transmit Data Register) is accessed.

SCI Status Register (SCSR)   A 68HC11 MCU built-in 7-bit status register used to keep track of the readiness of the receiver and/or the transmitter sections of the built-in UART.

Serial Communications Interface (SCI)   A section of the 68HC11 MCU that is accessible via port D. A built-in UART is used to perform asynchronous serial data communication between the MCU and an I/O device.

Serial Peripheral Interface (SPI)   A section of the 68HC11 MCU that is accessible via port D. This section of the MCU contains all of the circuitry necessary for the synchronous serial data communication between the MCU and an I/O device.

Software Keyboard Scanning   Upon reset of the MPU the keyboard monitor program, stored in ROM, continually scans the keyboard outputs until it senses that a key has been depressed. It then determines which key was depressed and takes appropriate action.

Space   A logic 0 level in serial data communications.

SPI Control Register (SPCR)   A 68HC11 MCU built-in 8-bit register used by both the serial communications interface and the serial peripheral interface systems. Bit DWOM (port D Wire-Or Mode) in particular determines whether port D outputs are normal or are in an open-drain configuration.

START Bit   Logic 0 level for a period of 1 bit time used in asynchronous serial data transmission to indicate the initiation of data transmission.

Start-of-Text (STX)   Special character code used in synchronous data communication.

STOP Bit   Logic 1 level for a period of 1 to 2 bit times used in asynchronous serial data transmission to indicate the termination of data word.

Sync Characters   Special character codes that are transmitted to a receiver in order to establish proper synchronization between the transmitter and the receiver.

Synchronous Serial Data Communication   Method of serial data communication in which blocks of data are transmitted continuously and where the transmitter is synchronized to the receiver through the use of special sync characters.

Two-Key Rollover   Technique whereby the keyboard monitor program incorporates checking to see that the first key depressed is released before scanning the keyboard for new key actuations.

UART   An IC that performs the function of interfacing between a parallel device (MPU) and a serial I/O device.

Video Display Terminal (VDT)   An I/O device consisting of a keyboard input and a video output.

QUESTIONS AND PROBLEMS

Section 9.1

1. Design the necessary circuitry for translating TTL logic levels (0, +5 V) to RS-232-C levels that are +12 V and −12 V for logic 0 and 1, respectively.
2. Design the circuitry for translating from RS-232-C to TTL.
3. Why should relays or optoisolators be used when an output port drives an ac load?

Section 9.2

4. Which of the following are *not* part of the standard asynchronous serial data format?
   (a) A START bit (0)   (b) 5 to 8 data bits   (c) A STATUS bit
   (d) One or more STOP bits   (e) An optional parity bit

5. Using the standard asynchronous serial format with 7 data bits, odd parity, and 2 STOP bits, draw the complete waveform for the transmission of the message "HELP."

6. If the transmission in Problem 5 is taking place at 1200 Baud, how long will it take for the complete message to be transmitted?

7. (a) Explain the difference between baud rate and data rate.
   (b) What is the data rate at which the transmission in Problem 5 is taking place?

Section 9.3

8. Which of the following are *not* part of a UART?
   (a) A serial receiver   (b) A serial transmitter
   (c) An internal baud-rate generator   (d) A bidirectional data bus buffer
   (e) Receive and transmit shift registers   (f) A memory address register
   (g) A parity checker

9. Describe the steps that take place when an MPU transmits a data word to a serial output device through a UART.

10. Describe the steps that take place when an MPU receives a data word from a serial input device through a UART.

11. How does the UART receiver section sync itself to the incoming serial data?

Sections 9.4–9.5

12. Name the *four* 6850 UART registers with which the MPU can communicate.

13. Which one of the following is *not* one of the four basic operations an MPU can perform on a UART?
    (a) Read the control register   (b) Read the status register
    (c) Write to the transmit data register   (d) Read from the receiver data register

14. Information that determines the serial transmission characteristics between a 6850 UART and an I/O device is in the UART's:
    (a) Status register   (b) Receive data register   (c) Transmit data register
    (d) Control register

15. If an MPU and a 6850 UART are set up for MPU-initiated conditional transfer, the MPU can determine if the 6850 UART has data for it by:
    (a) Reading and testing the status register
    (b) Reading and testing the receive data register
    (c) Reading and testing the control register
    (d) Reading and testing the transmit data register

16. What control word must the MPU send to the 6850 control register if the following operation is desired?
    9600 Baud using an external clock frequency of 614.4 kHz
    8 data bits
    Even parity
    1 STOP bit
    $\overline{\text{RTS}}$ = 0 and transmit interrupt disabled
    receiver interrupt disabled

17. Refer to Fig. 9.14. Assume that the microprocessor has previously written the word "5A" into the UART control register. Draw the serial waveform that is generated at the TxDATA output if the microprocessor then writes the word "C9" into the UART transmit data register (TxDR). Show the exact timing.

18. Refer to the flowchart of Fig. 9.15. Why is it necessary to read the status register contents before writing a new word into the TxDR for transmission? What would happen if this were not done? Remember that the microprocessor executes instructions in several microseconds.

19. Modify the circuit of Fig. 9.14 so that address 3001 is used to access the UART's control and status registers, and address 3000 is used to access RxDR and TxDR.

20. Refer to Fig. 9.14. Assume that the serial device that is interfaced to the 68HC11 MPU is a video display terminal (VDT) operating at 2400 Baud. The VDT uses a serial format of 7 data bits, an even parity bit, and 2 STOP bits. Write a program that will transmit the following message from the MPU to the VDT: "ARE YOU READY?" The ASCII codes for the characters can be assumed to be stored in memory starting at address 0300. The program should include steps to initialize the 6850 UART.

21. Modify the program of Problem 20 so that after the 68HC11 MPU transmits the message to the VDT, it waits for the operator to respond by hitting the "N" or "Y" keys (for No or Yes, respectively). When the MPU receives a character from the VDT, it should respond as follows:
    (a) If the character is anything other than "Y," the MPU retransmits the message and awaits a new response.
    (b) If the character is "Y," the MPU continues executing instructions in sequence.

Section 9.6

22. The 68HC11 MCU has its own built-in UART. Which of the 68HC11 MCU port pins can be used for the asynchronous serial communication interface between the MCU and an I/O device?

23. Write a program sequence that will enable the SCI section of the 68HC11 MCU for asynchronous serial communications.

24. Describe the function of the DDRD register of the 68HC11 MCU.

25. What effect does the state of the DWOM bit of the SPCR register have on the port D pins?

26. Describe the function of the RIE bit of the SCCR2 register.

27. Describe the function of the RDRF bit of the SCSR register.

28. Write a program sequence that will check whether or not a framing error was detected for the received character currently in the RDR.

29. Write a program sequence to clear the TDRE flag in the SCSR register.

30. Modify the program sequence of Example 9.6(b) so that a 2400 Baud rate can be used.

31. Which 68HC11 MCU register controls the character length that will be used during the asynchronous serial communication?

32. Modify the program sequence of Example 9.7 for the transmission of a message with an unknown number of characters. The first ASCII code of the message is stored at memory location C500 and the byte FF_{16} follows the last ASCII code in the message.

33. Modify the program sequence of Example 9.8 so that it checks for framing errors. If a framing error is detected, the MPU should stop checking for any more incoming ASCII codes, and leave the main program by jumping to a program sequence that will turn on an LED connected to port D pin 5.

Section 9.7

34. Compare asynchronous and synchronous serial data communications as to the following:
  (a) Which one uses START and STOP bits?
  (b) Which one uses special sync characters?
  (c) Which one has a transmission efficiency of about 98 percent?
  (d) Which one is best for high-speed transmission of large data blocks?
  (e) Which one has a protocol called BISYNC?

Sections 9.8–9.9

35. Refer to Fig. 9.18B. The MPU has programmed the 6850 UART for the following transmission parameters: 9600 Baud, 7 data bits, an odd parity bit, and 1 STOP bit. Draw the serial waveform at the input to the terminal when the MPU transmits the character "A."

36. Why is FSK used instead of pulses when data are transmitted over telephone lines?

37. Describe the functions performed by a modem.

38. Describe the three RS-232-C signals used most often by modems.

39. Refer to Fig. 9.20. Assume that the microcomputer programs the 6850 UART for the following transmission parameters: 4800 Baud, 8 data bits, no parity, and 2 STOP bits. Sketch the FSK waveform that is transmitted when the microcomputer sends the character "$" to the main computer.

40. What determines whether a modem is an originate modem or an answer modem? How does their operation differ?

41. Explain the difference between full-duplex and half-duplex communication.

42. State some of the advanced features available in smart modems.

Section 9.10

43. What is the function of the data direction register in the 6821 PIA?

44. The 6821 does not have a specific status register. Where, then, is status information stored for examination by the MPU?

45. Which of the following is *not* a feature of the 6821 PIA?
   (a) Programmability   (b) Handshaking   (c) Interrupt capability
   (d) Timer   (e) Parallel data handling

46. Refer to Fig. 9.23. Assume that a positive-going transition at CA1 sets the CA1 status flag in CRA. Draw a flowchart that shows the discrete steps the 68HC11 MPU has to execute to produce the following operation:
   (a) Initialize the printer.
   (b) Read the availability of the printer to receive the next ASCII character.
   (c) Send the next ASCII character to be printed out.

47. Describe the function of the Centronics interface signals $\overline{\text{ACKNLG}}$ and BUSY.

48. How does the printer of Fig. 9.23 know when the data at port B is a character it has not yet received?

Section 9.11

49. Which one of the following is *not* an advantage of interfacing an MPU to a keyboard using a software keyboard scanning technique as opposed to a hardware keyboard encoder?
   (a) Cheaper   (b) More reliable   (c) Faster   (d) Easier to modify

50. When interfacing a hexadecimal keyboard to an MPU using the software keyboard scanning technique:
   (a) A keyboard monitor program must be stored in RAM memory.
   (b) A keyboard monitor program must be stored on audio tape so that it can be loaded when needed.
   (c) A keyboard monitor program must be stored in ROM memory.
   (d) A keyboard monitor program must be entered each time power is applied.

51. Refer to Fig. 9.25. Assume that the MPU is executing the instruction LDAB $B810. Determine what result ends up in ACCB for each of the following situations:
   (a) The "D" key is down.   (b) The "8" key is down.
   (c) The "4" and "8" keys are down.   (d) The "4" and "5" keys are down.
   (e) No key is down.

52. Refer to Fig. 9.25. After executing the instruction LDAB $B801, the result is [**ACCB**] = 11111110. What key is down?

53. Write a program sequence for the keyboard interface of Fig. 9.25 that does the following:
   (a) Check for key "7" down.
   (b) If the "7" key is down, store 07 in address location C100 and then halt.
   (c) If the "7" key is not down, delay for 10 ms and repeat from step (a).

54. Describe how a keyboard program handles keyswitch bounce to ensure that the same key actuation is not detected more than once.

55. What is two-key rollover? How does a keyboard monitor program handle it?

56. The program below is written for the keyboard interface of Fig. 9.25. Its function is to send all 0s to an output port at address C700 only after the operator presses the "B" key followed by the "0" key. The program uses a 10-ms delay subroutine at C800.

Address	Label	Instruction code	Mnemonic
C100	START	B6	LDAA $B802
C101		B8	
C102		02	
C103		84	ANDA #$04
C104		04	
C105		26	BNE $C100
C106		F9	
C107		BD	JSR $C800
C108		C8	
C109		00	
C10A		B6	LDAA $B802
C10B		B8	
C10C		02	
C10D		84	ANDA #$04
C10E		04	
C10F		27	BEQ $C10A
C110		F9	
C111		B6	LDAA $B810
C112		B8	
C113		10	
C114		44	LSRA
C115		25	BCS $C111
C116		FA	
C117		7F	CLR $C700
C118		C7	
C119		00	
C11A	END	3E	WAI

Study this program and answer the following:
   (a) What is the function of the instructions at C100, C103, and C105?
   (b) What is the function of the instruction at C107?

(c) What is the function of the instructions at C10A, C10D, and C10F?

(d) What is the function of the instructions at C111, C114, and C115?

(e) Will this program send all 0s to the output port even if the "0" key is pressed before the "B" key is released?

57. Refer to Fig. 9.26. Port A has address C806 and port B has address C804. Write a program sequence that continuously scans the keyboard rows from top to bottom until it finds any key that is down. When it finds a key down, the program halts. (*Hint:* Use a shift operation on port B.)

Section 9.12

58. Refer to Fig. 9.31. Assume that the ASCII code for uppercase "E" is applied to the 2513 and the row select inputs are 010. The LOAD and CLK inputs to the shift register are shown in Fig. 9.34. Draw the serial output waveform.

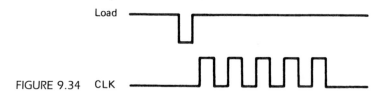

FIGURE 9.34   CLK

59. In the display system of Fig. 9.32, why are the two LSBs of the shift register loaded with 0s?

60. In the video display system of Fig. 9.32, which block contains information about all of the character positions on the CRT? Which block holds the actual pattern of dark and bright spots that are to be displayed on the CRT?

61. Why is the row select counter in Fig. 9.32 a MOD-10 counter when there are only seven rows in each character dot pattern?

Section 9.13

Refer to Figure 9.25 and to the Troubleshooting Case Study of section 9.13 for all the problems in this section.

62. What fault or faults in this circuit would cause keys 0, 4, 8, and C not to be responsive?

63. A technician has just built the circuit of Figure 9.25 and he is troubleshooting it with a logic analyzer. When no key is down, the monitor program scans the keyboard properly. However, the actuation of certain keys does not yield the expected results. The following are some examples of incorrect results:

When key "C" is pressed, accumulator A is loaded with $F7_{16}$ when LDAA $B808 is executed.

When key "9" is pressed, accumulator A is loaded with FB_{16} when LDAA $B810 is executed.

When key "4" is pressed, accumulator A is loaded with FD_{16} when LDAA $B808 is executed.

When key "E" is pressed, accumulator A is loaded with $F7_{16}$ when LDAA $B804 is executed.

When key "3" is pressed, accumulator A is loaded with FE_{16} when LDAA $B802 is executed.

(a) What is the most likely fault with this circuit? Explain.

(b) Describe the steps you would take in order to verify and fix the fault.

64. Assume that the *decoder circuitry* in this circuit belongs to the TTL logic family. Describe what would happen to the operation of the circuit of Figure 9.25 if the E signal from the MC68HC11A8 MCU became disconnected from the Enable input of the *decoder circuitry*.

Complete 68HC11 MCU Instruction Set

The following pages present a complete summary of each 68HC11 instruction. For each instruction, the summary includes: (1) a verbal description; (2) a symbolic description; (3) an indication of how the instruction will affect the various flags in the condition code register; (4) a table with instruction mnemonics, address modes, op codes, operand(s) used by the instruction, number of bytes of code, and number of clock cycles for execution. Following is a list of the nomenclature used in these descriptions.

(a) Operators

( )	= Contents of register shown inside parentheses
←	= Is transferred to
↑	= Is pulled from stack
↓	= Is pushed onto stack
•	= Boolean AND
+	= Arithmetic addition symbol except where used as inclusive-OR symbol in Boolean formula
⊕	= Exclusive-OR
×	= Multiply
:	= Concatenation
−	= Arithmetic subtraction symbol or negation symbol (2's complement)

(b) Registers in the MPU

ACCA = Accumulator A

ACCB = Accumulator B

ACCX = Accumulator ACCA or ACCB

ACCD = Double accumulator—accumulator A concatenated with accumulator B where A is the most significant byte

CCR = Condition code register

IX = Index register X, 16 bits

IXH = Index register X, higher order 8 bits

IXL = Index register X, lower order 8 bits

IY = Index register Y, 16 bits

IYH = Index register Y, higher order 8 bits

IYL = Index register Y, lower order 8 bits

PC = Program counter, 16 bits

PCH = Program counter, higher order (most significant) 8 bits

PCL = Program counter, lower order (least significant) 8 bits

SP = Stack pointer, 16 bits

SPH = Stack pointer, higher order 8 bits

SPL = Stack pointer, lower order 8 bits

(c) Memory and Addressing

M = A memory location (one byte)

M + 1 = The byte of memory at $0001 plus the address of the memory location indicated by "M"

Rel = Relative offset (i.e., the 2's complement number stored in the last byte of machine code corresponding to a branch instruction)

(opr) = Operand

(msk) = Mask used in bit manipulation instructions

(rel) = Relative offset used in branch instructions

(d) Bits 7–0 of the Condition Code Register

S = Stop disable, bit 7

X = X interrupt mask, bit 6

H = Half carry, bit 5

I = I interrupt mask, bit 4

N = Negative indicator, bit 3

Z = Zero indicator, bit 2

V = 2's complement overflow indicator, bit 1

C = Carry/Borrow, bit 0

(e) Notation used in CCR activity summary figures

− = Bit not affected

0 = Bit forced to 0

1 = Bit forced to 1

↕ = Bit set or cleared according to results of operation

$\downarrow$ = Bit may change from 1 to 0, remain 0, or remain 1 as a result of this operation, but cannot change from 0 to 1

(f) Notation used for operands

—	= Irrelevant data
ii	= One byte of immediate data
jj	= High-order byte of 16-bit immediate data
kk	= Low-order byte of 16-bit immediate data
hh	= High-order byte of 16-bit extended address
ll	= Low-order byte of 16-bit extended address
dd	= Low-order 8 bits of direct address $0000–$00FF
mm	= 8-bit mask (set bits correspond to operand bits which will be affected)
ff	= 8-bit forward offset $00 (0) TO $FF (255) (is added to index)
rr	= Signed relative offset $80 ($-127$) to $7F ($+127$) (offset relative to address following machine code offset byte)

(g) Notation used for # cycles

*	= Infinity or until reset occurs
**	= 12 cycles are used beginning with the op code fetch. A wait state is entered which remains in effect for any integer number of MPU E-clock cycle (n) until an interrupt is recognized. Finally, two additional cycles are used to fetch the appropriate interrupt vector (total = 14 + n)

ABA—Add Accumulator B to Accumulator A

Description Adds the contents of accumulator B to the contents of accumulator A and places the result in accumulator A. Accumulator B is not changed. This instruction affects the H condition code bit so it is suitable for use in the BCD arithmetic operations.

Operation

$$ACCA \leftarrow (ACCA) + (ACCB)$$

S	X	H	I	N	Z	V	C
—	—	$\updownarrow$	—	$\updownarrow$	$\updownarrow$	$\updownarrow$	$\updownarrow$

Mnemonic	Address mode	Op code	Operand(s)	# Bytes	# Cycles
ABA	Inherent	1B		1	2

ABX—Add Accumulator B to Index Register X

Description Adds the 8-bit unsigned contents of accumulator B to the contents of index register X (IX) considering the possible carry out of the low-order byte of the index register X; places the result in index register X (IX). Accumulator B is not changed. There is no equivalent instruction to add accumulator A to an index register.

Operation

$$IX \leftarrow (IX) + (ACCB)$$

S	X	H	I	N	Z	V	C
–	–	–	–	–	–	–	–

Mnemonic	Address mode	Op code	Operand(s)	# Bytes	# Cycles
ABX	Inherent	3A		1	3

ABY—Add Accumulator B to Index Register Y

Description Adds the 8-bit unsigned contents of accumulator B to the contents of index register Y (IY) considering the possible carry out of the low-order byte of the index register Y; places the result in index register Y (IY). Accumulator B is not changed. There is no equivalent instruction to add accumulator A to an index register.

Operation

$$IY \leftarrow (IY) + (ACCB)$$

S	X	H	I	N	Z	V	C
–	–	–	–	–	–	–	–

Mnemonic	Address mode	Op code	Operand(s)	# Bytes	# Cycles
ABY	Inherent	18 3A		2	4

ADC—Add with Carry

Description Adds the contents of the C bit to the sum of the contents of ACCX and M and places the result in ACCX. This instruction affects the H condition bit so it is suitable for use in the BCD arithmetic operations.

Operation

$$\text{ACCX} \leftarrow (\text{ACCX}) + (M) + (C)$$

S	X	H	I	N	Z	V	C
−	−	↕	−	↕	↕	↕	↕

Mnemonic	Address mode	Op code	Operand(s)	# Bytes	# Cycles
ADCA (opr)	A IMM	89	ii	2	2
	A DIR	99	dd	2	3
	A EXT	B9	hh ll	3	4
	A IND,X	A9	ff	2	4
	A IND,Y	18 A9	ff	3	5
ADCB (opr)	B IMM	C9	ii	2	2
	B DIR	D9	dd	2	3
	B EXT	F9	hh ll	3	4
	B IND,X	E9	ff	2	4
	B IND,Y	18 E9	ff	3	5

ADD—Add without Carry

Description   Adds the contents of M to the contents of ACCX and places the result in ACCX. This instruction affects the H condition code bit so it is suitable for use in the BCD arithmetic operations.

Operation

$$\text{ACCX} \leftarrow (\text{ACCX}) + (M)$$

S	X	H	I	N	Z	V	C
−	−	↕	−	↕	↕	↕	↕

Mnemonic	Address mode	Op code	Operand(s)	# Bytes	# Cycles
ADDA (opr)	A IMM	8B	ii	2	2
	A DIR	9B	dd	2	3
	A EXT	BB	hh ll	3	4
	A IND,X	AB	ff	2	4
	A IND,Y	18 AB	ff	3	5

Mnemonic	Address mode	Op code	Operand(s)	# Bytes	# Cycles
ADDB (opr)	B IMM	CB	ii	2	2
	B DIR	DB	dd	2	3
	B EXT	FB	hh ll	3	4
	B IND,X	EB	ff	2	4
	B IND,Y	18 EB	ff	3	5

ADDD—Add Double Accumulator

Description   Adds the contents of M concatenated with M + 1 to the contents of ACCD and places the results in ACCD. Accumulator A corresponds to the high-order half of the 16-bit double accumulator D.

Operation

$$ACCD \leftarrow (ACCD) + (M:M + 1)$$

S	X	H	I	N	Z	V	C
–	–	–	–	$\updownarrow$	$\updownarrow$	$\updownarrow$	$\updownarrow$

Mnemonic	Address mode	Op code	Operand(s)	# Bytes	# Cycles
ADDD (opr)	IMM	C3	jj kk	3	4
	DIR	D3	dd	2	5
	EXT	F3	hh ll	3	6
	IND,X	E3	ff	2	6
	IND,Y	18 E3	ff	3	7

AND—Logical AND

Description   Performs the logical AND between the contents of ACCX and the contents of M and places the result in ACCX.

Operation

$$ACCX \leftarrow (ACCX) \cdot (M)$$

S	X	H	I	N	Z	V	C
–	–	–	–	$\updownarrow$	$\updownarrow$	0	–

Mnemonic	Address mode	Op code	Operand(s)	# Bytes	# Cycles
ANDA (opr)	A IMM	84	ii	2	2
	A DIR	94	dd	2	3
	A EXT	B4	hh ll	3	4
	A IND,X	A4	ff	2	4
	A IND,Y	18 A4	ff	3	5
ANDB (opr)	B IMM	C4	ii	2	2
	B DIR	D4	dd	2	3
	B EXT	F4	hh ll	3	4
	B IND,X	E4	ff	2	4
	B IND,Y	18 E4	ff	3	5

ASL—Arithmetic Shift Left (same as LSL)

Description   Shifts all bits of the ACCX or M one place to the left. Bit 0 is loaded with a zero. The C bit in the CCR is loaded from the most significant bit of ACCX or M.

Operation

$$C \leftarrow \boxed{b7 \text{-----------} b0} \leftarrow \boxed{0}$$

S	X	H	I	N	Z	V	C
–	–	–	–	↕	↕	↕	↕

Mnemonic	Address mode	Op code	Operand(s)	# Bytes	# Cycles
ASL (opr)	EXT	78	hh ll	3	6
	IND,X	68	ff	2	6
	IND, Y	18 68	ff	3	7
ASLA	A INH	48		1	2
ASLB	B INH	58		1	2

ASLD—Arithmetic Shift Left Double Accumulator (same as LSLD)

Description   Shifts all bits of ACCD one place to the left. Bit 0 is loaded with zero. The C bit in the CCR is loaded from the most significant bit of ACCD.

Operation

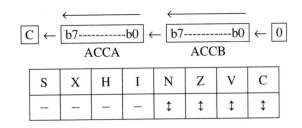

S	X	H	I	N	Z	V	C
–	–	–	–	$\updownarrow$	$\updownarrow$	$\updownarrow$	$\updownarrow$

Mnemonic	Address mode	Op code	Operand(s)	# Bytes	# Cycles
ASLD	INH	05		1	3

ASR—Arithmetic Shift Right

Description   Shifts all of ACCX or M one place to the right. Bit 7 is held constant. Bit 0 is loaded into the C bit of the CCR.

Operation

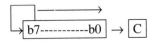

S	X	H	I	N	Z	V	C
–	–	–	–	$\updownarrow$	$\updownarrow$	$\updownarrow$	$\updownarrow$

Mnemonic	Address mode	Op code	Operand(s)	# Bytes	# Cycles
ASR (opr)	EXT	77	hh ll	3	6
	IND,X	67	ff	2	6
	IND,Y	18 67	ff	3	7
ASRA	A INH	47		1	2
ASRB	B INH	57		1	2

BCC—Branch if Carry Clear (same as BHS)

Description   Tests the state of the C bit in the CCR and causes a branch if C is clear.

Operation

$$PC \leftarrow (PC) + \$0002 + Rel \qquad If\ (C) = 0$$

S	X	H	I	N	Z	V	C
–	–	–	–	–	–	–	–

Mnemonic	Address mode	Op code	Operand(s)	# Bytes	# Cycles
BCC (rel)	REL	24	rr	2	3

BCLR—Clear Bit(s) in Memory

Description Clear multiple bits in location M. The bit(s) to be cleared are specified by 1s in the mask byte. All other bits in M are rewritten to their current state.

Operation

$$M \leftarrow (M) \cdot (\overline{PC+2})$$
$$M \leftarrow (M) \cdot (\overline{PC+3})\ (for\ IND,\ Y\ address\ mode\ only)$$

S	X	H	I	N	Z	V	C
–	–	–	–	$\updownarrow$	$\updownarrow$	0	–

Mnemonic	Address mode	Op code	Operand(s)	# Bytes	# Cycles
BCLR (opr)	DIR	15	dd mm	3	6
(msk)	IND,X	1D	ff mm	3	7
	IND,Y	18 1D	ff mm	4	8

BCS—Branch if Carry Set (same as BLO)

Description Tests the state of the C bit in the CCR and causes a branch if C is set.

Operation

$$PC \leftarrow (PC) + \$0002 + Rel \qquad If\ (C) = 1$$

S	X	H	I	N	Z	V	C
–	–	–	–	–	–	–	–

Mnemonic	Address mode	Op code	Operand(s)	# Bytes	# Cycles
BCS (rel)	REL	25	rr	2	3

BEQ—Branch if Equal to Zero

Description Tests the state of the Z bit in the CCR and causes a branch if Z is set.

Operation

$$PC \leftarrow (PC) + \$0002 + Rel \qquad If\ (Z) = 1$$

S	X	H	I	N	Z	V	C
–	–	–	–	–	–	–	–

Mnemonic	Address mode	Op code	Operand(s)	# Bytes	# Cycles
BEQ (rel)	REL	27	rr	2	3

BGE—Branch if Greater than or Equal to Zero

Description If the BGE instruction is executed immediately after execution of any of the instructions, CBA, CMP(A, B, or D), CP(X or Y), SBA, SUB(A, B, or D), the branch will occur if and only if the 2's-complement number represented by the ACCX was greater than or equal to the 2's-complement number represented by M.

Operation

$$PC \leftarrow (PC) + \$0002 + Rel \qquad If\ (N) \oplus (V) = 0$$
i.e., if (ACCX) ≥ (M)   (2's-complement "signed" numbers)

S	X	H	I	N	Z	V	C
–	–	–	–	–	–	–	–

Mnemonic	Address mode	Op code	Operand(s)	# Bytes	# Cycles
BGE (rel)	REL	2C	rr	2	3

BGT—Branch if Greater than Zero

Description   If the BGT instruction is executed immediately after execution of any of the instructions, CBA, CMP(A, B, or D), CP(X or Y), SBA, SUB(A, B, or D), the branch will occur if and only if the 2's-complement number represented by the ACCX was greater than the 2's-complement number represented by M.

Operation

$$PC \leftarrow (PC) + \$0002 + Rel \qquad \text{If } (Z) + [(N) \oplus (V)] = 0$$
$$\text{i.e., if } (ACCX) > (M) \qquad \text{(2's-complement "signed" numbers)}$$

S	X	H	I	N	Z	V	C
–	–	–	–	–	–	–	–

Mnemonic	Address mode	Op code	Operand(s)	# Bytes	# Cycles
BGT (rel)	REL	2E	rr	2	3

BHI—Branch if Higher

Description   If the BHI instruction is executed immediately after execution of any of the instructions, CBA, CMP(A, B, or D), CP(X or Y), SBA, SUB(A, B, or D), the branch will occur if and only if the unsigned binary number represented by the ACCX was greater than the unsigned binary number represented by M.

Operation

$$PC \leftarrow (PC) + \$0002 + Rel \qquad \text{If } (C) + (Z) = 0$$
$$\text{i.e., if } (ACCX) > (M) \qquad \text{(unsigned binary numbers)}$$

S	X	H	I	N	Z	V	C
–	–	–	–	–	–	–	–

Mnemonic	Address mode	Op code	Operand(s)	# Bytes	# Cycles
BHI (rel)	REL	22	rr	2	3

BHS—Branch if Higher or Same (Same as BCC)

Description   If the BHS instruction is executed immediately after execution of any of the instructions, CBA, CMP(A, B, or D), CP(X or Y), SBA, SUB(A, B, or D), the branch will occur if and only if the unsigned binary number represented by the ACCX was greater than or equal to the unsigned binary number represented by M.

Operation

$$PC \leftarrow (PC) + \$0002 + Rel \qquad If (C) = 0$$
i.e., if $(ACCX) \geq (M)$ (unsigned binary numbers)

S	X	H	I	N	Z	V	C
–	–	–	–	–	–	–	–

Mnemonic	Address mode	Op code	Operand(s)	# Bytes	# Cycles
BHS (rel)	REL	24	rr	2	3

BIT—Bit Test

Description Performs the logical AND operation between the contents of ACCX and the contents of M and modifies the condition codes accordingly. Neither the contents of ACCX nor M operands are affected.

Operation

$$(ACCX) \cdot (M)$$

S	X	H	I	N	Z	V	C
–	–	–	–	$\updownarrow$	$\updownarrow$	0	–

Mnemonic	Address mode	Op code	Operand(s)	# Bytes	# Cycles
BITA (opr)	A IMM	85	ii	2	2
	A DIR	95	dd	2	3
	A EXT	B5	hh ll	3	4
	A IND,X	A5	ff	2	4
	A IND,Y	18 A5	ff	3	5
BITB (opr)	B IMM	C5	ii	2	2
	B DIR	D5	dd	2	3
	B EXT	F5	hh ll	3	4
	B IND,X	E5	ff	2	4
	B IND,Y	18 E5	ff	3	5

BLE—Branch if Less than or Equal to Zero

Description   If the BLE instruction is executed immediately after execution of any of the instructions, CBA, CMP(A, B, or D), CP(X or Y), SBA, SUB(A, B, or D), the branch will occur if and only if the 2's-complement number represented by ACCX was less than or equal to the 2's-complement number represented by M.

Operation

$PC \leftarrow (PC) + \$0002 + Rel$ If $(Z) + [(N)\oplus(V)] = 1$

i.e., if $(ACCX) \le (M)$ (2's-complement signed numbers)

S	X	H	I	N	Z	V	C
–	–	–	–	–	–	–	–

Mnemonic	Address mode	Op code	Operand(s)	# Bytes	# Cycles
BLE (rel)	REL	2F	rr	2	3

BLO—Branch if Lower (Same as BCS)

Description   If the BLO instruction is executed immediately after execution of any of the instructions, CBA, CMP(A, B, or D), CP(X or Y), SBA, SUB(A, B, or D), the branch will occur if and only if the unsigned binary number represented by ACCX was less than the unsigned binary number represented by M.

Operation

$PC \leftarrow (PC) + \$0002 + Rel$ If $(C) = 1$

i.e., if $(ACCX) < (M)$ (unsigned binary numbers)

S	X	H	I	N	Z	V	C
–	–	–	–	–	–	–	–

Mnemonic	Address mode	Op code	Operand(s)	# Bytes	# Cycles
BLO (rel)	REL	25	rr	2	3

BLS—Branch if Lower or Same

Description   If the BLS instruction is executed immediately after execution of any of the instructions, CBA, CMP(A, B, or D), CB(X or Y), SBA, SUB(A, B, or D), the branch will occur if and only if the unsigned binary number represented by ACCX was less than or equal to the unsigned binary number represented by M.

Operation

$$PC \leftarrow (PC) + \$0002 + Rel \qquad \text{If } (C) + (Z) = 1$$
$$\text{i.e., if } (ACCX) \leq (M) \qquad \text{(unsigned binary numbers)}$$

S	X	H	I	N	Z	V	C
—	—	—	—	—	—	—	—

Mnemonic	Address mode	Op code	Operand(s)	# Bytes	# Cycles
BLS (rel)	REL	23	rr	2	3

BLT—Branch if Less than Zero

Description If the BLT instruction is executed immediately after execution of any of the instructions, CBA, CMP(A, B, or D), CP(X or Y), SBA, SUB(A, B, or D), the branch will occur if and only if the 2's-complement number represented by ACCX was less than the 2's-complement number represented by M.

Operation

$$PC \leftarrow (PC) + \$0002 + Rel \qquad \text{If } (N) \oplus (V) = 1$$
$$\text{i.e., if } (ACCX) < (M) \qquad \text{(2's-complement signed numbers)}$$

S	X	H	I	N	Z	V	C
—	—	—	—	—	—	—	—

Mnemonic	Address mode	Op code	Operand(s)	# Bytes	# Cycles
BLT (rel)	REL	2D	rr	2	3

BMI—Branch if Minus

Description Tests the state of the N bit in the CCR and causes a branch if N is set.

Operation

$$PC \leftarrow (PC) + \$0002 + Rel \qquad If (N) = 1$$

S	X	H	I	N	Z	V	C
–	–	–	–	–	–	–	–

Mnemonic	Address mode	Op code	Operand(s)	# Bytes	# Cycles
BMI (rel)	REL	2B	rr	2	3

BNE—Branch if Not Equal to Zero

Description   Tests the state of the Z bit in the CCR and causes a branch if Z is Clear.

Operation

$$PC \leftarrow (PC) + \$0002 + Rel \qquad If (Z) = 0$$

S	X	H	I	N	Z	V	C
–	–	–	–	–	–	–	–

Mnemonic	Address mode	Op code	Operand(s)	# Bytes	# Cycles
BNE (rel)	REL	26	rr	2	3

BPL—Branch if Plus

Description   Tests the state of the N bit in the CCR and causes a branch if N is Clear.

Operation

$$PC \leftarrow (PC) + \$0002 + Rel \qquad If (N) = 0$$

S	X	H	I	N	Z	V	C
–	–	–	–	–	–	–	–

Mnemonic	Address mode	Op code	Operand(s)	# Bytes	# Cycles
BPL (rel)	REL	2A	rr	2	3

BRA—Branch Always

Description Unconditional branch to the address given by the following formula, in which Rel is the relative offset stored as a 2's-complement number in the second byte of machine code corresponding to the branch instruction.

Operation

$$PC \leftarrow (PC) + \$0002 + Rel$$

S	X	H	I	N	Z	V	C
–	–	–	–	–	–	–	–

Mnemonic	Address mode	Op code	Operand(s)	# Bytes	# Cycles
BRA (rel)	REL	20	rr	2	3

BRCLR—Branch if Bit(s) Clear

Description Performs the logical AND of location M and the mask supplied with the instruction, then branches if the result is 0 (only if all bits corresponding to 1s in the mask byte are 0s in the tested byte).

Operation

$$PC \leftarrow (PC) + \$0004 + Rel \quad \text{If } (M) \cdot (PC + 2) = 0$$
$$PC \leftarrow (PC) + \$0005 + Rel \quad \text{If } (M) \cdot (PC + 3) = 0 \text{ (for IND, Y address modes only)}$$

S	X	H	I	N	Z	V	C
–	–	–	–	–	–	–	–

Mnemonic	Address mode	Op code	Operand(s)	# Bytes	# Cycles
BRCLR (opr)	DIR	13	dd mm rr	4	6
(msk)	IND,X	1F	ff mm rr	4	7
(rel)	IND,Y	18 1F	ff mm rr	5	8

BRN—Branch Never

Description Never branches. In effect, this instruction can be considered as a 2-byte NOP (no operation) requiring three cycles for execution. Its inclusion in the instruction set is to provide a complement for the BRA instruction. The instruction is useful during program debug to negate the effect of another branch instruction without disturbing the offset byte.

Operation

$$PC \leftarrow (PC) + \$0002$$

S	X	H	I	N	Z	V	C
—	—	—	—	—	—	—	—

Mnemonic	Address mode	Op code	Operand(s)	# Bytes	# Cycles
BRN (rel)	REL	21	rr	2	3

BRSET—Branch if Bit(s) Set

Description   Performs the logical AND of location M inverted and the mask supplied with the instruction, then branches if the result is 0 (only if all bits corresponding to 1s in the mask byte are 1s in the tested byte).

Operation

$PC \leftarrow (PC) + \$0004 + Rel$ If $(\overline{M}) \cdot (PC + 2) = 0$
$PC \leftarrow (PC) + \$0005 + Rel$ If $(\overline{M}) \cdot (PC + 3) = 0$ (for IND, Y address modes only)

S	X	H	I	N	Z	V	C
—	—	—	—	—	—	—	—

Mnemonic	Address mode	Op code	Operand(s)	# Bytes	# Cycles
BRSET (opr)	DIR	12	dd mm rr	4	6
(msk)	IND,X	1E	ff mm rr	4	7
(rel)	IND,Y	18 1E	ff mm rr	5	8

BSET—Set Bit(s) in Memory

Description   Set multiple bits in location M. The bit(s) to be set are specified by 1s in the mask byte (last machine code byte of the instruction). All other bits in M are unaffected.

Operation

$$M \leftarrow (M) + (PC + 2)$$
$$M \leftarrow (M) + (PC + 3) \text{ (for IND, Y address modes only)}$$

S	X	H	I	N	Z	V	C
–	–	–	–	$\updownarrow$	$\updownarrow$	0	–

Mnemonic	Address mode	Op code	Operand(s)	# Bytes	# Cycles
BSET (opr)	DIR	14	dd mm	3	6
(msk)	IND,X	1C	ff mm	3	7
	IND,Y	18 1C	ff mm	4	8

BSR—Branch to Subroutine

Description   The program counter is incremented by two (this will be the return address). The least significant byte of the contents of the program counter (low-order return address) is pushed onto the stack. The stack pointer is then decremented by one. The most significant byte of the contents of the program counter (high-order return address) is pushed onto the stack. The stack pointer is then decremented by one. A branch then occurs to the location specified by the branch offset.

Operation

PC ← (PC) + $0002	Advance PC to return address
↓ (PCL)	Push low-order return onto stack
SP ← (SP) − $0001	
↓ (PCH)	Push high-order return onto stack
SP ← (SP) − $0001	
PC ← (PC) + Rel	Load start address of requested subroutine

S	X	H	I	N	Z	V	C
–	–	–	–	–	–	–	–

Mnemonic	Address mode	Op code	Operand(s)	# Bytes	# Cycles
BSR (rel)	REL	8D	rr	2	6

BVC—Branch if Overflow Clear

Description   Tests the state of the V bit in the CCR and causes a branch if V is clear.

Operation

$$PC \leftarrow (PC) + \$0002 + Rel \qquad \text{If } (V) = 0$$

S	X	H	I	N	Z	V	C
—	—	—	—	—	—	—	—

Mnemonic	Address mode	Op code	Operand(s)	# Bytes	# Cycles
BVC (rel)	REL	28	rr	2	3

BVS—Branch if Overflow Set

Description   Tests the state of the V bit in the CCR and causes a branch if V is set.

Operation

$$PC \leftarrow (PC) + \$0002 + Rel \qquad \text{If } (V) = 1$$

S	X	H	I	N	Z	V	C
—	—	—	—	—	—	—	—

Mnemonic	Address mode	Op code	Operand(s)	# Bytes	# Cycles
BVS (rel)	REL	29	rr	2	3

CBA—Compare Accumulators

Description   Compares the contents of ACCA to the contents of ACCB and sets the condition codes, which may be used for arithmetic and logical conditional branches. Both operands are unaffected.

Operation

$$(ACCA) - (ACCB)$$

S	X	H	I	N	Z	V	C
—	—	—	—	↕	↕	↕	↕

Mnemonic	Address mode	Op code	Operand(s)	# Bytes	# Cycles
CBA	INH	11		1	2

CLC—Clear Carry

Description   Clears the C bit in the CCR.

Operation

$$C \text{ bit} \leftarrow 0$$

S	X	H	I	N	Z	V	C
—	—	—	—	—	—	—	0

Mnemonic	Address mode	Op code	Operand(s)	# Bytes	# Cycles
CLC	INH	0C		1	2

CLI—Clear Interrupt Mask

Description   Clears the interrupt mask bit in the CCR. When the I bit is clear, interrupts are enabled.

Operation

$$C \text{ bit} \leftarrow 0$$

S	X	H	I	N	Z	V	C
—	—	—	0	—	—	—	—

Mnemonic	Address mode	Op code	Operand(s)	# Bytes	# Cycles
CLI	INH	0E		1	2

CLR—Clear

Description   The contents of ACCX or M are replaced with 0s.

Operation

$$ACCX \leftarrow 0 \qquad \text{or:} \qquad M \leftarrow 0$$

S	X	H	I	N	Z	V	C
–	–	–	–	0	1	0	0

Mnemonic	Address mode	Op code	Operand(s)	# Bytes	# Cycles
CLR (opr)	EXT	7F	hh ll	3	6
	IND,X	6F	ff	2	6
	IND,Y	18 6F	ff	3	7
CLRA	A INH	4F		1	2
CLRB	B INH	5F		1	2

CLV—Clear 2's-Complement Overflow Bit

Description   Clears the 2's complement overflow bit in the CCR.

Operation

$$V \text{ bit} \leftarrow 0$$

S	X	H	I	N	Z	V	C
–	–	–	–	–	–	0	–

Mnemonic	Address mode	Op code	Operand(s)	# Bytes	# Cycles
CLV	INH	0A		1	2

CMP—Compare

Description   Compares the contents of ACCX to the contents of M and sets the condition codes, which may be used for arithmetic and logical conditional branching. Both operands are unaffected.

Operation

$$(ACCX) - (M)$$

S	X	H	I	N	Z	V	C
–	–	–	–	↕	↕	↕	↕

Mnemonic	Address mode	Op code	Operand(s)	# Bytes	# Cycles
CMPA (opr)	A IMM	81	ii	2	2
	A DIR	91	dd	2	3
	A EXT	B1	hh ll	3	4
	A IND,X	A1	ff	2	4
	A IND,Y	18 A1	ff	3	5
CMPB (opr)	B IMM	C1	ii	2	2
	B DIR	D1	dd	2	3
	B EXT	F1	hh ll	3	4
	B IND,X	E1	ff	2	4
	B IND,Y	18 E1	ff	3	5

COM—Complement

Description   Replaces the contents of ACCX or M with its 1's-complement. (Each bit of the contents of ACCX or M is replaced with the complement of that bit).

Operation
$$ACCX \leftarrow (\overline{ACCX}) = \$FF - (ACCX) \qquad or: \qquad M \leftarrow (\overline{M}) = \$FF - (M)$$

S	X	H	I	N	Z	V	C
–	–	–	–	↕	↕	0	1

Mnemonic	Address mode	Op code	Operand(s)	# Bytes	# Cycles
COM (opr)	EXT	73	hh ll	3	6
	IND,X	63	ff	2	6
	IND,Y	18 63	ff	3	7
COMA	A INH	43		1	2
COMB	B INH	53		1	2

CPD—Compare Double Accumulator

Description   Compares the contents of accumulator D with a 16-bit value at the address specified and sets the condition codes accordingly. The compare is accomplished internally by doing a 16-bit subtract of (M:M + 1) from accumulator D without modifying either accumulator D or (M:M + 1).

Operation

$$(ACCD) - (M:M + 1)$$

S	X	H	I	N	Z	V	C
–	–	–	–	$\updownarrow$	$\updownarrow$	$\updownarrow$	$\updownarrow$

Mnemonic	Address mode	Op code	Operand(s)	# Bytes	# Cycles
CPD (opr)	IMM	1A 83	jj kk	4	5
	DIR	1A 93	dd	3	6
	EXT	1A B3	hh ll	4	7
	IND,X	1A A3	ff	3	7
	IND,Y	CD A3	ff	3	7

CPX—Compare Index Register X

Description   Compares the contents of the index register X with a 16-bit value at the address specified and sets the condition codes accordingly. The compare is accomplished internally by doing a 16-bit subtract of (M:M + 1) from index register X without modifying either index register X or (M:M + 1).

Operation

$$(IX) - (M:M + 1)$$

S	X	H	I	N	Z	V	C
–	–	–	–	$\updownarrow$	$\updownarrow$	$\updownarrow$	$\updownarrow$

Mnemonic	Address mode	Op code	Operand(s)	# Bytes	# Cycles
CPX (opr)	IMM	8C	jj kk	3	4
	DIR	9C	dd	2	5
	EXT	BC	hh ll	3	6
	IND,X	AC	ff	2	6
	IND,Y	CD AC	ff	3	7

CPY—Compare Index Register Y

Description   Compares the contents of the index register Y with a 16-bit value at the address specified and sets the condition codes accordingly. The compare is accomplished internally by doing a 16-bit subtract of (M:M + 1) from index register Y without modifying either index register Y or (M:M + 1).

Operation

$$(IY) - (M:M + 1)$$

S	X	H	I	N	Z	V	C
—	—	—	—	$\updownarrow$	$\updownarrow$	$\updownarrow$	$\updownarrow$

Mnemonic	Address mode	Op code	Operand(s)	# Bytes	# Cycles
CPY (opr)	IMM	18 8C	jj kk	4	5
	DIR	18 9C	dd	3	6
	EXT	18 BC	hh ll	4	7
	IND,X	1A AC	ff	3	7
	IND,Y	18 AC	ff	3	7

DAA—Decimal Adjust ACCA

Description   If the contents of ACCA and the state of the carry/borrow bit C and the state of the half-carry bit H are all the result of applying any of the operations ABA, ADD, or ADC to binary-coded-decimal operands, with or without an initial carry, the DAA operation will adjust the contents of ACCA and the carry bit C in the CCR to represent the correct binary-coded-decimal sum and the correct state of the C bit.

S	X	H	I	N	Z	V	C
—	—	—	—	$\updownarrow$	$\updownarrow$	?	$\updownarrow$

Mnemonic	Address mode	Op code	Operand(s)	# Bytes	# Cycles
DAA	INH	19		1	2

DEC—Decrement

Description   Subtract one from the contents of ACCX or M. The N, Z, and V bits in the CCR are set or cleared according to the results of the operation. The C bit in the CCR is not affected by the operation.

Operation

$$\text{ACCX} \leftarrow (\text{ACCX}) - \$01 \qquad \text{or:} \qquad M \leftarrow (M) - \$01$$

S	X	H	I	N	Z	V	C
—	—	—	—	$\updownarrow$	$\updownarrow$	$\updownarrow$	—

Mnemonic	Address mode	Op code	Operand(s)	# Bytes	# Cycles
DEC (opr)	EXT	7A	hh ll	3	6
	IND,X	6A	ff	2	6
	IND,Y	18 6A	ff	3	7
DECA	A INH	4A		1	2
DECB	B INH	5A		1	2

DES—Decrement Stack Pointer

Description Subtract one from the stack pointer.

Operation

$$\text{SP} \leftarrow (\text{SP}) - \$0001$$

S	X	H	I	N	Z	V	C
—	—	—	—	—	—	—	—

Mnemonic	Address mode	Op code	Operand(s)	# Bytes	# Cycles
DES	INH	34		1	3

DEX—Decrement Index Register X

Description Subtract one from the index register X. Only the Z flag is affected.

Operation

$$\text{IX} \leftarrow (\text{IX}) - \$0001$$

S	X	H	I	N	Z	V	C
—	—	—	—	—	$\updownarrow$	—	—

Mnemonic	Address mode	Op code	Operand(s)	# Bytes	# Cycles
DEX	INH	09		1	3

DEY—Decrement Index Register Y

Description Subtract one from the index register Y. Only the Z flag is affected.

Operation

$$IY \leftarrow (IY) - \$0001$$

S	X	H	I	N	Z	V	C
–	–	–	–	–	$\updownarrow$	–	–

Mnemonic	Address mode	Op code	Operand(s)	# Bytes	# Cycles
DEY	INH	18 09		1	4

EOR—Exclusive-OR

Description Performs the logical exclusive-OR between the contents of ACCX and the contents of M and places the result in ACCX. (Each bit of ACCX after the operation will be the logical exclusive-OR of the corresponding bits of M and ACCX before the operation.)

Operation

$$ACCX \leftarrow (ACCX) \oplus (M)$$

S	X	H	I	N	Z	V	C
–	–	–	–	$\updownarrow$	$\updownarrow$	0	–

Mnemonic	Address mode	Op code	Operand(s)	# Bytes	# Cycles
EORA (opr)	A IMM	88	ii	2	2
	A DIR	98	dd	2	3
	A EXT	B8	hh ll	3	4
	A IND,X	A8	ff	2	4
	A IND,Y	18 A8	ff	3	5

Mnemonic	Address mode	Op code	Operand(s)	# Bytes	# Cycles
EORB (opr)	B IMM	C8	ii	2	2
	B DIR	D8	dd	2	3
	B EXT	F8	hh ll	3	4
	B IND,X	E8	ff	2	4
	B IND,Y	18 E8	ff	3	5

FDIV—Fractional Divide

Description   Performs an unsigned fractional divide of the 16-bit number in the D accumulator by the 16-bit denominator in the index register X and sets the condition codes accordingly. The quotient is placed in the index register X, and the remainder is placed in the D accumulator. The radix point is assumed to be in the same place for both the numerator and the denominator. The radix point is to the left of bit 15 for the quotient. The numerator is assumed to be less than the denominator. In the case of overflow (denominator is less than or equal to the numerator) or divide by zero, the quotient is set to $FFFF, and the remainder is indeterminate.

Operation

$$(ACCD)/(IX); IX \leftarrow Quotient, ACCD \leftarrow Remainder$$

S	X	H	I	N	Z	V	C
–	–	–	–	–	↕	↕	↕

Mnemonic	Address mode	Op code	Operand(s)	# Bytes	# Cycles
FDIV	INH	03		1	41

IDIV—Integer Divide

Description: Performs an unsigned integer divide of the 16-bit number in the D accumulator by the 16-bit denominator in the index register X and sets the condition codes accordingly. The quotient is placed in the index register X, and the remainder is placed in the D accumulator. The radix point is assumed to be in the same place for both the numerator and the denominator. The radix point is to the right of bit zero for the quotient. In the case of divide by zero, the quotient is set to $FFFF, and the remainder is indeterminate.

Operation

$$(ACCD)/(IX); IX \leftarrow Quotient, ACCD \leftarrow Remainder$$

S	X	H	I	N	Z	V	C
–	–	–	–	–	↕	0	↕

Mnemonic	Address mode	Op code	Operand(s)	# Bytes	# Cycles
IDIV	INH	02		1	41

INC—Increment

Description   Adds one to the contents of ACCX or M. The N, Z, and V bits in the CCR are set or cleared accordingly to the results of the operation. The C bit in the CCR is not affected by the operation.

Operation

$$ACCX \leftarrow (ACCX) + \$01 \qquad or: \qquad M \leftarrow (M) + \$01$$

S	X	H	I	N	Z	V	C
–	–	–	–	↕	↕	↕	–

Mnemonic	Address mode	Op code	Operand(s)	# Bytes	# Cycles
INC (opr)	EXT	7C	hh ll	3	6
	IND,X	6C	ff	2	6
	IND,Y	18 6C	ff	3	7
INCA	A INH	4C		1	2
INCB	B INH	5C		1	2

INS—Increment Stack Pointer

Description   Adds one to the stack pointer.

Operation

$$SP \leftarrow (SP) + \$0001$$

S	X	H	I	N	Z	V	C
–	–	–	–	–	–	–	–

Mnemonic	Address mode	Op code	Operand(s)	# Bytes	# Cycles
INS	INH	31		1	3

INX—Increment Index Register X

Description   Adds one to index register X. Only the Z flag is affected.

Operation

$$IX \leftarrow (IX) + \$0001$$

S	X	H	I	N	Z	V	C
–	–	–	–	–	↕	–	–

Mnemonic	Address mode	Op code	Operand(s)	# Bytes	# Cycles
INX	INH	08		1	3

INY—Increment Index Register Y

Description   Adds one to index register Y. Only the Z flag is affected.

Operation

$$IY \leftarrow (IY) + \$0001$$

S	X	H	I	N	Z	V	C
–	–	–	–	–	↕	–	–

Mnemonic	Address mode	Op code	Operand(s)	# Bytes	# Cycles
INY	INH	18 08		2	4

JMP–Jump

Description   A jump occurs to the instruction stored at the effective address. The effective address is obtained according to the rules for EXTended or INDexed addressing.

Operation

$$PC \leftarrow \text{Effective Address}$$

S	X	H	I	N	Z	V	C
—	—	—	—	—	—	—	—

Mnemonic	Address mode	Op code	Operand(s)	# Bytes	# Cycles
JMP (opr)	EXT	7E	hh ll	3	3
	IND,X	6E	ff	2	3
	IND,Y	18 6E	ff	3	4

JSR—Jump to Subroutine

Description   The program counter is incremented by three or by two, depending on the addressing mode, and is then pushed onto the stack, eight bits at a time, least significant byte first. The stack pointer points to the next empty location in the stack. A jump occurs to the instruction stored at the effective address. The effective address is obtained according to the rules for EXTended, DIRect, or INDexed addressing.

Operation

$PC \leftarrow (PC) + \$0003$	(for EXTended or INDexed, Y addressing) or:
$PC \leftarrow (PC) + \$0002$	(for DIRect or INDexed, X addressing)
$\downarrow (PCL)$	Push low-order return address onto stack
$SP \leftarrow (SP) - \$0001$	
$\downarrow (PCH)$	Push high-order return address onto stack
$SP \leftarrow (SP) - \$0001$	
$PC \leftarrow \text{Effective address}$	Load start address of requested subroutine

S	X	H	I	N	Z	V	C
—	—	—	—	—	—	—	—

Mnemonic	Address mode	Op code	Operand(s)	# Bytes	# Cycles
JSR (opr)	DIR	9D	dd	2	5
	EXT	BD	hh ll	3	6
	IND,X	AD	ff	2	6
	IND,Y	18 AD	ff	3	7

LDA—Load Accumulator

Description Loads the contents of memory into the 8-bit accumulator. The condition codes are set according to the data.

Operation

$$ACCX \leftarrow (M)$$

S	X	H	I	N	Z	V	C
–	–	–	–	$\updownarrow$	$\updownarrow$	0	–

Mnemonic	Address mode	Op code	Operand(s)	# Bytes	# Cycles
LDAA (opr)	A IMM	86	ii	2	2
	A DIR	96	dd	2	3
	A EXT	B6	hh ll	3	4
	A IND,X	A6	ff	2	4
	A IND,Y	18 A6	ff	3	5
LDAB (opr)	B IMM	C6	ii	2	2
	B DIR	D6	dd	2	3
	B EXT	F6	hh ll	3	4
	B IND,X	E6	ff	2	4
	B IND,Y	18 E6	ff	3	5

LDD—Load Double Accumulator

Description Loads the contents of memory locations M and M + 1 into the double accumulator D. The condition codes are set according to the data. The information from location M is loaded into accumulator A, and the information from location M + 1 is loaded into accumulator B.

Operation

$$ACCD \leftarrow (M:M + 1); ACCA \leftarrow (M), ACCB \leftarrow (M + 1)$$

S	X	H	I	N	Z	V	C
–	–	–	–	$\updownarrow$	$\updownarrow$	0	–

Mnemonic	Address mode	Op code	Operand(s)	# Bytes	# Cycles
LDD (opr)	IMM	CC	jj kk	3	3
	DIR	DC	dd	2	4
	EXT	FC	hh ll	3	5
	IND,X	EC	ff	2	5
	IND,Y	18 EC	ff	3	6

LDS—Load Stack Pointer

Description   Loads the most significant byte of the stack pointer from the byte of memory at the address specified by the program, and loads the least significant byte of the stack pointer from the next byte of memory at one plus the address specified by the program.

Operation

$$SPH \leftarrow (M), SPL \leftarrow (M + 1)$$

S	X	H	I	N	Z	V	C
–	–	–	–	$\updownarrow$	$\updownarrow$	0	–

Mnemonic	Address mode	Op code	Operand(s)	# Bytes	# Cycles
LDS (opr)	IMM	8E	jj kk	3	3
	DIR	9E	dd	2	4
	EXT	BE	hh ll	3	5
	IND,X	AE	ff	2	5
	IND,Y	18 AE	ff	3	6

LDX—Load Index Register X

Description   Loads the most significant byte of index register X from the byte of memory at the address specified by the program, and loads the least significant byte of index register X from the next byte of memory at one plus the address specified by the program.

Operation

$$IXH \leftarrow (M), IXL \leftarrow (M + 1)$$

S	X	H	I	N	Z	V	C
–	–	–	–	$\updownarrow$	$\updownarrow$	0	–

Mnemonic	Address mode	Op code	Operand(s)	# Bytes	# Cycles
LDX (opr)	IMM	CE	jj kk	3	3
	DIR	DE	dd	2	4
	EXT	FE	hh ll	3	5
	IND,X	EE	ff	2	5
	IND,Y	CD EE	ff	3	6

LDY—Load Index Register Y

Description   Loads the most significant byte of index register Y from the byte of memory at the address specified by the program, and loads the least significant byte of index register Y from the next byte of memory at one plus the address specified by the program.

Operation

$$IYH \leftarrow (M), IYL \leftarrow (M + 1)$$

S	X	H	I	N	Z	V	C
−	−	−	−	↕	↕	0	−

Mnemonic	Address mode	Op code	Operand(s)	# Bytes	# Cycles
LDY (opr)	IMM	18 CE	jj kk	4	4
	DIR	18 DE	dd	3	5
	EXT	18 FE	hh ll	4	6
	IND,X	1A EE	ff	3	6
	IND,Y	18 EE	ff	3	6

LSL—Logical Shift Left (same as ASL)

Description   Shifts all bits of the ACCX or M one place to the left. Bit 0 is loaded with a zero. The C bit in the CCR is loaded from the most significant bit of ACCX or M.

Operation

$$\boxed{C} \leftarrow \boxed{b7\text{----------}b0} \leftarrow \boxed{0}$$

S	X	H	I	N	Z	V	C
−	−	−	−	↕	↕	↕	↕

Mnemonic	Address mode	Op code	Operand(s)	# Bytes	# Cycles
LSL (opr)	EXT	78	hh ll	3	6
	IND,X	68	ff	2	6
	IND,Y	18 68	ff	3	7
LSLA	A INH	48		1	2
LSLB	B INH	58		1	2

LSLD—Logical Shift Left Double Accumulator (same as ASLD)

Description Shifts all bits of ACCD one place to the left. Bit 0 is loaded with zero. The C bit in the CCR is loaded from the most significant bit of ACCD.

Operation

$$C \leftarrow [\text{b7----------b0}] \leftarrow [\text{b7----------b0}] \leftarrow 0$$
$$\text{ACCA} \qquad\qquad \text{ACCB}$$

S	X	H	I	N	Z	V	C
–	–	–	–	↕	↕	↕	↕

Mnemonic	Address mode	Op code	Operand(s)	# Bytes	# Cycles
LSLD	INH	05		1	3

LSR—Logical Shift Right

Description Shifts all bits of the ACCX or M one place to the right. Bit 7 is loaded with a zero. The C bit in the CCR is loaded from the least significant bit of ACCX or M.

Operation

$$0 \rightarrow [\text{b7----------b0}] \rightarrow C$$

S	X	H	I	N	Z	V	C
–	–	–	–	0	↕	↕	↕

Mnemonic	Address mode	Op code	Operand(s)	# Bytes	# Cycles
LSR (opr)	EXT	74	hh ll	3	6
	IND,X	64	ff	2	6
	IND,Y	18 64	ff	3	7
LSRA	A INH	44		1	2
LSRB	B INH	54		1	2

LSRD—Logical Shift Right Double Accumulator

Description Shifts all bits of ACCD one place to the right. Bit 15 (MSB of ACCA) is loaded with zero. The C bit in the CCR is loaded from the least significant bit of ACCD (LSB of ACCB).

Operation

$$0 \rightarrow \boxed{b7\text{-----------}b0} \rightarrow \boxed{b7\text{-----------}b0} \rightarrow \boxed{C}$$

ACCA   ACCB

S	X	H	I	N	Z	V	C
–	–	–	–	0	↕	↕	↕

Mnemonic	Address mode	Op code	Operand(s)	# Bytes	# Cycles
LSRD	INH	04		1	3

MUL—Multiply Unsigned

Description Multiplies the 8-bit unsigned binary value in accumulator A by the 8-bit unsigned binary value in accumulator B to obtain a 16-bit unsigned result in the double accumulator D. Unsigned multiply allows multiple-precision operations. The carry flag allows rounding the most significant byte of the result through the sequence: MUL, ADCA #0.

Operation

$$ACCD \leftarrow (ACCA) \times (ACCB)$$

S	X	H	I	N	Z	V	C
–	–	–	–	–	–	–	↕

Mnemonic	Address mode	Op code	Operand(s)	# Bytes	# Cycles
MUL	INH	3D		1	10

NEG—Negate

Description   Replaces the contents of ACCX or M with its 2's-complement; the value $80 is left unchanged.

Operation
$$(ACCX) \leftarrow - (ACCX) = \$00 - (ACCX) \qquad \text{or:} \qquad (M) \leftarrow - (M) = \$00 - (M)$$

S	X	H	I	N	Z	V	C
—	—	—	—	↕	↕	↕	↕

Mnemonic	Address mode	Op code	Operand(s)	# Bytes	# Cycles
NEG (opr)	EXT	70	hh ll	3	6
	IND,X	60	ff	2	6
	IND,Y	18 60	ff	3	7
NEGA	A INH	40		1	2
NEGB	B INH	50		1	2

NOP—No Operation

Description   This is a single-byte instruction that causes only the program counter to be incremented. No other registers are affected. This instruction is typically used to produce a time delay. During debug, NOP instructions are sometimes used to temporarily replace other machine code instructions, thus disabling the replaced instruction(s).

S	X	H	I	N	Z	V	C
—	—	—	—	—	—	—	—

Mnemonic	Address mode	Op code	Operand(s)	# Bytes	# Cycles
NOP	INH	01		1	2

ORA—Inclusive-OR

Description Performs the logical inclusive-OR between the contents of ACCX and the contents of M and places the result in ACCX. (Each bit of ACCX after the operation will be the logical inclusive-OR of the corresponding bits of M and of ACCX before the operation.)

Operation

$$ACCX \leftarrow (ACCX) + (M)$$

S	X	H	I	N	Z	V	C
—	—	—	—	$\updownarrow$	$\updownarrow$	0	—

Mnemonic	Address mode	Op code	Operand(s)	# Bytes	# Cycles
ORAA (opr)	A IMM	8 A	ii	2	2
	A DIR	9 A	dd	2	3
	A EXT	BA	hh ll	3	4
	A IND,X	AA	ff	2	4
	A IND,Y	18 AA	ff	3	5
ORAB (opr)	B IMM	CA	ii	2	2
	B DIR	DA	dd	2	3
	B EXT	FA	hh ll	3	4
	B IND,X	EA	ff	2	4
	B IND,Y	18 EA	ff	3	5

PSH—Push Data onto Stack

Description The contents of ACCX are stored on the stack at the address contained in the stack pointer. The stack pointer is then decremented.

Operation

$$\downarrow ACCX, SP \leftarrow (SP) - \$0001$$

S	X	H	I	N	Z	V	C
—	—	—	—	—	—	—	—

Mnemonic	Address mode	Op code	Operand(s)	# Bytes	# Cycles
PSHA	A INH	36		1	3
PSHB	B INH	37		1	3

PSHX—Push Index Register X onto Stack

Description   The contents of index register X are pushed onto the stack (low-order byte first) at the address contained in the stack pointer. The stack pointer is then decremented by two.

Operation

$$\downarrow(IXL), SP \leftarrow (SP) - \$0001$$

$$\downarrow(IXH), SP \leftarrow (SP) - \$0001$$

S	X	H	I	N	Z	V	C
–	–	–	–	–	–	–	–

Mnemonic	Address mode	Op code	Operand(s)	# Bytes	# Cycles
PSHX	INH	3C		1	4

PSHY—Push Index Register Y onto Stack

Description   The contents of index register Y are pushed onto the stack (low-order byte first) at the address contained in the stack pointer. The stack pointer is then decremented by two.

Operation

$$\downarrow(IYL), SP \leftarrow (SP) - \$0001$$

$$\downarrow(IYH), SP \leftarrow (SP) - \$0001$$

S	X	H	I	N	Z	V	C
–	–	–	–	–	–	–	–

Mnemonic	Address mode	Op code	Operand(s)	# Bytes	# Cycles
PSHY	INH	18 3C		2	5

PUL—Pull Data from Stack

Description   The stack pointer is incremented. The ACCX is then loaded from the stack at the address contained in the stack pointer.

Operation

$$SP \leftarrow (SP) + \$0001, \uparrow(ACCX)$$

S	X	H	I	N	Z	V	C
–	–	–	–	–	–	–	–

Mnemonic	Address mode	Op code	Operand(s)	# Bytes	# Cycles
PULA	A INH	32		1	4
PULB	B INH	33		1	4

PULX—Pull Index Register X from Stack

Description   The index register X is pulled from the stack (high-order byte first), beginning at the address contained in the stack pointer plus one. The stack pointer is incremented by two in total.

Operation

$$SP \leftarrow (SP) + \$0001; \uparrow(IXH)$$
$$SP \leftarrow (SP) + \$0001; \uparrow(IXL)$$

S	X	H	I	N	Z	V	C
–	–	–	–	–	–	–	–

Mnemonic	Address mode	Op code	Operand(s)	# Bytes	# Cycles
PULX	INH	38		1	5

PULY—Pull Index Register Y from Stack

Description   The index register Y is pulled from the stack (high-order byte first), beginning at the address contained in the stack pointer plus one. The stack pointer is incremented by two in total.

Operation

$$SP \leftarrow (SP) + \$0001; \uparrow(IYH)$$
$$SP \leftarrow (SP) + \$0001; \uparrow(IYL)$$

S	X	H	I	N	Z	V	C
–	–	–	–	–	–	–	–

Mnemonic	Address mode	Op code	Operand(s)	# Bytes	# Cycles
PULY	INH	18 38		2	6

ROL—Rotate Left

Description   Shifts all bits of the ACCX or M one place to the left. Bit 0 is loaded from the C bit. The C bit is loaded from the most significant bit of ACCX or M.

Operation

$$\boxed{C} \leftarrow \boxed{b7\text{-----------}b0} \leftarrow \boxed{C}$$

S	X	H	I	N	Z	V	C
–	–	–	–	↕	↕	↕	↕

Mnemonic	Address mode	Op code	Operand(s)	# Bytes	# Cycles
ROL (opr)	EXT	79	hh ll	3	6
	IND,X	69	ff	2	6
	IND,Y	18 69	ff	3	7
ROLA	A INH	49		1	2
ROLB	B INH	59		1	2

ROR—Rotate Right

Description   Shifts all bits of the ACCX or M one place to the right. Bit 7 is loaded from the C bit. The C bit is loaded from the least significant bit of ACCX or M.

Operation

$$C \rightarrow \boxed{\text{b7-----------b0}} \rightarrow C$$

S	X	H	I	N	Z	V	C
−	−	−	−	↕	↕	↕	↕

Mnemonic	Address mode	Op code	Operand(s)	# Bytes	# Cycles
ROR (opr)	EXT	76	hh ll	3	6
	IND,X	66	ff	2	6
	IND,Y	18 66	ff	3	7
RORA	A INH	46		1	2
RORB	B INH	56		1	2

RTI—Return from Interrupt

Description   The condition code register, accumulators B and A, index registers X and Y, and the program counter will be restored to a state pulled from the stack. The X bit in the CCR may be cleared as a result of an RTI instruction but may not be set if it was cleared prior to execution of the RTI instruction.

Operation

$$SP \leftarrow (SP) + \$0001, \uparrow(CCR)$$
$$SP \leftarrow (SP) + \$0001, \uparrow(ACCB)$$
$$SP \leftarrow (SP) + \$0001, \uparrow(ACCA)$$
$$SP \leftarrow (SP) + \$0001, \uparrow(IXH)$$
$$SP \leftarrow (SP) + \$0001, \uparrow(IXL)$$
$$SP \leftarrow (SP) + \$0001, \uparrow(IYH)$$
$$SP \leftarrow (SP) + \$0001, \uparrow(IYL)$$
$$SP \leftarrow (SP) + \$0001, \uparrow(PCH)$$
$$SP \leftarrow (SP) + \$0001, \uparrow(PCL)$$

S	X	H	I	N	Z	V	C
↕	↓	↕	↕	↕	↕	↕	↕

Mnemonic	Address mode	Op code	Operand(s)	# Bytes	# Cycles
RTI	INH	3B		1	12

RTS—Return from Subroutine

Description   The stack pointer is incremented by one. The contents of the byte of memory, at the address now contained in the stack pointer, are loaded into the high-order 8 bits of the program counter. The stack pointer is again incremented by one. The contents of the byte of memory, at the address now contained in the stack pointer, are loaded into the low-order 8 bits of the program counter.

Operation

$$SP \leftarrow (SP) + \$0001, \uparrow(PCH)$$
$$SP \leftarrow (SP) + \$0001, \uparrow(PCL)$$

S	X	H	I	N	Z	V	C
—	—	—	—	—	—	—	—

Mnemonic	Address mode	Op code	Operand(s)	# Bytes	# Cycles
RTS	INH	39		1	5

SBA—Subtract Accumulators

Descriptions   Subtracts the contents of ACCB from the contents of ACCA and places the result in ACCA. The contents of ACCB are not affected. For subtract instructions, the C bit in the CCR represents a borrow.

Operation

$$ACCA \leftarrow (ACCA) - (ACCB)$$

S	X	H	I	N	Z	V	C
—	—	—	—	↕	↕	↕	↕

Mnemonic	Address mode	Op code	Operand(s)	# Bytes	# Cycles
SBA	INH	10		1	2

SBC—Subtract with Carry

Description   Subtracts the contents of M and the contents of ACCX and places the result in ACCX. For subtract instructions, the C bit in the CCR represents a borrow.

Operation

$$ACCX \leftarrow (ACCX) - (M) - (C)$$

S	X	H	I	N	Z	V	C
—	—	—	—	↕	↕	↕	↕

Mnemonic	Address mode	Op code	Operand(s)	# Bytes	# Cycles
SBCA (opr)	A IMM	82	ii	2	2
	A DIR	92	dd	2	3
	A EXT	B2	hh ll	3	4
	A IND,X	A2	ff	2	4
	A IND,Y	18 A2	ff	3	5
SBCB (opr)	B IMM	C2	ii	2	2
	B DIR	D2	dd	2	3
	B EXT	F2	hh ll	3	4
	B IND,X	E2	ff	2	4
	B IND,Y	18 E2	ff	3	5

SEC—Set Carry

Description   Sets the C bit in the CCR.

Operation

$$C \text{ bit} \leftarrow 1$$

S	X	H	I	N	Z	V	C
—	—	—	—	—	—	—	1

Mnemonic	Address mode	Op code	Operand(s)	# Bytes	# Cycles
SEC	INH	0D		1	2

SEI—Set Interrupt Mask

Description   Sets the interrupt mask bit in the CCR. When the I bit is set, all maskable interrupts are inhibited, and the MPU will recognize only non-maskable interrupt sources or an SWI.

Operation

$$I \text{ bit} \leftarrow 1$$

S	X	H	I	N	Z	V	C
–	–	–	1	–	–	–	–

Mnemonic	Address mode	Op code	Operand(s)	# Bytes	# Cycles
SEI	INH	0F		1	2

SEV—Set 2's-Complement Overflow Bit

Description   Sets the 2's-complement overflow bit in the CCR.

Operation

$$V \text{ bit} \leftarrow 1$$

S	X	H	I	N	Z	V	C
–	–	–	–	–	–	1	–

Mnemonic	Address mode	Op code	Operand(s)	# Bytes	# Cycles
SEV	INH	0B		1	2

STA—Store Accumulator

Description   Stores the contents of ACCX in memory. The contents of ACCX remain unchanged.

Operation

$$M \leftarrow (ACCX)$$

S	X	H	I	N	Z	V	C
–	–	–	–	↕	↕	0	–

Mnemonic	Address mode	Op code	Operand(s)	# Bytes	# Cycles
STAA (opr)	A DIR	97	dd	2	3
	A EXT	B7	hh ll	3	4
	A IND,X	A7	ff	2	4
	A IND,Y	18 A7	ff	3	5
STAB (opr)	B DIR	D7	dd	2	3
	B EXT	F7	hh ll	3	4
	B IND,X	E7	ff	2	4
	B IND,Y	18 E7	ff	3	5

STD—Store Double Accumulator

Description   Stores the contents of double accumulator ACCD in memory. The contents of ACCD remain unchanged.

Operation

$$M:M + 1 \leftarrow (ACCD); M \leftarrow (ACCA), M + 1 \leftarrow (ACCB)$$

S	X	H	I	N	Z	V	C
—	—	—	—	$\updownarrow$	$\updownarrow$	0	—

Mnemonic	Address mode	Op code	Operand(s)	# Bytes	# Cycles
STD (opr)	DIR	DD	dd	2	4
	EXT	FD	hh ll	3	5
	IND,X	ED	ff	2	5
	IND,Y	18 ED	ff	3	6

STOP—Stop Processing

Description   If the S bit in the CCR is set, then the STOP instruction is disabled and operates like the NOP instruction. If the S bit in the CCR is clear, the STOP instruction causes all system clocks to halt, and the system is placed in a minimum-power standby mode. All CPU registers remain unchanged. I/O pins also remain unaffected. Recovery from STOP may be accomplished by $\overline{\text{RESET}}$, $\overline{\text{XIRQ}}$, or an unmaskable $\overline{\text{IRQ}}$. When recovering from STOP with $\overline{\text{XIRQ}}$, if the X bit in the CCR is clear, execution will resume with the stacking operations for the $\overline{\text{XIRQ}}$ interrupt. If the X bit in the CCR is set, masking $\overline{\text{XIRQ}}$ interrupts, execution will resume with the op code fetch for the instruction that follows the STOP instruction (continue).

S	X	H	I	N	Z	V	C
–	–	–	–	–	–	–	–

Mnemonic	Address mode	Op code	Operand(s)	# Bytes	# Cycles
STOP	INH	CF		1	2

STS—Store Stack Pointer

Description Stores the most significant byte of the stack pointer in memory at the address specified by the program and stores the least significant byte of the stack pointer at the next location in memory, at one plus the address specified by the program.

Operation

$$M \leftarrow (SPH), M + 1 \leftarrow (SPL)$$

S	X	H	I	N	Z	V	C
–	–	–	–	↕	↕	0	–

Mnemonic	Address mode	Op code	Operand(s)	# Bytes	# Cycles
STS (opr)	DIR	9F	dd	2	4
	EXT	BF	hh ll	3	5
	IND,X	AF	ff	2	5
	IND,Y	18 AF	ff	3	6

STX—Store Index Register X

Description Stores the most significant byte of index register X in memory at the address specified by the program and stores the least significant byte of index register X at the next location in memory, at one plus the address specified by the program.

Operation

$$M \leftarrow (IXH), M + 1 \leftarrow (IXL)$$

S	X	H	I	N	Z	V	C
–	–	–	–	↕	↕	0	–

Mnemonic	Address mode	Op code	Operand(s)	# Bytes	# Cycles
STX(opr)	DIR	DF	dd	2	4
	EXT	FF	hh ll	3	5
	IND,X	EF	ff	2	5
	IND,Y	CD EF	ff	3	6

STY—Store Index Register Y

Description Stores the most significant byte of index register Y in memory at the address specified by the program and stores the least significant byte of index register Y at the next location in memory, at one plus the address specified by the program.

Operation

$$M \leftarrow (IYH), M + 1 \leftarrow (IYL)$$

S	X	H	I	N	Z	V	C
–	–	–	–	↕	↕	0	–

Mnemonic	Address mode	Op code	Operand(s)	# Bytes	# Cycles
STY (opr)	DIR	18 DF	dd	3	5
	EXT	18 FF	hh ll	4	6
	IND,X	1A EF	ff	3	6
	IND,Y	18 EF	ff	3	6

SUB—Subtract

Description Subtracts the contents of M from the contents of ACCX and places the result in ACCX. For subtract instructions, the C bit in the CCR represents a borrow.

Operation

$$ACCX \leftarrow (ACCX) - (M)$$

S	X	H	I	N	Z	V	C
–	–	–	–	↕	↕	↕	↕

Mnemonic	Address mode	Op code	Operand(s)	# Bytes	# Cycles
SUBA (opr)	A IMM	80	ii	2	2
	A DIR	90	dd	2	3
	A EXT	B0	hh ll	3	4
	A IND,X	A0	ff	2	4
	A IND,Y	18 A0	ff	3	5
SUBB (opr)	B IMM	C0	ii	2	2
	B DIR	D0	dd	2	3
	B EXT	F0	hh ll	3	4
	B IND,X	E0	ff	2	4
	B IND,Y	18 E0	ff	3	5

SUBD—Subtract Double Accumulator

Description   Subtracts the contents of M:M+1 from the contents of double accumulator D and places the result in ACCD. For subtract instructions, the C bit in the CCR represents a borrow.

Operation

$$ACCD \leftarrow (ACCD) - (M:M + 1)$$

S	X	H	I	N	Z	V	C
–	–	–	–	$\updownarrow$	$\updownarrow$	$\updownarrow$	$\updownarrow$

Mnemonic	Address mode	Op code	Operand(s)	# Bytes	# Cycles
SUBD (opr)	IMM	83	jj kk	3	4
	DIR	93	dd	2	5
	EXT	B3	hh ll	3	6
	IND,X	A3	ff	2	6
	IND,Y	18 A3	ff	3	7

SWI—Software Interrupt

Description   The program counter is incremented by one. The program counter, index registers Y and X, and accumulators A and B are pushed onto the stack. The CCR is then pushed onto the stack. The stack pointer is decremented by one after each byte of data is stored on the stack. The I bit in the CCR is then set. The program counter is loaded with the address stored at the SWI vector, and instruction execution resumes at this location. This instruction is not maskable by the I bit.

Operation

$$PC \leftarrow (PC) + \$0001$$
$$\downarrow(PCL), SP \leftarrow (SP) - \$0001$$
$$\downarrow(PCH), SP \leftarrow (SP) - \$0001$$
$$\downarrow(IYL), SP \leftarrow (SP) - \$0001$$
$$\downarrow(IYH), SP \leftarrow (SP) - \$0001$$
$$\downarrow(IXL), SP \leftarrow (SP) - \$0001$$
$$\downarrow(IXH), SP \leftarrow (SP) - \$0001$$
$$\downarrow(ACCA), SP \leftarrow (SP) - \$0001$$
$$\downarrow(ACCB), SP \leftarrow (SP) - \$0001$$
$$\downarrow(CCR), SP \leftarrow (SP) - \$0001$$
$$I \leftarrow 1, PC \leftarrow (SWI\ vector)$$

S	X	H	I	N	Z	V	C
—	—	—	1	—	—	—	—

Mnemonic	Address mode	Op code	Operand(s)	# Bytes	# Cycles
SWI	INH	3F		1	14

TAB—Transfer from Accumulator A to Accumulator B

Description Moves the contents of ACCA to ACCB. The former contents of ACCB are lost; the contents of ACCA are not affected.

Operation

$$ACCB \leftarrow (ACCA)$$

S	X	H	I	N	Z	V	C
—	—	—	—	↕	↕	0	—

Mnemonic	Address mode	Op code	Operand(s)	# Bytes	# Cycles
TAB	INH	16		1	2

TAP—Transfer from Accumulator A to Condition Code Register

Description Transfers the contents of bit positions 7–0 of accumulator A to the corresponding bit positions of the CCR. The contents of accumulator A remain unchanged. The

X bit in the CCR may be cleared as a result of a TAP instruction but may not be set if it was clear prior to execution of the TAP instruction.

Operation

$$CCR \leftarrow (ACCA)$$

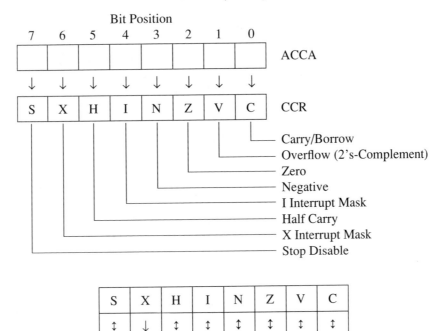

S	X	H	I	N	Z	V	C
↕	↓	↕	↕	↕	↕	↕	↕

Mnemonic	Address mode	Op code	Operand(s)	# Bytes	# Cycles
TAP	INH	06		1	2

TBA—Transfer from Accumulator B to Accumulator A

Description   Moves the contents of ACCB to ACCA. The former contents of ACCA are lost; the contents of ACCB are not affected.

Operation

$$ACCA \leftarrow (ACCB)$$

S	X	H	I	N	Z	V	C
—	—	—	—	↕	↕	0	—

Mnemonic	Address mode	Op code	Operand(s)	# Bytes	# Cycles
TBA	INH	17		1	2

TEST—Test Operation (Test Mode Only)

Description   This is a single-byte instruction that causes the program counter to be continuously incremented. It can be executed only while in the test mode. The MPU must be reset to exit this instruction. Code execution is suspended during this instruction. This is an illegal op code when not in test mode.

S	X	H	I	N	Z	V	C
–	–	–	–	–	–	–	–

Mnemonic	Address mode	Op code	Operand(s)	# Bytes	# Cycles
Test	INH	00		1	*

TPA—Transfer from Condition Code Register to Accumulator A

Description   Transfers the contents of the CCR to corresponding bit positions of accumulator A. The CCR remains unchanged.

Operation

$$ACCA \leftarrow (CCR)$$

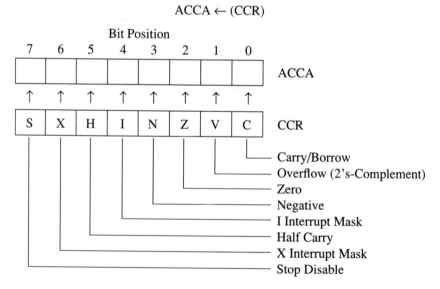

S	X	H	I	N	Z	V	C
–	–	–	–	–	–	–	–

Mnemonic	Address mode	Op code	Operand(s)	# Bytes	# Cycles
TPA	INH	07		1	2

TST—Test

Description   Subtracts $00 from the contents of ACCX or M and sets the condition codes accordingly. The subtraction is accomplished internally without modifying either ACCX or M.

Operation

$$(ACCX) - \$00 \qquad or: \qquad (M) - \$00$$

S	X	H	I	N	Z	V	C
–	–	–	–	↕	↕	0	0

Mnemonic	Address mode	Op code	Operand(s)	# Bytes	# Cycles
TST (opr)	EXT	7D	hh ll	3	6
	IND,X	6D	ff	2	6
	IND,Y	18 6D	ff	3	7
TSTA	A INH	4D		1	2
TSTB	B INH	5D		1	2

TSX—Transfer from Stack Pointer to Index Register X

Description   Loads the index register X with one plus the contents of the stack pointer. The contents of the stack pointer remain unchanged. After a TSX instruction, the index register X points at the last value that was stored on the stack.

Operation

$$IX \leftarrow (SP) + \$0001$$

S	X	H	I	N	Z	V	C
–	–	–	–	–	–	–	–

Mnemonic	Address mode	Op code	Operand(s)	# Bytes	# Cycles
TSX	INH	30		1	3

TSY—Transfer from Stack Pointer to Index Register Y

Description Loads the index register Y with one plus the contents of the stack pointer. The contents of the stack pointer remain unchanged. After a TSY instruction, the index register Y points at the last value that was stored on the stack.

Operation

$$IY \leftarrow (SP) + \$0001$$

S	X	H	I	N	Z	V	C
–	–	–	–	–	–	–	–

Mnemonic	Address mode	Op code	Operand(s)	# Bytes	# Cycles
TSY	INH	18 30		2	4

TXS—Transfer from Index Register X to Stack Pointer

Description   Loads the stack pointer with the contents of the index register X minus one. The contents of the index register X remain unchanged.

Operation

$$SP \leftarrow (IX) - \$0001$$

S	X	H	I	N	Z	V	C
–	–	–	–	–	–	–	–

Mnemonic	Address mode	Op code	Operand(s)	# Bytes	# Cycles
TXS	INH	35		1	3

TYS—Transfer from Index Register Y to Stack Pointer

Description   Loads the stack pointer with the contents of the index register Y minus one. The contents of the index register Y remain unchanged.

Operation

$$SP \leftarrow (IY) - \$0001$$

S	X	H	I	N	Z	V	C
–	–	–	–	–	–	–	–

Mnemonic	Address mode	Op code	Operand(s)	# Bytes	# Cycles
TYS	INH	18 35		2	4

WAI—Wait for Interrupt

Description   The program counter is incremented by one. The program counter, index registers Y and X, and accumulators A and B are pushed onto the stack. The CCR is then pushed onto the stack. The stack pointer is decremented by one after each byte of data is stored on the stack.

The MPU then enters a wait state for an integer number of MPU E-clock cycles. While in the wait state, the address/data bus repeatedly runs READ bus cycles to the address where the CCR contents were stacked. The MPU leaves the wait state when it senses any interrupt that has not been masked.

Upon leaving the wait state, the MPU sets the I bit in the CCR, fetches the vector (address) corresponding to the interrupt sensed, and instruction execution is resumed at this location.

Although the WAI instruction itself does not alter the condition code bits, the interrupt that causes the MCU to resume processing causes the I bit (and the X bit if the interrupt was XIRQ) to be set as the interrupt vector is being fetched.

Operation

$$PC \leftarrow (PC) + \$0001$$
$$\downarrow(PCL), SP \leftarrow (SP) - \$0001$$
$$\downarrow(PCH), SP \leftarrow (SP) - \$0001$$
$$\downarrow(IYL), SP \leftarrow (SP) - \$0001$$
$$\downarrow(IYH), SP \leftarrow (SP) - \$0001$$
$$\downarrow(IXL), SP \leftarrow (SP) - \$0001$$
$$\downarrow(IXH), SP \leftarrow (SP) - \$0001$$
$$\downarrow(ACCA), SP \leftarrow (SP) - \$0001$$
$$\downarrow(ACCB), SP \leftarrow (SP) - \$0001$$
$$\downarrow(CCR), SP \leftarrow (SP) - \$0001$$

S	X	H	I	N	Z	V	C
–	–	–	–	–	–	–	–

Mnemonic	Address mode	Op code	Operand(s)	# Bytes	# Cycles
WAI	INH	3E		1	**

XGDX—Exchange Double Accumulator and Index Register X

Description Exchanges the contents of double accumulator ACCD and the contents of index register X.

Operation

$$(IX) \leftrightarrow (ACCD)$$

S	X	H	I	N	Z	V	C
–	–	–	–	–	–	–	–

Mnemonic	Address mode	Op code	Operand(s)	# Bytes	# Cycles
XGDX	INH	8F		1	3

XGDY—Exchange Double Accumulator and Index Register Y

Description Exchanges the contents of double accumulator ACCD and the contents of index register Y.

Operation

$$(IY) \leftrightarrow (ACCD)$$

S	X	H	I	N	Z	V	C
–	–	–	–	–	–	–	–

Mnemonic	Address mode	Op code	Operand(s)	# Bytes	# Cycles
XGDY	INH	18 8F		2	4

		Op Code vs Instruction Cross Reference		
Op code	*Operands*	*Instruction*	*Address mode*	*Cycle*
00		TEST	INH	—
01		NOP	INH	2
02		IDIV	INH	41
03		FDIV	INH	41
04		LSRD	INH	3
05		ASLD/LSLD	INH	3
06		TAP	INH	2
07		TPA	INH	2
08		INX	INH	3
09		DEX	INH	3
0A		CLV	INH	2
0B		SEV	INH	2
0C		CLC	INH	2
0D		SEC	INH	2
0E		CLI	INH	2
0F		SEI	INH	2
10		SBA	INH	2
11		CBA	INH	2
12	dd mm rr	BRSET (opr) (msk) (rel)	DIR	6
13	dd mm rr	BRCLR (opr) (msk) (rel)	DIR	6
14	dd mm	BSET (opr) (msk)	DIR	6
15	dd mm	BCLR (opr) (msk)	DIR	6
16		TAB	INH	2
17		TBA	INH	2
18		(page 2 Switch)		
19		DAA	INH	2
1A		(page 3 Switch)		
1B		ABA	INH	2
1C	ff mm	BSET (opr) (msk)	IND, X	7
1D	ff mm	BCLR (opr) (msk)	IND, X	7
1E	ff mm rr	BRSET (opr) (msk) (rel)	IND, X	7
1F	ff mm rr	BRCLR (opr) (msk) (rel)	IND, X	7
20	rr	BRA (rel)	REL	3

		Op Code vs Instruction Cross Reference		
Op code	*Operands*	*Instruction*	*Address mode*	*Cycle*
21	rr	BRN (rel)	REL	3
22	rr	BHI (rel)	REL	3
23	rr	BLS (rel)	REL	3
24	rr	BCC/BHS (rel)	REL	3
25	rr	BCS/BLO (rel)	REL	3
26	rr	BNE (rel)	REL	3
27	rr	BEQ (rel)	REL	3
28	rr	BVC (rel)	REL	3
29	rr	BVS (rel)	REL	3
2A	rr	BPL (rel)	REL	3
2B	rr	BMI (rel)	REL	3
2C	rr	BGE (rel)	REL	3
2D	rr	BLT (rel)	REL	3
2E	rr	BGT (rel)	REL	3
2F	rr	BLE (rel)	REL	3
30		TSX	INH	3
31		INS	INH	3
32		PULA	INH	4
33		PULB	INH	4
34		DES	INH	3
35		TXS	INH	3
36		PSHA	INH	3
37		PSHB	INH	3
38		PULX	INH	5
39		RTS	INH	5
3A		ABX	INH	3
3B		RTI	INH	12
3C		PSHX	INH	4
3D		MUL	INH	10
3E		WAI	INH	14
3F		SWI	INH	14
40		NEGA	INH	2
43		COMA	INH	2
44		LSRA	INH	2
46		RORA	INH	2
47		ASRA	INH	2
48		ASLA/LSLA	INH	2
49		ROLA	INH	2
4A		DECA	INH	2
4C		INCA	INH	2
4D		TSTA	INH	2
4F		CLRA	INH	2
50		NEGB	INH	2
53		COMB	INH	2
54		LSRB	INH	2

Op code	Operands	*Op Code vs Instruction Cross Reference* Instruction	Address mode	Cycle
56		RORB	INH	2
57		ASRB/ASLB	INH	2
58		LSLB	INH	2
59		ROLB	INH	2
5A		DECB	INH	2
5C		INCB	INH	2
5D		TSTB	INH	2
5F		CLRB	INH	2
60	ff	NRG (opr)	IND, X	6
63	ff	COM (opr)	IND, X	6
64	ff	LSR (opr)	IND, X	6
66	ff	ROR (opr)	IND, X	6
67	ff	ASR (opr)	IND, X	6
68	ff	ASL/LSL (opr)	IND, X	6
69	ff	ROL (opr)	IND, X	6
6A	ff	DEC (opr)	IND, X	6
6C	ff	INC (opr)	IND, X	6
6D	ff	TST (opr)	IND, X	6
6E	ff	JMP (opr)	IND, X	3
6F	ff	CLR (opr)	IND, X	6
70	hh ll	NEG (opr)	EXT	6
73	hh ll	COM (opr)	EXT	6
74	hh ll	LSR (opr)	EXT	6
76	hh ll	ROR (opr)	EXT	6
77	hh ll	ASR (opr)	EXT	6
78	hh ll	ASL/LSL (opr)	EXT	6
79	hh ll	ROL (opr)	EXT	6
7A	hh ll	DEC (opr)	EXT	6
7C	hh ll	INC (opr)	EXT	6
7D	hh ll	TST (opr)	EXT	6
7E	hh ll	JMP (opr)	EXT	3
7F	hh ll	CLR (opr)	EXT	6
80	ii	SUBA (opr)	IMM	2
81	ii	CMPA (opr)	IMM	2
82	ii	SBCA (opr)	IMM	2
83	jj kk	SUBD (opr)	IMM	4
84	ii	ANDA (opr)	IMM	2
85	ii	BITA (opr)	IMM	2
86	ii	LDAA (opr)	IMM	2
88	ii	EORA (opr)	IMM	2
89	ii	ADCA (opr)	IMM	2
8A	ii	ORAA (opr)	IMM	2
8B	ii	ADDA (opr)	IMM	2
8C	jj kk	CPX (opr)	IMM	4
8D	rr	BSR (rel)	REL	6

Op code	Operands	Op Code vs Instruction Cross Reference Instruction	Address mode	Cycle
8E	jj kk	LDS (opr)	IMM	3
8F		XGDX	INH	3
90	dd	SUBA (opr)	DIR	3
91	dd	CMPA (opr)	DIR	3
92	dd	SBCA (opr)	DIR	3
93	dd	SUBD (opr)	DIR	5
94	dd	ANDA (opr)	DIR	3
95	dd	BITA (opr)	DIR	3
96	dd	LDAA (opr)	DIR	3
97	dd	STAA (opr)	DIR	3
98	dd	EORA (opr)	DIR	3
99	dd	ADCA (opr)	DIR	3
9A	dd	ORAA (opr)	DIR	3
9B	dd	ADDA (opr)	DIR	3
9C	dd	CPX (opr)	DIR	5
9D	dd	JSR (opr)	DIR	5
9E	dd	LDS (opr)	DIR	4
9F	dd	STS (opr)	DIR	4
A0	ff	SUBA (opr)	IND, X	4
A1	ff	CMPA (opr)	IND, X	4
A2	ff	SBCA (opr)	IND, X	4
A3	ff	SUBD (opr)	IND, X	6
A4	ff	ANDA (opr)	IND, X	4
A5	ff	BITA (opr)	IND, X	4
A6	ff	LDAA (opr)	IND, X	4
A7	ff	STAA (opr)	IND, X	4
A8	ff	EORA (opr)	IND, X	4
A9	ff	ADCA (opr)	IND, X	4
AA	ff	ORAA (opr)	IND, X	4
AB	ff	ADDA (opr)	IND, X	4
AC	ff	CPX (opr)	IND, X	6
AD	ff	JSR (opr)	IND, X	6
AE	ff	LSD (opr)	IND, X	5
AF	ff	STS (opr)	IND, X	5
B0	hh ll	SUBA (opr)	EXT	4
B1	hh ll	CMPA (opr)	EXT	4
B2	hh ll	SBCA (opr)	EXT	4
B3	hh ll	SUBD (opr)	EXT	6
B4	hh ll	ANDA (opr)	EXT	4
B5	hh ll	BITA (opr)	EXT	4
B6	hh ll	LDAA (opr)	EXT	4
B7	hh ll	STAA (opr)	EXT	4
B8	hh ll	EORA (opr)	EXT	4
B9	hh ll	ADCA (opr)	EXT	4
BA	hh ll	ORAA (opr)	EXT	4

Op code	Operands	Op Code vs Instruction Cross Reference Instruction	Address mode	Cycle
BB	hh ll	ADAA (opr)	EXT	4
BC	hh ll	CPX (opr)	EXT	6
BD	hh ll	JSR (opr)	EXT	6
BE	hh ll	LDS (opr)	EXT	5
BF	hh ll	STS (opr)	EXT	5
C0	ii	SUBB (opr)	IMM	2
C1	ii	CMPB (opr)	IMM	2
C2	ii	SBCB (opr)	IMM	2
C3	jj kk	ADDD (opr)	IMM	4
C4	ii	ANDB (opr)	IMM	2
C5	ii	BITB (opr)	IMM	2
C6	ii	LDAB (opr)	IMM	2
C8	ii	EORB (opr)	IMM	2
C9	ii	ADCB (opr)	IMM	2
CA	ii	ORAB (opr)	IMM	2
CB	ii	ADDB (opr)	IMM	2
CC	jj kk	LDD (opr)	IMM	3
CD		(page 4 Switch)		
CE	jj kk	LDX (opr)	IMM	3
CF		STOP	INH	2
D0	dd	SUBB (opr)	DIR	3
D1	dd	CMPB (opr)	DIR	3
D2	dd	SBCB (opr)	DIR	3
D3	dd	ADDD (opr)	DIR	5
D4	dd	ANDB (opr)	DIR	3
D5	dd	BITB (opr)	DIR	3
D6	dd	LDAB (opr)	DIR	3
D7	dd	STAB (opr)	DIR	3
D8	dd	EORB (opr)	DIR	3
D9	dd	ADCB (opr)	DIR	3
DA	dd	ORAB (opr)	DIR	3
DB	dd	ADDB (opr)	DIR	3
DC	dd	LDD (opr)	DIR	4
DD	dd	STD (opr)	DIR	4
DE	dd	LDX (opr)	DIR	4
DF	dd	STX (opr)	DIR	4
E0	ff	SUBB (opr)	IND, X	4
E1	ff	CMPB (opr)	IND, X	4
E2	ff	SBCB (opr)	IND, X	4
E3	ff	ADDD (opr)	IND, X	6
E4	ff	ANDB (opr)	IND, X	4
E5	ff	BITB (opr)	IND, X	4
E6	ff	LDAB (opr)	IND, X	4
E7	ff	STAB (opr)	IND, X	4
E8	ff	EORB (opr)	IND, X	4

Op code	Operands	Op Code vs Instruction Cross Reference Instruction	Address mode	Cycle
E9	ff	ADCB (opr)	IND, X	4
EA	ff	ORAB (opr)	IND, X	4
EB	ff	ADDB (opr)	IND, X	4
EC	ff	LDD (opr)	IND, X	5
ED	ff	STD (opr)	IND, X	5
EE	ff	LDX (opr)	IND, X	5
EF	ff	STX (opr)	IND, X	5
F0	hh ll	SUBB (opr)	EXT	4
F1	hh ll	CMPB (opr)	EXT	4
F2	hh ll	SBCB (opr)	EXT	4
F3	hh ll	ADDD (opr)	EXT	6
F4	hh ll	ANDB (opr)	EXT	4
F5	hh ll	BITB (opr)	EXT	4
F6	hh ll	LDAB (opr)	EXT	4
F7	hh ll	STAB (opr)	EXT	4
F8	hh ll	EORB (opr)	EXT	4
F9	hh ll	ADCB (opr)	EXT	4
FA	hh ll	ORAB (opr)	EXT	4
FB	hh ll	ADDB (opr)	EXT	4
FC	hh ll	LDD (opr)	EXT	5
FD	hh ll	STD (opr)	EXT	5
FE	hh ll	LDX (opr)	EXT	5
FF	hh ll	STX (opr)	EXT	5
18 08		INY	INH	4
18 09		DEY	INH	4
18 1C	ff mm	BSET (opr) (msk)	IND, Y	8
18 1D	ff mm	BCLR (opr) (msk)	IND, Y	8
18 1E	ff mm rr	BRSET (opr) (msk) (rel)	IND, Y	8
18 1F	ff mm rr	BRCLR (opr) (msk) (rel)	IND, Y	8
18 30		TSY	INH	4
18 35		TYS	INH	4
18 38		PULY	INH	6
18 3A		ABY	INH	4
18 3C		PSHY	INH	5
18 60	ff	NEG (opr)	IND, Y	7
18 63	ff	COM (opr)	IND, Y	7
18 64	ff	LSR (opr)	IND, Y	7
18 66	ff	ROR (opr)	IND, Y	7
18 67	ff	ASR (opr)	IND, Y	7

Op code	Operands	Op Code vs Instruction Cross Reference Instruction	Address mode	Cycle
18 68	ff	ASL/LSL (opr)	IND, Y	7
18 69	ff	ROL (opr)	IND, Y	7
18 6A	ff	DEC (opr)	IND, Y	7
18 6C	ff	INC (opr)	IND, Y	7
18 6D	ff	TST (opr)	IND, Y	7
18 6E	ff	JMP (opr)	IND, Y	4
18 6F	ff	CLR (opr)	IND, Y	7
18 8C	jj kk	CPY (opr)	IMM	5
18 8F		XGDY	INH	4
18 9C	dd	CPY (opr)	DIR	6
18 A0	ff	SUBA (opr)	IND, Y	5
18 A1	ff	CMPA (opr)	IND, Y	5
18 A2	ff	SBCA (opr)	IND, Y	5
18 A3	ff	SUBD (opr)	IND, Y	7
18 A4	ff	ANDA (opr)	IND, Y	5
18 A5	ff	BITA (opr)	IND, Y	5
18 A6	ff	LDAA (opr)	IND, Y	5
18 A7	ff	STAA (opr)	IND, Y	5
18 A8	ff	EORA (opr)	IND, Y	5
18 A9	ff	ADCA (opr)	IND, Y	5
18 AA	ff	ORAA (opr)	IND, Y	5
18 AB	ff	ADDA (opr)	IND, Y	5
18 AC	ff	CPY (opr)	IND, Y	7
18 AD	ff	JSR (opr)	IND, Y	7
18 AE	ff	LDS (opr)	IND, Y	6
18 AF	ff	STS (opr)	IND, Y	6
18 BC	hh ll	CPY (opr)	EXT	7
18 CE	jj kk	LDY (opr)	IMM	4
18 DE	dd	LDY (opr)	DIR	5
18 DF	dd	STY (opr)	DIR	5
18 E0	ff	SUBB (opr)	IND, Y	5
18 E1	ff	CMPB (opr)	IND, Y	5
18 E2	ff	SBCB (opr)	IND, Y	5
18 E3	ff	ADDD (opr)	IND, Y	5
18 E4	ff	ANDB (opr)	IND, Y	5
18 E5	ff	BITB (opr)	IND, Y	5
18 E6	ff	LDAB (opr)	IND, Y	5
18 E7	ff	STAB (opr)	IND, Y	5
18 E8	ff	EORB (opr)	IND, Y	5
18 E9	ff	ADCB (opr)	IND, Y	5
18 EA	ff	ORAB (opr)	IND, Y	5
18 EB	ff	ADDB (opr)	IND, Y	5
18 EC	ff	LDD (opr)	IND, Y	6
18 ED	ff	STD (opr)	IND, Y	6
18 EE	ff	LDY (opr)	IND, Y	6

Op code	Operands	Op Code vs Instruction Cross Reference Instruction	Address mode	Cycle
18 EF	ff	STY (opr)	IND, Y	6
18 FE	hh ll	LDY (opr)	EXT	6
18 FF	hh ll	STY (opr)	EXT	6
1A 83	jj kk	CPD (opr)	IMM	5
1A 93	dd	CPD (opr)	DIR	6
1A A3	ff	CPD (opr)	IND, X	7
1A AC	ff	CPY (opr)	IND, X	7
1A B3	hh ll	CPD (opr)	EXT	7
1A EE	ff	LDY (opr)	IND, X	6
1A EF	ff	STY (opr)	IND, X	6
CD A3	ff	CPD (opr)	IND, Y	7
CD AC	ff	CPX (opr)	IND, Y	7
CD EE	ff	LDX (opr)	IND, Y	6
CD EF	ff	STX (opr)	IND, Y	6

The 68HC11 MCU Block Diagram

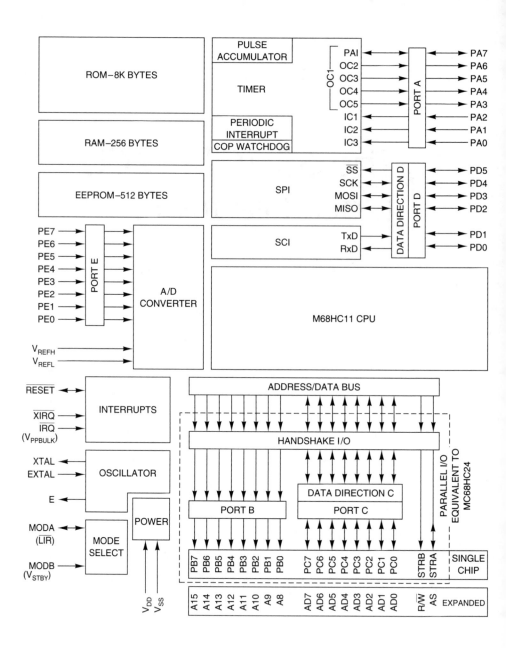

Appendix **C**

The 68HC11 MCU Register and Control Bit Assignments

Address	Bit 7	Bit 6	Bit 5	Bit 4	Bit 3	Bit 2	Bit 1	Bit 0		
$1000	Bit 7	—	—	—	—	—	—	Bit 0	PORTA	I/O Port A
$1001									Reserved	
$1002	STAF	STAI	CWOM	HNDS	OIN	PLS	EGA	INVB	PIOC	Parallel I/O Control Register
$1003	Bit 7	—	—	—	—	—	—	Bit 0	PORTC	I/O Port C
$1004	Bit 7	—	—	—	—	—	—	Bit 0	PORTB	Output Port B
$1005	Bit 7	—	—	—	—	—	—	Bit 0	PORTCL	Alternate Latched Port C
$1006									Reserved	
$1007	Bit 7	—	—	—	—	—	—	Bit 0	DDRC	Data Direction for Port C
$1008			Bit 5	—	—	—	—	Bit 0	PORTD	I/O Port D
$1009			Bit 5	—	—	—	—	Bit 0	DDRD	Data Direction for Port D
$100A	Bit 7	—	—	—	—	—	—	Bit 0	PORTE	Input Port E
$100B	FOC1	FOC2	FOC3	FOC4	FOC5				CFORC	Compare Force Register
$100C	OC1M7	OC1M6	OC1M5	OC1M4	OC1M3				OC1M	OC1 Action Mask Register
$100D	OC1D7	OC1D6	OC1D5	OC1D4	OC1D3				OC1D	OC1 Action Data Register
$100E	Bit 15	—	—	—	—	—	—	Bit 8	TCNT	Timer Counter Register
$100F	Bit 7	—	—	—	—	—	—	Bit 0		
$1010	Bit 15	—	—	—	—	—	—	Bit 8	TIC1	Input Capture 1 Register
$1011	Bit 7	—	—	—	—	—	—	Bit 0		
$1012	Bit 15	—	—	—	—	—	—	Bit 8	TIC2	Input Capture 2 Register
$1013	Bit 7	—	—	—	—	—	—	Bit 0		
$1014	Bit 15	—	—	—	—	—	—	Bit 8	TIC3	Input Capture 3 Register
$1015	Bit 7	—	—	—	—	—	—	Bit 0		
$1016	Bit 15	—	—	—	—	—	—	Bit 8	TOC1	Output Compare 1 Register
$1017	Bit 7	—	—	—	—	—	—	Bit 0		
$1018	Bit 15	—	—	—	—	—	—	Bit 8	TOC2	Output Compare 2 Register
$1019	Bit 7	—	—	—	—	—	—	Bit 0		
$101A	Bit 15	—	—	—	—	—	—	Bit 8	TOC3	Output Compare 3 Register
$101B	Bit 7	—	—	—	—	—	—	Bit 0		
$101C	Bit 15	—	—	—	—	—	—	Bit 8	TOC4	Output Compare 4 Register
$101D	Bit 7	—	—	—	—	—	—	Bit 0		
$101E	Bit 15	—	—	—	—	—	—	Bit 8	TOC5	Output Compare 5 Register
$101F	Bit 7	—	—	—	—	—	—	Bit 0		

Addr	Bit 7	Bit 6	Bit 5	Bit 4	Bit 3	Bit 2	Bit 1	Bit 0	Name	Description
$1020	OM2	OL2	OM3	OL3	OM4	OL4	OM5	OL5	TCTL1	Timer Control Register 1
$1021			EDG1B	EDG1A	EDG2B	EDG2A	EDG3B	EDG3A	TCTL2	Timer Control Register 2
$1022	OC1I	OC2I	OC3I	OC4I	OC5I	IC1I	IC2I	IC3I	TMSK1	Timer Interrupt Mask Register 1
$1023	OC1F	OC2F	OC3F	OC4F	OC5F	IC1F	IC2F	IC3F	TFLG1	Timer Interrupt Flag Register 1
$1024	TOI	RTII	PAOVI	PAII			PR1	PR0	TMSK2	Timer Interrupt Mask Register 2
$1025	TOF	RTIF	PAOVF	PAIF					TFLG2	Timer Interrupt Flag Register 2
$1026	DDRA7	PAEN	PAMOD	PEDGE			RTR1	RTR0	PACTL	Pulse Accumulator Control Register
$1027	Bit 7	—	—	—	—	—	—	Bit 0	PACNT	Pulse Accumulator Count Register
$1028	SPIE	SPE	DWOM	MSTR	CPOL	CPHA	SPR1	SPR0	SPCR	SPI Control Register
$1029	SPIF	WCOL		MODF					SPSR	SPI Status Register
$102A	Bit 7	—	—	—	—	—	—	Bit 0	SPDR	SPI Data Register
$102B	TCLR		SCP1	SCP0	RCKB	SCR2	SCR1	SCR0	BAUD	SCI Baud Rate Control
$102C	R8	T8		M	WAKE				SCCR1	SCI Control Register 1
$102D	TIE	TCIE	RIE	ILIE	TE	RE	RWU	SBK	SCCR2	SCI Control Register 2
$102E	TDRE	TC	RDRF	IDLE	OR	NF	FE		SCSR	SCI Status Register
$102F	Bit 7	—	—	—	—	—	—	Bit 0	SCDR	SCI Data (Read RDR, Write TDR)
$1030	CCF		SCAN	MULT	CD	CC	CB	CA	ADCTL	A/D Control Register
$1031	Bit 7	—	—	—	—	—	—	Bit 0	ADR1	A/D Result Register 1
$1032	Bit 7	—	—	—	—	—	—	Bit 0	ADR2	A/D Result Register 2
$1033	Bit 7	—	—	—	—	—	—	Bit 0	ADR3	A/D Result Register 3
$1034	Bit 7	—	—	—	—	—	—	Bit 0	ADR4	A/D Result Register 4
$1035 Thru $1038									Reserved	
$1039	ADPU	CSEL	IRQE	DLY	CME		CR1	CR0	OPTION	System Configuration Options
$103A	Bit 7	—	—	—	—	—	—	Bit 0	COPRST	Arm/Reset COP Timer Circuitry
$103B	ODD	EVEN		BYTE	ROW	ERASE	EELAT	EEPGM	PPROG	EEPROM Programming Control Register
$103C	RBOOT	SMOD	MDA	IRV	PSEL3	PSEL2	PSEL1	PSEL0	HPRIO	Highest Priority I-Bit Int and Misc
$103D	RAM3	RAM2	RAM1	RAM0	REG3	REG2	REG1	REG0	INIT	RAM and I/O Mapping Register
$103E	TILOP		OCCR	CBYP	DISR	FCM	FCOP	TCON	TEST1	Factory TEST Control Register
$103F	—	—	—	—	NOSEC	NOCOP	ROMON	EEON	CONFIG	COP, ROM, and EEPROM Enables

Answers to Selected Problems

▶ CHAPTER 1

1. (a) 22_{10} (c) 2313_{10}
  (b) 141_{10} (d) 983_{10}
2. (a) 100101_2 (d) 11001101_2
  (b) 1110_2 (e) 100100001001_2
  (c) 10111101_2
3. 255_{10}; 65535_{10}
4. (a) 483_{10} (c) 2047_{10}
  (b) 30_{10} (d) 175_{10}
5. (a) 73_8 (c) 1627_8
  (b) 564_8 (d) 200000_8
6. (a) 111100011_2 (c) 011111111111_2
  (b) 011110_2 (d) 010101111_2
7. (a) 26_8 (c) 4411_8
  (b) 215_8 (d) 1727_8
10. (a) 146_{10} (c) 14333_{10}
  (b) 422_{10} (d) 704_{10}
11. (a) $4B_{16}$ (c) 800_{16}
  (b) $13A_{16}$ (d) 6413_{16}
12. (a) 16_{16} (c) 909_{16}
  (b) $8D_{16}$ (d) $3D7_{16}$
13. (a) 10010010_2 (c) 0011011111111101_2
  (b) 000110100110_2 (d) 001011001101_2
14. (a) $65,536$ (b) $0000_{16} \rightarrow 0FFF_{16}$
16. (a) 01000111_{BCD}
  (b) 100101100010_{BCD}
  (c) 000110000111_{BCD}
  (d) $0100001001101000100101100010011_{BCD}$
17. 10 bits; 12 bits
18. (a) 9752_{10} (b) 184_{10}

21. Parity bit is leftmost bit
  (a) 110110110   (c) 111110111
  (b) 000101000
22. (a) 101110100
  (b) 000111000
  (c) 0000101100101
  (d) 11001001000000001
23. (a) 11100001   (c) 11111111
  (b) 01001100   (d) 11111110
24. (a) $+107_{10}$ (b) -18_{10} (c) -255_{10}
27. (a) No overflow   (c) Overflow
  (b) Overflow
28. (a) $BA9_{16}$ (c) $B01_{16}$
  (b) 255_{16} (d) 975_{16}

▶ CHAPTER 2

1. (a) 8   (b) 1
2. B (NAND)
3. A (NOR)
9. (a) 10 ns (t_s)   (b) 5 ns (t_H)
15. Reduce the number of IC pins
19. A–(2), B–(1), C–(4), D–(3)

▶ CHAPTER 3

2. (a) 131,072 bits or memory cells
8. 134,217,728 cells
9. 4,194,304 addresses; one per word

10. 64K × 4.
13. (a) $\overline{CS}$ = 1 produces Hi-Z outputs
    (b) Data out = 11101101
14. [A] = 1001
18. (a) 16,384 registers
    (b) 4 bits per register
    (c) Two 1-of-128 decoders are required.
23. By exposing it to ultraviolet (UV) light applied through a window on the chip
35. 26 pins
40. (a) 100 ns   (e) 30 ns
    (b) 30 ns   (f) 40 ns
    (c) 10 million   (g) 10 million
    (d) 20 ns
50. 16
51. 4; 16
57. (a) 32 words; 8-bits/word
    (b) RAMs 2 and 3
    (c) 00_{16} to $0F_{16}$; 10_{16} to $1F_{16}$

▶ CHAPTER 4

4. 20
10. 32 bit word size
12. Three consecutive memory locations
14. (a) 256   (b) 65,536   (c) 65,536
36. (a) 2   (d) 1
    (b) 22 READ; 0 WRITE   (e) 2
    (c) 3   (f) 0
40. (a) [A] = 02 and [C352] = 02
    (b) [A] = 00 and [C352] = FF
41. 18_{16}
49. (a) and (b)

▶ CHAPTER 5

3. (b)
4. (a) Address bus   (f) Data bus
   (b) Control bus   (g) Control bus
   (c) Address bus   (h) Address bus
   (d) Data bus   (i) Address bus and
   (e) Address bus   data bus
6. They are 90° out of phase.
8. (a) READ   (c) READ
   (b) WRITE
9. 4 READs and no WRITEs
10. (a) 3 READs and 1 WRITE
    (b) 3 READs and no WRITEs
    (c) 2 READs

13. <250 ns
16. (b) 32K of RAM
    (c) 14K of ROM
    (d) Max. number of I/Os = 2048
17. (a) 128; 8; 56   (b) 8; 3.5
18. 64; 4; C000-FFFF
19. 68HC11E9:ROM = 12K, EEPROM
    = 512, and RAM = 512
    68HC11A8: ROM = 8K, EEPROM
    = 512, and RAM = 256
20. 375A
21. Address 375A is on the 4K page that starts
    on address 3000
23. Module 0: 0000–03FF; Module 1:
    0400–07FF; Module 2: 0800–0BFF;
    Module 3: 0C00–0FFF
26. (a) 0400–07FF; 1400–17FF; 2400–27FF;
        3400–37FF; 4400–47FF; 5400–57FF;
        6400–67FF; 7400–77FF
    (b) $\overline{Y0}$ selects the same locations in the
        same RAM module.
28. (b) and (c)
30. ROM: 0000–2FFF; RAM: 5000–57FF
31. (a) 256 × 4
    (b) 256 × 8
    (c) 0000–00FF; 0100–01FF; 0200–02FF;
        0300–03FF
35. 800

▶ CHAPTER 6

1. ACCD; IX; IY; SP; PC; DAR
9. (d)
10. (b)
11. (b)
12. (d)
13. (b)
15. (c)
16. The addition produced a result outside of
    the range -128_{10} to $+127_{10}$.
19. 68HC11 MPU flags: S; X; H; I; N; Z; V; C;
    Z; N; S; H
20. (b)
21. (c)
22. [X] = 0 and [Y] = A4
23. (d)
24. (b)
26. [SP] = 01FE
29. (d)

30. (d)

40. **(a)** False   **(b)** True

▶ CHAPTER 7

2. **(a)** I   **(c)** N   **(e)** V   **(g)** H
    (b) Z   **(d)** C   **(f)** C   **(h)** S

3. I, C, and V

4. **(a)** Byte following op code
    (b) Address 007C
    (c) Address 57BB
    (d) Address 0200 + 3F = 023F

6. Extended

7. Inherent

8. Immediate

9. [ACCA] = 8F; [ACCB] = 00; [ACCD] = 8F00

10. Relative address mode

11. Indexed address modes

13. 13

14. **(a)** 8B   **(f)** 50   **(k)** 53
    (b) DB   **(g)** 70   **(l)** CD AC
    (c) 0A   **(h)** 09   **(m)** 3D
    (d) 18 A0   **(i)** 17
    (e) 8E   **(j)** 63

15. **(a)** 8B 20   **(h)** 09
    (b) DB 20   **(i)** 17
    (c) 0A   **(j)** 63 50
    (d) 18 A0 20   **(k)** 53
    (e) 8E 01 FF   **(l)** CD AC 45
    (f) 50   **(m)** 3D
    (g) 70 0A 44

16. No effect on the C flag: CLV, LDS, DEX, TBA; No effect on the Z flag: MUL

17. MUL = 10 clock cycles

19. Address; Label; Instruct code; Mnemonic; Comments

21. Change first instruction to LDS #$0286. Interchange PSHA and PSHB.

23. 0986

25. ABA; SUBA $0350; TAB (executed in that order)

26. ABA; TAB; LDAA $0350; SBA; STAA $0350 (executed in that order)

27. ABA; PSHB; TAB; LDAA $0350; SBA; STAA $0350; PULB (executed in that order)

28. **(a)** ACCA = 7C; N = 0; Z = 0; V = 0; C = 0

(b) ACCA = 00; N = 0; Z = 1; V = 0; C = 1

(c) ACCA = B1; N = 1; Z = 0; V = 1; C = 0

(d) ACCA = 7B; N = 0; Z = 0; V = 1; C = 1

(e) ACCA = 4E; N = 0; Z = 0; V = 1; C = 1

29. **(a)** ACCA = E8; N = 1; Z = 0; V = 0; C = 1

(b) ACCA = D6; N = 1; Z = 0; V = 1; C = 1

(c) ACCA = 39; N = 0; Z = 0; V = 0; C = 0

(d) ACCA = 6F; N = 0; Z = 0; V = 0; C = 0

(e) ACCA = 00; N = 0; Z = 1; V = 0; C = 0

30. **(a)** LDAA $51; ADDA $53; STAA $55; LDAA $50; ADCA $52; STAA $54; HLT (executed in that order)
    (b) SUM (H) = 65; SUM(L) = 89
    (c) SUM (H) = 03; SUM(L) = 02

34. LDAA $C080; ADDA $C081; DAA; STAA $C082 (executed in that order)

35. LDAA $C300; LDAB $C400; MUL; STD $C500 (executed in that order)

37. [ACCA] = 00   [ACCB] = F5
    [X] = 0010

39. LDAA $B800; ANDA #$3F (executed in that order)

40. LDAA $B800; ORAA #$C0 (executed in that order)

41. **(a)** LDAA $B800; SUBA #$63
    (b) LDAA $B800; EORA #$63

42. LDAA $B800; ANDA #$0F; EORA #$0F (executed in that order)

43. **(a)** E6, C = 0;   **(d)** E6, C = 0;
    (b) 3D, C = 0;   **(e)** 54, C = 1;
    (c) 3D, C = 0;   **(f)** 54BD, C = 0

47. **(a)** [ACCA] = 93;
    (b) [ACCB] = 00;
    (c) [X] = 3D00;
    (d) [SP] = 05A2;
    (e) [ACCB] = 00
    (f) [ACCA] = 94;
    (g) [3D00] = AA;
    (h) [ACCB] = FF

48. One way: STX $50; COM $50; COM $51; LDX $50

49. One way: STX $50; COM $50; COM $51; LDX $50; INX

50. 93

51. True

52. True

55. C4D1; C3D2

56. C69A

57. (a) C617;   (c) C640;
    (b) C6BA;   (d) C648

58. (a) 5A;   (d) 7F;
    (b) BD;   (e) BD (out of range)
    (c) FD;

59. Change the offset to 01 so that program will branch to C644. At 6C44, place at JMP $C700 instruction.

60. C200 LDAA $0900; ANDA #$28; BNE $C20B; CLRB; STAB $0A00; WAI

61. C200 LDAA $0900; ORAA #$AF; COMA; BNE $C20C; CLRB; STAB $0A00; WAI

62. 7000 CLR $C800; SBA; BHI $7009; COM $C800; WAI

63. Change BHI to BGT

66. (a) C500 BRCLR $35 $55 $C53A
    (b) C500 BRSET $F5 $AA $C53A

68. 0300 CBA; BHI $0333; BEQ $0333; BRA $0277

69. 0500 LDAB $F600; CMPB #$4E; BEQ $0530; CMPB #$59; BEQ $0550; JMP $0500

70. (a) BHI instruction will branch to C5DD
    (b) BEQ instruction will branch to C65E
    (c) BRA will branch to C676

72. C100 LDX $C500; CPX $C502; BEQ $C150; BHI $C160; BRA $C170

73. BITA does not alter [ACCA].

74. Branch to 0C60.

76. Branching will occur to 05D0.

77. (a) Branching will occur to 05C0.
    (b) Branching will occur to 05FF.

81. (a) C100 LDAA $A6; BSR $C160; STAA $A7; WAI
    (b) No

85. C200 LDX #$03D8; LDAA $00,X; STAA $C800; INX; CPX #$03FF; BNE $C203; WAI

87. Change instruction at C303 to LDX #$C9E0.
Change instruction at C30B to CPX #$CA56.

92. 14 microseconds

93. (a) 5.126 ms
    (b) Using the X register: 4.002 ms
        Using the Y register: 3.998 ms

94. For [X] = 0001: Delay = 1.0005 ms. For [X] = 0005: Delay = 4.9945 ms

95. 1. Change instruction LDX #$1388 to LDX #$1B58
    2. Change instruction LDX #$02BC to LDX #$03E8
    3. Change instruction LDX #$08FC to LDX #$0E74

98. Q_0 = 200 Hz; Q_1 = 100 Hz; Q_2 = 50 Hz squarewave; Q_3 = 25 Hz squarewave; Q_4 = 12.5 Hz squarewave; Q_5 = 6.25 Hz squarewave; Q_6 = 3.125 Hz squarewave; Q_7 = 1.5625 Hz squarewave

100. (a) $FFFF_{16}$ = $65{,}535_{10}$
    (b) RESET
    (c) LDD $100E: LDX $100E: LDY $100E

101. (a) 131.1 ms; 524.3 ms
    (b) When the TCNT counter cycles from FFFF to 0000
    (c) LDAA #$A0; STAA $1025

▶ CHAPTER 8

1. (b)

2. (c)

3. (d)

4. (c)

5. (b)

7. LDAA $8004; NEGA; STAA $8000

13. 1xxx xxxx; x1xx xxxx

16. ADR1, ADR2, ADR3, and ADR4

17. At address C00C change to LDAB #$10.

18. BSET $39, Y $40

20. Resolution or step-size of the A/D converter

22. (c)

26. (d)

30. Yes

36. e, a, b, d, f, and c

38. TIC3

39. LDAA #$1B; STAA $1021

40. The TFLG1 register at $1023. The TMSK1 register at $1022.

41. PA0 will function as an input port pin.

42. 5 KHz
43. Change instruction at address C10A to LDAA #$30.
46. [TCNT] = [TOC3]
47. **(a)** LDAA #$A8; STAA $1023
      (b) LDY #$1000; BCLR $23,Y $57
49. **(a)** F   **(c)** T   **(e)** F   **(g)** T
      (b) T   **(d)** F   **(f)** T
50. **(a)** Halt Steal   **(c)** TSC Steal
      (b) Halt Burst

▶ CHAPTER 9

4. (c)
6. 36.67 ms
7. (b) 1200 bits/s
8. (c) and (f)
13. (a)
14. (d)
15. (a)
16. 1A
22. PDO (R × D) and PD1 (T × D)

23. One possibility: LDAA #$0C; STAA $102D
29. LDAB $102E; STAA $102F
30. LDAA #$32; STAA $102B
31. SCCR1 at $102C
34. **(a)** A   **(c)** S   **(e)** S
      (b) S   **(d)** S
44. Control registers
45. (d)
49. (c)
50. (c)
51. **(a)** [ACCB] = xxxx1111
      (b) [ACCB] = xxxx1011
      (c) [ACCB] = xxxx1001
      (d) [ACCB] = xxxx1101
      (e) [ACCB] = xxxx1111
52. The STO key is down.
53. C200 LDAA $B802; ANDA #$02; BEQ $C20D; JSR $C000; JMP $C200; LDAA #$07; STAA; WAI
57. C200 SEC; LDAA #$7F; STAA $C804; LDAA $C806; INCA; BEQ $C20D; WAI; ROR $C804; JMP $C206

Index